G. O.

Jesus Said: "Follow Me

A General Outreach

&

Free Interpretation of the Sayings and Hymns

& The New Word

A Go Fish Ministries , Inc. Publication

G.O. F.I.S.H.

Jesus Said: *"Follow Me and I'll make you fishers of others."*

A General Outreach

&

Free Interpretation of the Sayings and Hymns & The New Word

A Go Fish Ministries Publication
By Sis. Kimberly M. Hartfield
Go Fish Logo designed by Sis. Kimberly M. Hartfield

Table of Contents

Introduction   p. 4
The Sayings   p. 6
The Hymns   p. 21
The Ten Commandments   p. 63
Matthew   p. 66
Mark   p. 92
Luke   p. 108
John   p. 134
Acts   p. 153
Romans   p. 176
I Corinthians   p. 186
II Corinthians   p. 196
Galatians   p. 202
Ephesians   p. 206
Philippians   p. 210
Colossians   p. 213
I Thessalonians   p. 215
II Thessalonians   p. 217
I Timothy   p. 219
II Timothy   p. 222
Philemon   p. 226
Hebrews   p. 227
James   p. 234
I Peter   p. 237
II Peter   p. 240
I John   p. 242
II John   p. 245
III John   p. 246
Jude   p. 247
Revelation   p. 248
Awake   p. 259
Personal Notes   p. 260
80 Day Summer Reading Plan   p. 271
Beatitudes   p. 272
Yeshua's Prayer   p. 273
About the Author   p. 274

A General Outreach

&

Free Interpretation of the Sayings and Hymns

Introduction

This Go Fish Ministries publication is a paraphrase of both the New Testament (The New Word) and the Proverbs and Psalms (Sayings and Hymns). Its main purpose is to present a simplified version to those who have difficulty understanding more traditional ones, especially children and teens. My inspiration was to give my own children a more understandable, easier to read text, and one that would encourage them and other young people to read the Word of God. Many Biblical versions were considered in the interpretation of this version, in which the starting point was the original King James Version. Other versions considered were the New King James Version, the Good News Bible, the Living Bible, the American Standard Version, the Revised Standard Version, and Others, along with a study of many of the original Hebrew words from the Strong's Concordance and Dictionary. The main departure from these common versions is the use of the proper Name of God, which is now commonly understood to be Yahweh. I now quote from the preface to *The New Oxford Annotated Bible Revised Standard Version* which states concerning the **Name of God**,

> "A major departure...is the rendering of the Divine Name...the term *Jehovah*; the King James Version had employed this in four places, but everywhere else, except in three cases where it was employed as part of a proper Name, used the English word *LORD* (or in certain cases *GOD*). . . While it is almost if not quite certain that the Name was originally pronounced *Yahweh*, this pronunciation was not indicated when the Masoretes added vowel signs to the consonantal Hebrew. To the four consonants *YHWH* of the Name, which had come to be regarded as too sacred to be pronounced, they attached vowel signs indicating that in its place should be read the Hebrew word *Adonai* meaning *Lord* (or *Elohim* meaning *God*)...The form *Jehovah* is of late medieval origin; it is a combination of the consonants of the Divine Name and the vowels attached to it by the Masoretes but belonging to an entirely different word. The sound of the Y is represented by J and the sound of W by V, as in Latin . . . **the word *Jehovah* does not accurately represent any form of the Name ever used in Hebrew . . . and is entirely inappropriate for the universal faith of the Christian Church."**

In light of these words and many hours of heartfelt prayer and study of the Scriptures, I've endeavored to bring back the use of the forgotten Name of God in this publication, and the use of the English word *Lord* has been replaced with *Savior*, in places where the use of YAHWEH was not employed. I've been tormented over whether or not this interpretation was the right thing to do, and I now believe with all my heart that I've done the perfect will of God. Yet, if I've rather entered into the permissive will of God, I now plead for God's mercy on my soul, as I've done it in ignorance rather than malice.

Another departure from the norm is the explicit use of the masculine form to denote the persons of the Godhead, noting that many of the Hebrew words implicating the Godhead are in feminine forms, in particularly Elohiym, which can denote God or Goddess. Where verses read He, Him, or His, many instances have been changed to read You, Your, or Yours, which doesn't denote a masculine or feminine Entity, but rather an androgynous Entity. Passages in the New Testament indicate that heavenly beings are neither male nor female, and I believe we can ascertain from these passages that God is neither masculine nor feminine or possibly has both qualities. Since human beings are made in the image of our Maker, and have both masculine and feminine hormones, and it is believed by most that God is complete in Self-existence, it is possible that God fully has both qualities. Since we have no way of knowing this for certain, I choose to use an androgynous descriptor of God in this text. In addition, since the word *man*, to some, no longer represents humanity in general as used to be the case for most people, I've changed the words *man, mankind*, and the like to more neutral forms, such as *humanity, people,* or *persons,* along with many of the systematically masculine wording such as *he, him,* and *his,*

4

to *they, them,* and *theirs* as the original Hebrew word (1931 Strong's) can be denoted as masculine, feminine, or androgynous (he, she, it, etc.).

Other passages which are antiquated by their wording and phrasing are given a more modern connotation than the original text would allow for. In every case that a change was made, several alternate texts were considered along with the original languages as denoted in the Strong's concordance and dictionary. Some verses were joined together, where the thought had been divided into separate verses in the KJV, when they were felt to be better understood by keeping the thought in one main sentence. Also the text has been put in paragraph form with the individual verses not being numbered, as I believe this can be a distraction when studying or reading the Word of God. Quotes have been placed in italics, as well.

With these departures in mind, I hope that this interpretation may be viewed as a help along with other translations in the great commission of Jesus Christ, my Savior. I hope to someday do additional interpretations of the Scriptures, but trust that I've done and will do only that which would be in God's perfect will. God Bless and Go Fish! Jesus said, *"Follow Me and I'll make you fishers of others."* Matthew 4:19.

Untitled
by

Rob Harshfield

5

The Sayings
(Proverbs)

1 [1-6] These are the sayings of Solomon, the son of David and ruler of Israel; So we can receive wisdom and learning in order to have a good understanding; To learn the teachings of wisdom, justice, judgment, and equality; To teach the uneducated and give the young knowledge and good judgment. A wise person will listen, and learn; and one of understanding will pay attention to wise guidance in order to understand a saying and its meaning, the words of smart people, and their wise sayings.

[7-9] The respect of Yahweh is the opening up of the mind to knowledge, but the untested and stupid reject knowledge and learning. Children, listen to the training of your parents, and don't ignore their words: They'll bring blessings and honor to you, and are as a prized medal around your neck.

[10-19] Children, if the sinful tempt you, don't agree to go with them. If they say, "*Come with us, let's hunt for someone to mug, and wait for a victim; Let's capture them, kill them, and send them to Hell. We'll find lots of valuables and fill our houses with their stuff; Join our gang and we'll all split the takings;*" Children, don't join their gang, but avoid them: They run to evil, and quickly shed innocent blood. Just like trying to catch a bird is useless, they wait for their own death, unknowingly stalking their own blood. Only greedy people that kill property owners for the takings act this way.

[20-23] Wisdom cries out to those in the streets: It cries out in public places, at the edge of the city limits: in the prominent places of the city, the voice of wisdom says, "*How long, you naive people, will you love ignorance? And ridiculers enjoy their hatred, and stupid people hate knowledge? Turn back at My warning; See, I'll give some of My spirit to you, revealing My words to you.*

[24-33] *I'll laugh at your misfortune, too because I called, and you refused; I reached out, and no one paid attention; I'll mock you when you are afraid because you've disregarded all my advice, and ignored my warnings. When great fear comes, and your destruction comes as a hurricane; when trouble and grief come on you, then you'll call on Me, but I won't answer; you'll quickly look for Me, but you won't find Me: For you hated knowledge, and didn't choose to show respect to Yahweh God. You ignored My direction and hated My correction, so you'll suffer the consequences of your own way, and be caught in your own plans: For the unconcern of the careless will kill them, and the wealth of stupid people will destroy them. If you listen to Me you'll live safely, and won't be upset by the fear of evil.*"

2 [1-9] Children, if you'll believe my words, and keep my teachings with you, so that you listen to these wise words, and apply your heart to understand them; Yes, if you look for knowledge, and ask questions to help you understand; if you look for it as riches, searching for it like hidden treasures, then you'll understand the respect of Yahweh God, and find the knowledge of God. Yahweh gives wisdom: the Words of God give knowledge and understanding. Yahweh gives a sound mind to godly people and helps those who walk honorably. Yes, God keeps the ways of judgment, and saves the way of those who believe, so you'll understand what's right, have good judgment, show equality, and follow every good way.

[10-22] When wisdom enters your heart, and knowledge is pleasing to your soul; good judgment will protect you and understanding will save you, in order to protect you from evil ways and from those that speak sinful things. They'll keep you safe from those who leave decent ways and do evil, and who have a good time doing evil things, enjoying the sinfulness of evil people, whose ways are crooked and who leave the true path. They'll save you from the ungodly, even from the ungodly that only tell people what they want to hear; who give up on the guidance of their youth, and forget the promises of God; whose houses lean toward death, and whose sidewalks lead to the dead. No one that stays with ungodly people ever returns to find the path of life. So walk in the ways of godly people, and keep the ways of the respectable, for godly people who are innocent will live and stay in the land, but the sinful will die out of the earth, and the offenders will be moved out of their place.

3 [1-6] Children, don't forget my words; but let your heart keep my teachings for more productive days, longer life, and peace. Don't let mercy and truth leave you. Place them around your neck like a prized medal, writing them in your heart, so that you'll find grace and have good understanding in the sight of God and humanity. Trust in Yahweh with all your heart; and don't trust your own understanding. Acknowledge God in everything you do, and Yahweh will guide your ways.

[7-12] Don't be wise in your own eyes: respect Yahweh, and stop doing evil, which will keep you strong and healthy. Honor Yahweh with all you have, and with the first of everything you get, so you'll be filled up, bursting out at the seams. Children, don't hate the correction of Yahweh; don't be tired of God's discipline, because Yahweh loves whoever is corrected; just like the parents do to the children they enjoy.

6

[13-20] Happy are those that find wisdom, the ones that understand, for its yield is better than a rich income, and making great wealth. It's more precious than expensive stones, and nothing that you can want can be compared to it. Watch and see; for longer days, riches, and honor will come with it. The ways of wisdom are enjoyable, and all its ways are peaceful. It's life to those who grab it and every one that keeps it will be happy. Yahweh has founded the earth with wisdom and has settled the heavens with understanding. The depths of the oceans quake and the clouds rain by the knowledge of God.

[21-26] Children don't lose sight of sound wisdom and good judgment. They're life to your soul, and health to your body, so you can walk in your way safely, never stumbling. When you lie down, you won't be afraid: yes, you'll lie down, and sleep soundly. Don't be afraid of unexpected fear, nor when the misery of the sinful comes, for Yahweh will be your confidence, and will keep you from being overcome.

[27-30] Don't keep back good from those you owe it to, when it's in your own power to do it. Don't say to your neighbor *"Go, and come back later, and I'll give it to you tomorrow"* when you know you have it right there. Don't plan evil against your neighbors, seeing they live peacefully beside you. Don't argue with anyone without a good cause, if they've done you no real harm.

[31-34] Don't be jealous of those that keep down others, and don't choose to follow their ways, for sinful people are disgraceful to Yahweh, but godly people are trusted with the secrets of God. The curse of Yahweh is on the houses of sinful people, but God's blessings are on the homes of godly people. Surely God looks down on those that make fun of others, but gives grace to those who have humility. The wise will be praised, but shame will come to stupid people.

4 [1-13] Listen, children, to the training of a parent, and pay attention to grasp my knowledge. I give you good guidelines, so don't give up on my words. Because I was my parents' child, young and very loved by them, they taught me also, and said to me: *Let your heart remember our words, keep our teachings, and live. Get wisdom and understanding, don't forget it, nor refuse to listen to our words. Don't give up on it, and it'll keep you safe, love it and it'll keep you. Wisdom is the most important thing; so get wisdom, and with all your power get understanding. Honor it, for if you hold on to it, it'll promote you and bring you honor. It'll make you a pleasure to see, and make you well known.* Listen, children, and learn my sayings; and you'll have many years in your life. I've taught you in the way of wisdom; I've led you in the right ways. When you walk, your steps won't be risky; and when you run, you won't stumble. Hold on to teaching and don't let it go, but keep it; for it's your very life.

[14-19] Don't follow the path of the sinful, and don't go with evil people. Avoid it, don't even pass by it, turn away from it, and go far away; for they won't sleep, unless they've made some trouble; and they lose sleep, unless they cause someone else to fall away. They live on evil, and violence. But the path of godly people is as the sunlight shining, which shines more brightly towards midday. The way of the sinful is as darkness, because they don't even know what they stumble over.

[20-27] Children, pay attention to my words; listen to my sayings. Don't lose sight of them; keep them in the depths of your heart, for they're life to those that find them, and health to every part of the body. Keep your heart with focus; for out of it are the matters of life. Put a disrespectful mouth away from you, and put filthy words far from you. Let your eyes focus, and look straight ahead of you. Think about the path your feet will take, and carefully choose everything you do. Don't turn right or left, but get off of every sinful path.

5 [1-14] Children, pay attention to my wisdom, and listen to my understanding, so that you can know good judgment, and that your words will be words of knowledge. For the words of the ungodly may be as sweet as honey and their mouths may be smoother than oil, but their end is as bitter as vinegar, sharp as a two-edged blade. Their feet lead them to death, their steps taking the path to Hell. Just in case you should wonder about the path of life, the ways of ungodly people change so much, you can't even know them. So listen to me now, children, and don't ignore the words of my mouth. Remove yourself far from ungodly people, and don't come near the door of their houses, or you'll give your honor to others, and your years to cruel people. Strangers will take your wealth and all the benefits of your work will wind up in the house of a stranger; You'll mourn at last, when your body and your life is used up, saying *"How I hated teaching, and my heart hated correction; I haven't obeyed the voice of my teachers, nor listened to those that warned me! I'm a disgrace to the eyes of everyone."*

[15-23] Love your own spouse, and be faithful to your mate. If you have children by others, your family ties will be scattered about. Let them only belong to you and your spouse, and not to another. Let your family be blessed, and celebrate with the spouse of your youth. Let your mate be loving and pleasing, and let only your spouse satisfy you sexually; and always be sexually satisfied with your mate's love. Why, children, would you want to be satisfied sexually by another, and hold on to a stranger? For the ways of humanity are seen by the eyes of Yahweh, who thinks about every choice we make. The sinful will be taken by their evil habits, and controlled by their own sins. They'll die without teaching, going astray in their great carelessness.

6 [1-5] Children, if you guarantee the debts of your friends, if you've made a commitment for a stranger, and you're caught by the words of your mouth, you've been taken by your own words. Do this now, children, to save yourself: when you come to your friend; go, humble yourself and plead to be released from the promise you made

7

to your friend. Don't close your eyes, nor go to sleep, until you deliver yourself as a deer from the hand of the hunter, and as a bird from the hand of the fowler.

[6-10] Go to the ant and think on its ways, and be wise, which having no guide, overseer, or ruler, stores up what it needs in the summer, and gathers its food in the harvest. How long will you sleep, lazy? When will you wake up from your sleep? A little sleep, a little slumber, a little folding of the hands to rest; so your poverty comes as a homeless drifter, and your need as an armed robber.

[12-15] Sinful and mischievous people have filthy mouths. They wink their eyes and speak with pacing feet, and teach with waving hands. They devise trouble with sinful hearts, always starting arguments; so their misfortune will come unexpectedly and they'll be ruined with no escape.

[16-19] Yahweh hates six things: yes, seven enrage God: A self-righteous look, a lying mouth, murdering hands, a sinful heart that imagines evil things, mischievous feet that are swift to run to trouble, a false witness that tells lies, and those that cause disagreements between members of a family.

[20-24] Children, keep these good things I say, and never give up on these words: Always unite them with your heart, and place them around your neck like a prized medal. When you go, they'll lead you; when you sleep, they'll keep you; and when you awake, they'll talk with you. For everything they say and the rules they make are a lamp and a light; and the lesson they teach, is the way of life to protect you from evil strangers and their lying words.

[25-29] Don't be attracted to an ungodly person in your heart; and don't let them tease you with their eyes, for by means of loose people, persons are brought to nothing, and the adulterers will pay with their very life. Can people put fire to their bodies, and their clothes not be burned? Can someone walk on hot ashes, and their feet not be burned? Those that behave adulterously are like this; whoever touches another's spouse won't be found innocent.

[30-35] Don't hate thieves, if they're stealing because they're hungry; but if they're caught, they must give back seven times whatever they took and will have to give everything they own if necessary. But whoever commits adultery is stupid because they destroy their own souls. They'll only get hurt and dishonor; and their shame won't ever be forgotten, because the person offended rages with jealousy. They won't spare you when they come to take revenge on you, and won't be persuaded or be at peace, even if you give them many gifts.

7 [1-5] Children, keep my words, and remember my teachings. Keep my rules, and live; keep my words as your favorite songs. Wear them as rings on your fingers; write them on the pages of your heart. Say to wisdom, you are my family; and call understanding your kin also, so that they can keep you from falling for the words of ungodly people, who only tell you what you want to hear.

[6-22] At the window of my house I looked through the glass and saw among the young people, some without good sense, who passing through the street near the corner, went to a house at dusk and again at midnight, where devious persons that were dressed in seductive clothes met them: (It was those who are loud and stubborn, never staying home, and that come into the streets to wait at the corners.) So they caught them, and kissed them, and with bold faces said to them, "*Today is our payday and we have plenty of food for a party. So we came to meet you, and now, we've found you. We've made our beds with fine linens and bedclothes, and perfumed them with fragrances. Come on; let's make love till morning, pacifying ourselves with our lovers. For our spouses aren't at home, and have gone out of town, taking their money with them, and won't be home for a few days.*" So with their seductiveness they caused those naive people to give in, coercing them with the words they wanted to hear. The young people followed after them like animals going to the slaughter, or as criminals to the correction of jail; till they contracted deadly diseases; and just like a bird rushes into a trap, they don't know that it will cost them their life.

[24-27] So listen to me now, children, and pay attention to my words. Don't let your heart turn to these ways and go astray, for they've wounded many: yes, many strong people have died by these ways. This way quickly leads to death and Hell.

8 [1-9] Doesn't wisdom cry out? And understanding call out? They stand at the top of the hills, and along the ways, crying out at the city limits, at the entrance of the city, at the opening of the doors of public places, saying "*I call to all people; and my voice is to the children of humanity. You immature and stupid people: know wisdom and have an understanding heart. Listen; What I say will be good and excellent things. What I say is the truth; for evil is a disgrace to me. All my words are in goodness; there's nothing evil or filthy in them. They're clear to those that understand, and right to those that want to find knowledge.*

[10-13] Receive my teachings, and don't look for money; look for knowledge rather than great wealth, for wisdom is better than expensive jewels and nothing you can want can be compared to it. I, wisdom, live with responsibility and find out the truth about shrewd lies. The respect of Yahweh is to hate evil, so I hate those who are proud and think too highly of themselves, the evil things they do, and the lies they tell.

[14-19] Counsel is Mine, and sound wisdom, so My understanding has strength. By Me, rulers reign and governments make laws of justice. By Me, those who rule in the governments, the dignitaries, and even all the judges of the earth, are in power. I love those that love Me; and those that look for Me while they're young will find

Me. Riches and honor are with Me; yes, lasting riches and goodness. My profit is better than gold, yes, than fine gold; and My income is better than great wealth.

[20-31] I lead in the way of goodness, clearly in the ways of good judgment, so that I can cause those that love me to gain assets; so that I can fill their treasuries. Before creation, I belonged to Yahweh. I existed from eternity, from the beginning, even before the earth was created. When there were no seas, I existed; when there were no rivers flowing with water, I came to be, even before the hills and mountains were settled . When God had not yet made the earth, or the fields, or even the smallest particle of the dust of the earth; when Yahweh prepared the heavens and set the extent of the oceans, I was there. When God created the clouds above and strengthened the sources of the oceans; when Yahweh gave the word to the sea that the waters shouldn't pass its limits; when God appointed the foundations of the earth, then I was beside Yahweh, as one brought up with God and I was a daily joy, always celebrating before the Creator; celebrating in the habitable part of the earth; and my joy was with the children of humanity.

[32-36] Now listen to me, children: for I'll bless those that keep my ways. Listen to my teaching, and be wise, and don't refuse it. I'll bless those that listen to me, all those that daily watch at my gateway, and wait at my doorposts. For whoever finds me finds life, and will obtain the grace of Yahweh. But those that sin against me wrong their own soul: all those that hate me will find death."

9 [1-12] Wisdom has built a House of God with seven pillars. The meat is ready, the wine is mixed, and the table is set. The maids have been sent out, who call out from the highest places of the city, "Whoever is ignorant, let them turn in here," and as for those that lack understanding, they say to them, "Come, eat the food of wisdom, and drink the wine it has mixed." Leave stupid people, and live; and follow the way of understanding. Those that try to warn a person who argues will only get shamed, and those that counsel a sinful one will be found guilty, so don't warn troublemakers, or they'll only hate you, but if you counsel wise people, they'll love you for it. Teach wise people, and they become wiser: teach godly people, and they grow in learning. The respect of Yahweh is to open up the mind to wisdom, and to have the knowledge of the holy is to have true understanding. For by this wisdom your days will prosper, and the years of your life will be increased. If you are wise, you'll be careful what you do, but if you show hatred, you alone will suffer for it.

[13-18] An ignorant person is loud, stupid, and knows nothing. They sit at the doors of their houses, in the prominent places of the city, to call to those who go by on their way, saying to them, "Whoever is naive, let them turn in here," and as for those that lack understanding, they say to them, "Stolen pleasures are sweet, and secret affairs are pleasant." But those stupid people don't know that the dead are there; and that the guests of those houses are in the depths of Hell.

10 [1-5] These are the sayings of Solomon. A wise child makes a parent glad, but a stupid one is a parent's heartache. Riches gained from evil actions will profit nothing, but goodness saves from death. Yahweh won't allow the soul of godly people to suffer need, but God throws away the possessions of the sinful. Those that act carelessly become poor, but the hands of the hard-working grow rich. Those that work hard are wise, but those that sleep while there's work to be done cause shame.

[6-10] Godly people are blessed, but violence is in the words of the sinful. The memory of godly people is blessed, but the name of the sinful will be forgotten. The wise of heart will learn, but an unwise person will quickly fall when they are accused and punished. Those that do what's right walk unquestionably, but those that do what's wrong will be exposed for who they are. Those that play pranks, winking their eyes and joking, only cause trouble, but an unwise person who is accused will unexpectedly fall.

[11-14] The words of a good person refresh the lives of those around them, but violence fills the words of the sinful. Hatred stirs up trouble, but love protects against all sins. Wisdom is found in the words of those that have understanding, but a good whipping is for the backside of those that have no understanding. The wise increase their knowledge, but the words of stupid people will soon destroy them.

[15-21] The wealth of rich people is their defense, but poverty destroys the poor. The actions of godly people bring life, but the practices of the sinful are evil. Those that keep the ways of a good up-bringing walk in the way of life, but those that refuse to be corrected greatly err. Those that hide hatred with lying words and character attacks are stupid. Sin is found in many words, but those that stop themselves from speaking too quickly are wise. The mouth of godly people is as great wealth, but the hearts of the sinful are worthless. The words of godly people nourish many, but stupid people die for lack of wisdom.

[22-26] The blessing of Yahweh makes people rich, and no sorrow comes with that treasure. It's amusing to a stupid person to cause trouble, but those of understanding have good judgment. Whatever the sinful fear will come to pass, but godly people will be given what they want. The sinful will be wiped out as they would by a passing hurricane, but godly people have a shelter with a strong foundation. As smoke is to the eyes or bitter drink to the tongue, so are lazy people to those that hire them.

[27-32] The respect of Yahweh will prolong days, but the years of the sinful will be cut short. The hope of godly people will be joy, but the prospects of the sinful won't last. The way of Yahweh is strength to godly people, but the sinful will be destroyed. Godly people will never be moved out of their place, but the sinful won't ever be

9

settled in the earth. The mouth of godly people is filled with words of wisdom, but the lying mouth won't have an answer. Godly people know what's acceptable to say, but the words of the sinful speak nothing but empty lies.

11 [1-9] Deceptive business practices are an offense to Yahweh, but fairness is pleasing. When someone has a proud look on their face, then shame soon follows, but those who don't think too much of themselves have wisdom. Goodness will be the guide of godly people, but the filthiness of the sinful will destroy them. Riches won't profit in the day of anger, but goodness delivers from death. The goodness of the godly will direct their steps, but the sinful will fall by their own sins. Goodness will save godly people, but the sinful will be taken in their own naughtiness. When sinful people die, their prospects will die with them and their hope passes away. Godly people are freed out of trouble, and the sinful ones take their place. The words of hypocrites destroy others, but through knowledge, godly people are freed from out of their troubles.

[10-13] The city celebrates when godly people do well, and when the sinful die, there's a joyous outcry. Cities are made known through the blessings of God's people, but they're overthrown by the words of the sinful. Those that lack wisdom hate others, but those of understanding hold their peace. A gossip reveals private matters, but those that are faithful won't tell things that aren't right to speak of.

[14-19] The people are overcome where there are no counselors, but with ample counselors there is wellbeing. Those that act as a guarantor for the ungodly will pay for it, and those who don't act as security have nothing to loose. Gracious people keep their honor as powerful people keep their riches. The merciful do well for their own soul, but cruel people trouble themselves. The sinful do lying things, but those who do what's right will certainly be repaid. As goodness brings life, so those that do what's evil bring about their own deaths.

[20-23] Yahweh is greatly offended by those that have sinful hearts, but those that do what's right are God's pleasure. Though hand joins in hand, the sinful won't go unpunished, but the children of godly people will have freedom. As a gold ring would be in a hog's snout, so are attractive people that are without good judgment. Godly people want good things only, but the prospects of the sinful are only looking for violence.

[24-27] There are those that give much, and yet increase all the more; and there those that keep more than necessary, but it only leads them to poverty. The generous soul will be made plentiful, and those that restore others will be restored themselves. The people will curse those that horde food, but those that sell it to them will be blessed. Those that are careful to look for good will obtain grace, but those that look for trouble will find it.

[28-30] Those that trust in their riches will fall like a winter leaf, but godly people will do well as a budding branch in spring. Those that trouble their own family will inherit nothing but the wind, and for their stupidity, they will serve smarter people than themselves. The harvest of godly people is life-giving; for those that win souls are very wise. Watch and see; if godly people are rewarded on the earth, how much more the ungodly sinners will be repaid in this life, as well.

12 [1-3] Whoever loves to be taught loves knowledge, but those that hate to be corrected are rebellious sinners. Godly people obtain the grace of Yahweh, but God will condemn those that make sinful plans against others. People won't be settled by doing evil, and godly people won't ever be moved out of their place.

[4-8] Honorable mates are a blessing to their spouses, but those that make them ashamed are very hurtful to their souls. The thoughts of the honorable are right, but the advice of the sinful is nothing but lies. The words of the sinful are deadly criticisms, but the words of godly people bring life. The sinful will be overthrown, and will die, but godly people will stay in their homes. People will be praised according to their wisdom, but those who have evil hearts will be hated.

[9-12] Those that are virtually unknown but employ a servant are better than those that make pretense and have need. Good people think on the lives of their animals, but the mercies of the sinful are nothing but cruelty. Those that work hard will be satisfied with their pay, but those that follow people who make empty promises lack understanding. The sinful want the profit of evil people, but the work of godly people pays well.

[13-20] Sinful people are trapped in the sinfulness of their own words, but godly people will overcome their troubles. People will be satisfied with the good their words bring, and the reward of their work will be given to them. The ways of stupid people may be right in their own eyes, but those that listen to good counsel are truly wise. A stupid person's anger is presently known, but a sensible person guards against the embarrassment of careless words. Those that speak truth show what's the right thing to do, but a liar shows the wrong thing to do. There are sinful people whose words pierce like a blade, but the words of wise people bring healthy emotions to everyone. The words of truth will be settled forever, but those who lie will only have their way a little while. Lies are in the hearts of those that imagine evil, but the counselors of peace have joy.

[21-23] No permanent damage will happen to godly people, but the sinful will be filled with their fair share of hurt. Yahweh hates liars, but those that are truthful are God's joy. A cautious person hides knowledge until the right time to make it known, but the heart of stupid people makes all its stupidity quickly known.

[24-28] The hand of a hard-working person will be promoted to leadership, but lazy workers will always be controlled. Sadness in the heart of people overwhelms them, but a good word makes them glad. Godly people are more worthy of praise than others, but evil ways will seduce the sinful. Lazy people don't roast what they take in

hunting, but the substance of hard-working people is precious. goodness is the way to life; and there is no death when you go that way.

13 [1-3] Smart children listen to their parent's teachings, but the disobedient ignore the wisdom of their parent's words. People will do well by the good their words bring, but the souls of the sinful will live on violence. Those that guard the words of their mouth will save their lives, but those that don't know how to keep their mouths closed will destroy themselves.

[4-9] The soul of the lazy wants everything and has nothing, but the soul of hard-working people will have plenty. Good people hate lying, but sinful people are hateful, and will come to shame. goodness keeps those that are good in the way, but evil overthrows the sinner. There are those that save up their money to become rich, yet they have nothing of real value, and there are those that give so sacrificially that they become poor, yet they have great riches. The rich will give all they have for a ransom to save their life, but the poor have no need of concern. The light of godly people burns brightly, but the fire of the sinful will be put out.

[10-12] Arguments come only by pride, but the well-advised have great wisdom. Wealth gotten by chasing after empty dreams will disappear, but those that earn by working hard will increase their income. Hope postponed makes one sick at heart, but when the wanted thing comes, it brings life-giving joy.

[13-19] Whoever hates the Word of Yahweh will be destroyed, but those that respect the Word of God will be rewarded. The words of the wise are the way to life, to escape from deadly traps. Good understanding gives grace, but the sinful will have a hard life. All sensible people will argue knowledgeably, but stupid people only show their stupidity. A lying news bearer falls into trouble, but a faithful spokesperson is a great help. Those that refuse to be taught will become poor and be ashamed, but those that listen to correction will be honored. When a goal is reached, it is sweet to the soul, but stupid people don't want to give up their evil ways.

[20-25] Those that walk with wise people will become smarter, but a friend of stupid people will be destroyed by lack of wisdom. Evil chases after the sinful, but good will be returned to godly people. Godly people leave an inheritance to their grandchildren, but the wealth of the sinful will be given to more honorable people. The poor make the food in their pantry last a long time, but there are those that starve by lack of judgment. The parents that neglect the discipline of their children don't really care about them, but those that love them punish them when necessary. Godly people eat to the satisfying of their soul, but the belly of the sinful will be hungry.

14 [1-4] Wise people build up their houses, but stupid people destroy them with their own hands. Those that live honestly respect Yahweh, but those who have filthy ways hate God. A sign of pride is in the words of stupid people, but the words of wise people save them. A place is clean where there aren't any animals, but wherever they are will prosper.

[5-9] A faithful witness won't lie, but a false witness will speak many lies. A troublemaker looks for wisdom, and doesn't find it, but knowledge comes easy to those of understanding. Leave the presence of stupid people, when you don't find the words of knowledge in them. The wisdom of the sensible is to understand their way, but stupid people are made stupid by their lying. Stupid people mock at sin, but godly people show grace to those who change their ways.

[10-14] No one can know a person's sadness but their own heart; and no one can intrude on someone else's joy. The houses of the sinful will be overthrown, but the home of godly people will do well. Sinful ways may seem right to people, but their end only brings death. Even in laughter, some hearts are sorrowful; and in the end, their partying is hopeless. The hearts of those who won't change their ways will be filled with their own evil, and godly people will be satisfied with themselves.

[15-19] Naive people believe every word they're told, but sensible people are cautious in their ways. Wise people fear and stop doing evil things, but stupid people rant and rave and are quite sure of themselves. Those who quickly get angry act stupidly, and those who make sinful plans are hated. The naive only get stupidity, but the sensible are rewarded with knowledge. The evil will be humbled before the good; the sinful are stopped at the gates of godly people.

[20-24] The poor are hated even by their own neighbors, but the rich will have many friends. It's a sin to hate your neighbor, but those that have mercy on the poor are happy. It's wrong to make evil plans, but mercy and truth will come to those that plan good things. Any kind of working will bring income, but only talking about it leads to poverty. The reward of wise people is their riches, but thoughtless people are stupid.

[25-30] A true witness frees souls, but a false witness speaks lies. The faithful have a strong confidence in Yahweh, and their children will have a safe place to live. The respect of Yahweh is the source of life, in which to escape from deadly traps. A ruler's honor is in the number of people who give them their support, but a government is destroyed by a lack of people to support them. Those that are slow to anger are of great understanding, but those who are quick tempered show nothing but their own stupidity. A sensible heart brings life to the body, but jealousy makes one wastes away.

[31-35] Those that keep down the poor blame their Creator, but those that honor God have mercy on the poor. The sinful are driven away in their evil, but godly people have the hope of everlasting life even in their death. Wisdom rests in the heart of those that have understanding, but those that stay with stupid people will be shown

11

to be stupid themselves. Goodness brings honor to a nation, but sin is a shame to any people. Wise people will be favored by rulers, but the anger of rulers will be against those who cause shame.

15 [1-5] A thoughtful answer calms anger, but severe words only stir it up. The mouths of wise people use knowledge rightly, but the words of stupid people pour out stupidity. The eyes of Yahweh are everywhere, seeing the evil and the good. A clean mouth is life-giving, but a filthy mouth abuses the spirit. Stupid people hate their parent's teaching, but those that think about a warning are sensible.

[6-10] Great wealth is in the home of godly people; but much trouble comes with the income of sinful people. The words of wise people give knowledge, but there is no knowledge in the heart of stupid people. The offerings of the sinful are an insult to God, but the prayers of godly people please Yahweh. The ways of the sinful are an insult to Yahweh, but God loves those who do what's right. Correction is dreadful to those that leave from God's way, and those that hate correction will die.

[11-15] If Hell and destruction are looked at closely by Yahweh, how much more then are the hearts of people? The disobedient never love those that warn them, and they won't go to wise people for advice. A happy heart makes a smiling face, but a heart full of sorrow shatters the spirit. The hearts of those that have understanding look for knowledge, but the words of stupid people live on stupidity. All the days of abused people are horrible, but those that have a happy heart always indulge on the good things in their heart.

[16-19] It's better to have little wealth with the respect of Yahweh than to have great treasure with much difficulty. It's better to have a dinner of herbs where love is, than to have a side of beef and hatred along with it. Angry people stir up trouble, but those who keep calm will quiet down arguments. The way of lazy people is blocked off like a hedge of thorns, but the way of godly people is a clear path.

[20-23] A wise child makes a parent glad, but stupid children hate their parents. Stupidity is funny to those who have no wisdom, but those of understanding do what's right. Good intentions will fall through without counsel, but with wise advisors one's purposes will come to pass. Their answers will make people happy: a word spoken at just the right time is so good!

[24-27] To the wise, the way of life is to look for heaven above, so that they can escape from Hell beneath. Yahweh will destroy the house of those who think they are better than others, but God will make the boundary of the single parent safe. The thoughts of the sinful are an insult to Yahweh, but the words of the innocent are pleasant. Those that are greedy for money will trouble their own household; but those that hate bribery will live.

[28-33] The hearts of godly people think before answering, but the words of angry people pour out sinful things. Yahweh is far away from the sinful, but hears the prayers of godly people. Joy in the eyes makes the heart celebrate, and a good word brings health. Those who listen to the correction of life are wise people. Those that refuse training hate their own soul, but those that listen to correction receive understanding. The teaching of wisdom shows respect for Yahweh; but you must humble yourself before gaining honor.

16 [1-6] The plans of the heart and the answers of the mouth are from Yahweh. The acts of human beings may be right in their own eyes; but Yahweh tests the intentions of their spirits. Commit every thing you do to Yahweh, and your thoughts will be settled. Yahweh, You've made all things for Yourself: yes, even sinful people for Judgment Day. All those who think they are better than others are an insult to Yahweh: though hand joins in hand, they won't go unpunished.

[6-9] By mercy and truth sin is removed, and by the respect of Yahweh people stop doing evil things. When a person's ways please Yahweh, even their enemies are at peace with them. It's better to have little wealth and do what's right than great income without any right to it. People's hearts plan their ways, but Yahweh directs all their steps.

[10-15] The words of wise rulers make fair judgments: their mouths never speak with poor judgment. Honesty in business practices comes from Yahweh: every fair business decision is directed by God. It's an insult to wise rulers to do evil: their reign is strengthened by doing what's right. Leaders take pleasure in good words; and God loves those that say what's right. The anger of rulers is like a death sentence, but a wise person will calm it down. Life is in the way a ruler looks at someone; and the ruler's grace is as a cloud bringing spring rain.

[16-19] It's so much better to get wisdom than gold and to get understanding rather than silver! The highway of godly people exits from the way of evil: those that keep going in the right direction will save their souls. Those who think themselves better than others will be ruined and brought down. It's better to have humility of spirit with those of lower class, than to divide lots of money with those who think they're better than others.

[20-25] Those that handle a matter wisely will find good, and whoever trusts in Yahweh will find peace. The wise-hearted will be called sensible and others will learn from their agreeable words. Understanding is a source of life to those that have it, but what stupid people learn is nothing but more stupidity. The heart teaches wise people what words to say. Pleasant words are agreeable to the soul, and bring health to the body. Though sinful ways may seem right to a person, the end of it only leads to death.

[26-30] Those that work are only working for themselves because their hunger drives them. Ungodly people stir up evil, and their words are like a fire that burns up everything. Sinful people start trouble, and gossips divide best

friends. Violent people tempt others, and lead them into ways that aren't good. They imagine sinful things, and use their words to bring the evil to pass.

[31-33] Silver hair is a crown of glory, if it is gotten by living right. Those that are even-tempered are better than the powerful; and those that rule their own spirit than those who can take a whole city hostage. Though the coin is flipped by chance, the side it lands on is guided by Yahweh.

17 [1-4] A scrap of food with peace is better than a house full of everything you need with trouble. A wise caretaker will manage a child that causes shame, and will have part of the inheritance among the children. Silver and gold are refined by heat, but Yahweh purifies the heart. A sinner listens to false words; and a liar listens to naughtiness.

[5-8] Whoever ridicules the poor blames their Creator, and those who are pleased about the bad things that happen to others won't go unpunished. Grandchildren are the honor of elderly people; and parents are the praise of their children. A great speech doesn't suit a stupid person any more than lying words do a ruler. A gift is as a precious stone in the eyes of the one that has it: wherever it turns up, it prospers.

[9-12] Those that overlook a sin look for love; but those that gossip about it can separate the closest of friends. A single correction enters more into a wise person than an hundred whippings into a stupid person. Evil people look only for rebellion, so an unmerciful spokesperson with bad news will be sent to them. A person is better off meeting a bear robbed of her cubs than meeting a stupid person with no sense.

[13-15] Whoever returns evil for good, evil will stay in their house. The beginning of trouble is like when one releases water out of a dam: so shut off hateful words before they gush out. Those who say that sinful people are right and the innocent are wrong, both of them are insults to Yahweh.

[16-18] Why will a stupid person pay any amount of money to get an education, yet learn nothing from it? A friend loves unconditionally, while families are born for trouble. People with no understanding shake hands, and put up collateral for their friends debts.

[19-21] Those that love sin also love trouble, and those that build high gates invite a break-in. Those who have sinful hearts find no good, and those who have filthy mouths get themselves into trouble. Those that bring along stupid people do it to their own sorrow, and the parents of a stupid child have no joy.

[22-25] A merry heart is good for your health like medicine, but continual depression is like a slow death. Wicked people give bribes in order to keep the law from being carried out fairly. Wisdom is the aim of those that have understanding; but a stupid person's eyes wander freely. Stupid children are a grief to their parents, and bitterness to those that gave birth to them.

[26-28] It isn't right to put good people in jail, nor to condemn officers for being fair. Those that have knowledge are careful with their words, and those of understanding are peaceful. Even stupid people that hold their peace are thought to be smart, and those that hold their tongues are believed to be people of understanding.

18 [1-3] Those that have set themselves apart search for wisdom and always brag about their knowledge trying to get what they want. Those who are stupid have no joy in understanding anything but their own heart. When sinful people come, then hatred also comes, and with their shame comes a warning.

[4-8] The words of a person's mouth are as dangerous as deep waters, but the wellspring of wisdom is like a flowing creek. It isn't good to accept the word of a sinful person, in order to judge godly people and overthrow them. A stupid person's words bring disagreements, and their mouths call for a whipping. The words of stupid mouths are the destruction and the trap of their own souls. The words of a gossip are as wounds, and cause ulcers to form in the inner parts of the belly.

[9-12] Those that are lazy in their work are like those who waste things. The Name of Yahweh is a strong refuge: godly people will safely hide in it. The rich people's wealth is their refuge; they're pride divides them from others like a high wall. The hearts of people are haughty before their destruction; but humility must come before honor.

[13-15] Those that answer a matter before they fully hear it, are stupid and it only brings shame on them. The strength of the spirit will keep a person safe in their illness; but a wounded spirit can save no one. The hearts of sensible people grasp knowledge and the ears of wise people listen for knowledge.

[16-18] A person who brings a gift will be allowed into the presence of great people. Those that take up their own cause first seem right; but someone else will come and investigate them thoroughly. The flip of a coin stops arguments, and decides between the most powerful.

[19-21] An offended family member is harder to be won over than a whole city and their disagreements are like the bars of a great house. A person's belly will be satisfied by what their own words say; they're filled with the results of their words. Life and death are in the power of one's words, and those that love the words of their own mouth will suffer the consequences of them.

[22-24] Whoever finds a spouse finds a good thing, and obtains the grace of Yahweh. The poor begs; but the rich answers them roughly. People that want to have friends must show themselves friendly, and God is a friend that sticks closer than blood kin.

13

19 [1-3] The poor who do what's right are better than those who are filthy in their words and act stupidly. It isn't good for a soul to be without knowledge; and those who act hastily will sin. The stupidity of people makes their ways evil, and their hearts fight against Yahweh.

[4-6] Wealth makes many friends; but the poor are separated even from their neighbors. A false witness that speaks lies won't go unpunished, nor escape. Many will ask for the grace of a ruler, and everyone is a friend to those that give gifts.

[7-9] If the whole family of a poor person hates them: how much more will their friends leave them? Even though they keep on calling them, they won't be answered by them. Those that receive wisdom love their own soul: those that keep their understanding will find good. A false witness won't be unpunished, and those that speak lies will eventually die and come to judgment.

[10-12] It isn't fitting for stupid people to enjoy themselves; much less for a subject to succeed to a position over a ruler. The good judgment of people holds back their anger; and it's to their praise to forgive a sin against them. The ruler's anger is as the loud roaring of a lion; but their grace is as refreshing as the dew on the grass.

[13-15] Stupid children are the misfortune of their parents, and the naggings of a spouse are like a faucet that always drips. A house and riches are the inheritance of parents and a sensible spouse is from Yahweh. Laziness brings a deep sleep; and a lazy person will suffer hunger.

[16-18] Those that keep the Words of Yahweh keep their own soul; but those that hate them will die. Those that give to the poor lend to Yahweh; and that which they have given, God will repay again. Correct your children while there is still hope, and don't let yourself spare them because of their tears.

[19-21] People of great anger will suffer punishment, but if you save them from the consequences, you'll have to do it over and over. Listen to counsel, and learn, so that you can be wise in the end of your days. There are many plans in a person's heart; Yet the Words of Yahweh will stand.

[22-24] People want kindness, and a poor person has more kindness than a liar. The respect of Yahweh leads to life, and those that have it will be satisfied and won't be visited with evil. Lazy people pat their bellies, and won't so much as bring their hand to their mouth again.

[25-29] Punish a troublemaker, and the youthful will beware: warn those that have understanding and they'll gain knowledge. Those that misuse and abuse their parents, chasing them away, are the children that cause shame and bring blame on them. Children, stop listening to false training that causes you to err from the words of knowledge. An ungodly witness mocks judgment, and the words of evil people live on sin. Judgment is prepared for troublemakers and whippings for the backsides of stupid people.

20 [1-3] Wine mocks people in the end and strong drinks make them rage. Whoever is deceived by alcohol is unwise. A fearsome ruler is as a roaring lion: whoever provokes one to anger sins against their own soul. It's an honor for people to end their fighting, but every stupid person will have the last word.

[4-6] Lazy people won't work because of the cold; so they'll beg on payday, and get nothing. Counsel in the heart of a person is like water in a deep well; but those of understanding will draw it out. Most people will brag loudly about their own goodness, but who can find a faithful person?

[7-9] People who are fair do what's right and their children will be blessed by them. A ruler that sits in the seat of judgment makes a person stop their evil ways with a look of the eyes. Who can say, I've made my heart clean, I'm innocent from my sin?

[10-12] Unequal pay and dishonest business practices are both an insult to Yahweh. Even children are known by their behaviors, whether their actions are innocent and right or not. Yahweh makes ears to hear and eyes to see.

[13-15] Don't love sleep, or you'll become poor; open your eyes and you'll be thankful for what you have. *This is no deal, this is no deal*, the buyers say, but when they leave, they brag to themselves that it was a real bargain. There is gold, and many rubies, but the words of knowledge are as precious as jewels.

[16-18] Take the shirt off the back of those that guarantee a debt for an untrustworthy person: take a payment from them for the ungodly. The food of lies is sweet to people; but later their mouths will be filled with grit. All purposes are settled by counsel, so only challenge someone with good advice.

[19-21] Those that gossip reveal private matters: so don't mix with those that only tell you what you want to hear. Whoever curses their parents, will be put out in the darkest night. An inheritance can be gotten hastily at the beginning; but it won't be blessed in the end.

[22-24] Don't say, "*I'll get even for the evil done to me*;" but wait on Yahweh to save you. Unequal pay is an insult to Yahweh; and dishonest business practices aren't good. A person's direction is of Yahweh; so how can they then understand their own way?

[25-27] It's a trap to those that take of that which is holy, and only after making a promise, ask about it. A wise ruler makes the sinful run away, and destroys them. The spirit of a person is the light of Yahweh, which searches the innermost soul.

14

[28-30] Mercy and truth saves rulers and their seats are upheld by mercy. Strength is the praise of young people, and the loveliness of elderly people is their grey heads. As the bruises of an injury disperses a wound: so a whipping cleanses the inmost soul.

21 [1-3] A ruler's heart is in the hand of Yahweh; it turns according to the will of God just like the water in a river. A person's ways may be right in their own eyes, but Yahweh thinks about what's in their heart. Doing what's right and having good judgment is more acceptable to Yahweh than making offerings.

[4-6] A self-important look, and a proud heart, and the behaviors of the ungodly, are all sinful. The thoughts of the careful produce much; but those that act too quickly will lack what they need. Treasures gotten by a lying mouth are useless to those who are insecure and only look for their own death.

[7-9] The thefts of the sinful will destroy them; because they refuse to recognize right from wrong. The ways of evil people are sinful and shocking, but the acts of the innocent are right. It's better to stay in a corner of the attic, than with an angry person in a fine house.

[10-12] The soul of the sinful hopes for evil to happen to others and they have no grace for them. When the troublemaker is punished, the youthful are made wiser, and when sensible people are taught, they receive knowledge. Good people wisely think on the household of the sinful: because God overthrows them for their evil.

[13-15] Whoever does not listen to the cry of the poor, will also cry, and won't be heard. A surprise gift pacifies strong anger as a bribe in the pocket prevents punishment. It's a pleasure to fair people to judge rightly, but destruction will come to those who practice sin.

[16-18] Those that wander from true knowledge will live as the dead. Those that love pleasure, wine, and fine foods will be poor and not rich. The sinful will take the punishment for honorable and godly people.

[19-21] It's better to stay in the countryside, than with an angry person who starts arguments. There are coveted treasures in the homes of wise people; but stupid people spend all their money on empty pleasures. Those that do what's right and have mercy will find life, justice, and honor.

[22-24] A wise person overwhelms the confidence of a strong person. Whoever guards the words of their mouth keeps their soul from trouble. Those that act in prideful anger are troublemakers who think themselves better than others.

[25-27] Lazy people refuse to work and their needs overwhelm them, while they greedily crave things all day long. But godly people give generously without sparing. The offerings of the sinful are an insult to God and all the more, when they bring it with lies.

[28-31] Though a false witness dies the people that heard the matter will continue to tell it. Sinful people have stubborn faces, but godly people change their ways when convinced of a wrong. There's no wisdom, nor understanding, nor counsel against Yahweh. Soldiers are prepared for the day of battle, but their safety is of Yahweh.

22 [1-4] Choose a good name rather than great riches, and loving grace rather than silver and gold. The rich and poor gather together because Yahweh is the Creator of them all. Sensible people foresee evil and leave, but the naive go on and are caught in their ignorance. Riches, honor, and life come by humility and the respect of Yahweh.

[5-7] The way of the sinful is always blocked, but those that keep their souls won't be stopped by anything. Train your children in the way they should go, and when they're old, they won't leave from it. The rich rule over the poor and the borrower is indebted to the lender.

[8-10] Those that keep on sinning are useless, and their strong anger won't get anything done. Those that are generous will be blessed; for they give of their own food to the poor. Throw out the troublemaker, and arguments will leave as well; yes, fighting and blame will end.

[11-13] The ruler will befriend those that love a heart of innocence for their graceful words. The eyes of Yahweh save the knowledgeable, and defeat the lies of the sinner. Lazy people say, "*There's danger outside; I'll be slain in the streets if I go out.*"

[14-16] The mouths of ungodly people are like deep graves in which those who Yahweh hates will fall in. Stupidity is fixed in the hearts of children; but a whipping will drive it out of them. Those that keep down the poor to increase their own riches, and those that bribe the rich, will surely become poor.

[17-21] Listen to me and hear the words of a wise person, and apply your heart to my knowledge. It's a pleasant thing if you keep them within you; they'll be restated by your own words. I've made them known to you today, so that your trust can be in Yahweh. Have I not written great things to you with counsel and knowledge, so that I might make you clearly know the words of truth and that You'll answer with the words of truth to those that ask of you?

[22-25] Don't steal from the poor, because they're poor; nor keep down the suffering in the city, because Yahweh will plead their case, and ruin the one that destroys them. Have no friendship with angry people; never go along with very angry people or you'll learn their ways, and your soul will be trapped.

15

[26-29] Don't be one of those who accepts credit, building up great debts. If you can't pay it back, they'll take away your own bed from under you. Don't ignore the rules, which your parents have set. Hard-working people will stand before rulers and many of their superiors.

23 [1-8] When you sit to eat with a superior, carefully think about what's before you and put a blade to your throat, if you are one with an appetite. Don't want their fine foods: for they're of no value. Don't work to get rich, but put an end to your own judgment. Don't set your eyes on that which you don't have, for riches certainly make themselves wings and fly away as an eagle toward heaven. Don't eat the food of those that have evil in their eyes, nor want their fine foods: For they are just as they think in their heart: "*Eat and drink*," they say to you; but their hearts aren't really with you. That which you've eaten you'll vomit up, and you'll lose your sweet words.

[9-11] Don't speak to stupid people: for they'll hate the wisdom of your words. Don't remove the old boundary lines; and don't break into the property of a single parent's child: For their Savior is powerful and will plead their case against you.

[12-16] Apply your heart to teaching, and your ears to the words of knowledge. Don't withhold firm discipline from your children: for if you whip them with a switch when they need it, they won't die. If you whip them with the switch to correct them, you'll save their soul from Hell. Children, if your heart is wise, my heart will celebrate. Yes, my control will relax and I'll be cheerful when your words speak good things.

[17-21] Don't let your heart be jealous of the sinful, but respect Yahweh always. For surely there's an end to evil things; and your expectation won't be a disappointment. Listen, children, and be wise, and guide your heart in the way of Yahweh. Don't be found among drunks or among riotous gluttons; because the drunkard and the glutton will both become poor, and for their laziness they will be clothed with rags.

[22-25] Listen to your parents who created you, and don't hate them when they're old. Find the truth, and don't throw it away; keep wisdom, teaching, and understanding, also. The parents of godly people will greatly celebrate, and those that have wise children will enjoy them. Your parents that created you will be glad and celebrate.

[26-28] Children, give me your heart, and let your eyes watch what I do. For adulterers are like a deep ditch; and the ungodly are like a narrow grave, all waiting for innocent victims, and increasing the sinful among the people.

[29-35] Those that drink wine and look for mixed drinks have misery and sorrow, are easily angered, and babble unintelligibly! They have wounds with no explanation and bloodshot eyes! So don't stare at red wine when it swirls and sparkles in the glass, because in the end it poisons like a snake, and hurts like a snakebite. Your eyes will see the ungodly, and your mouth will speak filthy things. You'll be as those that sink in the depths of the sea, like those that have gone to sleep in the crow's nest of a ship. "*They've injured me,*" you'll say, and "*I wasn't dizzy; they've beaten me, and I didn't feel it: when will I awake so I can have another drink.*"

24 [1-4] Don't be jealous of evil people, nor want to be with them, because their heart only destroys and they talk with mischievous words. A home is built through wisdom; and it is settled by understanding, and by knowledge the rooms will all be filled with pleasing and precious riches.

[5-9] Wise people are strong; yes, those with knowledge become stronger, because they challenge only with good advice, and with many counselors they're safe. Wisdom is too great for stupid people: they don't dare open their mouths in public. Those that plan ways to do evil will be called mischievous persons. Stupid thoughts are sinful, and troublemakers are an insult to everyone.

[10-12] You have little strength if you faint in the day of trouble. If you don't try to save those that are about to kill themselves, and those that are about to die; saying, "*See, we didn't know it;*" doesn't Yahweh who searches the heart think on it? And won't the God who keeps your soul know it and give to every person according to their own acts?

[13-14] Children, the knowledge of wisdom will be as sweet to your soul as eating honey or a honeycomb for it's sweet taste; and when you've found it, there'll be a sweet reward, and your expectations won't be disappointed.

[15-16] Sinners don't stalk outside the homes of godly people; don't destroy their resting place, because even if a good person falls seven times, they'll rise up again, while the sinful will wallow in their trouble. Don't celebrate when your enemy falls, and don't let your heart be glad whenever they stumble, or Yahweh will see it, and be displeased, and not be angry at them.

[19-20] Don't trouble yourself because of evil people, nor be jealous of the sinful, because there'll be no reward for them and their lives will be snuffed out like a candle. Children, respect Yahweh! Honor rulers and don't mess with those that are unpredictable, for their misfortune will come unexpectedly; and who knows what will ruin them?

[23-26] This is also said by smart people: *It isn't good to show favoritism to people that are being judged.* Those who say that sinful people are good will be cursed and nations will look down on them; but they'll be pleased and bless those that punish them. People will kiss the mouths of those that give a good answer.

[27-34] Put your outside work in order first, getting the land ready; then later prepare your home. Don't be a witness against others without cause; and don't lie to them. Don't say, "*I'll get even for what they have done to me and I'll do to them just what they did to me.*" I went by the property of a lazy person and by the home of someone

16

with no understanding; It was all grown over with weeds, and thorns covered the outside of it, and the fence was broken down. When I saw this and thought about it well, I looked on it, learning a lesson. A little sleep, a little slumber, a little folding of hands to rest: so your poverty comes as a homeless drifter; and your need as an armed robber.

25 [1-3] These are also the sayings of Solomon, which the people of Hezekiah, the ruler of Judah copied out. It's the glory of God to hide things, but the honor of rulers is to understand the matter. The hearts of rulers are as unsearchable as the heaven is for height, and as the earth is for depth.

[4-7] Melt the dross from the silver, and it will become finer. Take sinful people away from the presence of rulers, and the ruler's reign will be settled in goodness. Don't push yourself into the presence of rulers, and don't put yourself in the place of great people. It's better that it be said to you, "Come here;" than that you should be taken away from the presence of the ruler that you've just seen.

[8-10] Don't argue too hastily, or you won't know what to do in the end, when someone else has put you to shame. Argue your case with someone in person; and don't gossip about it to someone else, because those that hear it may put you to shame, and your infamy won't ever be lived down.

[11-13] A word truly spoken is like golden apples in a bowl of silver. As an earring with a pendant of fine gold, so is a wise warning on a respectful ear. As the cold snow is at harvest time, so are faithful messengers to those that send them because they refresh their soul.

[14-16] Whoever boasts themselves of an untrue talent are like the clouds and wind without any rain. A ruler is convinced when you don't give up, and a gentle word breaks their will. If you find honey, then eat as much as is necessary for you, or else you'll be too full and vomit it up.

[17-20] Leave your neighbor's house before they're tired of you, and hate you. People that lie against others are like a sledge hammer, a blade, and a sharp arrow. Having confidence in the unfaithful in time of trouble is like having a broken tooth, or a foot out of joint. Like those that take away a person's coat in cold weather, and as vinegar fizzes on baking soda, so are those that sing songs to a heavy heart.

[21-23] If your enemies are hungry give them food to eat, and if they're thirsty give them water to drink; because when you do, you'll make them hate you with a burning jealousy, but you'll be rewarded by Yahweh. Like the north wind drives rain away: an angry look will put an end to a back-talking mouth.

[24-28] It's better to stay in the corner of the attic, than with a difficult person in a fine house. As cold water is to a thirsty soul, so is good news from far away. A good person giving in to the sinful is as muddy as upset water, and as poisonous as a contaminated creek. As it isn't good for someone to eat too much honey, there is no honor for person looking for their own glory. Those that have no self-control are like an unprotected city without boundaries.

26 [1-9] Like snow is not wanted in summer and as rain is not wanted in harvest time, nor is it fitting to give respect to a stupid person. As the migrating bird, and as the soaring swallow, so punishment won't come without cause. A whip is for the horse, a bridle is for the ass, and a switch is for the backside of stupid people. Don't answer a stupid person to match their stupidity, or you'll also become like them. Give an answer to a stupid person to match their stupidity, or they'll become conceited. Those that send a message by the hand of a stupid person cuts off their own way and they'll soon be destroyed. As the legs of the lame are unequal, so is a report in the words of a stupid person. As those that tie a stone into a slingshot, so are those that give honor to a stupid person. As a thorn goes up into the hand of a drunkard, so is a story in the words of stupid people.

[10-12] The great God that formed all things repays stupid and sinful people, both. As dogs eat their own vomit, so stupid people return to their stupidity. Do you see all those know-it-alls? There's more hope of a stupid person than of them.

[13-17] The lazy say, "Trouble's coming; there's danger in the streets;" and as the door flips on its hinges, so lazy people turn over in their beds. The lazy pat their hand on their belly; but it's too much trouble for them to take another bite. The lazy think they're smarter than seven reasonable people. Those that pass by the arguments of others and interfere are like those who devil a dog when they pass by it.

[18-22] As a crazy person that throws deadly firebombs, so is a person that lies to others, and says, "I'm just joking!" Where there is no wood, the fire goes out: so trouble dies down where there's no gossip; but as coals added to burning coals, and wood added to fire; so is a divisive person that starts arguments. The words of a gossip are like ulcers in the belly.

[23-28] Insistent words with a misleading heart are like a piece of broken ceramic glazed with silver dross. Those that hate others are critical with their words and tell cruel lies. When they speak reasonably, don't believe them: for there are seven more shameful lies in their hearts. Those that cover hatred with lies will expose their evil to everyone. Whoever murders someone will only dig a grave for themselves; and a tombstone will fall back on the one who places it. A lying mouth attacks those it hates, and a mouth that only tells them what they want to hear will later destroy them.

27 [1-2] Don't brag about tomorrow; because you never know what a day may bring. Let someone else praise you and not your own mouth; allow a stranger to praise you and not your own words.

17

[3-5] A stupid person's anger is heavier than stone or wet sand. Rage is cruel, and anger is outrageous; but no one is able to stand before jealousy! Open rejection is better than secret love.

[6-8] The wounds of a friend are faithful; but an enemy's kiss is full of lies. A person who is full can't bear sweets; but anything is sweet to a hungry person. It's as dangerous for those that run away from home as it is for birds that stray from their nest.

[9-10] As fragrant oils and perfume make the heart joyful, so the cheerful counsel of a person's friend is sweet. Don't leave your own friend or your parent's friend alone in time of need, nor go into your family's home in the day of your misfortune. A close neighbor is better than a distant family member.

[11-12] Children, be wise, and make me happy, so that I can reply to everybody that criticizes me. If you are sensible people, you'll foresee trouble and get out of the way; but if you are naïve, you'll keep on going, and get only what you deserve.

[13-16] Take the shirt off the back of those that bail out untrustworthy people, and hold it for security from those that guarantee the debts of the ungodly. Those that loudly applaud their friends early in the morning will be cursed by them. A divisive person is very much like the constant dripping of a very rainy day: It's as useless to try to stop them as to try to stop the wind from blowing, or to catch oil in your hand.

[17-19] As metal sharpens metal; so are those that sharpen the attitudes of their friends. Whoever keeps the fig tree will eat its fruit: so those that work well for the owner of a company will be honored. As a face's reflection in the water, so the heart reflects the person.

[20-22] The eyes of a person are never satisfied, just like Hell and destruction are never full. As silver and gold are refined; so people will shine by the praise they receive. Though you whip a stupid person mercilessly, you can't beat their stupidity out of them.

[23-27] Be careful to know the state of your property, and look well to what you have, because riches aren't forever and don't pass down to every generation. But as sure as spring and summer bring in the harvest, if you budget a small amount for your clothing and a larger sum for your property, you'll have money enough for your food and for the upkeep of your family.

28 [1-3] Immoral people are anxious and run when no one is chasing them, but godly people are as bold as lions. Too many rulers make a nation rebel, but those of understanding and knowledge save it. A poor person that keeps down the poor is like a pouring rain which destroys food crops.

[4-8] Those that give up on the Word of Yahweh approve the sinful, but those that keep the Word of God challenge them about their wrongs. Evil people have no judgment, but people who look for Yahweh understand everything. Good poor people are better than evil rich people. Those who keep the Word of God are wise children, but those that are friends of riotous people shame their parents. Those that get richer by lending for interest and gaining unearned income will collect it only for others who will care for the poor.

[9-12] Even the prayers of those that don't listen to the Word of God are an insult to the Almighty. Whoever causes godly people to go astray in an evil way, will fall into their own trap, but godly people will find good things. Rich people think they know it all; but poor people who are smart thoroughly question them. When godly people celebrate, there's a great celebration, but when the sinful secretly rise to power, the people quietly disappear.

[13-14] Those that hide their sins won't prosper, but whoever admits and turns from them will have mercy. Those that always respect Yahweh are happy, but those that ignore the Word of God will get into trouble.

[15-16] As a roaring lion, and a raging bear; so are sinful rulers over poor people. The ruler that keeps down the people lacks understanding, but those that aren't greedy will prolong their days.

[17-18] People that violently murder any person will run from judgment till the day they die; so let no one help them. Whoever does well will be saved, but those who act in hateful ways will quickly fall.

[19-22] Those that work hard will have plenty of food, but those that follow after worthless people will have poverty enough. Faithful people will live with blessings, but those that want to get rich quickly aren't innocent. The favoritism of people is not good: for a small favor those people will go bad. Those who want to get rich quickly have eyes full of evil, and never think that poverty will come on them.

[23-28] Those that correct a person after a wrong will find more favor than those that only tell them what they want to hear. Whoever says it's no sin to steal from their parents are playing with destruction. Those that think themselves better than others stir up trouble, but those that put their trust in Yahweh will be richly rewarded. Those that trust in their own hearts are stupid, but whoever walks wisely will be saved. Those that give to the poor won't lack, but those that ignore them will have much trouble. When the sinful rise to power, people go into hiding, but when they die, godly people step up.

29 [1-2] Stubborn people, who have been corrected often, will be unexpectedly destroyed having no escape. When godly people are in power, the people celebrate, but when the sinful rule, the people mourn.

[3-5] Whoever loves wisdom causes their parents to celebrate, but those that keep company with loose people waste their living. By good judgment rulers make the land safe, but those that take bribes make it fall. People that only tell others what they want to hear set a trap for them.

18

[6-10] Evil persons will be trapped by their own sin, but godly people will sing and celebrate. Godly people think on the case of the poor, but the sinful don't even want to know about it. Rebellious people upset a city, but wise people calm their own anger. If a wise person argues with a stupid person there's no peace, whether they rage or laugh. Cruel people hate the good, but fair people look for the good.

[11-14] Stupid people speak their mind before hearing the whole story, but wise people listen and think before answering. If a ruler listens to lies, their staff members will be sinful as well. Yahweh gives light to the eyes of both the poor and the liars. The reign of rulers that faithfully judge the poor will be settled forever.

[15-17] A switch and correction give good judgment, but undisciplined children bring shame on their parents. When the sinful increase, sin multiplies, but godly people will live to see their downfall. Correct your children and they'll let you rest; yes, they'll give joy to your soul.

[18-21] Where there's no hope for the future, people will waste away and die, but those that keep their eyes on the Word of God are happy. An employee won't be corrected by words only, because they refuse to change their ways even when they understand. There's more hope of a stupid person than of those that speak too quickly. Those that carefully bring up their trainee as a young person will treat them like family in the end.

[22-27] An angry person stirs up trouble, and a furious person lives on sin. People's pride will bring them low, but honor will uphold the depressed in spirit. Whoever is an accessory to the crimes of a thief is their own worst enemy; and when they hear lying, they don't expose it for what it is. A person's fear controls them, but whoever puts their trust in Yahweh will be safe. Many look for the ruler's grace; but every person's judgment comes from Yahweh. Sinful people are an insult to fair-minded people, and those who live in a good way are an offense to the sinful.

30 [1-3] The words of Agur the son of Jakeh, the preaching that the people spoke to Ithiel and Ucal: Surely I'm more wild than anyone, and haven't the brain of a human being. I've no wisdom, nor do I have the knowledge of the holy.

[4] Who has gone up into heaven, or come down from it? Who has caught up the wind in their hands? Who has bound the waters in their clothes? Who has settled all the boundaries of the earth? What's God's Name, and what's the Firstborn's Name, if you can tell?

[5-6] All the Words of God are pure: You defend those that put their trust in You. Don't change the meaning of the Words of God, or you may be corrected and found to be a liar.

[7-9] Don't deny me these two things that I ask of You before I die: Take away from me self-importance and lies, and don't give me poverty or riches, but provide my food daily; If I'm too full, I might think I don't need You, and say, *Who is Yahweh?* But if I'm poor, I might steal, and misuse the Name of my God.

[10] Don't accuse an employee to their employer, or they'll curse you, and you may be found the guilty one.

[11-14] This generation curses their parents, and doesn't bless them. This generation is guiltless in their own eyes and yet isn't washed from the filthiness of their sins. This generation is so self-important they think they can do anything! This generation destroys the poor from the earth, and the needy from among the people.

[15-16] The bloodsucker has two children, always crying, "*Give, give.*" Three things are never satisfied, yes, four things won't ever have enough: The grave; and the barren womb; the thirsty earth; and an unquenchable fire.

[17] The one that disrespects a parent, and hates to obey them, will run away and die in a rough country and the birds will eat their body.

[18-19] There are three things which are too wonderful for me, yes, four which I can't even comprehend: The way an eagle soars through the air; the way a serpent slithers on a rock; the way a ship stays afloat in the midst of the sea; and the way a man loves a woman.

[20] The way of adulterous people is to eat and wipe their mouths, saying, "*We've done no evil.*"

[21-23] The earth is upset by three things, four things it can't bear: For an employee to be in control, for stupid persons to be full of food, for married people to be unlovable, and for employees that are due to inherit their employer's business.

[24-28] There are four things which are small on the earth, but are very wise: The ants, which aren't a strong species, yet they get everything they need ready in the summer; The mountain badgers that are quite feeble, yet make their homes in the cracks between the rocks; The locusts, which have no ruler, yet all fly in swarms; And the spider that makes a web even in the great houses of great people.

[29-31] There are three things that walk grandly, yes, four look splendid as they go about: A lion, which is the strongest among wild animals, and doesn't back off for anything; A greyhound; a ram also; and a ruler, who no one dares to rebel against.

[32-33] If you've stupidly lifted yourself up in pride, or if you've thought evil things, put your hand on your mouth, for just as churning milk makes butter, and a broken nose bleeds: so stirring up anger only brings trouble on yourself.

31 [1-9] These are the words of the ruler Lemuel, the preaching that his mother taught him. Oh, Child! Child of my womb! The child of my vows! Don't waste your strength on many lovers, nor give your ways to those things that destroy rulers. Child, it isn't for rulers to drink wine; nor for their children to drink strong alcohol, or they might

19

drink it, and forget the law, and their judgments misrepresent the troubled. Only give strong drinks to those that are about to die, and wine to those that have heavy hearts. Let them drink, and forget their poverty, not remembering their misery. Stand up for those that can't stand up for themselves, in the case of all those who are about to die. Speak for them and judge fairly the cases of the poor and needy.

[10-20] Who can find a worthy spouse, who is more valuable than riches? Their spouse's heart safely trusts in them, having no need to worry. They'll treat them well and not dreadfully every day of their life. They look for material goods and work willingly with their hands. They're like a buyer who gets food from far away places. They rise while it's still dark, and give it to their households and some to their employees as well. Thinking about a piece of property, they buy it and tend it with the work of their hands. They keep fit, strengthening their arms. They know what they produce is good, and they hardly even turn out the lights at night. They work with their hands, skillfully using their equipment. They give to the poor and reach out to the needy.

[21-31] They aren't afraid of the cold for their household: for they're all well clothed, having fine coats and quality clothing. Their spouses are well known when they sit among the leaders of the city. They supply fine merchandise, and bring it to the buyers to sell. They're strong and honorable; and will celebrate in the days ahead. They speak with wisdom and words of kindness. They look after their household well, and are never lazy. Their children will rise up and call them blessed; and their spouses will also praise them. Many spouses have done honorably, but these outshine them all. Favoritism is false, and attractiveness has no real value, but those who respect Yahweh will be praised. Give them the rewards of their hard work; and let their own acts be publicly honored.

The Old Hymns (Psalms)

Book 1

1 [1-6] Blessed are those who don't stand with the ungodly or take the advice of unrepentant sinners, nor sit with those who ridicule others, but their joy is in the Word of Yahweh; they think on Your Word day and night. They're like an evergreen tree growing by the river, that yields fruit in season; whatever they do will prosper. The ungodly aren't so, but are like trash that blows away in the wind. The ungodly or sinful won't stand in the judgment, or with good people. For Yahweh knows the way of godly people, but the way of the ungodly will come to an end.

2 [1-9] Why do the ungodly rage, and people imagine meaningless things? The rulers of the earth set themselves up, taking counsel together against Yahweh and against God's Anointed One, saying, *"Let's break away from them, and reject their influence on us."* You, oh God, who sits in heaven, will laugh: Yahweh will hate them. Then You'll speak to them in Your anger, and upset them with great unhappiness, saying, *"I've set My Savior on My holy hill of Jerusalem."* I'll declare the decree *"Yahweh has said to Me, You are My Firstborn; Today, I've brought You forth. Ask of Me, and I'll give You the peoples of the world for Your inheritance, and the furthermost parts of the earth for Your possession. You'll break them with a strong hand; You'll break them in pieces like a broken jug."*

[10-12] So be wise now, you who are in power: learn, you judges of the earth. Minister to Yahweh and celebrate with fear and trembling, showing a reverent respect. Kiss the Firstborn, or God may become angry, and you'll die in the way, when the anger of God is provoked only a little. Blessed are all those that put their trust in the Firstborn of God.

3 [1-4] *A Hymn of David, when he fled from Absalom his son.* Yahweh, how they've multiplied that trouble me! There are so many that stand up against me. There are so many that say of me, *"There's no help for you in God."* Selah! But You, oh Yahweh, keep me safe; You are my glory, for You lift my spirits. I cried out to Yahweh, who heard me from the holy hill of God. Selah!

[5-8] I lay down and slept, and then I awoke; for it was Yahweh who kept me safe. So I won't be afraid of all the people that have surrounded me and set themselves against me. Awake, oh Yahweh; save me, oh my God: for You've slapped all my enemies in the face; You've broken the teeth of the ungodly. Only Yahweh can save: Your blessings are on Your people. Selah!

4 [1-3] *To the first musician for stringed instruments, A Hymn of David.* Listen to me when I call, oh God, who helps me to do what's right: You've made me great when I was upset; have mercy on me, and hear my prayer. Oh children of humanity, how long will you turn my glory into shame? How long will you love meaningless things, and look for lies? Selah! But know that Yahweh has set apart those that are godly for God's own people: Yahweh, You'll hear me when I call on You.

[4-8] Stand in awe, and don't sin: think with your own heart when you're in your bed, and be still. Selah! Give your gifts of goodness, and put your trust in Yahweh. There are many that say, *"Who will show us what's good?"* Yahweh, shine the light of Your face on us. You've made my heart glad, even more than when my income increased. I'll lie down peacefully and sleep, because only You, oh Yahweh, can make me safe.

5 [1-6] *To the first musician for flutes, A Hymn of David.* Listen to the words of my prayer, oh Yahweh, think on my plans. Listen to my voice, my Savior, and my God: for I'll only pray to You. You'll hear my voice in the morning, oh Yahweh; in the morning I'll look up and pray to You, because You aren't a God that enjoys sinfulness, nor will You allow unrepentant sinners to come into Your presence. Stupid people won't stand in Your sight, because You hate all those who do evil. You'll destroy those who don't tell the truth, hating those bloodthirsty and lying people.

[7-12] But as for me, I'll come into the House of God in the greatness of Your mercy, and in awe of You, I'll worship in the holy House of God. Lead me, oh Yahweh, show me the right way. Because of my enemies; make Your way clear to me. There's no loyalty in their words; they're sinful to the core of their being; their mouths are as open graves, flattering others with their words. Destroy them, oh God; let them fall by their own counsels; throw them out for the sins they have stored up; for they've rebelled against You. But let all those that put their trust in You celebrate: let them shout for joy always, because You defend them: let them that love Your Name be joyful in You. You, oh Yahweh will bless godly people; with grace You'll come to their defense.

6 [1-5] *To the first musician for stringed instruments, A Hymn of David.* Oh Yahweh, don't warn me in Your anger, nor punish me in Your fury. Have mercy on me, oh Yahweh; for I'm weak: oh Yahweh, heal me; for my body is full of troubles. My soul is also very confused: oh Yahweh, but how long will You wait? Return, oh Yahweh, save my soul: oh save me for Your mercies' sake. For in death there's no memory of You: in the grave who will give You thanks?

[6-10] I'm tired of groaning; all night long I drench my bed with tears. My eyes are burning because of grief; they age because of all my enemies. Leave me alone, all you mean spirited people; for Yahweh has heard the

21

sound of my crying. Yahweh has heard my request; Yahweh will receive my prayer. Let all my enemies be ashamed and frustrated: let them turn back and be unexpectedly ashamed.

7 [1-5] ***A poem of David, which he sang to Yahweh, about the words of Cush, the Benjamite.*** Oh Yahweh my God, in You I put my trust: free me and save me from all those that abuse me, in case they tear my soul like a lion, ripping it in pieces, while there's no one to save me. Oh Yahweh my God, if I've done this thing; if there's sin in my hands; if I've done evil to those that were at peace with me; then let my enemies abuse my soul, and take it; yes, let them trample down my life on the earth, and lay my honor in the dust, even though I've released those who are my enemies without cause. Selah!

[6-8] Awake, oh Yahweh, in Your anger, raise Yourself up because of the fury of my enemies, and awake for me to the judgment that You've allowed, so the congregation of the church will surround You and for their sakes take back Your power. Yahweh will judge the people: judge me, oh Yahweh, according to what I've done right, and according to my honesty.

[9-17] Oh let the evil of the sinful come to an end; but set up good people: for those who do what's right, God tests the hearts and minds of godly people. My only defense is God, who saves good-hearted people. God judges godly people, but is always angry with the ungodly. If they don't change their ways, You'll sharpen and prepare Your weapons, making them ready. You've also prepared instruments of death; planning their aim against those who abuse me. See, they work with sin, having conceived trouble, and birthed lies. They made a grave, and dug it, and have fallen into the very hole they dug. The trouble they caused will comeback to them, and their violence will be repaid to them. I'll praise You, oh Yahweh according to Your goodness, and will sing praise to the Name of Yahweh, Most High.

8 [1-4] ***To the first musician on harp, A Hymn of David.*** Oh Yahweh, our God, how amazing is Your Name in the whole world! You've set Your glory above the heavens! You've ordained praise to boldly come out of the mouths of babies and nursing children, because of Your enemies, to stop their sinful judgments. When I think on Your heavens, the creations of Your hands, the moon and the stars, which You've put into place, I wonder, *"What is humanity, that You are mindful of us? And the children of humanity, that You visit them?"*

[5-9] For You've made us a little lower than the angels, and have crowned us with glory and honor. You give us power over the creations of Your hands; You've put everything in our control, the wild animals of the field, the birds of the air, and the fish of the sea, and whatever else lives in the seas. Oh Yahweh, our God, how amazing is Your Name in the whole world!

9 [1-7] ***To the first musician, to the tune of: To Die for the Son, A Hymn of David.*** I'll praise You, oh Yahweh, with my whole heart; I'll tell of all Your awesome acts. I'll be glad and celebrate in You: I'll sing praise to Your Name, oh Yahweh, Most High. When my enemies are turned back, they fall down as dead at Your presence. For You've maintained my right and my cause; You judged rightly from Your throne. You've corrected the ungodly, You've destroyed the sinful, and You've erased their name forever. Everything You've destroyed will come to an everlasting end, and You've destroyed the cities of Your enemies and their memory has died with them, but Yahweh will live forever and has prepared the throne for judgment.

[8-11] Yahweh will judge the world rightly, honestly ministering judgment to the people. Yahweh will be a refuge for those who are kept down, a safe haven in times of trouble. And those that know Your Name will put their trust in You: for You, oh Yahweh, haven't abandoned those that look for You. We sing praises to Yahweh, who inhabits Jerusalem: Tell the people everything Yahweh does.

[12-15] When blood is called for, Yahweh remembers those who have humility, never forgetting their cry. Have mercy on me, oh Yahweh; think on my trouble which I suffer of those that hate me, You, who have lifted me up from the doors of death, so that I can bring You praise in the public places of the people of Jerusalem: I'll celebrate in how You saved me. The ungodly are put in the grave that they made: in the trap which they hid, their own feet are taken.

[16-20] Yahweh, You are known by the judgment You make: the sinful are caught in the acts of their own hands. Selah! The sinful will have their share of Hell, along with all the nations that forget God. For the needy won't always be forgotten: the expectations of the poor won't lie dormant forever. Awake, oh Yahweh; don't let evil people win: let the ungodly be judged in Your sight. Put them in fear, oh Yahweh: that the leaders of nations will know themselves to be but human beings. Selah!

10 [1-10] Why are You so far off, oh Yahweh? Why do You hide Yourself in times of trouble? In their pride, the sinful abuse the poor, so let them be taken by their own plans they expect to happen to others. For the sinful bragged about what they wanted to happen, and approved the greedy ones, which Yahweh hated. The sinful, through their prideful ways, won't look for God, who isn't in their thoughts at all. Their ways are always dreadful; they can't understand Your judgments: they mocked at all of their enemies. They've said in their heart, I won't be upset: for I'll never have any trouble. Their mouths are full of cursing and lies and fraud: trouble and emptiness are in their words. They sit in the hang outs of the cities: in secret places they murder the innocent: their eyes are set against the poor to take advantage of them. They secretly wait as a lion in a den to catch the poor, catching them, when they lure them into their trap. They crouch, hiding themselves, so that the poor will fall by their strongest.

22

[11-18] They've said in their hearts, "*God has forgotten: the face of God is turned away and will never see it.*" Awake, oh Yahweh; oh God, lift up Your hand and don't forget those who have humility. Why do the sinful reject God? They've said in their hearts, "*Yahweh won't call for justice.*" You've seen it; You watch the trouble they cause and their spite in order to pay them back for what they've done: the poor put themselves in Yahweh's hands; You are the helper of the single parent's child. Break the strength of the ungodly evil ones: look for their evil till You find none left. Yahweh is the Savior forever and ever: the ungodly will all die out of the land. Yahweh, You've heard what those who have humility want: You prepare their heart; You listen, in order to do justice for the single parent's child and those who are kept down, so that the people of the earth can't keep down them any more.

11 [1-3] **To the first musician, A Hymn of David.** In Yahweh I put my trust, so why do you say to me, "*Fly away like a bird to the mountaintop?*" See, the sinful get their weapons ready, taking aim, so that they can secretly shoot at godly people. If they won't fight fair, what can godly people do?

[4-7] Yahweh, whose eyes see and watch the children of humanity, is in the holy House of God; yes, Yahweh's throne is in heaven. Yahweh tests godly people, but hates the sinful and those that love violence. Yahweh will rain fire and burning sulfur with a horrible downpour to catch the sinful, which will be only what they deserve. Yahweh, who isn't prejudiced, loves fairness; Certainly, God's face sees godly people.

12 [1-4] **To the first musician on lyre, A Hymn of David.** Help us, oh Yahweh; for the godly people are disappearing and the faithful are dying out from among the children of humanity. Evil people lie to others, talking with flattering words and a double heart. Yahweh will shut up all flattering words, and mouths that speak meaningless things, who have said, "*We'll win with our mouths; nothing but our own words rule over us!*"

[5-8] Yahweh says, "*Now I'll awake, because of those who are kept down of the poor and the sighing of the needy, and I'll make them safe from those that take advantage of them.*" The Words of Yahweh are good words: as silver tried in a furnace of earth, that has been purified seven times. You'll keep Your Word, oh Yahweh; You'll save them from this evil generation forever. When evil people are in power, the evil ones are everywhere.

13 [1-2] **To the first musician, A Hymn of David.** Will You forget me forever, oh Yahweh? How long will You hide Your face from me? How long will I counsel myself, my heart daily sorrowing? How long will my enemies have power over me?

[3-6] Listen to me and think about me, oh Yahweh, my God: lift up my eyes, before I die, or my enemy might say, "*I've won against you;*" and those that abuse me celebrate when I'm gone. But I've trusted in Your mercy; and my heart will celebrate in Your saving grace. I'll sing praises to Yahweh, because You've been gracious to me.

14 [1-3] **To the first musician, A Hymn of David.** Stupid people have said in their heart, "*There is no God.*" They're evil, and have done horrible things; none of them does any good. Yahweh looks down from heaven on the children of humanity, to see if anyone understands, and searches for God. They've all turned away, and are all together filthy. No one does any good; no, not even one.

[4-7] Are all those who keep on sinning stupid, who consume my people like eating a piece of bread, and never call on Yahweh? They're in great fear: for they know God only stays with godly people. The sinful shamefully disgrace all the plans of the poor, but Yahweh is their safe haven. Oh that the saving of Israel would come out of Jerusalem! When You, oh Yahweh, bring freedom back to Your people, they will all be glad and celebrate.

15 [1-5] **A Hymn of David.** Yahweh, who will grace Your House of God? Who will stay on Your holy hill? Those that are faultless, acting well, and who have honest hearts; Those that don't backstab, nor act badly toward others, nor accuse others falsely; and in whose eyes evil persons are judged as evil; but those that respect Yahweh are honored; Those that keep their promises without changing their minds, even when it hurts them; Those that lend out their money without charging interest, and don't take bribes against the innocent; Those that do these kinds of things will never be upset.

16 [1-4] **A Poem of David.** Keep me safe, oh God: for I place all my trust in You. Oh my soul, you've said to Yahweh, "*You are my God: my goodness is nothing without You; But all my joy is in the worthy ones, the saintly people, who are here on earth.*" Those who worship other things will have much sorrow: I'll never taste what they offer, nor speak their names with my mouth.

[5-11] Yahweh is my inheritance and my reward: You always keep what I've earned safe. The boundary lines are set for me in pleasant places; yes, I've a very good heritage. I'll bless Yahweh, who counsels my heart all night long. I keep Yahweh always before me: God is at my side, so I won't be upset. So my heart is glad and my soul celebrates: my body will rest in hope also; *for You won't leave My soul in Hell; nor will You let Your Holy One decay.* You'll show me the path of life: in Your presence is complete joy; at Your side is everlasting pleasure.

17 [1-5] **A Prayer of David.** Listen, oh Yahweh, pay attention the goodness of my cry, hear my prayer, words that aren't made in untruthfulness. Let me be judged in Your presence; let Your eyes see that things are fair. You've proved my heart; You've visited me in my dreams; You've tried me, and have found nothing; I've settled in my heart that my mouth won't sin. By Your Word, I've kept myself from the ways of the devil, as I thought about the words of other people. Keep me going in Your ways, so that my footsteps are sure.

23

[6-12] I've called on You, because I know You'll listen to me, God: so listen to me, and hear my prayer. Show Your awesome loving kindness, God, who saves by Your strong hand those who put their trust in You, from all those that rise up against them. Let me be favored in Your sight and hide me in the shade of Your Spirit, from the sinful who keep me down and from the deadly enemies that surround me. They speak proudly with their stubborn hearts. They've overcome me in my steps: crouching low; like young lions greedy for prey, and as if they were stalking in hidden places.

[13-15] Awake, oh Yahweh, disappoint them and overthrow them: save my soul from the sinful by Your judgment, from people which are in Your power, oh Yahweh, from the people of the world which have their portion in this life and whose belly You've filled with good things, who having many children, leave the rest of their inheritance to their grandchildren. As for me, I'll see Your face because I've done what's right, and I'll be satisfied when I awake with Your likeness.

18 [1-3] *To the first musician, A Hymn of David, the child of God, that spoke to Yahweh the words of this song in the day that God freed him from the hand of all his enemies, and from the hand of Saul, who said, "I love You, oh Yahweh, my strength."* Yahweh, You are my rock to stand on, and my refuge which surrounds me, and my deliverer from my enemies; my God, my strength, in whom I trust; my belt that protects me, the horn I blow to save me, and my safe haven. I'll call on Yahweh, who is worthy to be praised: so I'll be saved from my enemies.

[4-15] The sorrows of death overtook me, and the rush of ungodly people made me afraid. The sorrows of Hell overtook me: the traps of death captured me. In my trouble I called on Yahweh, and cried out to my God, who heard my voice out of the House of God, and listened to my cry. Then the earth quaked; the foundations of the hills were opened and shaken, because God was angry. Then God exhaled smoke and fire, in which the flames consumed everything ignited by them. God opened the heavens, coming down with dark smoke underneath, riding on a heavenly thing, and flying on the wind, making darkness the hiding place of God, with a cloak of dark waters and the thick clouds of the skies all around. But the brightness that surrounded God was followed by the thick clouds that passed, with hail stones and flashes of lightening. The noise of Yahweh rumbled in the heavens, and then the voice of the Most High God spoke through the hail stones and flashes of light. Yes, God sent out bolts of electricity, scattering the enemies, shooting out like flashes of lightning, and destroyed them. Then the outlets of water were seen, and the heart of the earth was uncovered at Your Word, oh Yahweh, from the release of Your exhaust.

[16-24] God sent from above, taking hold of me, and drawing me up out of much water, delivering me from my strong enemies, and from those who hated me, which were too strong for me, and who had shamed me in the day of my misfortune, but You, oh Yahweh, were my stay. You brought me out into a large place and freed me, because You delighted in me. Yahweh, You rewarded me according to my goodness; according to the cleanness of my heart You've repaid me, because I've kept the ways of Yahweh, and haven't done evil by not worshiping my God. For all Your Words were with me, and I didn't put any of them away from me. I was also good before You, and I kept myself from my sin. So You, oh Yahweh, have repaid me according to my goodness, according to the cleanness of my heart in Your eyes.

[25-30] With the merciful, You show Yourself to be merciful; with those who do what's right You show Yourself to be perfectly good; With the blameless You show Yourself to be blameless; and with those who won't change their ways You'll show Yourself to be unmercifully just. For You save the people who are abused; and bring down those who think they are better than others. You burn like a candle in my soul: Yahweh, my God, brightens my darkness. For by You I've run through a multitude of enemies; and by my God I've leaped over many barriers. The way of God is perfect: the Words of Yahweh have been tried: You are a covering to all those that trust in You.

[31-40] For who is God but Yahweh? or who can be a rock but our God? God provides me with strength, and makes my way perfect. Yahweh makes my feet like a deer's hoofs, and keeps me safe on my mountaintops. God teaches my hands to fight, so that my arms are strengthened. You've also covered me with Your saving grace, Your hand holds me up, and You come to my aid to make me great. You've multiplied my steps under me, so that my feet have never slipped. I've pursued my enemies, and overtaken them and I didn't turn back until they were all gone. I've wounded those that weren't able to rise, who were fallen under my feet. For You've provided me with the strength for all my struggles: You've subdued under me those that rose up against me. You've also given me the rulers of my enemies; that I might destroy those that hate me.

[41-45] They cried, but there was none to save them: they even cried to Yahweh, but You didn't answer them. Then I beat them as small as the dust before the wind and I threw them out as dust in the street. You've freed me from the hostility of those people; and You've given me control over them: a people that I never would have thought would be subject to me. As soon as they hear of me, they obey my orders: the ungodly submit themselves to me. The ungodly will lose heart, and be scared out of their hiding places.

[46-50] Yahweh lives; my rock is blessed; let praise come only to the God who saves me. It's God that takes revenge for me, and disciplines the people under me. You free me from those of my enemies who keep me down: yes, You lift me up above those that rise up against me: You've taken me away from violent people. So I'll give

24

thanks to You, oh Yahweh, among the people, and we'll sing praises to Your Name. You give great freedom and mercy to Your anointed ruler, David, and to his descendants forever.

19 [1-6] *To the first musician, A Hymn of David.* The heavens declare the glory of God; and the environment reveals all Your creations. Daily, its story is told, and nightly it shows all its wondrous knowledge. There's no dialect or language, where it can't be understood. Its announcement goes out through the whole world and calls out to the end of the world. You've set in it a covering for the light, which is as a bridegroom coming out of the wedding chamber, and celebrates as a champion running a race, going from one end of heaven to the other, its course all the way to the end of the sky, and nothing is untouched by its rays.

[7-10] The Word of Yahweh God is perfect, changing the soul: the commandments of Yahweh are sure, making the naive wise. The decrees of Yahweh are right, celebrating the heart: the testimony of Yahweh is pure, enlightening the eyes. The respect of Yahweh is holy, and lasts forever: the judgments of Yahweh are completely true and good. They're to be wanted more than gold, yes, more than much fine gold: They're sweeter also than honey and the honeycomb.

[11-14] Likewise, by them are Your children warned, and there's great reward in the keeping them. Who can understand their own errors? Cleanse me from my unknown faults. Keep me from the sins that I keep on doing also; don't let them have power over me: then I'll be good, and I'll be innocent from great sins. Let the words of my mouth, and the prayers of my heart, be acceptable in Your sight, oh Yahweh, my strength, and my Savior.

20 [1-5] *To the first musician, A Hymn of David.* Let Yahweh hear you in the day of trouble; Let the Name of God defend you; sending you help from the House of God, and strengthening you out of Jerusalem; and remember all your offerings, fully accepting your holy sacrifices; Selah! May Yahweh give you the hopes of your heart, and perfect all your plans. We'll celebrate when you're saved, and set up our signs in the Name of our God: May Yahweh God give you everything you ask for.

[6-9] Now I know that You save Your anointed and will answer from the holy heavens with a strong hand of lifesaving strength. Some trust in armored vehicles, and some in a swift means of transportation, but we'll trust in the Name of Yahweh, our God. They're fallen down, but we're raised up, and will stand strong in goodness. Give victory, oh Yahweh, let the leader hear us when we call.

21 [1-7] *To the first musician, A Hymn of David.* I'll celebrate in Your strength, oh Yahweh; how greatly I'll celebrate when You save me! You've given me the very thing my heart wanted, and haven't withheld any of my requests. Selah! For You amaze me with blessings of goodness: You set a golden crown on my head. I asked life of You, and You gave it to me, even everlasting life. My fame is made great in how You saved me; honor and majesty You've given me. For You've made me most blessed forever; You've made me very glad with Your look. For I trust in Yahweh, and through the mercy of the Most High God, I won't be upset.

[8-17] Your hand will find all Your enemies: Your strong hand will find all those that hate You. You'll make them as a fiery oven in the time of Your anger: Yahweh, You'll overcome them with Your anger, and the fire will consume them. You'll destroy their children from the earth, and their grandchildren from among the children of humanity. For they intended evil against You: they made mischievous plans, which they weren't able to do, so You'll make them turn back, when You prepare Your weapons against them. May You be made well-known, oh Yahweh, for Your mighty power: so we'll sing and praise Your victory.

22 [1-5] *To the first musician, to the tune of The Doe of the Dawn, A Hymn of David.* My God, My God, why have You left Me? Why are You so far from helping Me, and from the sound of My voice? Oh My God, I cry in the daytime, but You don't hear; and in the night and I'm still not silent. But You are holy, the One who lives in the praises of Your people. Our parents trusted in You: they trusted, and You saved them. They cried to You, and were set free: they trusted in You, and were never confused.

[6-10] But I'm a spineless creature, and no human being; blamed and hated by these people. All those that see Me laugh at me: sticking out their lips, shaking their heads saying, *"You trusted on Yahweh, thinking that God would save You: let Yahweh save You, seeing God delights in You."* But You are the One who took Me out of the womb: You made Me hope when I nursed on My mother's breasts. I was dedicated to You from the womb: You are My God from My conception.

[11-21] Don't be far from Me; for trouble is near; and there's none to help. Many strong ones have overtaken Me: and they have surrounded Me. Their mouths gape open at Me, as ravenous, roaring lions. I'm poured out like water, and all My bones are out of joint: My heart is like wax, melted in the midst of My bowels. My strength is dried up like a piece of pottery; and My mouth clings to My jaws; and You've brought Me into the dust of death. For these dogs have overtaken Me: the assembly of the sinful has enclosed Me: they pierced My hands and My feet. I can see all My bones as they look and stare at Me. They divided My clothes among them, and placed bets on My coat. But don't be far from Me, oh Yahweh: oh My strength, help Me quickly. Deliver My soul from the blade; My very life from the power of these sinners. Save Me from these lion's mouths: for You've heard Me cry out from the power of these brute wild animals.

[22-31] I'll declare Your Name to My people: in the midst of the congregation I'll praise You. You who respect Yahweh, all you children of God, praise, glorify, and respect God. Yahweh, You haven't hated them, nor hated the

25

troubles of those who are abused; nor have You turned Your face away from them; but when they cried to You, You heard. So I'll praise You in the great congregation: I'll pay My vows before those that respect You. Those with humility will eat and be satisfied: those that look for Yahweh will praise God and their spirit will live forever. Everyone in the world will remember and turn to Yahweh, and all the people of the nations will worship before You. For the ends of the earth are Yahweh's, and God rules among all the nations. All those that are living on the earth will eat and worship: all those who are buried in the earth will bow before You, none keeping their own soul alive. The children of generations yet to come will minister to You and be counted as children of God. They'll come and speak of Your goodness to a people that is still to be born in the future, saying that You alone have done all this.

23 [1-4] *A Hymn of David.* Yahweh, You are my life saver, so I need nothing else. I rest in a peaceful land, for You bring me to calm and refreshing waters. You revive my soul, leading me in the right direction for Your Name's sake. Yes, even if I walk through the deepest valley, in the darkest shadows, even to the brink of death, I won't be afraid of anything: for You always walk with me, leading, defending, and comforting me. You keep me safe in the sight of all my enemies, anointing me with Your Spirit as with oil; helping me until my blessings overflow. Your grace and mercy will certainly follow me for the rest of my life, and I'll stay in Your presence, oh Yahweh, forever.

24 [1-5] *A Hymn of David.* The earth is Yahweh's, and everything it is filled with; the whole world, and all those that live in it. For God has founded it on the seas, and settled it on the ocean floor. Who will ascend into the hill of Yahweh? Or who will stand in the Holy Sanctuary? The One who has clean hands, and an innocent heart; that hasn't been proud, or made lying promises. The One who will receive the blessing from Yahweh, and goodness from the God who saves.

[6-10] This is the generation of those that look for the Savior, that look for Your face, oh Jacob. Selah! Open the gates; open up the doors of eternity; and the glorious Savior will come in. Who is this glorious Savior? Yahweh, strong and mighty; Yahweh, victorious in crusades. Open the gates; open up the doors of eternity; and the glorious Savior will come in. Who is this glorious Savior? Yahweh, Leader of the heavenly hosts, is the glorious Savior. Selah!

25 [1-5] *A Hymn of David.* Oh Yahweh, I lift up my soul to You. Oh my God, I trust in You: Don't let me be ashamed, don't let my enemies triumph over me. Yes, let none that pray to You be ashamed; only let those who are immoral and without excuse be ashamed. Show me Your paths, oh Yahweh; teach me Your ways. Lead me in Your truth, and teach me: for You are the God who saves me; I pray to You all day long.

[6-10] Remember, oh Yahweh, Your tender mercies and Your love; which are everlasting. Don't remember the sins of my childhood, nor my rebellions: according to Your mercy, remember me for Your goodness' sake, oh Yahweh. Yahweh, You are the Good and Perfect One, who teaches the sinful in Your way. You guide those who have humility in their good judgments, and teach them the way of godliness. All the ways of Yahweh are mercy and truth to those that keep the Words of Your promises.

[11-16] For Your Name's sake, oh Yahweh, forgive my sins; for they're too many to count. Who are those that respect Yahweh? Yahweh, You'll teach them in the way You choose. Their souls will prosper; and their children will inherit the earth. Yahweh, Your secrets are with those that respect You, who reveals to them the truths of the Promise. My eyes are forever looking toward Yahweh; for You'll bring me out of trouble. Turn to me, and have mercy on me; for I'm lonely and abused.

[17-22] The troubles of my heart are multiplied: oh Yahweh, bring me out of my troubles. See all my misery and my pain; and forgive all my sins. Think about my many enemies; who hate me with a cruel hatred. Oh keep my soul, and save me: Don't let me be ashamed; for I put my trust in You. Let my goodness and my honesty save me; for I serve You. Redeem Your people, oh God, out of all their troubles.

26 [1-7] *A Hymn of David.* Judge me, oh Yahweh; for I've done what was right: I've trusted in You so I won't slip up. Watch me, oh Yahweh, and prove me; test my mind and my heart. For I see Your everlasting love, and I walk in Your truth. I haven't sat with people who think they are better than others, nor do I go with lying ones. I hate the gatherings of evildoers; and I won't sit with unrepentant sinners. I'll wash my hands in innocence: so I may come to Your altar, oh Yahweh: So that I can publish with a voice of thanksgiving, and tell of all Your wondrous acts.

[8-12] Yahweh, I've loved the environment of Your House of God, and the place where You are made known. Don't collect my soul with the sinful, or take my life with bloodthirsty people, whose hands are full of trouble and bribery. As for me, I'll do what's right, so free me and be merciful to me. My feet stand in a holy place: I'll bless Yahweh God in the congregation of the people.

27 [1-5] *A Hymn of David.* Yahweh is my light and the One who saves me; so who should I fear? Yahweh is the strength of my life; so what should I be afraid of? When the sinful, even my enemies and those who come against me, came to attack my body, they stumbled and fell. Though many should come against me, my heart won't fear: though disputes should rise against me, in this I'll be confident: I've wanted of Yahweh one thing and that I'll look for; that I can come into the House of God everyday of my life, to ask for and to see the loveliness of

Yahweh God in the House of God. For in the time of trouble You'll hide me in Your shelter: in the safe haven of Your House of God, You'll hide me and will set me up on a rock.

[6-11] And when I'm lifted up above my enemies who surround me, I'll offer in Your House of God, offerings of joy; I'll sing, yes, I'll sing praises to Yahweh. Listen, oh Yahweh, when I cry aloud: have mercy also on me, and answer me. When You said, *"Look for my face;"* my heart said to You, *"Your face, oh Yahweh, I'll look for."* Don't hide Your face far from me; Don't put the one who worship's You away in anger: You've been my help; Don't leave me, or give up on me, oh God, for You are the One who saves me. When my parents give up on me, then Yahweh will take me up. Teach me Your way, oh Yahweh, and lead me in a plain path, because of my enemies.

[12-14] Don't hand me over to the will of my enemies: for false witnesses have risen up against me, along with those who speak cruelly of me. I would have given up, if I hadn't believed I would see the goodness of Yahweh in the land of the living. Have courage and wait on Yahweh, and God will strengthen your heart: wait, I say, on Yahweh.

28 [1-5] *A Hymn of David.* Oh Yahweh, my rock, I'll cry to You: Don't be silent to me, because if You are, I'll be just like those that are buried in a grave. Listen to the sound of my prayer when I cry to You, when I lift up my hands toward Your holy House of God. Don't lead me away with the sinful, who speak peacefully to others, yet with lies and trouble waiting in their hearts. Punish them for what they've done, according to all the evil things they've done: reward them for their actions; give them just what they deserve; because they don't respect what You've done or the creations of the hands of Yahweh; destroy them forever.

[6-9] May Yahweh be blessed, because You've heard the sound of my prayer. Yahweh is my strength and my defense; my heart trusted in You, and I'm helped: so my heart greatly celebrates; and with my song I'll praise You. Yahweh, You are the strength of Your people, and the saving strength of Your anointed. Save Your people, and bless Your inheritance: provide for them and uphold them forever.

29 [1-5] *A Hymn of David.* Give to Yahweh, You, who are strong, give to Yahweh, the glory of your strength. Give to Yahweh the glory due to the Name of God; worship Yahweh in the loveliness of holiness. The voice of Yahweh is heard across the oceans: the God of glory rumbles, echoing over the seas. The voice of Yahweh is strong and majestic. The voice of Yahweh snaps the cedars into; yes, Yahweh snaps the cedars of Lebanon completely into.

[6-11] Yahweh makes the volcanoes erupt. The voice of Yahweh spews fiery flames. The voice of Yahweh shakes the desert; the countryside rumbles. The voice of Yahweh makes the doe to bear, and the forests to drop their leaves, and everyone tells of the glory of God in the House of God. Yahweh rules over the waves of the sea; yes, oh Yahweh sits a Savior forever. Yahweh, You give strength to Your people; Yahweh, You bless Your people with peace.

30 [1-6] *A Hymn sung at the dedication of the house of David.* I'll worship You, oh Yahweh; for You've held me up, and haven't allowed my enemies to celebrate over me. Oh Yahweh my God, I cried to You, and You've healed me. Oh Yahweh, You've raised up my soul from death: You've kept me alive, that I shouldn't be buried in the grave. Sing to Yahweh, You people of God, and give thanks when you remember the holiness of God. For God's anger lasts only a little while; but in God's grace is life: tears may last through the night, but joy comes with the new dawn. When I did well, I said, I'll never be upset.

[7-12] Yahweh, by Your grace You've made my mountain to stand strong: You hid Your face, and I was troubled. I cried to You and prayed, oh Yahweh: *What profit is there in my death, when I die? Shall the dust praise You? Will it declare Your truth? Listen, oh Yahweh, and have mercy on my soul: Yahweh, help me.* You've turned my sadness into dancing: You've taken my mourning clothes from me, and strengthened me with gladness; to the end that I can sing praise to You when I'm made known, and I won't be silent. Oh Yahweh my God, I'll give thanks to You forever.

31 [1-5] *To the first musician, A Hymn of David.* In You, oh Yahweh, I place my trust; let me never be ashamed: save me in Your goodness. Listen to me; save me quickly: be my rock, a safe haven to defend me. For You are my rock and my stronghold; so for Your Name's sake lead me, and guide me. Pull me out of the trap that's been secretly set for me: for You are my strength. Into Your hands I place My spirit: You've bought Me back, oh Yahweh, God of truth.

[6-10] I've hated those that honor empty lies, but I trust in Yahweh. I'll be glad and celebrate in Your mercy: for You've thought about my trouble; You've known my soul in hard times and haven't let me be caught by the hand of the enemy: You've let me go free. Have mercy on me, oh Yahweh, for I'm in trouble: my eyes are consumed with grief, yes, my soul and my body. For my life is spent with grief, and my years with sighing: my strength fails me because of my sin, and my body is consumed.

[11-14] I was accused by my enemies, but especially by my neighbors, and I was a fear to all my acquaintances: those that saw me outside fled from me. I'm forgotten as a dead person out of mind: I'm like a broken jar. I've heard the lies of many, fear being everywhere, while they all made their plans together against me, and planned how to take my life. But I trusted in You, oh Yahweh: I said, *"You are my God."*

27

[15-20] My time is in Your hand: save me from the hand of my enemies, and from those that abuse me. Make Your face to shine on me: save me for Your mercies' sake. Don't let me be ashamed, oh Yahweh; for I've called on You: let the sinful be ashamed, and let them be silent in the grave. Let lying words be put to silence; which proudly and critically speak dreadful things against godly people. Oh how great are Your mercies, which You've laid up for those who respect You; which You've created for those that trust in You from the children of humanity! You'll hide them in the shade of Your Spirit from the pride of humanity, secretly keeping them in a safe haven from the troubles of evil words.

[21-24] May Yahweh be blessed: for You've shown me Your awesome kindness when I was attacked in my city. For I said in my haste, *I'm hidden from Your eyes*: Yet You heard the voice of my prayer when I cried to You. Oh love Yahweh, everyone of God: for Yahweh saves the faithful, and amply repays those who think they are better than others. Have good courage, and God will strengthen Your heart, all You that hope in Yahweh.

32 [1-5] *A Hymn of David, A Poem of Teaching.* Blessed are those whose sins are forgiven, whose sins are covered. Blessed are the people to whom Yahweh doesn't accuse of sin, and in whose spirit there's no lies. When I kept silent, my body grew old through my loud crying all day long. For day and night Your hand was heavy on me: my sweat turned into the drought of summer. Selah! I acknowledged my sin to You, my sin I haven't hid. I said, "*I'll confess my sins to Yahweh*;" and You forgave the wrongs of my sin. Selah!

[6-11] For this, every one that is godly should pray to You while You can still be found: surely when the flood waters of the ocean waves rises; it won't come near to them. You are my hiding place; You'll save me from trouble; You'll surround me with songs of deliverance. Selah! Yahweh says, "*I'll train You and teach You in the way which You should go: I'll guide You with my watchful eye.*" So don't be like a horse or a mule, having no understanding, whose mouth must be harnessed with the bit and bridle, for anyone to come near you. The sinful will have many sorrows, but those that trust in Yahweh, will have mercy encamp around them. Be glad in Yahweh, and celebrate, you who are good, and shout for joy, all you goodhearted people.

33 [1-5] Celebrate in Yahweh, oh you good people: for praises are pleasant for godly people. Praise Yahweh with the harp: sing to God with the violin and all the stringed instruments. Sing to Yahweh a new song, playing skillfully and loudly. For the Words of Yahweh are right; and all the acts of God are done in truth. God loves goodness and judgment: the earth is full of the goodness of Yahweh.

[6-9] By the word of Yahweh the heavens were made, and all the host of them by the breath of God. God set the boundaries of the seas and the oceans in their places. Let the whole world respect Yahweh: let all the people of the world stand in awe of You. For You spoke and it was done; You said it, and it stood fast.

[10-15] Yahweh brings the counsel of the ungodly to naught, making their plans come to nothing. The counsel of Yahweh stands forever, the thoughts of God's heart to all generations. Blessed are the nations whose God is Yahweh, and the people that God has chosen for an inheritance. Yahweh looks from heaven and watches all the children of humanity. From the heavens You look on all the people of the earth. You make their hearts alike and think about all their acts.

[16-22] There's no ruler that is saved by the greatness of an army, neither is a strong person freed by great strength. It's an arrogant thing to depend on swift transportation for safety: and none will be saved by their great strength. See, the eyes of Yahweh are on those that respect God, on those that hope in God's mercy to save their soul from death, and to keep them alive when there's a lack of food. Our souls wait for Yahweh: You are our help and our defense. For our hearts will celebrate in You, because we have trusted in Your holy Name. Let Your mercy, oh Yahweh, be on us, according to our hope in You.

34 [1-7] *A Hymn of David, when God changed his behavior before Abimelech; who drove him away when he left.* I'll bless Yahweh at all times: Your praises will always be in my mouth. My soul will boast in Yahweh: those who have humility will be glad when they hear it. Oh glorify Yahweh with me, and let's make God's Name known together. I sought You, oh Yahweh, and You heard me, and freed me from all my fears. Their hoping faces looked to God, and weren't ashamed. The poor people cried, and Yahweh heard them, and saved them out of all their troubles. The angel of Yahweh encamps around those that respect God, and delivers them.

[8-14] Experience God and see that Yahweh is good: blessed are the people that trust in God. Respect Yahweh, people of God: for there's no lack to those that give their respect to God. Even young lions may lack, and suffer hunger, but those that look for Yahweh won't lack any good thing. Come, children, and listen to me: I'll teach you the respect of Yahweh. Who are those that want life, and want many days, so that they can see good times? Keep your mouth from evil, and your words from speaking lies. Stop doing evil, do good things, and keep looking for peace.

[15-22] Yahweh watches over godly people and listens to their cry. The face of Yahweh is against those that do evil, in order to remove any memory of them from the earth. Godly people cry, and Yahweh hears, and delivers them out of all their troubles. Yahweh comes near to those that have broken hearts; and saves those that have changed spirits. Many are the troubles of godly people, but Yahweh delivers them from every one of them. You keep safe all the bones of My body: none of them are broken. Evil will kill the sinful, and those that hate godly

28

people will be separated from them. Yahweh redeems the souls of the children of God, and none of those that trust in You will be separated.

35 [1-9] *A Hymn of David.* Plead my case, oh Yahweh, with those that dispute with me: fight against those that attack me. Take hold of Your weapons, and stand up for my help. Draw them out, and block the way of those that abuse me: say to my soul, *"I'll save you."* Let them be confused and put to shame, all those that look for my soul: make those that try to hurt me turn back and be brought to confusion. Let them be as trash in the wind, and let the avenging angel of Yahweh chase them. Let their way be dark and dangerous, and let the angel of Yahweh abuse them. They've hid a trap for me in a grave for no reason, which they've dug for my soul without cause. Let destruction come on them unexpectedly; and let the trap that they've hid catch them: into that very destruction let them fall. And my soul will be joyful in Yahweh: I'll celebrate when You save me.

[10-16] My very soul will say, oh Yahweh, who is like You, who delivers the poor from those who are too strong for them, yes, the poor and the needy from those that would ruin them? False witnesses rose up and accused me of things that I had nothing to do with. They rewarded me evil for good to the ruin of my soul. But as for me, when they were sick, I mourned and humbled my soul with fasting; and when my prayers returned unanswered, I behaved myself as though they had been my best friend or family: I grieved, as those that mourn for their own parents. But in my trouble they celebrated, and gathered themselves together: yes, these abusive people gathered themselves together against me, and I didn't know it; they come at me to no end: Like hypocritical troublemakers at a feast, they grit their teeth at me.

[17-22] My God, how long will You look on? Rescue my soul from their destructions, my very life from these wild animals. I'll give You thanks in the great congregations: I'll praise You among many people. Don't let those that are my enemies wrongfully celebrate over me; or let them, who hate me with no reason wink their eye. They don't speak peace, but make lying plans against the peaceful people in this land. Yes, they openly accused me, saying, *Aha, aha, we saw it.* You've seen this, oh Yahweh, so don't keep silent: oh God, don't be far from me.

[23-28] Awake Yourself, awake to judge my case, my God, my Savior. Judge me, oh Yahweh my God, according to Your goodness; and don't let them celebrate over me. Don't let them say in their hearts, "*Yes, this is exactly what we wanted:*" Don't let them say, "*We've put You in Your place.*" Let those that celebrate my hurt be ashamed and brought together in confusion: let those who make themselves great against me be decorated with shame and dishonor. Let those who favor my good cause shout for joy, and be glad: yes, let those who are pleased with the well-being of God's subject, say always, "*Let Yahweh be glorified;*" and my mouth will speak of Your goodness and of Your praise always.

36 [1-4] *To the first musician, A Hymn of David, the subject of Yahweh.* I say in my heart, concerning the evil of sinners, who have no respect for God in their eyes: "*They flatter themselves in their own eyes, until people find out how disgusting their sin is. The words of their mouth are full of sin and lies: they have stopped trying to be wise, or to do anything good. They devise trouble on their bed, setting themselves up in ways that aren't good; not hating evil.*"

[5-9] Your mercy, oh Yahweh, is stretched out like the heavens; and Your faithfulness is as far reaching as the clouds. Your goodness is as high as the great mountains; Your judgments are as deep as the oceans: oh Yahweh, You save both people and wild animals. How excellent is Your love, oh God! So the children of humanity put their trust in the shade of Your Spirit. They're greatly filled with the goodness of Your House of God; and You'll give them drink from the river of Your joy. You are the fountain of life: for it is by Your light that we see.

[10-12] Oh continue to love those that know You; and give Your goodness to goodhearted people. Don't let the prideful come against me, and don't let the sinful upset me. See there, those who practice sin have fallen down; and when they're down, they won't be able to get up again.

37 [1-7] *A Hymn of David.* Don't worry because of evildoers, or be jealous of those who practice sin, for they'll soon be cut down like the grass, and withered as a dry herb. Trust in Yahweh, and do good things; so that you'll stay in the land and not be hungry. Celebrate also in Yahweh; and God will give you everything your heart wants. Give your plans to Yahweh; trusting in God; and God will bring it to pass, and bring forward your goodness and your judgment as the light of midday. Rest in Yahweh, waiting patiently: Don't worry yourself because of those who prosper in their way, bringing sinful plans to pass.

[8-15] Cease from anger, and give up your rage: Don't allow yourself to do evil in any way. For evildoers will be moved out of their place, but those that pray to Yahweh, will inherit the earth. Just a little while longer, and the sinful won't exist: yes, you'll carefully think about their place, and it won't exist. But those who have humility will inherit the earth; and will enjoy themselves in a wealth of peace. The sinful plot against good people, and grit their teeth at them. My God will laugh at them: for God sees that their day is coming. The sinful have drawn out blades, and have weapons ready, to keep down the poor and needy, and to destroy those of good behavior. Their blade will enter into their own heart, and their weapons will be broken.

[16-22] A little that a good person has is better than the riches of many sinful people. The sinful will lose their control, but Yahweh upholds godly people. Yahweh knows the days of godly people, and their inheritance will be forever. They won't be ashamed in evil times, and in the days of need they will be satisfied. But the sinful will die,

29

and the enemies of Yahweh will be as a burning field: They will be consumed by smoke, and die out. The sinful borrows, and doesn't pay it back, but godly people show mercy, and give. For those who are blessed will inherit the earth; and those that are cursed will be moved out of their place.

[23-28] The steps of godly people are ordered by Yahweh, who delights in their way. Though they fall, they won't be all together disheartened: for You, oh Yahweh uphold them with Your strong hand. I've been young, and now I'm old; yet I haven't seen godly people given up on, or their children begging for food. They're ever merciful, and lend to those in need; and their children are blessed. Leave from evil, and do good things; and live forever, for Yahweh loves good judgment, and doesn't give up on the people of God; they're saved forever, but the children of the sinful will be moved out of their place.

[29-34] Godly people will inherit the land, and stay in it forever. The mouth of godly people speaks wisdom, and their words have good judgment. The Word of God is in their heart; so none of their steps will slip. The sinful watch godly people, and try to destroy them, but Yahweh won't leave them in their hand, nor condemn them when they're judged. Wait on Yahweh, and keep your way, and God will uplift you to inherit the land when the sinful are moved out of their place; Wait, you'll see it.

[35-40] I've seen the sinful in great power, and spreading themselves like an evergreen tree. Yet they passed away, and weren't there anymore: yes, I sought them, but they couldn't be found. Mark the godly, and watch them: for those people will end with a peaceful life. The sinful will be destroyed together in the end: they'll be completely moved out of their place. But the salvation of godly people is of Yahweh: You are their strength in the time of trouble. Yahweh, You'll help them and save them: You'll save them from the sinful, and free them, because they trust in You.

38 [1-7] *A Hymn of David, to bring to remembrance.* Oh Yahweh, don't warn me in Your anger or discipline me in Your heated rage. For You pierce my soul and Your hand puts great pressure on me. There's no wellness in my body because of Your anger; nor is there any rest in my body because of my sin. For my sins are over my head: as a heavy load, they're too heavy for me. My wounds have a stench and are rotten because of my stupidity. I'm troubled; I'm humbled greatly; I go about mourning all day long. For my insides are filled with a loathsome disease, and there's no soundness in my body.

[8-12] I'm very tired and broken: I've moaned because the bitterness of my heart. My God, all my requests are before You; and my complaints aren't hidden from You. My heart pants, my strength fails me: as for the light of my eyes, it's gone from me. My lovers and my friends stand away from my sores; and my kin people stand far off, as well. Those who look for my life set traps for me, and those that try to hurt me speak mischievous things, while planning their lies all day long.

[13-22] But I, as a deaf person, didn't hear; and I was as a dumb person that doesn't speak. So I was as those that don't hear, and in whose mouth is no shame. For I hope in You, oh Yahweh: You'll hear, oh Yahweh, my God. For I said, *"Listen to me, or they'll celebrate over me: whenever my foot slips, and magnify themselves against me. For I'm ready to break, and my sorrows are always before me. So, I'll tell of my sin; I'll be sorry for my sin."* But my enemies are lively and strong, and those that hate me are wrongfully multiplied. They that give back evil for good are also my enemies; because I follow the things that are good. Don't leave me, oh Yahweh: oh my God, don't be far from me. Help me quickly, oh my God, my salvation.

39 [1-5] *To the first musician, a laudatory, A Hymn of David.* I said, *"I'll be careful of my ways, that I don't sin with my mouth: I'll keep my mouth as if it was harnessed with a bridle, while the sinful are before me."* I was dumb with silence, I held my peace, even from speaking good things; and my sorrow troubled me. My heart was hot within me, and while I was thinking, I burned with fury and then spoke, *"Yahweh, make me to know my end, and the length of my days, whatever it is; so that I can know how frail I am. See, You've made my days short; and my age is as nothing before You: everyone at their best state is altogether dying."* Selah!

[6-11] Surely everyone walks in an arrogant show, uselessly storing up riches, not knowing who will get them. And now, my God, what do I wait for? My hope is in You. Free me from all my sins: don't make me the blame of stupid people. I was dumb, and didn't open my mouth; because it was You who did it. Remove this punishment from me, for I'm consumed by the blow of Your hand. You make attractiveness consume away like a moth eaten piece of clothing, when with a warning, You correct people for sin, and surely everyone is worthless. Selah!

[12-13] Listen to my prayer, oh Yahweh, and hear my cry; don't hold Your peace at my tears: for I'm like a stranger with You, and a wanderer, as all my ancestors were. Oh spare me, so that I can recover my strength, before I die, and live no more.

40 [1-4] *To the first musician, A Hymn of David.* I waited patiently for You, oh Yahweh; and You listened to me, and heard my cry. You brought me up out of a horrible pit, out of the muddy clay, and set my feet on a rock, and settled my way. You've put a new song in my mouth, even praises to my God: many will see it, and be warned, and will trust in Yahweh. Blessed are the people who make Yahweh their trust, and don't favor those who think they are better than others, nor those who turn aside to lies.

[5-10] Oh Yahweh, my God, many are the wonderful acts which You've done, and Your thoughts which are toward us can't be recalled in order to You: for if I tried to tell them all, they're more than I can count. You didn't

want sacrifice and offerings; You've opened my ears: sacrifice and offerings You never required. Then I said, "See, I come: in the volume of the book it's written of me, *I enjoy doing Your will, oh my God: yes, Your Words are within my heart. I've preached goodness in the great congregation, not holding back my words, oh Yahweh, for You know it. I haven't hid Your goodness in my heart; I've told Your faithfulness and Your saving grace: I haven't concealed Your love and Your truth from the great congregation.*

[11-17] Don't withhold Your tender mercies from me, oh Yahweh: let Your love and Your truth always save me. More evils than I can count have overtaken me, my sins have taken hold of me so that I'm not able to look up; They're more than the hairs of my head, so my heart fails me. Be pleased, oh Yahweh, to save me: oh Yahweh, hurry to help me. Let those who look for my soul to destroy it be ashamed and confused; let those that wish evil on me be driven back and put to shame. Let those that say to me, "*Aha, aha*" be deserted for the punishment of their shame. Let all those that look for You celebrate and be glad in You: let those who love the fact that You've saved them say always, "*oh Yahweh, let us make you known.*" But I'm poor and needy; yet my God thinks of me: You are my help and my deliverer; don't be long, oh my God.

41 [1-3] *To the first musician, A Hymn of David.* Blessed are those that have compassion on the poor: Yahweh will save them in their time of trouble. Yahweh will save them, keeping them alive and blessing them on the earth, and won't leave them to the will of their enemies. Yahweh will strengthen them on the bed of suffering, making up their beds in sickness.

[4-8] I said, *oh Yahweh, be merciful to me: heal my soul; for I've sinned against You. My enemies speak evil of me, so when will they die and their name die out?* And if they come to see me, they speak arrogant lies, collecting sins in their hearts, and when they go away, they tell it all. All that hate me whisper together against me, devising my hurt. They say that an evil disease is clinging to me; and now that I'm sick, they say I'll rise up no more.

[9-13] Yes, even My own close friend that I always trusted in, which ate of My food, has risen up against Me. But You, oh Yahweh, be merciful to Me, and raise Me up, that I can avenge Myself of them. By this I know, that You are gracious to Me, because My enemies won't triumph over Me. And as for Me, You uphold Me in My goodness, and set Me before Your face forever. May Yahweh be blessed, God of Israel, from eternity, to eternity. Amen and Amen.

Book 2

42 [1-4] *To the first musician, A Poem of Teaching, for the children of Korah.* As the deer pants after the waters of a stream, so my soul craves for You, oh God. My soul thirsts for You, for the living God: when will I come and appear before You? My tears have been my substance day and night, while they always say to me, *"Where is your God?"* When I remember these things, I pour my soul out within me: for I had gone in with the congregation, I went with them into Your House of God, Yahweh, with the voice of joy and praise, with all those that kept Your holyday.

[5-11] Why are you depressed, oh my soul? And why are you troubled in me? Hope in God: for I'll yet praise You when You look at me and help me. Oh my God, my soul is depressed within me: so I'll remember You all the times You helped me on my journey. Deep water calls to the rapids at the noise of Your waterfalls: all Your misty waves are washing over me. Yahweh, the commandment of Your love is with me in the daytime, and in the night Your song will be with me, and my prayer is to the God of my life. I'll say to God, my rock, *"Why have You forgotten me? Why do I go mourning because my enemy keeps me down?"* As if I had a blade in my body, my enemies accuse me, saying daily to me, *"Where is your God?"* Why are you depressed, oh my soul? And why are you troubled within me? Hope in God: for I'll yet praise You, who brings me health and happiness, You are my God.

43 [1-5] Judge me, oh God, and plead my case against an ungodly nation: oh save me from lying and unfair people. For You are the God of my strength: why do You throw me away? Why do I mourn because my enemy keeps me down? Oh send out Your light and Your truth: let them lead me; let them bring me to Your holy hill, and to Your House of God. Then I'll go to the altar of God, to Yahweh God with my great joy: yes, on the harp I'll praise You, oh Yahweh God, my God. Why are You depressed, oh my soul? And why are You troubled within me? Hope in God: for I'll yet praise You, who brings me health and happiness, You are my God.

44 [1-3] *To the first musician for the children of Korah, A Poem of Teaching.* We've heard with our ears, oh God, our parents have told us of the acts You did before in their days. How You drove out the ungodly with Your hand, and planted them; how You troubled the people, and threw them out. For they didn't get possession of the land by their own weapons, nor did their own strength save them, but the strong hand of Your power, and the way You looked at them and shined on them, because You had mercy on them.

[4-8] You are my Savior, oh God: give freedom to Your people. Through You, we will push back our enemies: through Your Name we will tread under those that rise up against us. For I won't trust in weapons, nor will my strength save me, but You've saved us from our enemies, and have put them to shame that hated us. We boast in God always, and we praise Your Name forever. Selah!

[9-14] But You've thrown us off, and put us to shame; and no longer go with our armies. You make us turn back from the enemy, and those who hate us take our things for themselves. You've given us to be like animals appointed for butchering; and have scattered us among the ungodly. You sell Your people for nothing, and don't increase Your wealth by their price. You make us an object of accusation to our neighbors, a ridicule and mockery to those that are around us. You makes us a byword among the ungodly, a shaking of the head among the people.

[15-19] My confusion is always before me, and the shame of my face has covered me, because of the voice of those that accuse and curse me; because of my enemy and punisher. All this has come on us; yet we haven't forgotten You, nor have we dealt falsely with Your Promise. Our hearts haven't left, nor have our steps declined from Your way; though You've greatly broken us in a land of dragons, and covered us with the shadow of death.

[20-26] If we've forgotten the Name of our God, or stretched out our hands to make ungodly things our objects of worship won't You know it? For You know all the secrets of the heart. Yes, for Your sake we're destroyed all day long, counted as animals for the slaughter. Awake, why do You sleep, oh my God? Awake, don't throw us off forever. Why do You hide Your face, and forget our misery and keep us down? For our souls are humbled to the dust: our bellies cling to the earth. Awake for our help, and free us for Your mercies' sake.

45 [1-7] *To the first musician on trumpet, for the children of Korah, A Poem of Teaching, A Wedding Song of loves.* My heart is trusted with a good thing: I speak of the things which I've written about the Savior: my words are from the pen of a poetic writer. You are most fair among the children of humanity: grace is poured into Your Words: so God has blessed You forever. Fasten your weapon on your thigh, oh Most High, with Your glory and Your majesty. And in Your majesty ride prosperously because of truth and gentleness and goodness; and Your hands will teach You awesome things. Your weapons are sharp in the heart of the Savior's enemies; by which the people fall under You. Your reign, oh God, is forever and ever: the reign of Your realm is a good reign. You love goodness, and hate evil: so God, Your God, has anointed You with the oil of gladness above all Your people.

[8-17] All your garments smell of spices, out of the ivory great houses, by which they've made You glad. Your children are among Your honorable people: Your bride will stand clothed in gold at Your side. Pay attention, oh children, think about it and listen; forget your own people, and your parent's house; For the One who is your Savior greatly wants your loveliness: so you should honor the Savior. And the children of the mountain nations will

32

be there with gifts; even the rich among the people will entreat Your favor. The children of the Savior are all glorious inside and out: their clothing is woven with threads of pure gold. They'll be brought to the Savior in clothing of fine needlework: their young followers will be brought to You, as well. With gladness and celebrating they'll be brought, entering into Your great house. Your children will replace Your ancestors, so that You can have crowned heads in the whole world. I'll make Your Name to be remembered in all generations, so the people will praise You forever and ever.

46 [1-3] *To the first musician for the children of Korah, A Song in soprano.* God is our safe haven and strength, here to help in all our stressful times. So we won't fear, even if the earth quakes and the islands fall into the sea; Even if the oceans roar and the ocean waves are stirred up, even if the volcanoes explosively erupt. Selah!

[4-7] There's a river, the streams of which will make glad the city of God, the holy place of the sanctuaries of the Most High. God is in the midst of the city, which will never be upset: God will soon help it. The ungodly raged, when their nations were upset: You spoke Your voice, and the earth melted. Yahweh, the Leader of heavenly hosts is with us; our God is our safe haven. Selah!

[8-11] Come see the acts of Yahweh! What misery You've made in the earth. You make wars to cease until the end of the earth; You break the weapons in half; You burn their vehicles in the fire, saying: *Be still, and know that I am God: I'll be praised among the ungodly; I'll be praised in the whole world.* Yahweh, the Leader of heavenly hosts is with us; our God is our safe haven. Selah!

47 [1-4] *To the first musician, A Hymn for the children of Korah.* Clap your hands everyone; shout to God with the voice of triumph. For Yahweh, the Most High is awesome; God is the great Savior over The whole world. You'll subdue the people under us, and the nations under our feet. You'll choose our inheritance for us, the greatness of the people that You've loved. Selah!

[5-9] You'll go up to the throne with a shout, oh Yahweh, with the sound of a trumpet. Sing praises to God, sing praises: sing praises to our Savior, sing praises. For God is the Savior of the whole world: Sing praises with understanding. God reigns over the ungodly, sitting on the throne of holiness. The rulers of the people are gathered together, even the people of God: for the boundaries of the earth belong to God: for You are very well known.

48 [1-3] *A Song and Hymn for the children of Korah.* You are Great, oh Yahweh, and greatly to be praised in the holy city, and in the holy mountain. The north side of the mount of Jerusalem, the city of the great Savior is a beautiful setting, the joy of the whole earth. God is known in their great houses as a safe haven.

[4-8] For rulers were assembled, passing by together. They saw it, wondering and troubled, and ran away. Fear took hold of them there, and pain, as a woman in childbirth. You break the ships of Tarshish with an east wind. As we have heard, so we have seen in the city of Yahweh, the Leader of heavenly hosts, in the city of our God: God will set it up forever. Selah!

[9-14] We've thought of Your love, oh God, in the midst of Your House of God. According to Your Name, oh Yahweh, so Your praises will ring to the ends of the earth: Your strong hands are full of goodness. Let the mount of Jerusalem celebrate; let the children of God be glad, because of Your judgments. Walk around Jerusalem, going around it, and telling about the towers of it. Mark well their defenses; think about their great houses, so that you can tell it to the generation which follows you. For this God is our God forever and ever: You'll be our Guide even to our death.

49 [1-4] *To the first musician, A Hymn for the children of Korah.* Listen to this, everyone; listen, everyone of the world: Those of both low and high class, rich and poor, together. I'll speak with wisdom; and my innermost thoughts will be of understanding. I'll listen to a story: I'll play my mysterious sayings on the harp.

[5-11] Why should I fear in the days of evil, when my sins are about to catch up with me and overcome me? Those that trust in their wealth, and boast themselves in the greatness of their riches; none of them can by any means free their own family members, nor give to God a ransom for them: For the redemption of their soul is precious, and forever finished, so that they should live forever, and not see evil. For they see that wise people die, likewise stupid people and the rebellious die, and leave their wealth to others. They believe that their lineage will continue forever, and that their resting places will be left for generations after them, calling their lands after their own names.

[12-14] Yet, even though people are honored, they won't stay, but are like the wild animals that die. Their way is stupidity: yet their children that follow them approve of their sayings. Selah! Like animals they're laid in their graves; death will live on them; and godly people will have dominion over them in the morning, their loveliness being consumed in the home of their grave.

[15-20] But God will free My soul from the power of the grave and will receive Me. Selah! Don't be afraid when someone is made rich and the fame of their house increases, because when they die they'll carry nothing with them and their fame won't follow them. Even though while they lived they blessed their own soul; as people will praise you when you do well for yourself, they'll go to their ancestors never seeing the light, and though they're honored, they don't understand that they're like the wild animals that die.

50 [1-6] *A Hymn of Asaph.* The mighty God, even Yahweh, has spoken, and called the earth from the rising of the sun to the setting of it. Out of Jerusalem, the perfection of loveliness, God has shined. Our God will come, and won't keep silent: a fire will consume before You, and it'll be very intense around You. You'll call to the heavens from above, and to the earth, so that You can judge Your people. *Gather My people together to Me, those that have made a Promise with Me by sacrificial offerings,* and the heavens will declare Your goodness: for You, God will be judge Yourself. Selah!

[7-15] Listen, oh My people, and I'll speak; I'll testify against You, My people: *"I am God, even Your God. I won't criticize you for your offerings or your sacrifices, which were to have been placed always before Me. I'll take no offering out of your house, nor sacrifices out of your assets. For all the creatures of the forest are mine, along with the cattle on a thousand hills. I know every bird of the mountains, and the wild animals of the fields are mine as well. If I were hungry, I wouldn't tell you: for the world is mine, and everything in it. Will I eat the meat of bulls, or drink the blood of goats? Offer to God thanksgiving; and pay your vows to the Most High: And call on Me in the day of trouble: I'll save you, and you'll make Me well-known."*

[16-23] But to the sinful God says, *"Seeing you hate teaching, and have thrown my words behind you, what do you have to do with My words, that you should let My Promise come out of your mouth? When you saw a thief, then you were an accomplice, and you've been with adulterers, also. You give your mouth to evil, and your words create lies. You sit and speak against your family; You slander your own mother's child. These things have you done, and I kept silent; you thought that I was altogether such a one as yourself, but I'll admonish you, and set them in order before your eyes. Now think about this, you who forget God; or I'll tear you in pieces, and there'll be none to save you. Whoever offers praise makes Me well-known, and all those who control their behaviors well, I, Yahweh God, will save."*

51 [1-4] *To the first musician, A Hymn of David, when Nathan the preacher came to him, after he had committed adultery with Bathsheba.* Have mercy on me, oh God, according to Your love, according to the greatness of Your tender mercies, forget my sins. Wash me thoroughly from my sin, and cleanse me, for I acknowledge my sins, which are always before me. Against You, and You only, have I sinned, doing this evil in Your sight; so that You'll be justified when You speak, and be clear when You judge.

[5-12] See, I was a sinner from my birth, and even from my conception. You want truth in my inmost mind, and in the secret parts of my soul You'll teach me wisdom. Cleanse me from my sins, and I'll be clean: wash me, and I'll be whiter than snow. Make me to hear joy and gladness; that the bones which You've broken can celebrate. Hide Your face from my sins, and forget them all. Create in me a new heart, oh God; and refresh Your spirit within me. Don't throw me out from Your presence; and don't take Your Holy Spirit from me. Bring me back the joy of when you first saved me; and Keep me freely with Your Spirit.

[13-17] Then I'll teach the sinful Your ways; and the sinful will be brought to You. Free me from the guiltiness of blood, oh God, You are the God who saved me, and my mouth will sing aloud of Your goodness. Oh my God, train my words; and my mouth will praise You. For You don't want sacrifice, or else I would give it; You don't celebrate in offerings. The only sacrifice that God requires is a broken spirit: a broken and a repentant heart, oh God, that, You won't hate.

[18-19] Do great things in Your good pleasure to Jerusalem: build up the walls of Jerusalem. Then You'll be pleased with the offerings of goodness, with both the small sacrifices and the large sacrifices: then they'll give offerings on Your altar.

52 [1-6] *To the first musician, A Poem of Teaching, A Hymn of David, when Doeg the Edomite came and told Saul, and said to him, David is come to the house of Ahimelech.* Why boast yourself in trouble, oh mighty ones? The goodness of God lasts everlastingly. Your mouths plan trouble; like a sharp razor, always lying. You love evil more than good; and lying rather than speaking what's good. Selah! You love all consuming words, oh you lying mouths. God will likewise destroy you forever, God will take you away, plucking you out of your homes, and uprooting you out of the land of the living. Selah!

[6-9] Godly people will see, and fear, and laugh at you, saying: *"So this is the people that refuse to make God their strength; but trusted in the abundance of their riches, and strengthened themselves in their evil."* But I'm like a green olive tree in Your House of God: I trust in the mercy of God forever and ever. I'll praise You forever, because You've done it, and I'll minister to Your Name, Yahweh; for it's good for Your people.

53 [1-3] *To the first musician, to the tune of The sickness, A Poem of Teaching, A Hymn of David.* Stupid people have said in their hearts, *"There is no God."* They're evil, and have done horrible sins: no one does good. God looked down from heaven on the children of humanity, to see if there were any that understand or look for God. All of them have turned away, and have become altogether filthy; there's none that does good, no, not one of them.

[4-6] Have the sinful any knowledge, who consume my people like they eat food? They've never even called on God. There they were in great fear, where there was nothing to fear: for You scattered the bodies of those that encamped against You: You've put them to shame, because You hated them. Oh that Israel would be saved out of Jerusalem! When You bring back Your people from captivity, they will celebrate and be glad.

54 [1-7] *To the first musician on the stringed instrument, A Poem of Teaching, A Hymn of David, when the Ziphims came and said to Saul, doesn't David hide himself with us?* Save me, oh Yahweh God, by Your Name, and judge me by Your strength. Listen to my prayer, oh God; hear my words. For the ungodly are risen up against me, and keep me down, looking for my soul: they don't keep God in their sight. Selah! See, God is my helper: You are with those that uphold my soul, and will repay evil to my enemies, destroying them with Your truth; so I'll freely sacrifice for You, praising Your Name, oh Yahweh; because it is so good. God has freed me out of all my trouble; and I've seen everything I wanted to happen to my enemies.

55 [1-8] *To the first musician on the stringed instrument, A Poem of Teaching, A Hymn of David.* Listen to me, oh God; and don't hide Yourself from my prayer. Pay attention to me, and listen to me: I mourn, complaining and groaning because of the voice of the enemy, because of the sinful who keep me down: for they place sin on me, and hate me in anger. My heart aches within me, and I'm scared to death. Fearfulness and trembling have come over me, and horror has overwhelmed me. So I said, *"Oh that I had wings like a dove! Then I could fly away, and be at rest."* See, then I would wander far off, and stay in the countryside. Selah! I would hasten my escape from the windy storm and fury.

[9-15] Destroy them, oh my God, and divide their tongues: for I've seen violence and trouble in this city. Day and night they go about on the borders of it: trouble and sorrow are in the midst of it also. Evil is in the midst of it: lies and more lies don't leave its streets. It wasn't an enemy that blamed me; for then I could have lasted it: nor was it those that hated me that magnified themselves against me; then I would have hid myself from them: But it was my equal, my guide, and my acquaintance. We took friendly encouragement from each other, and walked into Your House of God together. Let death seize on them, and let them go down quick into Hell: for evil is in their houses, and among them.

[16-21] As for me, I'll call on Yahweh God; and You'll save me. Evening, morning, and at noon, I'll pray, and cry aloud, and God will hear my voice. God has freed my soul in peace from the battle that was against me: for there were many with me. God will hear, and trouble them, even those that are old, because they haven't changed; They're unrepentant and don't respect God. Selah! They have used their hands against those that are at peace with them, breaking their promises. The words of their mouths were smoother than butter, but fighting was in their hearts: their words were softer than oil, yet they were as drawn blades.

[22-23] Give all your problems to Yahweh, and God will Keep you: God will never let good people be overturned. But You, oh God, will bring them down into the grave of destruction: bloodthirsty and lying people won't live out half their days; but I'll trust in You.

56 [1-7] *To the first musician, to the tune of Dove of the Silence, A Poem of David, when the Philistines took him in Goth.* Be merciful to me, oh God: for the people will overwhelm me; their fighting daily keeps me down. My enemies overwhelm me daily: for there are many that fight against me, Most High God, but whenever I'm afraid, I'll trust in You. In God, I'll praise Your Word; I've put my trust in God; I won't be afraid of what people might do to me. They change my words all day long: all their thoughts are evil towards me. They gather together, hiding themselves and marking my steps, while they wait for my very soul. Shall they escape by sin? No, You'll destroy them, oh God, in Your anger.

[8-13] You know where I've been and You've saved all my tears into Your bottle, and You've written them all down in Your book. When I cry to You, then my enemies turn back: God is for me; this I know. In God, I'll praise Your Word: in Yahweh God, I'll praise Your Word. In God, I've put my trust: I won't be afraid of what people might do to me. Your promises are on me, so I'll praise You, oh God. For You've freed my soul from death: won't You keep my feet from falling, so that I can walk before You in the light of life?

57 [1-4] *To the first musician, You must not destroy, A Poem of David, when he fled from Saul in the cave.* Be merciful to me, oh God, be merciful to me: for my soul trusts in You; yes, in the shade of Your Spirit I'll make my safe haven, until these misfortunes are over. I'll cry to Yahweh God Most High; to God who does all things for me. God will send from heaven, and save me from the accusations of those that try to overwhelm me. Selah! God will send mercy and truth. My soul is as if I were among lions, and I lie even among those that are set on fire with rage, even the children of humanity, whose teeth are as sharp as spikes and arrows, and their mouths speak as sharp blades.

[5-11] Be praised, oh Yahweh God, above the heavens; let Your glory be above the whole world. They've prepared a trap for my steps; my soul is humbled: they've dug a grave for me, into which they themselves are fallen. Selah! My heart is set, oh God, my heart is set: I'll sing and give You praise. Awake, my glory; awake, instruments and harp: I myself will awake early. I'll praise You, oh my God, among the people: I'll sing to You among the nations. For Your mercy stretches across the heavens and Your truth reaches to the clouds. Be praised, oh God, above the heavens: let Your glory be seen above the whole world.

58 [1-6] *To the first musician, You must not destroy, A Poem of David.* Do you indeed speak goodness, oh congregation? Do you judge uprightly, oh you children of humanity? Yes, in your heart you do evil; you measure the violence of your hands in the earth. The sinful are separated from the womb, going astray and speaking lies as soon as they're born. Their poison is like the poison of a serpent: like deaf snakes that stop their ears, which won't listen to the voice of charmers, charming ever so wisely. Break their teeth, oh God, in their mouth: break out the great teeth of the young lions, oh Yahweh.

[7-11] Let them melt away as waters which run always: when they ready their weapons, let them be as if they were cut in pieces. As a snail which melts, let every one of them pass away: just like the untimely birth of a stillborn baby. Before your pots can feel the heat from the burning thorns, God will take them away in living and burning anger as a furious hurricane. Godly people will celebrate when they see the vengeance: God will wash their feet in the blood of the sinful so that they'll say, *Truly, there's a reward for godly people: God is a God that judges in the earth.*

59 [1-4] ***To the first musician, You must not destroy, A Poem of David; when Saul sent, and watched the House of God to kill him.*** Free me from my enemies, oh my God: defend me from those that rise up against me. Free me from those who practice sin, and save me from bloodthirsty people. See, they lie in wait for my soul: the mighty are gathered against me; but not for my offense, nor for my sin, oh Yahweh. They run and prepare themselves unjustifiably: awake to help me, and see what they do.

[5-8] You, oh Yahweh, God of heavenly hosts, God of Your people, Israel, awake to visit all the ungodly: Don't be merciful to any sinful people. Selah! They return at evening, growling like dogs around the city. See, they're disgustingly loud with their mouth: sharpness is in their words: for that, they say, "*Who hears?*" But You, oh Yahweh, will laugh at them; You'll hate all the ungodly people.

[9-13] Because You are my strength, I'll minister to You: for You, God, are my defense. The God of my mercy will keep me and let me see the judgment on my enemies. Don't kill them, or my people will forget: scatter them by Your power; and bring them down, oh my God, our defense. For the sin of their mouth, the words they say, and for the cursing and lies which they speak, let them be taken in their pride. Consume them in anger, consume them so that they can't exist any longer, and let them know that God rules in Israel and even to the ends of the earth. Selah!

[14-17] And at evening let them return; and let them growl like dogs, going around the city. Let them wander up and down for meat, and howl if they aren't satisfied. But I'll sing of Your power; yes, in the morning I'll sing aloud of Your mercy: for You've been my defense and safe haven in the day of my trouble. To You, oh my strength, I'll sing: for God is my defense, and the God of my mercy.

60 [1-5] ***To the first musician on the trumpet of the congregation, A Poem of David, to teach; when he strove with Aram-naharaim and with Aram-zobah, when Joab returned, and struck twelve thousand of Edom in the valley of salt.*** Oh God, You've thrown us off, scattering us, You've been displeased; oh return to us again. You've made the earth tremble, breaking it: heal its division; for it quakes. You've shown Your people hard things: You've made us drink the wine of astonishment. You've given a banner to those that respect You, to be displayed because it bears the truth. Selah! Save with Your strong hand, and listen to me so that Your beloved can be freed.

[6-8] God has spoken in holiness; *I'll celebrate, I'll divide Shechem, and allot the valley of Succoth. Gilead is Mine, and Manasseh is Mine; Ephraim is also the strength of My head; Judah is My lawgiver; Moab is My wash pot; over Edom I'll place my shoe: Philistia, you'll triumph because of me.*

[9-12] Who will bring me into the strong city that will lead me into Edom? Won't You, oh God, who had thrown us off? And You, oh God, who didn't go out with our armies? Give us help from trouble because the help of people is no help at all. Through God, we'll have victory: for it's God that will bring down our enemies.

61 [1-4] ***To the first musician on stringed instrument, A Hymn of David.*** Listen to my cry, oh God; pay attention to my prayer. I'll cry to You from the ends of the earth, whenever my heart is overwhelmed: lead me to the Rock that is higher than I am. You've been a shelter for me, and a strong refuge from my enemies, so I'll stay in Your House of God forever: I'll trust in the protection of Your Spirit. Selah!

[5-8] For You, Yahweh, have heard my promises: You've given me the heritage of those that respect Your Name. You'll prolong my life, and my years will be as many generations. I'll live for God forever: Get Your mercy and truth ready, which saves me. I'll sing praise to Your Name forever, so that I'll keep my vows daily.

62 [1-4] ***To the first musician, to Laudatory, A Hymn of David.*** Truly my soul waits patiently on God, who saves me. God is my rock, who alone saves me. God is my only defense; so I won't be greatly upset. How long will you imagine trouble against me? Don't you know you'll be killed, every one of you: you'll be as a sagging wall, and as a leaning fence, because you make plans to throw me down from my greatness, enjoying telling your lies. And you bless me with your mouth, but inwardly you curse me. Selah!

[5-7] Wait patiently, my soul, on God; for my expectation is from God only. God is my rock, who alone saves me: God is my only defense; so I won't be greatly upset. God saves me and makes me known; God is the Rock of my strength. My safe haven is in God alone.

[8-12] Trust in God at all times; you people, pour out your hearts to God: God is a safe haven for us. Selah! Surely people of low class are full of emptiness, and people of high class are full of lies: to be weighed in the balance, they're altogether lighter than air. You people shouldn't trust in keeping others down, and become arrogant in thievery: even if your riches increase, don't set your heart on them. I've heard it said once or twice that

36

all power belongs to God. Mercy belongs also to You, oh my God: for You give to everyone according to their own acts.

63 [1-4] *A Hymn of David, when he was in the countryside of Judah.* Oh God, You are my God; I'll look for You early: my soul thirsts for You, my body longs for You in a dry and thirsty land where there's no water; so I'll see Your power and Your glory, like I've seen in Your House of God. Your love is better than life, so my words will praise You. I'll bless You as long as I live: I'll lift up my hands in Your Name, Yahweh.

[5-11] My soul will have everything I need; and my mouth will praise You with joyful words when I remember You while I lay in my bed, and think of You in the night. In the shade of Your Spirit I'll celebrate because You've been my help. My soul follows firmly after You: Your strong hand upholds me. But those that look for my soul, only to destroy it, will go to Hell. They'll fall by the blade and be a meal for foxes. But I'll celebrate victory in God; because every one that keeps the promises of God will celebrate, but the words of those that lie will soon end.

64 [1-5] *To the first musician, A Hymn of David.* Listen to my voice, oh God, in my prayer: save my life from the fear of my enemies. Hide me from the secret plans of the sinful; from the rebellion of those who practice sin: who sharpen their mouths like a blade, and get ready their weapons of bitter words, so they can secretly shoot at the godly, shooting at them unexpectedly, without fear. They encourage themselves in evil matters, talking together of secretly laying traps; They say, *"Who will see us?"*

[6-10] They search out sins, accomplishing a thorough search: the minds of every one of them, and their hearts, are beyond understanding. But God will unexpectedly repay them and they'll be wounded. So they themselves will fall by the words of their own mouth, and everyone that sees them will run away. And all people will respect, and declare the actions of God; for they'll wisely think about the acts of God. Godly people will celebrate in Yahweh, trusting in God; and all the goodhearted will praise God.

65 [1-4] *To the first musician, A Hymn, the Song of David.* We praise You, oh God, in Jerusalem, and to You God, we will keep our vows. You are the One who hears our prayers, to You everybody will come. My sins overtake me, yet You'll take them all away. Blessed are the people that You choose, and cause to come to You, so that they can stay in Your house: We'll be satisfied with the goodness of Your House of God, yes, Your holy House of God.

[5-8] By awesome things You'll answer us in goodness, oh God who saves us, who is the hope of everyone here and of those that are in faraway places across the sea. By Your strength, You set the mountains fast; being strengthened with Your power, which quiets the sound of the seas, the roaring of the waves, and the uproar of the people. And those who stay in the far off parts of the earth are afraid at Your signs: You make the dawn of the morning and the setting of the evening light to celebrate.

[9-13] You visit the earth, and water it: You greatly enrich it with the river of God, which is full of water: You prepare the grain, when You've so provided for it. You water the rows very much; settling the furrows of it, making it soft with rain showers and blessing its springing up. You crown the year with Your goodness; and Your ways always bring many blessings. You drop rain on the pastures of the countryside, and the little hills celebrate everywhere. The pastures are filled with herds; the valleys also are covered with grain; they shout for joy, and sing.

66 [1-4] *To the first musician, A Song or Hymn.* Let the whole land make a joyful sound to Yahweh God: Let them sing out the honor of Your Name and make Your praise glorious. Say to God, *How awesome You are in Your acts!* Through the greatness of Your power Your enemies submit themselves to You. The whole world will worship and praise You, singing to Your Name. Selah!

[5-9] Come and see the acts of God, which are awesomely done for the children of humanity. You turned the Red Sea into dry land, where they celebrated in God after going through the waters on foot. You rule by Your power forever, watching the nations; so don't let the rebellious make themselves great. Selah! Oh bless our God, everyone, and make the sound of God's praise be heard: Who keeps our souls alive, and doesn't let us fall.

[10-15] For You, oh God, have proved us, trying us, as silver is tried. You led us into a trap, making us miserable. You've caused people to rule over us, taking us through fire and through water, but You brought us out into a rich place. So I'll go into Your House of God with sacrifices, paying my vows to You, who spoke to me, when I was in trouble. I'll offer to You the wholeness of youth, with the aroma of strength; I'll give You my best sacrifices along with my offerings. Selah!

[16-20] Come and hear, all You that respect Yahweh God, and I'll declare what God has done for my soul. I cried aloud to God, and I praised God. If I allow sin in my heart, my God won't listen to me: but in truth You've heard me and listened to my prayers. Blessed be God, for You haven't turned away my prayer or Your mercy from me.

67 [1-2] *To the first musician on the stringed instrument, A Hymn or Song.* God be merciful to us, and bless us; and let the light of Your face shine on us; Selah! So that Your ways can be known on earth, and Your saving health among all the nations. Let the people praise You, oh God; let all the people praise You.

37

[4-7] Oh let the nations be glad and sing for joy: for You judge us rightly, and govern every nation on earth. Selah! Let the people praise You, oh God; let all the people praise You. Then the earth will be improved; and You, our own God, will bless us. You'll bless us; and the whole world will respect You, Oh God.

68 [1-4] ***To the first musician, A Hymn or Song of David.*** Awake God, let Your enemies be scattered: let them that hate You run from Your presence. Drive them away as smoke is driven away: as wax melts before the fire, so let the sinful die at the presence of God. But let godly people be glad, celebrating before God: yes, let them have a great time singing to God and celebrating before You, singing praises to Your Name and making You known, who journeys through the heavens by Your Name, Yahweh.

[5-8] God, in Your holiness, You are like a Parent to those who don't have a parent, and give judgment to the single parents. God puts the lonely ones in families: You bring out those who are kept down, but the rebellious stay in a dreary place. Oh God, when You went forward before Your people, Israel, when You marched with them through the countryside; Selah: The earth shook and the clouds descended at Your presence: even Sinai itself quaked at the presence of God, the God of Your people, Israel.

[9-13] You, oh God, sent much rain, by which You confirmed Your inheritance, when it was nearly destroyed. Your people stand in it: You, oh God, have provided Your goodness for the poor. My God gave the Word and those who published it were made great. Leaders of armed forces ran away, and those who stayed at home received the benefits. Though You've been as lifeless as a pot, yet you'll fly as the silver wings of a dove, with feathers of yellow gold.

[14-18] When the Almighty scattered rulers in it, it was white as the snow on Salmon. The hill of God is as the hill east of the Jordon River; as high as the hill Bashan, of Palestine. Why do you rise up, you high hills? This is the hill that God wants to stay in; yes, Yahweh will stay in it forever. The vehicles of God are twenty thousand, in which there are thousands of angels: my Savior God is among them, as in Mt. Sinai, in the holy place. You've gone up into heaven, leading those who were captive captive: You've received gifts for all people; yes, even for the rebellious also, so that my Savior God will live among them.

[19-26] Blessed be my Savior God, who daily fills us with blessings, even the God who saves us. Selah! The One who is our God is the God who saves us; and Yahweh, my Savior God, helps us escape from death. You'll wound the heads of Your enemies, and the scalps of those that still go on in their sin. My Savior God said, "*I'll bring back my people from Bashan, I'll bring my people back from the depths of the sea: so that your feet may walk in the blood of your enemies, and the mouth of your dogs in the same.*" They've seen Your ways, oh God; even the ways of my God, my Savior, in the House of God. The singers went first, with the instrument players following after; and among them, were the tambourine players. Bless You, oh God, in the assemblies, even my Savior God, from the beginning of Israel.

[27-31] There's little Benjamin with their ruler, the rulers of Judah and their council, the rulers of Zebulun, and the rulers of Naphtali. Your God has given you your strength: strengthen, oh God, that which You've already done for us. Because of Your House of God at Jerusalem, rulers will bring gifts to You. Punish those that fight, the great ones, along with the young people, till every one of them give themselves with monetary gifts, and You scatter the people that enjoy fighting. Leaders will come out of Egypt; Ethiopians will soon stretch out their hands to God.

[32-35] Sing to God, You nations of the earth; oh sing praises to Yahweh; Selah: To the Great One who rides on the heaven of heavens, which are everlasting; see, the mighty voice of God sounds out. Our strength is from You, God: Your greatness is above Your people, Israel, and Your strength is in the skies. Oh God, You are awesome coming out of Your holy places: it's You, God, who gives strength and power to Your people, Israel. God be blessed!

69 [1-4] ***To first musician on trumpet, A Hymn of David.*** Save me, oh God; for my soul is drowning. I'm sinking in deep mud, where I can't stand up: I'm in deep waters, where the floods overflow me. I'm tired of my tears: my throat is dry: my eyes grow weak while I wait for my God. Those that hate me for no reason are more than the hairs of my head: those that would destroy me, who are wrongfully my enemies, are mighty: so I've even restored to them that which I haven't taken.

[5-9] Oh God, You know my stupidity; and my sins aren't hid from You. Don't let Your people, oh Savior, God of the heavenly hosts, be ashamed for my sake: Don't let those that look for You become confused for my sake, oh God of Israel, because for Your sake I've been accused of many things and shame has covered my face. I'm as a stranger to my family members, and am as a foreigner to my brothers and sisters. For the passion of Your House of God has overwhelmed me; and the accusations of those that accused You are fallen on me.

[10-15] When I wept, and disciplined my soul with fasting, I was put down for it. I wore mourning clothes and I became a mockery to them. Those that sat in public spoke against me; and I was the song of drunks. But as for me, my prayer is to You, oh Yahweh, in an acceptable time: oh God, in the greatness of Your mercy listen to me, in the truth of Your saving grace. Pick me up out of the mud, and don't let me sink: let me be freed from those that hate me, and out of the flooding waters. Don't let the water overflow me, nor let the flood drown me, and don't let the grave shut its mouth on me.

38

[16-20] Listen to me, oh Yahweh; for Your love is good: turn to me according to the greatness of Your tender mercies, and don't hide Your face from Me; for I'm in trouble: listen to me quickly. Come near, and free my soul: save me from my enemies. You've known that I have been hated, shamed, and disrespected: my enemies are all before You. Their criticisms have broken my heart; and I'm very depressed: I looked for someone to feel sorry for me, but no one had any mercy; and for comforters, but I found none.

[21-26] They gave *Me* a bitter plant for *My* food; and in my thirst they gave *Me* sour vinegar to drink. Let their table trap them, and that which should have been for their welfare, let it become a snare. Blind their eyes, so that they don't see; and make their stomachs always rumble. Pour out Your righteous anger on them, and let Your great anger catch them. Let their surroundings be loneliness; and let no one stay in their house. For they abuse the one who You've struck down; and they take advantage of the grief of those that You've wounded.

[27-32] Add sin to their sin, and don't let them come into Your goodness. Let them be marked out of the book of the living, and not be written down with the names of godly people. But I'm poor and unhappy: let Your saving grace, oh God, make my place in heaven. I'll praise the Name of God with a song, and magnify Yahweh with thanksgiving. This pleases Yahweh better than sacrifices and offerings. The humble ones see this, and are glad, and the spirits of those that look for God will live.

[33-36] For You, Yahweh hear the poor, and don't hate those of Yours who are kept down. Let heaven and earth praise God, the seas, and every thing living in them. For God will save Jerusalem, and will build the cities of Judah: so that they can live there, and possess it. The children of Your people will also inherit it, and those that love the Name of Yahweh God will stay there.

70 [1-3] *To the first musician, A Hymn of David, to bring to remembrance.* Hurry, oh God, and save me; Hurry up and help me, oh Yahweh. Let those that try to destroy me be ashamed and confused: let those that hope for my harm be turned back and confused. Let their shame come back on them to repay those that say, "*Aha, aha.*"

[4-6] Let all those that look for You celebrate and be glad in You, and let those who love Your saving grace always say, "*Let God become well- known.*" But now I'm poor and needy, so hurry and come to me, oh God: You are my help and my Savior; oh Yahweh, don't be long.

71 [1-4] In You, oh Yahweh, I place my trust: let me never be confused. Free me in Your goodness, and help me escape: Listen to me, and save me. Be my safe haven, somewhere I can always go to. You've given Your Word to save me; for You are my rock and my defense. Free me, oh my God, out of the hand of the sinful, out of the hand of ungodly and cruel people.

[5-9] You are my hope, my Savior: You are my trust from my childhood. I've been held from the womb by You: You are the One that brought me safely out of my mother's womb: my praise will be always of You. Many wonder about me; but You are my strong safe haven. Let my mouth be full of Your praise and with Your honor all day long. Don't throw me off in my old age; Don't give up on me when my strength fails me.

[10-13] For my enemies speak against me; and those that wait around for my soul make their plans, saying to me, "*God has give up on you: we'll abuse and take you; for there's no one to save you.*" Oh God, don't be far from me: oh my God, hurry to help me. Let those that are enemies to my soul be confused and consumed; Let those that hope for my harm be shamed and disrespected.

[14-19] But I'll always hope in You, and will yet praise You even more. I'll tell of Your goodness and Your saving grace all day long; for I don't even know the extent of it. I'll go in the strength of the Savior God, making mention of Your goodness, and Yours only. Oh God, You've taught me from my childhood, and until now I've told everyone of all the amazing things You do. Now that I'm old and grey headed, oh God, don't give up on me; until I've made Your strength known to this generation, and Your power to every one that is to come. Your goodness is great also, oh God, who has done great things: oh God, who is like You!

[20-24] You, who have shown me severe and terrible troubles, will yet bring life to me, and will bring me up again from the depths of the earth. You'll make me greater and greater, and surround me with comfort. I'll praise You with the instruments, too, even Your truth, oh my God: I'll sing with the harp to You, oh Holy One of Israel. My soul, which You've bought back, will celebrate greatly whenever I sing my words to You. My mouth will talk of Your goodness also, all day long: for those who hope for my harm are confused and brought to shame.

72 [1-5] *A Hymn for Solomon.* Give the Ruler Your judgments, oh God, and Your goodness to the Ruler's Descendant, who'll judge Your people with goodness, and Your poor with good sense. The mountains and small hills will bring peace to the people, by Your goodness. The Savior who'll judge the poor people, saving the children of the needy, will destroy the one who keeps them down. They'll respect You as long as the sun and moon last, throughout all generations.

[6-9] The Savior will come down on the cut grass like rain: as the rain that waters the earth. In those days godly people will do well with a wealth of peace, as long as the moon lasts. You'll reign from sea to sea, also, and from the river to the whole world. Those that stay in the countryside will bow before You, the Savior, whose enemies will fall in the dust.

[10-14] The rulers of Tarshish and of the islands will bring presents: the rulers of Sheba and Seba will offer gifts. Yes, all rulers will fall down before the Savior: to whom all the nations will be subject, and who will save the poor and needy when they cry, sparing them and saving their souls, and also those that have no one to help them. Their blood will be precious in the Savior's sight, who will free their soul from lies and violence.

[15-20] And the Savior will live, who will be given of the gold of Sheba, and for whom continual prayer and praise will be made daily. There will be a handful of grain in the earth on the mountaintops; the fruit of it will shake like Lebanon, and they of the city will do well like grass of the earth. Your Most Holy Name, Yahweh, will last forever: Your Name will last as long as the sun; and the people will be blessed in You, all nations calling You blessed. May Yahweh be blessed, God, the God of Your people, Israel, who alone does wonderful things, and blessed be Your glorious Name forever, and may You be well-known in the whole earth; Amen, and Amen. The prayers of David the descendant of Jesse are ended.

Book 3

73 [1-6] *A Hymn of Asaph.* Truly God is good to Israel, to Your people who have clean hearts. But as for me, my feet had almost fallen; my steps had nearly slipped. I was jealous of stupid people, when I saw how well those sinful ones were doing. For death doesn't keep them out of trouble; their strength outlasts it. They don't suffer as other people; nor are they troubled as others are. So pride holds them like a chain and violence covers them like clothes.

[7-12] They keep getting more, even though they have more than a heart could hope for already. They're evil, talking proudly, and cruelly keep others down. They even speak against the heavens, as they walk through the earth. So their people return here, and take all their punishment for them. And they ask, *"How does God know?"* and, *"Does the Most High know it?"* See, these are the ungodly people that prosper in the world, which get more and more riches.

[13-20] Truthfully, I've cleansed my heart for no reason, and washed my hands in innocence. I've been troubled all day long, and disciplined every morning. If I say, *"I'll speak this;"* I would offend the whole generation of Your children. And when I knew this, it was too upsetting for me, until I went into the House of Yahweh God and understood what would happen to them in the end. Surely You put them in devious places, throwing them into ruin. In a moment, they're brought into misery! They're all together horrified. As a nightmare when a person awakes; so, my God, when You awake, You hate what you see.

[21-28] So my heart was grieved, and I was torn in my mind. I was so stupid and ignorant, like a dumb animal before You. Yet I stay with You, because You've held me by my hand. You'll guide me with Your wisdom, and afterward receive me up to heaven. Who have I in heaven but You? And there's no one on earth that I long for but You, God. My body and my heart fails, but You, God are the strength of my spirit, and my fortune forever. See, those that are far from You die: You destroy all those that are unfaithful to You. But it's good for me to draw near to God: I've put my trust in the Savior God, so that I can tell everyone of all Your acts.

74 [1-3] *A Poem of Teaching of Asaph.* Oh God, why have You left us forever? Why does Your anger burn against Your children? Remember Your people, which You've bought back long ago; the strength of Your inheritance, which You've freed; this mount Zion, where You've always been. Lift up Your feet from where You sleep and awake to see we're continually destroyed; See all the evil that the enemy has done in the House of God.

[4-8] Your enemies shout in the midst of Your congregations, setting up their flags for signs. People were famous if they had axed down thick trees, but now they break down its carved works at once with axes and hammers. They've thrown fire into Your House of God, polluting it by burning the resting place of Your Name, Yahweh, down to the ground. They said in their hearts, *"Let's destroy them"*, while burning up all the Houses of God in the land.

[9-12] We don't see our signs: there's not a preacher any more: nor are there any among us that knows how long. Oh God, how long will the enemy accuse us? Yahweh, will the enemy curse Your Name forever? Why do You withdraw Your hand, even Your strong hand? Take it out of Your lap. For You, God, are my Everlasting Savior, bringing Your saving grace in the midst of the earth.

[13-17] You divided the sea by Your strength: You broke the heads of the sea dragons in the oceans. You broke the heads of leviathan, the great dinosaur of the sea, in pieces, and gave them for meat to the people living in the countryside. You opened up the sources of water and the flood and dried up mighty rivers. The day is Yours; the night is Yours also; You made the sun and the moon. You set all the boundaries of the earth and made every season.

[18-23] Remember this, that the enemy has accused, oh Yahweh, and that stupid people have cursed Your Name. Oh don't give the soul of Your beloved to all the sinful people: Don't forget the poor of Your people forever. Keep Your promise: for the secret places of the earth are full of cruel territories. Don't let those who are kept down come back ashamed: let the poor and needy praise Your Name, Yahweh. Awake, oh God, plead Your own case: remember how stupid people accuse You daily. Don't forget the voice of Your enemies; the uproar of those that stand up against You keeps getting louder.

75 [1-5] *To the first musician, you must not destroy, A Hymn or Song of Asaph.* To You, oh God, we give thanks, to You we give thanks, for Your wondrous creations tell us that You are near. When I lead God's people I'll judge matters fairly. The earth and all of its people are broken, but I'll support it. Selah! I said to stupid people, *"Don't be stupid,"* and to the sinful, *"Don't be proud, lifting up your pride to heaven, and don't speak stubbornly."*

[6-10] Promotion comes neither from the east, nor from the west, nor from the south, but God is the judge, putting down one, and setting up another. For in the hand of Yahweh there's a penalty, and the wine of wrath is blood red; full of mixture; and God pours it out, but all the sinful of the earth will drink it, and even drink the sediment of it, as well. But I'll speak out forever; I'll sing praises to the God of Israel. All the strength of the sinful will be taken away; but the strength of godly people will be uplifted.

76 [1-7] *To the first musician on the stringed instrument, A Hymn or Song of Asaph.* God is known in Judah: Your Name is great in Israel. Your House of God is in Salem and Your resting place is in Jerusalem also.

There You break the bows and arrows, the shields, the blades, and the whole battle. Selah! You are more glorious and excellent than the mountains full of prey. The tough-hearted are spoiled, they've gotten their sleep, and none of the strong have found their strength. At Your teaching, oh God of Israel, both the driver and the horse are still. You, oh God, are to be feared, and who can stand in Your sight when You are angry?

[8-12] You, God, heard judgment from heaven; the earth feared, and stood still, when You arose to judgment, to save those of the earth with humility. Selah! Surely the people's anger will turn to praise You, and what's left of their anger You'll restrain. Vow, and pay what's due to Yahweh, Your God; let everyone around bring offerings to the One that ought to be respected. God will remove the spirit of the rulers: You're awful to the rulers of the earth.

77 [1-6] *To the first musician, to Laudatory, A Hymn of Asaph.* I cried aloud to God, to God with my own voice; and You listened to me. In the day of my trouble, when I ached all night with pain, which never stopped, and my soul refused to be comforted, I sought the Savior. I was troubled when I remembered God and complained, but my spirit was overwhelmed. Selah! You keep me awake: I'm so troubled that I can't even speak. I've thought about the past, the years long ago. I remembered my song in the night as I thought about it in my heart, my spirit carefully searching for it.

[7-12] I asked, *"Will the Savior throw me off forever? And will God be gracious no more? Is Your mercy completely gone forever? Will Your promises fail forever? Has God forgotten to be gracious? Have You shut up Your tender mercies in anger?"* Selah! And then I said, *"This is only what I deserved, but I remember the years the Most High was at my side."* I'll remember the acts of Yahweh: surely I'll remember Your wonders from the past. I'll think about all Your creations, and talk also of what You've done.

[13-20] Your way, oh Yahweh, is in the House of God: And who is as great as our God? You are the God that does wonders, showing Your strength among the people. You've bought back Israel, the descendants of Jacob and Joseph. Selah! The waters felt You, oh God, the waters felt You upset them and the depths were troubled as well. The clouds poured rain, the skies thundered, and Your lightening flashed also. The sound of Your thunder was in the heavens: the lightning lit up the world and the earth trembled and shook. Your way is in the sea; Your path is in the great oceans, and no one knows where You go. You led Israel like a herd of animals by the hand of Moses and Aaron.

78 [1-11] *A Poem of Teaching of Asaph.* Listen, oh my people, to my word: listen to the words of my mouth and I'll tell you a story, speaking of mysterious sayings of the past, which we have heard and known, and our parents have told us. We won't hide them from our children, and will show the praises of Yahweh to the next generation, along with the strength of God, and the wonderful things that God has done. For You left a testimony in Jacob, and made a law in Israel, which You told our parents to make them known to their children, so the generation to come would know them; And even their children that will be born to them to tell it to their children, so that they would put their hope in God, and not forget the acts of God, but keep Your commandments; and not be as their parents, who were a stubborn and rebellious generation, a generation that refused to change their hearts, and whose spirits weren't committed to God, as the children of Ephraim, being armed, and carrying weapons, turned back in the day of battle. They didn't keep the Promise of God, and refused to walk in Your Word, forgetting the acts of God, and the wonders that You had shown them.

[12-20] You did marvelous things in the sight of their parents, in the land of Egypt, in the field of Zoan. You divided the Red Sea, and allowed them to pass through it; making the waters to stand up as a mountain pass. You also led them with a cloud in the daytime, and through the night with the light of fire. You split the rock in the countryside, and gave them water to drink from a deep source. You, God brought streams of water out of the rock also, causing it to run down like rivers. And they sinned all the more against You by provoking the Most High God in the countryside. They tempted God in their hearts by asking for meat to satisfy their appetites. Yes, they even spoke against God and said, *"Can God furnish a table in the countryside? Look, God split the rock, so that the waters gushed out, and the streams overflowed; Can God give us food also? Can God provide meat for the people as well?"*

[21-33] Yahweh heard this, and was angry: so a fiery anger was kindled against Jacob, and anger also came up against Israel, because they didn't believed God, and didn't trust in Your saving grace, though You had told the clouds from above to open the doors of heaven, and had rained down manna on them to eat, and had given them of the grain of heaven. People ate the food of angels, and You, God, sent them enough meat to fill them. You caused an east wind to blow in the heavens, and powerfully brought in the south wind, raining meat on them as dust, and quail like the sand of the sea, and let them fall right in the middle of their camp, all around their tents. So they ate and were well filled, because You gave them what they wanted. They weren't kept from their appetites, but while their meat was yet in their mouths, the anger of God came down on them, and killed the fattest of them, and brought down the chosen people of Israel. For all this they still sinned, and didn't believe the wondrous acts of God, so You consumed their days with emptiness, and their years in trouble.

[34-39] But when You killed some of them, then the rest sought God, and they returned and soon asked for God. And they remembered that God was their Rock, the Most High God, their Savior. Yet they flattered You with their mouths, but lied to You with their words. Their hearts weren't right with God, nor were they committed to

Your Promise with them. But You, God, being full of compassion, forgave their sin, and didn't destroy them all: yes, many times You put aside Your anger, never stirring it up. For You remembered that they were only human; like a wind that passes away, and doesn't come again.

[40-51] How often they provoked You in the countryside, and grieved You in the desert! Yes, they turned back and tempted God, and limited what You, the Holy One of Israel, would do in their midst. They didn't remember God's hand, or the day when You freed them from the enemy. How God had made signs in Egypt, and wonders in the field of Zoan, turning their rivers into blood, making it so that they couldn't drink it. You sent different sorts of flies among them, which ate at them; and frogs, which destroyed them, giving their crops to the caterpillar, and their work to the locust also; destroying their vines with hail, and their sycamore trees with frost; destroying their cattle also in the hail, and their flocks with hot lightening bolts; throwing on them the fierceness of Your anger, all Your rage, righteous anger, and trouble, by sending evil angels among them; making way for Your anger; not sparing their soul from death, but giving their lives over to the deadly diseases; and striking all the firstborn in Egypt, their strongest rulers, in the Houses of Ham.

[52-61] But You made Your own people go forward like animals, guiding them in the countryside like a herd, leading them safely on, so that they weren't afraid, while the sea overwhelmed their enemies. You brought them to the border of Your House of God, even to this mountain, which the hand of God had bought. You also threw out the ungodly before them, and divided to them an inheritance by their families, and made the people of Israel to stay in their houses. Yet they tempted and provoked the Most High God, and didn't keep Your words, but unfaithfully turned back, doing just like their parents, who dishonestly turned away. They provoked God to anger with their places of worship, and made You jealous because of their worship of other things. When You, oh God, heard this, You were angry, and greatly hated Israel; so much that You forsook the House of God of Shiloh, the tent which You placed among the people, and allowed the Ark of the Promise to be taken into captivity, and the glory of God fell into the enemy's hand.

[62-66] You gave the people of God over to war; being angry with Your inheritance. The fire consumed their young people, even before they were married. Their preachers fell in war; and their survivors weren't allowed to mourn. Then the Savior awaked as one out of sleep, and like a drunk person who shouts, struck the rear of the enemy, and made them greatly ashamed.

[67-72] Moreover You refused the family of Joseph, and didn't choose the family of Ephraim, but chose instead the tribe of Judah, mount Zion, which God loved. And built Yahweh's House of God like high great houses, like the earth which You settled forever. You chose David also, who was Your worker, oh God, taking him from caring for the animals, and from following those that were pregnant with young, to feed Jacob, Your people, and Israel, Your inheritance. So David led them with a true heart; and guided them with skilful hands.

79 [1-5] *A Hymn of Asaph.* Oh God, the ungodly have come into Your inheritance, polluting Your holy House of God, and Jerusalem is in heaps. The dead bodies of Your children they have given for food to the birds of heaven, the bodies of Your saints to the wild animals of the earth. They have shed their blood like water around Jerusalem; and there was no one to bury them. We have become a curse to our neighbors, a mockery and the ridicule of those around us. How long, oh Yahweh? Will You be angry forever? Will Your jealousy burn like fire?

[6-9] Pour out Your anger on the ungodly that haven't known You, Yahweh, and on the nations that haven't called on Your Name, for they've destroyed Israel, and their homes. Oh don't remember our former sins: let Your tender mercies quickly stop us: for we're very humiliated. Help us, Yahweh, the God who saves us, for the glory of Your Name; save us and take away our sins, for Your Name's sake.

[10-13] Why should the ungodly say, "*Where is their God?*" Let God be known among the ungodly in our sight, by the avenging of the shed blood of Your people. Let the sighing of the captive come before You; according to the greatness of Your power save those that are about to die; and put blame into the lap of those who accused You seven times, my God. So we, Your people, those of Your realm, will give You thanks forever: We'll show Your praise to all generations.

80 [1-6] *To the first musician on the trumpet of the people, A Hymn of Asaph.* Listen, oh Shepherd of Israel, who leads the people of Joseph like a flock; You, oh God who stays between the angelic creatures, shine forward. Before Ephraim, Benjamin, and Manasseh, let Your strength rise up to come and save us. Return us to You, oh God, and cause Your face to shine on us; and we'll be saved. Oh Yahweh, God of heavenly hosts, how long will You be angry against the prayer of Israel? You feed them with the bread of sorrow; and give them many tears to drink. You make us a trouble to our neighbors, and our enemies laugh among themselves.

[7-11] Return us to You, oh God of heavenly hosts, and cause Your face to shine on us; and we'll be saved. You've brought a vine out of Egypt: You've thrown out the ungodly, and planted it. You made room for it, and caused it to take root deeply, and it filled the land. The hills were covered with the shadow of it, and its branches were like the good cedars. They sent them out to the sea, their branches to the river.

[12-19] Why have You then broken down their boundaries, so that all those which pass by pick on them? The wild boars in the woods waste it, and wild animals eat it. Return, we beg You, oh God of heavenly hosts: look down from heaven, and see; visit this vine and the vineyard which Your hand has planted, and the branch that

43

You made strong for Yourself. It's burned with fire and cut down, wilting at the look of Your face. Let Your hand be on Your chosen people, on the children of those that You made strong for Yourself. Revive us, so we won't turn away from You: and we'll call on Your Name. Return us to our former state, oh Yahweh, God of heavenly hosts, cause Your face to shine on us; and we'll be saved.

81 [1-5] *To the first musician on harp, a Hymn of Asaph.* Sing aloud to God, who is our strength, and make a joyful sound to the God of Israel. Take a hymn, and bring the tambourine, and the pleasant sounding harp, along with all the other instruments. Sound the trumpet at the new moon, in the time set aside for our formal holiday. For this was said for Israel, a law of the God of Israel. This was ordained by God for a witness in Joseph, when God went out through the land of Egypt, where I heard a language that I didn't understand.

[6-10] *I took the load from your shoulders and your hands were freed from the work. When you called in trouble, and I freed you; I answered you in the refuge of thunder: I proved you at the waters of Meribah. Selah! Listen, My people, and I'll testify to you: Israel, if you'll only listen to me; You will have no idols; nor are you to worship anything else but Me. I'm Yahweh, your God, which brought you out of the land of Egypt: open your mouth wide and I'll fill it.*

[11-16] *But My people wouldn't listen to My voice; and Israel wouldn't have Me. So I gave them up to what they themselves wanted, and they walked in their own ways. Oh that My people would have listened to me, and Israel would have walked in My ways! I would have quickly held back their enemies, and turned My strength against their enemies. Those who hate Yahweh should have obeyed Me: you shouldn't have quit. I would have fed you with the finest of the wheat, and I would have satisfied you with honey out of the rock face.*

82 [1-4] *A Hymn of Asaph.* God stands in the assembly of the mighty; God judges among the great ones. How long will you judge wrongly, and accept the persons of the sinful? Selah! Defend the poor and the survivors' children and do justice to the abused and needy. Deliver the poor and needy, removing them from the power of the sinful.

[5-8] They don't know or understand, walking on in darkness; and all the foundations of the earth are off course. I've said, "*You are gods; and all of you are children of the Most High God.* But you'll die as mere humans, and fall like one of the nobles. Awake, oh God, judge the earth: for You'll inherit all the people of the nations.

83 [1-4] *A Song or Hymn of Asaph.* Don't keep silence, oh God: Don't hold Your peace, and don't be still, oh God. See, Your enemies are in an uproar, and those that hate You have proudly put themselves in high places. They've craftily counseled against Israel, and consulted against Your mysterious ones. They've said, "*Come and let's destroy their nation so that the name of Israel will be forgotten.*"

[5-12] For with one consent they've planned together and are united against You: These worshipers of Edom, the Ishmaelites, Moabites, and the Hagarenes, the people of Gebal, and Ammon, and Amalek, and the Philistines along with the people of Tyre; The people of Assur also joined with them, who helped the descendents of Lot. Selah! Do to them as You did to the Midianites; and to Sisera, and as to Jabin, who died at Endor at the creek of Kison, and became as manure for the earth. Make their nobles like Oreb and Zeeb: yes, all their rulers as Zebah and as Zalmunna, who said, "*Let's take possession of the houses of God for ourselves.*"

[13-18] Oh my God, make them like the sagebrush; rolling as the stubble before the wind. As the fire burns through a forest, and as the flames set the mountains on fire; abuse them with Your tempest, and let Your storm make them afraid. Fill them with shame; so that they'll call Your Name, oh Yahweh. Let them be confused and troubled forever; yes, let them be ashamed and die, so that people can know that You alone, whose Name is Yahweh, are the Most High God over the whole earth.

84 [1-5] *To the first musician on harp, A Hymn for the children of Korah.* How agreeable are Your Houses of God, oh Yahweh, God of heavenly hosts! My soul longs, yes, even faints for the House of Yahweh, my heart and strength crying out for the living God. Yes, the sparrow and the swallow have found nests for themselves, where they can lay their eggs, even on Your altars, oh Yahweh, God of heavenly hosts, my Savior and my God. Blessed are those that stay in Your House of God and are still praising You. Selah! Blessed are the people whose strength is in You, in whose heart are their ways known.

[6-12] You, Who passing through the valley of Baca, make it spring up; with the rain filling the pools also. They go from one strength to another, every one of them in Jerusalem appearing before God. Oh Yahweh, God of heavenly hosts, hear my prayer; Listen, oh God of Israel. Selah! See, oh God, our defense, and look on the face of Your anointed. For a day in Your house is better than a thousand anywhere else. I had rather be a caretaker in the House of my God, than to stay in the house of evil. For Yahweh, my God, who gives grace and glory, is a light and a defense: God won't keep anything good from those who do what's right. Oh Yahweh, God of heavenly hosts, the people that trust in You are truly blessed.

85 [1-4] *To the first musician, A Hymn for the children of Korah.* Yahweh, You've been gracious to Your nation, Israel: You've given us back our freedom. You've forgiven the sin of Your people, covering them all. Selah! You've taken Your anger away, turning from all its fierceness. Turn us back to You, oh God who saves us, and let Your anger toward us come to an end.

44

[5-9] Will You be angry with us forever? Will You extend Your anger to all generations? Revive us again and let Your people celebrate in You! Show us Your mercy, oh Yahweh, and grant us Your saving grace. I'll hear what Yahweh God will speak, for You'll speak peace to Your people, to the saints of God, but don't let them turn again to stupidity. Surely the salvation of God is near those that respect You; so that You'll be well-known in our land forever.

[10-13] Mercy and truth have come together; goodness and peace have greeted each other with a kiss. Truth will spring out of the earth; and goodness will look down from heaven. Yes, Yahweh will give that which is good; and our land will produce its increase. Goodness will go before You; and will put us in the path of Your steps.

86 [1-5] *A Prayer of David.* Listen, oh Yahweh, listen to me; for I'm poor and needy. Save my soul; for I'm dedicated to You, oh my God; save me, the one who trusts in You. Be merciful to me, oh my God, for I cry to You daily. Let my soul celebrate: for I lift up my soul to You, oh my God. For You, my God, are good, and ready to forgive; and have great mercy to all those that call on You.

[6-10] Listen, oh Yahweh, to my prayer; and pay attention to what I ask. In the day of my trouble I'll call on You: for You'll answer me. Among the great ones there's none like You, oh my God; nor is there anything like Your creations. All the nations that You've made will come and worship before You, oh my God; and will glorify Your Name. For You are great, and do wonderful things: You, alone, are God.

[11-17] Teach me Your way, oh Yahweh, and I'll walk in Your truth: make my heart undivided to fully respect Your Name. I'll praise You, oh Savior, my God, with all my heart, and I'll glorify Your Name forever. For great is Your mercy toward me; You've freed my soul from the depths of Hell. Oh God, people who think they are better than me come against me, and violent gangs look for my soul; and haven't respected You. But You, oh my God, are a God full of compassion, gracious, patient, and have plenty of mercy and truth. Oh turn to me, and have mercy on me; give me Your strength, and save the child of one of Your people. Show me a token for good; that those who hate me can see it, and be ashamed: because You, oh Yahweh, have helped me, and comforted me.

87 [1-7] *A Hymn or Song for the children of Korah.* Yahweh, Your foundation is in the holy mountains. Yahweh, You love the gates of Jerusalem more than all the homes of Israel. Glorious things are spoken of the city of God. Selah! I'll make mention of Rahab and Babylon to those that know me, or Philistia, or Tyre, or Ethiopia; and they'll reply, "*I was born there.*" But of Jerusalem it'll be said, "*This one and that one was born there, and the Most High God will make it safe.*" Yahweh will count, when writing up its citizens, that I was born there. Selah! The singers as well as the players of instruments will be there: all my heart is in Jerusalem.

88 [1-6] *A Song or Hymn for the children of Korah, to the first musician, to The Sickness, to sing loudly, a poem of teaching of Heman, the Ezrahite.* Oh Yahweh, You're the God who saved me, and I've cried day and night before You. Let my prayer come before You; listen to my cry. My soul is full of troubles, and my life draws near to death. I'm counted as dead: I have no more strength: I'm given up like the dead, like one who has been killed and lies in the grave, that You remember no more, and they're removed from Your hand. You've laid me in the grave, in the depths of darkness.

[7-12] Your anger is hard on me, and You've tormented me with all Your pressure. Selah! You've put my acquaintances far away from me; You've made me an insult to them: I'm hiding, and I can't come out. My eyes cry because of my misery: Yahweh, I've called on You daily, I've stretched out my hands to You. Will You show wonders to the dead? Will the dead awake and praise You? Selah! Shall Your love be talked of in the grave; or Your faithfulness in death? Shall Your wonders be known in the dark and Your goodness in the land of forgetfulness?

[13-18] But to You I've cried, oh Yahweh; and in the morning my prayer will stop You. Yahweh, why do You throw my soul away? Why do You hide Your face from me? I've been abused and wanted to die from my childhood up, worrying and afraid from all my suffering. Your fierce anger overwhelms me; Your terrors have all but finished me. They came around me daily like water; together they overtook me. You put lover and friend, and even all my acquaintances far away from me where I can't even see them.

89 [1-4] *A poem of teaching of Ethan the Ezrahite.* I'll sing of the mercies of Yahweh forever, making known Your faithfulness to all generations. For I've said, "*Mercy will be settled forever: Your faithfulness will be honored even in heaven.*" As You've said, "*I've made a Promise with my chosen ones, I've sworn to David, who serves Me, I'll set up your descendents forever, and build up your reign in every generation.*" Selah!

[5-10] And the angels of heaven will praise Your wonders, oh Yahweh: Your faithfulness will be praised in the people of God, also. For who in heaven can be compared to Yahweh? Who among the children of the great ones can be likened to Yahweh? You are greatly respected among the people of God, and held in respect by all those that come to You. Oh Yahweh, God of the heavenly hosts, who is strong like You? Or who else has the faithfulness which surrounds You? You rule the raging sea and when its waves are troubled, You still them. You've divided the pride of Egypt in pieces as a dead one; You've scattered Your enemies with Your strength.

[11-14] The heavens and the earth are Yours, and the whole universe: You settled them all. You've created the north and the south: The mountains of Tabor and Hermon will celebrate, Your Name is written upon them. You

45

are strong and mighty: Your hand is lifted high. Justice and good judgment are the signs of Your reign: mercy and truth are with You.

[15-18] Blessed are those that know the joyful announcement of Your presence: They walk in the light of Your face, oh Yahweh. They celebrate all day in Your Name, and they're uplifted in Your goodness. For You are the glory of our strength, and our instruments sound out by Your grace. For Yahweh is our defense; and the Holy One of Israel is our ruler.

[19-26] Then in a vision You spoke to Your preacher, and said, "*I'll send help by a mighty one; I've lifted up a chosen one from the people. I've set up David, who serves Me; who I've anointed with My holy oil; and who I'll set up and strengthen. Who won't be threatened by the enemy; nor be troubled by the offspring of evil. And I'll put down his enemies before his face, and plague those that hate him. But My faithfulness and My mercy will be with him, and in My Name will the trumpet call be raised. I'll give him dominion in the sea, and in the rivers. And he will cry to Me, 'You are My Creator, My God, and the Rock, who saves me.'*

[27-37] *I'll make him as My Firstborn, higher than rulers on the earth. My mercy will keep him forever, and My Promise will stay with him. Also I'll make his descendents to last forever; and their reign as the everlasting days of heaven. If their children give up on My word, and don't walk in My judgments; If they break My decrees, and don't keep My commandments; Then I'll visit their sins with punishment and defeat. Yet I won't take My love from them all together, nor let My faithfulness fail them. I won't break My Promise, nor change what has gone out of My mouth. Once I swore by My holiness that I wouldn't lie to David. His descendents will last forever, and their reign as the sunlight. It'll be settled forever as the moon, as a faithful witness in heaven.*" Selah!

[38-44] But You've hated me and thrown me away, being angry with Your anointed. You've voided the Promise with me: You've undermined my reign, tossing my crown to the ground. You've broken down all my boundaries; You've brought my strongholds to ruin. All that pass by the way defeat me: my neighbors bring accusations against me. You've given strength to my enemies; You've made all my enemies celebrate. You've disabled my defenses, and haven't given me any victory. You've brought my glory to an end, and undermined my reign.

[45-52] You've shortened my childhood, covering me with shame. Selah! How long will You hide Yourself, oh Yahweh? Will Your anger burn like fire forever? Remember how short my time is. Have You made us all for nothing? Who is it that will stay, and not see death? Will God save any soul from the power of the grave? Selah! My God, where is Your former kindheartedness, which You swore to David in Your truth? Remember, my God, the accusations against me; how I bear in my heart the blame of all the great people, in which Your enemies have accused, oh Yahweh; in which they've blamed the ways of Your anointed. May Yahweh be blessed forever. Amen and Amen.

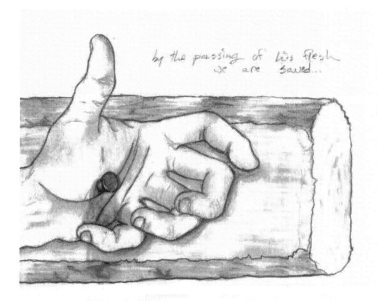

Book 4

90 [1-4] *A Prayer of Moses, the Preacher of God.* My God, You've been our resting place in all generations. Before the mountains were created, or before You had formed the earth and the universe, even from eternity, You are God. You turn us over to destruction; and say, *"Repent, you children of humanity."* For a thousand years in Your sight is only as yesterday when it's over and only as a watch in the night.

[5-10] You carry us away like in a flood; we're just as if we're asleep: in the morning we're like grass which grows up in the night. In the morning it does well, and grows up; in the evening it's cut down, and withers. For we're consumed by Your anger, and by Your anger we're troubled. You've exposed our sins; our secret sins are made clear in the light of Your face. For all our days are destroyed by Your anger: we spend our years as a story tale. We may live to be seventy years old; and if we're strong, maybe eighty years, yet even in our strength, is nothing but pain and sorrow; for it soon passes, and our souls soar away.

[11-17] Who knows the power of Your anger? Even those who respect You greatly fear Your anger. So teach us that our days are numbered, so that we can apply our hearts to know wisdom. Oh Yahweh, how long before You return to us? May You change Your mind when it concerns Your people. Oh comfort us with Your mercy soon, so that we can be glad and celebrate all our days. As many days as You've allowed us to be abused, and as many years as we have seen evil, make us happy. Let Your people see Your creations, and let Your glory appear to their children. And let the loveliness of Yahweh our God be reflected in our look, and may You inspire the creations of our hands in us; yes, You inspire the creations of our hands.

91 [1-6] The One who inhabits the secret place of the Most High will be in the shade of the Spirit of the Almighty. I'll say of Yahweh, *"God is my safe haven and my fortress, my God; in whom I'll trust."* Surely God will save You from the trap of the hunter, and from the dreadful pestilence. God will protect You, and in the Spirit of God You'll trust: the truth of God will be Your defense and weapon. You won't be afraid of terror by night, or of weapons that shoot by day, or for the pests that crawl about in darkness; or for any destruction that ruins at noon.

[7-16] A thousand will fall at Your side, and ten thousand on Your other side; but it won't come near You. With Your eyes only, You'll watch and see the punishment of the sinful, because You've made Yahweh, the Most High, who is my safe haven, Your resting place; No evil will befall You, nor will any deadly illness come near where You are, for the angels of God will have charge over You, to keep You in all Your ways. They'll bear You up in their hands, if You should stump Your foot on a stone. You'll stomp on the lion and the snake: the young lion and the dragon You'll trample under foot. And God said, *"Because You've set Your love on Me, I'll save You: I'll bring You to heaven, because You've known My Name. You'll call on Me, and I'll answer: I'll be with You in trouble; I'll save You, and bring You honor. With everlasting life I'll satisfy You, and show You My salvation."*

92 [1-5] *A Hymn or Song for the Holy day.* It's a good thing to give thanks to Yahweh, and to sing praises to Your Name, oh Most High, on a stringed instrument, on the lyre, and on the harp with a solemn sound, showing Your graciousness in the morning, and Your faithfulness every night. For You, oh Yahweh, have made me glad through Your actions: I'll triumph in what You do. Oh Yahweh, how great are Your acts! Your thoughts are very deep.

[6-9] A defiant person doesn't know; nor does a stupid person understand this. When the sinful grow like grass, and when all those who practice sin do well; it's they who are destroyed forever: But You, oh Yahweh, are Most High forever. See, Your enemies, oh Yahweh, Your enemies will die; all those who practice sin will be scattered.

[10-15] But You'll lift up my strength like the horn of a unicorn and anoint me with fresh oil. My eye will see what I asked of my enemies, and my ears will hear what I wanted of the sinful that rise up against me. Godly people will do well like the palm tree, and grow like a cedar in Lebanon. Those that are rooted in the House of God of Yahweh will do well in God's house. They'll still have children in their old age; They're healthy and do well to show that Yahweh is Good: God is my rock, in whom there's no evil.

93 [1-5] Yahweh reigns and is decorated with majesty; Yahweh is decorated with strength, which You restrain: the world is settled also, so that it can't be moved out of place. Your reign is settled from everlasting: You are Everlasting. The floods have risen up, oh Yahweh, the waters are roaring; the ocean waves rise up. Yahweh in heaven is stronger than the sound of many rushing waters, yes, than the strongest waves of the sea. Your words are very certain: holiness makes Your house beautiful forever, oh Yahweh.

94 [1-7] Oh Yahweh, God, revenge belongs to You; oh God, revenge belongs to You, show Yourself. Lift up Yourself, judge of the earth: repay those who think they are better than others with their punishment. Yahweh, how long will the sinful, how long will the sinful triumph? How long will they talk and speak harsh things; and all those who practice sin brag about themselves? They destroy Israel, oh Yahweh, and trouble Your heritage. They destroy the single parent and the foreigner, and murder the survivors' children. Yet they say, *"Yahweh won't see it, nor will the God of Israel care about it."*

[8-13] Understand, you defiant among the people, and you stupid ones; When will you get smart? Won't the One that created the ear hear it? Won't the One that formed the eye see it? Won't the One that punishes the ungodly correct them? Won't the One that teaches people knowledge know it? Yahweh knows the thoughts of all

people, that they're nothing. Those people that You discipline are blessed, oh Yahweh. You teach them out of Your Word, so that You can give them rest from the days of trouble, until the grave for the sinful is dug.

[14-18] For You, Oh Yahweh won't throw away Your people; neither will You give up on Your inheritance. But judgment will return to goodness, and all goodhearted people will follow it. Who will rise up for me against the evil ones; or who will stand up for me against the sinful ones? Unless Yahweh had been my help, my soul had almost lived in silence. When I said, "*My foot is slipping;*" Your mercy, oh Yahweh, held me up.

[19-23] In the multitude of my thoughts within me, Your comforts thrill my soul. Shall the reign of sin, which supports its trouble by law, have friendship with You? They gather themselves together against the souls of godly people, condemning innocent blood. But Yahweh is my defense; and my God is the foundation of my safe haven. God will bring on them the consequences of their own sin, and will destroy them in their own evil; yes, Yahweh our God will destroy them.

95 [1-7] Oh come, let's sing to Yahweh: Let's sing joyfully to the Rock who saves us. Let's come into God's presence with thanksgiving, making a joyful sound with hymns. For Yahweh is a great God, and Savior above all great ones. The deep places of the earth are in Your hands: the strength of the hills is Yours also. The sea is Yours, You made it, and Your hands formed the dry land. Oh come, let's worship and bow down: Let's kneel before Yahweh our maker. For You are our God; and we're the animals of Your pasture, and the lambs are cradled in Your arms.

[8-11] Today, if you'll hear the voice of God, who says: "*Don't be hardhearted, as the days I was provoked and tempted in the countryside: As when Your parents tempted Me, proved Me, and saw My miracles.* I was grieved forty long years with this generation, and said, "*These people are wrong in their hearts, and they don't know my ways:*" To whom I swore in my anger that they wouldn't enter into my restfulness.

96 [1-6] Oh sing to Yahweh a new song: sing to Yahweh, all you people of the earth. Sing to Yahweh, bless God's Name; Teach of God's salvation everyday. Tell the glory of God among the ungodly, the wonders of God among all people. For Yahweh is great, and to be greatly praised: God is to be respected above all great ones, because worshiping any of the great ones of the nations is idolatry, but Yahweh made the heavens. Honor and majesty are God's; strength and loveliness are in the House of Yahweh God.

[7-13] People of every race give to Yahweh, yes, give to Yahweh glory and strength. Give to Yahweh the glory due to the Name of God: bring an offering, and come into the house of God. Oh worship Yahweh in the loveliness of holiness: all you people of the earth respect God. Tell the ungodly that Yahweh reigns, so that the world will be settled and that it won't be moved out of place; and God will judge the people rightly. Let the heavens celebrate, and let the earth be glad; let the sea roar, and everything in it. Let the fields be joyful, and everything in them: then all the trees of the woods will celebrate before Yahweh, as well: for God comes, for God comes to judge the earth and will rightly judge the world and the people with truth.

97 [1-6] Yahweh reigns; let the people of the earth celebrate; let the masses of the islands be glad of it. Clouds and darkness are around You: goodness and judgment are the symbols of Your reign. A fire goes before You, and burns up Your enemies everywhere. Your lightning brightened the world: the people of earth saw, and trembled. The hills melted like wax at the presence of the Savior, at the presence of the Most High Savior of the whole earth. The heavens declare Your goodness, and everybody sees Your glory.

[7-12] Let all those that worship other things and brag to themselves of their idolatry be confused: worship Yahweh God, all you great ones. Jerusalem heard, and was glad; and the children of Judah celebrated because of Your judgments, oh Yahweh. For You, oh Yahweh, are high above the whole world: You are praised far above all great ones. You that love Yahweh, hate anything evil, for God saves the souls of the saints of God, delivering them out of the hand of the sinful. Light is allotted for godly people and gladness for goodhearted people. Celebrate in Yahweh, you who are good; and give thanks at the remembrance of God's holiness.

98 [1-3] *A Hymn.* Oh sing to Yahweh a new song; for God has done awesome things: Your strong hand and holy arm have claimed You the victory. Yahweh, You've made known Your saving grace: You've openly shown Your goodness in the sight of the ungodly. You've remembered Your mercy and Your truth toward the house of Israel: all the ends of the earth have seen how our God saves us.

[4-9] Make a joyful sound to Yahweh, all you people of the earth: make a loud sound and celebrate, singing praises. Sing to Yahweh with the harp; with the harp, and the song of a hymn. With the sound of trumpets and cornet make a joyful sound before Yahweh, the Savior. Let the sea roar and everything in it; the world, and all those who live in it. Let the floods slap its waves: let the hills be joyful together because of Yahweh; for God comes to judge the earth; God will judge the world and the people with goodness and with equality.

99 [1-5] Yahweh reigns; let the people tremble with the fear of the God who sits between the angelic creatures; let the earth be troubled. Yahweh is great in Jerusalem; and God is exalted above all the people. Let us praise Your great and awesome Name, Yahweh, because it's holy. The ruler's strength is to love good judgment; You set up equality, You carry out good judgment and goodness in Israel. We exalt You, oh Yahweh our God, and worship at the footstool of God; for You are holy.

48

[6-9] Moses and Aaron were among their priests, and Samuel was among those that call on Your Name; They called on Yahweh, and You answered them. You spoke to them in the cloudy pillar, and they kept Your words, and the laws that You gave them. You answered them, oh Yahweh our God: You were a God that forgave them, though You punished their evil behaviors. Exalt Yahweh our God, and worship at the holy hill; for Yahweh our God is holy.

100 [1-5] *A Hymn of praise.* Make a joyful sound to Yahweh, all you nations. Serve Yahweh with happiness: come before the presence of God with singing. Don't you know that Yahweh is God? You are the One that has made us, and not we ourselves; we're God's people, and the animals of Your pasture. We enter Your House of God with thanksgiving, and into Your presence with praise. Be thankful to God, and bless the Name of God. Yahweh is good, whose mercy is everlasting, and whose truth will last to all generations.

101 [1-4] *A Hymn of David.* I'll sing of mercy and judgment: to You, oh Yahweh, I'll sing. I'll behave myself wisely in a perfect way. Oh when will You come to me? I'll walk in my house with a perfect heart. I'll put no sinful thing before my eyes so that I won't get addicted to it: I hate what those that turn aside from Your way do. I won't have a sinful heart because I won't keep company with a sinful person.

[5-8] I'll take those who secretly lie about others from their place: I won't allow those that have a proud look and an arrogant heart to come near me. My eyes will be on the faithful of the land so that they can stay with me: those that walk in a perfect way, they'll be my people. Those that act dishonestly won't stay in my house: those that tell lies won't be in my sight long. Soon I'll ruin all the sinful of the land; so that I can remove all the sinful from the city of Yahweh.

102 [1-5] *A Prayer of the abused, when they're overwhelmed, and pour out their complaint before Yahweh.* Listen to my prayer, oh Yahweh, hear my cry. Don't hide Your face from me on the day when I'm in trouble; listen to me, answering me quickly on the day when I call. My days are gone like smoke, and my body is burned as a hearth. My heart is cut and withered like grass; so badly that I forget to eat my food. Because of the sound of my groaning my skin clings to my bones.

[6-11] I'm like a pelican of the countryside or like an owl of the desert. I watch, and am as a sparrow alone on the rooftop. My enemies accuse me all day; and those that are mad at me have sworn against me. For I've eaten ashes like food, and mixed my drink with tears, because of Your righteous anger and Your rage: for You've lifted me up, and thrown me back down. My days are like a shadow that fades; and I'm withered like grass.

[12-17] But You, oh Yahweh, will last forever; and all generations will remember You. You'll awake, and have mercy on Jerusalem: for the time of grace is theirs, yes, the set time has come. For we take pleasure in its stones, and favor the dust of its streets, so the ungodly will respect the Name of Yahweh and all rulers on the earth Your glory. When You build up Jerusalem, You Yahweh, Oh God, will appear in Your glory. God will have favor on the prayer of the poor, not hating to hear their words.

[18-22] This will be written for the generation to come, and the people born in the future will praise Yahweh. For God has looked down from the height of the House of God; even from heaven Yahweh has seen the earth; to hear the groaning of the prisoner, to free those that have been sentenced to death, to declare the Name of Yahweh in Zion, and Your praise in Jerusalem, when the people and the nations are gathered together to minister to Yahweh.

[23-28] You weakened my strength in the way, God, and shortened my days. So I said, "*Oh my God; don't take me away in the midst of my life: Your years are throughout all generations. From time everlasting You've laid the foundation of the earth, and the heavens are the creation of Your own hands. They'll all come to an end, but You'll last: yes, all of them will grow old like clothing; You'll change them as a garment, and they'll be changed: But You are the same, and Your years will have no end. The children of your people will last forever, and their children will be made known before You.*"

103 [1-5] *A Hymn of David.* Bless Yahweh, oh my soul; I bless Your holy Name with all that's in me. Bless Yahweh, oh my soul, and never forget all that God does for you: Who forgives all your sins and heals all your diseases; Who bought back your life from destruction and graces you with love and tender mercies; Who satisfies your mouth with good things; so that your youth is renewed like the eagle's strength.

[6-12] Yahweh executes goodness and judgment for all that are kept down. You've made known the ways of God to Moses, Your acts to the children of Israel. Yahweh, You are merciful and gracious, slow to anger, and have more than enough compassion. You won't always accuse: You won't keep Your anger forever. God, You haven't given us what we deserve for our sins; nor punished us according to our sins. Just as the heavens are high above the earth, so Your mercy toward those that respect You is great. As far as the east is from the west, God has taken our sins from us.

[13-22] Like parents pity their children, so You pity those that respect You, Yahweh. For God knows what we're made of and remembers that we're only dust. As for humans, their days are as grass: as flowers of the field, so they do well. The wind passes over them, and they're gone; and their beauty won't be seen in their place anymore. But the mercy of Yahweh is everlastingly on those that respect God; and the goodness of God is on their grandchildren; and on those who keep the Promise; and to those that remember to do the commandments.

49

The reign of Yahweh is ready in the heavens; Your power rules over all things. Bless Yahweh, you strong angels, which do the commandments when you hear to the sound of God's Word. Bless Yahweh, all you heavenly hosts; the ministers of God that do whatever God wants them to. Bless Yahweh, all creation everywhere: bless Yahweh, oh my soul.

104 [1-5] Bless Yahweh, oh my soul. Oh Yahweh my God, You are very great; You are decorated with honor and majesty, covering Yourself with light as with clothes: You, who stretches out the heavens like a curtain: Who lays the shafts of Your chambers in the waters and makes the clouds Your vehicle, moving on the wings of the wind: Who makes the angels spirits; and Your ministers to shine like flaming fire: Who laid the foundations of the earth, so that it wouldn't ever be moved out of its place.

[6-11] You covered it with the floods as with clothes: the waters stood above the mountain tops. At Your command it fled; at the voice of Your thunder it rushed away. It goes up by the mountains and goes down by the valleys to the place which You've made for it. You've set a boundary that it can't pass over; that it won't cover the earth again. God sends the creeks into the valleys, which flow among the hills. God gives drink to every beast of the field: even the wild donkeys quench their thirst.

[12-17] The birds of heaven which sing among the branches have their nests beside them. God waters the hills from the heavens: the earth is satisfied with everything Your creation provides. God, You cause the grass to grow for the cattle, and herbs for the people's benefit, so that all of them can get food from the earth; And wine that makes the people's hearts glad, and oil to make their faces shine, and food to strengthen their hearts. The trees of Yahweh, You, God, have planted; the cedars of Lebanon, where the birds make their nests, and the fir trees that are the home of the stork are all full of sap.

[18-23] The high hills are a safe haven for the wild goats; and the rocks for the rabbits. God, You appointed the moon for the seasons and the sun goes down at its proper time. You make darkness, and the night comes in which all the wild animals of the forest creep out. The young lions roar after their prey, and look for their meat from God. The sun rises, they gather together, and lay down in their dens. People go to their work and to their place of employment until the evening.

[24-30] Oh Yahweh, how many are Your creations! In wisdom You've made them all: the earth is full of Your treasures. So is this great and wide sea, in which are innumerable living things, both small and great. There go the ships and there's leviathan, that great dinosaur of the sea that You've made to play in it. These all wait for You to give them their meat in due season. They gather whatever You give them: You open Your hand, and they're all filled with good things. You hide Your face, and they're troubled: You take away their breath, and they die, and return to the dust. You send Your spirit, they're created, and You renew the face of the earth with them.

[31-35] Yahweh will be made known forever: You'll celebrate in Your creation, oh Yahweh. God, You look on the earth, and it quakes: God, You touch the volcanoes, and they smoke. I'll sing to Yahweh as long as I live: I'll sing praises to my God as long as my spirit exists. My thoughts of You will be sweet: I'll celebrate in Yahweh God. Let the sinful be removed from the earth, and let them be no more. Bless You, oh Yahweh, oh my soul. Praise Yahweh!

105 [1-6] Oh give thanks to Yahweh; calling on the Name of God and make known God's acts among the people. Sing to God, sing hymns to God: talk of all the wondrous acts of God. Celebrate in the Holy Name: let the heart of them that look for Yahweh celebrate. Look for the strength of Yahweh: look for Yahweh's face forever. Remember the awesome acts that God has done; the wonders, and the judgments of God's mouth; Oh you children of Abraham, God's subject, children of Jacob, God's chosen.

[7-15] God is Yahweh, our God, who judges all the people of the earth. You've remembered Your Promise forever, the word which You told to a thousand generations, which You made with Abraham, and gave Your oath to Isaac; and confirmed the same to Jacob for a law, and to Israel for an everlasting Promise, saying, "*To You I'll give the land of Canaan, the lot of Your inheritance,*" when they were only a few people in number; yes, very few, and the ungodly were in it as well. When they went from one nation to another, from one people to another; God let no one do them wrong: yes, God corrected rulers for their sakes, saying, "*Don't touch my anointed, and do no harm to my preachers.*"

[16-22] Moreover God called for a famine on the land, withering the whole stalk of grain. God sent someone before them, even Joseph that was sold for a slave, whose feet they hurt with shackles when he was bound in iron until the time that God's Word came, the Word of Yahweh, to try Joseph. The ruler of the people sent word to let Joseph go free. The ruler then made Joseph the head manager of all their lands and substance; to imprison the rulers as he wanted and teach wisdom to the governors.

[23-29] Israel came into Egypt; and Jacob traveled to the land of Ham. God increased their people greatly; and made them stronger than their enemies. God turned the Egyptians' hearts to hate their people, to deal deviously with their children. God sent Moses, God's own minister; and Aaron who also had been chosen, who showed the signs of God among them, and wonders in the land of Ham. God sent darkness, and made it very dark; and they didn't rebel against the Word of God. God turned their waters into blood, and killed their fish.

50

[30-36] Their land was troubled with frogs in abundance, even in the chambers of their rulers. God spoke, and there came different sorts of flies, and lice in all their coasts. God gave them hail for rain, and flaming fire in their land. God struck their vines also and their fig trees; and broke the trees of their coasts. God spoke, and the locusts came, and caterpillars, so many they couldn't be counted, which attacked all the herbs in their land, and ate all the produce of their ground. God struck also all the firstborn in their land, the first of all their strength.

[37-45] God brought them forward with silver and gold, and there was not one frail person among them. Egypt was glad when they left, because they feared them. God spread a cloud for a covering; and fire to give light in the night. The people asked, and God brought quails, and satisfied them with the food of heaven. God split open the rock, making water gush out and run in dry places like a river. You remembered Your holy promise, and Abraham, God's subject. You brought forward Your people with joy, and Your chosen ones with gladness, giving them the lands of the ungodly, and they inherited the work of another people; so that they could learn Your words, and keep Your laws. Praise Yahweh!

106 [1-5] Praise Yahweh! Oh give thanks to Yahweh; for God is good: for Your mercy lasts forever. Who can tell of the mighty acts of Yahweh? Who can show all Your honor? Those that judge wisely are blessed; and those that practice good ways all the time are blessed as well. Remember me, oh Yahweh, with the grace that You give to Israel: oh visit me with Your saving grace, so that I can see the good of Your chosen ones, and celebrate in the gladness of Your nation, and triumph with Your inheritance.

[6-11] We've sinned along with our parents; we've sinned, doing evil. Our parents didn't understand Your wonders in Egypt; they didn't remember the greatness of Your mercies; but provoked You at the Red Sea. Yet, You saved them, God, for Your Name's sake, that You'll make Your mighty power to be known. You divided the Red Sea also, and it was dried up and led them through the depths, as through the countryside. And You saved them from the hand of those that hated them, and bought them back from the hand of their enemies, which the waters overcame till there was none left.

[12-18] Then they believed Your Words and sang Your praise. But they soon forgot Your acts and didn't wait for Your counsel, complaining excessively in the countryside, and tempting God in the desert. And You gave them their requests; but sent sadness into their soul. They were jealous of Moses and Aaron, the saints of Yahweh, also in the camp. The earth opened up and swallowed Dathan, and buried the followers of Abiram. And a fire was kindled in the middle of them, burning up those sinful ones.

[19-23] They made a golden calf in Horeb, and worshipped the molten image, changing their glory into the likeness of an ox that eats grass. They forgot God their savior, which had done great things in Egypt; wondrous acts in the land of Ham, and awesome things by the Red Sea. So You said that You would destroy them, yet if Moses, Your chosen, hadn't begged for mercy before You to turn away Your anger, You would have destroyed them all.

[24-31] Yes, they hated the promised land and didn't believe Your Word; but complained in their homes and didn't listen to the voice of Yahweh. So You lifted up Your hand against them, to overthrow them in the countryside: To overthrow their children also among the nations, and to scatter them in the lands. They joined themselves also to the false god, Baal-peor, and ate offerings made for the dead. So they provoked You to anger with their inventions, and a deadly illness came on them. Then Phinehas stood up with wise judgment, so the deadly illness was stopped. And that was counted to him for goodness for all generations forever.

[32-38] They angered You also at the waters of trouble, so that it went ill with Moses for their sakes, because they provoked his spirit, so that he spoke unwise words. They didn't destroy the nations, who Yahweh told them to wipe out: But intermixed with the ungodly, and learned their evil ways. They served other things, which were a trap to them. Yes, they sacrificed their own children to demons, shedding innocent blood, even the blood of their own children, so that they sacrificed to the false gods of Canaan, polluting the land with blood.

[39-42] So they were made filthy with their own acts, and went lustfully after their own inventions. Your anger, Yahweh, was kindled against Your people, so much that You hated Your own inheritance. And You gave them into the hand of the ungodly; and those that hated them had rule over them. Their enemies also kept them down, and they were brought into subjection under their hand.

[43-48] Many times You saved them, oh God; but they provoked You with their words, and they were humbled for their sin. Yet, You regarded their misery, oh God, when You heard their cry, remembering Your Promise with them, and repented according to the greatness of Your mercies. You made them also to be pitied of all those that carried them captives. Save us, oh Yahweh, our God, and gather us from among the ungodly, to give thanks to Your holy Name, and to triumph in Your praise. May Yahweh be blessed, God of Israel, from everlasting to everlasting, and let all the people say, *Amen.* Praise Yahweh!

Book 5

107 [1-5] Oh give thanks to Yahweh, for God is good: Your mercy lasts forever. Let those who are saved by Yahweh say that God has bought them back from the hand of the enemy, and gathered them out of the lands, from the east, from the west, from the north, and from the south. They wandered alone in the countryside, finding no city to stay in, their souls fainting in hunger and thirst. Then they cried to Yahweh in their trouble, and God freed them out of their troubles. And God led them forward by the right way so that they could go to live in a city. Oh that people would praise You, Yahweh for the goodness of God, and for Your wonderful actions toward the children of humanity!

[9-15] For God satisfies the longing soul, and fills the hungry soul with goodness. God brought down the hearts of those that sit in darkness and in the shadow of death with hard work. They're bound in misery and shackles because they rebelled against the Words of God, and condemned the counsel of the Most High; and when they fell down, there was no one to help. Then they cried to Yahweh in their trouble, and God saved them out of it all. God brought them out of darkness and the shadow of death, breaking open their shackles. Oh that people would praise You, Yahweh for Your goodness, and for Your wonderful actions toward the children of humanity!

[16-22] For God has broken the gates of brass, and cut the bars of iron in half. Stupid people are made miserable because of their offenses, and their sins. They hate all kinds of meat, drawing near even to the gates of death. Then they cry to Yahweh in their trouble, and God saves them out of it all. God sent word, and healed them, and saved them from destruction. Oh that people would praise You, Yahweh for Your goodness, and for Your wonderful actions toward the children of humanity! Let them sacrifice the offerings of thanksgiving, declaring Your actions with celebrations.

[23-32] Those that go down to the sea in ships, that do business in the great oceans, see the acts of Yahweh and the wonders in the oceans. For You command, and raise the stormy winds that lifts up the waves of the sea. They mount up to the heaven and go down again to the depths: their souls are upset because of trouble. They drift back and forth, and stagger like drunks, and are at their wit's end. Then they cry to Yahweh in their trouble, and You bring them out of it all. You calm the storm, and still the waves. Then they're glad because the waves are quiet; so You bring them to the harbor where they wanted to go. Oh that people would praise You, Yahweh for Your goodness, and for Your wonderful actions toward the children of humanity! Let them exalt You also in the congregation, and praise You in the meetings of the elders.

[33-43] God turns rivers into barren countryside and the creeks into dry ground; a fruitful land into barrenness, for the evil of those that stay in it. God turns the countryside into pools of water, and dry ground into creeks of water. And there God makes the hungry to stay, so that they can build a place to live in; and plant the fields, and plant the vineyards, which produce their fruits. God blesses them also, so that they're multiplied greatly; and doesn't let their animals decrease in number. Again, they're diminished and brought low by those keeping them down, their misery, and sorrow. God pours out hatred on rulers, and causes them to wander in the countryside, where there's no way out. Yet God uplifts the poor from their misery, and makes their families as large as a flock. Godly people will see it, and celebrate, and all sin will stop coming from their mouths. Whoever is wise, and will observe these things, will understand the love of Yahweh.

108 [1-6] *A Song or Hymn of David.* Oh God, my heart is fixed; I'll sing and give praise, even with my triumph. Awake, stringed instruments and harp: I myself will awake early. I'll praise You, oh Yahweh, among the people, and I'll sing praises to You among the nations. For Your mercy is as wide as the heavens and Your truth stretches up to the clouds. Be praised, oh God, above the heavens, and Your glory above the whole world; Save with Your strong hand, and answer me, so that Your beloved can be freed.

[7-13] God, You've spoken in Your holiness; *"I'll celebrate, as I divide Shechem, and give out the valley of Succoth. Gilead is mine; Manasseh is mine; Ephraim also is the strength of my head; Judah is my lawgiver; I'll wash myself at Moab; I'll lay out my shoes over Edom; I'll triumph over Philistia."* Who will bring me into the strong city? Who will lead me into Edom? Will You not, oh God, who has thrown us off? And won't You, oh God, go forward with our people? Give us help from our troubles, for what help people give is useless. Through God we'll do valiantly, for it is God that will trample down our enemies.

109 [1-5] *To the first musician, A Hymn of David.* Don't hold Your peace, oh God of my praise, for the mouths of the sinful and the mouths of the lying are opened against me, speaking against me with their lies. They overtook me with words of hatred; and fought against me wrongly. Even though I gave them my love, they're my enemies, but I give myself to prayer. They've rewarded me evil for good, and hated me for my love to them.

[6-16] So set a sinful person over them, and let Satan stand at their side. When they're judged, let them be condemned, and let their prayer become sin. Let their days be few; and let others take their places. Let their children be orphaned, and their spouses become survivors. Let their children always be tramps, and beg: let them look for food out of their gloomy places also. Let thieves take everything they have; and let the ungodly ruin all their efforts. Let none be there to extend mercy to them, nor let there be any to help their orphaned children. Let them have no grandchildren; and in the generation following let their name be forgotten. Let the sin of their parents be remembered by Yahweh; and don't let their sins be forgotten. Let them always be ashamed before Yahweh, so that God can remove their memory from the earth, because they didn't show mercy, but persecuted the poor and needy people, that they would even destroy the broken hearted.

[17-20] As they loved cursing, so let it come to them; and as they didn't enjoy their blessings, so let it be far from them. As they decorated themselves with cursing like putting on the clothes they wear, so let it come into them like the water they drink, and like the rich foods they eat. Let it be to them as the clothes that cover them, or like the belt they wear. Let this be the punishment from Yahweh of my enemies, those who speak evil against my soul.

[21-25] But do for me, oh Yahweh, my God, for Your Name's sake: because Your mercy is good, save me. I'm poor and needy, and my heart is broken. I'm gone like the passing shadow when it fades: I'm tossed up and down as the locust in the wind. My knees tremble from fasting; and my body is thin. I was a disgust to them when they looked on me and shook their heads.

[26-31] Help me, oh Yahweh my God: oh save me according to Your mercy, so that they can know that this is Your hand; that You, oh Yahweh, have done it. Let them curse me, but when You bless me they'll awake and be ashamed; and let me celebrate. Let my enemies be covered with shame, and let them cover themselves with their own confusion, as with a shroud. I'll greatly praise Yahweh with my mouth; yes, I'll praise You among the people. God will stand at the side of the poor, to save them from those that would condemn their souls.

110 [1-7] *A Hymn of David.* Yahweh said to my God, *Sit at My side, until I make Your enemies Your footstool.* Yahweh, You'll send the rod of Your strength out of Jerusalem: so take control in the midst of Your enemies. Your people will support You in the day of Your rule; in the beauty of holiness from the breaking of day You'll have the freshness of Your youth. Yahweh has sworn, and won't repent; *"You are a priest forever after the order of Melchizedek."* Yahweh at Your side will strike through rulers in the day of God's anger. You'll judge the ungodly, filling their places with the dead bodies; You'll wound the rulers over many countries, and drink of the creek in the way: so will You lift up Your head.

111 [1-5] Praise Yahweh! I'll praise Yahweh with my whole heart, in the congregation of the godly, when the people gather together. The creations of Yahweh are great, sought out by all those that have pleasure in them. Your actions are honorable and worthy of praise, and your goodness lasts forever. You've made your wonderful acts to be remembered: Yahweh is gracious and full of compassion. You've given food to those that respect You: God will be ever mindful of our Promise.

[6-10] You've shown Your people the power of Your acts, so that You can give them the inheritance of the ungodly. The acts of Your hands are true and Good; all Your commandments are sure, standing fast forever and ever, and are done in truth and honesty. God, You saved Your people, authorizing the Promise forever: Your Name is holy and worthy of respect. The respect of Yahweh is the beginning of wisdom: all those that do Your commandments have a good understanding: Your praise lasts forever.

112 [1-5] Praise Yahweh! Blessed are those that respect Yahweh, the ones that joy greatly in Your commandments. Their children will be mighty on earth, for the lives of godly people will be blessed. Wealth and riches will be in their houses; and their goodness will last forever. There will arise light in the darkness for godly people because they're gracious, and full of compassion and goodness. Godly people show grace, and lend, always guiding their affairs with good judgment.

[6-10] They'll never be upset, and will always be remembered. They won't be afraid of bad news, for their hearts are fixed on Yahweh. Their hearts are set, and not afraid, until they see justice come to their enemies. They'll be given honor because they have given to the poor; their goodness lasts forever. The sinful will see it, and be grieved; and will grate their teeth, pining away until everything they want dies out.

113 [1-4] Praise Yahweh! Praise, oh people of Yahweh, praise the Name of Yahweh. Blessed be the Name of Yahweh from this time forward and forever. From the dawning of the sun to the setting of the same, Yahweh's Name is to be praised. Yahweh, You are Savior over all nations, and Your glory is above the heavens.

[5-9] Who is like You, oh Yahweh our God, who inhabits heaven, and who comes down to see the things that are in heaven, and in the earth! And who picks up the poor out of the dust, and lifts the needy out of the manure pile; so that You can put them with rulers, even with the rulers of Your people. You even make the barren to keep house, and to be a joyful mother of children. Praise Yahweh!

114 [1-7] When Israel went out of Egypt, the house of Jacob from a strange speaking foreign people; Judah was their House of God, and Israel their dominion. The Red Sea saw it and pulled back: the Jordan river was driven back. The mountains and the little hills trembled. What upset you, oh sea, that you pulled back? And you Jordan, that was driven back? And you mountains and little hills that trembled? Tremble earth, at the presence of the Savior, at the presence of our God, which turned the rock into a pool of water, the flint-rock into a stream of water.

115 [1-7] Not to us, oh Yahweh, not to us, but to Your Name give glory, for Your mercy, and Your truth's sake. Why should the ungodly say, "*Where is their God now?*" But our God is in the heavens: You've done whatever You pleased. Their idolatry is their silver and gold, the things made from human hands. They have mouths, but don't speak, and eyes, but don't see: They have ears, but don't hear, and noses, but don't smell: They have hands, but don't hold anything, and feet, but don't walk: nor do they speak through their mouth.

[8-13] Those that make them are as dumb as they are and so is every one that trusts in them. Oh Israel, trust in Yahweh: God is our help and our defense. Oh house of Aaron, trust in Yahweh: God is our help and our defense. You that respect Yahweh trust in Yahweh: God is your help and your defense. Yahweh has been thinking of us: God will bless us; God will bless the house of Israel; God will bless the house of Aaron. God will bless those that respect Yahweh, both small and great.

[14-18] Yahweh will increase you more and more, you and your children. You are blessed of Yahweh which made heaven and earth. The heavens, even the heavens, are Yahweh's, but the earth God has given to the children of humanity. The dead don't praise Yahweh, or anyone that goes down into the silence of the grave. But we'll bless Yahweh now and forever. Praise Yahweh.

116 [1-6] I love Yahweh because God has heard my voice and my prayer. I'll call on God as long as I live because Yahweh has listened to me. The sorrows of death overtook me, and the pains of Hell got hold of me and I found nothing but trouble and sorrow. Then I called on the Name of Yahweh; *oh God, I beg You, save my soul.* Yahweh is gracious and good; yes, our God is merciful. Yahweh saves the naive: for I was brought low and God helped me.

[7-14] Return to your rest, oh my soul; for Yahweh has dealt bountifully with you. For You've freed my soul from death, my eyes from tears, and my feet from falling; and I'll walk with Yahweh in the land of the living. I believed, so I've spoken: I was greatly tormented because I said in my haste, everyone is a liar. What will I give to Yahweh in exchange for all the blessings granted me? I'll take the reward of Your saving grace, and call on the Name of Yahweh. I'll pay my vows to Yahweh now in the presence of all Your people.

[15-19] The death of the people of God is precious in the sight of Yahweh. Oh Yahweh, truly I belong to You; I belong to you, and I'm the child of one who belongs to You: You've freed me from everything that kept me down. I'll offer to You the sacrifice of thanksgiving, and will call on the Name of Yahweh. I'll pay my vows to Yahweh now in the presence of all Your people. Praise Yahweh in the House of God, in the midst of Jerusalem!

117 [1-2] Praise Yahweh, all you nations: praise God, everyone. God's merciful kindness has blessed us greatly, and the truth of Yahweh lasts forever. Praise Yahweh!

118 [1-4] Oh give thanks to Yahweh; for God is good: Your mercy lasts forever. Let Israel say now, "*Your mercy lasts forever.*" Let the house of Aaron say now, "*Your mercy lasts forever.*" Let those who respect Yahweh say now, "*Your mercy lasts forever.*"

[5-11] I called on Yahweh in my trouble: You answered me, and set me in a large place. Yahweh is on my side, so I won't fear: What can humans do to me? Yahweh takes my side with those that help me: so I'll see justice on those that hate me. It's better to trust in Yahweh than to put your faith in any other. It's better to trust in Yahweh than to put your faith in the government. All nations overtook me, but in the Name of Yahweh, I'll destroy them. They overtook me; yes, they overtook me, but in the Name of Yahweh, I'll overcome them.

[12-16] They overtook me like bees; they're quenched as a fire of thorns: for in the Name of Yahweh, I'll overcome them. They've pushed me roughly so that I would fall, but Yahweh helped me up. Yahweh is my

strength and song, and is my saving grace. The sound of celebration and salvation are in the houses of godly people: the strong hand of Yahweh is valiant. The strong hand of Yahweh is glorious: the strong hand of Yahweh is valiant.

[17-23] I won't die, but I'll live to tell the acts of Yahweh. Yahweh has greatly disciplined me, but hasn't let me die yet. Open to me the gates of goodness, this gate of Yahweh, in which godly people will enter, and I'll also go in praising Yahweh. I'll praise You: for You've heard me, and are my saving grace. The stone which the builders refused has become the main cornerstone. This is Yahweh's doing; it's awesome in our eyes.

[24-29] This is the day which Yahweh has made; in which we'll celebrate and be glad. Save now, I beg You, oh Yahweh: I beg You, send now prosperity, oh Yahweh. Blessed be the One that comes in the Name of Yahweh: we have blessed You from the House of God of Yahweh. God is Yahweh, who has shown us light: we will lay our sacrifices on top of the altar. You are my God, and I'll praise You: You are my God, so I'll exalt You. Oh give thanks to Yahweh; for God is good: for Your mercy lasts forever.

119 [1-8] Those who walk purely in the way of the Word of Yahweh are blessed. Those that keep Your words, and that look for God with their whole heart are blessed. They don't sin, because they walk in the ways of God. You've told us to carefully keep Your guidelines. Oh that my ways were always aimed to do what You tell me! When I have respect for all Your words then I won't be ashamed. And when I've learned Your good judgments I'll praise You with an honest heart. I'll follow Your directions: oh don't all together give up on me.

[9-16] Young people cleanse their way by paying attention to Your Word. I've sought You with my whole heart: oh don't let me wander from Your words. I've treasured Your Word in my heart, so that I won't sin against You. You are blessed, oh Yahweh: teach me Your words. I've told of all Your judgments with my words. I've celebrated in the way of Your words, as much as in riches. I'll think on Your guidelines, and have respect for Your ways. I'll be joyful in Your words; I won't forget Your Word.

[17-24] Bless me, so that I can live, and keep Your Word. Open my eyes, so that I can see wondrous things from out of Your Word. I'm a foreigner in the earth; don't hide Your words from me. My heart breaks all the time, longing for Your judgments. You've corrected those that are cursed, who stopped following Your words. Free me from accusations and hatred; for I've kept Your words. Leaders sat and spoke against me, but I reflected on Your words. Your words are my joy and my counselors.

[25-32] My soul clings to the dust: revive me according to Your Word. I've confessed my ways, and You heard me: now teach me Your words. Help me understand the way of Your guidelines: so I can talk of all Your wondrous acts. My soul faints for heaviness: strengthen me according to Your Word. Remove from me lying ways, and graciously give me Your Word. I've chosen the way of truth and followed Your judgments. I've stuck to Your words, oh Yahweh, so don't shame me. When You enlarge my heart, I'll quickly follow all of Your words.

[33-40] Teach me, oh Yahweh, the way of Your words; and I'll keep it to the end of my days. Give me understanding, and I'll keep Your Word, yes, studying it with my whole heart. Make me walk in Your words; for my joy is in them. Lean my heart toward Your words, and never to greed. Turn my eyes away from seeing worthless things; and revive me in Your way. Keep Your Word in me, the one who is faithful to You. Turn my shame away which I fear: for Your judgments are good. See, I've longed after Your guidelines, so revive me in Your goodness.

[41-48] Let Your mercies come to me also, oh Yahweh, even Your saving grace, according to Your Word, so I'll have something to say to those that accuse me: for I trust in Your Word. And don't take the word of truth out of my mouth all together; for I've hoped in Your judgments. So I'll keep Your Word always and forever. I'll walk in freedom, for I look for Your guidelines. I'll speak of Your words before rulers, and won't be ashamed. I'll celebrate in Your words, which I've loved. I'll lift up my hands to Your words also, which I've loved; and I'll think about them.

[49-56] Help me, Your worker, to remember Your Word, on which You've caused me to hope. This is my comfort in my misery: Your Word has revived me. People who think they are better than me have greatly disrespected me: yet I haven't given up on Your Word. I remembered Your past judgments, oh Yahweh; and have comforted myself. I'm horrified by the sinful that give up on Your Word. Your Words have been my songs in the House of God through out life's journey. I've remembered Your Name, oh Yahweh, in the night, and have kept Your Word. This I was able to do, only because I followed Your guidelines.

[57-64] Oh Yahweh, You are my lot in life, so I've said that I'd keep Your Words. I asked for Your grace with my whole heart, so be merciful to me according to Your Word. I thought on my ways, and turned my ways to Your words. I didn't delay, but quickly followed Your words. Evil gangs of people have robbed me, but I haven't forgotten Your Word. At midnight I'll rise to give thanks to You, because of Your good judgments. I'm a friend of all those that respect You, and of those that keep Your guidelines. The earth, oh Yahweh, is full of Your mercy: teach me Your words.

[65-72] You've dealt with me well, oh Yahweh, according to Your Word. Teach me good judgment and knowledge, for I've believed Your words. Even before I was abused, I went astray, but now I've kept Your Word. You are good, and do good things; so teach me Your words. People who think they are better than me have told lies against me, but I'll keep Your guidelines with my whole heart. Their hearts are full of emptiness; but I have joy

in Your Word. It has worked out for my good that I've been abused; because I learned Your words from my suffering. Your Word is better than a wealth of riches to me.

[73-80] Your hands have created me and designed me, so give me understanding to learn Your words. Those that respect You will be glad when they see me; because I've hoped in Your Word. I know, oh Yahweh, that Your judgments are right, and that You have allowed me to be abused in faithfulness. Let Your merciful kindness, I pray, be for my comfort according to Your Word to me. Let Your tender mercies come to me so that I can live, for Your Word is my joy. Let those people who think they are better than others be ashamed; for they dealt harshly with me for no reason, but I'll reflect on Your guidelines. Let those that respect You turn to me, and those that have known Your words. Let my heart know Your words well, so that I won't be ashamed.

[81-88] My soul faints for Your saving grace, but I hope in Your Word. I grow old as I wait for Your Word, saying, "When will You comfort me?" For I'm smudged like a bottle in the smoke; yet I don't forget Your words. How long are the days of Your worker? When will You execute judgment on those that abuse me? People who think they are better than me, who don't follow after Your Word, have tried to make me fall. All Your commandments are faithful, but they abuse me wrongfully; so help me. They almost took me from this earth; but I never left Your guidelines. Revive me out of Your love; so I'll keep Your Word.

[89-96] Oh Yahweh, Your Word is forever settled in heaven. Your faithfulness is to all generations, for You've created the earth, and it's still here. They continue today according to Your laws, for everything follows Your plan. Unless Your Word had been my joy, I would have died in my misery. I'll never forget Your guidelines, for You've revived me with them. I'm Yours, save me; for I've searched out Your guidelines. The sinful have waited to destroy me, but I'll believe Your words. I've seen all good things come to an end, but Your words outlast them all.

[97-104] Oh how I love Your Word! It's in my thoughts all day long. You, through Your words, have made me wiser than my enemies, for they're ever with me. I understand more than all my teachers, because I think on Your words. I understand more than the wise ones of the past, because I keep Your guidelines. I've kept myself from going any evil way, so that I can keep Your Word. I haven't left from Your judgments, for it was You who taught them to me. How sweet are Your Words! Yes, sweeter than honey to the taste! Through Your guidelines I've come to understand, and so I hate every way that is untrue.

[105-112] Your Word shines its light for my feet and brightens my pathway. I promised that I'll keep Your good judgments, and I'll do it. I'm abused very much: revive me, oh Yahweh, according to Your Word. Accept, I beg You, the offerings of my mouth, which are of my own free will, oh Yahweh, and teach me Your judgments. My soul is always at risk in my own hands: yet I don't forget Your Word. The sinful have tried to trap me: yet I haven't stopped following Your guidelines. Your words I've taken as an inheritance forever, for they're my heart's joy. My heart is set to do Your words always, even to the end of my days.

[113-120] I hate those who think themselves better than others, but I love Your Word. You are my refuge and my defense, so I hope in Your Word. Leave me alone, you evil people, for I'll keep the words of my God. Keep me according to Your Word so that I can live and not be ashamed of my hope. Keep me, and I'll be safe, and I'll have respect for Your words always. You've crushed all those that stopped following Your words for the falseness of their lies. You throw away all the sinful of the earth like trash, so I love Your words. My body trembles for fear of You; and I'm afraid of Your judgments.

[121-128] I've given good judgments and justice so don't leave me to those who come against me. Be my security for good and don't let those who think they are better than me put me down. I grow old waiting for Your saving grace, and for the word of Your goodness. Deal with me according to Your mercy, and teach me Your words. Because I'm Your worker, give me understanding so that I can know Your words. It's time for You to act, oh Yahweh, for they've made Your Word of no effect. I love Your words more than riches, yes, even more than the finest gold. I highly respect all Your guidelines concerning all the things which are right; and I hate every way that is false.

[129-136] Your words are wonderful, so my soul keeps them. The opening of Your Word gives light, bringing understanding to the naïve, so I expectantly waited, longing for Your Word. Yahweh, look on me, and be merciful to me, as You used to do to those that loved Your Name. Guide my steps by Your Word, and don't let any sin have control of me. Free me from those who would keep me down, and I'll keep Your guidelines. Let Your face smile on me, while You teach me all Your words. My eyes flow rivers of tears, because others don't keep Your Word.

[137-144] You are good, oh Yahweh and Your judgments are good as well. Your Words are good and true. I'm overpowered by my passion, because my enemies have forgotten Your Words. Your Words are perfect, so I love them. I'm unimportant and hated, yet I don't forget Your guidelines. Your goodness is an everlasting goodness, and Your Word is the truth. Trouble and grief have overwhelmed me, yet Your words are my delight. The goodness of Your words is everlasting, so give me understanding, and I'll live.

[145-152] I cried with my whole heart, "Listen to me, oh Yahweh and I'll keep Your words." I cried to You, "Save me, and I'll keep Your words." The dawning of the morning was slow in coming, and I cried, "I hoped in Your Word." My eyes don't sleep in the night as I think on Your Word. Listen to my voice according to Your love,

oh Yahweh, revive me according to Your judgment. Those who try to cause trouble are chasing after me, being far from Your Word. You are near, oh Yahweh; and all Your Words are truth. I've always known that You created Your words to last forever.

[153-160] Think on my misery and save me, for I haven't forgotten Your Word. Plead my case and save me; revive me according to Your Word. Your saving grace is far from the sinful, for they don't follow Your words. Great are Your tender mercies, oh Yahweh, so revive me according to Your judgments. I have many who come against me, who are my enemies; yet I don't reject Your words. I saw the sinful and was grieved, because they haven't kept Your Word. Think about how I love Your guidelines, and revive me, oh Yahweh, according to Your love. Your Word is true from the beginning of creation, and every one of Your good judgments will last for eternity.

[161-168] Leaders have abused me wrongly, but my heart is in awe of Your Word. I celebrate in Your Word, as one that finds great treasure. I hate and look down on lying, but I love Your Word. I praise You seven times a day because of Your good judgments. Those who love Your Word have great peace, and nothing offends them. Yahweh, I've hoped for Your saving grace and followed Your commandments. I've kept Your words, which I love very much. I've kept Your guidelines and Your words, for You know all my ways.

[169-176] Let my cry come to Your hearing, oh Yahweh; give me understanding according to Your Word. Let my prayer be heard by You and save me according to Your Word. My words will speak Your praise, when You've taught me all Your words. My mouth will tell of Your Word, for all Your words are good. Let Your hand help me, for I've chosen Your ways. I've longed for Your saving grace, oh Yahweh; and Your Words are my joy. Let my soul live, and it'll praise You; and let Your judgments help me. I've gone astray like a lost animal; find me, for I haven't forgotten Your words.

120 [1-7] *A Song of Ascents.* In my trouble I cried to Yahweh, and God heard me. Deliver my soul, oh Yahweh, from lying words and lying mouths. What penalty will be given or what punishment will be done to those who lie? The consequence of their ways will be the weapons of their own mouths which destroy others. Why must I stay here, staying in this house? My soul has lived too long with those that hate peace. My aim is peace, but when I speak of it, they only want to fight.

121 [1-8] *A Song of Ascents.* I'll set my eyes on the mountains of God, from where my help comes. My help comes from Yahweh God, who made heaven and earth. God won't let your foot slip, because the One that keeps you won't sleep. See, the One that keeps Israel, the people of God, won't slumber, nor sleep. Yahweh is your keeper; Yahweh will overshadow you. The sunlight won't expose you by day, nor will the moon by night. Yahweh will save you from all evil, yes, God will save your soul. Yahweh will save you when you leave out and when you enter any place from this time forward, and forever.

122 [1-9] *A Song of Ascents of David.* I was glad when they said to me, "*Let's go into the House of God of Yahweh.*" Our feet will stand within Your gates, oh Jerusalem. Jerusalem is a city that is built tightly together, where the people go up, that is, the people of Yahweh, to give the testimony of Israel, and to give thanks to the Name of Yahweh. For there, the seat of judgment is set, the reign of the house of David. Pray for the peace of Jerusalem; for those who love it will prosper. Let peace be within its walls, and prosperity within its great houses. For my family and friends' sakes, I'll say now, "*Let peace be on Jerusalem.*" I'll look for its good, because of the House of God of Yahweh, our God.

123 [1-4] *A Song of Ascents.* I lift up my eyes to You, the One who lives in the heavens. See, as the eyes of people look to their overseers for direction, and as the eyes of daughters to their mother; so our eyes look to Yahweh our God, until God has mercy on us. Have mercy on us, oh Yahweh, have mercy on us, for we're much disgraced. Our souls are greatly shamed by those that have an easy life, and by their proud hatred of us.

124 [1-8] *A Song of Ascents of David.* If it hadn't been for Yahweh being on our side, let Israel say now; if it hadn't been for Yahweh being on our side, when people rose up against us, and when their anger was hot against us, they would have quickly overcome us. When the waters would have overwhelmed us, then the river would have gone over our heads. Yes, the flood waters would have gone over our heads. May Yahweh be blessed, who hasn't let us be overcome. Our souls escaped as a bird out of the hunter's trap; for the trap was broken, and we've escaped. Our help is in the Name of Yahweh, who made heaven and earth.

125 [1-5] *A Song of Ascents.* Those that trust in Yahweh will be as mount Zion, which can't be shaken and will always be there. As the mountains that surround Jerusalem, so Yahweh surrounds the people of God from now to eternity. For the rule of the sinful won't stay in the land given to godly people; or else they would be tempted to sin. Do good things, oh Yahweh, to those that are good, to those whose hearts are good. As for those that practice crooked ways, Yahweh will take them away with the sinful, but let peace stay on Israel.

126 [1-6] *A Song of Ascents.* When Yahweh released the people of Jerusalem from captivity, we were in a dream-like state. We were filled with laughter, and singing, and then we said among the ungodly, "*Yahweh has done great things for us. Yahweh has done great things for us; for which we're glad.*" Free us again from the captivity of our sin, oh Yahweh, as the streams that flow in the south. Those that plant seeds of tears will pick a harvest of joy. Those that go on with the precious seed of repentance will doubtless come again with celebrating, bringing a good harvest with them.

127 [1-5] ***A Song of Ascents for Solomon.*** Unless Yahweh builds the house, those that build it work for nothing. Unless Yahweh keeps the city, the night watchman stays awake for no reason. It's of no use for you to rise up early, or to sit up late, only to worry about your own sorrows; for God gives sleep to those who are beloved. See, children are the inheritance of Yahweh, and the child in the womb is God's gift. As a strong hunter powerfully handles weapons; so the children of their youth are their strength. Those who have lots of children will be happily rewarded; and they won't be publicly shamed, but will have an answer to their enemies' accusations.

128 [1-6] ***A Song of Ascents.*** Every one that respects Yahweh is blessed, all those who walk in the ways of God. You'll eat from the work of your hands and be happy, and it'll be well with you. Your spouse will be as a fruitful vine beside your house and Your children will sprout up like olive plants around your table. See, the people that respect Yahweh will be blessed. Yahweh will bless you out of Zion, and you'll see the good of Jerusalem all the days of Your life. Yes, you'll see your grandchildren, and peace in Israel.

129 [1-8] ***A Song of Ascents.*** Many times they have abused me from my childhood, God's people can now say: Many times they have abused me from my childhood; yet they haven't overcome me. The farmers plowed on my back, making long furrows. God is good, for Yahweh has cut the cords of the sinful in half. Let those that hate Jerusalem all be confused and turn back. Let them be as the grass on the housetops, which withers before it grows up, and in which the mowers don't fill their hands; or those that bind sheaves fill their hearts. And those who go by won't say, *"The blessing of Yahweh be on You: bless You in the Name of Yahweh."*

130 [1-8] ***A Song of Ascents.*** Out of the depths of my soul I've cried to You, oh Yahweh. My God, hear my voice; let Your ears listen to the sound of my prayer. If You, oh Yahweh, should keep a record of sins, oh my God, who could stand before You? But forgiveness is with You, so that You can be respected. I wait for Yahweh, my soul waits, and it's in Your Word that I hope. My soul watches for the Savior more than those that watch for the morning; yes I say, more than those that watch for the morning. Let Israel hope in Yahweh; for with Yahweh there's more than enough mercy to buy us back from our sin. And God will free Israel from all their sins.

131 [1-3] ***A Song of Ascents of David.*** Yahweh, my heart isn't proud, nor do my eyes look down on anyone; nor do I exercise myself in great matters or in things too brilliant for me. Surely I've behaved and comforted myself, as a weaned child: even my soul is as a weaned child. Let Israel hope in Yahweh now and forever.

132 [1-7] ***A Song of Ascents.*** Yahweh, remember all the troubles of David: How he swore to Yahweh, and vowed to the mighty God of Israel, *"Surely I won't come into the safety of my house, nor go to my bed; I won't let my eyes sleep or even close my eyelids, until I discover a place for Yahweh, a house for the mighty God of Jacob."* See, we heard of it at Ephratah and found it in the fields of the woods. So we'll go into the House of God and worship at the footstool of God.

[8-12] Arise, oh Yahweh, into Your resting place; You, and Your powerful craft. Let Your priests shine with Your goodness; and let the people of God celebrate loudly. For Your worker, David's sake, don't turn the face of Your anointed away. Yahweh has sworn in truth to David, and won't break this promise, *"I'll set on Your throne One of your own descendants. If your children will keep My Promise and My testimony that I'll teach them, their children also will sit on your throne continuously."*

[13-18] For Yahweh has chosen Jerusalem; God has wanted it for a resting place saying, *"This is My resting place; I'll stay here forever; for this is what I've wanted. I'll bless what they have even more, satisfying the poor with food. I'll also cover the priests with My saving grace, and the people of God will loudly celebrate. There I'll make the strength of David to grow: I've chosen My Anointed One to reflect My glory, whose enemies I'll cover with shame, but the crown of the One I anoint will outshine them all."*

133 [1-3] ***A Song of Ascents of David.*** See how good and pleasant it is for the family of God to be together as one! It's like the precious oil on Aaron's head, that ran down on his beard, flowing all the way down to the skirts of his garments; As the dew of Mt. Hermon, that fell on the mountains of Jerusalem: for there Yahweh gave the blessing of everlasting life.

134 [1-3] ***A Song of Ascents.*** Bless Yahweh, everyone who worships by night in the house of God. Lift up your hands in the House of God, and worship Yahweh, who made heaven and earth, and who will bless you from Jerusalem.

135 [1-5] Praise Yahweh! Praise the Name of Yahweh; Praise God, oh people of Yahweh. All you who worship in the house of Yahweh, in the sanctuary of the house of our God, praise Yahweh; for Yahweh is good: Sing praises to the Name of God, which sounds sweet to our ears. Yahweh, You have chosen Jacob for Yourself and Israel for Your particular treasure. I know that Yahweh is great, and that our God is above all great ones.

[6-12] Whatever Yahweh wanted was done in heaven, and on earth, in the seas, and in every deep place. God causes the water to evaporate, rising from all over the earth; God makes the lightning in the rain; God brings the wind out of its places in heaven: Yes, God who struck the firstborn of Egypt, both people and beast; and who sent signs and wonders in Egypt, on Pharaoh, and on all his people; and who struck great nations and slaughtered rulers; Sihon ruler of the Amorites, and Og ruler of Bashan, and all the nations of Canaan, giving their land for an inheritance, a heritage to the people of Israel.

[13-21] Your Name, oh Yahweh, lasts forever; and You will be remembered, oh Yahweh, throughout all generations. For You, Yahweh will judge Your people, and will be compassionate toward Your children. The ungodly worship their statues of silver and gold, creations of human hands, having mouths, but not speaking; having eyes, but not seeing; having ears, but not hearing; nor is there any life in them. Those that make them are as dumb as they are, and so is every one who trusts in them. Bless Yahweh, oh house of Israel: bless Yahweh, oh house of Aaron: Bless Yahweh, oh house of Levi, and all you who respect God, bless Yahweh. May Yahweh be blessed from out of Zion, whose resting place is at Jerusalem. Praise Yahweh!

136 [1-9] Oh give thanks to Yahweh; for God is good: for the mercy of God is forever. Oh give thanks to the God of all great ones: for the mercy of God is forever. Oh give thanks to the Savior of Saviors: for the mercy of God is forever. To the One, who alone does great wonders: for the mercy of God is forever. To the One that by wisdom made the heavens: for the mercy of God is forever. To the One that brought the earth out of the waters: for the mercy of God is forever. To the One that made the great lights: for the mercy of God is forever: The sunlight to rule by day: for the mercy of God is forever: The moon and starlight to rule by night: for the mercy of God is forever.

[10-21] To the One that struck Egypt's firstborns: for the mercy of God is forever: And brought Israel out from among them: for the mercy of God is forever: With a strong hand, and with an out stretched arm: for the mercy of God is forever. To the One, who divided the Red Sea into two parts: for the mercy of God is forever: And made Israel to pass through the midst of it: for the mercy of God is forever: But overthrew Pharaoh and his army in the Red Sea: for the mercy of God is forever. To the One, who led the people of God through the countryside: for the mercy of God is forever. To the One, who struck great rulers: for the mercy of God is forever: And killed famous rulers: for the mercy of God is forever: Sihon ruler of the Amorites: for the mercy of God is forever: And Og the ruler of Bashan: for the mercy of God is forever: And gave their land for a heritage: for the mercy of God is forever.

[22-26] Even a heritage to the people of God, to Israel: for the mercy of God is forever. Who remembered us in our humility: for the mercy of God is forever: And has bought us back from our enemies: for the mercy of God is forever. Who gives food to everyone: for the mercy of God is forever. Oh give thanks to the God of heaven: for the mercy of God is forever.

137 [1-6] We sat down and wept by the rivers of Babylon, when we remembered Jerusalem. We hung our harps on the willows beside it. For there, those that carried us away captive, demanded us to sing a song to amuse them, saying, "*Sing us one of the songs of Jerusalem.*" How can we sing Yahweh's song in a foreign land? If I forget Jerusalem let my hands forget their skill. If I don't remember you; if I don't prefer Jerusalem above my favorite enjoyment, let my tongue cling to the roof of my mouth.

[7-9] Remember, oh Yahweh, the children of Edom in the day of Jerusalem; that said, "*Destroy it, destroy it, even to the foundation of it*". Oh children of Babylon, who will be destroyed, God, who punishes you as you've punished us, will be joyful. God will be joyful, who revenges us against you and your children.

138 [1-3] *A Hymn of David.* I'll praise You with my whole heart: I'll sing praise to You before the great ones. I'll worship toward Your holy House of God and praise Your Name, Yahweh, for Your love, and for Your truth, because You've glorified Your Word even above Your Name. In the day when I cried, You answered me, and built me up with strength in my soul.

[4-8] All rulers on the earth will praise You, oh Yahweh, when they hear Your Words. Yes, they'll sing in the ways of Yahweh: for great is the glory of Yahweh. Though Yahweh is the Savior, God respects those who have humility, but barely knows those who think they are better than everyone else. Though I'm in trouble where I walk, You'll revive me. You'll stretch out Your hand against the rage of my enemies, and Your strong hand will save me. Yahweh will complete everything that concerns me, for Your mercy, oh Yahweh, is forever; so don't give up on the creation of Your own hands.

139 [1-6] *To the first musician, A Hymn of David.* Oh Yahweh, You've examined me, and know me well. You know when I sit down and when I get up; You understand my thoughts from where You are. You come to me whether I am awake or asleep, and know all my ways. There isn't a word in my mouth, oh Yahweh, that You don't thoroughly know. You've come behind me and before me, and laid Your hand on me. Such knowledge is too wonderful for me; it's so wonderful, I can't even imagine it.

[7-12] Where can I go away from Your spirit? Or where can I run from Your presence? If I go up into heaven, You are there, or if I make my bed in Hell, You are even there. If I were to leave first thing in the morning, and live on an island in the farthest part of the sea; even there Your hand will lead me, and Your strong hand will hold me. If I say, "*Surely the darkness will cover me,*" even the night will be light around me. Yes, the darkness won't hide me from You; but the night would shine as the light of day, because to You, the darkness and light are both alike.

[13-16] You've made my mind passionate for You, protecting me from my mother's womb. I'll praise You; for I'm powerfully and wonderfully made: Your creations are awesome; as my soul knows so well. My essence wasn't hid from You, when I was conceived in private, and so interestingly created. Your eyes saw my substance, while I

59

was still imperfect; and all my members were noted in Your book, which were formed each in their turn, before any of them were even formed.

[17-24] How precious and how great, oh God, are Your thoughts to me! If I should count them, they're more numerous than the grains of sand: and when I awake, I'm still with You. Surely You'll destroy the sinful, oh God: *so leave me alone, you bloodthirsty people.* For they speak wickedly against You, and Your enemies vainly misuse Your Name. Don't I hate them, oh Yahweh, those that hate You? And am not I grieved with those that rise up against You? I hate them with complete hatred, counting them my own enemies. Look me over, oh God, and see my heart; question me, and know my thoughts. See if there is any sinfulness in me, and lead me to eternity.

140 [1-5] *To the first musician, A Hymn of David.* Free me, oh Yahweh, from evil people: save me from the violent people who imagine trouble in their hearts; and always gang up for a fight. They've sharpened their tongues like the fangs of a serpent, whose poison is in their words. Selah! Keep me, oh Yahweh, from the hands of the sinful; save me from violent people who want to stop what I do. People who think they are better than me have hid their traps for me, spreading a net in the wayside and ropes with a noose to hang me. Selah!

[6-13] I said to Yahweh, "*You are my God, so hear the voice of my prayer, oh Yahweh. Oh God, my Savior, the strength of the grace that saves me, You've protected me in the days of fighting. Yahweh, don't give the sinful what they want and don't further their sinful plans; or they'll praise themselves. Selah! Let the trouble of their own words fall on the heads of those that surround me. Let them be thrown into a fire with burning coals falling on them; or into deep pits in which they can't get out of again. Don't let those who speak evil become well known in the earth: let evil hunt violent people and overthrow them. I know that Yahweh will uphold the case of the abused, and the right of the poor. Surely godly people will give thanks to Your Name, and always stay in Your presence.*"

141 [1-4] *A Hymn of David.* Yahweh, I'm crying to You: hurry to me; hear my voice, when I cry to You. Let my prayer be set before You like burning incense; and my uplifted hands as the evening sacrifice. Watch my mouth, oh Yahweh, set a guard on the doors of my lips and keep them. Don't let my heart lean toward anything evil, to do what is sinful with those who practice sin, and don't let me share in their excesses.

[5-10] If godly people punish me; it'll be a kindness, and if they warn me; it'll be excellent ointment, which won't harm me, for even in their troubles, I'll yet pray for them. When their judges are overthrown in rough places, they'll finally acknowledge that my words are good. Our bones are scattered at the mouth of the grave, as when wood lay chopped and split on the ground. But my eyes look to You, oh God, my Savior: my trust is in You, so don't leave my soul without hope. Keep me from the traps which they've set for me, and from the noose of those who practice sin. Let the sinful fall into their own traps, while I escape out of them.

142 [1-4] *A poem of teaching of David; A prayer when he was in the cave.* I cried to You, Yahweh, praying aloud to You. I made my complaints to You, telling You all my troubles. When my spirit was overwhelmed inside me, then You knew my way. They secretly set a trap for me in the way that I walked. I looked to my side, but there was no one that knew me: safety failed me and no one cared for my soul.

[5-7] I cried to You, oh Yahweh: saying, "*You are my safe haven and my lot in life. Pay attention to me; for I'm greatly humbled: save me from those who try to hurt me; for they're stronger than I am. Bring my soul out of its prison, so that I can praise Your Name: let godly people surround me; for You greatly help me always.*"

143 [1-6] *A Hymn of David.* Listen to my prayer, oh Yahweh, listen to my prayer. In Your faithfulness and goodness answer me. And don't judge Your worker, for in Your sight, no one living would be justified. For the enemy has abused my soul and has beaten my life down to the ground, making me stay in darkness, as those that are dead. My spirit is overwhelmed inside me and my heart is lonely. I think on everything You've done as I remember the days of the past; I reflect over all Your hands have done. I raise my hands up to You, my soul thirsting after You, as the dry land thirsts for water. Selah!

[7-12] Listen to me soon, oh Yahweh; my spirit fails, so don't hide Your face from me, or I'll be like a dead person. Cause me to hear Your loving voice in the morning; for I trust in You. Cause me to know the way I should walk; for I lift up my heart to You. Free me, oh Yahweh, from my enemies, for I run to You to protect me. Teach me to do Your will; for You are my God: Your Spirit is good; lead me into the way of honesty. Revive me, oh Yahweh, for Your Name's sake; and bring my soul out of trouble for Your goodness' sake. And by Your mercy take away my enemies, and destroy all those that torment my soul; for I'm Your faithful worker.

144 [1-4] *A Hymn of David.* May Yahweh be blessed, who is my strength, who teaches me how to fight: My goodness and my stronghold; my strong tower that protects me; my defense, the God in whom I trust forever, and that quiets my people for me. Yahweh, what are human beings, that You take note of them! Or the children of humanity, that You take account of them! People are as nothing, for their days are as a shadow that passes away.

[5-9] Open Your heavens, oh Yahweh, and come down: You touch the mountains and they smoke. Make lightning, shooting out Your lightening bolts; scatter them and destroy them. Send Your hand from above; free me, and save me out of the floods, from the hand of the ungodly, whose mouths speak proudly, and their hands are hands of falsehood. I'll sing a new song to You, oh God: on a musical instrument and an instrument of ten strings I'll sing praises to You.

[10-15] It's You, who gives saving grace to rulers, who freed David, Your worker, from the hurtful blade. Free me, and save me from the hand of the ungodly, whose mouths speak proudly, and their hands are hands of falsehood: So that our sons and daughters can be as young plants who have grown up; or as corner stones, polished like those on a great house: So that our cabinets can be full, holding all kinds of stuff; and that our animals can bring forth thousands and ten thousands in our streets: So that our cattle can be strong to work; and that there be no thieves breaking in, nor our people going out; and that there be no complaining in our streets. Those kind of people are blessed; yes, the ones, whose God is Yahweh, are blessed.

145 [1-7] *David's Hymn of praise.* I'll worship You, my God, my Savior; and I'll bless Your Name forever and ever. All day long I'll bless You; and I'll praise Your Name forever and ever. Yahweh is great, and deserves to be greatly praised: Your greatness is unsearchable. One generation will praise You to another, telling of Your mighty acts. I'll speak of the glorious honor of Your majesty, and of Your wondrous creations. And people will speak of the power of Your awesome acts, and I'll tell them how great You are. They'll remember Your great goodness, and will sing of Your goodness.

[8-13] Yahweh is gracious, and full of compassion; slow to anger, and of great mercy. Yahweh is good to all: You have tender mercy for all Your creations. All Your creations will praise You, oh Yahweh; Your people, Israel, will bless You as well. They speak of the glory of Your realm and talk of Your power, so that they can make Your mighty acts known and the glorious majesty of Your dominion to the children of humanity. Your realm is an everlasting realm, and Your power lasts throughout all generations.

[14-21] Yahweh holds up all those that fall, and lifts up all those that are humbled. The eyes of all people will look to You, because You give them their food in due season. You open Your hand, and give every living thing what it needs. Yahweh, You are good in all Your ways and holy in all Your acts. Yahweh, You're near to all those that call on You, yes, to all those who call on You in truth. You give those that respect You what they want, hearing their cry, and saving them. Yahweh, You save all those that love You, but all the sinful You'll destroy. My mouth will speak the praise of Yahweh; Let everyone bless Your holy Name forever and ever.

146 [1-7] Praise Yahweh! Praise Yahweh, oh my soul. As long as I live I'll praise Yahweh: I'll sing praises to my God as long as I have any being. Don't put your trust in the government, nor in the children of humanity, in whom is no help at all. Their breath leaves them, they return to the earth; and in that very day their thoughts vanish. Happy are those that have God for their help, whose hope is in Yahweh their God: Who made heaven and earth, the sea, and all that is in them and who keeps truth forever: Who gives good judgment for those who are put down, who gives food to the hungry. Yes, Yahweh sets the prisoners free.

[8-10] Yahweh opens the eyes of the blind and raises those that are humbled, because Yahweh loves godly people. Yahweh keeps the foreigner safe; God relieves a single parent's child and the survivor, but God upsets the way of the sinful. Yahweh will reign forever; yes even Your God, oh Zion, *New Jerusalem*, to all generations. Praise Yahweh!

147 [1-6] Praise Yahweh! For it's good to sing praises to our God; It's pleasant and praise is beautiful. You build up Jerusalem, Yahweh, gathering together the outcasts of Your people, Israel. God heals the brokenhearted, binding up their wounds. God tells the number of the stars, calling them all by Name. Great is our God, and of great power, whose understanding is endless. Yahweh lifts up those with humility, and casts down the sinful.

[7-12] Sing to Yahweh with thanksgiving; sing praise on the harp to our God, who clothes the heavens with clouds, and prepares rain for the earth, and makes the grass grow on the mountains. God gives the wild animals their food, and the young ravens that cry. God doesn't delight in the strength of the horse, or take pleasure in their legs. Yahweh, You take pleasure in those that respect You, in those that hope in Your mercy. Praise Yahweh, oh *New* Jerusalem; Praise your God, oh Zion.

[13-20] For God has strengthened the bars of your gates; God has blessed your children within you. God makes peace all around you, and fills you with the finest of wheat. God sends forward the commandment on earth: Your Word acts very swiftly. You give snow like wool, scattering the frost like ashes. You scatter ice like bread crumbs: who can stand before the cold? You send out the word, and melt them, causing the wind to blow, and the waters to flow. You show Your Word to Jacob, Your words and judgments to Your people, Israel. You haven't dealt this way with any other people, and as for Your judgments, others have never known them. Praise Yahweh!

148 [1-6] Praise Yahweh! Praise Yahweh from the heavens: Praise God in the heights of heaven. Praise God, all you angels: Praise God, with all the heavenly hosts. Praise God, sun and moon: Praise God, all you stars of light. Praise God, heaven of heavens, and waters above the heavens. Let them praise the Name of Yahweh: for God spoke, and they were all created. God settled them forever and ever, making a law which won't ever pass away.

[7-14] Praise Yahweh from the earth, you dragons in the depths of the oceans: Fire and hail, snow and vapors, and the stormy wind, all fulfill God's word. Mountains and hills, fruitful trees and cedars, wild animals and cattle, reptiles and birds, the rulers of the earth, and all people, the nobles and all the judges of the earth, both young and old people, and even little children: Let them all praise the Name of Yahweh: for God's Name alone is

excellent; Your glory is above the earth and heaven. You uphold the strength of Your people, the praise of all Your saintly people; even the children of Israel, a people near to Your heart. Praise Yahweh!

149 [1-4] Praise Yahweh! Sing to Yahweh a new song, with praises in the congregation of the saints of God. Let Israel celebrate in the One that made them: let the children of Zion, the New Jerusalem, be joyful in their Savior. Let them praise God's Name in the dance: let them sing praises to God with the tambourine and harp. For Yahweh takes pleasure in the people of God, making those with humility known by God's saving grace for them.

[5-9] Let the saints of God be joyful in glory: let them sing aloud on their beds. Let their mouths lift up the praises of God, and give them a double-edged blade to execute vengeance on the nations, and bring punishments on the peoples, to bind their rulers with chains, and their nobles with iron shackles; All the people of God have the honor of executing on them the written judgment. Praise Yahweh!

150 [1-6] Praise Yahweh! Sing praises to God in the House of God: We Praise You, God, in Your great heaven! We praise You for Your mighty acts: We praise You because of Your perfect power. We praise You with the sound of the trumpet: We praise You with the instruments and harp. We praise You with the tambourine and dance: We praise You with stringed instruments and organs. We praise You on the loud cymbals: We praise You on the high sounding cymbals. Let every thing that has breath praise Yahweh. Praise Yahweh!

62

The Ten Commandments

Deuteronomy 5:6-21

1 Yahweh said, I am Yahweh your God... Don't worship anything else but Me.

2 Don't make an idol of any kind or a false god of anything in the heavens, on the earth, or in the sea. Don't bow down to them or worship them because I, Yahweh your God, am a jealous God, who passes the parents' faults down to the children up to the third and fourth generation of those who hate Me, but forgiving many generations of those who love and keep My Laws.

3 Don't use the name of Yahweh your God with disrespect. Yahweh won't let anyone go unpunished who misuses God's name.

4 Remember the Seventh Day and keep it set aside to worship, as Yahweh your God told you. You may do all your work in six days, but the seventh day is the Day of Rest of Yahweh your God. On that day no one may do any work.

5 Respect your father and mother," as Yahweh your God told you, so you'll live a long life and God may bless you in the land Yahweh your God is giving you.

6 Don't kill anyone.

7 Don't be sexually unfaithful to your spouse.

8 Don't steal anything.

9 Don't tell lies about anyone."

10 Don't want what someone else has. Don't want their spouse, their house, their land, their workers, their animals, or anything else that belongs to someone else."

Illustration by Rock Hartfield
©2005

The
New Word
For All God's
People

A Go Fish Ministries Publication

The New Word According to Matthew

The Family Tree of Yeshua the Christ (Royal Line of David)

1 [1-17] This is the book of the family tree of Yeshua the Christ, who was the descendent of David, who was the descendent of Abraham. Abraham had Isaac; and Isaac had Jacob; and Jacob had Judah and his siblings; and Judah had Perez and Zerah by Tamar; and Perez had Hezron; and Hezron had Aram; and Aram had Aminadab; and Aminadab had Nahshon; and Nahshon had Salmon; and Salmon had Boaz by Rahab; and Boaz had Obed by Ruth; and Obed had Jesse; and Jesse had David, the ruler of Israel; and David had Solomon by the survivor of Urias; and Solomon had Rehoboam; and Rehoboam had Abijah; and Abijah had Asa; and Asa had Jehoshaphat; and Jehoshaphat had Joram; and Joram had Uzziah; and Uzziah had Jotham; and Jotham had Ahaz; and Ahaz had Hezekiah; and Hezekiah had Manasseh; and Manasseh had Amon; and Amon had Josiah; and Josiah had Jechoniah and his siblings, about the time they were taken captive and carried away to Babylon. After they were brought there, Jechoniah had Shealtiel; and Shealtiel had Zerubbabel; and Zerubbabel had Abiud; and Abiud had Eliakim; and Eliakim had Azor; and Azor had Zadoc; and Zadoc had Achim; and Achim had Eliud; and Eliud had Eleazar; and Eleazar had Matthan; and Matthan had Jacob; and Jacob had Joseph, the husband of Mary, who gave birth to Yeshua, who is called the Christ. So all the generations from Abraham to David were fourteen generations; and from David until the Babylonian captivity were fourteen generations; and from the Babylonian captivity until the Christ were fourteen generations.

The Conception and Birth of Jesus

[18-25] Now this is how the birth of Yeshua the Christ happened: When Mary, the mother of the Christ, was engaged to Joseph, she became pregnant with the Child of the Holy Spirit before they were married. Then Joseph, her future husband being a good person, and not willing to make a public example out of her, was thinking about secretly breaking the engagement. But while he thought about it, the angel of God appeared to him in a dream, saying, *"Joseph, descendent of David, don't be afraid to take Mary as your wife because her baby was conceived by the Holy Spirit. And she'll have a child, and you're to call the Child's name Yeshua because this child will save God's people from their sins."* Now all this happened, so that what was spoken of by the great preacher of God would happen, who said, *a young girl who has never had sexual relations will become pregnant, and will have a child, and they'll call the Child's name Immanuel, which means, God is with us.* Then Joseph, being awakened from sleep, did as the angel of God had told him, and took Mary in marriage, but didn't have sexual relations with her until after she had given birth to her first child: and Joseph called the Child's name Yeshua, which means *God saves.*

The Astronomers and Herod

2 [1-10] Now when Yeshua was born in Bethlehem of Judea in the days when Herod ruled, three astronomers came from the east to Jerusalem, asking, *"Where is the One that was born to be Ruler of the Jews? We've seen a new star in the east, and have come to worship the new Ruler."* So when Herod, who was then ruling, heard this, he was very uneasy, and all the people of Jerusalem, as well. So he gathered all the leading priests and the religious leaders together, and asked them where the Christ was to have been born. And they told him, *"In Bethlehem of Judea because the Word says by the great preacher, 'and you, Bethlehem, in the land of Judah, aren't the least among the royalty of Judah because a Governor will come from you, to rule My people Israel.'"* Then Herod, who had called the astronomers in secret, cautiously asked them about what time the star had appeared. Then he sent them to Bethlehem, saying, *"Go and search carefully for the young Child; and when you've found the Child, come and tell me, so that I can come and show my respect also."* So when they had heard what Herod said, they left; and the star, which they saw in the east, moved in front of them, till it came and stood over the place where the young Child was. When they saw the star, they were greatly overjoyed.

The Astronomers with Yeshua

[11-12] And when they had come into the house, they saw Mary with the young Child and bowed down, and worshipped the Child: and when they had opened their treasures, they presented to them gifts of gold, frankincense, and myrrh. And being warned of God in a dream not to return to Herod, they went back another way to their own country.

Escape into Egypt

[13-15] And when they had left, the angel of Yahweh appeared to Joseph in a dream, saying, *"Get up, and take the young Child and Mary, and run away into Egypt, and stay there until I bring word because Herod will try to kill the Child."* And when they got up, he took them by night and escaped into Egypt, staying there until the death of

Herod, so that the Words which were spoken of God by the great preacher would happen, which says, "*I've called my Child out of Egypt."*

Herod Kills the Children

[16-18] Then Herod, who saw that he had been tricked by the astronomers, was very angry, and sent guards to kill all the male children two years old and under in Bethlehem, and the surrounding areas, according to the time which the Astronomers had told him of it. Then what was spoken of by Jeremiah, the great preacher, happened, who said, "*In Rama, near Bethlehem, a voice of great grief was heard, with screaming and crying, Rachel crying for her children, who wouldn't be comforted, because they were dead."*

The Nazarene

[19-23] But when Herod was dead, an angel of God appeared to Joseph in a dream while in Egypt, saying, "*Get up and take the young Child and Mary, and go back to the land of Israel because the ones who wanted to kill the young Child are dead now."* So Joseph got up, and took them back into the land of Israel. But when he heard that Archelaus ruled in Judea in place of his father Herod, they were afraid to go there: So being warned of God in another dream, they turned aside into the country of Galilee: And they came and lived in a city called Nazareth, so that it would happen which was spoken by the great preachers, "*The Child will be called a Nazarene."*

John the Baptist

3 [1-12] Now in those days, John the Baptist came preaching in the countryside of Judea, saying, "*Change your evil ways because the realm of heaven is about to come."* I am the one that was spoken of by the great preacher Isaiah, saying, "*The voice of one calling out in the countryside will clear the way for Yahweh God, making the way plain."* And John had clothing of camel's hair, with a leather belt around the waist; and ate locusts and wild honey. Then the people of Jerusalem went out to him, along with all Judea, and the whole countryside around Jordan, and were baptized by him in the Jordan River, admitting all their sins. But when John saw many people from the religious sects coming to be baptized, he said, "*You snakes! Who warned you to escape from the coming judgment? If so, don't just say you're sorry, change your evil ways: And don't think to yourselves, Abraham is our ancestor because I tell you, that God is able to create more children for Abraham even from these stones. Now the axe is laid to the root of the trees: so every tree which doesn't make good fruit will be cut down, and put into the fire. I baptize you with water as a symbol of your changed life: but the One that comes after me is greater than I, whose shoes I'm not even worthy to carry: The Christ will baptize you with the fire of the Holy Spirit: Who holds the separating fan, and will carefully clear the floor, gathering the wheat into the storage room; but burning up the waste with a great fire."*

John Baptizes the Christ

[13-17] Then Yeshua came from Galilee to the Jordan to John to be baptized. At first John refused saying, "*I need to be baptized by you, and here you are coming to me?"* But Yeshua said, "*Do it this way now because it's right to do it this way."* Then John baptized Yeshua. And when Yeshua was baptized, coming straight up out of the water, John saw the heavens open up, and the Spirit of God coming down like a dove, and landing on Yeshua: And a voice from heaven said, "**This is My Child, who I love and I am so pleased with You."**

The Temptation of Christ

4 [1-11] Then Yeshua was led by the Spirit up into the countryside to be tempted by the devil. So after Yeshua had gone without food forty days and forty nights, the Christ was very hungry. Then the devil came to tempt Yeshua, saying, "If you're really the Child of God, order these stones to become bread." But Yeshua answered, "*It's written, 'No one can live by bread alone, but by every word that God says'."* Then the devil took the Christ up into Jerusalem, the holy city, and set Yeshua on top of the Place of Worship, and said, "If you're really the Child of God, jump down from here because the Word says, '*God's angels will be in charge of You: and they'll pick you up in their hands, if you should ever stumble over a stone.'"* And Yeshua answered, "*It's also written; 'You should never tempt Yahweh your God.'"* Then, the devil took the Christ up into a very high mountain, showing Yeshua all the countries of the world, and all of their amazing realms; saying, "I'll give you all of this, if you'll only bow down and worship me." But Yeshua said, "*Get away from Me, Satan; the Word says, 'You'll worship Yahweh your God, and will serve only Yahweh.'"* Then the devil left and God's angels quickly came and ministered to the Christ.

The Christ's Ministry Begins

[12-17] Now when Yeshua heard that John had been put in jail, the Christ went into Galilee; and leaving Nazareth, came and stayed in Capernaum, which is on the sea coast, in the borders of Zebulun and Naphtali, so that it would happen which was spoken of by Isaiah the great preacher, saying, "*In the land of Zebulun and Naphtali, beside the sea, and beyond Jordan, in Galilee, where the other peoples live; The people who were*

67

surrounded by darkness saw a great light; and a light has shined for those who lived under the shadow of death." From then on Yeshua began to preach saying, *"Change your evil ways, because the power of heaven is here."*

Calling the Followers

[18-25] And Yeshua, walking by the Sea of Galilee, saw two brothers, Simon Peter and Andrew, throwing a net into the sea because they were fishers. So Yeshua called out to them, *"Follow Me and I'll make you fishers of others."* Then suddenly, they left their nets, following the Christ. And going on from there, Yeshua saw two more brothers, James and John, two of the children of Zebedee, in a ship with Zebedee their father, mending their nets; and called out to them also. And they, too, suddenly left their ship and their father, following the Christ. Then Yeshua went all around Galilee, teaching in their worship services, and preaching the New Word of heaven, and healing all kinds of sicknesses and diseases among the people. And Yeshua became famous throughout all Syria: and they brought all the sick people, who had many different diseases and pains, and those who were overcome by evil spirits, and those who had mental illnesses, and those who were paralyzed; and Yeshua healed them all. And great crowds of people from Galilee, from Decapolis, from Jerusalem, from Judea, and from beyond Jordan followed the Christ.

The Sermon on the Mount

5 [1-12] And seeing the crowds, Yeshua went up on a mountain: and when the Christ had sat down, the followers came, too: And Yeshua began to speak, and taught them all, saying, *"Blessed are those whose spirits are disheartened because the power of heaven is now theirs. Blessed are those who grieve because they'll be in good spirits now. Blessed are those who are gentle because the earth will be given to them. Blessed are those who hunger and thirst for goodness because they'll be filled with it. Blessed are those who have compassion because they'll be given compassion in return. Blessed are those whose hearts are innocent because they'll see God. Blessed are those who are peacemakers because they'll be called the children of God. Blessed are those who are abused for the sake of goodness, because the power of heaven is now theirs. Blessed are you, when people hate you, and mistreat you, and say all kinds of evil things against you falsely, for My sake. Celebrate, and be very happy because your reward in heaven will be great because they also abused the great preachers who came before you.*

Salt and Light

[13-16] *You're like the salt of the earth: but if the salt loses its flavor, how can it flavor anything? It isn't good for anything, but to be thrown out, and walked on. You're also like the light of the world. A city built on a hill can't be hid. Nor would anyone light a candle and hide it, but they would put it on a candle holder; so that it gives light to everyone in the house. So let your light shine for others, so that they can see what good things you've done, and praise your God who is in heaven.*

[17-20] *Don't think that I've come to put an end to the law of God, or the great preachers' prophesies: I haven't come to end them, but to complete them. The truth is, until heaven and earth come to an end, not one comma or one period will be taken from the Word of God, till everything is complete. So whoever breaks the least part of the Word, and teaches others to do so, that person will be the least important in heaven: but whoever will do and teach it, that person will be called great in heaven. I tell you, that unless your goodness is greater than the goodness of the religious leaders, you'll never get into heaven.*

The Dangers of Judgment

[21-26] *You've heard it said by the old ones, '"Don't kill; and whoever kills will be in danger of judgment': But I tell you, that whoever is angry with another without cause will be in danger of judgment: and whoever says to another, 'You godless idiot,' will be in danger of being sued at law: but whoever says, 'You godless idiot,' will also be in danger of the Hell fire. So if you bring your gift to the altar, and remember that another has something against you; Leave your gift there at the altar, and go first and make up with the other person, and then come and offer your gift. Come to an agreement quickly with those who come against you, while you're with them; or they may bring you to the judge, and the judge will hand you over to the officer, who will put you in jail. The truth is, you'll by no means be freed, till you've paid every cent of your fine.*

Sexual Sin

[27-32] *You've heard it said by the old ones, 'Don't be sexually unfaithful in your marriage': But I tell you, that whoever thinks of someone in a sexual way who isn't their spouse has done a sexual sin in their heart already. And if your eyes cause you to suffer in sin, don't use them because it's better for you that you not be able to use one of your members, and not that your whole body be thrown into Hell. And if your hand causes you to suffer in sin, don't use it because it's better for you that you not use one of your members and not that your whole body be thrown into Hell. It has been said, 'Whoever divorces their spouse, should give them a writ of divorcement': But I*

tell you, that whoever divorces their spouse, except for sexual unfaithfulness, causes them to be sexually unfaithful: and whoever marries that person who is divorced is being sexually unfaithful as well.

Breaking Promises

[33-37] Again, you've heard it said by the old ones, 'Don't break your promises, but do everything you promise to God': But I tell you, don't make promises at all; not by heaven, because it's God's throne; Nor by the earth, because it's God's footstool; nor by Jerusalem, because it's the City of God. Nor should you swear by your head, because you can't make one hair white or black. So let your yes be yes, and your no be no, because whatever you say more than this is of evil.

Do More Than is Expected

[38-42] You've heard it said, 'An eye for an eye, and a tooth for a tooth': But I tell you that you shouldn't fight back against evil; but whoever hits you on your right cheek, turn to them the other cheek also. And if anyone sues you at law and takes away your coat, let them have your shirt also. And whoever orders you to go a mile, go with them two miles. Give to anyone who asks of you, and don't keep from anyone that would borrow from you.

Always Do What's Right

[43-48] You've heard it said, 'Love your neighbor, and hate your enemy'. But I tell you, love those who come against you, bless those who curse you, do good to those who hate you, and pray for those who shamefully use and mistreat you; so that you can be the children of your God who is in heaven, because God makes the sun to rise on the bad and the good, and sends rain on those who are fair and those who aren't. Because if you only love those who love you, what have you gained? Don't the sinners even do this? And if you only respect your loved ones, what more do you do than others? Don't the sinners even do that? So always do what's right, just as your God, who is in heaven always does what's right.

Tithing Should be Private

6 *[1-4] Be sure that you don't give your gifts openly, to be seen by others: otherwise you'll have no reward from your God who is in heaven. So when you give your gifts, don't tell it to everyone, like a fake does in a worship service and in the streets, so that they can be thought highly of by others. The truth is, they've already gotten all the reward they'll get. But when you give your gifts, don't let others know what you do: Let your gifts be private: and your God who sees in secret will reward you openly.*

The Christ Teaches How to Pray

[5-8] And when you pray, you shouldn't be like a fake, because they love to pray standing in the places of worship and on the street corners, so that they can be seen by others. The truth is, they've already gotten all the reward they'll get. But you, when you pray, come into your private room, and when you've shut your door, pray to your God secretly; and your God who sees in secret will openly reward you. But when you pray, don't use meaningless repetitions, as the ungodly do because they think that they'll be heard for all their talking. So don't be like them because your God knows what your needs are, even before you ask for them.

Yeshua's Prayer

[9-13] So pray like this: Yahweh, our God in heaven, Your Name is Holy. May Your everlasting realm come soon. May Your will be done on earth, just as it's done in heaven. Give us what we need for today. And forgive our sins, as we forgive those who sin against us. Help us not to sin when we're tempted, but free us from evil, because the power and the victory of Your Realm is forever. So be it!

The Importance of Forgiving Others

[14-15] If you forgive others their sins, your God in heaven will also forgive you, but if you don't forgive others their sins, nor will your God forgive your sins.

Fasting Should be Private

[16-18] Besides this, when you go without food for a religious reason, don't be like fakes, who disfigure their faces with a sad look, so that they can appear to others to be going without. The truth is; they've already gotten all the reward they'll get. But you, when you go without food for a religious reason, anoint your head with oil, and wash your face; so that you don't appear to others to be going without, but secretly to your God; and your God, who sees in secret, will openly reward you.

Your Heart is Where You put Your Money

[19-23] Don't store up wealth for yourselves on earth, where moths and rust will destroy it all, and where thieves can break in and steal everything: But store up wealth for yourselves in heaven, where neither moth nor rust can destroy it, and where thieves won't break in to steal it. Your heart is where you put your money. The eye is the light of the body, so if your eye is set on the light of goodness, your whole body will be full of light. But if your eye is set on evil, your whole body will be full of darkness. So if the light that is in you is dimmed, how great that darkness will be!

Don't Worry, God Will Take Care of You

[24-33] No one can serve two rulers because they'll either hate one and love the other; or else, they'll hold on to one and hate the other. You can't serve both God and money. So I tell you, don't worry about your livelihood, what you'll eat, or what you'll drink; or what you'll wear. Isn't life more than food and the body more than clothing? The birds of the air neither plant nor pick, nor do they store up food; but still your God in heaven takes care of them. Aren't you worth more than they are? Which of you by thinking about it can add one hour or one day to your life? And why do you worry about your clothing? Consider the lilies of the field, how they grow; they don't work nor weave: And still, I tell you, that even Solomon in all his glory wasn't decorated like one of them. So if God clothes the grasses of the fields this way, which grow today, and are dead by tomorrow, won't God clothe you that much more? Don't you have any faith? So don't worry, saying, 'What will I eat?' Or, 'What will I drink?' Or, 'What am I going to wear?' Those who are earthly worry about all this, but your God in heaven knows that you need these things. So first find the goodness of the realm God; and all these other things will be given to you as well. Don't worry about what tomorrow may bring because tomorrow will worry about itself. There's enough evil in one day without worrying about another.

Be Careful of Judging People Unfairly

7 [1-5] Don't be quick to judge, so that you won't be judged this way. Because with whatever judgment you judge others, you'll be judged in this way, too: and with whatever measure you use, you'll be measured with it, too. Why do you believe that the splinter in another's eye is worse than the stake that is in your own eye? Or how can you say to another, 'Let me pull the splinter out of your eye, when there's a stake in your own eye?' You fake, first take the stake out of your own eye; and then you can see clearly to take the splinter out of another's eye.

Be Careful Who You Give To

[6] Don't give anything set aside for a holy purpose to those who fight against God, nor give your valuables to them, or they won't appreciate it, and they'll turn around and resent you for it.

Ask, and It'll Be Given To You

[7-12] Ask, and it'll be given to you; search, and you'll find it; knock, and the door will be opened for you. Everyone that asks will get what they ask; and those who search will find; and for those who knock, the door will be opened. How many of you, who if your child asks for bread, would give them a stone? Or if they asked for a fish, would you give them a snake instead? If you then, who are evil by nature, know how to give good gifts to your children, how much more will your God in heaven give good things to those who ask for them? So everything that you would want someone to do to you, you do that to them because this is what God's Word and the great preachers have always taught us.

Only One Way

[13-14] Go in at Heaven's Gate, because the gate of Hell is wide open, and many go that way to be destroyed: But because there's only one way that leads to life and that way is hard, only a few will find it.

Knowing the Difference Between the Good and Bad

[15-20] Beware of false teachers, who come to you looking as gentle as a lamb, but inwardly they're selfish and greedy wolves. You'll know them by what they do. Do people gather grapes from thorns, or figs from weeds? Every good tree makes good fruit; but a bad tree makes bad fruit. A good tree can't make bad fruit, nor can a bad tree make good fruit. Every tree that doesn't make good fruit will be cut down, and put into the fire. So you'll know them by what they do.

Do God's Will

[21-23] Not everyone who calls Me, Christ, will come into heaven; but only those who do the will of God in heaven. Many will say to Me in that day, 'Christ, haven't we preached in Your Name? And in Your Name put out evil spirits? And in Your Name done many amazing things?' And then I'll tell them, 'I don't know you! Get away from Me, you who are always doing evil.'

The Solid Foundation

[24-28] So whoever hears My teachings, and does them, that person is like a wise person, who built their house on a rock: And the rain came down, and the floodwaters rose, and the winds blew, and beat that house; but it didn't fall because its foundation was built on solid rock. And everyone that hears My teachings, and doesn't do them, is like a stupid person, who built their house on the sand: And the rain came down, and the floodwaters rose, and the winds blew, and beat that house; and it fell: And it was totally destroyed!" And then, when Yeshua had finished these teachings, the people were amazed by them, because Yeshua taught them as someone with power, and not as the other religious leaders.

A Leper Healed

8 [1-4] When Yeshua had come down from the mountain, great crowds followed along. And then a person with leprosy came and begged the Christ, saying, *"Christ, if You want to, You can heal me."* And Yeshua reached out, and touched them, saying, *"I want to; be healed."* And suddenly the leprosy was healed. And Yeshua said, *"See that you don't tell anyone; but go and show yourself to the priest, and offer the gift that Moses said to give, to show them what you say is true."*

The Faith of a Soldier

[5-13] And when Yeshua went to Capernaum, a soldier came pleading, asking, *"Christ, my worker lies paralyzed at home, and in great pain."* And Yeshua said, *"I'll come and heal your worker."* But the soldier answered, *"Christ, I'm not worthy for you to come under my roof. Just say the word, and I know my worker will be healed. I too am someone with power, having guards under me. I say to one, Go, and the soldier goes; and to another, Come, and that soldier comes; and to my worker, Do this, and the worker does it."* So when Yeshua heard this, the Christ was amazed, saying to those who followed, *"The truth is, I haven't found a faith so great, no, not in all of Israel. I tell you, that many will come from the east and west, and will sit down with Abraham, Isaac, and Jacob, in heaven. But the children of the satanic realm will be put out into utter darkness where they'll be crying and gritting their teeth."* And Yeshua said to the soldier, *"Go now; and it'll happen just like you believed it would."* And the Centurion's worker was healed at that very time.

Peter's Mother-in-Law healed

[14-17] Then when Yeshua came into Peter's house, the Christ saw Peter's wife's mother sick in bed with a fever. So Yeshua touched her hand and the fever left her; and she got up, and took care of them all. When the evening came, people brought many that were overcome by evil spirits, and the Christ freed them from them with a word, and healed all that were sick. So what was spoken by Isaiah the great preacher, saying, *"The Christ took on our weaknesses, and healed our sicknesses,"* happened in this way.

[18-22] Now when Yeshua saw great crowds surrounding them, the Christ told the faithful followers to go by boat to the other side. And a certain religious leader came, saying to Yeshua, *"Christ, I'll follow you wherever you go."* And Yeshua said, *"The foxes have holes, and the birds of the air have nests; but I have nowhere to call home."* And another follower said to Yeshua, *"Christ, let me wait until my parents die so I can bury them."* But Yeshua said, *"You follow Me; and let those who are spiritually dead bury their dead."*

The Christ Calms the Storm

[23-27] And when the Christ went in a ship, the most faithful followers came along. A great storm came up in the sea, so bad that the ship was covered with the waves. But the Christ was sleeping, so the followers came, and awoke Yeshua, saying, *"Christ, save us or we'll all be destroyed."* So the Christ answered, *"Why are you so afraid, don't you have any faith?"* Then the Christ got up, and told the winds and the sea to *"Be still";* and there was a great calm. They were all amazed, saying, *"What kind of person is this that even the wind and the sea obeys?"*

The Gergesenes

[28-34] And when they came to the other side into the country of the Gergesenes, two people overcome by evil spirits came out of the tombs, who were so fierce that no one could pass by that way. And they called out, saying, *"What do we have to do with you, Yeshua, Child of God? Have you come here punish us before our time?"* And there was a herd of many pigs feeding a good way off from them. So the evil spirits begged Yeshua, saying, *"If you put us out, let us go into the herd of pigs."* And the Christ said, *"Go."* And when they had come out, they went into the herd of pigs, and the whole herd ran madly down a steep cliff into the sea, and drowned in the waters. And those who kept them ran off, and went into the city, and told everyone everything that had happened to the ones who had been overcome by the evil spirits. Then the whole city came out, and when they saw the Christ, they begged Yeshua to leave their coasts.

A Paralytic Healed

9 [1-8] And then Yeshua went back to the ship, and crossed over the sea, and came back. And they brought someone paralyzed, lying on a bed to the Christ. So, Yeshua, seeing their faith said to the paralyzed one; *"Child, be happy; your sins are forgiven you."* And some of the religious leaders said, *"This person shows disrespect to God."* And Yeshua knowing what they were thinking said, *"Why do you think evil in your hearts? Is it easier to say, 'Your sins are forgiven you'; or to say, 'Get up, and walk?' But so that you can know that I have the power on earth to forgive sins,"* (then the Christ said to the paralyzed one,) *"Get up, pick up your bed, and go home."* And the paralyzed one got up, and went home. But when the crowds saw it, they were amazed, and praised God, who had given such power to Yeshua.

Matthew Called

[9] And as the Christ left from there, Yeshua said to someone, named Matthew, who was sitting where the taxes were collected, *"Follow Me."* And Matthew got up, and followed Yeshua.

Eating With Sinners

[10-13] And then, as Yeshua was eating a meal in the house, many tax collectors and sinners came and sat down with the Christ and the followers. And when the religious leaders saw it, they said to the followers, *"Why does your Christ eat with tax collectors and sinners?"* But on hearing that, Yeshua answered, *"Those who are well don't need a doctor, but only those who are sick. But you go and learn what this means, 'I want mercy, and not a sacrifice'; because I haven't come to call those who do good things, but sinners to change their ways."*

On Fasting

[14-17] Then the followers of John came, asking, *"Why do we and the religious leaders go without food for religious reasons often, but your followers don't go without food at all?"* And Yeshua answered, *"Can those who are with the bridal party cry, as long as the bride and groom are with them? But the time will come, when the bridal party will be taken from them, and then they'll go without food and cry. No one puts a new piece of cloth on an old piece of clothing, for what was put in to patch it up will shrink and pull on the tear, and make it worse. Neither does anyone put new wine into old bottles, or else the bottles will break, and the wine will spill out, and the bottles will be broken. But they put new wine into new bottles, and both are kept safely.*

Woman Healed of Bleeding Disorder And A Young Girl Brought Back to Life Again

[18-26] While the Christ spoke this to them, there came a certain ruler, and bowed before Yeshua, saying, *"My daughter is just about dead now: but come and lay your hand on her, and she'll live again."* And Yeshua got up and followed along, and so did the followers. Then a woman, who suffered with a flow of blood for twelve years, came up behind Yeshua, and touched the hem of the Christ's clothing, saying to herself, *"If I can only touch the clothing of the Christ, I'll get well."* But Yeshua turned around, and seeing her, said, *"Daughter, be in good spirits now; your faith has made you well."* And the woman was healed at that very time. Then coming into the ruler's house, and seeing the musicians and the people crying, the Christ told them, *"Get out of the way, the girl isn't dead, but is only sleeping."* And they all disrespectfully laughed. But when everyone was put out, the Christ went in, and took her by the hand and the girl got up. And this story became famous all over the countryside.

Sight Brought Back to the Blind

[27-31] And when Yeshua left there, two people who were blind followed along, crying, and saying, *"Heir of David, have mercy on us."* And when the Christ came into the house, those who were blind came also: and Yeshua answered, *"Do you believe that I am able to do this?"* And they said, *"Yes, Christ."* So the Christ touched their eyes, saying, *"As your faith is, let it happen to you, now."* And their eyes began to see; and Yeshua told them clearly, saying, *"Don't tell anyone."* But when they left, they made it famous throughout the whole country.

Speech Brought Back to the Dumb

[32-35] As they went out, someone brought to the Christ a person who couldn't speak and who was overcome by an evil spirit. And when the evil spirit was put out, the person who was dumb spoke: and the crowds were amazed, saying, *"Nothing like this has ever been seen in all of Israel!"* But the religious leaders said, *"This person puts out evil spirits by the ruler of the evil spirits."* And Yeshua went throughout all the cities and towns, teaching in their worship services, and preaching the New Word of the realm of God, and healing every sickness and every disease among the people.

Few Workers

[36-38] But when Yeshua saw the crowds, the Christ had compassion for them, because they were weak, and were scattered out, as animals having no keeper. Then Yeshua said to the followers, *"The harvest is great, but the truth is, the workers are few; So pray that the God of the harvest will send workers to gather it in."*

The Twelve Followers Given Power

10 [1-4] And calling the twelve followers, the Christ gave them power over evil spirits to put them out, and to heal all kinds of sicknesses and diseases. Now the names of the twelve followers are these: The first, Simon Peter, and Andrew, his brother; James and John, the sons of Zebedee; Philip, Bartholomew; Thomas, Matthew, the tax collector; James, the son of Alphaeus, Lebbaeus, who was called Thaddaeus; Simon, from Canaan, and Judas Iscariot, who handed over the Christ.

[5-15] These twelve Yeshua sent out, and told them, saying, *"Don't go to the cities of the other peoples, or into any city of the people of mixed heritage; but instead go to the lost ones of the house of Israel. As you go, preach, saying, Heaven is here. Heal the sick, heal those with leprosy, give life to the dead, and put out evil spirits. You've been given everything freely, so give to them freely. Don't give money for your personal expenses, nor for your journey, nor bring two coats, nor extra shoes, nor even staples because workers are worthy of the food they eat. And whatever city or town you come to, ask who in it is worthy; and stay there until you leave that place. And when you come into a house, say hello to those there. And if they're worthy, let your peace come on them: but if they aren't worthy, let your peace return to you. And whoever won't accept you, nor hear your words, when you leave out of that house or city, shake the dust off your feet. The truth is, it'll be more tolerable for the land of Sodom and Gomorrah in the day of judgment than for that city.*

You Will Be Hated by Others for Christ's Sake

[16-25] *I send you out as tamed animals to a bunch of wolves: so be as wise as snakes, and harmless as doves. But beware of the others because they'll bring you to the courts, and punish you; and you'll be brought to governors and rulers for My sake, for a witness against them. But when they arrest you, don't worry about how or what you'll speak because it'll be given to you at that very time what to say. Because it isn't you who speaks, but the Spirit of your God who speaks in you. And siblings will hand over siblings to death, and the parents, the children: and the children will go up against their parents, and cause them to be put to death. And you'll be hated by everyone because of My Name: but those who are faithful to the end will be saved. But when they mistreat you in one city, run to another. The truth is, you won't have gone to all the cities of Israel, till I come. The follower isn't better than the teacher, nor the worker better than the owner. It's enough for the followers to be like the teacher, and the workers to be like their owner. If they've called the owner of the house by the name of the devil, how much more they'll call the children of the household names!*

Pick Up Your Cross And Follow Me

[26-39] *So don't be afraid of them because there isn't anything covered, that won't be uncovered; and secret, that won't become known. What I tell you in secret, you speak openly: and what you hear whispered in your ear, preach at the top of your voice. And don't be afraid of those who can kill the body, but aren't able to kill the soul: but instead fear God, who is able to destroy both soul and body in Hell. Aren't two sparrows sold for a small coin? Not one of them will fall on the ground without your God knowing it. But the very hairs of your head are all numbered. So don't be afraid, you're worth much more than many sparrows. So whoever says that they know Me to others, I'll also say that I know them to My God who is in heaven. But whoever denies that they know Me to others, I'll also say that I don't know them to My God who is in heaven. Don't think that I've come to send peace on the earth: I didn't come to send peace, but instead disagreement. I've come to set children at odds against their parents, and in-law against in-law. And those who come against you will be those of your own home. Whoever loves their parents more than Me isn't worthy of Me: and whoever loves their children more than Me isn't worthy of Me. And whoever doesn't pick up and carry their own cross of suffering, and follow after Me, isn't worthy of Me. Whoever tries to save their life will lose it: and whoever willingly gives up their life for my sake will save it.*

Accept Yeshua, accept God

[40-42] *Whoever accepts you accepts Me, and whoever accepts Me accepts the God who sent Me. Whoever accepts a great preacher in the name of a great preacher will get a great preacher's reward; and whoever accepts a good person in the name of a good person will get a good person's reward. And whoever gives a cup of cold water to drink to anyone, only in the name of a follower of Christ, the truth is; they'll not lose their reward."*

The Followers of John Question Yeshua

11 [1-6] And then, when Yeshua had finished teaching the twelve followers, the Christ left there to teach and preach in their cities. Now when John, who was in the prison, had heard about the things Christ did, he sent two followers to ask, *"Are you the One who is to come, or do we look for another?"* Yeshua answered, *"Go and tell John again the things you hear and see: Those who are blind see, and those who are paralyzed walk, those with leprosy are healed, and those who couldn't hear can hear again, the dead are given life, and those who are poor have the New Word preached to them. Whoever isn't offended by Me is blessed."*

[7-15] And as they went, Yeshua began to say to the crowds about John, *"What did you go out into the countryside to see? A reed shaken in the wind? But what did you go out to see? A person clothed in soft furs? Those who wear soft furs are in rulers' palaces. But what did you go out to see? A great preacher? Yes, I tell you, and more than just a great preacher, because this is the one, of whom the Word says, I send My messenger before You, who will clear Your way for You. The truth is, among all those who are born of women, there hasn't been one greater than John the Baptist: but in the same way, whoever is least important in the realm of heaven is greater than John is. And from the days of John the Baptist until now, heaven is at war, and the evil ones are trying to take it by force. Because all the great preachers and God's Word preached until John. And if you'll accept it, this is Elijah, who was to come. If anyone will accept this, let them accept it.*

[16-19] *But what should I say this people is like? They are like children sitting in the shopping centers, and calling to their friends, saying, 'We've played to you, and you didn't dance; we've cried to you, and you haven't cried for us'; because John didn't come eating or drinking, and they say, 'He's got an evil spirit.' Then I came, both eating and drinking, and they say, look, a pig, and a drunk, a friend of tax collectors and sinners. But children are made right by their own thinking.*

[20-24] *Then Yeshua began to call out curses against the cities in which most of the amazing things had happened, because they didn't change their evil ways: You'll be sorry, Chorazin! You'll be sorry, Bethsaida! If the amazing things, which have happened in you, had been done in Tyre and Sidon, they would have changed their ways long ago, crying in mourning clothes and putting ashes on their heads. But I tell you, it'll be more tolerable for Tyre and Sidon at the day of judgment, than for you. And you, Capernaum, which is praised even to heaven, will be brought down to Hell because if the amazing things, which have been done in you, had been done in Sodom, it would have been here until today. But I tell you that it'll be more tolerable for the land of Sodom in the day of judgment, than for you."*

God's Plan Revealed to the Undoubting

[25-27] At that time Yeshua said, *"I thank You, God, Ruler of heaven and earth, because you've hidden this from the wise and the cautious, and have made it known to undoubting children. Just the same, God, because it seemed good in Your sight, all things are given to Me by You: and no one knows Me, but God; nor does anyone know God, but Me, and those to whom I make You known.*

Rest in God's Work

[28-30] Come to Me, all you that work hard and carry heavy loads, and I'll give you rest. Take responsibility for My work, and learn about Me, because I am gentle and humble in heart and you'll find rest for your souls. Because my work is easy, and my load is light."

The Seventh Day Teachings Challenged

12 [1-8] At that time Yeshua went through the grain on a Day of Worship; and the followers were hungry, so they began to take the grain to eat. But when the religious leaders saw it, they said, *"Your followers are doing what isn't right to do on a Day of Worship."* But the Christ answered, *"Haven't you read what David did, when he and his followers were hungry? How they went in the house of God, and ate the bread, which wasn't right for any of them to eat, but only for the priests? Or haven't you read in the Word of God, how that on Days of Worship, the priests in the Place of Worship don't keep its rules, and are without fault? But I tell you that there's One greater than the Place of Worship in this place. But if you had known what this means, I want mercy, and not sacrifice, you wouldn't have accused the guiltless. Because I am the Ruler of even a Day of Worship."*

Doing Good on the Seventh Day

[9-13] And when they left there, the Christ went into their worship service, and there was someone whose hand was paralyzed. And they asked Yeshua in order to make an accusation, *"Is it right to heal on Days of Worship?"* So the Christ answered, *"Who is there among you, who has an animal, which falls into a hole on a Day of Worship, won't take hold of it, and pull it out? How much more then is a human being better than an animal? So it's right to do what's good on Days of Worship."* Then Yeshua said to the person, *"Give Me your hand."* And the person did; so it was given back well, just like the other one.

Yeshua Heals the Crowds

[14-21] Then the religious leaders went out, and held a court against Yeshua, discussing how to get rid of the Christ. But when the Christ knew it, Yeshua left there and healed all of the great crowds following along, telling

74

them not to tell it: So that it would happen which was spoken by Isaiah the great preacher, saying, *"I'll give My Spirit to My Helper, whom I've chosen; the One I Love, in whom My soul is very pleased: Who will show mercy to the other peoples. Who won't fight, nor cry out; nor whose voice will anyone hear in the streets. Who won't break someone who is already bruised, and won't smother a person who still has a spark of hope, till victory comes in the judgment. And the other peoples will trust in the Name of My Christ."*

Christ Speaks on Evil Spirits

[22-30] Then someone who was overcome by an evil spirit, who was blind, and dumb was brought to the Christ, who healed them, so that the one who was blind and dumb both spoke and saw. And all the people were amazed, saying, *"Isn't this the Heir of David?"* But when the religious leaders heard it, they said, *"This person doesn't put out evil spirits by anything but the devil's own power, the ruler of the evil spirits."* And Yeshua knowing what they were thinking, answered, *"When the people of a country are divided that country will be destroyed; and every city or family that is divided won't survive. So if Satan puts out Satan, and the devil is divided against the devil; then how can the devil's realm stand? And if I, by the devil put out evil spirits, by whom do your children put them out? So they'll be your judges. But if I put out evil spirits by the Spirit of God, then the realm of God has come to you now. Or else how can someone come into a strong person's house, and take what they own, unless that person first tie up the strong person? and then the other will take what they own. Whoever isn't with Me is against Me; and whoever doesn't gather souls with Me scatters them out.*

The Unforgivable Sin

[31-37] *I tell you, all kind of sin and disrespect of God will be forgiven humanity: but the disrespect and rejection of the Holy Spirit won't be forgiven them. And whoever speaks a word against Me, it'll be forgiven them: but whoever speaks against the Holy Spirit, it won't be forgiven them, not in this world, nor in the world to come. Either say that the tree is good, and its fruit's good; or else say the tree is bad, and its fruit's bad because the tree is known by its fruit. You snakes, how can you, being naturally evil, speak good things? The mouth speaks from what's in the heart. A good person out of the good things of their heart speaks good things: and an evil person out of the evil things in their heart speaks evil things. But I tell you, that people will give account for every casual word that they speak in the day of judgment. By your words you'll be made right, and by your words you'll be accused."*

The Sign of Jonah

[38-45] Then some of the religious leaders and those of the religious sects answered, saying, *"Teacher, we would like to see a sign from you."* But the Christ answered them, *"An evil and unfaithful people look for a sign; but no sign will be given to it, but the sign of the great preacher Jonah: because as Jonah was three days and three nights in the belly of a whale; so I'll be three days and three nights in Hell, which is in the heart of the earth. Those of Nineveh will rise up in judgment of this people, and will accuse it: because they changed their ways at the preaching of Jonah; And One greater than Jonah is here. The ruler of the south will stand up in the judgment of this people, and will accuse it because she came from the distant parts of the earth to hear the wisdom of Solomon; And One greater than Solomon is here. When an evil spirit has gone out of someone, it walks through dry places, looking for rest, and not finding it. Then it says, 'I'll return to the place I came from'; and when it comes back, it finds that house empty, cleaned, and decorated. Then it goes, and brings seven other spirits more evil than itself, and they come and stay there: and the last state of that person is worse than the first. It'll be like this for this people also."*

Who is My Family?

[46-50] While still talking to the people, Yeshua's mother and family stood outside, hoping to speak with the Christ. Then someone said, *"Your mother and family stand outside, hoping to speak with you."* But the Christ said to the one who said it, *"Who is My mother? And who is My family?"* And the Christ reached out toward the followers, saying, *"This is My family! Because whoever does the will of My God, who is in heaven, is My family."*

The Story of the Seeds

13 [1-9] That same day Yeshua went out of the house, and sat on the seashore. And great crowds were gathered around, so the Christ went and sat in a ship; and the whole crowd stood on the shore. And the Christ spoke many things to them in stories, saying, *"A farmer went out to plant; And when the farmer planted, some seeds fell beside the rows, and the birds came and ate them. Some fell on stony places, where they didn't have much earth: and they came up quickly, because they weren't deep enough. But when the sun was up, they were scorched and wilted away, because the roots were too shallow. And some fell in thorny places; and the thorns came up, and choked them out. But others fell into the good ground, and made fruit, some a hundred times as much, some sixty times as much, and some thirty times as much. Whoever will accept this, let them accept it."*

[10-17] And the followers came, and asked, *"Why do you speak to them in stories?"* So Yeshua answered them, *"Because you're able to know the secrets of heaven, but they aren't able to know them. Whoever has the truth, more will be given, and they'll be richly blessed: but whoever doesn't have the truth, even what they have will be taken away. So I speak to them in stories: because seeing they don't see; and hearing they don't hear, nor do they understand it. And the Word, which was given ahead of time by Isaiah comes true by them, which said, 'By hearing you'll hear, and won't understand; and seeing you'll see, and won't realize it: because this people's heart has grown hard, and their ears are hard of hearing, and their eyes they've closed; in case at some time they would see with their eyes, and hear with their ears, and understand with their heart, and be changed, and I heal them.' But your eyes are blessed, because they see: and your ears, because they hear. The truth is, that many great preachers and other good people have wanted to see what you see, and haven't seen it; and to hear what you hear, and haven't heard it.*

[18-23] *So understand the story of the farmer. When anyone hears the Word of the realm of God, and doesn't understand it, then the evil one comes, and takes away what was planted in their heart. These are the ones that the seed fell beside the rows. But those who get the seed that fell into stony places, are those who hear the Word, and accept it with joy; Yet they have no root, only lasting for a little while, because when troubles or discrimination comes up because of the Word, they're offended by it. Also those who get the seed that fell in the thorns are those who hear the Word; but the cares of this world, and the false hope of riches, choke out the Word, and they become unfruitful. But whoever gets the seed that fell in the good ground are those who hear the Word, and understand it; who also make fruit, and produce, some a hundred times, some sixty, some thirty."*

The Good Seed and the Bad Seed

[24-30] And Yeshua told them another story, saying, *"Heaven is like the One who planted good seed in the fields: But while the farmhands slept, the enemy came and planted weeds among the wheat, and went away. But when the blade came up, and made fruit, then the weeds came up also. So the farmhands came, saying to the farmer, 'Didn't you plant good seed in your field? Where did the weeds come from then?' So the farmer answered, 'An enemy has done this.' The farmhands said, 'Do you want us to go and gather them up?' But the farmer said, 'No; in case when you gather up the weeds, you uproot the wheat with it. Let both grow together until the harvest: and at harvest time I'll say to the pickers, Gather together the weeds first, and put them in bundles to burn: then gather the wheat into my barn.'"*

[31-32] Then Yeshua told them another story, saying, *"Heaven is like a grain of mustard seed, which someone took, and planted in the field, which is certainly among the smallest of all seeds: but when it grows, it's the greatest among herbs, and becomes a small tree, so that even the birds of the air come and nest in its branches."*

[33-42] And Yeshua told them another story; *"Heaven is also like the yeast, which a woman mixed in three cups of meal, till the whole dough was leavened."* All this Yeshua spoke in stories; and never spoke to the crowds without a story: so that it would happen which was spoken by the great preacher, saying, *"I'll speak in stories; telling things which have been kept secret from the beginning of the world."* Then Yeshua sent the crowd away, and went into the house: and the followers came, saying, *"Tell us the meaning of the story of the weeds in the field."* So Yeshua answered, *"I am the One who plants the good seed; The field is the world; the good seed are the children of the realm of God; but the weeds are the children of the evil one; The enemy that planted them is the devil; the harvest is the end of the world; and the pickers are the angels. As the weeds are gathered and burned in the fire; so it'll be in the end of this world. Then I'll send out my angels, and they'll gather out of this world everything that causes sin, and all those who keep on sinning; And will put them into a great fire: where they'll be crying and gritting their teeth in pain. Then those who do good will shine as the sun in the realm of their God. Whoever will accept this, let them accept it.*

Hidden Treasure and the Pearl of Great Price

[44-46] *Again, heaven is like a treasure hid in a field; which when someone has found it, they hide it again, and for joy they go and sell everything they have to buy that field. Again, heaven is like a salesperson that was looking for good pearls: Who, when they had found one pearl that was worth more than all the others, went and sold all the others and bought it.*

The Fish Net

[47-52] *Again, heaven is like a net that was let down into the sea, and caught all kinds of fish: Which, when it was full, they drew it to shore, and sat down, and gathered the good into containers, but threw the bad ones away. So it'll be at the end of the world: the angels will come, and divide the good from the bad, and will put them into the great fire: where they'll be crying and gritting their teeth in pain."* Then Yeshua asked, *"Do you understand all this?"* So they answered, *"Yes, Christ."* Then Yeshua said, *"So all those who are taught of the heavenly realm are like those who are homeowners, which bring both new and old things to use out of the wealth of things they own."*

A Great Preacher Without Honor

[53-58] And then, when Yeshua had finished these stories, they all left there together. And when they came to Yeshua's own hometown, the Christ taught them in their worship services, so that the people were amazed, saying, *"Where does Yeshua get this wisdom, and do these amazing things? Isn't this the carpenter's child? Isn't Mary Yeshua's mother? and James, Joses, Simon, and Judas, the brothers of Yeshua? And aren't Yeshua's sisters all with us, too? Where has this person gotten all this?"* And they were greatly offended by the Christ. But Yeshua answered, *"A great preacher isn't without honor, except in their own town, and their own home."* And the Christ couldn't do many miracles there because of their unbelief.

Herod Kills John the Baptist

14 [1-14] At that time Herod, the ruler, heard of Yeshua, who was now famous. And said to those working for him, *"This must be John the Baptist; who has come back to life to do all these amazing things!"* He said this because he had taken John, and put him in prison for Herodias' sake, who had been married to Philip, his brother, because John had said, *"It isn't right for you to be married to her."* And when he wanted to put John to death, he wouldn't, being afraid of the people, because they saw him as a great preacher. But on the celebration of Herod's birthday, the daughter of Herodias danced for him, greatly pleasing him. Upon which he promised, swearing to give her whatever she would ask. And she, being told by her mother, said, *"Give me John the Baptist's head on a plate, right here."* And the ruler was sorry: but, because he had sworn it, and because of those who were there, he ordered it to be given to her. And they sent, and beheaded John in the prison. And John's head was brought on a plate, and given to the girl: and she brought it to her mother. And the followers came, and picked up the body, and buried it, and went and told Yeshua. So when Yeshua heard it, the Christ left there alone by ship into a deserted place: and when the people had heard it, they followed along on foot out of the cities. And Yeshua came out of the ship and seeing a great crowd, had compassion for them, and healed their sick.

Yeshua Feeds the Five Thousand

[15-21] Then when it was evening, the followers came saying, *"This is a deserted place, and it's late; send the crowd away, so that they can go into the towns, and buy food."* But Yeshua answered, *"They don't need to leave; you give them something to eat."* But they said to Yeshua, *"We only have five small loaves, and two fish here."* So the Christ said, *"Bring them here to Me."* Then the Christ told the crowd to sit down on the grass, and took the five loaves, and the two fish, and looking up to heaven, blessed, and broke it, and gave it to the followers, and the followers gave it to the crowd. They all ate, and were full: and the followers took up twelve baskets full of the scraps that were left over. There were about five thousand men who had eaten, besides the women and children.

Walking on the Water

[22-33] And suddenly the Christ told the followers to get into a ship, and go to the other side, but Yeshua stayed behind to send the crowds away. And when the crowds had gone away, Yeshua went up on a mountain alone to pray. When the evening came, the Christ was alone there. But the ship was now in the middle of the sea, being tossed by the waves because the wind was blowing hard against it. And late that night Yeshua went out to them, walking on the sea. And when the followers saw the Christ walking on the sea, they were afraid, saying, *"It's a ghost;"* and they screamed in fear. But suddenly, Yeshua spoke to them, saying, *"It's okay; it's only Me; Don't be afraid."* And Peter answered, *"Christ, if it's really You, call me to come to You on the water."* So Yeshua said, *"Come on."* And when Peter got down out of the ship, he walked on the water to go to Yeshua. But when he saw how strong the wind was, he was afraid; and beginning to sink, he screamed, saying, *"Christ, save me."* And suddenly Yeshua gave him a hand and caught him, saying, *"Don't you have any faith? Why did you doubt?"* And when they got into the ship, the wind stopped. Then those who were in the ship came and worshipped the Christ, saying, *"It's true! You're the Child of God."*

[34-35] And when they had crossed over, they came into the land of Gennesaret. When the people there knew of them, they sent word into the whole countryside all around, and brought all that were diseased to Yeshua; begging just to touch the hem of the Christ's clothing: and all those who touched it were made completely well.

Human Way of Life

15 [1-9] Then the religious leaders and the ministers from religious sects, who were from Jerusalem, came to Yeshua saying, *"Why do your followers not keep the way of life of the elders? They don't wash their hands when they eat."* But Yeshua answered them, *"Why do you also not keep the Word of God by your way of life? God said, 'Honor your parents: And whoever curses their parents, let them die in their punishment.' But you say, whoever says to their parents, 'What I might have given to you I've given as a gift to the church'; And doesn't honor their parents, they'll be excused. So you've made the Words of God to have no effect by your way of life. You fakes, Isaiah was right about you, saying, 'This people speaks of Me with their mouth, and honors Me with their words;*

but their hearts are far from Me. Their worship of Me is empty, teaching human standards for the principles of God's word.'"

[10-20] And Yeshua called the crowd, saying to them, *"Now, listen and understand: It isn't what goes into the mouth that makes someone sick; but it's what comes out of the mouth that makes someone sick."* Then the followers came, saying, *"Don't you know that the religious leaders were offended when they heard this?"* But the Christ answered, *"Every plant, which My God in heaven hasn't planted, will be moved out of their place. Stay away from them: they're blind leaders of the blind. And if those who are blind lead those who are blind, both will fall in the ditch."* Then Peter said, *"What does this story mean?"* So Yeshua said, *"Do you, too, still not understand? Don't you understand that whatever comes into the mouth goes into the belly, and then out in the waste? But the things which go out of the mouth come from the heart; and that is what makes the person sick, because out of the heart go evil thoughts, murders, sexual unfaithfulness, other sexual sins, thefts, lies, and disrespect for God: These are the things which make someone sick: but to eat with unwashed hands doesn't really make someone sick."*

The Canaanite Woman

[21-28] Then Yeshua left there, and went into the coasts of Tyre and Sidon. And a woman of Canaan came out of the coasts, and called out, saying, *"Have mercy on me, Christ, Heir of David; my daughter is completely overcome with an evil spirit."* But Yeshua didn't say a word to her. Then the followers came and begged, saying; *"Send her away, she won't stop calling out to us."* So the Christ answered her saying, *"I am only sent to the lost ones of the house of Israel."* Then she came and begged, saying, "Christ, help me." But the Christ answered, *"It isn't right to take the children's bread, and give it to the dogs."* But she said, *"That's true, Christ, but still, the little dogs eat the scraps from their owners' table."* Then Yeshua answered to her, *"Woman, your faith is great: so you'll get what you've asked for."* And her daughter was healed at that very time.

Feeding the Four Thousand

[29-31] And Yeshua left there, and came near the Sea of Galilee; and went up on a mountain, and sat down there. And great crowds came there, having with them those that were crippled, blind, dumb, hurt, and many others, and put them down at Yeshua' feet; who healed them all: So much so, that the crowds were amazed when they saw those who were dumb speak; those who were hurt get well; those who were unable to stand walk; and those who were blind see: and they praised the God of Israel.

[32-38] Then Yeshua called the followers over, saying, *"I am concerned about the crowd, because they have stayed with Me three days now, and haven't had anything to eat: and I won't send them away, while they willingly go without food, in case they faint on the way."* And the followers asked Yeshua, *"Where would we get enough bread in the countryside, to give to all these people?"* So Yeshua asked them, *"How many loaves do you have?"* And they said, *"Seven, and a few little fish."* And Yeshua told the crowd to sit down on the ground. Then the Christ took the seven loaves and the fish, giving thanks, and breaking them up, and gave it to the followers, who then gave it to the crowd. So everyone in the crowd ate, and was full. Then the followers picked up seven baskets full of the scraps that were left over. And those who ate were four thousand people, beside the women and children. Then Yeshua sent away the crowd, and went to the ship, coming into the coasts of Magdala.

The Sign of Jonah

16 [1-5] Then the ministers from the religious sects came also, trying to tempt Yeshua, and wanted to see a sign from heaven. So Yeshua answered them, *"When it's evening, you say, 'It'll be fair weather because the sky is red.' And in the morning, 'It'll be bad weather today because the sky is red and lowering.' You fakes, you understand the signs of the sky; but you can't understand the signs of the times! An evil and unfaithful people look for a sign; but the only sign you'll get is that of the great preacher Jonah."* And Yeshua left them and went to another place. And when the followers had come to the other side, they saw that they had forgotten to take bread.

The Leaven of the Religious Sects

[6-12] Then Yeshua said, *"Be cautious of the leaven of these religious sects."* And they argued among themselves, asking, *"Is it because we forgot the bread?"* On hearing it, Yeshua answered, *"You people have such little faith. Why do you question among yourselves, because you forgot the bread? Don't you understand, nor remember the five loaves of the five thousand and how many baskets of scraps you took up? Nor the seven loaves of the four thousand, and how many baskets you took up? How can you still not understand that I didn't speak to you about bread, but that you should be cautious of the teachings of the ministers from the religious sects?"* Then they understood that Yeshua wanted them not to beware of the leaven of bread, but of the teachings of the ministers from the religious sects.

Peter's Confession

[13-20] When the Christ came into the coasts of Caesarea Philippi, Yeshua asked the followers, *"Who do people say that I am?"* And they answered, *"Some say that you're John the Baptist; some, Elijah; and others, Jeremiah, or one of the other great preachers."* Then Yeshua asked, *"But who do you say that I am?"* And Simon Peter answered, *"You're the Christ, the Child of the Living God."* And Yeshua answered, *"You're blessed, Simon Barjona, because nothing human has made this known to you, but the God I am from, who is in heaven. And I say also to you, that you're Peter, a little rock, and on this rock, I'll build the church of My people, and the gates of Hell won't overcome it. And I'll give to you the power of the realm of heaven: and whatever you put a stop to on earth will be stopped in heaven: and whatever you free on earth will be freed in heaven."* Then Yeshua told the followers, *"Tell no one that I am the Christ."*

The Foretelling of the Death and Rising Again of the Christ

[21-23] From then on, Yeshua began to tell the followers, how that the Christ must go to Jerusalem, and suffer many things because of the elders and leading priests and the rest of the religious leaders, and be killed, and come back to life again on the third day. Then Peter took hold of Yeshua, and began to argue, saying, *"Don't even think about it, Christ: this won't happen to you."* But Yeshua turned; saying to Peter, *"Get away from Me, Satan: you offend Me because you don't want the things that God wants, but what you, as a human being, wants."*

Forget Yourself and Follow Christ

[24-28] Then Yeshua said to the followers, *"If anyone wants to follow Me, let them forget themselves, and pick up their crosses, and follow Me, because whoever wants to save their life will lose it: and whoever gives up their life for My sake will find it. What profit is there to someone, if they gain the whole world, and lose their own soul? Or what would someone give up to save their soul? I'll come in the glory of My God with My angels; and then I'll judge everyone for what they've done. The truth is, there are some right here, who won't see death, till they see Me coming in My Reign."*

Yeshua with Moses and Elijah

17 [1-13] And after six days Yeshua took Peter, James and John, the brothers, and brought them up to a high mountain alone, and the Christ was changed in front of them: whose face shined as the sun, and whose clothing was as white as the light. Then Moses and Elijah appeared to them and were talking with Yeshua. Then Peter said to Yeshua, *"Christ, it's good for us to be here: if you want, let's make three memorials here; one for You, one for Moses, and one for Elijah."* But while he was speaking, a bright light in the midst of a cloud moved over them: and a voice came from the cloud, which said, ***"This is My Child, who I love and am so pleased with; Listen to Yeshua."*** When the followers heard it, they dropped to the ground, and were very afraid. But Yeshua came and touched them, saying, *"Get up, and don't be afraid."* And when they looked up, they saw no one but Yeshua. And as they came down from the mountain, Yeshua told them, *"Don't tell anyone what you saw until I've come back to life again from the dead."* And the followers asked, *"So why do the religious leaders say that Elijah must come back first?"* And Yeshua answered, *"The truth is, Elijah will come first, and turn everyone back to the truth. But I tell you that Elijah has already come, and they didn't know it, but have done to him what they wanted to do. And I'll also suffer like this by them."* Then the followers understood that Yeshua spoke to them of John the Baptist.

An Only Child Healed from Seizures

[14-21] And when they had come back to the crowd, someone came to them, kneeling down, and saying, *"Christ, have mercy on my child because the child has seizures, and suffers greatly and often falls into the fire, or into the water. I brought the child to your followers, but they couldn't help."* Then Yeshua answered, *"You faithless and evil people, how long will I be here and have to put up with you? Bring the child here to Me."* And Yeshua ordered the evil spirit to come out of the child; and it went out: and the child was healed at that very time. Then the followers came to Yeshua alone, and asked, *"Why couldn't we make it go out?"* And Yeshua answered, *"Because of your unbelief. The truth is, if you have faith, even as small as a grain of mustard seed, you can say to this mountain, move from this place to that place; and it'll move; and nothing will be impossible for you. But, this kind will only go out by prayer and willingly going without food.*

Peter Goes Fishing

[22-23] And while they stayed in Galilee, Yeshua said, *"I'll soon be handed over into the other people's hands and they'll kill me, and the third day I'll come back to life again."* And the followers were very sad.

[24-27] Afterwards, when they had come to Capernaum, tax collectors came to Peter, asking, *"Doesn't your leader pay taxes?"* So Peter said, *"Yes."* And when they came into the house Yeshua knew what he was about to say, and asked, *"What do you think, Simon? Who do the rulers of the earth take taxes from? From their own people, or from foreigners?"* And Peter answered, *"From foreigners."* So Yeshua said, *"Then the children are free.*

But just the same, in case we should offend them, go to the water, and go fishing, taking up the first fish that you catch; and when you open its mouth, you'll find a piece of money: take it, and give it to them for us."

Like a Little Child

18 [1-6] At this time the followers came to Yeshua, saying, *"Who is the greatest in the realm of heaven?"* And Yeshua called a little child to come, and set the child in the middle of them, and said, *"The truth is, unless you're changed and become like little children, you won't get into heaven. So whoever becomes as undoubting as this little child, they'll be the greatest in heaven. And whoever helps one such little child in My Name helps Me. But whoever hurts the faith of one of these little ones who believe in Me, it would better for that person to be dropped in the sea with a weight around their neck and be put to death.*

The World is Full of Sorrow

[7-14] *The world is full of sorrow because of wrongdoing! Bad things will always happen; but the person who hurts someone's faith will be very sorry! So if your hand or foot causes you to sin, don't even use them, as if they were cut off, because it's better for you to live disabled, instead of having two hands or two feet and be thrown into the everlasting Hell fire. And if your eye causes you to sin, don't use it, as if it had been put out, because it's better for you to live with one eye, instead of two and be thrown into Hell's flames. Be sure that you don't hate even one of these little ones, because I tell you that their angels always see the face of My God in heaven. I've come to save what was lost. So what do you think? If someone has a hundred animals in their herd, and one of them goes off somewhere, don't they leave the ninety-nine, and go to look for the one that has gotten lost? And if they find it, the truth is; they'll celebrate more because of that one animal, than of the ninety-nine which didn't go off. Just the same, it isn't the will of your God, who is in heaven, that even one of these little ones would be lost.*

On Church Discipline

[15-20] *Besides this, if someone sins against you, go and tell them their fault between you and them alone: if they hear you, you've gained them back. But if they won't listen to you, then take one or two more with you, that every word can be witnessed by two or three others. And if they won't listen to them either, tell it to the church. If they won't listen to the church, treat them as an ungodly person or a tax collector. The truth is, whatever you say on earth, whether to put a stop to something or to cause something to happen, that will be done in heaven, too. Again, I tell you, that if two of you agree on earth about anything they ask, it'll be done for them by My God, who is in heaven, because where two or three come together in My Name, I am there in Spirit with them, too."*

On Forgiveness

[21-22] Then Peter asked, *"Christ, how often can another Christian sin against me, and I still forgive them? Seven times?"* But Yeshua answered, *"Not just seven times: but, seventy times seven.*

[23-35] *Heaven is like a certain owner, who kept a record of what all the workers owed. And when the owner had taken account, one worker was brought in, who owed the owner ten thousand dollars. But the worker had nothing to pay, so the owner told the other workers to sell everything that worker had, so the payment could be made. But the worker bowed down, and begged the owner to have patience, and it would all be paid back. So then, the owner of that worker had compassion, and released the worker from the debt that was owed. But then, that same worker went out, and finding another coworker, which owed the first worker a hundred dollars: and grabbed the other worker by the throat, saying, 'Pay me everything that you owe me.' And that coworker bowed down, and begged, saying, 'Have patience with me, and I'll pay you everything.' But the first worker wouldn't listen and had the other thrown in jail, till the debt could be paid. So when their coworkers saw what had happened, they were very upset, and came and told the owner everything that had happened. Then the owner, called the first worker in saying, 'You've done a very evil thing. I forgave you all your debt, because you wanted me to: Shouldn't you also have had compassion on your coworker, just as I had mercy on you?' And the owner was angry, and handed that worker over to be punished, till the dept was paid in full. So My God in heaven will do this to you, too, if you don't forgive the sins of one another from your hearts."*

On Divorce

19 [1-2] And then, when Yeshua had finished telling these stories, they went from Galilee, and came into the coasts of Judea beyond Jordan. Great crowds followed along; and were healed by the Christ there.

[3-9] Then the religious leaders came also, trying to tempt Yeshua and asked, *"Is it right for someone to divorce their spouse for any reason?"* And the Christ answered them, *"Haven't you read, that in the beginning, God, who made humanity, made them male and female, and said, because of this, a person will leave their parents, and will stay faithful to their spouse: and the two of them will be as one body? So they're not just two people, but one body. So what God has joined together, let no one separate."* So they asked Yeshua, *"Then why did Moses tell us to give a writ of divorcement, and allow divorce?"* Then Yeshua answered, *"Moses let you*

divorce your spouses because of your unforgiving hearts: but from the beginning, it wasn't this way. And I tell you, whoever divorces their spouse, unless it's for their spouse's sexual sin, and marries another, takes part in sexual sin themselves: and whoever marries someone who is divorced takes part in sexual sin, too."

Only Some are Able to Remain Sexually Pure
[10-12] The followers said to Yeshua, "If that's the case of the person who marries, then it isn't good to marry." But Yeshua answered, *"Some people can't accept this, but only those to whom it's given. Because there are some people who are not able to be sexual, who were born that way from birth: and there are some who are not able to be sexual, who were made that way by others: and there are some, who have kept themselves sexually pure for heaven's sake. Whoever can accept this, let them accept it."*

Let the Little Children Come to Me
[13-15] Then some little children were brought to the Christ, who laid hands on them to bless them, and to pray for them. But the followers scolded those who brought them, so Yeshua said, *"Let the little children come to Me, and don't forbid them, because the realm of heaven is full of little ones like them."* So the Christ laid hands on them, and left there.

The Wealthy Young Person
[16-22] And someone came asking, *"Good Teacher, what good thing may I do, that I may have everlasting life?"* And the Christ answered, *"Why are you asking Me about what's good? There's only One who tells us what's good, and that is God: so if you want everlasting life, do what the Words of God tell you to do."* So the young person asked, *"What words?"* So Yeshua said, *"Don't murder, don't take part in sexual sin, don't steal, don't tell lies about someone, honor your parents, and love others as yourself."* So the young person said, *"I've done all this from my youth up: so what do I still lack?"* Then Yeshua answered, *"If you want to be complete, go and sell whatever you have, and give to those who are poor, and then you'll have wealth in heaven. Then come and follow Me."* But the young person went away very sorrowful when he heard that, because he was very wealthy.

It's Very Hard for a Rich Person to Get into Heaven
[23-26] Then Yeshua said to the followers, *"The truth is, it'll be very hard for a rich person to go to heaven. And I tell you again, it's easier for a camel to be completely unloaded and squeeze through the smallest gate, than for a rich person to come into the realm of God."* When the followers heard that, they were amazed, saying, *"Then who can be saved?"* But Yeshua looked at them, saying, *"Anything that's impossible for human beings alone; is possible with God's help."*

You will be Rewarded for Whatever You Give Up
[27-30] Then Peter said, *"You know that we've given up everything, and followed you; so what will we get?"* And Yeshua answered, *"The truth is, that you who have followed Me, when I sit on the throne of My victory in the new life, you'll also sit on twelve thrones, judging the twelve family groups of Israel. And everyone that has given up homes, or brothers, or sisters, or father, or mother, or spouse, or children, or lands, because of My Name, will get a hundred times that much, and will have everlasting life, as well. But many of those who are first now will be last then; and those who are last now will be first then.*

The Owner of the Garden
20 [1-16] *Heaven is like someone who is an owner of a garden, who went out early in the morning to hire workers. And when the owner had agreed with the workers for a day's pay, they went to the garden. Then the owner went out about nine o'clock, and saw others in the shopping center who weren't working, and said, 'Go to the garden also, and whatever is right I'll give you.' So they went, also. Then again, the owner went out about twelve o'clock noon and three o'clock in the afternoon, and did the same. And about five o'clock, the owner went out, and found others not working, saying to them, 'Why haven't you been working all day?' So they answered, 'Because no one has hired us.' So the owner said, 'Go to the garden also; and whatever is right I'll give you.' So when evening came, the owner of the garden said to the manager, 'Call the workers, and give them their pay, starting from the last ones hired to the first ones hired.' And when those who were hired at five o'clock came, they all got a full day's pay. But when the first to be hired came, they expected to have gotten more; but they all got the same amount. And when they had gotten it, they grumbled to the owner of the house, saying, 'These last ones hired have only worked one hour, and you've made them equal to us, who have worked through the heat of the day.' But the owner said to one of them, 'Friend, I've done you no wrong: didn't you agree with me for that amount? Take what's yours and leave: I'll give to these last ones hired just as I gave to you. Isn't it right for me to do what I want with my own money? Are you angry, because I'm good?' So those who are last will be first and those who are first will be last, because many will be called, but few are chosen."*

81

The Foretelling of Christ's Death and Rising to Life Again

[17-19] And Yeshua, going up to Jerusalem, took the twelve followers aside on the way, saying to them, *"We're going up to Jerusalem now; and I'll be handed over to the leading priests and to the religious leaders, and they'll accuse Me and sentence Me to death, and will deliver Me to the Romans, who will mock Me, and beat Me, and put Me to death. But on the third day, I'll come to life again."*

Whoever Wants to be Great, Must Minister to the Needs of Others

[20-29] Then the mother of Zebedee's children came with her children, bowing, and wanting something of Yeshua. And the Christ said to her, *"What do you want?"* So she said, *"Let my two children sit, one on your right side, and the other on the left, when You come into power."* But Yeshua said to them, *"You don't know what you're asking. Are you able to accept the cup that I have to drink, and to be baptized with what I have to suffer?"* And they answered, *"We are."* Then Yeshua said, *"You certainly will drink it with Me, and you'll be baptized as I am: but to sit beside Me, on My right and on My left, isn't Mine to give, but it'll be given to those it's prepared for by My God."* And when the other ten heard it, they were resentful of them. But Yeshua called them over, saying, *"You know that the rulers of the other peoples control them, and those who are great have power over them, also. But it won't be this way among you. Whoever wants to be great among you, must minister to others needs; And whoever wants to be a leader among you, they must work the hardest for you: Just as I didn't come to be ministered to, but to minister to others, and to give My life as the payment for the debts of others' sins."* Then as they left Jericho, a great crowd followed along.

Two Blind Beggars Healed

[30-33] And two blind beggars sitting by the roadside, when they heard that Yeshua passed by, called out, saying, *"Have mercy on us, Christ, Heir of David."* And the crowd scolded them, because they wanted them to be quiet, but they called out all the more, saying, *"Have mercy on us, Christ, Heir of David."* And Yeshua stood still, and called them, saying, *"What do you want Me to do for you?"* So they said, *"Christ, we want You to make our eyes able to see."* So Yeshua had compassion on them, and touched their eyes: and suddenly their eyes could see, and they followed along.

Yeshua's Entry into Jerusalem

21 [1-11] When they came near Jerusalem, and had come to Bethphage, to the Mount of Olives, then Yeshua sent two of the followers, saying to them, *"Go into the town near by, and soon you'll find a donkey tied up, and a foal with her: untie them, and bring them to Me. And if anyone says anything to you, say, 'The Christ needs them;' and they'll send them right away."* And it happened like this, so that everything would happen which was said by the great preacher, saying, "Tell the daughter of Zion, your Ruler comes to you, gentle, and sitting on a young donkey, yes, the foal of a donkey." And the followers went, doing as Yeshua told them, and brought the donkey, and the foal, and laid their clothes across its back, and they put Yeshua on it. And a very great crowd spread their clothes down on the road; others cut down branches from the palm trees, and placed them down on the road. And the crowds that went along followed, calling out, saying, *"Save us, now, Heir of David!: Blessed is the One who comes in the Name of Yahweh God; Save us, now! O Highest One!"* And when they came into Jerusalem, all the city was excited, saying, *"Who is this?"* And the crowd said, *"This is Yeshua, the great preacher from Nazareth of Galilee."*

The Angry Christ

[12-16] And Yeshua went into the House of God, and put out all those who bought and sold in the Place of Worship, and turned over the bankers' tables, and the seats of those who sold doves, and said, *"It's written, My House will be called the House of prayer; but you've made it a place of thieves."* And those who were blind and unable to walk came to Yeshua in the Place of Worship; and the Christ healed them. But when the leading priests and religious leaders saw the amazing things that the Christ did, and the children calling out in the Place of Worship, and saying, *"Save us, now, Heir of David;"* they were very displeased, and asked, *"Don't you hear what they're saying?"* And Yeshua answered, *"Yes; haven't you ever read, 'You've put praises in the mouths of little ones and nursing babies?'"*

The Fig Tree

[17-22] And the Christ left them, and went out of the city into Bethany; and stayed there. Now in the morning, Yeshua, who was coming back into the city, was hungry. And seeing a fig tree on the way, the Christ came up to it, and finding nothing but leaves on it, said, *"Let no fruit grow on it from now on."* And the fig tree died right then. And when the followers saw it, they were amazed, saying, *"Look how suddenly the fig tree died!"* And Yeshua said to them, *"The truth is, if you have faith, and don't doubt, you won't just do things like what happened to the fig tree,*

but if you say to this mountain, 'move, and go into the sea;' it'll happen as well. And you'll get whatever you ask for in prayer, if you truly believe it."

Who Gave You this Power?

[23-27] And when they came into the Place of Worship, the leading priests and the elders of the people came in as the Christ was teaching, and asked, *"By what right do you do this? And who gave you this power?"* And Yeshua answered them, *"I'll ask you something, too, which if you can tell me, I'll also tell you by what power I do this. Where did the baptism of John come from? Was it from heaven, or did it come from human ideas?"* And they argued among themselves, saying, *"If we say, from heaven; then Yeshua will say to us, 'Why didn't you believe him then?' But if we say, from human ideas; we fear the people because they all believe John was a great preacher."* So they said to Yeshua, *"We don't know."* And the Christ answered, *"Then neither will I tell you by what power I do this."*

The Two Rebellious Children

[28-32] So what do you think? Someone had two children; and came to the first one, saying, 'Go work today in my garden.' And the child answered, 'I won't go': but later thought differently, and went to work anyway. And then the person came to the second child, saying the same. And that child answered, saying, 'I'll go', but didn't. Which of the two did what was wanted of them?" So they answered Yeshua, *"The first."* Then Yeshua said, *"The truth is, that the tax collectors and the whores will go into the realm of God before you, because John came to you with the way of goodness, and you wouldn't believe it: but the tax collectors and the whores believed it: and you, even when you knew it, didn't change your mind later, and believe.*

The Land Owner and the Farmers

[33-46] *Listen to another story: There was a certain landowner, who planted a garden, and built a wall all around it, and dug a winepress in it, and built a guard tower. The landowner rented it out to farmers, then went into a far country. When time for the fruit came near, the owner sent some workers to the farmers to get the grapes. But the farmers took the workers, and beat one, and killed another, and stoned another. Then again, the owner sent other workers besides the first ones: and the farmers did the same to them. So last of all, the landowner's own heir was sent to them, the owner thinking, 'They'll respect my own heir.' But when the farmers saw the owner's heir, they said among themselves, 'This is the heir; come, let's kill the heir, and we'll take the inheritance.' And they brought the heir out of the garden, who they killed. So when the owner of the garden comes, what do you think will happen to those farmers?"* And they said to Yeshua, *"The owner will miserably kill those evil farmers, and will rent out the garden to other farmers, who will give the grapes when they're in season."* So Yeshua answered, *"Didn't you ever read in the Words, 'The stone which the builders rejected will become the head cornerstone: this is Yahweh's doing, and we're so amazed? So I say to you, the realm of God will be taken from you, and given to a nation who will produce the fruit. And whoever falls on this stone will be broken: but whoever the stone falls on, will be crushed to pieces."* And when the leading priests and religious leaders heard those stories, they realized that Yeshua was speaking of them. But when they tried to take Yeshua, they were afraid of the crowd, because the people believed the Christ was a great preacher.

The Marriage Supper

22 [1-10] And Yeshua spoke to them again with stories, saying, *"The realm of heaven is like a certain ruler, who planned a supper for a child, who was to be married. The ruler sent out workers to call those who were asked to the wedding, but none of them would come. So once again, the ruler sent out other workers, saying, 'Tell those who have been asked, I've prepared my dinner: the meat is done, and everything is ready: come to the marriage, now.' But they made excuses, and left, one going to their farm, and another to their sales goods. Some even took the workers, and treated them cruelly, and killed them. But the ruler heard it, and was angry: and sent out guards to kill those murderers, and burn up their city. Then the ruler said to the workers, 'The wedding is ready, but those who were asked weren't worthy. So go into the streets, and as many as you find, call to the marriage. So those workers went out into the streets, and gathered together all that they found, both bad and good. So the wedding had many guests.*

[11-14] *And when the ruler came in to see the guests, and seeing some there which didn't have on the wedding clothing, the ruler said, 'Friends, how did you come in here, not having on the wedding clothing?' And they were speechless. Then the ruler said to the workers, 'Tie up their hands and feet, and take them away, and put them into the darkness outside; where they'll be crying and gritting their teeth,' because many are invited, but few are chosen."*

On Paying Taxes and Tithes

[15-22] Then the religious leaders left and planned together how to confuse Yeshua's words. So they sent out their own followers along with Herod's people to Yeshua, saying, *"Christ, we know that you're honest, and teach the way of God in truth, nor do you care what anyone thinks because you don't consider what others say. So tell us, what do you think about this? Is it right to give taxes to the ruling government, or not?"* But Yeshua knew their evil plan, saying, *"Why do you tempt Me, you fakes? Show me the money.* So they showed Yeshua a coin. Then Yeshua asked them, *"Whose picture and name is this?"* And they answered, *"The Ruler's."* Then Yeshua answered them back, *"So pay your taxes to the government; and pay to God the part of your money that belongs to God."* And they were amazed, and left when they heard what Yeshua said.

No Sexuality in the Afterlife

[23-33] This same day some from the religious sects came, who say that there's no afterlife, and asked, *"Christ, Moses said, if someone dies, having no children, another will marry their spouse, and give her children. Now there were with us seven brothers: and the first, who had gotten married, died, and having no child, left his spouse to another. It was the same way with the second also, and the third, up to the seventh. And last of all, the woman died also. So when we come to life again, whose spouse will she be of the seven, because they all had her?"* So Yeshua answered them, *"You're wrong, not knowing the Word, or the power of God, because when we come to life again, we won't be sexual and live in marriage, but we'll be neither male, nor female, as the angels of God in heaven. But speaking of the coming to life again of the dead, haven't you read what was spoken to you by God, saying, 'I am the God of Abraham, and the God of Isaac, and the God of Jacob?' God isn't the God of the dead, but God is the God of the living."* And when the crowds heard this, they were amazed at this teaching.

The Greatest Rule

[34-40] But when the religious leaders had heard that Yeshua had put the religious sects to silence, they gathered together. Then one of them, which was a student of the law, asked a question to tempt Yeshua, saying, *"Christ, what is the greatest rule in the Word of God?"* And Yeshua said, *"'Love Yahweh, your God, with all your spirit, with all your soul, and with all your mind.' This is the first and greatest rule. And the second is very much like it, 'Love others as you love yourself.' All of the Word of God and the Words of great preachers are based on these two rules."*

Christ David's Descendant

[41-46] While the religious leaders were gathered together, Yeshua asked them, *"What do you think of the Christ? Whose descendant is the Christ?"* And they said to Yeshua, *'The descendant of David."* So Yeshua asked, "How then did David in spirit call the Christ, Christ, saying, Yahweh God said to my Christ, sit beside Me, till I make those who come against you a place to rest Your feet? So if David called the Christ, Christ, how is the Christ David's descendant?" And no one was able to answer a word, nor did anyone dare ask Yeshua any more questions from that day on.

Yeshua Tells of the Guilt of the False Religious Leaders

23 [1-12] Then Yeshua spoke to the crowd, and the followers, saying, *"The religious leaders and those in the religious sects sit in the judgment seat of Moses, so whatever they tell you to do, do it; but don't do what they do, because they tell you to do it, but don't do it themselves. They make rules that are very hard to follow, and order others to follow them; but they themselves won't even try to follow them. But everything they do, they do to be seen by others: they wear ornamental religious jewelry and impressive religious clothing, and love the best places at the dinners of religious celebrations, and the best seats in the places of worship, and greetings in the shopping centers, and to be called 'Teacher, Teacher' by others. But don't be called Teacher because only One is your Teacher, Me, the Christ; and you're all equals. And don't call any religious leader Father on earth because the One who is in heaven is who we come from. And don't be called superior because I, the Christ am your only superior. But whoever wants to be greatest among you must be willing to work the hardest. And whoever wants to be praised must become the lowest worker; and whoever puts themselves in the lowest position will be raised to a higher position.*

[13-15] *But you'll be sorry, all you religious leaders and those in the religious sects, you fakes! You slam heaven's doors in the face of others and you won't even go in yourselves, nor will you let those who are trying to go in, get in. Yes, you'll be sorry you religious leaders and those in the religious sects. You're all fakes! You take what little money a death survivor has, and say long prayers just for show: so you'll surely get the greater punishment. Yes, you'll be sorry, you religious leaders and those in the religious sects, you fakes! You'll travel over land and sea to get one convert, and when they're converted, you make them two times as much a child of Hell than you yourselves are.*

[16-22] *Yes, you'll be sorry you, you blind leaders, who say, 'Whoever swears by the Place of Worship, hasn't done anything wrong; but whoever swears by the offering of the Place of Worship, is responsible for their oath!' You're thoughtless and blind leaders because which is greater, the offering, or the Place of Worship that blesses the offering? And you say, 'Whoever swears by the altar hasn't done anything wrong; but whoever swears by the gift that is on it, is guilty.' You're thoughtless and blind leaders because which is greater, the gift, or the altar that blesses the gift? So whoever swears by the altar, swears by it, and by everything on it. And whoever swears by the Place of Worship, swears by it, and by the God whose Spirit is in it. And whoever swears by heaven, swears by the throne of God, and by the God who sits on it.*

[23-33] *Yes, you'll be sorry you religious leaders and those in the religious sects, you fakes! You pay a part of even the smallest amount of spices, and have left out doing the most important things, like making good judgments, having mercy, and being faithful. You should do this, but not leave the other things undone. You blind leaders, who won't break the least important rule in the least way, and yet you ignore all the most important ones. Yes, you'll be sorry, you religious leaders and those in the religious sects, you fakes! You obey the Word of God outwardly, but inside you're full of lies and selfishness. You blind religious leaders, first obey the Word of God inwardly, and then you'll appear to do it outwardly, as well. Yes, you'll be sorry, you religious leaders and those in the religious sects, you fakes! You're like the beautiful grave markers of a burial place, which appear very beautiful, but are only markers of graves full of dead peoples' bones, and rotting corpses. Just like this, you, too, appear good to others outwardly, but you're full of lies and sin inside. Yes, you'll be sorry, you religious leaders and those in the religious sects, you fakes! Because you build great memorial places for all the great preachers, and decorate the graves of those who've done great things, and say, 'If we had lived in the days of our ancestors, we wouldn't have killed the great preachers.' You then are witnesses yourselves, that you're the children of those who killed the great preachers. And you certainly measure up to your ancestors. You snakes, you bunch of snakes, how can you ever escape the punishment of Hell?*

[34-39] *I'll send you great preachers, and wise ones, and writers of the Word: and some of them you'll kill and torture; and some of them you'll beat in your places of worship, and chase them like criminals from city to city, so that all the guilt of the blood shed on the earth of those who followed God can come on you, from the blood of Abel to the blood of Zachariah, child of Barachias, who was killed between the Place of Worship and the altar. The truth is, all this guilt will come on this generation of people. Oh Jerusalem, Jerusalem, you who kill all the great preachers, and murder those who are sent to warn you! How often I wanted to gather your children together, like a hen gathers her chicks under her wings, and you wouldn't let me! So you see your house is now empty. I tell you, I won't come to you again, till you say, 'Blessed is the One who comes in the Name of Yahweh.'"*

Destruction of the Temple Foretold

24 [1-2] And Yeshua went out, and left the Place of Worship: and as they left, the followers pointed out the great buildings of the Place of Worship. And Yeshua answered, *"Do you see this? The truth is, there won't be one stone left on another, that won't be out of place."*

The End Times

[3-14] And as they sat on the Mount of Olives, the followers came secretly, asking the Christ, "Tell us when this will happen and how will we know of your second coming, and of the end of the world?" So Yeshua answered them, *"Be sure that no one misleads you, because many will come in My Name, saying, 'I am the Christ,' misleading many people. And you'll hear of wars and news of more wars, but don't be uneasy because all this must happen. It's not the end of time yet. Nation will come against nation, and land against land. There will be a great lack of food, and deadly diseases, and natural disasters, in many different places. All this is just the beginning of trouble. Then they'll arrest you to be punished, and will kill you, and you'll be hated by all nations because of My Name. At that time, many will be offended by Christianity, and will lie to one another, and will hate one another. And many untruthful preachers will come, misleading a great many people. And because wrongs will be greatly increased, many people won't know how to love others. But whoever doesn't give up, even to the end of time, those are the ones who will be saved. Then when this New Word of the realm of God is told in the whole world for a witness to all nations; the end of time will come.*

The Antichrist

[15-28] *So when you see the antichrist, spoken of by Daniel, the great preacher, standing in the holy place, (whoever reads, let them understand), then let those who are in Israel escape into the mountains of Judea, and let those who are on the roof not come down to get anything out of their homes, nor let those who are in the field go back to get their clothes. And those who are pregnant with babies, and those who are breastfeeding in those days will have great sorrow! But pray that you don't have to run in the winter, nor on a Day of Worship, because at that time great troubles will come, like there's never been since the beginning of time till now, no, nor ever will. And unless those days are stopped short, no one would be saved: but for the sake of the chosen ones those days will*

85

be shortened. Then if anyone says to you, 'Look, here is the Christ', or 'The Christ is there'; don't believe it, because false Christs, and false teachers will come one and do many amazing things; so that they would even mislead the chosen ones of God, if it were possible. But listen, I've told you the truth. So if they say to you, 'The Christ is in the desert'; don't go: or 'The Christ is in a secret place'; don't believe it, because as you see the lightning strike in the east, and flash even to the west; so you'll see My coming. And when you see all the dead, you'll see the buzzards gather.

The Powers of Heaven Shaken

[29-35] And right after all these troubles, the sun will become dark, and the moon won't have any light, and the stars will fall from heaven, and all the heavenly bodies will be shaken out of place: And then the sign of My coming will appear in heaven, and all the families of the earth will cry, and they'll see Me coming in the clouds of heaven with great power and bright light. And I'll send My angels with a great sound of a trumpet, and they'll gather together My chosen ones from every direction, from one end of heaven to the other. And now learn what the story of the fig tree means; When the branch of the fig tree is still tender, and puts out leaves, you know that summer is near: So you, too, when you see all this happening, know that the time of My coming is near, so very near. The truth is, the generation in which this happens won't pass, till everything I said will happen. Heaven and earth will come to an end, but My Words won't ever die out.

Like a Thief in the Night

[36-51] But no one knows of that day and hour, no, not even the angels of heaven, but only Yahweh, My God. But as the days of Noah were, so too will My coming be. Just like the days before the flood, they were eating, drinking, and getting married, until the day that Noah went into the ark, and they didn't know a thing until the flood came, and drowned them all. So too will My coming be. Then two people will be working in the field; one will be taken up, and the other left behind. Two others will be working at the workshop; one will be taken up, and the other left behind. So watch, because you don't know when your Christ will come! If the owners of a house had known the time the thief would come, they would have watched, and wouldn't have let their house be broken into. So be ready, too, because I am coming when you least expect it. So then, who is a faithful and wise worker, who has been made overseer of the household, to give those of the household food at just the right time? Blessed is that worker, who when I come, I find doing My work. The truth is, that I'll make them overseer over all My goods. But if there are workers who are evil and say in their hearts, it's not time yet; And begin to abuse their coworkers, and to eat and drink with the drunks; The Owner will come in a day when their not watching, and at a time that they won't know of, and will cut them off, and will give them their due punishment in Hell with the other fakes: where they'll be crying and gritting their teeth.

The Ten Virgins

25 [1-13] The Realm of Heaven is like ten virgins who have never been sexually active, who took their lamps, and went out to meet the bridal party. And five of them were wise, but five were stupid. Those who were stupid took their lamps, but forgot to take oil with them. But the wise took oil in their bottles along with their lamps. And while they waited for the bridal party, they all fell asleep. And at midnight, someone called out, 'The bridal party is coming; go out to meet them.' Then they all got up, and started getting their lamps ready. But those who were stupid said to those who were wise, 'Give us some of your oil; our lamps have gone out.' But those who were wise said, 'We can't; there won't be enough for both us and you: go buy some for yourselves.' And while they went to buy some, the bridal party came; and those who were ready went in with them to the marriage ceremony and the door was shut. Then the other virgins came later, saying, 'Open the door; Open the door.' But the one who opened the door answered, 'The truth is, I don't even know who you are.' So watch, because you don't know the day or the hour I'll come.

The Traveling Owner

[14-30] And heaven is like an owner traveling to a far away country, who called the workers giving them everything to manage. And one was given five valuable coins, to another, two, and to another, one; to each one of them for their different abilities; and then the owner left soon afterwards. Then the one who had gotten the five coins went and traded with the coins, and got five more coins. And the one who had gotten two, gained another two, as well. But the one who had gotten only one coin went and dug a hole in the ground, and hid the owner's money. So after a long time the owner came, and took account of them. And so the one who had gotten five coins came and brought the other five coins also, saying, 'Boss, You gave me five coins and I've gained five more coins.' The owner said, 'Well done, you're a good and faithful worker: you've been faithful over a few things, so I'll make you manager over many things: Come into My house and celebrate with Me.' And the one who had gotten two coins came saying, 'Boss, You gave me two coins and I've gained two more coins beside them.' And the owner said, 'Well done, you're a good and faithful worker; you've been faithful over a few things, so I'll make you

manager over many things: Come into My house and celebrate with Me.' Then the one who had gotten only one coin came saying, 'Boss, I knew you that you were a hard person, making profit from others, and collecting from where others have done business: So I was afraid, and went and hid your coin in the earth: See, here is what's yours.' So the owner answered said, 'You are a bad and lazy worker, you knew that I make profit from others, and collect from where others have done business: So you should have put My money in the bank, and then at My coming I would have gotten My own with interest. Take the coin from this worker, and give it to the one that has ten coins.' So to everyone that has earned something, more will be given, and they'll become rich: but from those who haven't earned anything, even what they have will be taken away. And the unprofitable worker will be put into the blackest darkness: where they'll be crying and gritting their teeth.

The Judgment of the Good and the Bad

[31-46] And when I come in My victory, and all the holy angels with Me, then I'll sit on My throne of glory: And all nations will gather to Me: and I'll separate them from one another, as a keeper divides one kind of animal from another: And I'll put the good ones on the right side of Me, but the bad ones on the left. Then I'll say to those on the right side, 'Come, you who are blessed of My God, inherit the realm of God prepared for you from the beginning of the world: Because I was hungry, and you gave Me food; I was thirsty, and you gave Me drink; I was a stranger, and you took Me in; Naked, and you clothed Me; I was sick, and you visited Me; I was in prison, and you came to Me. Then those who do good will answer, saying, 'Christ, when did we see You hungry, and feed You? Or thirsty, and gave You something to drink? When did we see You as a stranger, and take You in? Or naked, and clothe You? Or when did we see You sick, or in prison, and come to You?' And I'll answer and say to them, 'The truth is, as much as you've helped one of the least of these My children, you've helped Me.' Then I'll say to those on the left hand 'Go away from Me, you cursed ones, into the everlasting fire, which was prepared for the devil and the evil spirits: because I was hungry, and you gave Me nothing to eat; I was thirsty, and you gave Me nothing to drink; I was a stranger, and you didn't take Me in; naked, and you didn't clothe Me; sick, and in prison, and you didn't visit Me.' Then they'll also answer, saying, 'Christ, when did we see You hungry, or thirsty, or a stranger, or naked, or sick, or in prison, and didn't help You?' Then I'll answer them, saying, 'The truth is, as much as you didn't help one of the least of these, you didn't help Me.' And these will go away into everlasting punishment: but those who did right will go into everlasting life."

Yeshua is anointed at Bethany

26 [1-5] And then, when Yeshua had finished all these stories, the Christ said to the followers, "You know that the celebration of the Passover is in two days, and I'll be handed over and sentenced to death on a cross." Then the leading priests and the religious leaders and the elders of the people gathered together at the great house of Caiaphas, the leading priest and discussed how to take and kill Yeshua secretly. But they said, "Not on the celebration day, in case the people start an uproar."

[6-13] Now when Yeshua was in Bethany, in the home of Simon, a person who had leprosy, a woman came in having an alabaster jar of very expensive perfumed oil, and poured it on Yeshua's head, while they were eating a meal. But when the followers saw it, they resented it, saying, "Why was this wasted?" because this perfume might have been sold for a lot of money, and given to those who were poor. Then Yeshua, realizing their resentment, answered, "Why are you bothering this woman? She's done a very good thing for Me. You'll always have those who are poor with you; but I won't be here forever. When she poured this perfume on My body, she did it for My coming burial. The truth is, whenever this New Word is preached in the whole world, what this woman has done for Me, will be told for a memorial of her also."

Judas Plans to Hand Yeshua Over to the Priests

[14-16] Then one of the twelve, called Judas Iscariot, went to the leading priests, and asked them, "What will you give me if I hand over Yeshua to you?" And they promised him thirty pieces of silver. And from then on Judas looked for a chance to hand over the Christ.

The Passover Supper

[17-25] Now on the first day of the celebration of unleavened bread the followers came to Yeshua, asking, "Where would you like us to get ready to eat the Passover?" And the Christ said, "Go into the city, and say to a certain person, 'The Christ said, My time is here; I'll keep the Passover with My followers at your home.'" And the followers did as Yeshua had told them; and they got ready for the Passover. Now when the evening came, Yeshua sat down with the twelve. And as they ate, the Christ said, "The truth is, that one of you will hand Me over." And they were very upset, so all of them began to ask the Christ, "Is it me?" Yeshua answered, "Whoever dips their hand in the dish with Me will be the one who hands Me over. I go as the Word says of Me: but the one who hands Me over will be very sorry! It would have been better for that person if they had never been born." Then Judas, which handed over the Christ, asked, "Christ, is it me?" And Yeshua answered, "It's just as you say."

87

[26-35] And as they were eating, Yeshua took the loaf bread, and blessed it, and broke it apart, giving some to each of the followers, saying, *"Take this and eat it all; this is a memorial of My body."* And then Yeshua took the cup, and gave thanks, and gave it to them, saying, *"Each of you drink some of it, because this is a memorial of My blood for the New Word, which will be shed for taking away the sins of many people. But I tell you, I won't drink wine again, until the day when I drink it anew with you in the realm of God."* And when they had sung a hymn, they went out to the Mount of Olives. Then Yeshua said, *"Every one of you will leave Me alone tonight because the Word says, 'When the keeper is taken, the herd will be scattered.' But after I come to life again, I'll go to meet you in Galilee."* Then Peter said, *"Even if everyone else leaves you, I won't ever leave you."* But Yeshua said, *"The truth is, that tonight, before the rooster crows, you'll say that you don't know Me three times."* Peter said, *"Even if I should die with you, I still won't say that I don't know you!"* And all the followers said the same thing.

Prayer in the Garden
[36-46] Then Yeshua came with them to a garden, called Gethsemane, saying to the followers, *"Sit here, while I go and pray over there."* But the Christ took Peter, James and John along, and becoming very sad, said, *"My soul is so sad, I'm about to die: stay here, and pray with Me."* And Yeshua went a little farther, laid face down, and prayed, saying, *"My God, if it's possible; don't let this happen to Me: but just the same, don't let it be as I want, but as You want."* And then Yeshua came to the followers, and finding them sleeping, said to Peter, *"Couldn't you even pray with Me an hour? Watch and pray, so that you won't be tempted. Even if the spirit's willing, the body is weak."* And the Christ went away the second time, and prayed, saying, *"My God, if this must happen to Me, I want whatever You want to be done."* And the Christ came and found them sleeping again because they were very tired. So Yeshua left them, and went away again, and prayed the third time, saying the same words. Then the Christ came to the followers, saying to them, *"You might as well sleep, now. See, it's time now, and I am given into the hands of sinners. Get up, we have to go. See, the one who is handing Me over is here, now."*

Yeshua Arrested
[47-56] And while Yeshua was still speaking, Judas, one of the twelve, came with a great crowd, who had swords and sticks, from the leading priests and elders of the people. Now Judas, who handed over the Christ, gave them a sign, saying, *"The One who I greet with a kiss is the One to hold on to."* And then Judas came up to Yeshua, saying, *"Hello, Teacher"*; and kissed the Christ. And Yeshua said, *"Friend, why have you come?"* Then they came, taking hold of Yeshua, and took the Christ. And one of those who was with Yeshua drew a sword, and struck one of the leading priest's workers, and cut off his ear. Then Yeshua said, *"Put your sword back in its place, because anyone who uses a sword will be killed by a sword. Don't you know that I can pray to My God right now, and God would quickly send Me more than twelve thousand angels? But then, how would the things take place that God's Words' said would?"* And at that time Yeshua said to the crowds, *"Have you come out to take Me with swords and sticks as if I were a thief? I sat with you daily in the Place of Worship, teaching and you didn't take Me then."* But all this happened, so that the words of the great preachers would happen. Then all the followers left the Christ, and ran away.

Yeshua Brought to Caiaphas
[57-68] And those who had taken Yeshua led the Christ away to Caiaphas the leading priest, where some of the religious leaders and the elders were gathered. But Peter followed along far off and went to the leading priest's great house, and went in, and sat with the workers, to see what would happen. Now the leading priests, the elders, and all the court looked for false witnesses against Yeshua, in order to put the Christ to death; But they found no one. Even though many false witnesses came, still they found no one. At last, two false witnesses came, and said, *"This person said, 'I am able to destroy the House of God, and build it again in three days.'"* And the leading priest got up, saying, *"Don't you have anything to say? What is this that these people speak against you?"* But Yeshua didn't say anything. And the leading priest said, *"I ask you to swear by the Living God, if you're the Christ, the Child of God."* Then Yeshua said, *"It's just as you say: but just the same, I tell you, later, you'll see Me sitting on the throne of God's power, and coming in the clouds of heaven."* Then the leading priest tore his clothes, saying, *"This person has spoken disrespectfully of God; Why do we need any more witnesses? Now you've heard for yourselves this disrespect of God. So what do you think we should do?"* And they answered, *"This person is guilty of death."* Then they spit in the Christ's face, and beat the Christ; and others slapped the Christ with the palms of their hands, saying, *"Tell us, Christ, who hit you?"*

The Rooster Crows
[69-75] Now Peter, who was sitting outside the great house was asked by a girl, *"Aren't you one of those who was with Yeshua of Galilee?"* But he denied it to everyone there, saying, *"I don't know what you're talking about."* And when he had gone into the porch, another girl saw him; saying to those who were there, *"This person was with Yeshua of Nazareth, too."* And again he denied knowing the Christ, and cursing, he said, *"I swear I don't*

know that person!" And after a while those who stood around came to Peter, saying, *"Surely you're one of them; the way you speak gives you away."* Then Peter began to curse and to swear, saying, *"I don't know who that person is."* And suddenly the rooster crowed. And Peter remembered the Words of Yeshua, who had said, *"Before the rooster crows, you'll say you don't know Me three times."* And Peter left there, and cried with great sorrow.

The Christ brought to Pilate

27 [1-10] When the morning came, all the leading priests and elders of the people, were planning to put the Christ to death. They tied up and led Yeshua away to Pontius Pilate the governor. Then Judas, who had handed over the Christ, when he saw that the Christ was to be sentenced to death, changed his mind about it all, and brought the thirty pieces of silver back to the leading priests and elders, saying, *"I've sinned and handed over innocent blood."* And they said, *"What is that to us? You see to that."* And Judas threw down the pieces of silver in the Place of Worship, and went and hung himself. And the leading priests took the silver pieces, saying, *"It isn't right to put them into the treasury, because it's the price of blood."* So they came up with a plan, and bought with it the potter's field, to bury strangers in. And that field is called, *The field of blood*, even today. And what was spoken of by Jeremiah, the great preacher, happened, who wrote, "and they took the thirty pieces of silver, the value of the One who was priced, whom those of the children of Israel put a price on; and gave them for the potter's field, as Yahweh told me."

[11-18] And as Yeshua stood in front of the governor, Pilate asked the Christ, saying, *"Are you the Ruler of the Jews?"* And Yeshua said, *"It's just as you say."* And Yeshua, being accused by the leading priests and elders, didn't say anything. Then Pilate asked the Christ, *"Don't you hear what all they're saying about you?"* But Pilate was greatly amazed because the Christ never answered a word. Now at the time of their celebration, the governor usually freed a prisoner, whoever the people wanted him to. And they had then a notable prisoner, called Barabbas. So when they were gathered together, Pilate, knowing that it was for jealousy that they had brought the Christ to him, asked, *"Who do you want me to free to you? Barabbas, or Yeshua, which is called the Christ?"*

Pilate's Wife

[19-23] When he sat down on the judgment seat, his wife sent word to him, saying, *"Don't have anything to do with the punishment of that person, because I've had horrible dreams today because this person is innocent."* But the leading priests and elders won over the crowd to ask for Barabbas, and have Yeshua killed. So the governor asked them again, *"Which of the two do you want me to free to you?"* They answered, *"Barabbas."* So Pilate asked, *"Then what should I do with Yeshua, who is called Christ?"* And they all said to him, *"Put Yeshua to death!"* And the governor said, *"Why, what evil has this person done?"* But they called out all the more, saying, *"Put Yeshua to death!"*

[24-27] When Pilate saw that he couldn't change their minds, and that everything was in disorder, he took a bowl of water, and washed his hands in front of the crowd, saying, *"I am innocent of the blood of this good person: you see to it."* Then all the people said, *"May the guilt of this person's blood be on us, and on our children."* Then he freed Barabbas to them: and when he had ordered Yeshua to be beaten, he handed the Christ over to them to be put to death.

[28-33] Then the guards of the governor took Yeshua into the common hall, and the whole troop gathered together. They stripped Yeshua, and then put a scarlet robe on the Christ. And making a crown of thorns, they put it on Yeshua's head, and put a reed in the Christ's right hand: and bowed down on their knees, and mocked, saying, *"Hello, Ruler of the Jews!"* And they spit on Yeshua, and took the reed, and hit the Christ on the head with it. And after they had mocked Yeshua, they took the robe off, and put the Christ's own clothing back on, and led the Christ away to be put to death.

Yeshua on the Cross

[32-37] And as they came out, they found someone by the name of Simon from Cyrene, and told him to carry the cross. And when they had come to a place called Golgotha, which means, *The Place of the Skull*, they offered the Christ sour wine mixed with a strong drug. But when Yeshua had tasted it, the Christ wouldn't drink it. And after putting Yeshua on a cross, they divided the clothes of the Christ, and placed bets on them: so that it would happen which was spoken by the great preacher, "They divided My clothes among them, and placed bets on them." And sitting down, they watched the Christ hanging there; And they put up over the Christ's head their accusation written, *"This is Yeshua, The Ruler of the Jews."*

Two Criminals

[38-49] Then there were two criminals being put to death on each side of Yeshua. And those who passed by hated the Christ, shaking their heads, and saying, *"You said that you could destroy the Place of Worship, and build it again in three days, so save yourself. If you're the Child of God, come down from the cross."* Also the leading priests were mocking the Christ, along with the religious leaders and elders, saying, *"You saved others;*

why can't You save Yourself. If You're the Ruler of Israel, come down from the cross right now, and we'll believe You. You trusted in God; let God set You free now, if God will have You," because Yeshua had said, "I am the Child of God." The two criminals also, which were put to death with the Christ, said the same.

Yeshua Dies on the Cross

[45-50] Now from noon till three o'clock it was dark everywhere. And about three o'clock Yeshua called out, saying, "Eli, Eli, lama sabachthani?" which means, "My God, My God, why have You left Me?" And some of those who stood there, when they heard that, said, "This One calls for Elijah." And suddenly one of them ran, and took a sponge, and filled it with sour wine, and put it on a reed, and gave the Christ a drink. Then the rest said, "Wait, let's see whether Elijah will come or not." And calling out again with a loud voice, the Christ gave up the Spirit.

[51-55] And at that very time the curtain in the Place of Worship was torn in two from the top to the bottom; and there was an earthquake that opened up the rocks; and the graves began to open; and many of those who had died came to life again, and after they had come to life again, came out of their graves and went into the Holy City of Jerusalem, appearing to many. Now when the guards who were watching Yeshua saw the earthquake, and what had happened, they were very afraid, and one of them said, "It's true, this was the Child of God."

The Christ Buried in a New Tomb

[55-61] And many women were there, watching from far off, who had followed Yeshua from Galilee, and had ministered to the Christ, among which was Mary Magdalene, and Mary, the mother of James and Joses, and Salome, the mother of James and John, the wife of Zebedee. And when the evening came, a rich person of Arimathaea, who was named Joseph, who was also a follower of Yeshua, went to Pilate, and begged for the body of the Christ. Then Pilate ordered the body to be given to him. And when Joseph had taken the body, and wrapped it in a clean linen cloth, he laid it in his own new tomb, which had been cut out of the rock; and a great stone was rolled in front of the door of the tomb, and then he left. And Mary Magdalene, and the other Mary, was sitting across from the tomb.

[62-66] Now the next day, which followed the day of the preparation, the leading priests and religious leaders came together to Pilate, saying, "Sir, we remember when Yeshua was still alive, that liar said, 'After three days I'll come to life again.' Order guards to watch the tomb until the third day, in case the followers come by night, and steal the body away, and say to the people, the Christ is alive from the dead: so the last lie will be worse than the first one." So Pilate answered, "You can stand guard: Go, and make it as safe as you can." So they went, and made sure the tomb was secure, sealing the stone, and standing guard.

The Women See the Risen Christ

28 [1-10] As Saturday night ended and it began to dawn on Sunday morning, Mary Magdalene and the other Mary came to see the tomb. And there was a great earthquake because the Angel of God came down from heaven, and rolled back the stone from the door, sitting on it. And the Angel's appearance was as bright as lightning, whose clothing was as white as snow: And the guards shook with fear, frozen stiff like the dead. And the angel said to the women, "Don't be afraid because I know that you're looking for Yeshua, who was put to death. But Yeshua isn't here because the Christ is alive, as was foretold. Come and see the place where the Christ lay. And go quickly, and tell the followers that the Christ has come back alive from the dead; Who's going to come to you in Galilee; where you'll see the Christ: Listen to what I've told you." And they went quickly from the tomb, fearful, but with great joy; and ran to bring word to the followers. And as they went to tell the followers, Yeshua met them, saying, "Hello!" And they came and worshipped the Christ holding Yeshua by the feet. Then Yeshua said, "Don't be afraid, but go and tell my followers that I am going into Galilee, and they'll see Me there."

The Guards Bribed

[11-15] Now when they were going, some of the guards came into the city, and told the leading priests everything that had happened. And when they were together with the elders, and had gotten their advice, they gave a large sum of money to the guards, telling them to say, "The followers came by night, and stole the body away while we slept." And they told them, "If this should come to the governor's ears, we'll prove it to him, and keep you safe." So they took the money, and did as they were told: and these words are commonly told among the Jews even today.

The Mission of the Followers

[16-20] Then the eleven followers went away into Galilee, up on a mountain where Yeshua had told them to go. And when they saw Yeshua, they worshipped the Christ: but some of them doubted. And Yeshua came and spoke to them, saying, "I've been given all power in heaven and in earth. So go, and make followers of all people, baptizing them in the Name of Yahweh God, and of Yeshua the Christ, and of the Holy Spirit: Teaching them to remember and do everything I've told you: And I am always with you, even to the end of time. So be it!"

The New Word According to Mark

John the Baptist

1 [1-8] This is the beginning of the New Word of Yeshua the Christ, the Child of God. As the Word says in the great preachers, *"I send my messenger before you, who will get Your way ready for You. The voice of one calling out in the countryside will get ready the way of Yahweh God, and make the way plain."* John baptized in the countryside, and preached the baptism of a changed life to save people from their sins. All of Judea, and those of Jerusalem, went out to John and were all baptized by him in the Jordan River, admitting their sins. Now John was clothed with camel's fur, and wore a leather belt around his waist; and ate locusts and wild honey. John preached, saying, *"Someone is coming after me who is greater than I am, the lace of whose shoes I am not even worthy to bend down and untie. Yes, I have baptized you with water: but the Christ will baptize you with the Holy Spirit."*

The Baptism of Yeshua

[9-13] At that time Yeshua came from Nazareth of Galilee, and was baptized by John in the Jordan River. As soon as Yeshua came up out of the water, John saw the heavens open up, and the Spirit of God coming down on the Christ like a dove. And a voice came from heaven, saying, *"You're My Child, who I love and I am so pleased with You."* Then suddenly the Spirit led Yeshua out into the countryside. Christ was there in the countryside forty days, being tempted by Satan; and was with the wild animals; and the angels ministered to the Christ.

Fishers of Others

[14-20] Now after John was put in prison, Yeshua came into Galilee, preaching the New Word of the realm of God saying, *"Now is the time, the realm of God is here: change your evil ways, and believe the New Word."* As the Christ walked by the sea of Galilee, Yeshua saw Simon and Andrew, who were brothers, throwing a net into the sea because they were fishers. So Yeshua said to them, *"Follow Me, and I'll make you fishers for people."* They suddenly left their nets, and followed along. And when they had gone a little farther, they saw James, the Child of Zebedee, and John his brother, who also were in a ship fixing their nets. And then the Christ called out to them: and they left their father, Zebedee, in the ship with the hired workers, and followed along.

Yeshua Casts Out Evil Spirits

[21-28] They went into Capernaum; and then on a Day of Worship, the Christ went in the Place of Worship, and began teaching. The people were amazed at the teachings of Yeshua, because the Christ taught them as One who had power, and not as the religious leaders. And there was someone full of evil spirits in their worship service, who called out, saying, *"Leave us alone; we don't want anything to do with you, Yeshua of Nazareth. Have you come to get rid of us? I know who you are, the Holy One of God."* And Yeshua scolded them, saying, *"Be quiet, and get out of him."* And when the evil spirits left the man, they called out with a loud voice, and came out of him. And everyone was amazed, so that they asked among themselves, *"What is this? What New Word is this? This person orders even the evil spirits with such power that even they obey."* And suddenly Yeshua became famous throughout the whole region around Galilee.

Peter's Mother-in Law Healed

[29-31] And then, when they had come out of the Place of Worship, Yeshua went in the house of Peter and Andrew, along with James and John. But Peter's wife's mother was sick with a fever, so they told the Christ about her. And the Christ came and took her by the hand and lifted her up; and suddenly the fever left her, and she served them all.

[32-34] And at evening, when the sun had set, they brought all that were diseased, and those who were overcome by evil spirits to the Christ. And the whole city gathered together at the door. And the Christ healed many that were sick of different diseases, and put out many evil spirits; and wouldn't let the evil spirits speak, because they knew that Yeshua was the Christ.

[35-39] And in the morning, getting up a long while before the day, the Christ went out to a solitary place to pray. And Simon and those who were with them followed after the Christ. And when they had found Yeshua, they said, all the others are looking for you. And the Christ answered, *"Let's go to the other towns, so that I can preach there also, because this is why I came."* And the Christ preached in their worship services throughout all Galilee, and put out many evil spirits.

A Leper Healed

[40-45] And someone who was a leper came, kneeling down, and begged the Christ saying, *"If you want to, you can make me well."* And Yeshua, with great care, reached out, and touched the person, saying, *"I do want to;*

get well." And as soon as the Christ had spoken, the leprosy disappeared, and the person was healed. Then the Christ clearly warned the person, and sent them away, saying, *"Don't tell anyone: but go and show yourself to the priest, and offer whatever Moses told you to for your healing, as a witness to them."* But that person went out, and told it to everyone, spreading it everywhere, so that Yeshua couldn't even go into the city openly anymore, but stayed out in countryside: and the people came to the Christ from everywhere.

A Paralyzed Person Walks
2 [1-12] They went to Capernaum again after a few days. Soon everyone found out the Christ was in the house, and quickly gathered together, so that there wasn't any room to get in, no, not even room at the door. So as the Christ preached the Word to them, four people came carrying a paralyzed person. And when they couldn't get near the Christ for the crowd, they tore open the roof where the Christ was: and when they had broken it up, they let down the bed with the paralyzed person in it. When Yeshua saw their faith, the Christ said to the one who was paralyzed, *"Child, your sins are forgiven you."* But there were some of the religious leaders sitting there, and questioning in their hearts, *"Why does this person speak disrespectfully of God? Who can forgive sins but God?"* And suddenly when the Christ's Spirit realized that they questioned it within themselves, Yeshua answered, *"Why do you question Me in your hearts? Is it easier to say to the paralyzed, Your sins are forgiven you; or to say, Get up, and pick up your bed, and walk? But so that you can know that I have the power on earth to forgive sins,* (the Christ said to the paralyzed,) *I tell you, get up, and pick up your bed, and go home."* So the paralyzed person got up quickly, picked up the bed, and walked out in front of them all. Everyone was so amazed, and praised God, saying, "We've never seen anything like this!"

Matthew Called
[13-17] And they went out again to the seashore; and the whole crowd followed along, and the Christ taught them. As they passed by, the Christ saw Matthew, son of Alphaeus, sitting where the taxes were collected, and said, *"Follow Me."* So Matthew got up and followed Yeshua. Then, as Yeshua was eating a meal in the home of Matthew, many tax collectors and sinners sat together with Yeshua and the followers because there were many, and they had all followed along. And when the religious leaders and the ministers from the religious sects saw them eat with tax collectors and sinners, they said to the followers, *"Why does Yeshua eat and drink with tax collectors and sinners?"* So Christ, who had heard it, answered, *"Those who are well don't need a doctor, but only those who are sick. I didn't come to those who are good, but to call sinners to change their ways."*

On Fasting
[18-22] The followers of John and of the religious leaders would go without food for religious reasons, so they came to ask, "Why do we, the followers of John, and the religious leaders go without food, but your followers don't?" And Yeshua answered, *"Can the friends of the bridal party go without food, while the bridal party is with them? As long as the bridal party is with them, they can't go without food. But the time will come, when the bridal party will be gone, and then they'll go without and pray at that time. No one sews a piece of new cloth on old clothes: or else the new piece that covered up the hole would shrink and tear the old, and the hole would be worse than before. And no one puts new wine into old bottles: or else the new wine would burst the bottles, spilling the wine, and breaking the bottles. New wine must be put into new bottles."*

Questions About the Seventh Day
[23-28] And then, as they went through the grain fields on a Day of Worship; the followers began to take the grain as they went along. And the religious leaders said, "Why do they do what isn't right to do on a Day of Worship?" And the Christ answered, *"Haven't you ever read what David and those who were with him did, when they had need, and were hungry? How they went into the House of God in the days of Abiathar, the leading priest, and ate the bread, which isn't right for anyone to eat but the priests?"* And the Christ said, *"The Seventh Day was made for people, and not people for the Seventh Day: So I have power over the Seventh Day also."*

A Plan to Kill the Christ
3 [1-6] Then they came again into the Place of Worship; and there was someone there who had a deformed hand. They watched to see whether Yeshua would heal the person on a Day of Worship; because they wanted something with which to accuse the Christ. And the Christ said to the person who had the deformed hand, *"Stand up."* And Yeshua asked, *"Is it right to do good on Days of Worship, or to do evil? To save life, or to kill?"* But they didn't say anything. And when the Christ had looked around at them all with anger, being upset by their uncaring hearts, the Christ said to the person, *"Stretch out your hand."* And the person stretched it out: and the hand was made well just like the other one. And the religious leaders went out, and quickly made a plan against Yeshua with Herod's people, deciding how to kill the Christ.

93

Yeshua Heals the People

[7-12] So Yeshua left with the followers to go to the sea. A great crowd from Galilee followed along, with those from Judea, Jerusalem, Idumaea, from beyond Jordan; and those around Tyre and Sidon also. So the crowd came out to Yeshua, when they had heard what great things the Christ did. So Christ spoke to the followers, telling them that a small ship should wait near by, in case the crowd began to overtake them. Yeshua had healed many; and all those who were sick crowded forward to try to touch the Christ. Whenever evil spirits came near the Christ, they bowed down, calling out, *"You're the Child of God."* So Christ strictly told them not to say that.

The Twelve Sent Out

[13-21] And the Christ went up on a mountain, calling the people to come up one at a time. Then whoever the Christ wanted came up. Later, Yeshua set apart twelve followers, to come along, and sent them out to preach, and gave them the power to heal sicknesses, and to put out evil spirits: Simon, who was called Peter; James, the son of Zebedee, and John, the brother of James, who they nicknamed Boanerges, which means the sons of thunder: Andrew, Philip, Bartholomew, Matthew, Thomas, James, the son of Alphaeus, Thaddaeus, Simon, from Canaan, and Judas Iscariot, who later handed over the Christ. Then they all went into a house, but the crowd came together again, so that they couldn't even eat a meal. When Yeshua's own family heard it, they went out to take the Christ, because they thought that Yeshua was crazy.

The Unforgiveable Sin

[22-30] And the religious leaders who came down from Jerusalem said, *"The devil is in this One, and by the ruler of the evil spirits, this One puts out evil spirits."* And the Christ called them over, saying to them, using stories, *"How can Satan put out Satan? If a country is divided against itself, that country won't stand. And if a house is divided against itself, that house won't stand. And if Satan comes against Satan, and is divided, then the devil won't stand and will be destroyed. No one can come into a strong person's house, and take their things, unless they first tie up the strong person; and then they'll take their things. The truth is, all sins will be forgiven humanity, even being disrespectful to God, no matter how they dishonor and disrespect God: But whoever rejects the Holy Spirit will never have forgiveness, but is in danger of being damned forever."* The Christ had said this because they said that Yeshua had an evil spirit.

The Family of Christ

[31-35] Then Yeshua's family came, and standing outside, they sent word to the Christ to come there. And the crowd sat around Yeshua, so someone said, your family is outside looking for you. And Yeshua answered, *"Who is My family?"* And the Christ looked around at those who sat around, saying, *"See, this is My family! Whoever does the will of God is My family."*

Four Kinds of Earth

4 [1-9] And then the Christ began to teach on the seashore again, and a great crowd gathered around, so that they had to get into a ship, and sit in the sea; and the whole crowd was on the seashore. Christ taught them many things through stories, saying to them in these teachings, *"Listen carefully; a farmer went out to plant: And then, as the farmer planted, some seeds fell beside the rows, and the birds of the air came and ate it up. And some fell on stony ground, where it didn't have much earth; and it sprang up quickly, because it wasn't very deep: But when the sun came up, it scorched because the root wasn't deep enough, and wilted away. And some fell among thorns, and the thorns grew up, and choked them, and they made no fruit. And others fell on good ground, and made fruit that grew big and increased; and made more fruit, some thirty times as much, and some sixty times as much, and some a hundred times as much."* And the Christ said, *"If anyone will accept this, let them accept it."*

[10-13] And when they were alone, the twelve and a few other followers asked the Christ about the story. And Yeshua answered, *"You're allowed to know the secrets of the realm of God: but to those who are outside of it, all this is told in stories: So that seeing they will see, but not realize what they see; and hearing they will hear, but not understand what they hear; in case they at some time would change their ways, and their sins be forgiven them."* Then Yeshua said, *"Don't you understand this story? Then how will you ever understand all the rest of My stories?*

[14-20] *The farmer is the one who spreads the New Word. And the ones that fell beside the rows are those who the Word was planted in; but when they heard it, Satan came quickly, and took the Word away that was planted in their hearts. And the ones which are planted on stony ground are those who, when they heard the Word, gladly accepted it at first; But they have no root in themselves, and so only last for a little while: and later, when suffering or discrimination comes up for the Word's sake, they're suddenly offended. And the ones who are planted among thorns are those who hear the Word, but the worries of this world, and the falseness of riches, and the wants of other things are let in, and choke the Word out, and it becomes unfruitful. And those who are planted on good ground are the ones who hear the Word, and accept it, and make fruit, some thirty times as much, some sixty times as much, and some a hundred times as much."*

[21-29] Then Christ Yeshua said, *"Is a candle brought out only to be put somewhere it can't be seen? No, it's to be set on a candle holder. There isn't anything hid, which won't become plain; nor anything kept secret, that won't become known. If anyone will accept this, let them accept it."* Then Yeshua said, *"Be sure to use what you hear: because with whatever measure you use it, it'll be measured to you again. To you that hear, that much more will be given to you. Whoever uses what they have, more will be given to them: and whoever doesn't use what they have, even what they have will be taken from them."* And then Yeshua said, *"So the realm of God is like when someone puts seed in the ground; But while they are going to sleep at night and awaking by day, the seed springs up and grows, without anyone knowing how. The earth makes fruit by itself; first the leaf, then the stalk, after that the grain. But when the fruit's ripe, the crop is harvested quickly, because the fruit's ready."*

[30-36] And then the Christ asked, *"To what can we compare the realm of God? Or with what story can we compare it? It's like a grain of mustard seed, which, when it's planted in the earth, is the smallest of all the seeds in the earth: But when it's planted, it grows up, and gets bigger than all the other herbs, and grows big branches; so that the birds of the air can nest under its shadow."* And Yeshua spoke the New Word to them with many stories like this, as they were able to understand it. Yeshua never spoke to them without a story: but when the Christ was alone with the followers, everything was explained to them.

Christ Calms the Sea

[35-41] And this same day, when the evening came, the Christ said, *"Let's go over to the other side."* And when Yeshua had sent the crowd away, they took the Christ over in the ship. And there were other little ships with them, too. Then a great windstorm came up, and the waves beat so hard into the ship, that it began to fill up. And the Christ was in the back of the ship, sleeping on a pillow, so they awoke Yeshua, saying, *"Christ, don't you care if we drown?"* And the Christ got up, and ordered the wind and the sea, saying, "Calm down and be still!" And suddenly the wind stopped, and a great calm came. And the Christ said to them, *"Why are you so afraid? Don't you have any faith?"* And they were very afraid, saying to one another, *"What kind of person is this, who even the wind and the sea obey?"*

Wild Man Healed

5 [1-10] Then they came over to the other side of the sea, into the country of the Gadarenes. And when they came out of the ship, suddenly someone who lived among the tombs and had an evil spirit came out of the tombs and met them. No one could hold him, no, not even with chains. He had been chained up often with shackles and chains, and the chains had been taken off by him, and the shackles broken in pieces. He was so wild, no one could tame him. Night and day, he stayed in the mountains, and in the tombs, crying and cutting himself with stones. But when he saw Yeshua still far off, he ran and bowed down to the Christ, and called out with a loud voice, saying, *"What do I have to do with you, Yeshua, Child of the Most High God? I beg you by God, not to make me suffer."* And the Christ said, *"Come out of this person, you evil spirit."* And Yeshua asked, *"What is your name?"* And the evil spirit said, *"My Name is Legion because there are many of us."* And they begged the Christ not to send them away out of the country.

[11-14] Now near the mountains there was a large herd of pigs feeding. So all the evil spirits begged the Christ, saying, *"Let us go into the pigs, and stay in them."* So Yeshua the Christ said that they could. And the evil spirits went out of the man, and into the pigs: and the whole herd ran fiercely over a cliff into the sea, (it was about two thousand;) and was drowned in the sea. And those who fed the pigs ran away, and told the story all over the countryside and in the city. And the people went out to see what it was that happened.

[15-20] And they came to Yeshua, and saw the one who had the legion of evil spirits, sitting clothed, and in his right mind: and they were very afraid. And those who saw it told them what happened to the one who was overcome by the evil spirit, and also what happened to the pigs. And the people began to beg the Christ to leave out of their coasts. And when they went back to the ship, the one who had been overcome by the evil spirit begged to come with them. But Yeshua wouldn't let him, saying, *"Go home to your friends, and tell them what great things God has done for you, and how God has had compassion on you."* And he went, and began to tell the great things Yeshua had done for him in Decapolis: and all the others were amazed.

A Little Girl and a Woman Healed

[21-24] And when Yeshua was over on the other side again, a great many people gathered to them: and they were near the sea. Then when one of the leaders of the places of worship, Jairus by name, saw them, he fell at Yeshua's feet, and begged the Christ, saying, *"My little daughter is at the point of death: I beg you come and lay your hands on her, so that she'll be healed; and she'll live."* And Yeshua went with him; with many people following along, and pushing them.

[25-34] And a certain woman, who had a flow of blood for twelve years, and had let many doctors do many things to her, and had spent everything she had, but wasn't any better, and instead grew worse, who had heard of Yeshua, came up behind the Christ in the crowd, and touched the Christ's clothing, thinking to herself, *"If I can

only touch the clothes of the Christ, I'll get well." And suddenly the flow of her blood was stopped; and she felt in her body that she was healed. And Yeshua, suddenly knowing in the Spirit that power had gone out, turned around to the crowd, saying, "Who touched my clothes?" And the followers said, "You see the crowd pushing behind you, and you ask, 'Who touched me?'" And the Christ looked around to see who had done it. And the woman fearing and trembling, knowing what happened to her, came and bowed down in front of the Christ, and told them the truth of it all. And the Christ said to her, "Daughter, your faith has made you well; go in peace, and be free of your disease."

[35-43] While the Christ was speaking, someone came from the house of Jairus, who said, "Your daughter is dead: don't bother the Christ any more." As soon as Yeshua heard what was said, the Christ said to Jairus, "Don't be afraid, only believe." And no one was allowed to follow them, but Peter, James, and John, his brother. And they came to the house of Jairus, and saw the disorder, and those who were mourning and crying. And when they came in, the Christ asked, "Why are you so upset, and crying? The girl isn't dead, but only sleeping." And they laughed disrespectfully at the Christ. But when Yeshua had put them all out, the Christ took the parents of the girl, and those who were with them, and went in where the girl was lying. And Yeshua took the girl by the hand saying to her, "Talitha cumi; which is to say, Young lady, I tell you to get up." And suddenly the girl got up and walked around, who was twelve years old. And everyone was very amazed. And the Christ told them clearly to tell no one; and told them to give her something to eat.

Yeshua is Rejected by Friends and Family

6 [1-6] When Yeshua and the followers left from there, they went back to Yeshua's home town. And when a Day of Worship came, Yeshua began to teach in the Place of Worship: and many who were listening were amazed, saying, "Where has Yeshua gotten this wisdom from? And what gift has been given to Yeshua, who is doing all these amazing things?" Isn't this the carpenter, the Child of Mary? Aren't James, Joses, Judah, Simon, and the sisters all Yeshua's siblings?" And everyone was offended at the Christ. But Yeshua said, "A great preacher isn't without honor, except in their own country, and among their own kin, and in their own home." And the Christ couldn't do any powerful work's there, except laying hands on a few sick folk, and healing them. And the Christ was amazed because of their unbelief. So Yeshua went around the towns, teaching.

The Twelve Sent Out

[7-11] And the Christ called the twelve, and began to send them out two by two; and gave them power over evil spirits; And told them to take nothing for their journey, except only a walking stick, with no backpack, no food, and no money in their bag, but to wear sandals, and not to put on two coats. And the Christ said, "Whatever town you go to, come into a house and stay there till you leave from that place. And whoever won't accept you, nor listen to you, when you leave there, shake the dust off of your feet for a witness against them. The truth is; it'll be better for Sodom and Gomorrah in the day of judgment, than for that city."

John the Baptist Beheaded

[12-20] And they went out, and preached to the people to change their evil ways. And they put out many evil spirits, and anointed many that were sick with oil, and healed them. And Herod, the ruler, had heard of Yeshua; (for the Christ's name was famous:) so he said that John the Baptist had come back to life, and that is why the Christ could do all those amazing things. Others said that the Christ was Elijah. And others said that Yeshua was a great preacher, or like one of the great preachers. But when Herod heard it, he said, "It's John, who I beheaded and has come back to life." Herod himself had sent out and taken John, and put him in prison for Herodias' sake, his brother Philip's wife, because he had married her. John had said to Herod, 'It isn't right for you to have your brother's wife." So Herodias resented John, and would have killed him; but she couldn't, because Herod respected John, knowing that he was a good person and a holy one, and watched him; and when he heard John, he did many things, and heard him gladly.

[21-29] And a day came, when Herod made a supper on his birthday to those of high standing, the highest ranking captains, and leading people of Galilee; And when the daughter of Herodias came in and danced, pleasing Herod and everyone there, the ruler said to the girl, "Ask me for whatever you want, and I'll give it you." And he swore to her, "Whatever you ask me for, I'll give it to you, even to half of my country." So she went out, saying to her mother, "What should I ask for?" And she conveniently took the opportunity saying, "The head of John the Baptist." And she came in suddenly to the ruler, saying, "I want you to give me the head of John the Baptist on a plate." And the ruler was very sorry; but because he had promised, and because of all those who were there, he wouldn't tell her no. So suddenly, the ruler sent an executioner, and ordered the head to be brought: so he went and beheaded John in the prison, and brought his head on a plate, and gave it to the girl: and the girl gave it to her mother. And when the followers heard it, they came and took the body, and laid it in a tomb.

Christ Feeds Five Thousand

[30-34] Then the followers came back together to Yeshua, and told the Christ everything, both what they had done, and what they had taught. And the Christ answered, *"Come alone into the countryside, and rest a while,"* because many people were coming and going, and they hadn't even had time to eat. So they secretly went into a deserted place by ship. But all the people saw them leaving, and many knew the Christ, and ran there on foot from all the cities, and went to them, and came together to where the Christ was. And when Yeshua came out, and saw many people, the Christ had compassion on them, because they were like animals without a keeper. So the Christ began to teach them many things.

[35-40] And when the day was almost over, the followers came, saying, *"This is a deserted place, and the day is almost over: Send them away, so they can go into the countryside and towns around here, to buy food, because they don't have anything to eat."* But Yeshua answered them, *"You feed them."* And they said, *"It would take two hundred days of work worth of bread to feed them all!"* So Yeshua answered, *"How many loaves do you have? Go and see."* And when they knew, they said, *"Five, and two fish."* And the Christ told them to make everyone sit down in large groups on the grass, which was green because it was early spring. And they sat down in groups of hundreds and fifties.

[41-46] And when the Christ had taken the five loaves and the two fish, looking up to heaven, Yeshua blessed it, and broke the loaves, and gave them to the followers to give to the people; and the two fish Yeshua divided between them all. And everyone ate until they were full. And they took up twelve baskets full of bread and fish scraps. There were about five thousand people. Then suddenly, Yeshua made the followers get in the ship, and go to the other side to Bethsaida, while sending away the people. And after sending them all away, the Christ went up on a mountain to pray.

Christ Walks on the Water

[47-52] And when evening came, the ship was in the middle of the sea, and the Christ was alone on the land. And Yeshua saw them having a hard time rowing because the wind was coming against them. So about 3 o'clock in the morning, in the middle of the night, the Christ came to them, walking on the sea, intending to pass by them. But when they saw the Christ walking on the sea, they thought it was a ghost, and screamed, and were very scared. And suddenly, Yeshua answered, *"Calm down, it's Me; Don't be afraid."* And when the Christ climbed up into the ship with them, the wind stopped. They were more amazed than ever, and wondered greatly about it. They didn't even think about the miracle of the loaves because they couldn't believe what had just happened.

[53-56] And when they had crossed over, they came into the land of Gennesaret, and came to the shore. And when they had come out of the ship, suddenly everyone knew it was the Christ, and ran throughout that whole region all around, and began to bring out all those that were sick in beds to where they had heard that the Christ was. And wherever Yeshua went, whether in towns, cities, or the country, they laid the sick in the streets, and begged to touch the Christ, even if only the edge of the Christ's clothing. And whoever touched the Christ got well.

The Religious Leaders Question the Christ

7 [1-13] Then some of the religious sects and some of the religious leaders came to Yeshua from Jerusalem. And when they saw some of the followers eat without washing their hands, they found fault with them. The religious leaders and all the rest of the Jews won't eat, unless they wash their hands first, keeping the way of life of the elders. And when they come from the shopping center, they won't eat unless they wash up first. And they have many other ways of life, which they've come to keep, such as washing dishes and tables. Then the religious leaders and the ministers from the religious sects asked Yeshua, *"Why don't your followers live by the way of life of the elders, but instead, don't wash their hands?"* The Christ answered them, *"Isaiah said rightly of you fakes, as the Word says, which was given ahead of time. These people honor me with their words, but their hearts are far from me. But their worship is empty, teaching the teachings of humanity as the Teachings of God. Ignoring the Teachings of God, you keep the way of life of humanity, such as washing dishes: and many other things like this."* And Yeshua said, *"You reject the Law of God full well, so that you can keep your own way of life. Moses said, Honor your parents; And whoever curses their parents, let them be put to death. But you say they won't be punished if someone says to their parents, It's a gift to God, whatever you might have gotten from me. So you don't let them do what they should for their parents any more, which makes the Word of God of no effect by this way of life, which you've taught: and many other things like this that you do."*

[14-23] And when the Christ had called all the people to come, Yeshua said, *"Listen carefully to Me, everyone of you, and understand: There isn't anything from outside of someone, that coming into them can make them filthy. It's the things which come out of them, which make the person filthy. If anyone will accept this, let them accept it."* And when the Christ went in the house from the people, the followers asked about this teaching. And Yeshua answered them, *"Do you, too, still not understand? Don't you realize that whatever goes into a person from outside, it can't make them filthy; because it doesn't go into their heart, but into the belly, and goes out into the waste, taking away everything?"* And then the Christ said, *"What comes out of a person is what makes the*

person filthy. It's from within, out of the person's heart, that evil thoughts, unfaithfulness, sexual sins, murders, thefts, greed, evil, lies, loose living, evil imaginations, disrespect for God, pride, and stupidity come: All these evil things come from within, and make the person filthy."

A Greek Woman's Daughter Healed
[24-30] And from there Yeshua got up, and went into the borders of Tyre and Sidon, and went in a house, and didn't want anyone to know it: but the Christ couldn't be hid. Then a woman, whose young daughter had an evil spirit, heard of the Christ, and came and fell at Yeshua's feet. The woman was a Greek, a Syrophenician by nation; and she begged the Christ to make the evil spirit go out of her daughter. But Yeshua said to her, "The children must be fed first. It isn't right to take the children's food, and give it to the dogs." But she answered, "Yes, Christ: but still the little dogs eat of the children's crumbs under the table." And the Christ said to her, "Because you've said this, go; the evil spirit has gone out of your daughter." And when she came to her house, she found that the evil spirit was gone, and her daughter was lying quietly on the bed.

A Deaf and Dumb Person Healed
[31-37] And again, leaving from the coasts of Tyre and Sidon, they came to the sea of Galilee, in the middle of the coasts of Decapolis. And someone brought to the Christ a person who was deaf, and had a problem with their speech; and they begged the Christ to lay hands on them. So the Christ took the one who couldn't hear aside from the crowd, and put fingers into the person's ears, and then the Christ spit, and touched the person's tongue; And looking up to heaven, the Christ breathed deeply, saying, "Ephphatha," that is, "Open up." And suddenly the person's ears began to hear, and the speech problem was healed, and the person spoke clearly. And the Christ told them not to tell anyone: but the more Yeshua told them not to, the more they told it; And everyone was more amazed than ever, saying, "Everything the Christ has done is good. The Christ has made both those who are deaf to hear again, and the dumb to speak again."

Christ Feeds Four Thousand
8 [1-9] The crowd being very great at that time, and having nothing to eat, Yeshua called the followers, saying to them, "I am concerned about the crowd, because they've been with me for three days now, and don't have anything to eat: And if I send them away hungry to their own homes, they'll faint on the way because many came from far away." And the followers answered, "How can anyone satisfy all these people with food out here in the countryside?" And the Christ asked them, "How many loaves do you have?" And they answered, "Seven." Then the Christ told the people to sit down on the ground and took the seven loaves, and gave thanks, and broke it, and gave it to the followers to give to them. Then they gave it to the people. And they had a few small fish, so the Christ blessed it, and told the followers to give it to them also. So everyone ate until they were full: and the followers took up seven baskets of scraps. And those who had eaten were about four thousand. Then the Christ sent them away.

Beware of the Teachings of Religious Sects
[10-13] And quickly the Christ went in a ship with the followers, and came into parts of Dalmanutha. And the religious leaders came out, and began to question the Christ, looking for a sign from heaven, to tempt Yeshua. And the Christ breathed deeply in the spirit, saying, "Why do these people look for a sign? The truth is; no sign will be given to this people." And the Christ left them, and going into the ship again, went to the other side.

[14-21] Now the followers had forgotten to take bread, and they didn't have more than one loaf with them in the ship. Then Christ told them, saying, "Be careful of the leaven of the religious leaders, and of the leaven of the ruler." And they argued among themselves, saying, "It's because we don't have any bread." And when Yeshua realized it, the Christ said, "Why are you arguing about not having any bread? Don't you realize, nor still understand? Is your heart still full of doubt? You have eyes, don't you see? And you have ears, don't you hear? And don't you remember when I broke the five loaves among five thousand, how many baskets full of scraps you picked up?" They answered, "Twelve." "And when I broke the seven among four thousand, how many baskets full of scraps you picked up? And they said, "Seven." Then the Christ said, "Then how is it possible that you still don't understand?"

A Blind Person Sees
[22-26] And when they got to Bethsaida; a blind person was brought to Yeshua, and begged to be touched by the Christ. So Yeshua took the one who was blind by the hand and led them out of the town; and when the Christ had spit on the person's eyes, and laid hands on them, asked if the person saw anything. And they looked up, saying, "I see people as trees, walking." After that the Christ laid hands on the person's eyes again, and told them to look up, and then that person was healed, and saw everything clearly. And the Christ sent them home, saying, "Don't go into the town, nor tell anyone in the town."

Yeshua is the Christ

[27-33] And Yeshua went with the followers, into the towns of Caesarea Philippi: and on the way asked the followers, *"Who do other people say that I am?"* And they answered, *"John the Baptist: but some say, Elijah; and others, one of the great preachers."* So the Christ asked, *"But who do you say that I am?"* And Peter answered, *"You're the Christ."* And Yeshua told them not to tell this to anyone. Then Yeshua began to tell them, saying, *"I must suffer many things, and be rejected by the elders, the leading priests, and religious leaders, and be killed, and after three days I'll come to life again."* And the Christ told them this openly. But Peter took the Christ aside, and began to argue about it. But the Christ turned around and looked on the followers, and scolded Peter, saying, *"Leave Me alone, Satan, because you don't want what God wants, but what human beings want."*

Carry Your Own Cross and Follow Me

[34-38] And later, when Yeshua had called the followers and the rest of the people to come also, the Christ said, *"Whoever wants to follow Me, has to forget what they want, and carry their own cross, and follow Me. Whoever wants to save their life will lose it; but whoever is willing to lose their life for My sake and the New Word's sake, they'll save it. What good will it do someone, if they get everything they want in this life, and lose their own soul? Or what wouldn't someone give up in exchange for their soul? So whoever is ashamed of Me and of My Words in the unfaithful and sinful people of this time; I'll be ashamed of them also, when I come in the victory of God with the holy angels."*

9 [1] Then Yeshua said, *"The truth is, that some of those who are standing here, won't taste of death, till they've seen the realm of God come with power."*

Elijah and Moses Appear with the Christ

[2-13] And after six days Yeshua took Peter, James, and John, and led them up on a high mountain alone by themselves. Then the Christ was suddenly changed right in front of them. And the Christ's clothing was shining brightly, as white as snow; like no cleaner on earth can whiten them. And Elijah and Moses appeared to them: and they were talking with Yeshua. And Peter said to Yeshua, *"Christ, it's good that we're here with you. Let's make three memorial stones; one for you, one for Moses, and one for Elijah."* He didn't know what to say because they were very afraid. Then a cloud overshadowed them, and a voice came out of the cloud, saying, *"This is My Child, who I love: Listen to Yeshua."* And suddenly, when they looked around, they saw no one but Yeshua with them anymore. And as they came down from the mountain, Yeshua told them, *"Don't tell anyone what you've seen, till I've come to life again from the dead."* And they kept those words to themselves, questioning one another about what the Christ meant by coming to life again from the dead. And they asked the Christ, saying, *"Why do the religious leaders say that Elijah must come first?"* And Yeshua told them, *"The truth is, Elijah will come first, and explain everything; and tell what the Word says of Me, that I must suffer many things, and become of no importance. But I tell you that Elijah has already come, and they did to him whatever they wanted to, as the Word says of him."*

An Only Child Healed from Seizures

[14-19] And when Yeshua came back to the followers, the Christ saw a great crowd around them, and the religious leaders arguing with them. And when all the people saw the Christ, they were very excited, and suddenly ran to greet Yeshua. Christ asked the religious leaders, *"What are you arguing with them about?"* And someone in the crowd answered, *"Christ, I've brought You my child, who is taken with an evil spirit and can't speak; And whenever it overcomes my child with seizures, the child foams at the mouth, and clenches his teeth, and faints. I spoke to your followers and asked them to put it out; but they couldn't."* So the Christ answered, saying, *"You faithless people, how long must I be with you? How long do I have to put up with you? Bring the child to Me."*

[20-27] And when they brought the child to Yeshua, suddenly, the spirit overcame him; and threw him down, and the child wallowed on the ground foaming at the mouth. And Yeshua asked the child's parent, *"How long ago was it since this began to happen?"* And he answered, *"Since he was a young child. And often it has put the child into the fire, and into the water, and almost killed him: but if you can do anything, have compassion on us, and help us."* So Yeshua said, *"If you believe, everything is possible for those who believe."* And suddenly, the parent of the child cried out with tears, saying, *"Christ, I do believe; but help my unbelief."* When Yeshua saw that the people came running together, the Christ took control over the evil spirit, saying to it, *"You dumb and deaf spirit, I order you to come out of this child, and don't come into him anymore."* And the spirit cried, and struggled very much, and came out of the child: and the child was like a dead person; so that many said, *"The child is dead."* But Yeshua took the child by the hand and lifted him up; and the child got up.

[28-29] And when they came into the house, the followers privately asked, *"Why couldn't we put the spirit out?"* And the Christ answered, *"The only way this kind will go out is by willingly going without food to pray."*

The Death of Christ Foretold

[30-37] And they left there, and went through Galilee; but the Christ didn't want anyone to know it. And Yeshua said to the followers, *"I'll be given into the hands of others, and they'll kill Me; and after I'm killed, I'll come to life again on the third day."* But they didn't understand what the Christ told them, and were afraid to ask about it. Then they went to Capernaum. The Christ asked them, while they were in the house, *"What was it that you argued about among yourselves on the way?"* But they didn't say anything because on the way they had argued among themselves about who would be the greatest of them. And the Christ sat down, and called the twelve, saying to them, *"If anyone wants to be first, that one will be last of all, and will work for everyone."* And Yeshua picked up a child, and set the child in the middle of them: saying to them, *"Whoever accepts one child like this in My Name, accepts Me: and whoever accepts Me, accepts not only Me, but the One who sent Me."*

Punishment will come to Those who hurt Little Ones

[38-50] And John said to Yeshua, "Christ, we saw someone putting out evil spirits in Your Name, but they don't follow along with us, so we told them to stop." But Yeshua said, *"Don't stop them because there's no one who does a miracle in My Name, who can lightly speak evil of Me. Whoever isn't against us is with us. And whoever gives you a cup of water to drink in My Name, because you belong to Christ, the truth is, they'll certainly get their reward. But whoever hurts one of these little ones who believe in Me and causes them to loose faith, it would be better for that person to have a large stone hung around their neck, and be drowned in the sea. So if your hand offends you, don't use it as if it was cut off: It's better for you to live disabled, than having two hands and go to Hell, to the everlasting fire, where the worms never die, and the fire never goes out. And if your foot offends you, don't use it as if it was cut off: It's better for you to live disabled, than have two feet to be put into Hell, to the everlasting fire: where the worms never die, and the fire never goes out. And if your eye offends you, don't use it as if it was put out: It's better for you to come into the realm of God disabled, than having two eyes and be put into the Hell fire: where the worms never die, and the fire never goes out. Everyone will be tested with fire, and every sacrifice will be flavored with salt. Salt is good: but if the salt has no flavor, what will you season it with? So have the flavor of goodness in yourselves, and have peace with one another."*

On Divorce and Remarriage

10 [1-9] And they left there, and went into the coasts of Judea by the far side of the Jordan. The people came to the Christ again there; who taught them, as usual. And the religious leaders came to tempt the Christ, and asked Yeshua, *"Is it right for someone to divorce their spouse?"* And the Christ answered them, *"What did Moses tell you?"* And they said, *"Moses allowed us to write a writ of divorcement, and to divorce."* So Yeshua answered them, *"Moses wrote you this principle because of your unforgiving hearts. But from the beginning of creation God made humanity male and female. And because of this, they're to leave their parents, and come together in marriage; And the two of them becomes as one body: so that they're not two anymore, but are as one body. So whoever God has put together, no one should separate."*

[10-12] And later in the house the followers asked the Christ again about the same thing. And Yeshua answered, *"If a man divorces his wife, and marries another, he sins sexually against her. And if a woman divorces her husband and is married to another, she takes part in sexual sin, as well."*

Let the Children Come

[13-16] And the people brought young children to the Christ, hoping that the Christ would bless them, but the followers scolded those that brought them. Yeshua saw it, and was greatly displeased, saying to them, *"Let the little children come to Me, and don't stop them, because the realm of God is full of little ones like these. The truth is, whoever won't come to the realm of God with undoubting faith as a little child, they won't come in."* And the Christ picked them up, laid hands on them, and blessed them.

The Rich Young Person

[17-22] And when they had gone out into the way, someone came running, and kneeled down, asking, "Good Christ, what can I do to get everlasting life?" And Yeshua said, *"Why do you call Me good? No one is good but God. You know God's teachings, Don't do any sexual sin, Don't kill, Don't steal, Don't lie about someone, don't cheat, Honor your parents."* And the young person answered, "Christ, I have done all this from my youth up." Then Yeshua lovingly looked at the young person, and said, *"There's only one thing that you lack: go and sell whatever you've got, and give to those who are poor, and you'll have wealth in heaven: then come, pick up your cross, and follow Me."* And the young person, who was very rich, was sad and went away grieved because of what the Christ had said.

[23-27] And Yeshua looked around, saying to the followers, *"Those, who have riches, will have a hard time coming into the realm of God!"* And the followers were amazed at these words. But Yeshua said again, *"Friends,*

it's very hard for those who trust in riches to come into the realm of God! It's easier for a camel to be completely unloaded and go through the eye of a needle, that is, the smallest gate, than for a rich person to come into the realm of God." And they were amazed more than ever, saying among themselves, "Then who can be saved?" And Yeshua looking on them said, "This may be impossible for human beings, but not with God, because everything is possible with God."

The Blessings of Those Who Follow Christ

[28-31] Then Peter said to Christ, "See; we've left everything, and have followed you." And Yeshua answered, "The truth is, there's no one that has left a house, or brothers, or sisters, or father, or mother, or spouse, or children, or lands for My sake, and the New Word's, that won't get a hundred times that much more now in this life, homes, brothers and sisters, parents and children, and lands, but not without suffering discrimination; and in the world to come everlasting life. But many that are first will be last; and the last will be first."

The Death of Christ Foretold Again

[32-34] And they were going up to Jerusalem and on the way, Yeshua went ahead of them: and as they followed, they were shocked and afraid, because the Christ took the twelve again, and began to tell them what things would happen, saying, "We're going up to Jerusalem; I'll be handed over to the leading priests there, and to the religious leaders. They'll accuse Me of being worthy of death, and will deliver Me to the Romans: And they'll mock and beat Me, and spit on Me, and will kill Me; but the third day I'll come to life again."

Being First Means to Serve All

[35-45] And James and John, the children of Zebedee, came, saying, "Christ, we want you to do us a favor." And the Christ answered, "What do you want Me to do for you?" So they said, "Let us sit one on your right side, and the other on your left, when you come in your victory." But Yeshua answered, "You don't know what you ask: can you go through what I have to go through? and suffer what I have to suffer?" And they said, "We can." And Yeshua answered, "You certainly will go through what I have to go through; and suffer as I do: But to sit beside Me isn't Mine to give; but it'll be given to those for whom it's prepared." And when the other ten heard it, they resented James and John. But Yeshua called them over, saying to them, "You know that those who rule over the other peoples use control over them; and their leaders use power over them. But it won't be like that among you: but whoever wants to be great among you, will be your minister. And whoever of you wants to be a leader, will work for everyone else, even as I didn't come to be ministered to, but to minister to others, and to give My life in order to pay the debts of many."

Blind Bartimaeus

[46-52] And they came to Jericho and as the Christ went out of Jericho with the followers and a great number of people, blind Bartimaeus, the child of Timaeus, sat beside the street begging. And when he heard that it was Yeshua of Nazareth, he began to cry out, and say, "Yeshua, Descendant of David, have mercy on me." And many told him to be quiet: but he called out a great deal more, "Descendant of David, have mercy on Me." And Yeshua stood still, and told him to be called. And they called the one who was blind, saying to him, "It's okay, get up; the Christ is calling for you." And tossing aside his outer clothing, he got up, and came to Yeshua. And Yeshua asked, "What do you want Me to do for you?" So the one who was blind said, "Christ, I want to see again." So Yeshua said, "Go now; your faith has made you well." And suddenly he could see again, and followed Yeshua on the way.

Yeshua Rides into Jerusalem on a Foal

11 [1-11] And when they came near Jerusalem, to Bethphage and Bethany, at the Mount of Olives, the Christ sent out two of the followers, and said, "Go into the next town now: and as soon as you go in it, you'll find a foal tied, in which no one has ever rode. Untie it, and bring it here. And if anyone asks you, "Why are you doing this?" say that "Yeshua the Christ needs it;" and they'll send it." And they left, and found the foal tied by the door outside in a place where two roads met; and they untied it. And certain of those who stood there asked, "Why are you untying the foal?" So they answered just as Yeshua had told them to: and so they let them go. And they brought the foal to Yeshua, and put their outer coats on it; and the Christ rode on it. And many spread their coats down on the road and others cut down palm branches off the trees, and spread them down on the road. And those who went ahead, and those who followed, called out, saying, "Save us! Blessed is the One who comes in the Name of Yahweh God! Blessed is the realm of God, the Heir of David, the One that comes in the Name of Yahweh God: Oh save us, Highest One." And Yeshua went into Jerusalem, and into the Place of Worship. Then after the Christ had looked around at everything, and when the evening had come, the Christ went out to Bethany with the twelve.

The Angry Christ

[12-14] And the next day, when they had come from Bethany, the Christ was hungry. So seeing a fig tree a little way off having leaves, the Christ came up to it, thinking that there might be fruit on it. And coming to it, the Christ didn't find anything but leaves on it because it wasn't time for the figs yet. So Yeshua said to it, *"No one will eat fruit from this tree ever again."* And the followers heard it.

[15-19] Then they came to Jerusalem. Yeshua went into the Place of Worship, and began to throw out all those who sold and bought in the Place of Worship, throwing over the tables of the bankers, and the seats of those who sold doves; and wouldn't let anyone carry anything through the Place of Worship. Christ said, *"Isn't it written, My house will be called the house of prayer by all nations? But you've made it a place for thieves."* And the religious leaders and leading priests heard it, and looked for a way to get rid of Yeshua, being afraid of the Christ, because all the people were so amazed at the Christ's teachings. And when evening came, they went out of the city.

[20-26] And in the morning, as they passed by it, they saw that the fig tree had dried up from the roots. And Peter, reminding them, said, *"Christ, the fig tree that you cursed has died."* And Yeshua answered, *"You must have faith in God, because the truth is, that whoever says to this mountain, "Move, and go into the sea;" and doesn't doubt in their heart, but believes that the things which they say will happen; whatever they say will happen. So I tell you, when you pray, whatever you want, believe that you'll get it, and you'll get just what you wanted. And when you stand praying, you must forgive, if you have something against someone, so that Yahweh, your God who is in heaven, can also forgive you your sins. But if you don't forgive, neither will your God who is in heaven forgive your sins."*

The Christ Questioned by the Religious Leaders

[27-33] And they came again to Jerusalem: and as they were walking into the Place of Worship, some of the leading priests came up to them, along with the religious leaders, and the elders, and asked the Christ, *"By what power do you do this? Who gave you the power to do it?"* And Yeshua answered them, *"I'll also ask you a question, and if you can answer me, then I'll tell you by what power I do this. The baptism of John, was it from heaven, or of human origin? Answer Me."* And they argued among themselves, saying, *"If we say, from heaven; Yeshua will say, 'Why didn't you believe him then?' But if we say, Of human origin; we fear the people because they all count John as a great preacher."* So they answered Yeshua, *"We don't know."* And Yeshua answered, *"Then neither will I tell you by what power I do this."*

The Farmer's Own Child Sent

12 [1-12] And Yeshua began again to speak to them by stories, saying, *"Someone planted a garden, and built a wall around it, and dug a place for the winepress, and built a guard tower, and rented it out to farmers, and went into a far country. At the end of the season the owner sent to the farmers a worker, to get some of the fruit of the garden from the farmers, who they caught and beat, and sent away empty-handed. Then the owner sent to them another worker; and they threw stones at this one, who they wounded in the head, and shamefully sent away. And again the owner sent another; and they killed that one, and many others; beating some, and killing some. So still having one child, the owner's own child who was greatly loved, the owner sent the heir at last to them also, saying, 'They'll respect my child.' But those farmers said among themselves, 'This is the heir; come, if we kill the heir, the inheritance will be ours.' And they took the heir out of the garden and killed the heir. So what will the owner of the garden do? The owner will come and kill the farmers, and will give the garden to others. Haven't you read this Word: The stone which the builders rejected has become the first cornerstone: This was God's doing and it's amazing in our eyes?"* And they looked for a way to take Yeshua prisoner, but were afraid of the people because they knew that the Christ had told the story about them. Then Christ left them, and went away.

On Paying Taxes and Tithes

[13-17] Then they sent to the Christ some of the religious leaders and some of Herod's people, to try to find fault in the Christ's words. And when they had come, they said to Yeshua, *"Christ, we know that you're honest, and don't care what anyone thinks because you don't consider what others say, but teach the way of God in truth: Is it right to pay taxes to the ruling government, or not? Do we pay it or not?"* But the Christ, knowing they were trying to find some fault, answered, *"Why do you try to tempt Me? Bring Me a coin, so that I can see it."* And they gave a coin to Yeshua. Then the Christ asked, *"Whose picture and name is this?"* And they said, "The ruler's." Then Yeshua said, *"Then pay your taxes to the government and give to God the part of your money that belongs to God."* And they were amazed at that answer.

No Sexuality in the Afterlife

[18-27] Then some of the religious sects came, which say no one will come to life again; and asked, "Christ, Moses wrote to us, if someone dies, and leaves their wife behind without children, that another would take their wife, and give her children. Now there were seven people: and the first took a wife, and dying left no children. And the second took her, and died, without leaving any children: and the third the same. And all seven had her, and left no children: last of all the woman died also. When we come to life again in the afterlife, whose wife will she be, because all seven had her for a wife? And Yeshua answered, *"You're wrong, because you don't know the Word, nor the power of God. When we come to life from the dead, we won't be sexual and live in marriage; but are neither male nor female, as the angels are in heaven. And speaking of the dead coming to life again: haven't you read in the book of Moses, how God spoke in the bush, saying, 'I am the God of Abraham, and the God of Isaac, and the God of Jacob?' God isn't the God of the dead, but the God of the living: so you're very wrong."*

[28-34] And one of the religious leaders came up, and having heard them discussing it, and perceiving that the Christ had answered them well, asked the Christ, *"Which is the most important rule of all?"* And Yeshua answered, *"The most important of all the rules is, 'Hear, Oh Israel; God, our God, is One God: Love Yahweh, your God with all your spirit, and with all your soul, and with all your mind, and with all your strength:' this is the first rule. And the second is like it, namely this, 'Love others as yourself.' There's no other rule greater than these."* And the religious leader said, "You've answered well, Christ, You've said the truth because there's One God; and there's no other god but Yahweh, our God: And to love God with all the spirit, and with all the understanding, and with all the soul, and with all the strength, and to love others as yourself, is more than all the offerings and sacrifices one could give." And when Yeshua saw that he had answered carefully, the Christ said, *"You aren't far from the realm of God."* And no one dared to ask Yeshua any more questions after that.

Christ is David's Descendant

[35-37] While teaching in the Place of Worship Yeshua asked, *"How can the religious leaders say that the Christ is the Descendant of David? If David himself said by the Holy Spirit, Yahweh God said to My Christ, sit beside Me, till I make those who come against you a place to rest Your feet. So David himself called the Christ, Christ; so how can the Christ be the descendant of David?"* And the common people gladly listened to Yeshua.

False Religious Leaders

[38-40] And the Christ taught them, saying, *"Beware of the religious leaders, which love to go around in impressive clothing, and love greetings in the shopping centers, and the best seats in the places of worship, and the best places at the dinners of religious celebrations: But who take what little money the poor death survivors have, and for a pretence make long prayers. They'll get the greater punishment."*

The Survivor's Small Coin

[41-44] And Yeshua sat next to the treasury, and watched how the people put money into the treasury. Many that were rich put in much. And there came a certain poor survivor, and she threw in two small coins. And the Christ called the followers over, saying to them, *"The truth is that this poor survivor has given more than anyone else who has given to the treasury, because all they did was to give from what they had extra; but she gave from out of her need and put in all that she had, even all her living."*

The End Times Foretold

13 [1-8] And as they went out of the Place of Worship, one of the followers said, *"Christ, look at these stones and the buildings here!"* And Yeshua answered, *"You see these great buildings? There won't be one stone left on another, that won't be out of place."* As they sat on the Mount of Olives next to the Place of Worship, Peter, James, John, and Andrew asked privately, *"Tell us when this will happen? And what signs will we have when all this begins to happen?"* And Yeshua answering them said, *"Be careful, in case anyone tries to mislead you, because many will come in My Name, saying, I am the Christ; and will mislead many people. When you hear of wars and news of wars, don't be upset because things like this will happen; but the end won't come yet. But nation will fight against nation, and land will fight against land. There will be earthquakes in different places, and there will be a great lack of food in some places and other troubles like this. These things are just the beginning of trouble.*

[9-13] *But be careful for yourselves because they'll arrest you, and bring you to courts; You'll be beaten in the places of worship, and you'll be brought before great rulers for My sake, and for a witness against them. The New Word must first be published throughout the whole world. So when they take away your freedom, and arrest you, don't worry ahead of time about what you'll say, nor think about it: but whatever is given to you at that time, speak it, because it isn't you that speaks, but the Holy Spirit in you. Now brothers and sisters will hand over their own siblings to death, and the parent, the child; and children will turn against their parents, and will cause them to be put to death. You'll be hated by everyone because of My Name: but whoever is faithful to the end will be saved.*

[14-23] *But when you see the antichrist, spoken of by Daniel the great preacher, standing where it shouldn't, (let those who read understand) then let those who are in Judea escape to the mountains. Those who are on the rooftop shouldn't go down into the house, nor go in to take anything out of their house. And those who are in the field shouldn't turn back to pick up their clothing. There will be great trouble for those who are with child, and who are breastfeeding in those days! And pray that your escape isn't in the winter, because there will be great trouble in those days, such as never before, from the beginning of creation, which God created, to this time, nor ever will be. And unless God shortens those days, no one would be saved: but God will shorten those days for the sake of those who God has chosen. So if anyone says to you, 'Look, here is the Christ;' or, 'The Christ is there;' don't believe them, because false Christs and false teachers will come, and will show great signs and amazing things, to fool, even the chosen ones if that were possible. So listen carefully: I've told you all this ahead of time.*

[24-30] *But in those days, after all that trouble, the sun will be darkened, and the moon won't have its normal light, and the stars of heaven and the other heavenly bodies will be shaken out of their places. Then they'll see Me coming in the clouds with great power and bright light. Then I'll send My angels, and will gather together the chosen ones from every direction, from the ends of the earth to the ends of heaven. Now learn the story of the fig tree: When its branch is still tender, and puts out its leaves, you know that summer's near. So in this way, when you see all this happening, know that the time is near, so very near. The truth is that the people of this time won't pass away, till everything is finished. Heaven and earth will come to an end: but My Words won't ever end.*

[32-37] *But of that day and hour no one knows, no, not the angels in heaven, nor Me, but only Yahweh God. Listen carefully, watch and pray because you don't know when that hour will come. It's like someone taking a far journey, which left their house, and gave work orders to each of their workers and told the caretaker to watch. So watch because you don't know when the owner of the house will come, at evening, or at midnight, or at dawn, or later on in the day: In case it so happens that, coming suddenly, the owner finds you sleeping. And what I tell you, I say to all who come after you, so watch!"*

Mary Anoints the Christ

14 [1-2] Two days later the Passover celebration of unleavened bread came: and the leading priests and the religious leaders looked for a way to take Yeshua secretly, and put the Christ to death. But they said, *"Not on the celebration day, in case the people cause an uproar."*

[3-9] And in Bethany in the house of Simon, one of those with leprosy who was healed, as they were eating a meal, a woman, named Mary, came having an alabaster jar of very precious perfumed oil of spikenard; and she broke open the jar, and poured it on the Christ's head. And some of those there resented it, thinking to themselves, *"Why was this perfume wasted like this? It might have been sold for almost a years worth of pay, and been given to those who are poor."* And they hatefully whispered about her. And Yeshua said, *"Leave her alone; why are you bothering her? She's done a good thing for Me. Those who are poor will always be with you, and whenever you can, do something good for them: but you won't always have Me with you. She's only done what she could: she came ahead of time to anoint my body for burying. The truth is, wherever this New Word is preached throughout the whole world, this thing that she's done will be spoken of for a memorial of her, too."*

Judas Betrays the Christ

[10-11] And Judas Iscariot, one of the twelve, went to the leading priests, to see if he could hand the Christ over to them. And when they heard it, they were happy, and promised to give him money. So after that he watched for the right time to hand over the Christ.

The Last Supper

[12-21] And on the first day of unleavened bread, when they killed the Passover sacrificial animals, the followers said, *"Where do you want us to go and get ready to eat the Passover?"* And the Christ sent out two of the followers, saying to them, *"Go into the city, and you'll find someone carrying a pitcher of water: follow them. And wherever they go in, say to the owner of the house, 'The Christ asks, Where is the guestroom, where I'll eat the Passover with my followers?' And they'll show you a large upper room furnished and prepared: get everything ready for us there."* And the followers went out, and came into the city, and found it all just as the Christ had said: and they got everything ready for the Passover. And in the evening the Christ came with the twelve followers. And as they sat and ate, Yeshua said, *"The truth is, one of you who eats with Me will hand Me over."* And they became very sad, saying to the Christ one by one, *"Is it I?"* and another said, *"Is it I?"* And the Christ answered them, *"It's one of you twelve, who dips his bread in the dish with Me. I'll certainly go, just as the Word says of Me: but the person who hands Me over will be very sorry! It would better for that person to have never been born."*

[22-24] And as they ate, Yeshua took the bread, and blessed it, breaking it in pieces to give to them, saying, *"Take this and eat it: this is a memorial of My body."* And the Christ took the cup, and after giving thanks, gave it to the followers: and they all drank of it. And the Christ said, *"This is a memorial of My blood, which is shed for many*

people, and for the New Word. The truth is, I'll drink no more wine, until the day that I drink it anew in the realm of God."

The Christ Prays in the Garden of Gethsemane

[26-31] And when they had sung a song, they went out to the Mount of Olives. And Yeshua said, *"You'll all leave me alone tonight because the Word says, When the Keeper is taken, the herd will be scattered. But after I have come back to life, I'll come to you in Galilee."* But Peter said, *"Even if everyone else leaves you, I won't."* And Yeshua said, *"The truth is that this very day, even tonight, before the rooster crows twice, you'll say you don't even know Me three times."* But he spoke all the more strongly, *"Even if I were to die with you, I would never say I don't know you in any way."* And all the others said the same.

[32-42] And they came to a place which was named Gethsemane: and Yeshua said to the followers, *"Sit here, while I pray."* And the Christ took along Peter, James, and John, and began to be very uneasy and sad. Then the Christ said, *"My soul is so sad I'm about to die: stay here and watch."* And the Christ went ahead a little, and fell on the ground, and prayed that if it were possible, the time might pass without any harm. And the Christ prayed, *"My Yahweh God, everything is possible to You; please don't let this happen to Me: but don't let happen what I want, but only what You want."* And the Christ came back and found them sleeping, saying to Peter, *"Simon Peter, are you sleeping? Couldn't you watch one hour? Watch and pray, in case you're tempted. The truth is, the spirit's willing, but the body's weak."* And again the Christ went away, and prayed, speaking the same words. And when Yeshua came back, the Christ found them sleeping again, (because they were very tired,) nor did they know what to answer the Christ. And the Christ came the third time, saying to them, *"You might as well sleep now, and take your rest. It's enough, It's time now; I'm handed over into the hands of sinners. Get up, let's go; The one who hands Me over is here."*

The Christ is Taken

[43-45] And suddenly, while the Christ was still speaking, Judas came, who was one of the twelve, and with him a great crowd with swords and sticks, from the leading priest and the religious leaders and the elders. And the one who handed over the Christ had told them a sign, saying, *"The One who I kiss, that is the One to take away."* And as soon as they came, he went over, saying, *"Teacher, Teacher;"* and kissed the Christ on the cheek.

[46-52] And they took hold of Yeshua, trying to take the Christ away. But one of those who were with the Christ drew a sword, and cut off the ear of one of the leading priest's workers. Then Yeshua said, *"Have you come out with swords and sticks to take Me like a thief? I was with you, teaching daily in the Place of Worship, and you didn't take Me then: but everything the Word says must happen."* And all those who were with the Christ left and ran away. And I followed along, having quickly tied a towel around my naked body; and those who took Yeshua tried to take me, too: But the linen cloth came off in their hands, and I ran away from them naked.

The Christ Taken Before the Priests

[53-59] And they led Yeshua away to the leading priest: and with them were gathered all the leading priests and the elders and the religious leaders. So Peter followed along far off, even to the great house of the leading priest: and sat with the workers, and warmed himself by the fire. Then the leading priests and all the court looked for a witness against Yeshua in order to put the Christ to death; but found none, because many told lies about the Christ, but their statements didn't agree together. And some got up, and told lies about the Christ, saying, *"We heard Yeshua say, 'I'll tear down this Place of Worship that was made by humans, and within three days, I'll build another not made by humans."* But their statements didn't agree together.

[60-65] And the leading priest stood up in the middle of them, and asked Yeshua, saying, *"Don't you have anything to say? Don't you hear what they're saying about you?"* But the Christ didn't say anything, and kept quiet. Again the leading priest asked, *"Are you the Christ, the Child of the Blessed One?"* And Yeshua said, *"I am: and you'll see Me sitting with the power of God, and coming in the clouds of heaven."* Then the leading priest tore his clothes, saying, *"Why do we need any more witnesses? You've heard this disrespect of God: what do you think?"* And they all said the Christ was guilty of death. And some began to spit on and cover Yeshua's face, and to beat the Christ, saying, *"Preach":* and they all slapped Yeshua with the palms of their hands.

Peter Denies Knowing the Christ

[66-72] And as Peter was downstairs in the great house, one of the workers of the leading priest came down. When she saw Peter warming himself, she looked at him, saying, *"You, too, were with Yeshua of Nazareth."* But Peter denied it, saying, *"I don't know who or what you're talking about."* And they went out onto the porch; and the rooster crowed. Then another girl saw Peter again, and began to say to those who stood around, *"This is one of them."* And Peter denied it again. And a little while later, those who stood by said to Peter again, *"Surely you're one of them because you're a Galilaean, and your speech proves it."* But Peter began to curse and to swear, saying, *"I don't even know who you're talking about."* And the rooster crowed the second time. And Peter

remembered what Yeshua had said, *"Before the rooster crows twice, you'll say you don't know me three times."* And when he remembered it, he cried miserably.

Christ Sent to Pilate

15 [1-5] As soon as it was morning the leading priests talked with the elders and religious leaders and the whole court, and tied up Yeshua, and carried the Christ away to Pilate. So Pilate asked Yeshua, *"Are you the Ruler of the Jews?"* And the Christ answered, *"I am who you say."* And the leading priests accused the Christ of many things: but Yeshua didn't say anything. So Pilate asked the Christ again, saying, *"Don't you have anything to say? Listen to all this they say against you."* But Yeshua still didn't say anything; so that Pilate was amazed.

[6-14] Now at the celebration Pilate usually freed one prisoner to the people, whoever they wanted. So there was someone named Barabbas, which was chained up with those who had made an uprising, and who had murdered someone in the uprising. So the crowd called out, asking Pilate to do as he had always done for them. But Pilate answered, saying, *"Don't you want me to free to you the Ruler of the Jews?"* because he knew that the leading priests had brought the Christ because of their jealousy. But the leading priests won over the people to ask Pilate to free Barabbas to them. And Pilate answered again, asking them, *"Then what do you want me to do to Yeshua, whom you call the Ruler of the Jews?"* And they called out again, *"Put Yeshua to death!"* Then Pilate answered, *"Why, what evil has this person done?"* And they called out all the more, *"Put Yeshua to death!"*

[15-20] And so Pilate, wanting to please the people, freed Barabbas to them, and handed over Yeshua, who had been beaten, to be put to death. And the guards led the Christ away into the judgment hall; and they called together all the guards. And they clothed Yeshua with a purple robe, and platted a crown of thorns, and put it on the Christ's head, and began to make fun of Yeshua, saying, "Hello, Ruler of the Jews!" And they hit Yeshua on the head with a reed, and spit on the Christ, and bowing their knees mockingly worshiped. And later, they took off the purple robe, and put Yeshua's own clothes back on, and led the Christ out to be put to death.

Christ on the Cross

[21-28] And they ordered someone named Simon, a Cyrenian from Africa, who passed by as he was coming out of the country, who was the parent of Alexander and Rufus, to carry the cross. And they brought them to a place named Golgotha, which means *The Place of the Skull.* And they gave the Christ sour wine mixed with a strong drug to numb the pain: but the Christ refused it. And when they had put the Christ on the cross, they divided the clothes of Yeshua, placing bets on them, to see what each one would get. And it was about nine o'clock in the morning, when they put Yeshua on the cross. And their accusation was written above Yeshua, which said, *THE RULER OF THE JEWS.* And they put two criminals on two other crosses; One on the right, and the other on the left. And the Word came true, which said, *"and the Christ was counted as a lawbreaker."*

[29-32] And those who passed by mocked the Christ, shaking their heads, and saying, *"Ah, you who could destroy the Place of Worship, and build it again in three days, save yourself, and come down from the cross."* The leading priests mocking said the same thing among themselves, along with the religious leaders, saying, *"You saved others; but You can't save Yourself."* If You're the Christ, the Ruler of Israel, come down now from the cross, so that we can see and believe."* And even those, who were on the other crosses, mocked the Christ.

The Christ's Last Words

[33-38] And when noon came, darkness covered the whole land until three o'clock. And at three o'clock Yeshua called out with a loud voice, saying, *"Eloi, Eloi, lama sabachthani?"* which means, *"My God, My God, why have you left Me?"* And some of those who stood there, when they heard it, said, *"This One is calling Elijah."* And one of them ran and filled a sponge full of sour wine, and put it on a reed, and gave the Christ a drink, saying, *"Be still; let's see whether Elijah comes or not."* Then Yeshua called out, and gave up the Spirit. And at that very time the curtain of the Place of Worship was torn in two all the way from the top to the bottom.

[39-41] And the soldier, who stood next to the Christ, heard that, and saw that Yeshua was dead, and said, *"It's true, this person was the Child of God."* And there were also women watching a little way off: among whom was Mary Magdalene, and Mary the mother of James, the younger, and of Joses, and Salome; (Who also, when Yeshua was in Galilee, followed along, and ministered to the Christ;) and many other women who came along with the Christ to Jerusalem.

Joseph Asks For Christ's Body

[42-47] Then when the evening came, because it was Friday, the preparation day, that is, the day before the Seventh Day, Joseph of Arimathaea, an honorable person, who also watched for the realm of God, came, and went bravely in to Pilate, and asked for the body of Yeshua. And Pilate was amazed that the Christ was already dead: and calling a soldier, asked whether the Christ had been dead very long. And when Pilate was told by the soldier, he gave the body of Christ to Joseph, who bought fine linen, and took the body down, and wrapped it in

the linen, and laid it in a tomb which was cut out of a rock, and rolled a stone in front of the door of the tomb. And Mary Magdalene and Mary the mother of Joses watched to see where the Christ was laid.

The Christ Comes to Life Again

16 [1-8] And when Saturday was over, Mary Magdalene, and Mary the mother of James, and Salome, had bought sweet spices, to come and anoint the body. And very early, at dawn, on Sunday morning, they came to the tomb. And they asked among themselves, *"Who'll roll the stone away from the door of the tomb for us?"* And when they looked, they saw that the stone was already rolled away, which was very large. And going into the tomb, they saw a young person sitting on the right side, clothed in a long white robe; and they were afraid. And the angel answered, *"Don't be afraid: If you're looking for Yeshua of Nazareth, who died on the cross: the Christ has come to life again and isn't here. Look at the place where the Christ was laid. Go now, and tell the followers, and Peter that the Christ will come to you in Galilee, who you'll see for yourselves, and who told you all of this ahead of time."* And they quickly went out, and ran away from the tomb because they were very afraid and amazed: but they didn't say anything to anyone because they were so afraid.

[9-13] Now when Yeshua had come to life again early on Sunday morning, the Christ appeared first to Mary Magdalene, from whom seven evil spirits had been put out. And she went and told those who had been with the Christ, as they mourned and cried. And when they had heard that the Christ was alive, and had been seen by her, they didn't believe it. After that the Christ appeared in the form of another to two of them, as they walked, and went into the country. And they went and told it to the rest, who didn't believe them either.

[14-18] And later, the Christ appeared to the eleven as they were eating a meal, and scolded them for their unbelief and stubborn hearts, because they didn't believe those who had seen Yeshua after coming back to life. And the Christ said to them, *"Go to all the countries of the world, and preach the New Word to everyone. Whoever believes and is baptized will be saved; but whoever doesn't believe will be damned to Hell. And these signs will follow those who believe; In My Name they'll put out evil spirits; They'll speak in new languages; They'll pick up deadly snakes; and if they drink any deadly poison, it won't hurt them; and they'll lay hands on the sick, who will get well."*

[19-20] So then, after Yeshua had spoken to them, the Christ went up into heaven, and sat on the right side of God's throne. And they all went out, and preached every where, Christ working with them, and confirming the New Word with many signs following them. So be it!

The New Word According to Luke

1 [1-4] Because many have taken it upon themselves to write an account of the things which are believed by us without a doubt, just as they were given to us by those, who from the beginning, were eyewitnesses, and ministers of the New Word; It seemed good to me also, having had a clear understanding of this from the very beginning, to write to you an account, in the order that it happened, Theophilus, so that you might know, without a doubt, the things that you've been taught.

Zachariah's Vision

[5-10] In the days of Herod, the ruler of Judea, there was a priest named Zacharial of the line of Abijah, whose wife, Elisabeth, was of the line of Aaron. They were both good in the sight of God, following all the teachings of God without fault. But they didn't have a child, because Elisabeth hadn't been able to get pregnant, and they were both very old now. And then, while it was Zachariah's turn to keep the duty of the priest's office to God, as was the priests' way of life, he was to burn incense when he went into the Place of Worship of God. And a large crowd of people were praying outside at this time.

[11-17] An angel of God appeared to him standing on the right side of the altar of incense, and when Zachariah saw the angel, he was uneasy, and afraid. So the angel said, *"Don't be afraid, Zachariah, because your prayer has been heard; and your wife Elisabeth will carry a child for you, and you'll call the child's name John. And you'll have great joy and happiness; and many will celebrate at his birth. And the child will be great in the sight of God, and won't drink wine, nor alcohol of any kind; and will be filled with the Holy Spirit, even before he is born. John will turn many of the children of Israel back to Yahweh their God, and he will go ahead of the Christ in the spirit and power of Elijah, to turn the hearts of the parents to the children, and the disobedient ones to the wisdom of being good; to get the people ready for the Christ."*

[18-25] And Zachariah said to the angel, *"How will I know? I am very old, and my wife is very old, too."* And the angel answered, *"I am Gabriel, who stands in the presence of God; and have been sent to speak to you, and to tell you this New Word. Because you didn't believe my words, which will happen when the time is right, you'll be dumb, and not able to speak, until the day that this happens."* The people outside waited for Zachariah, and wondered why he stayed so long in the Place of Worship. And when he came out, he couldn't speak to them, but they realized that he had seen a vision in the Place of Worship because he waved to them, but still couldn't speak to them. And then, when he had finished his duties, he went home. And after that, his wife Elisabeth became pregnant and kept herself hidden five months, saying, *"God has looked on me and done this to me in order to take away my disrespect among the people."*

Gabriel Appears to Mary

[26-29] Now when Elisabeth was in her sixth month, the angel Gabriel was sent from God to a city of Galilee, called Nazareth, to a young girl, named Mary, who had never had sexual relations before, and who was engaged to someone named Joseph, of the house of David. So the angel came to her, saying, *"Hello, you who are greatly favored; God is with you; You're the most blessed among all women."* And when she saw the angel, she was uneasy at this greeting, wondering what kind of greeting it was.

[30-37] The angel said to her, *"Don't be afraid, Mary, because you've been especially chosen by God. And you'll become pregnant, and have a Child, and will call the Child's name Yeshua, who will be great, and will be called the Child of the Most High God. Yahweh God will give the throne of the lineage of David to the Child, who is the rightful Heir: And the Child will reign over the lineage of Jacob forever; and there will be no end to the reign of the Christ.* Then Mary said to the angel, *"How can this be, since I haven't had sexual relations with anyone yet?"* So the angel said to her, *"The Holy Spirit will visit you, and the power of God will make it possible for you: so that the Holy One which you'll give birth to will be called the Child of God. And your cousin Elisabeth, who couldn't have a child, is also six months pregnant with a child, even in her old age. Nothing is impossible for God.* So Mary said, *"I am God's helper; so let it happen to me just as you've said."* Then the angel left her.

Mary Visits Elizabeth

[39-45] So Mary got up, and quickly went into the countryside, into a city of Judah, going to the house of Zachariah, and greeted Elisabeth. When Elisabeth heard Mary's greeting, the baby jumped in her womb. Suddenly Elisabeth was filled with the Holy Spirit, and she spoke loudly, saying, *"You're the most blessed among women, and blessed is the Child inside you. And why is it that the mother of my Christ would come to me? As soon as I heard the sound of your voice, the baby jumped for joy inside me. And you're blessed because you believed, because everything you were told by God will certainly happen."*

[46-56] And Mary said, *"My soul greatly blesses Yahweh, my God, and my spirit celebrates in God my Savior, because God has considered my low place, and from now on, every generation will say that I'm blessed, because the Most Powerful has done great things to me! Holy is the Name of Yahweh! God's mercy is on those who honor and respect God, from one people to the next. The God, who has shown mighty strength, has confused the proud in the thoughts of their hearts. The God, who has put the powerful down from their places, has lifted up those in low places. The God, who has filled the hungry with good things, has sent the rich away empty handed. The One who has helped Israel, in remembrance of the mercy of God, as God told our ancestors, Abraham, and the descendants of Abraham forever."* So Mary stayed with Elisabeth about three months, and then went home.

John the Baptist is Born

[57-66] Now the time for Elisabeth to give birth came; and she had a son. All her neighbors and her cousins had heard how God had shown great mercy to her and celebrated with her. Then, on the eighth day, when they came to cut the flesh of the foreskin of the child; and they called him Zachariah, after his father, Elisabeth said, *"No; he will be called John."* And they said to her, *"None of your kin is called by that name."* So they made signs to Zachariah, to see what he wanted him called. And he asked for a writing tablet, and wrote, saying, *"His name is John."* So everyone was amazed. Then Zachariah was suddenly able to speak, and praised God. So everyone that lived around them was amazed: and told all these stories throughout all the countryside of Judea. All those who heard them kept them in their hearts, saying, *"What a child this will be!"* So God's hand was with him.

[67-80] And the child's father, Zachariah was filled with the Holy Spirit, and praised God, saying, *"Blessed is Yahweh, the God of Israel, who has visited and saved the people, and has brought us the way to be saved from the lineage of David, God's helper; As God spoke by the mouth of the great holy preachers, which have been coming since the beginning of the world: that we would be saved from our enemies, and from the hand of all who hate us, to give us the mercy promised to our ancestors, and to remember the promise of the holy agreement of God; The promise which God swore to our ancestor Abraham, that we would be taken out of the hand of our enemies so that we can serve God without fear, in faithfulness and goodness before God, all the days of our life. And you, child, will be called the great preacher of the Highest because you'll go before the face of the Christ to get the way ready; To teach God's people how to be saved by the forgiveness of their sins, through the tender mercy of our God; by which the Dawn of Heaven has visited us, to give light to those who live in darkness and are about to die, and to show us the way of peace."* And the child grew, becoming strong in spirit, living in the countryside till the day he was made known to Israel.

Christ is Born

2 [1-5] In those days, Caesar Augustus ordered everyone to be taxed. (And this tax was first collected when Cyrenius was governor of Syria.) So everyone went to be taxed, each family to their home town. And Joseph went up from Galilee, out of the city of Nazareth, into Judea, to the city of David, which is called Bethlehem; (because he was of the lineage of David :) To be taxed with Mary, to whom he was engaged , being great with child.

[6-14] While they were there, it was time for her to give birth. And she had her firstborn child in a stable, and wrapped the baby in strips of cloth, and laid it in the animal's food trough; because there was no room for them in the inn. And in this country, there were animal keepers staying in the fields, keeping watch over their herds by night. And the angel of God came to them, and the light of God shone all around them: so they were very afraid. And the angel said, *"Don't be afraid because I bring you good news of great joy, which will be for all people. There has been born today in the city of David, a Savior for you, who is the Christ of God. And this will be a sign to you; You'll find the baby wrapped in strips of cloth, lying in the animal's food trough, in a stable."* And suddenly, a crowd of the heavenly hosts was with the angel, praising God, and saying, *"Praise to God, the Most High, who sends peace on earth, and goodness for all people."*

[15-20] And then, as the angels went away from them back into heaven, the animal keepers said to one another, *"Let's go to Bethlehem, now, and see for ourselves this thing that has happened, which God has sent the angel to tell us."* So they went quickly, and found Mary and Joseph, with the baby lying in the animal's food trough. And when they had seen it, they told everyone what they had been told about this child. And all those who heard the story were amazed at the things which they were told by the animal keepers. But Mary remembered all this, and thought about it, keeping it in her heart. So the animal keepers went back, worshipping and praising God for everything that they had seen and heard, just as it was told them.

Simeon and Anna Praise the Christ Child

[21-24] And when eight days had ended, the time came to cut the flesh of the foreskin of the Christ Child, who was named Yeshua, which was the name given ahead of time by the angel before Mary had become pregnant. And when the days of her rest had ended for the law of Moses, they went to Jerusalem to present the Child to God; (As the Word of God says, "Every firstborn male will be called holy to God;") And to offer a sacrifice for what is said in God's Word, a pair of doves, or a pair of young pigeons.

[25-35] And there was someone in Jerusalem, whose name was Simeon; who was good and dedicated, waiting for the comfort of Israel: and who had been blessed with the Holy Spirit. It was revealed to him by the Holy Spirit, that he wouldn't see death, until he had seen the Christ of God. So being led by the Spirit into the Place of Worship, when the parents brought the Child Yeshua in, to do as God's Word said, which was their way of life, he picked the Child up, and blessed God, saying, *"God, now let Your worker go in peace, for Your Word, because my eyes have seen Your saving grace, which you've prepared even before Your people were created; A light to give light to the other peoples, and the light of Your people Israel."* And Joseph and Mary were amazed at all the things he said. And Simeon blessed them, saying to Mary, the Child's mother, *"This Child is set apart for the rising and fall of many people in Israel; and for a sign which will be badly talked about; (Yes, your own soul will be pierced through, too,) so that the secret thoughts of many hearts will be seen by all."*

[36-40] And there was another person named Anna, a great preacher, the daughter of Phanuel, of the family of Aser: who was of a great age, and had only lived with a husband for seven years from the time she was married; She was his survivor, about eighty-four years old, who never left from the Place of Worship, but served God by willingly going without food and praying night and day. And she coming in at that instant gave thanks in this way to God, and spoke of God to all those who wanted to be saved in Jerusalem. So when they had done everything as God's Word says, they came back to Galilee, to their own home town of Nazareth. And the Christ Child became strong in body, mind, and spirit: and God's grace was on Yeshua.

Yeshua, the Child

[41-45] Now Mary and Joseph went to Jerusalem every year at the celebration of the Passover. And when Yeshua was twelve years old, they went up to Jerusalem, as was their way of life, during the celebration. But when it was over, as they came back, the Child Yeshua stayed behind in Jerusalem; but Joseph and Mary didn't know it. And they, thinking Yeshua was in the group of people traveling along, walked a day's journey; then looked for Yeshua among their kin people and those known by them. But when they couldn't find Yeshua, they came back to Jerusalem, looking there.

[46-52] Then, after three days of searching, they found Yeshua in the Place of Worship, sitting in the middle of the teachers, both hearing them, and asking them questions. And all that heard the Child were amazed at the Christ's understanding and answers. And when they saw Yeshua, they were amazed: and Yeshua's mother said, *"Child, why have you done this to us? Your father and I have looked everywhere for you and have been so worried about you."* So Yeshua answered, *"Why were you looking for Me? Didn't you know that I would be doing the work of My God, who I am from?* But they didn't understand what Yeshua had said. So Yeshua came down with them, and went to Nazareth, and obeyed them: but Mary remembered all this, keeping it in her heart. And Yeshua grew in mind and body, and was loved by God and people.

John Baptizes the Christ

3 [1-9] Now in the fifteenth year of the reign of Tiberius Caesar, Pontius Pilate being governor of Judea, and Herod being governor of Galilee, and another governor, Philip, of Ituraea and of Trachonitis, and Lysanias, the governor of Abilene, Annas and Caiaphas being the leading priests, the Word of God came to John, the child of Zachariah, in the countryside. So John came into all the country around the Jordan river, preaching the baptism of a changed life to save them from their sins, just as the Word says in the book of Isaiah, the great preacher, saying, *"The voice of one calling out in the countryside will get the way of Yahweh God ready, and make the way plain. Every valley will be filled, every mountain and hill will become level; the crooked will become straight, and the rough ways will become smooth; Everyone will see the One God sent to save us."* Then John said to the crowd that came out to be baptized, *"You snakes! Who warned you to escape from the coming judgment? Don't just say your sorry, but change your evil ways, and don't think to yourselves, Abraham is our ancestor because I tell you, that God is able to create more children for Abraham even from these stones. The axe is laid to the root of the trees now: so every tree which doesn't make good fruit will be cut down, and put in the fire."*

[10-17] So the people asked John, saying, *"What should we do then?"* And John answered them, *"Whoever has two coats, let them give to those who have no coat; and whoever has food, let them do the same."* Then the tax collectors came also to be baptized, saying, *"John, what should we do?"* And John answered, *"Take no more than what you're told to."* And the guards asked John the same, saying, "And what should we do?" So John answered, *"Don't hurt anyone, nor accuse anyone falsely; and be satisfied with your pay."* And as the people were in expectation, and everyone wondered about John in their hearts, whether he was the Christ or not; John said to them all, *"I baptize you with water as a symbol of your changed life: but the One that comes after me is greater than I, whose shoes I am not even worthy to loosen: The Christ will baptize you with the fire of the Holy Spirit: Who holds the fan, and will carefully purge the floor, gathering the wheat into the grain storage; but burning up the waste with never ending fire."*

[18-22] And John preached to the people with many other encouragements. But Herod, the governor, was disapproved of by John for Herodias, his brother Philip's wife, and for all the evil things which Herod had done. So

because of this, on top of everything else, he put John in prison. Now when all the people were baptized, and Yeshua, having been baptized, too, was praying, when the heavens opened, and the Holy Spirit came down in the bodily shape of a dove, landing on Yeshua. Then a voice came from heaven, which said, *"You're My Child, who I love; I am so pleased with You."*

Christ's Physical Lineage (Family Line of Joseph)

[23-38] And Yeshua was about thirty years old, being (as was thought) the child of Joseph, which was the child of Heli, which was the child of Matthat, which was the child of Levi, which was the child of Melchi, which was the child of Janna, which was the child of Joseph, which was the child of Mattathiah, which was the child of Amos, which was the child of Nahum, which was the child of Esli, which was the child of Naggai, which was the child of Maath, which was the child of Mattathiah, which was the child of Semei, which was the child of Joseph, which was the child of Judah, which was the child of Joannas, which was the child of Rhesa, which was the child of Zerubbabel, which was the child of Shealtiel, which was the child of Neri, which was the child of Melchi, which was the child of Addi, which was the child of Cosam, which was the child of Elmodam, which was the child of Er, which was the child of Jose, which was the child of Eliezer, which was the child of Jorim, which was the child of Matthat, which was the child of Levi, which was the child of Simeon, which was the child of Judah, which was the child of Joseph, which was the child of Jonan, which was the child of Eliakim, which was the child of Melea, which was the child of Menan, which was the child of Mattathah, which was the child of Nathan, which was the child of David, which was the child of Jesse, which was the child of Obed, which was the child of Boaz, which was the child of Salmon, which was the child of Nahshon, which was the child of Aminadab, which was the child of Aram, which was the child of Hezron, which was the child of Perez, which was the child of Judah, which was the child of Jacob, which was the child of Isaac, which was the child of Abraham, which was the child of Terah, which was the child of Nahor, which was the child of Saruch, which was the child of Ragau, which was the child of Peleg, which was the child of Heber, which was the child of Shelah, which was the child of Cainan, which was the child of Arphaxad, which was the child of Shem, which was the child of Noah, which was the child of Lamech, which was the child of Methuselah, which was the child of Enoch, which was the child of Jared, which was the child of Mahalalel, which was the child of Cainan, which was the child of Enosh, which was the child of Seth, which was the child of Adam, which was the child of God.

The Temptation of Christ

4 [1-13] So Yeshua being full of the Holy Spirit came back from the Jordan River, and was led by the Spirit into the countryside, to be tempted by the devil forty days. And Yeshua, who ate nothing during that time, was hungry later. So the devil said, *"If You're the Child of God, tell this stone to become bread."* But Yeshua answered, saying, *"It's written, that a person shouldn't live by bread alone, but by all the Words of God."* And the devil, taking Yeshua up to a high mountain, showed the Christ all the countries of the world in a moment of time. And the devil said, *"I'll give you control of all this, and all the victory over what has been given to me; I can give it to whoever I want. So if you'll worship me, all of it will be Yours."* But Yeshua answered, *"Leave Me alone, Satan, because the Word says, You must worship Yahweh, your God, and serve Yahweh only."* So then Satan brought Yeshua to Jerusalem, to a high point on the Place of Worship, saying, *"If You're the Child of God, jump down from here: because the Word says, God will give the angels charge over you, to keep you safe: And in their hands they'll pick you up, in case you ever trip over a stone."* But Yeshua answered, *"It's written, You shouldn't tempt, Yahweh, your God."* And when all the temptations were over, Satan left the Christ for a while.

The Christ's Ministry Begins

[14-20] Then Yeshua went back by the power of the Spirit into Galilee: and word went out about the Christ through the whole area. So Yeshua taught in their worship services, being praised by all. Then Yeshua came to Nazareth, where the Christ had been brought up. As their way of life was, Yeshua went into the Place of Worship on a Seventh Day, and stood up to read. The book of the great preacher Isaiah was given to Yeshua. So the Christ opened the book, finding the place where it was written, *"The Spirit of God is on Me, who has anointed Me to preach the New Word to those who are poor; and has sent Me to heal the brokenhearted, to preach freedom to those who are enslaved, to give back sight to those who are blind, to set free those who are abused, to preach that now is the right time to believe God."* Then the Christ closed the book, and gave it back to the minister, and sat down. And all those who were in the Place of Worship stared at Yeshua.

[21-32] So the Christ said, "Today, what this Word says has happened in your hearing." And all who witnessed this were amazed at the gracious words which came out of Yeshua's mouth. But they asked, *"Isn't this Joseph's child?"* So Yeshua answered, *"You'll certainly tell Me this saying, 'Doctor, heal yourself: whatever we've heard that was done in Capernaum, do also here in your country.'"* And then Yeshua said, *"The truth is, no great preacher is accepted in their own country. The truth is, many widows were in Israel in the days of Elijah, when it didn't rain for three and a half years, when a great hunger went throughout the whole land; But Elijah was sent to none of them,*

except to Sarepta, a city of Sidon, to a woman who was a widow. And many lepers were in Israel in the time of Elijah, the great preacher; and none of them were healed, except Naaman the Syrian." And everyone in the Place of Worship, when they heard this, were angry and got up, leading the Christ out of the city and to the edge of the hill that their city was built on, to throw Yeshua down headfirst. But passing through the middle of them, Yeshua got away, and came down to Capernaum, a city of Galilee, and taught them on the Days of Worship. And they were amazed at Yeshua's teachings, because the Christ spoke with power.

Christ Puts An Evil Spirit Out

[33-37] In the Place of Worship there was someone who had an evil spirit, and called out with a loud voice, saying, *"Leave us alone; what have we to do with You, Yeshua of Nazareth? Have You come to get rid of us? I know who You are; You're the Holy One of God."* But Yeshua scolded it, saying, *"Be quiet, and get out of this person."* So when the evil spirit had thrown the person down in the middle of them, it came out, without hurting the person. Then everyone was amazed, and said among themselves, *"What a powerful word this is! Yeshua orders the evil spirits with power and control, and they obey."* So Yeshua became well known all over the countryside.

The Christ Heals

[38-44] Then Yeshua left from the Place of Worship, and went to Simon's house. Simon's wife's mother had a high fever; and they begged the Christ to heal her. So Yeshua stood over her, and told the fever to leave; and it left her. Then suddenly she got up and served them all. Now when the sun was setting, all those who had anyone sick, with many different diseases, brought them to the Christ; who laid hands on them, and healed them all. And evil spirits came out of many, calling out, and saying, *"You're the Christ, the Child of God."* But Yeshua wouldn't let them speak because they knew that Yeshua was the Christ. And in the morning, the Christ left, going into a deserted place. But the people looked for the Christ, and came, and stayed with Yeshua, so that the Christ couldn't leave them. But Yeshua told them, *"I must preach about the realm of God to other cities also, because this is why I was sent."* And the Christ preached in all the places of worship of Galilee.

Christ Calls Peter

5 [1-11] As the people crowded in to hear the Word of God, the Christ, who stood beside Lake Gennesaret, saw two ships standing by the lake: but the fishermen were washing their nets and had left them. So Yeshua went in one of the ships, which was Simon Peter's, and asked him to go out a little from the shore. The Christ sat down, and taught the people from the ship. Now when the Christ had finished speaking, Yeshua said to Peter, *"Go out into the deep water, and let down your nets for a catch."* But Peter answered, *"Christ, we've worked all night, and haven't caught a thing: but because you say so, I'll put the net down one more time."* And when they had done it, they caught so many fish that their net almost broke. So they waved to their partners, who were in the other ship, to come and help them. When they came, they filled both ships up so much that they began to sink. When Peter saw it, he dropped down at Yeshua' knees, saying, *"Christ, go away from me; I am a sinful person!"* He said this because they were all so amazed at how many fish they had caught: And so were James and John, the sons of Zebedee, who were partners with Peter. So Yeshua said to Peter, "Don't be afraid; from now on you'll be catching other people." And when they had docked their ships, they left everything, and followed along with Yeshua.

Christ Heals a Leper

[12-16] And then, when they were in a certain city, someone who had leprosy, seeing Yeshua, dropped to the ground and begged, saying, "Christ, if only You want to, You can make me well! So the Christ reached out, and touched the leper, saying, *"I want to: Get well."* Then suddenly the leprosy was gone, so the Christ said to the person, *"Tell no one: but go, and show yourself to the priest, and offer what Moses told you to for your healing, for a witness to them."* But word of Yeshua went out all the more and great crowds came together to listen, and to be healed by the Christ of all their sicknesses. So the Christ often went alone into the countryside to pray.

A Paralyzed Person Walks

[17-26] On a certain day, as the Christ was teaching, there were religious leaders and teachers of the Word of God sitting near, which had come out of every town of Galilee, Judea, and Jerusalem. The power of God was with Yeshua to heal those in need, so some people brought a person who was paralyzed in a bed. They looked for a way to bring them in, to put at Yeshua's feet, but when they couldn't find a way to bring the person in because of the crowd, they went up on the rooftop, and let the person down on the bed to Yeshua through the roof, right in the middle of the crowd. And when the Christ saw their faith, Yeshua said, *"Your sins are forgiven you."* So the religious leaders and those of the religious sects began to question, saying, *"Who is this who speaks disrespectfully of God? Only God can forgive sins!"* But when Yeshua realized what they were thinking, the Christ said, *"Why do you question Me in your hearts? What is easier to say, Your sins are forgiven you; or to say, Get up and walk? But so you can know that I have the power on earth to forgive sins,* (the Christ said to the paralyzed

112

one) *I tell you, Get up, and pick up your bed, and go home."* And suddenly, the person got up in front of them, and picked up the bed, and went home, praising God all the way. And everyone was amazed, and praised God, and were filled with fear, saying, *"What strange things we've seen today!'*

Christ Calls Matthew

[27-32] Then the Christ went out, and saw a tax collector, named Matthew, sitting where the taxes were collected, so Yeshua said to him, *"Follow Me."* And Mathew left everything, got up, and followed along. And there was a dinner held at Mathew's home: and a great many tax collectors and others were there. But the religious leaders and those in the religious sects spoke against the followers, asking, *"Why do you eat and drink with tax collectors and sinners?"* And Yeshua answered, *"Those who are well don't need a doctor; but only those who are sick. I didn't come to those who are good, but to sinners to tell them to change their ways."*

[33-35] So they said, *"Why do the followers of John often go without food, and pray, and those of the religious leaders, too; but Your followers eat and drink?"* And the Christ answered, *"Can you make the friends of one of the bridal party go without food, while the bridal party is with them? But the time will come, when the bridal party will be gone, and then they'll go without food at that time."*

[36-39] And then the Christ told them a story, saying, *"No one puts a piece of a new cloth on old clothes; because then the new cloth would shrink and make a bigger tear, and the new piece wouldn't match the old cloth. And no one puts new wine into old bottles; or else the new wine would burst and break the bottles, and be spilled out. But new wine must be put into new bottles so both are safely kept. And no one, having drunk old wine, suddenly wants new, because they say, 'The old wine is better'."*

The Seventh Day

6 [1-5] And then on the next Day of Worship, they went through the grain fields; and the followers took the grain, rubbing it in their hands, and ate it. So some of the religious leaders asked, *"Why do you do what isn't right to do on the Days of Worship?"* And Yeshua answered, *"Haven't you ever read what David did, when he was hungry, and those who were with him; How he went into the house of God, taking and eating the bread, and gave to those who were with him, too; which isn't right for anyone to eat but the priests?"* Then Yeshua said, *"I am also the ruler of the Seventh Day."*

[6-12] And then on another Seventh Day, Yeshua went to the Place of Worship to teach: and there was someone there whose hand was paralyzed. The religious leaders and the ministers from the religious sects watched to see whether Yeshua would heal on a Day of Worship in order to accuse the Christ of something. But the Christ knew what they were thinking, saying to the person who had the paralyzed hand, *"Get up, and stand out in the middle."* So the person got up and stood in the middle of them. Then Yeshua said, *"I ask you one thing; Is it right on Days of Worship to do good, or to do evil? to save a life, or to end it?"* And looking around on them all, Yeshua said to the person, *"Stretch out your hand."* And the person did so: and the hand became well just like the other one. So all the religious leaders were full of anger; and discussed with one another what to do to Yeshua. And then one day, the Christ went up on a mountain to pray, and stayed up all night in prayer to God.

[13-19] So when it was day, Yeshua called all the followers: and the Christ chose twelve out of them, who were called to lead the followers; Simon, (who the Christ called Peter,) Andrew, his brother, James, John, Philip, Bartholomew, Matthew, Thomas, James, the son of Alphaeus, Simon called Zelotes, Thaddaeus, the brother of James, and Judas Iscariot, which also was the one who later handed the Christ over. So Yeshua came down with them, and stood in the field, with the crowd of followers, and another great crowd of people out of all Judea and Jerusalem, and from the sea coast of Tyre and Sidon, who came to hear the Christ, and to be healed of their diseases; And those who were suffering with evil spirits were healed, too. So the whole crowd looked for a way to touch the Christ because the power to heal came out of Yeshua and healed them all.

Sermon on the Mountainside

[20-26] Then the Christ looked on all the followers, saying, *"Blessed are those who are poor because you'll have the realm of God. Blessed are you that hunger now because you'll be filled. Blessed are you that cry now because you'll laugh. Blessed are you, when others hate you, and when they keep you from their company, and accuse you, and call you evil, because of My Name. Celebrate in that day, and leap for joy because your reward in heaven is great! Their ancestors treated the great preachers in this way, too. But those who are rich will be sorry! They've gotten their comfort already. You who are full will be sorry because you'll hunger. You who laugh now will be sorry because you'll cry sorrowfully. When everyone speaks well of you, you'll be sorry! So did their ancestors to all the false teachers.*

[27-38] *But I tell everyone of you who are listening, love those who come against you out of their own choosing, do good to those who hate you, bless those who curse you, and pray for those who shamefully misuse you. And to those who slap you on one cheek offer them the other one, too; and those who take away your shirt, don't tell them not to take your coat, too. Give to everyone that asks to borrow something from you; and of those*

who take your belongings away, don't ask them for it again. And as you want others to do to you, do the same to them, too. If you love those who love you, what have you done that deserves thanks? Even sinners love those that love them. And if you do good to those who do good to you, what have you done that deserves thanks? Even sinners do that. And if you lend to them of whom you hope to get something back, what have you done that deserves thanks? Even sinners lend to sinners, to get it back again. But love those who come against you, and do good, and lend, hoping for nothing back again; and your reward will be great, and you'll be the children of the Highest because God is kind even to ungrateful and evil people. So have compassion, as your God also has compassion. Don't judge people wrongly, and you won't be judged wrongly either. Don't criticize others, and you won't be criticized either. Forgive, and you'll be forgiven: Give, and it'll be given to you; like a good measure of flour, pressed down, and shaken together, and running over, will others put what you need into your lap, because with the same measurement that you measure with, it'll be measured back to you again."

[39-49] Then the Christ told a story to them, "Can someone who is blind lead another who is blind? Won't they both fall into the ditch? The follower isn't any better than the teacher: but everyone who wants to be complete will be as the teacher. And why do you believe that the splinter that is in another's eye is worse than the stake that is in your own eye? So how can you say to another, 'Let me pull out the splinter that is in your eye', when you yourself can't see the stake that is in your own eye? You fake, first pull the stake out of your own eye, and then you can see clearly to pull out the splinter that is in another's eye. A good tree doesn't make bad fruit; nor does a bad tree make good fruit: A tree is known by its fruit. And you don't gather figs from thorns, nor do you gather grapes from briars. A good person out of the good things of their heart does what is good; and an evil person out of the bad things of their heart does what is evil, because they speak and act out of what is kept in their heart. And why do you call me, Christ, Christ, and don't do the things which I say? Whoever comes to Me, and hears My Words, and does them, I'll show you to whom they're like: They're like someone who built a house, and dug deep, and laid the foundation on a rock: and when the flood came up, the water beat strongly on that house, but couldn't shake it because it was built on a rock. But whoever hears what I say, and doesn't do it, is like someone that built a house on the earth, without a proper foundation; which the waters beat strongly against, and suddenly it fell; and that house was totally destroyed."

Christ Heals the Worker of an Officer

7 [1-10] Now when the Christ had finished all the teachings to the people, they went to Capernaum. There, a certain officer's worker, who was very dear to the officer, was sick, and about to die. So when the officer heard that Yeshua had come, he sent the elders of the Jews, begging for Yeshua to come and heal the worker. And when they came to Yeshua, they started begging, saying, "The one who has asked this is worthy for this request to be done: because he loves our nation, and has built us a Place of Worship." Then Yeshua went with them. And when the Christ wasn't far from the house, the officer sent some friends, saying, "Christ, don't trouble yourself, because I am not worthy for you to come in to my house: Nor did I believe myself to be worthy to come to you: but if You'll just say the word, I know my worker will be healed. Because I also am someone who has been given power, having guards under me, and I say to one, 'Go', and they go; and to another, 'Come', and they come; and to my workers, 'Do this', and they do it." When the Christ heard this, Yeshua was amazed, and turned around, saying to the people that followed along, "I tell you, I haven't found this great a faith, no, not in all Israel." And those who were sent, returning to the house, found the worker who had been sick well again.

Christ Raises the Dead

[11-18] Then the next day they went into a city called Nain; and many of the followers and other people went with them. Now when they came near the gate of the city, there was a dead person being carried out, the only child of a mother, and she had lost her husband also: and many people of the city were with her. When the Christ saw her, Yeshua had compassion on her, saying to her, "Don't cry" and came and touched the casket: and those who carried it stood still. The Christ said, "Young one, I tell you, Get up." And the one who was dead sat up, and began to speak. So the Christ gave the mother back her child alive. And a fear came over all the people: but they praised God, saying, a great preacher has risen up among us; and God has visited us. So the fame of Yeshua spread throughout all Judea, and throughout the whole region. And the followers of John told him of all this.

John the Baptist Questions Yeshua

[19-23] John called two followers and sent them to Yeshua, saying, "Are you the One who was to come? or do we look for someone else?" And when they had come to the Christ, they said, "John, the Baptist, has sent us to you, saying, 'Are you the One who was to come? or do we look for someone else?'" And in that same time the Christ healed many with sicknesses and diseases, and with evil spirits; and many who were blind were able to see again. Then Yeshua answered, "Go now, and tell John what you've seen and heard; how that those who are blind see, those who are paralyzed walk, those with leprosy are healed, those who are deaf can hear again, those who

are dead come to life again, and the New Word is preached to those who are poor. Those who aren't offended by Me are blessed."

[24-30] When the followers of John had gone, the Christ began to speak to the people about John, "What did you go out into the countryside to see? A reed shaking in the wind? But what did you go out to see? A person clothed in soft furs? Those who are richly clothed, and have many delicacies, are in rulers' courts. But what did you go out to see? A great preacher? Yes, I tell you, and much more than a great preacher. This is the one who the Word speaks about, I send my messenger before you, who will get your way ready for you. I tell you, among all those who have ever been born, there isn't a preacher greater than John the Baptist: but whoever is least in the realm of God is greater than even this." And when all the people heard this, even the tax collectors praised God, because they had been baptized by John. But the religious leaders and the ministers from the religious sects rejected the will of God for themselves, not having been baptized by John.

[31-35] Then the Christ said, "How can I describe this generation of people? and what are they like? They're like children sitting in the shopping center, calling one another, saying, We've played music for you, and you haven't danced; we've cried to you, and you haven't cried with us. John the Baptist came, neither eating bread, nor drinking wine; and you say, 'He has an evil spirit.' I come eating and drinking; and you say, 'Look, this person is a pig, and a drunk, a friend of tax collectors and sinners!' But children are made right by their own thinking."

Mary Anoints the Christ

[36-50] And one of the religious leaders wanted Yeshua to eat with them. So they went into the house, and sat down to eat. And a woman of the city, who was a sinner, when she knew that Yeshua was eating a meal in that house, brought an alabaster box of perfume, and stood crying at the Christ's feet, and began to wash Yeshua's feet with her tears, and wiped them with her hair, and kissed the Christ's feet, and anointed them with the perfume. Now when the religious leader who had asked the Christ to join them saw it, he thought to himself, "If you're really a great preacher, You would've known who and what kind of woman this is, who is a sinner." And Yeshua said, "Simon, I have something to say to you." And he said, "Christ, tell me." So the Christ said, "There was a certain creditor who had two debtors. One owed more than a year's pay, and the other about two month's worth. And when neither of them had anything to pay it back with, the creditor forgave them both. Tell Me then, which of them will love the creditor most?" Simon answered, "I think the one who was forgiven the most." And Yeshua said, "You're right," and turning toward the woman, said to Simon, "Do you see this woman? I came here, and you didn't give me any water to wash My feet, but she's washed My feet with her tears, and wiped them with the very hairs of her head. You didn't greet Me with a kiss, but this woman hasn't stopped kissing My feet since the time I came in. You didn't anoint My head with oil, but this woman has anointed My feet with perfumed oil. Why I tell you, her sins, which are many, are forgiven because she loved much, but those who are forgiven little, love little." And the Christ said to her, "Your sins are forgiven." And those who were eating the meal with them began to think to themselves, "Who is this that forgives sins, too?" And the Christ said to the woman, "Your faith has saved you; go in peace."

Women Follow Christ

8 [1-3] Then later, Yeshua and the twelve went throughout every city and town, preaching and telling the New Word of the realm of God. And certain women, who had been healed of evil spirits and other sicknesses, Mary called Magdalene, who was freed of seven evil spirits, and Joanna, the wife of Chuza, Herod's manager, and Susanna, and many other women, who gave for the needs of the Christ out of their own things.

Four Kinds of Hearts

[4-15] When many people were gathered together, and had come to them out of every city, Yeshua told a story: "A farmer went out to plant the seed: and as the farmer planted, some fell beside the rows; and it was overrun, and the birds of the air ate it. And some fell on rocky ground; and as soon as it came up, it wilted away, because it lacked water. And some fell among thorns, which sprang up with it, and choked it off. And others fell on good ground, and sprang up, and bare fruit, some a hundred times as much." And Yeshua ended the story by saying, "If anyone will accept this, let them accept it." And the followers asked, saying, "What does this story mean?" So the Christ said, "You're allowed to know the secrets of the realm of God: but others are told in stories; that seeing, they won't see, and hearing, they won't understand. Now the story is this: The seed is the Word of God. Those that fell beside the rows are those who hear; then the devil comes, and takes the Word out of their hearts, or else they would believe and be saved. Those that fell on the rocky ground are those, who, when they hear, believe the Word with joy; but they have no root, which for a while believe, but in time of temptation fall away. And what fell among thorns are those, which, when they've heard, go out, and are choked with the cares and riches and pleasures of this life, and their fruit never ripens. But those that fell on the good ground are those, who, with an honest and good heart, having heard the Word, do it, and make fruit, waiting for it with patience.

115

[16-18] *No one, when they have lit a candle, covers it up, or puts it under a bed; but they set it on a candle holder, so that those who come in can see the light. Nothing is secret that won't become known, nor anything hid that won't be seen and be brought out in the open. So be careful when you listen because whoever understands, will be given more; and whoever doesn't, even what they seem to have, will be taken away from them.*"

The Christ's Family

[19-21] Then Yeshua's mother and brothers came, but couldn't get in for the crowd. So it was told Yeshua by someone who said, *"Your mother and brothers are outside, hoping to see You."* And the Christ answered, *"My family members are those who hear the Word of God, and do it."*

Christ Calms the Storm

[22-26] Now on a certain day, the Christ went into a ship with the followers: saying to them, *"Let's go over to the other side of the lake."* So they started out. But as they sailed, Yeshua fell asleep: and a storm of wind came up on the lake; and the boat was full of water, and they were in danger. So they went and woke Yeshua up, saying, *"Christ, Teacher, we'll be destroyed."* Then the Christ got up, and said to the wind and the raging water, *"Be still":* and it stopped, and everything calmed down. And the Christ asked, *"Don't you have any faith?"* And they, being afraid, were amazed, saying to one another, *"What kind of person is this, who tells even the winds and water what to do, and they do it!"* Then they arrived at the country of the Gadarenes, which is next to Galilee.

Christ Casts Out Evil Spirits into the Pigs

[27-36] When they went ashore, someone met them from out of the city, who had evil spirits for a long time, and wore no clothes, nor lived in any house, but stayed in the tombs. When this person saw Yeshua, they called out, and bowed down on their knees, and with a loud voice said, *"What I have to do with You, Yeshua, Child of the Most High God? I beg you, don't make me suffer."* (Christ had told the evil spirit to come out of the person because it had often taken control of the person: who was kept with chains and shackles; but who had broken them, and was driven by the evil spirit into the countryside.) And Yeshua asked, *"What is your name?"* And the evil spirits said, *"Legion":* because many evil spirits were in the person. And they begged the Christ not to make them go out into the deep. But there was a herd of many pigs feeding on the mountain: so they begged the Christ to let them go into the pigs. So Yeshua let them. Then the evil spirits went out of the person, and into the pigs: and the whole herd ran madly down a cliff into the lake, and was drowned. When those who fed them saw what had happened, they ran away, and told this all over the city and countryside. Then all the people went out to see what happened; and came to Yeshua, and found the person, out of whom the evil spirits had gone, sitting at the feet of Yeshua, clothed, and in a right mind: and they were very afraid. So those who had seen it told them how the one who was overcome by the evil spirits was healed.

[37-40] Then the whole crowd of people from the countryside of Gadarenes begged the Christ to go away from them because they were very afraid: so the Christ and the followers went back to the ship, and came back again. Now the person out of whom the evil spirits had gone begged to go with them: but Yeshua sent the person away, saying, *"Go back to your own home, and tell all the great things God has done for you. So the person left, and told throughout the whole city the great things that Yeshua had done."* And then, when Yeshua got back, the people were very happy because they had been waiting for the Christ.

A Woman with a Bleeding Problem Healed

[41-48] Then someone named Jairus came, who was a leader of the Place of Worship: and who bowed down at Yeshua' feet, and begged the Christ to come home with him: because he had only one daughter, who was about twelve years old, and she lay dying. But as they went the people crowded them. And a woman having a bleeding problem for twelve years, who had spent everything she had on doctors, but couldn't be healed by any of them, came up behind them, and touched the edge of Yeshua's clothing: and suddenly she was healed. Then Yeshua said, *"Who touched me?"* When all denied it, Peter and those who were with Yeshua said, *"Christ, the crowd is swarming and pressing you, and you say, 'Who touched Me?'"* And Yeshua said, *"Somebody touched Me because I know that power has gone out of Me."* So when the woman saw that she was found out, she came trembling, and falling down in front of the Christ, she told the Christ and all the people why she had touched the Christ and how she was suddenly healed. And the Christ said to her, *"Daughter, be in good spirits now: your faith has made you well; go in peace."*

A Young Girl Healed

[49-56] And while they were speaking, someone came from the Place of Worship's leader's house, saying to them, *"Your daughter is dead; don't bother the Teacher anymore."* But when Yeshua heard it, the Christ answered, saying, *"Don't be afraid: only believe, and she'll get well."* And when they came into the house, Yeshua let no one go in, but Peter, James, John, and the parents of the girl. And everyone cried, and grieved for her: but the Christ said, *"Don't cry; she isn't dead, but only sleeping."* And they laughed disrespectfully at the Christ,

knowing that she was dead. So the Christ put them all out, and took her by the hand and called her, saying, *"Young lady, get up."* Then her spirit came into her again, and she suddenly got up. The Christ told them to give her something to eat. Her parents were amazed: but the Christ told them not to tell anyone what had happened.

The Twelve Sent Out

9 [1-6] Then Yeshua called the twelve followers together, and gave them power over all the evil spirits, and the power to heal diseases, sending them to preach about the realm of God, and to heal the sick. And the Christ said to them, *"Take nothing for your journey, neither walking sticks, nor bag, nor food, nor money; nor two sets of clothes. And whatever house you come into, stay there until you leave that place. And whoever won't accept you, when you go out of that city, shake off the very dust from your feet for a witness against them."* So they left, and went through the towns, preaching the New Word, and healing every where.

Herod Wants to See the Christ

[7-9] Now Herod the governor heard of all that happened by them: and was confused, because it was said by some, that John had come back to life; And by some, that Elijah had appeared; and by others, that one of the great old preachers had come back to life again. And Herod said, *"John, I have beheaded: but who is this that I am hearing these things about?"* And Herod wanted to see the Christ.

The Feeding of the Five Thousand

[10-17] And when the followers came back, they told the Christ all that they had done. Now the Christ secretly went with them into a deserted place outside the city of Bethsaida. But when the people knew it, they followed along: so the Christ welcomed them, and told them of the realm of God, and healed those who needed to be healed. When the day was almost over, the twelve came, saying, *"Send the crowd away, so that they can go into the towns and country around here, and stay, and get food because we're out here in this deserted place."* But the Christ answered, *"You give them something to eat."* But they said, *"We only have five loaves of bread and two fish; unless we go and buy food for all these people."* There were about five thousand people, so the Christ said to the followers, *"Make them sit down in groups, by fifties."* So they made them all sit down. Then the Christ took the five loaves and the two fish, and looking up to heaven, blessed it, and broke it up, and gave to the followers to give to the crowd. So they ate, and were all filled: and twelve baskets of scraps were taken up that were left over.

Peter's Confession

[18-21] And later, as Yeshua was praying alone with the followers, the Christ asked them, *"Who do the people say that I am?"* So they answered, *"John the Baptist; but some say, Elijah; and others say, that one of the great old preachers is here back to life again."* Then the Christ asked, *"But who do you say that I am?"* And Peter answered, *"The Christ of God."* And Yeshua clearly warned them, telling them not to tell anyone; saying, *"I must suffer many things, and be rejected by the elders and leading priests and religious leaders, and be killed, and be raised to life again on the third day."*

[23-27] And Yeshua said to them all, *"If anyone wants to come after me, let them forget themselves, and pick up their cross of suffering daily, and follow Me. Because whoever wants to save their life will lose it: but whoever is willing to lose their life for My sake, will save it. What good does it do someone, if they gain the whole world, and lose their soul, or is lost? Whoever is ashamed of Me and of My Words, I'll be ashamed of them, when I come in My own victory, and in My God's, with all of the holy angels. The truth is, some that are standing here won't taste of death till they see the realm of God."*

Elijah and Moses Appear with the Christ

[28-36] About eight days after that, Yeshua took Peter, John, and James, and went up on a mountain to pray. As Yeshua prayed, the way the Christ's face looked was changed, and the clothes the Christ wore were glowing white. And two other people talked with the Christ, who were Moses and Elijah: Who appeared in their changed bodies, and spoke of the Christ's death which would happen at Jerusalem. But Peter, John, and James were very tired: and when they awoke, they saw Yeshua changed, along with the two others that stood with the Christ. And then, as they left, Peter said to Yeshua, *"Christ, it's good that we're here: let's make three memorial stones; one for You, one for Moses, and one for Elijah"* not knowing what he said. While he was speaking, a cloud came, overshadowing them: and as they went into the cloud, they were very afraid. And a voice came out of the cloud, saying, *"This is My Child, who I love: Listen to Yeshua."* And when the voice was gone, Yeshua was alone with them. And they kept it secret, telling no one in those days any of the things which they had seen.

An Only Child Healed from Seizures

[37-45] On the next day, when they had come down from the mountain, many people met them. Then someone out of the crowd called out, saying, *"Christ, I beg you, look at my child, who is my only child."* And then a

117

spirit overtook the child, which hardly left the child without hurting him, who suddenly called out; and foamed at the mouth again. *"I begged your followers to put the spirit out; but they couldn't."* So Yeshua answered, *"You faithless and evil people, how long will I be with you, and have to put up with you? Bring your child here."* And as they were still coming, the evil spirit threw the child down, who had a fit. So Yeshua ordered the evil spirit to come out, and healed the child, and handed him back over to the parent. And everyone was amazed at the wonderful power of the Christ. But while they were all still wondering about what Yeshua did, the Christ said to the followers, *"Listen very carefully to these words because I'll be handed over to the others very soon."* But they didn't understand what the Christ said, and they didn't realize what the Christ meant, but they were afraid to ask about it.

Who will be Greatest?

[46-50] Then later they got in an argument about which one of them would be the greatest. And Yeshua, knowing the very thoughts of their hearts, took a child, and set it in the middle of them, and said, *"Whoever accepts this child in My Name accepts Me: and whoever accepts Me accepts the One who sent Me because whoever seems least important among you all now, will be great in heaven."* Then John asked, *"Christ, we saw someone putting out evil spirits in Your Name; and we told them not to, because they don't follow along with us."* But Yeshua answered, *"Don't tell them not to, because those who aren't against us are for us."*

[51-56] And then, when the time came for the Christ to be taken up, Yeshua decidedly left for Jerusalem, sending messengers to go on ahead: who went into a town of the Samaritans, a people of mixed race, to get ready for the Christ. But they didn't accept the Christ because they knew Yeshua had decided to go on to Jerusalem. And when the followers, James and John, saw this, they said, *"Christ, do you want us to order fire to come down from heaven, and burn them up, just like Elijah did?"* But the Christ turned, and scolded them, saying, *"You don't know what kind of spirit you have. I haven't come to take peoples' lives, but to save them."* So they went on to another town.

[57-62] And then, as they went down the road, someone said, *"Christ, I'll follow you wherever you go."* But Yeshua answered, *"Foxes have holes, and the birds of the air have nests; but I don't have anywhere to lay My head."* And then the Christ said to another one, *"Follow Me."* But that one said, *"Christ, let me first go and bury my parents."* So Yeshua said, *"Let those who are spiritually dead bury their dead: but you go and preach the realm of God."* And then another person said, *"Christ, I'll follow you; but let me go and tell those at home goodbye first."* And Yeshua said, *"No one, having started their work, and looking back at their past life, is fit for the realm of God."*

The Seventy Followers Sent Out

10 [1-15] Later, Yeshua chose seventy other followers also, and sent them on ahead by twos into all the cities and towns, wherever the Christ was to go. Then the Christ said to them, *"The truth is, the harvest is great, but the workers are few: so pray that the God of the harvest will send out workers into the harvest. Now go: I am sending you out as lambs to the wolves. Don't carry a moneybag, or a backpack, or shoes: and don't stop to say hello to anyone on the way. And whatever house you come into, first say, 'Peace be to this house.' If a child of peace is there, your peace will rest on it: if not, it'll come back to you again. Stay in the same house, eating and drinking whatever they give you because the workers are worthy of their hire. Don't go from house to house. Whatever city you come into, if they accept you, eat whatever is set before you: and heal the sick that are in it, and say to them, 'The realm of God has come near you.' But whatever city you come into, if they don't accept you, go out into the streets, and say, 'Even the very dust of your city, which cleaves on us, we wipe off as a witness against you, but in spite of this you can be sure that the realm of God has come near you.' But I tell you, that it'll be more tolerable in that day for Sodom, than for that city. You'll be sorry, Chorazin! You'll be sorry, Bethsaida! If the amazing things, which have been done in you had been done in Tyre and Sidon, they would have changed their ways long ago, sitting and crying in mourning clothes and ashes. But it'll be more tolerable for Tyre and Sidon at the judgment, than for you. And you, Capernaum, which are praised to heaven, will be thrown down to Hell. Whoever hears you, hears Me; and whoever hates you, hates Me; and whoever hates Me hates the very One who sent Me."*

Satan has Fallen

[17-24] Later, the seventy came back with joy, saying, *"Christ, even the evil spirits have to do what we say in Your Name."* And Christ answered, *"I watched Satan fall from heaven like lightening. So I've given you power to stomp on snakes and scorpions, and over all the power of the enemy: nothing will hurt you in any way. Just the same, don't celebrate because the spirits have to do what you say; but instead celebrate, because your names are written in heaven."* Then Yeshua celebrated in spirit, saying, *"I thank You, Yahweh God, Ruler of heaven and earth, that you've hid this from the wise and careful, and have revealed it to babies. Just the same, God, because it was good in Your sight, everything is given to Me by You: and no one knows Me, but You, God; and no one knows You, God, but Me, whom You sent, and those to whom I reveal You."* Then the Christ turned to the followers privately, saying, *"Blessed are the eyes which see the things that you see, because I tell you, that many great preachers and rulers have wanted to see and hear what you see and hear, and haven't seen it or heard it."*

118

The Good Samaritan

[25-37] And a certain student of the law stood up, tempting Yeshua, saying, *"Christ, what can I do to have everlasting life?"* And Christ answered, *"What does the Word of God say? What do you think it says?"* And the student of the law answered, *"Love Yahweh, your God with all your spirit, with all your soul, with all your body, and with all your mind; and love others as you love yourself."* So the Christ said, "You're right: so do this and you'll live." But wanting to make himself appear to be good, he said to Yeshua, *"And who should I love?"* So Yeshua told a story, saying, *"Someone went down from Jerusalem to Jericho, and thieves beat that person, tearing their clothes off and leaving them for dead. And by chance a certain priest came that way: and when the priest saw the person who had been attacked, that priest walked by on the other side of the road. Then another religious leader passed by coming to that place, and looking at the person, walked by on the other side of the road. But someone from the city of Samaria, who was taking a trip, came to where the person was: and that mixed-race Samaritan saw the person, and had compassion, who went to the person, dressing the wounds, pouring in oil and alcohol, and took the person on his own horse, bringing them to an inn, and taking care of that person. The next day the Samaritan left, giving some money to the host, saying, 'Take care of this person; and whatever it costs more than this, I'll repay you when I come back.' So which of these three, do you think, showed love to the one who was attacked by the thieves?"* And the student of the law said, *"The one who cared for the person."* Then Yeshua said, *"Go, and do the same."*

Mary and Martha

[38-41] Now it so happened, as they were going, that they went into a certain town, where a woman named Martha had taken them into her house. And she had a sister, Mary, who also sat at Yeshua's feet, listening to the Words of the Christ. But Martha was busy with all the serving, and came to Yeshua, saying, *"Christ, don't you care that my sister has left me to serve all alone?"* Tell her to help me. And Yeshua answered, *"Martha, Martha, you're upset and worried about too many things, but there is only one thing that's really needed: Mary has chosen what's good and that won't be taken away from her."*

Christ's Teaches How to Pray

11 [1-4] As Christ was praying in a certain place, when they stopped, one of the followers said, *"Christ, teach us to pray, as John also taught his followers."* And Yeshua answered, *"When you pray, say: Yahweh, Our God in heaven, Your Name is Holy. May Your everlasting realm come soon. May what You want be done on earth, as it's done in heaven. Give us what we need today. And forgive our sins as we also forgive everyone that has sinned against us. And help us not to sin when we're tempted; but free us from all evil."*

Ask and It Will Be Given to You

[5-13] Then Yeshua said, *"Who among you that has a friend, if you went to them at midnight, and asked, 'Friend, let me borrow three loaves of bread; because a friend of mine has come to me on a trip, and I don't have anything to give them?' And the friend inside the house answers and says, 'Don't bother me: the door is already locked, and my children are asleep in bed with me and I can't get up to give it to you.' I tell you, even if the friend won't get up and give it to you, because you're their friend, still if you keep on knocking they'll get up and give you whatever you need. So I tell you, ask, and it'll be given to you; look for it, and you'll find it; knock, and it'll be opened to you. Because everyone that asks gets what they ask for; and whoever looks for something will find it; and to those who knock it'll be opened to them. If a child asked for a piece of bread from any of you that is a parent, would you give them a stone? Or if they ask for a fish, would you give them a snake? Or if they asked for an egg, would you offer them a scorpion? If you then, being evil by nature, know how to give good gifts to your children: wouldn't your God in heaven give the Holy Spirit to those who ask even more than this?"*

Christ Speaks on Evil Spirits

[14-26] Then the Christ was putting out an evil spirit, and it was dumb. And when the evil spirit had gone out, the dumb person was able to speak; and the people were amazed. But some of them said, *"This person puts out evil spirits by the power of the devil, the leader of the evil spirits."* And others, trying to tempt the Christ, looked for a sign from heaven. But the Christ, knowing what they were thinking, said, *"When the people of a country are divided against themselves the country will be destroyed; and when a family is divided against itself, that family won't survive. If Satan fights against the evil spirits, how could that realm survive? You say that I put out evil spirits by the devil. But if I put out evil spirits by the devil, by whom do your children put them out? So they'll be your judges. But if I put out evil spirits with the Spirit of God, the realm of God has come to you without a doubt. When a strong person who is armed watches over their house, whatever they own is safe: But when someone stronger than that comes and overpowers them, that person will take all the swords that the owners trusted to keep them safe, and take whatever they own. Whoever isn't with Me is against Me: and whoever doesn't gather souls with*

119

Me scatters them out. When an evil spirit has gone out of someone, it walks through dry places, looking for rest; but finding none, it says, 'I'll return to the house where I came from.' And when it comes, it finds it swept and decorated. Then it goes, and brings along seven more spirits which are more evil than itself, which come in, and stay. Then the last state of that person is worse than the first."

The Eye is the Light of the Body

[27-36] And then, as the Christ spoke this, a certain woman out of the crowd lifted up her voice, saying, "Blessed is the womb that birthed you, and the breasts which you've sucked." But the Christ said, "Yes, but more importantly, blessed are those who hear the Word of God, and do it." And when the people were crowded together, the Christ began to say, "This is an evil people that look for a sign; but they won't be given any sign, but the sign of Jonah, the great preacher. Just as Jonah was a sign to the Ninevites, so I'll be a sign to this people also. The queen of the south will stand up in the judgment with others of this people, and accuse them because she came from the farthest parts of the earth to hear the wisdom of Solomon; and someone greater than Solomon is here. The people of Nineveh will stand up in the judgment with this people, and will accuse them because they changed their ways at the preaching of Jonah; and someone greater than Jonah is here. No one, when they have lit a candle, puts it in a secret place, nor under a basket, but on a candle holder, so that those who come in can see the light. The eye is the light of the body, so when your eye is set on the light of goodness, your whole body is full of light also; but when your eye is set on the darkness of evil, your body is full of darkness also. So be sure that your spiritual light isn't dimmed. If your whole body is full of light, having no dark purpose, the whole body will be full of light, as when a shining candle gives you light."

Christ Speaks On Giving

[37-44] As the Christ spoke, a certain religious leader begged Yeshua to dine with him: so the Christ went in, and sat down to eat. And when the religious leader saw it, he was surprised that Yeshua hadn't washed before dinner. So Yeshua said, "Now you religious leaders wash the outside of the cup and plate; but your inside is full of evil and greediness. You're so thoughtless, didn't the One who made the outside also make the inside? You should give a part out of whatever you have; and you'll be clean both inside and out. But you'll be sorry, you religious leaders! You give a part of even the smallest amounts of herbs, but you overlook fair judgment and God's love: you should do this, but not leave the other things undone. You'll be sorry, you religious leaders! You love the best seats in the places of worship, and love to be greeted in the shopping centers. You'll be sorry, you religious leaders and those of you in the religious sects, you fakes! You're like hidden graves that people walk over and don't even know they're there."

[45-54] Then one of the religious leaders, said, "Christ, what you say accuses us also." And the Christ said, "You'll be sorry also, you religious leaders! because you give others rules that are hard to keep, and you yourselves don't even try to keep them. You'll be sorry! You build the memorial tombs of the great preachers, and your own ancestors killed them. The truth is, you're witnesses of the fact that you accept the actions of your ancestors because they in fact killed them, and you build their memorials. So the wisdom of God said, 'I'll send them great preachers and followers, and they'll kill and mistreat some of them: So that the blood of all the great preachers, which was shed from the beginning of the world, can be required of this people; From the blood of Abel to the blood of Zachariah, who was killed between the altar and the Place of Worship: The truth is, it'll be required of this people. You'll be sorry, you religious leaders! You've hidden away the key of knowledge; You didn't come in yourselves, and you even stopped those who were trying to come in." As the Christ said this to them, the religious leaders and the religious sects began to question Yeshua, to try to get the Christ to speak of many things, waiting to catch something in which they could put blame on the Christ.

The Unforgiveable Sin

12 [1-12] In the mean time, when there was an innumerable crowd of people gathered together, so that they trampled on one another, the Christ began to say to the followers first of all, "Beware of the untruthful leaven of the religious ones, because there isn't anything covered, that won't become known; nor hid, that won't be found out. So whatever you've spoken in darkness will be heard in the light; and what you've whispered in private will be called out on the rooftops. I tell you My friends, don't be afraid of those who can kill the body, and after that can do no more. I tell you whom you should fear: Fear the One, who has power to put your soul in Hell when you're dead; yes, I tell you, Honor and respect Yahweh God. Aren't five sparrows sold for two small coins, and not one of them is forgotten by God? Even the very hairs of your head are all numbered. So don't be afraid: you're worth more than many sparrows. I tell you, too, whoever admits that they know Me to others, I'll admit that I know them in the presence of the angels of God: But whoever says they don't know me to others, I'll say I don't know them in the presence of the angels of God. And whoever speaks a word against Me, can be forgiven: but those who reject the Holy Spirit won't be forgiven. And when they bring you to religious ones, courts, and rulers, don't think about what you'll answer, or what you might say, because the Holy Spirit will show you what to say at that very time."

120

Beware of Greed

[13-21] Then one out of the crowd said, *"Christ, tell my brother to divide the inheritance with me."* But Christ said, *"Who made me a judge or an overseer over you?"* And then Christ answered, *"Be careful and beware of greed because a person's life isn't made up of what they have."* And then Christ told a story to them, saying, *"The land of a certain rich person produced a great crop, so that person thought, 'What can I do, because there's no room to store my crops? I know; I'll do this: I'll tear down my barns, and build bigger ones; and then I'll have room for all my crops and stuff. And I'll say to myself, I've got enough stored up for many years to come; eat, drink, rest, and have fun.' But God said, 'You idiot, tonight your soul will be taken from you and then who will get everything you saved up?' This is the way it'll be for whoever saves up wealth for themselves, and aren't rich in God."*

Don't Worry About Worldly Things

[22-30] Then Christ said to the followers, *"So I tell you, don't worry about your life, what you'll eat; nor for the body, what you'll put on. Life is more than food, and the body is more than clothing. Think about the ravens, which neither plant nor pick; nor store anything up; and God takes care of them: how much better you are than the birds! And who by worrying can add one inch to their height? If you then aren't able to do this least little thing, why do you worry about all the rest? Consider the lilies that grow: they don't work, they don't plant; and still I tell you, that all Solomon's riches didn't make him as beautiful as one of these. So then, if God clothes the grasses this way, which is in the field today, and wilts away in the heat by tomorrow; how much more will God clothe you, who have such little faith? So don't worry about what you'll eat, or what you'll drink, nor doubt in your mind, because worldly people do this. Your God in heaven knows that you need these things.*

[31-40] *But instead, put your mind on the realm of God; and all this will be given to you, too. Don't be afraid, little flock because it's your God's good will to give you the realm of God. Sell whatever you have, and give your gifts to God and others; work for the wealth that never gets old, a wealth in the heavens that never runs out, where no thief comes near, nor any moth harms because your heart is wherever your wealth is. Always be ready to go, night or day; and you yourselves, be like those that wait till their owner returns from the wedding; who comes and knocks, so that they can quickly open the door. Blessed are those who are watching when I come. The truth is, that even I'll get ready, and make them sit down to eat, and will come out and serve them. And if I come late at night or early in the morning, and find them waiting, they'll be blessed. Know this, if the owners of the house had known when the thief would come, they would have watched, and not have let their house be broken into. So you be ready also because I'll come at a time when you won't be expecting Me."*

Be Ready

[41-48] Then Peter said, *"Christ, are you speaking this story just to us, or to everyone?"* And Christ said, *"Who is that faithful and wise caretaker, whom the owner will put over the household, to give them what they need at just the right time? Blessed is that worker, whom when the owner comes back, finds working hard. The truth is, I tell you, that the owner will make them a ruler over everything. But if that worker says in their heart, 'My owner puts off coming;' and begins to abuse the workers and working girls, and to eat and drink, and gets drunk; The owner of that worker will come in a day when the worker isn't watching, and at a time when the worker won't know it, and will punish the worker with death in the judgment of unbelievers. And that worker, which knew the owner's will, but didn't get ready, nor do what the owner wanted, will be badly punished. But whoever didn't know what the owner wanted, and did things worthy of punishment, will only be punished a little, because a lot will be expected of whoever is given a big job: and to whoever has been trusted with a lot, more will be expected of them.*

[49-53] *I have come to send fire on the earth and long for it to be lit already! But I have a baptism to be baptized with; and am troubled till it's over! Do you think that I've come to bring peace on earth? I tell you, no; but instead, I'll cause disagreements: because from now on there will be five in a house divided, three against two, and two against three. Father against son and son against father; mother against daughter, and daughter against mother; mother-in-law against daughter-in-law, and daughter-in-law against mother-in-law."*

[54-59] Then Yeshua said to the people, *"When you see a cloud come up out of the west, quickly you say that a rain shower is coming; and so it does. When you see the south wind blow, you say that it's going to be hot; and it's hot. You fakes, you understand the face of the sky and of the earth; but why don't you understand this time? Yes, and why don't you yourselves judge what's right? When you're on the way to go to court with your enemy, try your best to settle your argument; in case they take you to the judge, and the judge hands you over to the officer, and the officer puts you in jail. I tell you, you won't leave there, till you've paid the very last cent of your fine."*

Story of the Fig Tree

13 [1-5] At that time, some came and told Yeshua of the Galilaeans, who Pilate had killed while they were making sacrifices, mixing their own blood with that of the sacrifices. Then Yeshua said, *"Do you think that these people were greater sinners than anyone else, because they suffered like this? I tell you, no: but, unless you change your evil ways, you'll all be destroyed like this. Or those eighteen, on whom the tower in Siloam fell, and* killed them, do you think that they were greater sinners than anyone else that lived in Jerusalem? I tell you, no: but, unless you change your evil ways, you'll all be destroyed like this."

[6-10] Then the Christ told them this story, too; "Someone had a fig tree planted in their garden and came and looked for some fruit on it, but didn't find any. Then the owner said to the gardener, 'I've looked for fruit on this fig tree for three years now, and haven't found any: cut it down; why should it take up space?' But the gardener answered, 'Leave it alone this year, till I'll dig around it, and fertilize it: If it makes fruit, good: but if not, then after that I'll cut it down as you say.' And the Christ was teaching in one of the places of worship on the Seventh Day.

A Woman Healed on the Seventh Day

[11-17] There was a woman who had a problem for eighteen years, and was humped over, and couldn't lift herself up by any means. When the Christ saw her, Yeshua called her, saying to her, "Woman, you're freed from your problem." And when the Christ laid hands on her, she was suddenly able to straighten up, and praised God. But because Yeshua had healed on a Seventh Day, the leader of the Place of Worship said to the people with resentment, "There are six days in the week to work, so come and be healed on those days, and not on a Day of Worship." So Christ said then, "You fake, doesn't each one of you let your animals out of their stalls, and lead them to water on the Seventh Day? So shouldn't I help this woman, being a daughter of Abraham, whom Satan has made to suffer these eighteen years, be freed from this condition on a Day of Worship?" And when the Christ had said this, all the enemies of Yeshua were ashamed. So all the people celebrated for the amazing things that had happened because of the Christ.

The Realm of God

[18-30] Then the Christ said, "What is the realm of God like? And to what can I compare it? It's like a grain of mustard seed, which someone took and planted in their garden; It grew, and became a great tree; so much that even the birds of the air could live in its branches." Then the Christ said, "What is the realm of God like? It's like yeast, which a woman mixed in three cups of flour, till it was all leavened." And then the Christ went through all the cities and towns, teaching, and going toward Jerusalem. Then someone said, "Christ, are there only a few that will be saved?" And the Christ answered, "Work hard to come in the right way at the gate, which is narrow, because many, I tell you, will want to come in, but won't be able. When the owner of the house has gotten up, and shut the door, and you begin to gather outside, knocking at the door, saying, 'Christ, Christ, open the door to us;' then the owner will answer saying to you, 'I don't even you know who you are.' Then you'll begin to say, 'We've celebrated in your presence, and you've taught in our streets.' But the owner will say, 'I tell you, I don't even know who you are; go away, you sinful people.' And you'll be crying and gritting your teeth, when you see Abraham, Isaac, and Jacob, and all the great preachers, in the realm of God, and you yourselves put out. And they'll come from east, west, north, and south, and will sit down in the realm of God. And some of those who were last will be first then, and some of those who were first will be last then."

Herod Threatens the Christ

[31-35] This same day some of the religious leaders came, saying to the Christ, "Get out, and leave here because Herod will kill you." But Christ answered, "Go, and tell that sly one, I'll put out evil spirits and heal today, tomorrow, and the third day I'll be finished. In the same way, I must walk today, tomorrow, and the next day because a great preacher can't be killed outside of Jerusalem. Jerusalem, Jerusalem, you who kill the great preachers, and stone those who are sent to you; how often I would have gathered your children together, as a mother hen gathers her chicks under her wings, but you wouldn't come! Your house is left to you empty, and the truth is, you won't see Me, until the time comes when you'll say, 'Blessed is the One who comes in the Name of Yahweh God.'"

Healing on a Day of Worship

14 [1-6] And then, one of the important religious leaders watched as the Christ went into his house to eat on a Day of Worship. And someone came to the Christ, who was very swollen with fluid in the body. So Yeshua said to the religious leaders and the ministers from the religious sects, asking, "Is it right to heal on a Day of Worship?" But they didn't answer. So the Christ healed the person, and let them go; And said, "Which of you, if you had a donkey or a cow that had fallen into a hole, wouldn't quickly pull them out, even on a Day of Worship?" And again, they couldn't answer the Christ's question.

Be Humble

[7-11] So Yeshua told a story to those which were asked, when the Christ noted how they chose the best places; saying to them, "When you're asked to a wedding by someone, don't sit down in the best places; in case a more honorable person than you is also asked by them; And then the one who asked you, comes and says to you, 'Let this person have your place;' and then, with shame, you have to go to a less important place. But when

122

you're asked, go and sit down in a less important place; so that when the one who asked you comes, they can say to you, 'Friend, come sit over here.' Then you'll be praised in front of all those who sit to eat with you. Whoever puts themselves in a higher place will be shamed; and whoever humbles themselves will be praised."

[12-14] Then Yeshua said this to the one who had asked the Christ to come and eat, "When you give a dinner or a supper, don't just call your friends, nor your family, nor your other kin people, nor your rich neighbors, because they'll also ask you to a dinner, and repay the favor. But when you give a dinner, call those who are poor, or hurt, or disabled, or blind. Then you'll be blessed even though they can't repay you, because you'll be repaid when those who are good come back to life again."

The Great Supper

[15-24] When someone who was eating with them heard this, they said, "Blessed is the One who eats in the realm of God." Then the Christ answered, "Someone made a great supper, and asked many to come, sending their worker at supper time to say to those who were asked, 'Come because everything is ready now.' But they all, in agreement, began to make excuses. The first said, 'I've bought a piece of land and have to go and see it: Please, excuse me.' And another said, 'I've bought five pairs of cattle, and have to prove them: Please, excuse me.' And another said, 'I've just gotten married, and so I can't come.' So the worker came, and told the owner this. Then the owner of the house, being angry said to the worker, 'Go quickly out into the streets and roads of the city, and bring here all those who are poor, hurt, disabled, and blind.' And the worker said to the owner, 'I've done as you've told me, and there's still more room.' So the owner said to the worker, 'Go out into the highways and the roads, and beg them to come in, so that my house can be filled. Because I tell you that not one of those others who were asked will taste of my supper.'"

Count the Cost

[25-35] And great crowds went along with the Christ: who turned, saying to them, "If anyone comes to Me, and doesn't hate their parents, and spouse, and children, and brothers, and sisters, yes, and even their own life also, they can't be My follower. Whoever doesn't carry their own cross, and come after Me, can't be My follower. Would any of you, intending to build a house, not sit down first, and count the cost, to see whether or not you had enough to finish it? In case, after you've laid the foundation, you aren't able to finish it, and all that see it begin to mock you, saying, 'This person began something, and wasn't able to finish it.' Or what ruler, going to make war against another, doesn't sit down first, and consider whether they are able with ten thousand to fight those who come against them with twenty thousand? Or else, while the other is still a great way off, they send an ambassador asking for conditions of peace. So in this way, whoever doesn't turn away from everything, can't be My follower. Salt is good: but if the salt has lost its saltiness, how can it season anything? It's not fit for the land, nor even for the compost; but only to be thrown out. If anyone will accept this, let them accept it."

Finding the One That's Lost

15 [1-9] Then all the tax collectors and sinners came near to hear the Christ. The religious leaders and the ministers from the religious sects spoke against the Christ, saying, "This person accepts sinners, and eats with them." So Christ told this story to them, saying, "Which one of you, if you had a hundred animals, and lost one, wouldn't leave the ninety-nine in the countryside, and go after the one that's lost, until you find it? And when you find it, lay it across your shoulders, and celebrate. And when you come home, call together all your friends and neighbors, saying to them, 'Celebrate with me because I've found my animal that was lost.' I tell you that the same kind of joy will be in heaven over one sinner that changes their ways, more than over ninety-nine good people, who don't need to change their ways."

[8-10] "And who, having ten silver coins, if they lose one, wouldn't get a light, and search the house, and look carefully till they find it? And when they find it, call their friends and neighbors together, saying, 'Celebrate with me because I've found the silver coin that I had lost.' In this way, I tell you, the angels of God will have great joy over one sinner that changes their ways."

The Lost Child

[11-32] Then the Christ told them this story, "Someone had two children. The younger of them said to the parent, "Give me my share of the inheritance now." So the parent gave the inheritance to the younger one. A few days later, the younger child gathered everything together, and took a journey into a far country, and when the child got there, wasted it all with selfish living. And when the child had spent it all, a great shortage of food came to that land; and the child began to be in need. So the child went to work for a citizen of that country; who sent them into their fields to feed the pigs. And the child almost would have eaten what the pigs ate, because no one gave the child anything to eat. And when the child thought about it, thinking, 'How many of my parent's hired workers have enough food, with some to spare, and I am dying of hunger! I'll go back home to my parent, and say to them, I've sinned against heaven, and you, and I'm not worthy to be called your child: but make me as one

of your hired workers.' So the child got up, and went home to their parent. So when the child was still a great way off, the parent saw them, and had compassion, and ran, and hugged the child's neck, and kissed them. And the child said, 'I've sinned against heaven, and in your sight, and I'm not worthy to be called your child.' But the parent said to the workers, 'Bring out the best clothes, and put it on my child; and put a ring and shoes on the child: And butcher the fatted calf, and kill it; and let's eat, and celebrate, because my child was dead, and is alive again; and was lost, and now is found.' And they began to celebrate. Now the older child was in the field: and coming home, got near the house, and heard music and dancing. So that child called one of the workers, and asked what was the meaning of all this. And the worker said, 'Your younger brother has come home; and your parent has killed the fatted calf, because the child has returned safe and sound.' And the older child was angry, and wouldn't go in: so the parent came out, and begged the child to come in. So the older one said to the parent, 'Look, I've worked for you many years, and I've never disobeyed your word: and still, you never even gave me a baby goat, that I might have a party with my friends: But as soon as that child came home, who has spent your living on whores, you killed the fatted calf. So the parent said, 'Child, you've always been with me, and all that I have is yours. But it's right to celebrate, and be happy because this child was dead, and is alive again; and was lost, and now is found.'"

The Story of the Bad Manager

16 [1-12] The Christ also said to the followers, *"There was a certain rich person, which had a manager who was accused of having wasted their goods. So they called them, saying, 'How come I am hearing this about you? Give an account of your management or you can no longer be my manager.' Then the manager thought, 'What will I do? My owner will take away my job. I can't dig; and I'm ashamed to beg. I know what to do. When I'm fired from the management, I'll go to those who owe my owner.' So the manager called everyone of the owner's debtors, saying to the first, 'How much do you owe my owner?' And that one said, a hundred dollars worth of oil. So the manager said, 'Take your bill, and sit down quickly, and change it to fifty.' Then the manager said to another, 'and how much do you owe?' And that one said, 'a hundred dollars worth of wheat.' So the manager said, 'Take your bill, and change it to eighty.' And the owner applauded the bad manager, because the manger had wisely gotten out of trouble by giving them a good discount. The people of this world are more dishonest than the children of light. So I tell you, make godly friends with your earthly money; so that, when you die, you'll be accepted into the heavenly realm along with them. Whoever is faithful with a little is faithful also with a lot. And whoever is unfaithful with a little will also be unfaithful with a lot. So if you haven't been faithful in the world's money, who will trust you with the true riches? And if you haven't been faithful in what belongs to another, who will give you anything for your own?"*

Serve God, Not Money

[13-17] "No worker can serve two employers because either they'll hate one, and love the other; or else they'll be faithful to one, and hate the other. You can't serve God and worship money, too." And the religious leaders also, who were very selfish, heard all this, and mocked what Yeshua had said. So the Christ said, *"You're the ones who try to make yourselves appear good to others; but God knows your hearts. What's highly valued among humanity is evil in the sight of God. Humanity has had the Word of God and the great preachers up until John came, and since that time, the realm of God has been preached about, and everyone is trying to get into it. But it's easier for heaven and earth to pass, than one small point of the Word of God to fail. So whoever divorces their spouse, and marries another, takes part in sexual sin: and whoever marries someone that is divorced takes part in sexual sin, as well.*

Lazarus and the Rich Person

[19-31] *There was a certain rich person, who was clothed in fine clothes, and fared well every day: And there was a certain beggar named Lazarus, who lay at the gate, and was full of sores, hoping to be fed with the crumbs which fell from the rich person's table. And besides this, the dogs came and licked the beggar's sores. And then the beggar died, and was carried by the angels to Abraham. Then the rich person also died, and was buried. And the rich person opened their eyes up in Hell, and suffering, saw Abraham far off, and Lazarus near by, too. So the rich person cried saying, 'Abraham, have mercy on me, and send Lazarus to dip the tip of his finger in water, and cool my tongue because I am suffering in this flame.' But Abraham said, 'Child, remember that you in your lifetime had good things, and Lazarus had evil things: but now Lazarus is comforted, and you're suffering. And besides all this, there's a great gulf fixed between us and you: so that those who would pass from here to you can't; nor can those who would come from there pass to us.' Then the rich person said, 'I beg you, then, send Lazarus to my family to tell them: because I have five brothers, in case they also come into this place of suffering.' And Abraham said, 'They have Moses and the great preachers; let them hear them.' But the rich person said, 'No, Abraham: but if someone went to them from the dead, they'll change their evil ways.' And Abraham said, 'If they won't hear Moses and the great preachers, they won't be won over, even though someone rose from the dead."*

Abusers Will be Punished

17 [1-10] Then Yeshua said to the followers, *"It would be impossible for abuses not to happen: but sorrow will surely come to those who hurt others! It would better for them to have a large stone hung around their neck, and be drowned in the sea, than to hurt one of these little ones. Watch out for yourselves: If someone sins against you, confront them; and if they change their evil ways, forgive them. And if they sin against you seven times in a day, and seven times in a day turn back to you, saying, I'll change my evil ways; forgive them."* And the followers said to Christ, *"Help us to have more faith."* So Christ said, *"If you have faith even as small as a grain of mustard seed, if you said to this sycamore tree, 'Be moved out of your place, and be planted in the sea;' it would obey you. But which of you, having a worker plowing or feeding cattle, would say to them, when they've come in from the field, 'Go and sit down to eat?' But wouldn't you say to them instead, 'Get my supper ready, and get ready to serve me, till I've finished my meal; and then you can eat'? Would you thank that worker because they did what they were told? I don't think so. So it's the same with you, when you've done all that you're told, say, 'We're worthless workers: we've only done what was our duty to do.'"*

Ten People Healed, One Returns with Thanks

[11-19] And then, as they went on to Jerusalem, they passed through the middle of Samaria and Galilee. And as they came to a certain town, ten lepers met them, who stood off away from them: And they called out, saying, *'Yeshua, Christ, have mercy on us.'* And seeing them, the Christ said, *"Go show yourselves to the priests."* As they went, they were healed, and one of them, who saw that he was healed, turned back, and praised God with a loud voice, and fell face down at Yeshua's feet, giving thanks: and it was a mixed-race Samaritan. So Yeshua said, *"Weren't there ten healed? So where are the other nine? Didn't any come back to give praise to God, except this stranger?"* So Christ said, *"Get up, and go: your faith has healed you."*

The End Times

[20-37] Now when the religious leaders asked the Christ when the realm of God would come, Yeshua answered, *"The realm of God isn't something you see: Nor will people say, Look here! or, Look there! because the realm of God is what's inside you."* Later the Christ said to the followers, *"The time will come, when you'll wish to see one of these days with Me, but you won't see it. And people will say to you, 'Look here;' or, 'Look there:' but don't go with them, nor follow after them, because I'll be like the lightning that flashes from one side heaven and shines to the other side of heaven in the day of My return. But first I must suffer many things, and be rejected by the people. And just as it was in the days of Noah, so it will be also in the day of My return. People ate and drank, and were married and given in marriage, until the day that Noah went in the ark, and the flood came, and killed them all. The same also as it was in the days of Lot; they ate, they drank, they bought, they sold, they planted, and they built; But the very day that Lot went out of Sodom, God rained fire and sulfur down from heaven, and killed them all. In the same way, it'll also be this way on the day when I am made known. In that day, whoever is on the rooftop, and their stuff is in the house, don't go down to get it: and whoever is in the field, don't go back. Remember Lot's wife. Whoever tries to save their life will lose it; and whoever is willing to lose their life will save it. I tell you, on that night there will be two people on one bed; and one will be taken, and the other left behind. Two women will be working together; and one will be taken, and the other left behind. Two men will be out in the field; and one will be taken, and the other left behind."* And they asked, "Where, Christ?" And Yeshua answered, *"Wherever the body is, the birds of prey will be gathered together there."*

Keep Praying

18 [1-8] And Yeshua told a story to them so that people would always pray, and not give up hope; So the Christ said, *"There was a judge in a city, who wasn't afraid of God, nor cared about what people thought either: And there was a widow in that city, who came to the judge, saying, 'Punish my enemy.' And the judge wouldn't for a while: but later thought, 'Though I'm not afraid of God, nor do I care what anyone thinks; Yet because this widow bothers me, I'll get justice for her, or if she keeps coming, she'll wear me out.'"* And then Yeshua said, *"Listen to what the evil judge said. Won't God do justice for the chosen ones, who cry out to God day and night, though God waits along time to answer them? I tell you that God will bring justice for them suddenly. And yet, when I come, will I find any faith left on the earth?"*

The Religious Leader and the Tax Collector

[9-14] Christ told this story to certain people who trusted in themselves that they were good, but hated others: *"Two people went into a Place of Worship to pray; One was a religious leader, and the other a tax collector. The religious leader stood and prayed to himself, 'God, I thank you, that I'm not like others are, cheats, evil ones, sexually unfaithful, or like this tax collector. I go without food twice a week, I always give a part of what I have.' And the tax collector, standing far off, wouldn't even look up to heaven, but hit himself on the chest, saying, 'God,*

be compassionate to me a sinner.' I tell you, this person went home made right instead of the other because everyone who thinks too highly of themselves will be ashamed; and whoever humbles themselves will be praised."

Let the Children Come

[15-17] And the people brought babies to Yeshua, also, hoping that the Christ would bless them: but when the followers saw it, they scolded them. But Yeshua called them over, saying, *"Let the little children to come to Me, and don't tell them not to come, because the realm of God is filled with such as these. The truth is, whoever won't come into the realm of God with the undoubting faith of a little child, won't come in at all."*

Put Christ First

[18-30] Then a certain ruler asked Yeshua, saying, *"Good Christ, what do I need to do to have everlasting life?"* And Yeshua said, *"Why do you call Me good? No one is good, except One, and that is God. You know the Words of the Law: Don't do any sexual sin, don't kill, don't steal, don't lie about someone, and honor your parents."* And the ruler said, *"I've done all this from my youth up."* Now when Yeshua heard this, the Christ said, *"Yet still, you lack one thing. Sell everything you own, and give to the poor, and you'll have wealth in heaven: and come, follow Me."* But the ruler, hearing this, was very sorrowful because he was very rich. Yeshua saw that he was very sorrowful, and said, *"How hard it is for those who have riches to come into the realm of God! It's easier for a camel to be completely unloaded and squeeze through the eye of a needle, that is, the smallest gate, than for a rich person to come into the realm of God."* And those who heard it said, *"Who can be saved then?"* And the Christ said, *"The things that are impossible for people, are possible with God."* Then Peter said, *"Look, we've left everything, and followed you."* And Yeshua answered, *"The truth is, there's not one of you who has left a house, or parents, or siblings, or a spouse, or children, for the realm of God's sake, who won't get much more in this life, and in the world to come, everlasting life."*

The Death of Christ Foretold

[31-34] Then the Christ took the twelve away from the others, saying to them, *"We're going up to Jerusalem, and everything that is written by the great preachers about Me will happen. I'll be handed over to the other peoples, and mocked, and treated hatefully, and spit on: And they'll beat Me, and put Me to death: and the third day I'll come to life again."* But they didn't understand any of this: the Christ's words were unclear to them, and they didn't remember any of what the Christ had said.

The Blind Sees

[35-43] And then as they came near Jericho, a certain blind person sat begging beside the road. Hearing the crowd pass by, the blind person asked what it meant. And the people told him, that Yeshua of Nazareth was passing by. So he called out, saying, *"Yeshua, Child of David, have mercy on me."* And those who were ahead of him scolded him, telling him to be quiet: but he called out all the more, *"Child of David, have mercy on me."* And Yeshua stood still, and told the people to bring the person who was blind there: and when he came near, the Christ asked, *"What do you want Me to do to you?"* And he said, *"Christ, that I can have my sight."* And Yeshua said, *"Believe that you'll see: your faith has saved you."* And suddenly, he got his sight back and followed along, worshipping God: and all the people, when they saw it, gave praise to God.

Christ Eats at the House of Zaccaeus

19 [1-10] Then Yeshua came and passed through Jericho, where there was someone named Zaccaeus, which was the leader among the tax collectors, and who was rich. Now Zaccaeus looked for a way to see who Yeshua was; but couldn't for the crowd, because he was short. So he ran, and climbed up into a sycamore tree to see Yeshua, because the Christ was about to pass by that way. And when Yeshua came to that place, the Christ looked up, and saw him, saying, *"Zaccaeus, come down quickly; I want to stay at your house today."* So he quickly came down, and welcomed the Christ joyfully. And when the people saw it, they all spoke against it, saying, *"The Christ has gone to be the guest of a sinner!"* And Zaccaeus stood up, saying, *"Christ, I'll give half of everything I own to the poor; and if I've taken anything from anyone by false claim, I'll give them back four times as much."* And Yeshua said, *"Today, you and your family are saved, because you also are a child of Abraham. This is why I've come to find and save those who are lost."*

The Story of the Workers and the Coins

[11-27] As they heard this, Yeshua told another story, because Jerusalem was near by, and because they thought that the realm of God was just about to happen. So the Christ said, *"Someone of great respect went far away to accept the rule of a country, and to return; who called ten workers, and gave them ten coins, saying to them, do business till I come back. But the citizens hated this person, and sent a message, saying, 'We won't have you reign over us.' And then the ruler came back, having taken rule over the country, and called the workers*

126

to whom he had given the money, in order to know how much each had gained by trading. Then the first came, saying, 'Ruler, your coin has gained ten more.' And the Ruler said, 'Well done, you're a good worker, and because you've been faithful in a very little, you'll have power over ten cities.' And the second came, saying, 'Ruler, your coin has gained five coins.' And the Ruler said the same to this one, 'You also will be over five cities.' And another came, saying, 'Ruler, here is your coin, which I've saved wrapped in a napkin because I was afraid of you, because you're a harsh person: you take what you didn't put down, and pick what you don't plant.' And the Ruler said, 'I'll judge you by your own words, you evil worker. You knew that I was a harsh person, taking what I haven't put down, and picking what I didn't plant: Why then didn't you put my money into the bank, so that at my coming I might have gotten my own back with interest?' And the Ruler said to those who stood by, 'Take the coin, and give it to the one who has ten coins.' (And they said, 'Ruler, he has ten coins already.') I tell you, that everyone which has something will be given more; and those who haven't got much, even what they have will be taken away from them. And all my enemies, who didn't want me to reign over them, bring them here to me, and kill them."

Christ Rides into Jerusalem on a Donkey

[28-40] And when Yeshua had said this, the Christ went on ahead, going up to Jerusalem. And then the Christ came near Bethphage and Bethany, at the Mountain called the Mount of Olives, and sent two of the followers, saying, "Go into the town up ahead of you; and when you get there, you'll find a foal tied up, on which no one has ever sat before. Untie it, and bring it here. And if anyone asks you, 'Why are you untying it?' Say to them, 'because the Christ needs it.'" And those who were sent left, and found it just as the Christ had told them. And as they were untying the foal, the owners of it asked, "Why are you untying the foal?" So they said, "The Christ needs it." And they brought it to Yeshua: and laid some of their clothes on the foal, and Yeshua sat on it. And as the Christ went, they spread their clothes down on the road. And when the Christ came near the slope of the Mount of Olives, the whole crowd of followers began to celebrate and praise God with a loud voice for all the amazing things that they had seen; saying, "May the One who is coming be blessed, a Ruler that comes in the Name of Yahweh God: peace in heaven, and victory to the Highest." And some of the religious leaders from among the crowd said, "Christ, tell your followers not to do that." But the Christ answered them, saying, "I tell you that if these were to be quiet, the stones would cry out."

[41-48] And Yeshua came near, and saw the city, and cried over it, saying, "If you had only known, even in this your time now, the things which would give you peace! But now they're hid from you. The time will come, that those who come against you will put a siege around you, and surround you, and keep you closed off from every direction, and will level you to the ground, along with your people; and they'll not leave in you one stone in its place; because you didn't know it when I visited you." And as they went into the Place of Worship, the Christ began to throw out all those who were buying and selling in it; saying to them, "It's written, 'My house is the house of prayer': but you've made it a place of thieves." So the Christ taught daily in the Place of Worship. And the leading priests, the religious leaders, and the leaders of the people looked for a way to kill Yeshua; but they couldn't find a way to do it, because all the people came to hear the Christ.

The Christ Questioned by the Religious Leaders

20 [1-8] On one of those days, as the Christ taught the people in the Place of Worship, and preached the New Word, the leading priests and the religious leaders, along with the elders, came and asked the Christ, saying, "Tell us, by what right do you do this? Who gave you this right?" So the Christ answered them, saying, "I'll ask you something, too; and you tell Me: Was the baptism of John from heaven, or of human origin? And they argued among themselves, saying, "If we say, 'From heaven;' then Yeshua will say, 'Then why didn't you believe?' But if we say, 'Of human origin;' all the people will stone us because they believe that John was a great preacher." So they said that they didn't know. And Yeshua answered, "Then neither will I tell you by what right I do this."

The Story of the Farmers

[9-18] Then the Christ began to tell the people this story; "Someone planted a garden, and rented it out to farmers, and went into a far off country for a long time. And at the end of the season the owner sent a worker to the farmers, to collect the fruit of the garden, but the farmers beat and sent the worker away empty-handed. And again the owner sent another worker, who they beat, treating shamefully, and sent this one away empty-handed, too. And again the owner sent a third, who they wounded and put out, too. Then the owner of the garden said, 'What will I do? I'll send my own child, who I love. It may be that when they see the heir, they'll show respect.' But when the farmers saw the heir, they argued among themselves, saying, 'This is the heir: come, if we kill the heir, the inheritance will be ours.' So they went outside of the garden, and killed the heir. So what will the owner of the garden do to them? The owner will come and kill these farmers, and will give the garden to others." And when they heard it, they said, "Never!" And watching them, the Christ said, "Then what is this that is written, the same stone which the builders rejected will become the first cornerstone? And whoever falls on that stone will be broken; but whoever it falls on, will be ground to dust."

127

On Paying Taxes and Tithes

[19-26] So the leading priests and the religious leaders began at that very time, to look for a way to take the Christ; but they were afraid of the people because they realized that the Christ had told this story about them. So they watched the Christ, and sent out spies, who would pretend to be good people, in order to hear some word, that they might use to hand over the Christ to the power and control of the governor. So they asked Yeshua, saying, *"Christ, we know that you say and teach what is right, nor do you care what anyone says, so teach us the way of God: Is it right for us to give taxes to the ruling government, or not?"* But the Christ realized their craftiness, and answered, *"Why do you try to tempt Me? Show Me a coin. Whose picture and name does it have?"* And they answered, *"The Ruler's."* Then the Christ answered, *"So pay your taxes to the government, and give the part of your money to God that belongs to God."* And they couldn't grasp the Christ's words in front of the people: and were amazed at the answer, and didn't say anything.

No Sexuality or Marriage in the Afterlife

[27-38] Then some of the religious sects came, which don't believe that there's any afterlife; and asked, saying, *"Christ, Moses wrote to us, 'If someone dies, having a spouse, and they die without children, that another should take their spouse, and give them children.' There were seven people: and the first took a spouse, and died without children. And the second took her as a spouse, and died childless. And the third took her; and in this same way all seven also: and they left no children, and died. Last of all the woman died also. So when they come to life again whose spouse will she be because all seven had her in marriage?"* So Yeshua answered, *"The people of this world marry, and are given in marriage: But those who are thought worthy to obtain that world, and the coming to life again from the dead, won't be sexual or live in marriage: Neither will they die any more because they'll be like the angels; and are the children of God, being the children of the new life. And as to those who are dead coming to life again, even Moses showed at the bush, when God was called the God of Abraham, the God of Isaac, and the God of Jacob, that God isn't a God of the dead, but of the living because all live to God."*

Christ David's Descendant

[39-44] Then some of the religious leaders said, *"Christ, you've answered well."* After that they dared not ask any more questions at all. So Yeshua asked them, *"How do they say that Christ is David's descendant? When David himself said in the book of Songs, Yahweh God said to My Christ, sit beside Me, till I make those who come against you a place to rest your feet. So then, if David called the Christ, Christ, how is the Christ David's descendent?"*

False Religious Leaders

[45-47] Then in the presence of all the people the Christ said to the followers, *"Beware of the religious leaders, which want to walk around dressed in impressive clothing, and love greetings in the shopping centers, and the best seats in the places of worship, and the best places at celebration dinners; which take survivors' money, and for a show make long prayers: these will get the greater punishment."*

The Survivor's Coins

21 [1-4] Then the Christ looked up, and saw the rich people throwing their money into the treasury. And then the Christ saw a certain poor survivor throwing in two small coins, also. So the Christ said, *"The truth is, this poor survivor has put in more than all of them. All of these have put into God's offering out of their wealth, but she has put in all the living that she had, even in her need.*

The End Times

[5-9] And as some spoke of the Place of Worship, how it was decorated with beautiful stones and metals, the Christ said, *"As for this which you see, the time will come, in which there won't be left one stone on another, that won't be put out of its place."* So they asked Yeshua, saying, *"Christ, but when will this happen? And what sign will there be when this is about to happen?"* And Yeshua answered, *"Be sure that you aren't lied to because many will come in My Name, saying, 'I am Christ;' and 'The time is near': but don't follow them. When you hear of wars and rebellions, don't be frightened because this must happen first; but the end isn't yet."*

[10-19] Then Yeshua said, *"Nation will make war with nation, and country will fight country. Great earthquakes will be in many different places, a great lack of food, and deadly diseases; Then there will be fearful sights and great signs from heaven. But before all this, people will take and mistreat you, and hand you over to the religious leaders, putting you in jails. You'll be brought to rulers and leaders because of My Name, and it'll give you a time to tell others about Me. So settle it in your hearts, not to think about what you'll say, because I'll give you a word of wisdom, with which all those who come against you won't be able to dispute nor argue. You'll be handed over by parents, siblings, kinfolks, and friends; and they'll put some of you to death. You'll be hated by all people because of My Name, but a hair of your head won't be destroyed. If you have patience, you'll keep your souls.*

128

The Destruction of Jerusalem

[20-24] *When you see Jerusalem surrounded by armies, then know that it's destruction is near. Those who are in Judea should escape to the mountains; and those who are in the middle of it should leave; and those who are in the countryside shouldn't go back into it, because these are the days of its punishment, so that everything which is written will happen. But those with child and those who are breastfeeding will be sad in those days! For there will be great suffering in the land and rage toward this people. They'll be killed in war, and those left will be taken captive into all nations. Jerusalem will be overrun by the nations of the world, until their time is up.*

[25-28] *And then there will be signs in the sun, moon, and stars; and the nations on earth will have great troubles, with confusion; even the waves of the sea will be uprising; People's hearts will fail them for fear, and for watching what is going to happen on the earth because the forces of heaven will be out of balance. And then they'll see Me coming in a cloud with great power and bright light. And when this begins to happen, then look up, and lift up your heads because you'll be saved very soon."*

The Story of the Fig Tree

[29-33] And then the Christ told them a story; *"Watch the fig tree, and all the trees; When you see the buds begin to shoot out, don't you know for yourselves that summer is near. So in this same way, when you see all this happening, know that the realm of God is near. The truth is, the people of this time won't die out, till all of it happens. Heaven and earth will come to an end: but My Words won't ever come to an end.*

[34-38] *And watch yourselves, in case your hearts ever be overcome with partying, drunkenness, and the cares of this life, or that day will come on you unexpectedly, because it will come on everyone on the whole face of the earth like a sudden trap. So always watch and pray, so that you may be thought worthy to escape all this that will happen, and to stand with Me."* And Yeshua was teaching in the Place of Worship in the day time; and at night went out, staying on the mountain that is called the Mount of Olives. And all the people came early in the morning to the Place of Worship to hear the Christ.

The Passover Supper

22 [1-6] Now the celebration of unleavened bread came near which is called the Passover. And the leading priests and religious leaders were looking for a way to take the Christ secretly because they were afraid of the people. Then the spirit of Satan went into Judas, named Iscariot, being one of the twelve, who left, and talked with the leading priests and captains, to decide how to turn the Christ over to them. And they were pleased, and promised to give Judas money. So he promised to look for a way to turn the Christ over to them without the crowd being there.

[7-13] Then the day of unleavened bread came, when the Passover animals would be killed. So Yeshua sent Peter and John, saying, *"Go, and get the Passover meal ready for us, so that we can eat."* And they asked, *"Where do you want us to get it ready?"* So the Christ answered, *"Right when you get to the city, someone carrying a pitcher of water will meet you; follow them into the house they go into. And say to the owner of the house, the Christ said to ask you, 'Where is the guestroom, where I may eat the Passover with My followers?' And they'll show you a large furnished upper room: get everything ready there."* So they went, and found it just as the Christ had said: and they got the Passover meal ready.

[14-20] And when the time came, Christ and the twelve followers sat down. And Yeshua said, *"I've longed to eat this Passover with you before I suffer, because I tell you, I won't eat it any more, until I eat it in the realm of God."* And the Christ took the cup, and gave thanks, saying, *"Take this, and share it among yourselves. I tell you, I won't drink wine anymore, until the realm of God comes.* Then Yeshua took bread, giving thanks, and breaking it, and gave it to them, saying, *"This is the symbol of My body that is being given for you. Do this to remember Me."* And after supper, the Christ took the cup, and said, *"This cup is the symbol for My blood, which is shed for you in the New Word."*

[21-23] But the hand of the one who will hand Me over is with Me on the table. And the truth is, I go, as it was decided: but sorrow is coming to the one who hands Me over! So they began to ask, who among them, would do this.

Who will be the Greatest?

[24-30] And there was an argument among them, about which of them would be the greatest. So the Christ said, *"The rulers of the other peoples use control over them; and those who use power over them are called governors. But you won't do this: whoever wants to be greatest among you, should be like the younger; and whoever leads, like the one who serves, because which is greater, the one who sits to eat, or the one who serves? Isn't it the one who sits to eat? Yes, but I am among you as One who serves. You're the ones who have stayed with Me through all My troubles. So I give you a realm, just as My God has given one to Me; so that you can eat and drink at My table in My Realm, and sit on the judgment thrones of the twelve families of Israel."*

129

Peter will be Tempted

[31-38] And the Christ, said, *"Peter, Peter, Satan wants to have you, so that you can be tested: But I've prayed for you, that your faith doesn't fail. So when your faith comes back, strengthen the others."* And Peter said, *"Christ, I am ready to go with you, both to jail, and even to death."* But the Christ said, *"I tell you, Peter, the rooster won't crow today, before you'll say that you don't even know Me three times."* Then Yeshua said, *"When I sent you without a moneybag, backpack, or shoes, did you lack anything?"* And they answered, "Nothing." Then Christ said, *"But now, whoever has a money bag, let them take it, and their backpack: and whoever has no weapon, should sell their extra clothing, and buy one. I tell you, that what has been written about Me, 'and the Christ was thought of as a lawbreaker,' must happen to Me, because the things written about Me have a purpose."* And they said, *"Christ, we have two swords."* And Yeshua said, *"That's enough."*

The Christ is Betrayed

[39-46] Yeshua and the followers came out, and went to the Mount of Olives as they were used to doing. When they got there, Yeshua said, *"Pray, so that you won't be tempted."* The Christ withdrew from them about a stone's throw away, and kneeling down, prayed, *"Yahweh God, if You will allow it, don't let this happen to Me; but don't let happen what I want to be done, but what You want."* And an angel from heaven appeared to Yeshua, in order to strengthen the Christ. And the Christ, being greatly troubled, prayed harder: so much that the sweat was like great drops of blood falling on the ground. So the Christ getting up from prayer, and coming back to the followers, found them sleeping for sorrow, and asked, *"Why are you sleeping? Get up and pray, in case you're tempted."*

[47-53] And while the Christ was speaking, a crowd came up, along with Judas, who was one of the twelve. Then Judas started to kiss Yeshua. But Yeshua said, *"Judas, are You betraying Me with a kiss?"* When those who were with the Christ saw what was about to happen, they said, *"Christ, should we use our swords?"* And one of them cut off the right ear of the worker of the leading priest. And Yeshua answered, *"Let this happen, too."* And the Christ touched the ear, and healed it. Then Yeshua said to the leading priests, and the religious leaders of the Place of Worship, and the elders, which had come to them, *"Have you come out with swords and sticks like you'd come against a thief? When I was with you in the Place of Worship daily, you didn't put your hands on Me: but this is your time, and the time for the power of darkness."*

Peter Denies the Christ

[54-62] Then they took Yeshua, leading the Christ into the house of the leading priest. Peter followed far off behind them. And when they had made a fire in the middle of the hall, and had sat down together, Peter sat down with them. But a certain girl was watching as he sat down by the fire, and carefully looking at him, said, *"This one was with Yeshua, too."* And Peter denied it, saying, *"Woman, I don't even know this person."* And after a little while another person saw Peter, and said, *"You're one of them, too."* But Peter answered, *"I am not."* Then about an hour later, someone else swore to it, saying, *"It's the truth, this person was with them, too, because he's a Galilaean."* And Peter said, *"People, I don't even know what you're talking about."* And suddenly, while Peter was speaking, the rooster crowed. And Yeshua turned, and looked straight at Peter. And Peter remembered the Words of Yeshua, how the Christ had said, *"Before the rooster crows, you'll say that you don't know Me three times."* So Peter left there, and cried with great sorrow.

Christ Mocked by the Priests

[63-71] And those who were keeping Yeshua mocked and hit the Christ. And then when they had blindfolded the Christ, they struck Yeshua on the face, and said, *"Tell us who hit you."* And they spoke against the Christ many other disrespectful things. Then as soon as it was day, the elders of the people, the leading priests, and the religious leaders all came together, and led Yeshua into their court, saying, *"If You're the Christ, tell us!"* And Yeshua answered, *"If I tell you, you won't believe Me: And if I also ask you something, you won't answer Me, nor let Me go. But later, I'll sit in judgment with the power of God."* So they all said, *"Then, are you the Heir of God?"* And the Christ answered, *"You say it, because I am."* So they said, *"Why do we need any more witnesses? We've heard it ourselves, from this person's own mouth!"*

Christ Goes to Pilate

23 [1-7] Then they all got up, and took the Christ to Pilate. They began to accuse the Christ, saying, *"We found this person leading the people astray, forbidding them to pay taxes to the government, and claiming to be the Christ, a Ruler."* So Pilate asked, *"You are the Ruler of the Jews?"* And the Christ answered, *"It's just as you say."* Then Pilate said to the leading priests and to the people, *"This person has done nothing wrong."* But they were greatly angered, saying, *"This One stirs up the people, teaching throughout all Judea, all the way from Galilee to here."* So when Pilate heard of Galilee, he asked if the Christ were a Galilaean. And as soon as he knew that it was Herod's place to judge the matter, he sent the Christ to Herod, who was in Jerusalem at that time.

130

Christ Sent to Herod

[8-12] Then when Herod saw Yeshua, he was very happy because he had wanted to see the Christ for long time, having heard many things, and hoped to see the Christ do a miracle. So he asked many times; but the Christ didn't answer. And the leading priests and religious leaders stood by, accusing the Christ. Then Herod, along with his guards, clothing Yeshua in a beautiful robe, disrespectfully mocked the Christ, sending Yeshua back to Pilate. And that very day Pilate and Herod became friends together, though they were enemies before.

Pilate Finds Christ Innocent

[13-26] So Pilate, who had called together the leading priests, the rulers, and the people, said, *"You've brought this person to me, as One that leads the people astray: But I, having questioned this person, have found no fault as to these accusations. No, nor Herod either, because I sent you to him; and this person has done nothing worthy of death. The punishment is done, so I'll free Yeshua to you* (because he was required to free someone to them at the celebration.) And the people called out all at once, saying, *"Take Yeshua away, and free Barabbas"* (who was put in jail for a certain rebellion made in the city, and for murder.) So Pilate, wanting to free Yeshua, asked them again, but they called out, saying, *"Put Yeshua on a cross, put Yeshua on a cross."* And Pilate asked them the third time, *"Why, what evil has this person done? I've found no cause for death: so I'll punish and let Yeshua go."* And instantly, they called out for Yeshua to be put to death. And their voices overpowered Pilate's. So Pilate set the punishment as they wanted it, and freed to them the one who was put in jail for rebellion and murder, whom they had wanted; but gave Yeshua over to their will. And as they led the Christ away, they ordered someone named Simon, a Cyrenian, coming out of the country, to carry the cross, following after Yeshua.

Two Thieves with Christ

[27-33] And a great many people, including women followed along, who also grieved for the Christ. But Yeshua turning to them said, *"Daughters of Jerusalem, don't cry for me, but cry for yourselves, and for your children, because the days are coming, in the which they'll say, 'Blessed are those who never gave birth, and the breasts which never nursed a baby.' Then they'll begin to say to the mountains, 'Fall on us;' and to the hills, 'Cover us.' If they do this when the tree is green, what will be done when it's dry?"* And there were two others, too, law breakers, led with the Christ to be put to death. And when they had come to the place of the skull, which is called Calvary, they put Yeshua to death, along with the law breakers, one on the right side, and the other on the left.

[34-37] Then Yeshua said, *"God, forgive them because they don't know what they are doing."* And they divided the Christ's clothing, and placed bets on them. And the people stood watching. And the rulers also with them mocked the Christ, saying, *"You saved others; so save Yourself, if You're the Christ, the Chosen of God."* And the guards also mocked Yeshua, coming and offering the Christ sour wine, and saying, *"If You're the Ruler of the Jews, save Yourself."* And a title was written also over the Christ in letters of Greek, Latin, and Hebrew, *This is the Ruler of the Jews.*

[39-45] And one of the law breakers who was hung also mocked the Christ, saying, *"If You're the Christ, save Yourself and us."* But the other one scolded him, saying, *"Don't you honor and respect God, seeing you're judged in the same way? And we, justly, because we're only getting what we deserve for our actions: but this person hasn't done anything wrong."* And he said to Yeshua, *"Christ, remember me when You come into Your realm."* And Yeshua said, *"The truth is, today you'll be with Me in the Garden of Paradise."* And about noon, darkness came over all the earth until about three o'clock. And when the sun was darkened, the curtain of the Place of Worship was torn in half.

Christ's Last Words

[46-49] And when Yeshua had called out, having said, *"God, I give My Spirit to You,"* the Christ gave up the Spirit. Now when one of the guards saw what happened, he praised God, saying, *"The truth is, this really was a good person!"* And all those who had come together to see this, and who were watching everything that had happened, hit their breasts, and left. And all those who had known the Christ, and the women who had followed along from Galilee, stood far off, watching all of this.

Joseph Asks for Christ's Body

[50-56] And there was someone named Joseph, a person from Arimathaea, a city of the Jews, who was a good and fair person: (who hadn't consented to the words and actions of them;) and who also waited for the realm of God. This person went to Pilate, and begged for the body of Yeshua. So he took it down, and wrapped it in linen, and laid it in a tomb that was cut out of stone, and in which no one had ever been laid to rest. And that day was the preparation day, and the Seventh Day was nearing. The women, which came with the Christ from Galilee, followed, and watched the tomb, and saw how the body was laid. And they went home, and got the spices and perfumes ready; and rested on the Day of Worship according to the Word of God.

131

Christis Alive!

24 [1-12] Now very early on Sunday morning, they came to the tomb, bringing the spices which they had prepared, and a few others were with them. And they found the stone rolled away from the tomb. So they went in, and didn't find the body of the Christ Yeshua. And then, as they were very confused about it, two people stood next to them in shining white clothes: And as they were afraid, and bowed down their faces to the earth, the two asked, "Why are you looking for One who lives among the dead? The Christ isn't here, but is risen: remember how the Christ spoke to you while still in Galilee, saying, 'I must be given into the hands of sinful people, and be put to death, and the third day come to life again?'" And they remembered the Words of the Christ, and came back from the tomb, and told all this to the eleven, and to all the rest who were there. It was Mary Magdalene, and Joanna, and Mary, the mother of James, and some other women that were with them, who told this to the followers. But their words seemed to the followers as story-tales, so they didn't believe them. Then Peter got up and ran to the tomb; and stooping down, saw the linen clothes put by themselves, and went, wondering to himself, about what had happened.

Christ Appears to the Followers

[13-26] And two of them went that same day to a town called Emmaus, which was from Jerusalem about seven miles. And they talked together of all this which had happened. And then, while they talked and reasoned together, Yeshua came near, and walked with them. But they didn't know it was the Christ. And the Christ asked, *"What kind of stories are these that you've told to each other, as you were walking, and why are you so sad?"* And one of them, whose name was Cleopas, answered, *"Are you the only stranger in Jerusalem that doesn't know the things which have happen there in these days?"* And the Christ asked, *"What things?"* And they said, *"About Yeshua of Nazareth, who was a great preacher, powerful in words and actions before God and all the people: And who the leading priests and our rulers caused to be accused, and put to death, and have put the Christ to death. But we trusted that it was the One who would have saved Israel: and besides all this, today, is the third day since all this has happened. Yes, and also, some of the women of our company amazed us, which went early to the tomb; And when they didn't find the body, they came, saying, that they had also seen a vision of angels, who said that the Christ was alive. And some of those who were with us went to the tomb, and found it just as the women had said: but didn't see the Christ."* Then the Christ said, *"You thoughtless, and slow of heart to believe all that the great preachers have spoken: Shouldn't Christ have suffered this, and have victory?"*

[27-35] And beginning at Moses and all the great preachers, Yeshua explained all the Words about the Christ. And as they came near the town, where they were going: the Christ pretended to want to go further. But they pleaded with Yeshua, saying, *"Stay with us, it's just about evening, and the day is almost over."* So the Christ went in to stay with them. And then, as Yeshua was eating a meal with them, the Christ blessed and broke the bread, and gave it to them. Then suddenly they understood, and knew it was Yeshua; and then the Christ disappeared. So they said to each other, *"Didn't our hearts burn within us, while the Christ talked with us on the way, and explained the Word to us?"* And they got up right then, and went back to Jerusalem, and found the eleven and those who were with them all gathered together, and who were saying, *"The Christ has truly come to life again, and has appeared to Peter."* Then the two of them told what had happened to them on the road, and how the Christ was known of them in the breaking of the bread.

[36-49] And as they were speaking, Yeshua appeared in the middle of them, saying to them, *"Be at peace."* But they were terrified and afraid, and thought that they had seen a spirit. So the Christ said, *"Why are you so upset? And why do you doubt in your hearts? See My hands and My feet, It's Me: Touch Me, and see, because a spirit doesn't have a body and bones, as you see that I have."* And when the Christ had said this, they saw Yeshua's hands and feet. And while they still couldn't believe it for joy, and were so amazed, the Christ asked, *"Do you have any food here?"* And they gave the Christ a piece of a broiled fish and honeycomb. So Yeshua took it, and ate it in front of them. And then said, *"These are the words which I spoke to you, while I was still with you, so that everything would happen, which was written in the Words of Moses, and in the Words of the great preachers, and in the Songs about Me."* Then the Christ opened their minds to understand the Words, and said, *"Just as it was written, it was right that Christ would suffer, and come to life from the dead on the third day: And that a change of ways and freedom from sins would be preached in the Name of Yeshua among all the nations, beginning at Jerusalem. And you're witnesses of this. So I send the promise of My God, who I am from, to you. But stay in the city of Jerusalem, until you're given the power from Heaven."*

Christ Carried Into Heaven

[50-53] Then the Christ led them out as far as to Bethany, and with uplifted hands, blessed them. And then, while Yeshua blessed them, the Christ was taken from them, and carried up into heaven. And they worshipped the Christ, and went back to Jerusalem with great joy, staying in the Place of Worship continually, praising and blessing God. So be it!

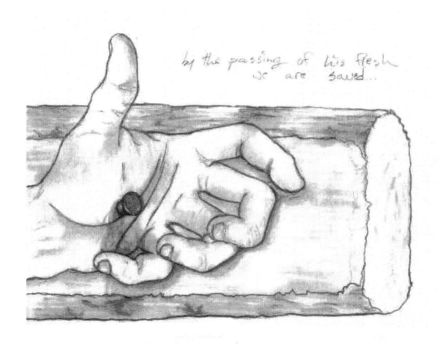

The New Word According to John

The Spoken Word
1 [1-5] The Word was at the beginning of creation, and the Word was with God, and the Word was God. This same Word was active in the creation with God. Everything was made by the Voice of the Spoken Word; and nothing that was made was made without the Voice of the Spoken Word. Life was in the Spoken Word; and the Life was the Light of humanity. And the Light shined in the darkness; but the darkness didn't know it.

John's Witness of the Light
[6-14] There was someone sent from God, whose name was John. And John came to be a witness, to be a truthful witness of the Light, so that all people might believe. John wasn't the Light, but was sent to be a truthful witness of the Light. This was the True Light, which gives light to everyone that comes into the world. The Spoken Word, who brought the world into being, was in the world, but the world didn't know it. The Word came into the world, but the world didn't accept the Spoken Word. But those who accepted the Spoken Word were given the power to become the children of God, that is, all those who believe on the Name of the Spoken Word of God: Who wasn't born by blood relation, nor by physical means, nor by human means, but by God. And the Spoken Word became human, and lived among us, (and we saw the miracle, the miracle of the First and Only One Born of God,) full of grace and truth.

Yeshua the Christ
[15-18] John gave witness to the Spoken Word, calling out, "This was the One of whom I said, the One coming after me is better than me because this One existed before me. And we've all been given grace and more grace from the gifts of this One. Though the Word of God's Law was given by Moses, the Word of grace and truth came by Yeshua the Christ. No one has ever seen God; but the First and Only One Born of God, who is in the heart of God, and has told us of God."

The Voice of One Calling out in the Countryside
[19-28] And this is what John said, when the Jews sent priests and religious leaders from Jerusalem to ask, *"Who are you?"* John said, and didn't deny it; but clearly said, *"I am not the Christ."* So they asked John, *"Then who are you, Elijah?"* But John answered, *"I am not."* Then they asked, *"Are you the great preacher?"* But again, John said, *"No."* So they asked again, *"Tell us who you are then, so that we can give an answer to those who sent us. What do you say of yourself?"* Then John said, *"'I am the voice of one calling out in the countryside to get the way ready for Yahweh God, making the way plain',* as the great preacher Isaiah said." And those who were sent were of the religious leaders. So they asked John, *"Why do you baptize then, if you aren't the Christ, nor Elijah, nor the great preacher?"* And John answered, saying, *"I baptize with water: but there stands One among you, whom you don't know; This is the Christ, who is coming after me, and is better than me, whose shoe laces I am not even worthy to undo."* And this happened in Bethabara beyond Jordan, where John was baptizing.

John Baptizes the Christ
[29-34] The next day John saw Yeshua coming to him, and said, *"See, the Christ, the Lamb of God, who takes away the sin of the world. This is the One of whom I said, 'Someone is coming after me who is better than me and who existed before me.'* But I didn't know who it was until it was to become known to Israel, so I came baptizing with water." Then John said, *"I saw the Spirit coming down from heaven like a dove, and it rested on Yeshua. And I didn't know who it would be: but the One who sent Me to baptize with water told me, 'The One who you see the Spirit coming down and resting on will be the One who baptizes with the Holy Spirit.' And I saw, and say that this is the One Born of God."*

Calling the Disciples - Andrew and Peter
[35-42] Again the next day John was standing with two followers; And looking at Yeshua, who was walking by, said, *"See, the Christ, the Lamb of God!"* So when the two followers heard John speak, they followed Yeshua. Then Yeshua turned, and seeing them following, asked, *"What do you want?"* And they asked, *"Rabbi,"* (which means, Teacher) *"where are you staying?"* So the Christ answered them, saying, *"Come and see."* So they went and saw where the Christ was staying, and stayed there for the rest of the day because it was about four o'clock. And one of the two who heard John speak, and followed along, was Andrew, Simon Peter's brother, who found his own brother, Simon, first, saying, *"We've found the Messiah"*, (which means, the Christ) and brought him to Yeshua. And seeing them, the Christ said, *"You're Simon, the son of Jonas: you'll be called Peter,"* (which means, a rock.)

134

Calling the Disciples - Philip and Nathanael

[43-51] The next day Yeshua went out into Galilee, and found Philip, saying, *"Follow Me."* Now Philip was from Bethsaida, the same city Andrew and Peter were from. Then Philip found Nathanael, and said, *"We've found the Christ, who Moses and the great preachers wrote about in God's Law, Yeshua of Nazareth, the Child of Joseph."* And Nathanael said, *"Can anything good come out of Nazareth?"* So Philip said, *"Come and see."* And seeing Nathanael coming, Yeshua said of him, *"See, a true Israelite, who always speaks the truth!"* And Nathanael asked, *"How do you know me?"* So Yeshua answered, *"I saw you when you were under the fig tree, before Philip found you."* And Nathanael answered, *"Teacher, You are the Child of God and the Ruler of Israel."* So Yeshua said, *"Just because I said, 'I saw you under the fig tree', you believe? You'll see even greater things than this."* And the Christ said, *"The truth is; later you'll see heaven open, with the angels of God coming down to Me and going back up from Me."*

The First Miracle

2 [1-11] On the third day, Yeshua's mother was at a wedding in Cana of Galilee, in which Yeshua and the followers were also invited. And when they needed more wine, Yeshua's mother said, *"They have no wine."* But Yeshua said to her, *"Woman, what does that have to do with you and Me? My time isn't here yet."* So Yeshua's mother said to the workers, *"Whatever Yeshua says to you, do it."* And there were six stone jars sitting there, the kind the Jews use for washing, containing several gallons each. Then Yeshua said, *"Fill up the jars with water."* So they filled them up to the brim. And then Yeshua told them, *"Dip some out now, and carry it to the host of the celebration."* So they did. And when the host of the celebration had tasted the water that had turned to wine, and didn't know where it came from: (but the workers which dipped the water knew;) the host of the celebration called the groom, and said, *"Everyone sets out the good wine first; and when everyone has drunk well, then they put out what is worse: but you've kept the good wine until now."* So what Yeshua did in Cana of Galilee was the first amazing miracle, which made the followers believe that Yeshua was the Christ.

The Angry Christ

[12-17] Later, the Christ, the Christ's mother and family members, and the followers all went down to Capernaum, where they stayed for several days. And it was the Jews' Passover, so Yeshua went up to Jerusalem. Then finding sales people and bankers sitting in the Place of Worship, the Christ braided a whip of small cords, and drove them all out of the Place of Worship, along with the animals; overthrowing the tables, and dumping out the bankers' money; and said to those who sold doves, *"Take all this out of here; and don't make My God's house a place of business."* And the followers remembered that it was written, *"The passion of Your house has overcome Me."*

[18-21] Then the Jews asked, *"What proof can you show us, seeing what you've done?"* So Yeshua answered them, saying, *"Destroy this sanctuary, and in three days I'll raise it up."* Then the Jews said, *"It took forty-six years to build this Place of Worship! Will you rebuild it in three days?"* But Yeshua was talking about the sanctuary of the Christ's body. And when the Christ had come back to life, the followers remembered what Yeshua had said and believed the Writings.

[23-25] Now when they were in Jerusalem at the Passover on the celebration day, many believed in the Name of Yeshua, when they saw all the amazing things which the Christ did. But knowing all people and how they are, Yeshua didn't trust them, not needing to hear anyone say anything about them.

The New Birth

3 [1-13] There was someone named Nicodemus, from the religious leaders, who was a ruler of the Jews: This person came to Yeshua by night, saying, *"Teacher, we know that you're a teacher from God, because no one can do these amazing things that you do, unless God is with them."* And Yeshua answered, *"The truth is, unless a person is born anew, they can't see the realm of God."* So Nicodemus asked, *"How can someone be born when they're old? Can they go into their mother's womb a second time, and be born anew?"* So Yeshua said, *"The truth is, unless a person is born of water and of the Spirit, they can't come into the realm of God. What is born of the body is physical; but what is born of the Spirit is spiritual. So don't be surprised that I said to you, you must be born anew. The wind blows where it wants to, and you hear the sound of it, but can't tell where it comes from, nor where it goes: Everyone that is born of the Spirit is like this."* So Nicodemus asked, *"How is this?"* And Yeshua answered, *"Can you be a leader of Israel, and not know this? The truth is, we speak about what we know, and tell others about what we've seen; and you don't believe us. If I've told you about earthly things, and you don't believe it, how will you believe what I tell you about heavenly things? No one has gone up to heaven, but the One who came down from heaven, even the very One who is in heaven.*

[14-17] And just as Moses lifted up the snake in the countryside, I must also be lifted up, so that whoever believes in Me won't be destroyed, but will have everlasting life. And God, who loved the world so much, gave us

the only One Born of God, that whoever believes in the Christ, wouldn't be destroyed, but would have everlasting life. But God didn't send the Christ into the world to judge the world; but that the world might be saved through belief in the Christ.

[18-21] Whoever believes on the Christ isn't damned: but whoever doesn't believe is already damned, because they haven't believed in the Name of the only One Born of God. And this is why they're damned in judgment; the light has come into the world, but humanity loved darkness instead of light, because their actions were evil. Because everyone that does evil things hates the light, and won't come into the light, or their actions would be discovered. But whoever does what is true comes into the light, so that it is clear to all that their actions have been done in God."

Jews Question John about Jesus

[22-36] Later, Yeshua came with the followers into the land of Judea; and stayed there with them, and baptized. And John was also baptizing in Aenon, near Salem, because there was a lot of water there. So they came, and were baptized, because John hadn't been put in jail, yet. Then a question came up between some of John's followers and the Jews about baptism. And they came to John, saying, "Teacher, everyone is going to be baptized by the One who was with you at the Jordan, the One who you told us about." So John answered, "No one can have anything, unless it's given to them from heaven. You yourselves know that I said, I am not the Christ, but that I have been sent before the Christ. The One who is getting married gets the spouse: but the best friend, which stands by, celebrates greatly because of the voice of the One who marries: so my joy is complete. The Christ must become more important, but I must become less important. The One who comes from above is above all: and the one who is of the earth is earthly, and speaks of earthly things: but the One who comes from heaven is above all. And tells us what has been seen and heard by that One; but no one believes it. But whoever believes what the Christ says, knows that God is true. The One whom God has sent speaks the Words of God because God has given the Spirit in full to the Christ. Yahweh loves Yeshua, and has given everything into the Christ's hand. Whoever believes on Yeshua the Christ, has everlasting life: and whoever doesn't believe in the Christ won't see life; but the judgment of God is on them."

Woman at the Well and the Samaritans

4 [1-6] Knowing that the religious leaders had heard that Yeshua made and baptized more followers than John, (Though Yeshua didn't baptize, but only the followers,) the Christ left Judea, and went back to Galilee, going through Samaria. Then they came to a city of Samaria, called Sychar, near the piece of land that Jacob gave to Joseph. Now Jacob's well was there, so Yeshua, being tired from the long walk, sat on the well about noon.

[7-15] Then a woman from Samaria came there to get water: so Yeshua asked her, "Give Me a drink," (because the followers had gone on to the city to buy food.) Then the woman of Samaria answered, "How come you, being a Jew, ask me to give you a drink, who am I a woman from Samaria? Jews don't have anything to do with Samaritans of mixed-race. So Yeshua answered her, "If you knew the gift of God, and who it is that said to you, Give me a drink; you would have asked of Me, and I would have given you living water." So the woman said, "Sir, you have nothing to get it with, and the well is deep: so then, where do you have that living water? Are you greater than our ancestor Jacob, who gave us this well, and drank out of it, along with the children and cattle?" So Yeshua answered, "Whoever drinks this water will always thirst again, but whoever drinks the water that I give them will never thirst; but the water that I give them will be in them as a well of water springing up into everlasting life." Then the woman said, "Sir, give me this water, so that I won't be thirsty, nor have to come here to get it."

[16-26] And Yeshua said to her, "Go, call your husband and come back here." But the woman answered, "I don't have a husband." So Yeshua said to her, "You said rightly, I don't have a husband: because you've had five husbands; and the one you have now isn't even your husband: in that you said rightly." So the woman said, "Sir, I realize now that you're a great preacher. Our ancestors worshipped on this mountain; but you Jews say that Jerusalem is the place where we ought to worship." So Yeshua said to her, "Woman, believe me, the time is coming, when you won't worship God on this mountain, nor at Jerusalem. You don't even know what you worship: but we know what we worship because it is through the Jews that people are saved. But the time is coming, and now is, when the true worshippers will worship God in spirit and in truth because Yahweh God wants worship from this kind of people. God is Spirit: and those who worship God must worship God in spirit and in truth." Then the woman said, "I know that the Messiah is coming, which is called the Christ: and will tell us everything then." So Yeshua said to her, "I, the One who is speaking to you, am the Christ."

[27-30] At this time, the followers came, and were amazed that the Christ talked with the woman: but still no one said, "What do you want?" or, "Why are you talking with her?" Then the woman left her water jar, and went back into the city, saying to all the people, "Come and see someone who has told me everything that I ever did: isn't this the Christ?" Then they went out of the city, and came to the Christ.

[31-38] In the mean time, the followers begged Yeshua, saying, "Christ, eat." But Yeshua answered, "I've got food to eat that you don't know of." So the followers asked one another, "Has anyone brought Yeshua anything to

eat?" And Yeshua answered, *"My food is to do what the One who sent Me wants Me to do, and to finish God's work. So don't say, 'There are still four months, and then the harvest will be ready?' I tell you, look up, and see that the fields are all ready to be harvested. And whoever collects the harvest will get paid, and gathers fruit to everlasting life, so that both those who plant and those who pick it can celebrate together. And this saying is true, One plants, and another picks. I sent you to pick from what you've not worked on: other people worked, and you joined them in their work."*

[39-42] And many of the Samaritans of that city believed on the Christ because of the Words of the woman, who told us truthfully, "The Christ told me everything that I ever did." So when the Samaritans had come, they begged the Christ to stay with them: so the Christ stayed there two days. And many more believed because of the Christ's own words, who said to the woman, "Now we believe, not because of your saying, but because we've heard the Christ for ourselves, and know for sure that this is the Christ, the Savior of the world."

The Second Miracle

[43-54] Now after two days the Christ left there, and went into Galilee. And Yeshua told us truthfully, that great preachers have no honor in their own country. Then when the Christ came into Galilee, the Galilaeans accepted Yeshua, having seen everything that the Christ did at Jerusalem at the celebration because they also went to the celebration. So Yeshua came back into Cana of Galilee, where the water was turned to wine. And there was someone of high standing, whose child was sick at Capernaum, who had heard that Yeshua had come out of Judea into Galilee. So this person went to the Christ, and begged the Christ to come down, and heal the child, who was at the point of death. Then Yeshua answered, *"Unless you people see signs and amazing things, you won't believe any other way."* Then the person begged, *"Sir, come down or my child will die."* So Yeshua said, *"Go now; your child lives."* And that person believed the Words that Yeshua had spoken, and left. And some workers came to the person, who was going back down, saying, *"Your child lives;"* Who then asked them the time when the child began to get well. And they said, *"Yesterday, at one o'clock the fever left the Child."* So the person knew that it was at the very time that Yeshua had said, *"Your child lives":* so the whole family believed. This is the second miracle that Yeshua did, when the Christ came out of Judea into Galilee.

Miracle at Bethesda

5 [1-9] Later there was a celebration of the Jews; and Yeshua went up to Jerusalem. Now at Jerusalem, by the animal market, there's a pool, which is called in the Hebrew language Bethesda, having five columned porches, where a great many people, who were disabled, blind, unable to walk, or had other disabilities, lay waiting for the moving of the water, because whoever stepped in first after the water stirred, was healed of whatever trouble they had when an angel went down at a certain time into the pool, and stirred the water. And there was someone there, who was disabled for thirty-eight years. So when Yeshua saw them lying there, and knew that they had been that way a long time, the Christ asked, *"Would you like to become well?"* But the helpless person answered, *"Sir, when the water is stirred, I don't have anyone to help me into the pool: but while I am coming, someone else steps down before me."* Then Yeshua said, *"Get up, pick up your bed, and walk."* And suddenly the person was healed, and picked up their bed, and walked. That day was on the Seventh Day.

[10-16] So the Jews said to the one that was healed, *"You can't carry your bed; It's a Day of Worship!"* And that person answered, the One who made me well told me, *"Pick up your bed, and walk."* Then they asked, *"Who said to you, 'Pick up your bed, and walk?'"* And the one who was healed didn't know who it was because Yeshua had left from the crowd that was there. But later, Yeshua saw that person in the Place of Worship, and said, *"Now that you're well: don't sin any more, or something worse may come to you."* Then the person went and told the Jews that it was Yeshua who had done it, so the Jews mistreated Yeshua, and looked for a way to kill the Christ, because it had been done on a Day of Worship.

Christ's Judgment and the Afterlife

[17-29] So Yeshua told them, *"The One I came from has been working until now, so I have been working."* So the Jews looked for a way to kill the Christ all the more, because Yeshua hadn't only broken the law of the Day of Worship, but said also, "I am from God," which made Yeshua equal with God. Then Yeshua answered, saying, *"The truth is, I can't do anything of Myself, but what I see God do, I do, because whatever God does, I do in the same way. God loves Me, and shows Me everything that is done: and God will show Me greater things than these, so that you can wonder about it. Just as God brings the dead to life again, and gives them the breath of life; in the same way I'll give life to whoever I want. God judges no one, but has given all judgment to Me, so that all people would honor Me, just as they honor God. Whoever doesn't honor Me doesn't honor God, who has sent Me. The truth is, whoever hears My Word, and believes on the One who sent Me, has everlasting life, and won't be damned to Hell, but will go from death to life. The truth is, the time is coming, and now is, when the dead will hear the voice of the Christ of God: and those who hear will live. As God is life; so God has given Me life in Myself, and has given Me power to give judgment also, because I am the Christ. Don't wonder about this because the time is*

137

coming, in which those who are dead in their graves will hear My voice, and will come out; those who have done good will come to life again and live; and those who have done evil will be damned in the afterlife.

The Four Witnesses

[30-35] I can do nothing of My own self: but as I hear, I judge: and My judgment is fair, because I don't do what I want, but what the God who has sent Me wants. If I only give witness of Myself, My witness isn't true. But there's another that tells the truth about Me; and I know that this witness of Me is true. You sent to John, who gave witness of the truth, though I don't accept what a person says: but I say this that you might be saved. John was a burning and shining light: and for a while you wanted to celebrate in that light.

[36-38] But there's a greater witness of Me than John because the work that My God has given Me to finish, the very things that I do, are a truthful witness of Me, that I have been sent by God. And My God, who has sent Me, has given witness of Me. You haven't even heard the voice of God once, nor seen what God looks like. And you don't have God's Word in you because you don't believe the One God has sent to you.

[39-47] You search the Words because you think you have everlasting life in them: but they're the very words which tell of Me. But you won't come to Me, that you might have life. I get no honor from you people. But I know that you don't have God's love in you. I am come in the Name of God, and you don't accept Me: but if someone else comes in their own name, you'll accept them. How can you believe, who get honor from one another, but don't want the honor that comes from God? And don't think that I'll accuse you to God: but there's one who does accuse you, Moses, the very one in whom you trust. If you had believed Moses, you would have believed Me because Moses wrote of Me. But if you don't believe those Writings, how will you believe My Words?"

The Bread and Fish

6 [1-14] Later, Yeshua sailed across the sea of Galilee, which is the Sea of Tiberias. And a great crowd followed along, because they saw all the amazing things which the Christ did for those who were diseased. So Yeshua went up on a mountain, and sat there with the followers, the Passover, a celebration of the Jews, being near. Then when Yeshua looked up, and saw a great many coming to them, the Christ said to Philip, "Where can we buy bread, so that they can eat?" But the Christ said this to test them, already knowing what would happen. Then Philip answered, "More than half a year's wage worth of bread isn't enough, even if everyone takes just a little." Then another of the followers, Andrew, Simon Peter's brother, said, "There's a little boy here, who has five loaves of barley bread, and two little fish: but how can they feed so many?" Then Yeshua said, "Make the people sit down." Now there was a lot of grass in that place, so the people sat down, which numbered about five thousand. Yeshua took the loaves; and when the Christ had given thanks, gave it to the followers, and the followers to those who were sitting down; and they all had as much of the bread and the fish as they wanted. Then when they were full, the Christ said to the followers, "Gather up the scraps that are left over, so that nothing is wasted." So they gathered them together, and filled twelve baskets with the scraps of the five barley loaves, which were over and above what had been eaten. And the people, when they had seen the miracle that Yeshua did, said, "It's true, this is the great preacher that was to come into the world!"

The Christ Walks on the Water

[15-21] So realizing that the people would come, making the Christ their Ruler by force, Yeshua went back up on a mountain alone. When evening came, the followers went down to the sea, got in a ship, and rowed across the sea toward Capernaum. It was dark, but Yeshua still hadn't come to them. Then the waves rose up from a storm wind. And when they had rowed about three or four miles, they saw Yeshua walking on the water, and coming near the ship: so they were very afraid. But the Christ called out, "It's Me; don't be afraid." Then they willingly took the Christ into the ship: and the ship was suddenly at the land where they were heading.

[22-24] The next day, the people which stood on the other side of the sea saw that there was no other boat there, except the one that the followers had come in, and that Yeshua hadn't got into the boat and left with the followers, because the followers had left alone. But other boats had come from Tiberias, near the place where they ate the bread, after the Christ had given thanks. So when the people saw that Yeshua wasn't there, nor the followers, they also took shipping, and came to Capernaum, looking for Yeshua.

Bread From Heaven

[25-29] And when they had found the Christ on the other side of the sea, they asked, "Teacher, when did you come here?" And Yeshua answered, "The truth is, you look for Me, not because you saw the amazing things, but because you ate the bread, and were filled. But don't just work for the food that ruins, but for the spiritual food that lasts to everlasting life, which I'll give to you because I have the blessing of My God." Then they asked, "What do we need to do, so that we might do the work of God?" And Yeshua answered, saying to them, "The work of God is that you believe on the One who God has sent."

[30-40] Then they asked the Christ, *"What sign will you show us then that we can see, and believe you? What will you do? Our ancestors ate the bread from heaven in the desert; as the Word says, God gave them bread from heaven to eat."* Then Yeshua answered, *"The truth is, Moses didn't give you that bread from heaven; but My God gives you the true bread from heaven, because the bread of God is the One who comes down from heaven, and gives life to the world."* Then they said, *"Christ, give us this bread to have forever."* And Yeshua answered, *"I am that bread of life: whoever comes to Me will never hunger; and whoever believes on Me will never thirst. But I say to you that even though you've seen Me, you still don't believe. Everyone that God gives Me will come to Me; and I won't ever put out those who come to Me, because I came down from heaven, not to do what I want, but what the One who sent Me wants. And this is what God who has sent Me wants; that I would lose none of all I have been given, but would bring them to life again at the last day. And this is what the One who sent Me wants, that everyone who sees and believes on the Christ, will have everlasting life: and I'll bring them to life at the last day."*

[41-45] Then the Jews spoke against the Christ for saying, *"I am the bread which came down from heaven."* And they said, *"Isn't this Yeshua, the Child of Joseph, whose parents we know? Why then does Yeshua say, I came down from heaven?"* So Yeshua said to them, *"Don't whisper among yourselves. No one can come to Me, unless the God who sent Me calls them: and I'll bring them to life at the last day. It's written in the Words of the great preachers, 'and they'll all be taught of God.' So everyone that has heard, and learned of God, comes to Me.*

[46-51] Not that anyone has seen God; but the only One who has seen God is the One who is of God. The truth is, whoever believes on Me has everlasting life. I am that bread of life. Your ancestors ate the bread from heaven in the countryside, and are dead now. But this is the bread which comes down from heaven, which when someone accepts it, they won't die. I am the living bread which came down from heaven: if anyone eats this bread, they'll live forever: and the bread that I give is My body, which I give for the life of the whole world."*

[52-58] So the Jews argued among themselves, saying, *"How can someone give us their body to eat?"* Then Yeshua answered, *"The truth is, unless you eat of My body, and drink of My blood, you won't have life in you. Whoever eats My body, and drinks My blood, has everlasting life; and I'll bring them to life at the last day. The truth is, My body is spiritual food, and My blood is spiritual drink. Whoever accepts My body, and My blood, lives in Me, and I in them. As the Living God has sent Me, and I live by God, so, whoever is fed by Me, will live by Me. This is that bread which came down from heaven. Not as your ancestors ate the bread from heaven, and are dead, but whoever eats of this bread will live forever."*

[59-65] The Christ said this in the Place of Worship, while teaching in Capernaum. So many of the followers, when they had heard this, said, *"This is hard to hear; who can understand it?"* And when Yeshua knew that the followers spoke against it, the Christ asked, *"Does this offend you? What if you see Me go up to where I came from? It's the Spirit that gives life; the body is good for nothing: I speak to you with Life-giving words, which are spirit. But there are some of you who still don't believe."* And Yeshua, knowing from the beginning who wouldn't believe, knew who it was that would hand the Christ over. So Christ said, *"So I said to you, that no one can come to Me, unless they were called of My God."*

Peter's Confession

[66-71] From then on many of the followers went back home, and didn't follow along any more. So Yeshua asked the twelve, *"Will you go away, too?"* Then Simon Peter answered, *"Christ, who would we go to? Only You speak the Words of everlasting life. We believe and are sure that You're the Christ, the One Born of the Living God."* So Yeshua said, *"Didn't I choose the twelve of you, and even one of you has an evil spirit?"* Yeshua spoke of Judas Iscariot, the son of Simon, because it was him who would hand over the Christ, being one of the twelve.

The Unbelief of Christ's Family

7 [1-9] Later, Yeshua walked in Galilee, not going in the towns of the Jews, because they waited for a chance to kill the Christ. Now, it was the Jews' celebration of harvest huts, so some of the Christ's family members said, *"Leave here, and go to Judea, so that your followers there can also see what you've done and what you do, because no one does anything in secret, who wants to become known to the public. If you really do these things, show yourself to the world."* Not even Yeshua's own family members believed in the Christ. Then Yeshua answered, *"My time isn't here yet: but your time is always right now. The world doesn't hate you; but it hates Me, because I tell them that what they've done is evil. Go on up to this celebration: but I won't go now because it's not My time yet."* So the Christ told them this and stayed behind in Galilee.

The Heavenly Teacher

[10-13] But when they had gone on up, the Christ went up also to the celebration, though not in the open, but in secret. The Jews were looking for the Christ at the celebration, saying, *"Where is that One?"* And everyone was whispering about the Christ, some saying, *"The Christ is a good person"*, and others saying, *"No; but this One misleads the people."* But no one spoke openly of the Christ for fear of the Jews.

139

[14-19] Now about the middle of the celebration Yeshua went up into the Place of Worship, and was teaching. And the Jews were wondering, saying, *"How does this person understand letters, having never been taught?"* So Yeshua answered, saying, *"My teaching isn't Mine, but is from the One that sent Me. If anyone wants to do what God wants, they'll know whether these words are of God, or whether I speak for Myself. Whoever speaks for themselves looks for their own praise; but whoever wants praise for the One who sent them, this person is true, and no ungodliness is in them. Didn't Moses give you the Word of God, and still none of you keep it? Why do you go about trying to kill Me?"*

[20-24] So the people answered, *"You've got an evil spirit: who is going around trying to kill you?"* So Yeshua said to them, *"I've done one work, and you all wonder. Moses gave you the practice of cutting the flesh of the foreskin, not because it's of Moses, but of the ancestors, and you even cut the flesh of people on a Day of Worship. If someone can be cut on a Day of Worship, so that the Words of Moses won't be broken; why are you angry at Me, because I've made someone well on a Day of Worship? Don't judge by the way something appears, but use good sense."*

[25-31] Then some of those from Jerusalem said, *"Isn't this the One they want to kill? But this person speaks without fear, and they don't say anything. Do the rulers really know that this is the very Christ? But we know where this person comes from; and no one will know where the Christ comes from."* Then Yeshua called out in the Place of Worship while teaching, saying, *"You both know Me, and you know where I am from: I am not come of Myself, but the One who sent Me is true, whom you don't know. But I know this One because I am from God, and God has sent Me."* Then they looked for a way to take the Christ; but no one dared, because it wasn't the right time. And many of the people believed on the Christ, asking, *"When the Christ comes, will anyone do more amazing things than what this person has done?"*

The Living Water

[32-39] The religious leaders heard the people whispering these things; and they sent officers to take the Christ. Then Yeshua said, *"For a little while yet, I am with you, and then I'll go to the One who sent Me. You'll look for Me, but won't find Me; and where I am, you can't come."* Then the Jews said among themselves, *"Where can Yeshua go, that we can't find? To those scattered among the other peoples, and teach them? What kind of saying is this, 'You'll look for Me, and won't find Me'; and 'Where I am, there you can't come?'* So in the last day, the greatest day of the celebration, Yeshua stood up and called out, saying, *"If anyone is thirsty, let them come to Me, and drink of My Words. Whoever believes on Me, as the Word has said, 'Out of their spirit will flow rivers of living water."* (But Yeshua spoke this of the Holy Spirit, which hadn't yet been given to those who would believe on the Christ, who hadn't been raised from the dead yet.)

[40-44] So many of the people, when they heard this saying, said, *"It's true, this is the Great Preacher."* But others said, *"This is the Christ."* And some asked, *"Will the Christ come out of Galilee? Hasn't the Word said that the Christ comes from the line of David, from the town of Bethlehem, where David was born?"* So there was a disagreement among the people about the Christ. Some of them would have taken the Christ; but no one dared .

[45-53] Then the officers went back to the leading priests and the religious leaders; and they asked, *"Why haven't you brought Yeshua?"* The officers said, *"No one has ever spoken like this person."* Then the religious leaders asked them, *"Have you also lost your minds? Have any of the rulers or the religious leaders believed this person? But these people who don't know the Word of God are cursed."* And Nicodemus said, (the one who came to Yeshua by night, being one of them) *"Does our law judge anyone, before it hears them, and knows what's been done?"* So they asked, *"Are you also of Galilee? Search, and see that no great preacher comes out of Galilee."* And everyone left and went home.

The Woman Caught in Sexual Sin

8 [1-11] Then Yeshua went to the Mount of Olives. And early in the morning Yeshua came into the Place of Worship again, so all the people came and sat down, and the Christ taught them. Then the religious leaders and those from the religious sects brought to Yeshua a woman caught in the act of sexual sin; and when they had put her in the middle of the room, they said to Yeshua, *"Teacher, this woman was caught in sexual sin, in the very act. Now Moses in the Word of God told us, that these kinds of people must be stoned to death, but what do You say?"* But they said this, tempting Yeshua, so that they would have something in which to accuse the Christ. But Yeshua bent over, and with a finger wrote on the ground as though not hearing them. So when they asked the Christ again, Yeshua stood up, answering them, *"Whoever has never sinned among you, let them be the first to throw a stone at her."* And Yeshua bent over again, and wrote on the ground. And those who heard it, being convicted by their own consciences, went out one by one, from the oldest, even to the last youngest: and Yeshua was left alone, with the woman standing in the middle of the room. So when Yeshua got up, seeing no one but the woman, the Christ said to her, *"Woman, where are your accusers? Has no one accused you?"* So she answered, *"No one, Christ."* And Yeshua said to her, *"Nor do I accuse you. Go, but don't sin any more."*

The Light of the World

[12-18] Then Yeshua spoke to them again, saying, *"I am the light of the world. Whoever follows Me won't walk in darkness, but will have light for the way of life."* So the religious leaders said, *"Just because you say so, doesn't make it true."* So Yeshua answered, *"Though I say so Myself, still My record is true because I know where I came from, and where I go; but you can't tell where I came from, nor where I go. You judge by what you see; I judge no one. But still if I judge, My judgment is true because I am not alone, but it is I and the One who sent Me. It's also written in your law, that if two people say something is true, then it's the truth. I am One that says what I say of Myself is true, and the One that sent Me tells the truth about Me, too."*

[19-27] Then they asked, "Where is the One who sent You?" So Yeshua answered, *"You neither know Me, nor the One who sent Me. If you had known Me, you would have known the One who sent Me also."* These words Yeshua spoke in the treasury room, while teaching in the Place of Worship, so no one tried to take the Christ because it wasn't the right time yet. Then Yeshua said to them again, *"I go away, and you'll look for Me, but will die in your sins; and where I go, you can't come."* Then the Jews asked, *"Will you kill yourself?"* for saying, *"Where I go, you can't come."* Christ answered, *"You're from below; I am from above. You're of this world; but I am not of this world. So I said to you, that you'll die in your sins because if you don't believe that I am the Christ, you'll die without forgiveness for your sins."* Then they asked, *"Who are you?"* So Yeshua answered, *"The One who I said I was from the beginning. I have many things to say about you and to judge: but the One who sent Me is true; and I tell the world only what I've heard from that One."* But they didn't understand that the Christ spoke to them of God.

The Truth will Make You Free

[28-32] Then Yeshua said, *"When you've lifted Me up, then you'll know that I am the Christ, and that I do nothing of Myself; but as My God has told Me, I say this. And the One who sent Me is with Me. God hasn't left Me alone because I always do what pleases God."* As Yeshua said these words, many believed on the Christ. Then Yeshua said to the Jews who believed, *"If you stay in My Word, then you are My true followers; and you'll know the truth, and the truth will make you free."*

[33-47] And they answered, *"We're from Abraham's family, and have never served anyone, so how can you say, 'You'll become free?'"* So Yeshua answered, *"The truth is, whoever is doing sinful things is the servant of that sin. And the servant doesn't live in the house forever, but only the true Child lives there forever. So if the Child makes you free, you'll be truly free. I know that you're of Abraham's family; but you try to kill Me, because you don't accept My Word. I say only what I've seen with the One I came from; and you do what you've seen with who you came from."* Then they said, *"We come from Abraham."* But Yeshua answered, *"If you were Abraham's children, you would do what you've seen of Abraham. But now you try to kill Me, because I have told you the truth, which I've heard of God. Abraham didn't do like this. You do what the One you came from does."* Then they said, *"We weren't born of unfaithfulness; we've come from only One, who is God."* So Yeshua said, *"If God was who you came from, you would love Me because I came from God; nor did I come of Myself, but God sent Me. Why don't you understand what I say? It's because you can't hear My Words. You come from the devil, and what the devil wants, you'll do. The devil was a murderer from the beginning, and didn't stay in the truth, because there's no truth in the devil. When someone tells a lie, it's spoken out of themselves because they're a liar, and the one they're from is a liar, too. And because what I say is true, you don't believe Me. Who of you can prove Me a sinner? And if I speak the truth, why don't you believe Me? Whoever is of God hears the Word of God, so you who can't hear them, aren't of God."*

[48-59] Then the Jews said, *"Didn't we say rightly that you're a Samaritan, and have an evil spirit?"* Then Yeshua answered, *"I don't have an evil spirit; but I honor My God, and you dishonor Me. And I don't want praise for Myself: but there's One who wants it and judges. The truth is, if anyone keeps My Word, they won't see death."* Then the Jews said, *"Now we know that you have an evil spirit. Abraham is dead, and all the great preachers; and you say, 'If someone keeps My Word, they won't see death.' Are you greater than our ancestor Abraham, who is dead, and the great preachers who are dead? Who do you think you are?"* And Yeshua answered, *"If I honor Myself, My honor is nothing. It's My God that honors Me; who you say is your God, yet you don't know God. But I know God: and if I were to say, I don't know God, I'd be a liar like you: but I know God, and keep God's Word. Your ancestor Abraham wanted to see My day, and saw it, and was happy."* Then the Jews said, *"You aren't even fifty years old, and have you seen Abraham?"* And Yeshua answered, *"The truth is, before Abraham was, I Am."* Then they picked up stones to throw at Yeshua, but the Christ hid, and so passed by, going through the middle of them, and went out of the Place of Worship.

One Born Blind Healed

9 [1-7] And passing by, Yeshua saw someone who was blind from birth. And the followers asked, *"Christ, who sinned, this person, or the parents, to cause this blindness at birth?"* So Yeshua said, *"Neither has this person, nor the parents sinned; but it happened so that God's work would be seen in him. I must do the work of the One who sent Me, while there's still time. The time is coming, when it'll be too late to work. As long as I am in the world, I*

141

am the light that shows the way to the world." And after saying this, the Christ spat on the ground, and made clay out of the spit, rubbing it on the eyes of the person who was blind, and saying, *"Go, wash in the pool of Siloam,"* (which means, sent). So the person who was blind left, and washed, and came back seeing.

[8-12] So the neighbors, and those who had seen this person before, said, *"Isn't this the one who sat and begged?"* Some said, *"Yes, it is;"* but others said, *"It looks like the one who was blind."* So the one who had been blind said, *"It's me."* So they asked, *"How can you see?"* So he answered, *"Someone named Yeshua made clay, and rubbed it on my eyes, and said to me, 'Go to the pool of Siloam, and wash;' so I went and washed, and I could see."* But when they asked, *"Where is this One?"* he said, *"I don't know."*

[13-17] Then they brought the one who had been blind to the religious leaders, because it was a Day of Worship when Yeshua had made the clay, and healed his eyes. So the religious leaders asked him, *"How are you able to see?"* who answered, *"Yeshua put clay on my eyes, and I washed, and now I see."* So some of the religious leaders said, *"Yeshua isn't of God, because this person doesn't keep the Day of Worship."* But others said, *"How can someone that is a sinner do such amazing things?"* So there was a disagreement among them. Then they asked the one who had been blind, *"What do you think of this person that has made you see?"* who answered, *"Yeshua is a great preacher."*

[18-23] But the Jews didn't believe that this person had been blind, and could now see, until they called the parents of the one whose eyes had been healed. They asked them, saying, *"Is this your child, who you say was born blind? Then how does he now see?"* And they answered, "We know that this is our child, who was born blind, but as to how, we don't know; or who has done it, we don't know: ask him; we don't need to speak for someone who's an adult now." They said this, because they were afraid of the Jews, and because the Jews had already agreed that if anyone said that Yeshua was the Christ, they would be put out of the Place of Worship. So they said, "Our child is old enough to speak for himself."

[24-34] Then they called the one that had been blind again, saying, *"Give God the praise: we know that this person is a sinner;"* who answered, *"Whether this One is a sinner or not, I don't know: but one thing I know, that I was blind, and now I see."* Then they asked again, *"What did Yeshua do to you? How are your eyes able to see?"* And he answered, *"I've told you already, and you didn't listen, so why do you want to hear it again? Will you also become followers?"* Then they hated him, and said, *"You're the follower; but we're followers of Moses. We know that God spoke to Moses: as for Yeshua, we don't know where this person is from."* Then he asked them, *"Why is this so important, that you don't know from where Yeshua is from, who has still healed my eyes? Now we know that God doesn't hear sinners; but if anyone is a worshipper of God, and does what God's wants, God hears them. Since the world began, it has never been heard that someone healed the eyes of one that was born blind. If Yeshua isn't of God, how could this person do anything?"* But they answered, *"You were fully born in sin, and you dare to teach us?"* And they put him out.

[35-41] And Yeshua, who had heard that they had put that person out, found him, and asked, *"Do you believe on the Child of God?"* So that person asked, *"Who is it, that I might believe on them?"* And Yeshua said, *"You've already seen them, and it's the One who is speaking to you, now."* So he said, *"Christ, I believe!"* and bowed and worshipped Yeshua. And Yeshua said, *"I am come into this world for judgment, that those who don't see might see; and that those who see might become blind."* And some of the religious leaders which were with them heard this, and asked, *"Are we blind also?"* So Yeshua answered, *"If you didn't understand you wouldn't be sinning; but since you say, "We understand; you are sinning."*

The Good Keeper

10 [1-6] *"The truth is, whoever doesn't come in by the gate into the pen, but climbs up some other way is a thief and a burglar. But the One who comes in by the gate is the Keeper of the animals. The gatekeeper opens the gate for the Keeper; and the animals hear the Keeper's voice: who calls their own animals by name, and leads them out. And the Keeper who lets out the animals, goes before them, and the animals follow because they know their Keeper's voice. The animals won't follow a stranger, but will run away from them because they don't know the voice of strangers."* Yeshua told this story to them, but they didn't understand what the story meant.

[7-18] Then Yeshua said again, *"The truth is, I am the gate for the animals. Whoever has come before Me are thieves and burglars; but the animals didn't go to them. I am the gate, so if anyone comes in by Me, they'll be saved, and will go in and out, and find land. The thief only comes to steal, kill, and hurt: I am come so that they'll have life, and that they'll have the best life possible. I am the Good Keeper, and the Good Keeper gives their own life for their animals. But whoever is a hired hand and not the Keeper, who doesn't own the animals, and sees the wolf coming, will leave the animals, and run away. Then the wolf takes some, and scatters all the other animals. The hired hand runs away, because they're a hired hand and doesn't really care about the animals. I am the Good Keeper, and know My animals, and I am known by those who are Mine. As God knows Me, in the same way I know God; and I give My life for those who are Mine. And I have others, which aren't from this pen. I must also bring them, and they'll know My voice; and there will be one pen, and One Keeper. My God loves Me, because I*

give My life, so that I might live again. No one takes it from Me, but I give it Myself. I have the power to give it, and I have the power to take it again. I have this promise from My God."

[19-21] So there was another disagreement among the Jews because of these stories. And many of them said, *"Yeshua has an evil spirit, and is crazy; why do you listen to that One?"* But others said, *"These aren't the Words of someone who has an evil spirit. Can an evil spirit make someone who is blind see?"*

One Being

[22-30] And it was the celebration of the dedication at Jerusalem, during the winter, when Yeshua walked in the Place of Worship in Solomon's porch. Then the Jews came to the Christ, saying, *"How long will you make us doubt? If you're the Christ, tell us clearly?"* So Yeshua answered, *"I've told you already, and you didn't believe Me: what I do in Yahweh's Name, is a truthful witnesses of Me. But you don't believe, because you aren't Mine, as I said to you. Those who are Mine hear My voice, and I know them, and they follow Me: And I give them everlasting life; and they'll never die, nor will anyone take them out of My hand. My God, which gave them to Me, is greater than all; and no one is able to take them out of My God's hand. Yahweh God and I are One Being."*

[31-38] Then the Jews picked up stones again, wanting to kill the Christ. So Yeshua said, *"I've shown you many good works from My God, so for which of them do you stone Me?"* And the Jews answered, *"We don't stone you for a good work; but for disrespect of God; and because you, being human, make yourself God."* Then Yeshua asked, *"Isn't it written in your law, 'I said, you're gods?' If God called them gods, to whom the Word of God came, and that Word can't be broken; How can you say of the One, who God has set apart, and sent into the world, You show disrespect for God; because I said, I am the Child of God? If I don't do what is of My God, then don't believe Me. But if I do, even if you don't believe Me, believe what I've done: so that you can know, and believe that God is in Me, and I am in God."*

[39-42] So they looked for a way to take Yeshua again: but the Christ escaped from them and went away again beyond Jordan into the place where John first baptized; and stayed there. And many came to Christ, saying, *"John didn't do any miracle, but everything that John said of You was true."* So many believed on the Christ there.

Lazarus Brought Back to Life

11 [1-6] Now someone named Lazarus was sick, who was of Bethany, the town of Mary and her sister Martha. (It was the same Mary who anointed the Christ with perfume, and wiped the Christ's feet with her hair, whose brother Lazarus was sick.) So Lazarus's sisters sent word to Yeshua, saying, *"Christ, the one you love is sick."* But hearing that, Yeshua said, *"This sickness won't end in death, but is for God's praise, that the Child of God might be made known by this."* Now Yeshua loved Martha, her sister, and Lazarus, but hearing that Lazarus was sick, the Christ stayed two more days in the place they were at.

[7-16] Then after that, the Christ said to the followers, *"Let's go into Judea again."* And the followers asked, *"Christ, the Jews were just looking for a way to kill You; and You want to go there again?"* So Yeshua answered, *"Aren't there twelve hours in a day? If someone waits to walk in the daylight, they won't stumble, because they see the light of the world. But if someone goes ahead and walks in the darkness of night, they'll stumble, because they have no light."* Then the Christ said, *"Our friend Lazarus is sleeping; but I go, so that I can wake him up."* Then the followers said, *"Christ, if he's sleeping, that's good."* The Christ had spoken of the death of Lazarus, but they thought that Yeshua had spoken of resting in sleep, so Yeshua said clearly, *"Lazarus is dead, and I am happy for your sakes that I wasn't there, so that you can believe; So let's go."* Then Thomas, who is called the Twin, said to the followers, *"Let's go, too, that we may die with Yeshua."*

[17-27] Then when Yeshua got there, the Christ found out that Lazarus had been in the grave four days already. Now Bethany was very near, only about two miles away from Jerusalem, so many of the Jews came to Martha and Mary, to comfort them about their brother. Then Martha, as soon as she heard who was coming, went and met Yeshua, but Mary still stayed in the house. And Martha said to Yeshua, *"Christ, if You had been here, my brother wouldn't have died, but I know, that even now, whatever you ask of God, God will give it to You."* So Yeshua said to her, *"Your brother will come to life again."* Then Martha said, *"I know that he will come to life again in the new life at the last day."* But Yeshua said to her, *"I am the One who gives life again; I am the new life. Whoever believes in Me, even though they were dead, they'll still live; and whoever lives and believes in Me will never die. Do you believe this?"* And she said, *"Yes, Christ: I believe that You're the Christ, the Child of God, the One who would come into the world."*

[28-35] And when she had said this, she went, and secretly called Mary her sister, saying, *"The Teacher is here, and wants you."* And as soon as she heard that, Mary quickly got up, going to the Christ. Now Yeshua hadn't come into the town yet, but was still there where they had met. Then the Jews who were with Mary in the house, and comforted her, when they saw her suddenly get up and go out, followed her, saying, *"She's going to the grave to cry there."* Then when Mary came to where Yeshua was, and saw the Christ, she bowed down at the Christ's feet, saying, *"Christ, if You had been here, my brother wouldn't have died."* So when Yeshua saw her

143

crying, and the Jews who came with her also crying, the Christ mourned in the spirit, and was upset, and said, *"Where have you laid Lazarus?"* So they said, *"Christ, come and see."* And Yeshua cried.

[36-46] Then the Jews said, *"Look how much Yeshua loved him!"* And some of them said, *"Couldn't this person, which opened the eyes of those who are blind, have kept this person from dying?"* So Yeshua, mourning in the spirit again, came to the grave, which had a stone covering it. Then Yeshua said, *"Take away the stone."* But Martha, the sister of the one who was dead, said, *"Christ, by this time he stinks, being dead for four days."* So Yeshua said to her, *"Didn't I say to you, that if you'd believe, you'd see the victory of God?"* Then they moved the stone from the cave where the body was laid. Yeshua looked up, saying, *"God, I thank You that You've heard Me. I know that You always hear Me, but because of the people here, I said it, so that they can believe that You've sent Me."* After that, the Christ called out loudly, saying, *"Lazarus, come out."* And the one who was dead came out, tied up hand and foot with graveclothes, and whose face was tied up with a cloth. So Yeshua said, *"Untie him, and let him go."* Then many of the Jews which came to Mary, and had seen the things which Yeshua did, believed on the Christ. But some of them went to the religious leaders, and told them what Yeshua had done.

The Leading Priest Foretells Yeshua's Death

[47-54] Then the leading priests and the religious leaders gathered a court, saying, *"What do we do? Yeshua does so many amazing things. If we let this go on, everyone will believe in this One: and the Romans will come and take us out of our place and destroy our nation."* And one of them, named Caiaphas, being the leading priest that year, answered, *"You don't know anything at all, nor know that it's necessary for us, that One person dies for the people, so that the whole nation won't be destroyed."* And he didn't speak this of himself, but being the leading priest that year, he foretold that Yeshua was about to die for that nation; And not for that nation only, but also so that the Christ would gather together the children of God that were scattered about into one family. Then from that day on, they planned together to put the Christ to death. So Yeshua didn't walk among the Jews openly anymore; but left there to a place near the countryside, into a city called Ephraim, and stayed there with the followers.

[55-57] And the Jews' Passover was near, so many went from the countryside up to Jerusalem for the Passover, to purify themselves. Then they looked for Yeshua, and spoke among themselves, as they stood in the Place of Worship, *"Do you think that Yeshua will come to the celebration at all?"* because both the leading priests and the religious leaders had given a word, that if anyone knew where Yeshua was, to tell them, so that they could catch the Christ.

The Anointing of Yeshua at Bethany

12 [1-8] Then six days before the Passover, Yeshua came to Bethany, where Lazarus was, who had been dead but was brought back to life again by the Christ. And Martha was serving them supper there, and Lazarus was one of those who sat at the table with the Christ. Then Mary, who had taken a pound of perfumed oil of spikenard, which was very expensive, anointed the feet of Yeshua, wiping them with her hair; and the whole house was filled with the smell of the perfume. Then one of the followers, Judas Iscariot, Simon's son, who was about to hand over the Christ, said *"This perfume could've been sold for almost a year's wage; Why wasn't it sold and given to those who are poor?"* But he said this, not that he cared for those who are poor; but because he was a thief, and took some of what was put in the moneybag. Then Yeshua said, *"Leave her alone; she's done this for the day of My burial. You'll always have those who are poor with you; but you won't always have Me."*

The Plan to Kill Lazarus

[9-11] Many people of the Jews knew that the Christ was there: but they didn't come for Yeshua's sake only, but to see Lazarus also, whom the Christ had raised from the dead. So the leading priests planned to put Lazarus to death, as well, because many of the Jews went away, and believed on Yeshua because of him.

The Entry into Jerusalem

[12-19] On the next day many people that had come to the celebration, when they heard that Yeshua was coming to Jerusalem, took branches of palm trees, and went out to meet the Christ, and called out, "Save us now! Blessed is the Ruler of Israel that comes in the Name of Yahweh." And when Yeshua had found a young donkey, and sat on it; as the Word says, *"Don't be afraid, daughter of Zion: your Ruler comes, sitting on an donkey's foal."* The followers didn't understand this at the time, but when Yeshua came to life again, they remembered that this was written about the Christ, and that this had happened. So the people that were there when the Christ called Lazarus out of the grave, and brought him back from the dead, told everyone about it. Because of this, the people also came out, because they had heard that the Christ had done this miracle. Then the religious leaders said among themselves, *"Don't you know that you haven't done a thing? The whole world is following after this Yeshua!"*

[20-22] And there were certain Greeks among those who came up to worship at the celebration. And one of them came to Philip, who was of Bethsaida of Galilee, and asked, saying, *"Sir, we want to see Yeshua."* So Philip went and told Andrew, and then Andrew and Philip went together and told Yeshua.

The Seed of Grain

[23-27] But Yeshua said, *"It's time for Me to die now and come back to life. The truth is, unless a grain of wheat is put into the ground and dies, it's only one grain; but if it dies, it will make much more. Whoever loves their life will lose it; and whoever hates their life in this world will keep it to everlasting life. If anyone wants to serve Me, let them follow Me; Where I am, My worker will be there also. If anyone serves Me, My God will honor them. My soul is uneasy now; but what can I say? God, save Me from this time: No, but I came to this time for this very reason."*

Yahweh Speaks from Heaven

[28-36] *"Yahweh God, bring praise to Your Name."* Then a voice came from heaven, saying, *"I've both made it known, and will make it known again."* And some of the people that stood by, heard it, and said that it had thundered, but others said, *"An angel spoke to Yeshua."* So Yeshua said, *"This voice didn't come because of Me, but for your sakes. Now, this world will come to judgment, and then, the ruler of this world will be put out. And if I am lifted up from the earth, I'll draw all people to Myself."* And this was said to signify how the Christ was to die. So the people asked, *"But we've heard out of the Word of God that the Christ lives forever, so why do you say, 'I must be lifted up?' What are you talking about?"* Then Yeshua answered, *"The Light is with you for just a little while longer. Walk while you have the Light, in case darkness overcomes you; because whoever walks in darkness doesn't know where they're going. Believe in the Light, while you have it, so that you can be the children of Light."* After speaking this, the Christ went and hid from them.

The Blindness of Unbelievers

[37-43] Even though the Christ had done so many amazing things for them, many still didn't believe on Yeshua; so that the saying of Isaiah the great preacher would happen, which said, "God, who has believed us? And to whom has the strength of Yahweh God been made known?" So they couldn't believe, because Isaiah had said again, "God has blinded their eyes, and made their hearts full of doubt; so that they don't see with their eyes, nor understand with their heart, and be changed, and healed." Isaiah said this when he saw God's glory, and spoke of it. But in the same way, many among the leading rulers believed on the Christ; but loving the praise of others more than the praise of God, and because of the religious leaders, they didn't say so or they would be put out of the Place of Worship.

Judgment on Those Who Reject Christ

[44-50] Then Yeshua said, *"Whoever believes on Me, doesn't believe on Me only, but on the One who sent Me. And whoever sees Me sees the One who sent Me. I am come like a light into the world, so that whoever believes on Me wouldn't live in darkness. And if anyone hears My Words, and doesn't believe, I don't judge them because I didn't come to judge the world, but to save the world. Yet, whoever rejects Me, and doesn't accept My Words, will be judged by the Word that I've spoken, which will judge them in the last day; because I haven't spoken of Myself; but of the God who sent Me, who gave Me a Word, what I would say, and what I would speak. And I know that God's Word is everlasting life, so whatever I speak, I say just as God told Me."*

Washing the Feet of the Followers

13 [1-5] Before the celebration of the Passover, knowing that the time had come to leave this world and go back to God, the Christ loved the people of God, which were in the world, to the end. Now supper being over, the devil's spirit put it into the heart of Judas Iscariot, Simon's son, to hand over the Christ. And knowing that God had put everything into the Christ's own hands, and that the Christ came from God, and went to God; Yeshua arose from supper, and with clothes laid aside, took a towel, and got ready; pouring water into a basin, and began to wash the followers' feet, and to wipe them with the towel to get them ready.

[6-17] Then as the Christ came to Simon Peter: Peter asked, *"Christ, are you going to wash my feet?"* So Yeshua answered, *"What I do you don't know now; but you'll understand afterwards."* But Peter said, *"You're not washing my feet."* So Yeshua said, *"If I don't wash your feet, you can have nothing to do with Me."* So then Simon Peter said, *"Christ, then don't wash my feet only, but my hands and my head, as well!"* And Yeshua said, *"Whoever is washed only needs to wash their feet, but is clean everywhere else: and you're clean, but you aren't all clean."* And knowing who would hand over the Christ; Yeshua had said, *"You aren't all clean."* So the Christ, who had washed their feet, and dressed, and sat down again, asked, *"Do you know what I've done to you? You call Me Teacher and Christ: and you say well, because so I am. If then, being your Teacher and Christ, I've washed your feet, you also ought to wash one another's feet, because I've given you an example, that you would*

145

do as I've done to you. The truth is, the worker isn't greater than the owner; nor is the One who is sent greater than the One who sent them. If you know this and do it, you'll be happy.

Yeshua Identifies Judas

[18-22] *I don't speak of you all. I know whom I've chosen; but so that this Word will happen, 'The one who eats bread with Me is ready to kick Me down;' I tell you before it comes, so that when it's happened, you can believe that I am the One. The truth is, whoever accepts the one I send accepts Me; and whoever accepts Me accepts the One who sent Me."* Having said this, being uneasy in spirit, Yeshua told us truthfully, saying, *"I am telling you the truth, that one of you will hand Me over."* Then the followers looked at one another, wondering who the Christ spoke about.

[23-30] Now there was one of the followers leaning on the Christ, whom Yeshua loved. So Simon Peter waved to him, to ask who it was of whom the Christ had spoken. Then, leaning back on Yeshua, he asked, *"Christ, who is it?"* And Yeshua answered, *"It's the one that I'll give a piece of bread, when I've dipped it."* And the Christ dipped a piece of bread, and gave it to Judas Iscariot, the son of Simon. And after the piece of bread was dipped, Satan overcame him. Then Yeshua said, *"What you do, do quickly."* Now no one at the table knew why the Christ had said this to him, some of them thinking, because Judas had the moneybag, that Yeshua had said to buy what was needed for the celebration; or, to give something to those who are poor. Then having taken the piece of bread, Judas suddenly went out, it being night.

The New Word

[31-35] So, when he had gone out, Yeshua said, *"Now I'll be made known, and God will be made known in Me. If God be made known in Me, God will also make Me known in God's own self, and will make Me known soon. Little children, I am with you for just a little while longer. You'll look for Me, and as I said to the Jews, 'Where I go, you can't come'; so now I tell you. A New Word I give to you, that you love one another; Just as I've loved you, you also love one another. If you love one another, by this, all people will know that you're My followers."*

Peter's Denial Foretold

[36-38] Simon Peter asked, *"Christ, where are You going?"* And Yeshua answered, *"Where I go, you can't follow Me now; but you'll follow Me later."* Then Peter said, *"Christ, why can't I follow you now? I'll give my own life for Your sake."* So Yeshua asked, *"Will you really give your life for My sake? The truth is, the rooster won't crow, till you've said you don't even know Me three times."*

No One Comes to God but by Me

14 [1-7] *"Don't let your hearts be upset by anything: If you believe in God, believe in Me, too. There are many places to live in My God's house: I'd have told you if it weren't true. I go to get a place ready for you. And if I go to get a place ready for you, I'll come back, and bring you to Myself; so that where I am, you may be there, also. And you know where I am going, and you know the way."* Then Thomas asked, *"Christ, we don't know where you're going; so how can we know the way?"* And Yeshua answered, *"I am the way, the truth, and the life! No one comes to God, but by Me. If you had known Me, you would have known My God also: and from now on, you know God, and have seen God."*

[8-14] Then Philip said, *"Christ, show us God, and it will be enough."* But Yeshua answered, *"Have I been with you this long, and you still don't know Me, Philip? Whoever has seen Me has seen God; so how can you say then, 'Show us God?' Don't you believe that I am in God, and God in Me? The words that I speak to you, I don't speak of Myself: but the God who lives in Me, does the things that you've seen. Believe Me, that I am in God, and God in Me: or else believe Me for the sake of the very things you've seen Me do. The truth is, whoever believes on Me, they'll do the things that I do, also; and they'll do even greater things than these; because I go to My God. And whatever you ask in My Name, that I'll do, so that God can be made known in Me. If you ask anything in My Name, I'll do it.*

Yeshua Promises the Comforter

[15-21] *If you love Me, keep My Words. And I'll pray to God, who will send you another Comforter, who can stay with you forever; the Spirit of Truth; Whom the world can't accept, because it's the One who it doesn't see, nor know: but who you know because it's the One who lives with you, and who will be in you. I won't leave you helpless: I'll come to you. In just a little while, and the world will see Me no more; but you'll see Me, because I live, and you'll live also. At that time you'll know that I am in My God, and you in Me, and I in you. Whoever has My Words, and keeps them, that is who loves Me; and whoever loves Me will be loved of My God, and I'll love them, and will make Myself known to them."*

[22-31] Then Judas, not Iscariot, asked the Christ, *"How is it that you'll make yourself known to us, and not to the world?"* Yeshua answered, *"If someone loves Me, then they'll keep My Words: and My God will love them, and We'll come to them, and make Our home with them. Whoever doesn't love Me doesn't keep My Words: and the Word which you hear isn't My own, but is God's, who sent Me. I've told you this, being still here with you. But the Comforter, which is the Holy Spirit, whom God will send in My Name, will teach you everything, and help you remember what I've said to you. I leave peace with you, but it's My peace I give to you: I don't give you as the world gives. Don't let your heart be upset by anything, nor let it be afraid. You've heard how I said to you, 'I go away, and come back again to you.' If you loved Me, you'd celebrate, because I said, 'I go to God, because My God is greater than I.' And now I've told you before it happens, so that when it happens, you might believe. From now on, I won't talk much with you because the ruler of this world is coming, and has nothing to do with Me. But that the world can know that I love God; and just as God gave Me Word, so I do. Get up, it's time to go from here.*

The Vine and the Branches
15 [1-6] *I am the true vine, and My God is the Farmer. Every branch in Me that doesn't make fruit is cut away: and every branch that bears fruit, is pruned, so that it can make more fruit. Now you're already saved through the Word which I've spoken to you. So live in Me, and I'll live in you. As the branch can't make fruit by itself, without the vine; neither can you, unless you live in Me. I am the vine, you're the branches: Whoever lives in Me, and I in them, makes much fruit; but you can't do anything without Me. So if someone doesn't live in Me, they're cut off like a branch, and will wither; and they're gathered together to be put into the fire, and burned.*

Ask Anything in My Name
[7-12] *If you live in Me, and My Words live in you, you may ask whatever you want, and it'll be done for you. In this, My God is made known, so that you'll make much fruit; and you'll be My followers. As God has loved Me, I have loved you, so live in My love. If you keep My Words, you'll live in My love, just as I've kept the Word of God, and live in God's love. I've told you this, that My joy might live in you, and that you may have complete joy. This is My Word, that you love one another, as I've loved you.*

Yeshua calls us Friends
[13-17] *No one has greater love than when someone gives up their own life for their friends. You're My friends, if you do what I tell you. From now on I won't call you workers because a worker doesn't know what the owner does: but I've called you friends because everything that I've heard of My God I've told you. You haven't chosen Me, but I've chosen you, and set you apart, so that you would go and make fruit, and that your fruit would live: so that whatever you ask of God in My Name, it will be given to you. I tell you this, so that you'll love one another.*

We are Hated by the World
[18-27] *If the world hates you, you know that it hated Me before it hated you. If you were of the world, the world would love its own: but because you aren't of the world, and I've chosen you out of the world, the world hates you. Remember what I said to you, 'The worker isn't greater than the owner.' If they've abused Me, they'll also mistreat you; but if they've kept My Word, they'll keep yours also. But they'll do all this to you because of My Name, because they don't know the One who sent Me. If I hadn't come and spoken to them, they wouldn't have sinned, but now there's no excuse for their sin. Whoever hates Me hates My God also. If I hadn't done among them the things which no one else has done, they wouldn't have sinned, but now they've seen and hated both Me and My God. But this happened so that the Word would happen that is written in their Words, "They hated Me without a cause." But the Comforter will come, whom I'll send to you from God, the Spirit of Truth, who comes from God, and who will tell others of Me: And you are truthful witnesses, because you've been with Me from the beginning.*

The Rejection of the Followers Foretold
16 [1-6] *I've told you this, so that you won't be offended. They'll put you out of the places of worship. Yes, the time is coming, that whoever kills you will think that they're helping God. And they'll do this to you, because they don't know God, nor Me. But I've told you this, that when the time comes, you'll remember that I told you about them. I didn't say this to you at first, because I was with you. But now I am going away to the One who sent Me; and none of you asks Me, 'Where are you going?' And now, because I've said this to you, your heart is sad.*

The Spirit of Truth
[7-16] *Just the same, the truth is, that it's necessary for you that I go away because if I don't go away, the Comforter won't come to you; but if I leave, I'll send the Comforter to you. And the Comforter is coming, who'll convict the world of sin, and of My goodness, and of judgment. Of sin, because they don't believe on Me; Of My goodness, because I go to My God, and you won't see Me any more; And of judgment, because the ruler of this world is judged. I still have many things to say to you, but you can't understand them all now. But when the*

147

Comforter is here, this Spirit of Truth will help you to know what's true, not speaking of Its Own Self; but whatever the Comforter hears, that the Comforter will speak and will show you things to come. The Comforter will make Me known, taking of what's Mine, and showing it to you. Everything that God has is Mine: so I said that the Comforter will take of Mine, and will show it to you. In just a little while, you won't see Me: and again, in just a little while, you'll see Me, because I go to God."

[17-27] Then some of the followers said among themselves, *"What does the Christ mean by, 'In just a little while, you won't see Me: and again, in just a little while, you'll see Me: because I go to God?'"* So they said, *"What does it mean, 'In a little while?' We don't know what the Christ meant."* Now Yeshua knew that they wanted to ask, so the Christ said to them, *"Are you asking among yourselves about what I said, 'In a little while, you won't see Me: and again, in a little while, you'll see Me?' The truth is, that you'll cry and mourn, but the world will celebrate: and you'll be sorrowful, but your sorrow will be turned into joy. A woman who's in labor suffers, because her time is here: but as soon as she's given birth, she doesn't remember the suffering any more, for the joy that she's brought a child into the world. So now you'll have sorrow: but I'll see you again, and your heart will celebrate, and no one will take your joy from you. And in that day you won't have to ask Me anything. The truth is, whatever you ask God in My Name, God will give it to you. Up to now, You haven't asked anything in My Name, so ask, and you'll get what you ask for, that you can have complete joy. I've told you this in strange sayings: but the time is coming, when I won't speak to you any more in strange ways, but I'll explain clearly about God. At that time you'll ask in My Name: and I don't say to you, that I'll pray to God for you because God's Own Self loves you, because you've loved Me, and have believed that I came from God. I came from God, and am come into the world: but again, I leave the world, and go to God."*

Overcoming the World

[29-33] Then the followers said, *"See, now you're speaking clearly, and aren't speaking in strange sayings. Now we're sure that you know everything, and that we don't need to ask anything of you: by this, we believe that God is who You came from."* Then Yeshua answered, *"Do you believe now? The time is coming, yes, and is now here, that you'll be scattered, everyone on their own, and will leave Me alone: but still I am not alone, because God is with Me. I've said this to you, so that in Me you might have peace. You'll always have troubles in the world, but be happy; because I've overcome the world."*

One God, One Family

17 [1-8] These words Yeshua spoke, looking up to heaven, saying, *"Yahweh God, it's time now; Make your Child known, that your Child may also make You known: As you've given Me power over everyone, to give everlasting life to whoever You've given to Me. And this is everlasting life, that they may know You, Yahweh, the only true God, and Me, Yeshua the Christ, whom You've sent. I've made You known on the earth: I've finished the work which You gave Me to do. And now, God, make Me known along with Your Own Name with the glory which I had with You before the world was. I've made Your Name clear to all those which You gave Me out of the world. They were Yours, and You gave them to Me; and they've kept Your Word. Now they've known that everything that You've given Me is of You, because I've given to them the Words which You gave to Me; and they've accepted them, and have truly known that I came from You, and they've believed that You sent Me.*

[9-13] *I pray for them, though I don't pray for the whole world, but only for those who You've given Me because they're Yours. And all Mine are Yours, and Yours are Mine; and I am made known through them. And now I am no more in the world, but they are in the world, and I come to You. Holy God, keep through Your Own Name those whom You've given Me, that they can be one, as We are One. While I was with them in the world, I kept them in Your Name, Yahweh: those that You gave Me I've kept, and none of them is lost, but the one who was forever damned; so that everything in the Word would happen. And now I come to You; and this I speak in the world, so that they'll have My complete joy in themselves.*

[14-23] *I've given them Your Word; and the world has hated them, because they aren't of the world, just as I am not of the world. I don't pray that you would take them out of the world, but that you would keep them from the evil in it. They aren't of the world, just as I am not of the world, so set them apart through Your truth: Your Word is truth. As You've sent Me into the world, in the same way I've also sent them into the world. For their sakes I set Myself apart, so that they also might be set apart through the truth. I don't pray for these alone, but for those who will also believe on Me through their word; so that they can all be one; as You, God, are in Me, and I in You, so that they also can be one in Us: and that the world may believe that You've sent Me. The glory, which You gave Me, I've given to them; so that they can be one, just as We are One: I in them, and You in Me, so that they can be made one family; and that the world can know that You've sent Me, and have loved them, as You've loved Me.*

[24-26] *God, I also want those whom You've given Me, to be with Me where I am; so that they can see My victory, which you've given Me because You loved Me before the beginning of the world. Good God, the world hasn't known You: but I've known You, and these have known that You've sent Me. And I've told them Your Name, Yahweh, and will tell it: that the love in which You've loved Me can be in them, and I in them."*

The Garden of Gethsemane

18 [1-6] After the Christ had spoken these words, Yeshua went out with the followers over the creek Cedron, coming into a garden. And Judas, which handed over the Christ, knew the place, because Yeshua often went there with the followers. So Judas then, having gotten troops and officers from the leading priests and religious leaders, came there with lanterns and torches and swords. And Yeshua, knowing everything that would come about, went to them, saying, *"Who are you looking for?"* So they answered, *"Yeshua of Nazareth."* And Yeshua said, *"I am that One."* And Judas also, who had turned Yeshua over, stood with them. Then as soon as the Christ had said, *"I am that One",* they all went backward, falling to the ground.

[7-14] Then the Christ asked them again, *"Who are you looking for?"* And they said, *"Yeshua of Nazareth."* So Yeshua said, *"I've told you that I am that One: so if you're looking for Me, let all these go;"* so that the saying would happen, which the Christ spoke, *"I have lost none of those who You gave Me."* Then Simon Peter, having a sword, took it out and cut off the right ear of the leading priest's worker, whose name was Malchus. Then Yeshua said to Peter, *"Put your sword in its sheath: shouldn't I suffer the things which My God has given Me to suffer?"* Then the troop, the captain, and the officers of the Jews took and tied up Yeshua, leading the Christ away to Annas first, because he was father-in-law to Caiaphas, who was the leading priest that year. Now Caiaphas was the one, who said to the Jews, that it was necessary that one person would die for the people.

Peter Denies Knowing Yeshua

[15-18] And Simon Peter followed Yeshua, and so did another follower: that follower was known to the leading priest, and went in with Yeshua into the hall of the leading priest. But Peter stood outside the door. Then that other follower went out, which was known to the leading priest, and spoke to the girl that kept the door, bringing Peter in. Then she said to Peter, *"Aren't you also one of this person's followers?"* But Peter said, *"I am not."* And the workers and officers stood there, who had made a fire of coals because it was cold and warmed themselves: and Peter stood with them, and warmed himself.

The Leading Priests Question Yeshua

[19-24] The leading priest then asked Yeshua about the followers, and of the Christ's teachings. So Yeshua answered, *"I spoke openly to the world; I taught in all the places of worship, where the Jews always go; and I haven't said anything in secret. Why do you ask Me? Ask those who heard what I've said: they know what I said."* And when the Christ had said this, one of the officers which stood by slapped Yeshua with the palm of his hand saying, *"You dare answer the leading priest that way?"* Then Yeshua answered, *"If I've spoken any evil, be a truthful witnesses of the evil: but if well, why do you hit Me?"* Then Annas sent the Christ tied up to Caiaphas the leading priest.

Peter's Final Denial

[25-27] And Simon Peter stood and warmed himself. So they asked him, *"Aren't you also one of the followers?"* But Peter denied it, saying, *"I am not."* Then one of the workers of the leading priest, being kin to the one whose ear Peter cut off, asked, *"Didn't I see you in the garden with Yeshua?"* Then Peter denied it again, and suddenly the rooster crowed.

Pilate and Yeshua

[28-32] Then they led Yeshua from Caiaphas to the hall of judgment, being early; but they themselves didn't go into the judgment hall, or they would be ruined and not be able to eat the Passover. So then Pilate went out to them, saying, *"Of what do you accuse this person?"* And they answered, *"If this One wasn't a criminal, we wouldn't have brought this person to you."* Then Pilate said to them, *"You take and judge this One by your law."* So the Jews said, *"It isn't right for us to put anyone to death;"* so that what Yeshua had said, would happen, about what death the Christ would die.

[33-40] Then Pilate went in the judgment hall again, and asked Yeshua, saying, *"Are you the Ruler of the Jews?"* And Yeshua answered, *"Do you say this thing of yourself, or did others tell you about Me?"* Then Pilate asked, *"Am I a Jew? Your own nation and the leading priests have given You to me: what have you done?"* So Yeshua said, *"My realm isn't of this world: if My realm were of this world, then My workers would fight, so that I wouldn't be given to the Jews: but My realm is not here now."* So Pilate asked, *"Are you a Ruler then?"* And Yeshua answered, *"You say that I am a Ruler. For this reason I was born, and for this cause I came into the world, that I would be a witness to the truth. Everyone that knows the truth hears My voice."* And Pilate asked, *"What is truth?"* And when he had said this, he went out again to the Jews, saying to them, *"I find no fault at all in this person. But you have a way of life, that I free someone to you at the Passover, so would you like me to free to you the Ruler of the Jews?"* Then they all cried out again, saying, *"Not this One, but Barabbas."* And Barabbas was a criminal.

The Guards Mock Yeshua

19 [1-7] Then Pilate had Yeshua beaten. And the guards platted a crown of thorns, and put it on Yeshua's head, and put a purple robe on the Christ, saying, *"Hello, Ruler of the Jews!"* as they slapped Yeshua with their hands. So Pilate went out again, saying to them, *"I am bringing Yeshua out to you, so that you can know that I find no fault in this person."* Then Yeshua came out, wearing the crown of thorns, and the purple robe. And Pilate said, *"Look at this person?"* So when the leading priests and officers saw the Christ, they called out, saying, *"Put this One to death, put this One to death."* So Pilate answered, *"You do it, because I find no fault in this person."* But the Jews said, *"We have a law, and by our law this One ought to die, because this person claimed to be the Child of God."*

[8-12] So when Pilate heard that, he was all the more afraid; And went back into the judgment hall, saying to Yeshua, *"Where are You from?"* But Yeshua didn't answer. So Pilate asked, *"Why don't you speak to me? Don't you know that I have the power to put you to death, or the power to free you?"* Then Yeshua answered, *"You could have no power at all against Me, unless it were given to you from above, so whoever has given Me to you has the greater sin."* And from then on Pilate looked for a way to free the Christ. But the Jews called out, *"If you let this person go, you aren't Caesar's friend; whoever claims to be a Ruler speaks against Caesar."*

[13-16] So when Pilate heard that, he had Yeshua brought out, and sat down in the judgment seat in a place that is called the Pavement, but in the Hebrew, Gabbatha. And it was the preparation of the Passover, and about noon, when he said to the Jews, *"See, your Ruler!"* But they called out, *"Away with this One, away with this One, put this person to death."* Then Pilate asked, *"Do I put your Ruler to death?"* And the leading priests said, *"We have no Ruler but Caesar."* Then he gave the Christ to them to be put to death. And they took and led Yeshua away.

Christ on the Cross

[17-22] And the Christ, carrying the cross, went out to a place called *"The Place of a Skull,"* which is called in the Hebrew *"Golgotha"*: Who they put to death, along with two others, one on either side, with Yeshua in the middle. And Pilate wrote a title, and put it on the cross. And the writing was *"Yeshua of Nazareth, The Ruler of the Jews."* Then many of the Jews read this title because the place where Yeshua was put to death was near the city, and it was written in Hebrew, Greek, and Latin. Then the leading priests of the Jews said to Pilate, *"Don't write, 'The Ruler of the Jews'; but that this One said, I am Ruler of the Jews."* But Pilate said, *"I've written what I've written."*

The Soldier's Divide the Christ's Clothes

[23-24] Then the guards, when they had put Yeshua on the cross, took the Christ's clothes, and made four parts, giving to every soldier a part; and also the Christ's coat, but the coat was without seam, woven from the top throughout. So they said among themselves, *"Let's not tear it, but place bets for it, to see whose it will be;"* so that the Word would happen, which said, *"They divided my clothing among them, and they placed bets for My coat."* And so the guards did this.

The Christ's Mother

[25-27] Now Yeshua's mother stood there by the cross, with her sister, Mary, the spouse of Cleophas, and Mary Magdalene. So seeing her with the follower standing by, whom the Christ loved, Yeshua said, *"Mother, look, this is your child!* Then the Christ said to the follower, *"Look, this is your mother!"* And from that time on, that follower took her to his own home.

Christ Gives Up the Spirit

[28-37] Later, knowing that everything had now happened, that was said in the Word should happen, Yeshua said, *"I'm thirsty."* Now there was a bottle full of sour wine, so they filled a sponge with it, and put it on a hyssop reed, and put it to the Christ's mouth. After taking the wine, the Christ, giving up the Spirit, said, *"It's done;"* whose head then bowed. So the Jews, because it was the preparation day, (for that Day of Worship was a holy day) begged Pilate that their legs be broken, and that they be taken away so that the bodies wouldn't stay on the crosses on a Day of Worship. Then the guards came, and broke the legs of the first, and then of the other who were put on crosses along with the Christ. When they came to Yeshua, and saw that the Christ was dead already, they didn't break them: But when one of the guards pierced the Christ's side with a spear, blood and water gushed out. And the one who saw it told it, and what they say is true: and they know what they said is true, so that you might believe. And this happened, so that what was written in the Word would happen, *"Not a bone of the Christ will be broken."* And again another Word said, *"They'll look on the One whom they pierced."*

Yeshua's Burial

[38-42] And then Joseph of Arimathaea, being a follower of Yeshua, but secretly for fear of the Jews, begged Pilate to let him take away the body of Yeshua: so Pilate said that he could. Then he came and took the body of Yeshua. And Nicodemus came also, who first came to Yeshua by night, and brought a mixture of myrrh and aloes, about a hundred pounds. Then they took the body of Yeshua, and wound it in linen cloths with the spices, as is the Jews way to bury someone. Now near the place where the Christ was put on the cross, there was a garden; and in the garden a new tomb, in which no one had ever been laid. So they laid Yeshua there because of the Jews' preparation day and because the tomb was near there.

Mary Magdalene Sent to the Followers

20 [1-10] Mary Magdalene came to the tomb early on Sunday morning when it was still dark, and saw the stone moved away from the tomb. Then she ran, and came to Simon Peter, and to the other follower, whom Yeshua loved, saying to them, *"They've taken away the Christ out of the tomb, and we don't know where they've laid the body."* So Peter went out, and that other follower, and came to the tomb. And both of them ran together: but the other follower outran Peter, and came to the tomb first. And stooping down, and looking in, he saw the linen clothes there; but still didn't go in. Then Simon Peter came following him, and went into the tomb, and saw the linen clothes lying there, with the napkin that was around the Christ's head, not lying with the linen clothes, but folded up in a place by itself. Then that other follower also went in, which came first to the tomb, and saw it, and believed. But they still didn't know the Word, that the Christ must come to life again from the dead. Then the followers went back to their own homes.

[11-18] But Mary stood outside the tomb crying: and as she cried, she stooped down, and looked into the tomb, and saw two angels in white sitting, one at the head, and the other at the feet, where the body of Yeshua had lain. And they said to her, *"Woman, why are you crying?"* So she answered, *"Because they've taken my Christ away, and I don't know where they've put the body."* And when she had said this, she turned around, and saw the Christ standing there, but didn't know that it was Yeshua. Then Yeshua said to her, *"Woman, why are you crying? Who are you looking for?"* And she, thinking it to be the gardener, said, *"Sir, if you've taken the body from here, tell me where you've put it, and I'll take it away."* Then Yeshua said to her, *"Mary!"* And she turned around, saying, *"Rabboni;"* which means, *"Teacher."* And Yeshua said to her, *"Don't touch Me yet because I am still not gone up to God: but go to My followers, and say to them, I go up to the One I am from, and the One you're from; to My God, and to your God."* So Mary Magdalene came and told the followers that she had seen the Christ, who had spoken this to her.

Receiving the Holy Spirit

[19-23] Then the same day at evening, being Sunday, when the doors were shut where the followers were gathered for fear of the Jews, Yeshua came and stood in the middle, saying to them, *"Be at peace!"* And after the Christ had said this, they saw Yeshua's hands and side. Then the followers were happy, when they saw the Christ. And then Yeshua said again, *"Be at peace: just as My God has sent Me, I am sending you, too."* And the Christ said this, then breathed on them, saying to them, *"Take the Holy Spirit: Whoever's sins you forgive, they're forgiven them; and whoever's sins you keep, they're kept."*

The Doubting Thomas

[24-30] But Thomas, one of the twelve, called the Twin, wasn't with them when Yeshua came. So the other followers told him, *"We've seen the Christ."* But he said, *"Unless I see the print of the nails in Yeshua's hands, and put my finger into them, and put my hand into Yeshua's side, I won't believe it."* And eight days later the followers were again inside, and Thomas was with them. Then Yeshua came, the doors being shut, and stood in the middle, saying, *"Be at peace."* Then the Christ said to Thomas, *"Touch Me here with your finger, and see My hands; and touch Me here with your hand and put it into My side: and don't be faithless, but believe."* And Thomas answered, *"My Christ and my God."* Then Yeshua said, *"Thomas, you believed because you've seen Me: those who haven't seen are blessed, because they've still believed."*

[30-31] And Yeshua, truly, did many other signs in the presence of the followers, which aren't written in this book. But these things are written, so that you might believe that Yeshua is the Christ, the Child of God; and that believing, you might have life in the Name of Yeshua.

Peter and the Followers Go Fishing

21 [1-3] Later Yeshua appeared again to the followers at the Sea of Galilee; and this is the way it happened: Simon Peter, and Thomas, called the Twin, and Nathanael of Cana in Galilee, and the sons of Zebedee, and two other of the followers were all together. Then Simon Peter said, *"I'm going fishing."* Then the others said, *"We're going, too."* So they went out, and quickly got in a ship; but that night they caught nothing.

151

[4-8] Now at sunrise, Yeshua stood on the shore, but the followers didn't know yet that it was Yeshua. Then Yeshua called out, *"Children, did you catch anything?"* And they answered, *"No"*. So Yeshua called out, *"Throw out the net on the right side of the ship, and you'll catch some."* So they threw it out, and then they weren't able to pull it in for all the fish. So the follower whom Yeshua loved said to Peter, *"It's the Christ."* Now when Simon Peter heard that it was Christ, he put on his fisher's coat, because he was naked, and dove into the water. And the other followers came in a little ship, not being far from land, but only about a hundred yards or so, dragging the net with the fish.

[9-14] Then as soon as they had come to land they saw the coals of a fire there, with fish and bread laid on it. And Yeshua said, *"Bring some of the fish you caught."* So Simon Peter went and drew the net to land full of huge fish, a hundred and fifty-three: but still the net wasn't broken even though there were so many. Then Yeshua said, *"Come and eat."* And knowing that it was the Christ, none of the followers dared ask, *"Who are you?"* Then Yeshua came, and took bread, and gave them some, along with the fish. Now this is the third time that Yeshua appeared to the followers, after the Christ had come back to life.

Peter's Threefold Duty

[15-19] So when they had eaten, Yeshua asked Simon Peter, *"Peter, son of Jonah, are you sure that you love Me, even more than these here?"* Then Peter answered, *"Yes, Christ; you know that I love you."* Then the Christ said, *"Feed My new followers."* Then Yeshua asked again the second time, *"Peter, son of Jonah, have you really made up your mind to love Me?"* Then Peter said, *"Yes, Christ; you know that I truly love you."* Then the Christ said, *"Guide My young followers."* Then Yeshua asked the third time, *"Peter, son of Jonah, do you truly love Me?"* And Peter was saddened because the Christ had asked for the third time, *"Do you love Me?"* So Peter said, *"Christ, you know everything; you know that I truly love you."* And Yeshua said, *"Be faithful to My older followers."* The truth is, when you were young, you made yourself ready, and went wherever you wanted to go: but when you're old, you'll reach out for help, but someone else will get you ready, and take you where you don't want to go."* The Christ spoke this, signifying what kind of death Peter would die for God's glory. And after this, the Christ said, *"Follow Me."*

The Follower Who Yeshua Loved

[20-25] Then Peter, turning around, saw the other follower, whom Yeshua loved, following along; which also was the one who leaned back on the Christ at supper, saying, *"Christ, who is it that will turn You over to them?"* So Peter said to Yeshua, *"Christ, and what will this follower do?"* So Yeshua answered, *"If I want this one to stay till I come, what is that to you? You follow Me."* Then it spread among the Christians, that that follower wouldn't die: but Yeshua didn't say to them that the follower wouldn't die; but only, *"If I want this one to stay till I come, what is that to you?"* This is the one who tells us of this, and who wrote this: and we know that this is a true story. And there are many other things also, which Yeshua did, and which, if they were all written, I think that even the world itself couldn't contain the books that would be written about it. So be it!

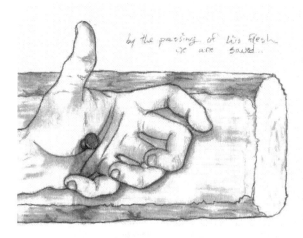

by the passing of his flesh we are saved...

152

The Acts of the Followers

1 [1-8] The earlier work I made for you, Theophilus, told of all that Yeshua began to do and teach, until the day in which the Christ was taken up, after the Christ, through the Holy Spirit, had told the followers, whom Yeshua had chosen, what to do: To whom also the Christ appeared alive after suffering death on the cross, by many unmistakable proofs, being seen of them forty days, and speaking of the things concerning the realm of God: And being gathered together with them, the Christ said, *Don't leave from Jerusalem, but wait for the promise of Yahweh God, who I am from. You've heard me say, John truly baptized with water; but you'll be baptized with the Holy Spirit a few days from now.* So when they had come together, they asked, saying, "Christ, will you now give Israel back again the realm of God?" But the Christ answered, "*It isn't for you to know the days or periods of time, which are all in the power of Yahweh God. But you'll have power, after the Holy Spirit comes on you: and you'll be My witnesses both in Jerusalem, and in all Judea, and in Samaria, and even to the farthest parts of the world.*"

[9-14] And when Yeshua had spoken this, even as they watched, the Christ was taken up in the sky, with a cloud blocking their sight. And as they kept on looking toward heaven as the Christ went up, two messengers stood by them in white clothing; Who said, "*You people of Galilee, why are you standing here staring up into heaven? This same Yeshua, which has been taken up from you into heaven, will come again in the same way as you've seen the Christ go into heaven.*" Then they came back to the city from the Mount of Olives, which is a Seventh Day's walk from Jerusalem. And when they had come in, they went upstairs into an upper room, where Peter, James, John, Andrew, Philip, Thomas, Bartholomew, Matthew, James, the child of Alphaeus, Simon, the Zealot, and Judas, the brother of James, were. They all came together with one heart, praying and making requests, along with the women, Mary, the mother of Yeshua, and with the other Christians.

Matthias Chosen

[15-26] And in those days Peter stood up in the middle of the followers, (about a hundred and twenty all together) saying, "*Christians, this Word had to have been completed, which the Holy Spirit spoke by the mouth of David about Judas, who was the guide to those who took Yeshua. "He was included in our number, and had taken part in this ministry."* (Now Judas bought a field with the profit of his sin; and falling headfirst, his body burst open, and all his insides fell out. And everyone who lives in Jerusalem knew this; so that field is called in their language, Aceldama, which means, Field of Blood.) "*The Word says in the book of Psalms, "Leave his home empty, and let no one live in it: and let someone else take up his work."* So which of these others who have been with us all the time that Christ Yeshua went in and out among us, beginning from the baptism of John, to that same day that the Christ was taken up from us, must be set apart to be a witness with us of the Christ's coming to life again?" So they chose two, Joseph, who is called Barsabas, who was nicknamed Justus, and Matthias. And they prayed, saying, "*You, Christ, who knows the hearts of everyone, show us which of these two You've chosen, who will take part in the leadership of this ministry, from which Judas by sin fell, that he might go where he belonged.*" And they threw their lots to see who would be chosen; and the lot fell on Matthias; who was numbered along with the other eleven leaders.

Peter's Sermon on the Day of Pentecost

2 [1-13] And when the day of Pentecost had come, they were all in the same place together with one heart. And suddenly a loud noise from heaven, like a very strong wind, filled the whole house where they were sitting together. And they all saw what looked like split languages of fire, which came to rest on each of them. And everyone was filled with the Holy Spirit, and began to speak with other languages, as the Spirit gave them words. And many people were staying at Jerusalem, both Jews, and other dedicated people, from all over the world. Now when they heard the noise sound out, the crowd came together, and were confused, because everyone heard them speaking in their own language. And everyone was amazed and wondered about it, saying to one another, "*Aren't all these who are speaking Galilaeans? So how do we hear them in our own languages, which came from where we were born? Parthians, Medes, Elamites, those who live in Mesopotamia, Judea, Cappadocia, Pontus, Asia, Phrygia, Pamphylia, Egypt, Libya near Cyrene, and strangers of Rome, Jews and converts, Cretes and Arabians, we all hear them speak of the amazing things God has done in our own languages.*" And everyone was amazed, and wondered, asking one another, "*What does this mean?*" Others mocking them said, "*These people are drunk on new wine.*"

[14-21] But Peter, standing up with the eleven, spoke out, saying to them, "*You people of Judea, and all you that live at Jerusalem, let this be known to you, and listen carefully to My Words: because these people aren't drunk, like you think. You can see it's only nine o'clock in the morning. But this is what was spoken by the great preacher Joel; And in the last days, says God, I'll pour out of My Spirit on all people: and your sons and your daughters will preach, and your young people will see visions, and your old people will dream dreams: And on My*

male and My female workers I'll pour out of My Spirit in those days; and they'll all preach: And I'll show amazing things in heaven above, and signs in the earth beneath; blood, and fire, and smoky vapors: The sun will be turned into darkness, and the moon will shine blood red, till that great and notable day of Yahweh God comes: And whoever will call on the Name of Yahweh God will be saved.

[22-36] You people of Israel, hear these words; Yeshua of Nazareth, someone who lived among you and who was approved by God by the amazing and wonderful signs, which God did among you through Yeshua, as you yourselves also know: This person, being given by the unchangeable direction and foreknowledge of God, you've taken, and by evil hands have put to death on the cross: Whom God has brought back to life, having been freed from the sufferings of death, because it wasn't possible for the Christ to be held by it. And David speaks about the Christ, saying, I saw the Christ before my face, who is always beside me, so that I wouldn't be shaken: So my heart celebrated, and my voice was happy; and my body will also rest in hope: because you won't leave my soul in Hell, nor will you let your Holy One decay. You've made known to me the ways of life; you'll make me full of joy when you come. Everyone, let me speak to you freely of our ancestor David, who's both dead and buried, and whose tomb is with us to today. David, being a great preacher, knew that God had sworn to him with a promise, that from one of his own descendants, the Christ would be raised up to sit on his throne; So knowing this, David spoke of the new life of Christ, that the Christ's soul wasn't left in Hell, nor was the Christ's body decayed. This Yeshua, God has brought back to life, in which we are all witnesses. So being lifted up on the right side of God, and having gotten the promise of the Holy Spirit from God, the Christ has poured it out upon us, which is what you now see and hear. David hasn't gone up into the heavens: but said himself, Yahweh God said to my Christ, "Sit beside Me, until I put your enemies under your feet." So let all the house of Israel know without a doubt, that God has made that same Yeshua, whom you've put to death, both Ruler and Christ."

[37-40] Now when the people heard this, their hearts were greatly saddened, saying to Peter and to the rest of the followers, "Everyone, what should we do?" Then Peter answered, "Change your evil ways, and all of you be baptized in the Name of Yeshua the Christ for the forgiveness of sins and you'll get the gift of the Holy Spirit. The promise is to you, and to your children, and to all who are to come, whoever Yahweh God will call." And with many other words, Peter talked to them and strongly encouraged them, saying, "Save yourselves from the evil of the people of this time."

All Things Together In Common

[41-47] Then those who gladly accepted his word were baptized: and this same day about three thousand souls were added to their numbers. And they faithfully stayed in the followers' teachings, breaking bread and praying in loving friendship. And every soul feared and wondered at many amazing things and signs that had happened by the followers. And everyone that believed had all things together in common; And sold their possessions and goods, and divided them out to everyone, as they had need. And continuing daily with one heart in the Place of Worship, and breaking bread from house to house, they ate their food with happiness and undivided hearts, praising God, and having favor with all the people. And God gave to the church daily all who would be saved.

The Crippled Walks

3 [1-11] Now Peter and John went up together into the Place of Worship at the time of prayer, being three o'clock. And someone unable to walk from birth was carried and laid daily at the gate of the Place of Worship which is called Beautiful, to ask for money of those who went in the Place of Worship; Who seeing Peter and John about to go into the Place of Worship asked for a gift. And Peter, looking at him with John, said, "Look at us." And he looked up to them, expecting to get something from them. Then Peter said, "I don't have any money; but what I have I give to you: In the Name of Yeshua the Christ of Nazareth, get up and walk." And they took him by the right hand, and lifted him up: and suddenly his feet and ankle bones were made strong. And jumping up, he stood up and walked, and came with them into the Place of Worship, walking, leaping, and praising God. And all the people saw him walking and praising God: And they knew that it was the one who sat waiting for gifts at the Beautiful gate of the Place of Worship: and they were amazed and wondered at what had happened to him. And as the person who was unable to walk and was healed held Peter and John, all the people, who were greatly amazed, ran together to them in the porch that is called Solomon's.

[12-18] And when Peter saw it, he said to the people, "People of Israel, why are you so amazed at this? Why are you staring at us, as though by our own power or goodness we had made this person walk? The God of Abraham, Isaac, and Jacob, the God of our ancestors, has made Yeshua, God's Christ, known; whom you gave up, and denied in the presence of Pilate, when he had decided to let the Christ go. But you denied the Holy and Godly One, and wanted a murderer to be freed to you instead; And you killed the One who has the power of life, which God has brought back to life from the dead; in which we're all witnesses. And through faith in the Christ's name, this person was made strong, whom you see and know: yes, the faith in the name of Yeshua, which is through the Christ, has given this person complete healing in the presence of you all. And now, people, I

154

understand that you did it in ignorance, as your rulers also did. But those things, which God had showed by the words of all the great preachers, that Christ would suffer, have now happened.

[19-26] So change your evil ways, and turn back to God, that your sins can be forgiven, so that the times of refreshing will come from the presence of God; And God will send Yeshua the Christ, which was preached to you: Whom heaven must keep until the time when everything will be made right, which God has spoken by the mouth of all the great holy preachers since the world began. The truth is, Moses said to the ancestors, Yahweh your God will raise up to you a great preacher out of your own people, like me; Listen to whatever is said to you by this One. Every soul, which won't listen to that great preacher, will be completely separated from among the people. Yes, and all the great preachers from Samuel and those that follow after, whoever has spoken, has foretold of these days. You're the children of the great preachers, and of the promised agreement which God made with our ancestors, saying to Abraham, 'and your descendant will bless all the families of the earth.' God, having brought back Yeshua the Christ to life, sent the Christ to you first to bless you, by turning all of you away from your uncontrolled actions."

Peter and John Jailed

4 [1-4] And as they spoke to the people, the priests, and the leader of the Place of Worship, and those of the Religious sects, came to them, being upset that they taught the people, and preached through Yeshua the coming to life again from the dead. So they took them, and put them in a holding cell till the next day because it was now evening. But many of those who heard the Word believed; and the people numbered about five thousand.

[5-12] And then the next day, their rulers, the elders, the religious leaders, Annas, the leading priest, Caiaphas, John, Alexander, and all those who were kin to the leading priest, were gathered together at Jerusalem. And when they had put them in the middle, they asked, "Who gave you the power to do this?" Then Peter, filled with the Holy Spirit, answered, "You rulers of the people, and elders of Israel, If we're being questioned today about the good thing we did for the helpless person, who was made well; Let it be known to all of you, and to all the people of Israel, that it was by the Name of Yeshua the Christ of Nazareth, whom you put to death, and whom God raised from the dead, that this person stands here before you made completely well. This is the stone that was not chosen by you builders, which has now been chosen for the most important cornerstone. Nor can we be saved by any other because there's no other name under heaven given to humanity, by which we can be saved.

[13-22] Now when they saw that Peter and John had no fear, and realized that they were untaught and without knowledge, they were amazed and took note that they had been with Yeshua. And seeing the person who was healed standing with them, they couldn't say anything against it. So they told them to leave the courtroom, and they talked among themselves, saying, "What are we going to do to these people? There's no doubt that a notable miracle has been done by them. It's plain to all who live in Jerusalem; and we can't deny it. But so that it spread no further among the people, let's strictly warn them not to speak to anyone in this name again." And they called them, and told them not to speak at all, nor teach in the Name of Yeshua. But Peter and John asked them, "Which is right in the sight of God? To listen to you more than to God, what do you say? We can't say anything but what we've seen and heard." So when they had further threatened them, they let them go, finding no way to punish them, because of the people. And everyone praised God for what happened, because the person on whom this miracle of healing was done was more than forty years old.

Peter and John Released

[23-30] And being let go, they went to their own company, and told all that the leading priests and elders had said. And when they heard that, they called out to God with one heart, saying, "Yahweh, You are God, who has made heaven and earth, and the sea, and everything that is in them: Who by the mouth of Your worker David has said, 'Why did the ungodly rage, and the people imagine meaningless things? The rulers of the earth stood up, and the rulers were gathered together against Yahweh God, and against God's Christ.' The truth is, both Herod, Pontius Pilate, the people of Israel, and all the other peoples were gathered together against Your Holy One Yeshua, whom You've anointed, to do whatever You decided was to be done. And now, God, listen to their threatening: and help Your workers speak Your word without fear. Let us be Your healing hands, let there be great signs, and let amazing things be done by the Name of Your Holy One, Yeshua."

All Things Together In Common

[31-37] And when they had finished praying, the place where they were gathered together shook strongly; and everyone was filled with the Holy Spirit, and they spoke the Word of God without fear. And all of those who believed were of one heart and of one mind: no one said that anything they had was their own; but they had all things together in common. And the followers spoke with great power about the coming to life again of Christ Yeshua: and great grace was on them all. No one lacked anything among them because whoever had lands or homes sold them, and brought whatever they got from the things that were sold, and laid it down at the followers' feet: and everyone was given according to their needs. And Joses, who by the followers was nicknamed

Barnabas, which means "the child of comfort," and Matthew, from the country of Cyprus, sold the land they owned, and brought the money, and laid it at the followers' feet.

Ananias and Sapphira Lie

5 [1-11] Someone named Ananias, along with Sapphira, his spouse, sold some land, but kept back part of the price. With Sapphira being in on it, he brought a certain part, and laid it at the followers' feet. But Peter said, *"Ananias, why has Satan filled your heart to lie to the Holy Spirit, and to keep back part of the price of the land? Wasn't it yours as long as you owned it? And after it was sold, wasn't it in your own power? Why have you planned this thing in your heart? You haven't lied to human beings, but to God."* And when Ananias heard these words, he fell down, and died: and great fear came on all those who heard about it. And some young people got up, wound him up, carried him out, and buried him. Then about three hours later, Sapphira, not knowing what had happened, came in. And Peter said to her, *"Tell me whether you sold the land for this much?"* And she said, *"Yes, for that much."* Then Peter said to her, *"How is it that you've agreed together to tempt the Spirit of God? The feet of those who buried your husband are at the door, and will carry you out as well."* Then suddenly she fell down at their feet, and died: and the young people came in, and found her dead, and carried her out, and buried her by her husband. And great fear came on all the church, and on whoever heard this.

Peter's Shadow

[12-16] And the followers did many great signs and amazing things among the people; (and everyone was with one heart in Solomon's porch. But none of the rest dared to join them, even though the people thought highly of them. And more and more, both men and women believed in Christ and were added to their numbers.) So much so, that they brought the sick out into the streets, and laid them on beds and pallets, that Peter's shadow might at least overshadow some of them as he passed by. A crowd also came out of the cities around Jerusalem, bringing sick folks, and those who were suffering with evil spirits: and they were all healed.

Peter and the Followers Released from Jail by an Angel

[17-28] Then the leading priest and all those of the religious sect who were with him were filled with resentment, and took the followers, and put them in the common prison. But the angel of God opened the prison doors that night, and brought them out, saying, *"Go, stand, and speak in the Place of Worship to the people all the Words of this life."* And when they heard that, they went in the Place of Worship early in the morning, and taught. But when the leading priest and those who were with him came, they called the court together and all the elders of the children of Israel and sent to the prison to have them brought. But when the officers came, they didn't find them in the prison, and came back, and told them, saying, *"The truth is, we found the prison shut tight, and the guards standing outside the doors: but when we had opened them, we found no one inside."* Now when the leading priest and the captain of the guard of the Place of Worship, and the other priests heard this, they wondered what would happen next. Then someone came and told them, saying, *"Those people you put in prison are standing in the Place of Worship, and teaching the people."* Then the captain and the officers went and brought them without violence because they were afraid, thinking the people might try to kill them. And when they had brought them, they brought them before the court: and the leading priest asked them, saying, *"Didn't we clearly tell you that you shouldn't teach in this name? And you've filled all Jerusalem with your teachings, and intend to bring this person's blood on us."*

[29-32] Then Peter and the other followers answered, *"We must obey God, not people. The God of our ancestors brought Yeshua back to life, which you hung on a cross and killed. The Christ was lifted up to God's own right side to be a Ruler and a Savior, to give the people of Israel a chance to change their ways, and be freed from sins. And we're Christ's witnesses of this; and so is the Holy Spirit, whom God has given to those who accept the Christ."*

Beaten for Christ's Sake

[33-42] When they heard that, they were so angry they planned to kill them. Then someone stood up in the court, a Religious leader, named Gamaliel, a teacher of the Word of God, who had a good reputation among all the people, and told them to put the followers out for a little while; Who said, *"You people of Israel, be very careful what you intend to do with these people. Someone named Theudas once came, bragging about himself and claiming to be somebody important; to whom about four hundred people joined themselves: who was put to death; and all who followed him were scattered out, and brought to nothing. Later someone named Judas of Galilee came in the days of the taxing, and drew many people after himself, who was also killed; and all who followed him were scattered. And now I tell you, don't do anything to these people, and leave them alone because if these words or this work is of human origin, it'll come to nothing: But if it's of God, you can't stop it; and you may even find yourselves to be fighting against God."* And they all agreed with him: and when they had called the followers, and beaten them, they told them not to speak in the Name of Yeshua, and let them go. And they went from the

presence of the court, with joy that they were counted worthy to suffer shame for the name of Christ. And they didn't stop teaching and preaching about Yeshua the Christ, but spoke daily in the Place of Worship, and in every house.

Stephen Chosen

6 [1-4] And in those days, when the number of followers was growing, the Grecian followers secretly complained against the Hebrew followers, because their widows were being neglected in the daily ministry. Then the twelve called all the followers to them, saying, *"It isn't right that we neglect spreading the Word of God to serve tables. So, Christians, pick out from among you seven people known to be honest and respectable, who are full of the Holy Spirit and wisdom, whom we can appoint over this business, so we may continue to pray, and to do the ministry of the Word."*

[5-8] And this pleased the whole crowd, so they chose Stephen, someone full of faith and of the Holy Spirit, Philip, Prochorus, Nicanor, Timon, Parmenas, and Nicolas, a convert of Antioch. They brought them before the followers, who prayed for them, and laid their hands on them. And the Word of God spread; and the number of the followers in Jerusalem grew daily; and a great many of the Jewish priests accepted the faith. And Stephen, full of faith and power, did wonderful and amazing things among the people.

[9-15] Then some of the local worshipers from the Church of the Free People, Cyrenians, Alexandrians, and those of Cilicia and Asia, began arguing with Stephen. But they weren't able to speak against the wisdom and the spirit of Stephen. Then they secretly told some to say, *"We've heard this person speak disrespectful words against Moses, and against God."* So they stirred up the people, the elders, and the religious leaders, who came to take Stephen and brought him to the court. The false witnesses said, *"This person won't stop speaking disrespectful words against this holy place, and the Word of God: We've heard him say that this Yeshua of Nazareth will destroy this place, and will change the way of life which Moses gave us."* And all that sat in the court, stared intently at Stephen, whose face shown like the face of an angel.

Stephen Martyred

7 [1-10] Then the leading priest asked, *"Is this so?"* And Stephen said, *"Everyone, listen carefully; The God of victory appeared to our ancestor Abraham, who was still in Mesopotamia, before he lived in Haran, and said, 'Get out of your country, and go away from your family, and go the land which I'll show you.' Then Abraham came out of the land of the Chaldaeans, and lived in Haran: and from there, when his father died, God moved Abraham's family into this land in which you now live. But God gave him no inheritance in it, no, not even enough to set a foot on. But still God promised to give it to the descendants of Abraham for a possession, when Abraham still had no child. And God said that the descendants would live in a foreign country, which would make slaves of them, and treat them cruelly for four hundred years. 'And then I'll judge the nation who enslaves them,' God said: 'and after that they'll come out of that country, and serve Me in this place.' And God gave them the sign of the promised agreement, which was the cutting of the male foreskin. So Abraham had Isaac, and cut his flesh on the eighth day; and Isaac had Jacob; and Jacob had the twelve leaders of the families of Israel, who acted in jealousy, and sold Joseph into Egypt. But God was with him, and freed him from all his troubles, and gave him favor and wisdom in the sight of Pharaoh, the ruler of Egypt, who made him governor over Egypt and his whole house.*

[11-22] *Now a drought came over all the land of Egypt and Canaan, with great suffering, so that our ancestors had no food. But when Jacob heard that there was grain in Egypt, our ancestors were sent the first time. Then when they were sent a second time, Joseph was made known to his brothers; and Joseph's family was made known to Pharaoh. Then Joseph sent, and called Jacob to come, and all their family, seventy-five people in all. So Jacob went down into Egypt, where he and our ancestors died, and whose bones were carried back into Shechem, and laid in the tomb that Abraham bought from the children of Hamor, the leader of Shechem. But when the time came near for the promise to take place, which God had sworn to Abraham, the people grew and grew in Egypt, till another ruler came, which didn't know Joseph. This Pharaoh was very cruel to our people, and treated our ancestors horribly, making them throw their babies in the river and kill them. Moses was born at this time, and was a beautiful baby, and was nursed in his parent's house three months: And when Moses was put out, Pharaoh's daughter found him, and brought him up as her own child. And Moses was taught in all the wisdom of the Egyptians, and was powerful in words and in actions.*

[23-36] *And when Moses was forty years old, it came into his heart to go see the children of Israel. And seeing one of them being beaten, he defended them, and took revenge for the one who was hurt, and killed the Egyptian. He thought the Hebrews would understand how that God would free them through him: but they didn't understand. And the next day he came up to two of them as they argued, and wanted to help them make peace again, saying, 'People, you're family; Why are you fighting one another?' But the one who did the other wrong pushed him away, saying, 'Who made you a ruler and a judge over us? Will you kill me, as you did the Egyptian yesterday?' When he said this, Moses ran away, and became a stranger in the land of Midian, where he had two children. And after another forty years, an angel of God appeared to him in the countryside of Mount Sinai in a flame of fire in a bush.*

157

When Moses saw it, he was amazed at the sight: and as he came nearer, he heard the voice of God say, 'I am the God of your ancestors, the God of Abraham, the God of Isaac, and the God of Jacob.' Then Moses was so afraid that he dared not look. Then God said to him, 'Take your shoes from off your feet because the place where you're standing is holy ground. I've seen the suffering of My people in Egypt, and I've heard their crying, and I am come down to free them. And now come, I'll send you back to Egypt.' This Moses whom they rejected, saying, 'Who made you a ruler and a judge?' was the same person God sent to be their leader to free them by the power of the Angel who appeared to him in the bush. So Moses led them out, showing them amazing things for forty years, with signs in the land of Egypt, in the Red sea, and in the countryside.

[37-50] This is the same Moses, who said to the children of Israel, 'Yahweh your God will send you a great preacher out of your own people, like me; Listen to this One.' This is the One who was in the meeting place in the countryside with the angel which spoke to him in Mount Sinai, and with our ancestors who got the words of life to give to us. But our ancestors wouldn't accept him, rejected Moses, and turned their hearts back to Egypt again, saying to Aaron, 'Make us gods to go with us. As for this Moses, who brought us out of the land of Egypt, we don't even know what has happened to him.' And they made a golden calf in those days, and offered sacrifices and celebrated in the false worship of something made by their own hands. So God turned away from them, and let them worship the planets and stars of heaven; as the Word says in the book of the great preachers, 'House of Israel, did you give Me animals to be killed and sacrifices those forty years in the countryside? You took up the worship of Molech, and worshiped the star of your god Remphan; things which you made yourselves to worship them: so I'll carry you far away beyond Rome.' Our ancestors had the Place of Worship in the desert as a witness of God's Word, who had told Moses to make it the way that God had shown it to him. Our ancestors that came afterwards brought it in with Joshua into the land of the other peoples, whom God drove out before them. It was used until the time of David, who found favor with God, and wanted to find a Place of Worship for the God of Jacob that wouldn't be moved. But Solomon built the house of God, though the Most High God doesn't live in places of worship made by humans; as the great preacher once said, 'God said, Heaven is My throne, and the earth is where I rest My feet, so what kind of house will you build Me to rest in? Haven't I made all this Myself?'

[51-60] You stubborn people are uncleansed in your heart and ears, you always reject the Holy Spirit: you do just as your ancestors did. Have any of the great preachers not been abused by your ancestors? They've put to death all those who told them of the coming of the Christ; And now, you, who have the Word of God by the gift of angels, and haven't kept it, have handed over and murdered Yeshua the Christ." When they heard this, they were deeply angered, and they ground their teeth at him. But Stephen, being full of the Holy Spirit, stared up into heaven, and saw the light of God, and Yeshua standing on the right side of God, and said, "I see heaven opened up, and the Christ standing on the right side of God." Then they yelled loudly, and stopped listening, and ran at him all together, and put him out of the city, and stoned him to death, laying down their clothes at a young man's feet, whose name was Saul. And they stoned Stephen while he called on God, saying, "Christ Yeshua, take my spirit." And he kneeled down, and called out with a loud voice, "Christ, don't hold this sin against them." And after he said that, he fell dead.

Saul Persecutes the Church

8 [1-8] Now Saul agreed to Stephen's death. And at that time the church at Jerusalem was greatly discriminated against; so much that everyone except the followers were scattered throughout all the areas of Judea and Samaria, but some dedicated people carried Stephen to be buried, and mourned greatly over him. As for Saul, he made havoc of the church, going into every Christian home, putting both men and women into prison. So those who were scattered out went every where preaching the New Word. Then Philip went down to the city of Samaria, and preached about Christ to them. And the people listened to what Philip spoke with one heart, because they both heard and saw the amazing things which he did. Evil spirits, calling out with loud voices, came out of many that were overcome by them, and many who were paralyzed, and that were unable to walk, were healed, also. There was great joy in that city.

Simon, the Witch, is Converted

[9-24] But there was someone, named Simon, who used witchcraft before in that same city, and fooled the people of Samaria, making out that he was someone great. Everyone in the city listened to him, from the youngest to the oldest, saying, "This person is the great power of God." And they had great respect for him, because he had fooled them with his witchcraft for so long. But when they believed Philip's preaching about the things of the realm of God, and the Name of Yeshua the Christ, they were baptized, both men and women. Then Simon himself also believed, and when he was baptized, he stayed with Philip, and was amazed, watching all the amazing things and signs which had happened. Now when the followers who were at Jerusalem heard that Samaria had accepted the Word of God, they sent Peter and John to them: Who, when they had come down, prayed for the Holy Spirit to come on them: (because the spirit hadn't fallen on any of them yet; they were only baptized in the Name of Christ Yeshua.) Then they laid their hands on them, and the Holy Spirit came on all of them. And when Simon saw that

through laying on of the followers' hands the Holy Spirit was given, he offered them money, saying, *"Give me this power, too, so that whoever I lay hands on can get the Holy Spirit."* But Peter said, *"Your money will be destroyed along with you, because you think that the gift of God can be bought with money. You can't have any part in this, because your heart isn't right in the sight of God. Change your evil ways, and pray to God that maybe what you thought in your heart can be forgiven you. I realize that you have a spirit of bitterness, and are being controlled by sin."* Then Simon said, *"Pray to God for me, that what you've just said won't happen to me."*

Phillip Baptizes the Queen's Worker

[25-40] And when they had told us the truth and preached the Word of God, they went back to Jerusalem, preaching the New Word in many of the Samaritan towns, which were of mixed race. And an angel of God spoke to Philip, saying, *"Get up, and go south, toward the way that goes down from Jerusalem to Gaza, which is deserted."* So he got up and went, coming to someone who was from Ethiopia, one of Queen Candace's helpers, who had great power and was in charge of all her wealth. He had come to Jerusalem to worship, and was returning, sitting in a chariot reading from Isaiah, the great preacher. Then the Spirit said to Philip, *"Go near, and catch up to this chariot."* And Philip ran up to it, and heard the person reading from the great preacher Isaiah, saying, *"Do you understand what you're reading?"* And he answered, *"How can I, unless someone explains it to me?"* And he asked Philip to come up and sit with him. He was reading in the Word at this place, *"The Christ was led as an animal to slaughter; and like a dumb lamb to its shearer, who didn't cry out: The Christ was humbled, whose judgment was taken away. Who will tell of the Christ's people? The Christ's life was taken from the earth."* And the person asked Philip, saying, *"Who does the great preacher speak about? of himself, or of some other person?"* Then Philip began to speak at the same place, and preached about Yeshua to him. And as they went on, they came to a place with water, so the person asked Phillip, *"Look, here's some water; what's keeping me from being baptized?"* And Philip answered, *"If you believe with all your heart, you can."* And the person said, *"I believe that Yeshua the Christ is the Child of God."* They told the chariot to stop, and both of them went down into the water; and Phillip baptized him. And when he had come up out of the water, the Spirit of God caught Philip, away and he never saw him again, but went on with great joy. And Philip was brought to Azotus, so passing through, he preached in all the cities, till he came to Caesarea.

Saul Sees the Christ

9 [1-9] And Saul, still threatening to slaughter the followers of God, went to the leading priest, and asked for letters to send him to Damascus to the places of worship, and that if he found any of this way, whether they were men or women, to arrest them and bring them to Jerusalem. And as he journeyed, coming near Damascus, a bright light suddenly shined from heaven all around him. He fell to the earth, and heard a voice saying, *"Saul, Saul, why are you trying to hurt me?"* And he said, *"Who are you, Christ?"* And the Christ said, *"I am Yeshua, who you are trying to hurt: isn't it hard for you to fight against My prods?"* And trembling and amazed Saul said, *"Christ, what do you want me to do?"* And the Christ said, *"Get up, and go into the city, and you'll be told there what you must do."* And the others who went with him stood speechless, hearing a voice, but not seeing anyone. And Saul got up from the ground; and when his eyes opened, he couldn't see anything. So they led him by the hand, bringing him into Damascus. And he couldn't see for three days, nor did he eat or drink anything.

Saul's Ministry Begins

[10-22] And there was a certain follower at Damascus, named Ananias; and God said to him in a vision, *"Ananias."* And he answered, *"I am here, Christ."* And the Christ said, *"Get up, and go to the street named Straight, and ask in the house of Judas for someone called Saul of Tarsus, because he prays, and has seen in a vision someone named Ananias coming in, and putting his hand on him to give him sight again."* Then Ananias said, *"Christ, I've heard by many of this person, and how much evil he has done to your people at Jerusalem: And now he has power from the leading priests to arrest all that call on Your Name."* But the Christ said, *"Go now because he's has been chosen by Me, to bring My Name to the other peoples, and rulers, and the children of Israel: but I'll show him the great things he must suffer because of My Name."* And Ananias left, and went to the house, and putting his hands on Saul said, *"Brother Saul, Christ Yeshua, who appeared to you down the road as you came, has sent me, that you might see again, and be filled with the Holy Spirit."* And suddenly something like scales fell from his eyes and he could see then. He got up, and was baptized right then. And after he had eaten, he was strengthened. Then Saul stayed a few days with the followers at Damascus. Then suddenly, he began to preach about Christ in the places of worship, that Yeshua was the Child of God. Everyone who heard him was amazed, saying, *"Isn't this the one who killed all those who called on this name in Jerusalem, and came here for that very reason, to arrest them and bring them to the leading priests?"* But Saul increased all the more in strength, and shamed the Jews which lived at Damascus, proving that Yeshua was, in fact, the Christ.

[23-31] And after a long time had passed, the Jews planned to kill him, but Saul found out about their plan. They watched the gates day and night to kill him, but the followers took him by night, and let him down a window

159

in the city wall in a basket. Then when Saul came to Jerusalem, he tried to join the followers, but everyone was afraid of him, and didn't believe that he was really a follower. But Barnabas took him, and brought him to the followers, and told them how he had seen Christ on the road, and that the Christ had spoken to him, and how he had preached without fear at Damascus in the Name of Yeshua. So he was with the followers at Jerusalem, coming and going with them. And he spoke without fear in the Name of Christ Yeshua, and argued with the Greeks, who tried to kill him. So when the Christians found out, they brought him down to Caesarea, and sent him to Tarsus. Then the churches had rest throughout all Judea, Galilee, and Samaria, and grew. And walking in the fear of God, and in the comfort of the Holy Spirit, their numbers grew greatly.

Peter raises Tabitha from the Dead

[32-43] And then, as Peter passed throughout all quarters, he came down to the Christians who lived at Lydda, also. And Peter found someone named Aeneas there, who had been bed-ridden for eight years, and was paralyzed. And Peter said, *"Aeneas, Yeshua the Christ makes you well: Get up, and make up your bed."* And suddenly, he got up. And everyone that lived at Lydda and Saron saw him, and turned to Christ. Now at Joppa, there was a certain follower named Tabitha, which means Dorcas. This woman was always doing good things and loved everyone. And then in those days, she got sick, and died, who they had washed, and lay in an upstairs room. And so as Lydda was near Joppa, the followers had heard that Peter was there, so they sent two people, hoping that Peter would come quickly. So Peter got up and went with them, and when he came, they brought him to the upstairs room. All the widows stood around crying, and showing him the coats and clothes which Dorcas had made, while she was alive. But Peter put them all out, and kneeling down to pray, turned to the body and said, *"Tabitha, Get up."* And she opened her eyes, and when she saw Peter, she sat up. And Peter gave her his hand and helped her up. Then he called in all the Christians and widows, and showed them that she was alive. And it was made known throughout all Joppa; and many believed in the Christ. And then Peter stayed for a long time in Joppa with someone named Simon, who was a tanner.

Peter's Vision

10 [1-8] There was someone in Caesarea named Cornelius, a soldier of the Italian band. He was a dedicated person, who believed in God along with his whole family, who gave many gifts to the people, and always prayed to God. He saw clearly in a vision at about three o'clock in the afternoon, an angel of God coming to him, and saying, "Cornelius." And when he saw it, he was afraid, saying, "What is it, Christ?" And the angel said, *"Your prayers and your gifts have gone up as a memorial to God. Now send to Joppa, and call for someone named Simon, whose is called Peter, who lives with another named Simon, who is a tanner, whose house is by the sea shore: he'll tell you what you need to do."* And when the angel who spoke to Cornelius was gone, he called two of his household workers, and a dedicated soldier of those who waited on him continually; And when he told this to them, he sent them to Joppa.

[9-18] The next day, as they went on their journey, and came near the city, Peter went up on the rooftop to pray about noon: And he became very hungry, and would have eaten: but while it was being made, he fell into a trance, and saw heaven open up. And something like a great sheet knotted at its four corners came down to him, which was let down to the earth. All kinds of four-footed animals of the earth, wild animals, insects, and birds of the air were in the sheet. And a voice spoke to him, saying, *"Get up, Peter; kill, and eat."* But Peter said, "No, Christ, I've never eaten anything that is common or bad for me." And the voice spoke to him again the second time, *"What God says is good, don't call evil."* This happened three times, and then the sheet was taken up again into heaven again. Now while Peter was wondering what this vision that he had seen meant, those who were sent from Cornelius had asked where Simon's house was, and stood at the gate, asking whether Simon, who was nicknamed Peter, lived there.

[19-33] While Peter thought about the vision, the Spirit said, *"Three people are looking for you. So get up, and go down stairs. Go with them, doubting nothing because I've sent them."* Then Peter went down to those who were sent to him from Cornelius; saying, *"I'm the One you're looking for. Why have you come?"* And they said, "Cornelius, the soldier, a good person, who believes God, and has a good name among the whole nation of the Jews, was told by God through a holy angel to call you to come to his home to hear what you have to say." Then he called them in, asking them to stay for the night. The next day Peter went away with them, along with some Christians from Joppa, who went with them. And the next day they came to Caesarea. Cornelius was waiting for them, and had called all his kin people and close friends together. And as Peter was coming in, Cornelius met them, and bowed down at his feet, and worshipped him. But Peter lifted him up, saying, stand up; *"I'm just a man, myself."* And as he talked with them, they went in, and found that many people had come together. So Peter said, *"You know how it's not proper for a Jew to keep company, or come to the house of someone from another nation; but God has shown me that I shouldn't call anyone common or evil. So I came to you without arguing, as soon as I was sent for: So I ask why you've sent for me?"* And Cornelius said, *"Four days ago I was going without food until this time; and at three o'clock I was praying in my house, and someone came to me in bright clothing, and*

said, 'Cornelius, your prayer is heard, and your gifts are remembered in the sight of God. So send to Joppa, and call Simon, whose nickname is Peter, who lives in the house of someone named Simon, who is a tanner by the sea shore. When he comes, he'll speak to you.' So I sent to you right away; and it's good that you've come. So now that we're all here before God, we want to hear everything that God has told you."

[34-43] Then Peter began telling them, "The truth is, I realize now that God doesn't favor one person over another: But in every nation whoever believes God, and does good things, is accepted by God. The word which God sent to the children of Israel, preached peace by Yeshua the Christ, who is the Christ of all. That Word, I say, and you know, was published throughout all Judea, beginning from Galilee, after the baptism which John preached. God anointed Yeshua of Nazareth with the Holy Spirit and with power: who went about doing good, and healing all that were kept down by the devil, because God was with the Christ. And we're witnesses of everything which the Christ did both in the land of the Jews, and in Jerusalem; whom they hung on a cross and killed. But God brought the Christ back to life on the third day, who was openly seen; Not by all the people, but to the witnesses chosen by God, those of us who ate and drink with Yeshua after the Christ rose from the dead. And the Christ told us to preach to the people, and to tell others that it's Yeshua who was chosen by God to be the Judge of both those alive and dead. All the great preachers have witnessed that through the Name of Christ, whoever believes in Yeshua the Christ will be forgiven of their sins."

[44-48] While Peter was speaking these words, the Holy Spirit fell on all those who heard it. And the Jews who came with Peter and were believers were amazed, knowing that the gift of the Holy Spirit was given to the other peoples also, when they heard them speak with other languages, and praising God. Then Peter said, "Can anyone deny them water, that these people shouldn't be baptized, who have gotten the Holy Spirit just as we did?" And Peter told them to be baptized in the Name of Christ. Then the people asked them to stay a few days.

Peter Tells the News at Jerusalem

11 [1-10] And the followers and the Christians from Judea heard that the other peoples had also heard the Word of God. And when Peter came up to Jerusalem, those who were of the Jews argued with him, saying, "You went to those who are not of us, and ate with them." But Peter went over the story from the beginning, and explained it to them in order, saying, "I was in the city of Joppa praying and in a trance when I saw in a vision something like a large sheet come down, which was let down from heaven by its four corners; and it came down to me. And when I looked at it, I thought about it, and saw four-footed animals of the earth, wild animals, insects, and birds of the air. And I heard a voice saying to me, 'Get up, Peter; kill and eat.' But I said, 'No, Christ; I have never eaten anything common or bad for me.' But the voice from heaven said to me again, 'What God says is good, don't call evil.' And this happened three times: and it was all taken back up into heaven again.

[11-18] And suddenly there were three people, who had already come to the house where I was, and who were sent from Caesarea to me. And the Spirit wanted me to go with them, without doubting anything. Besides this, these six Christians came with me, and we went in to the person's house, who told us how he had seen an angel in his house, which said, 'Send to Joppa, and call for Simon, whose nickname is Peter; Who will tell you words, by which you and all your house will be saved.' And as I began to speak, the Holy Spirit fell on them, just as it did on us at the beginning. Then I remembered the words of Christ, who said, 'The truth is, John baptized with water; but you'll be baptized with the Holy Spirit.' So then, as God gave them the same gift, who believed on Yeshua the Christ, as we ourselves got; who was I that I could go against God?" When they heard this, they didn't say anything else, but praised God, saying, "Then God has also given to the other peoples a chance to change their ways to have life without end."

The Followers Called Christians

[19-30] Now those, who were scattered out from the discrimination that rose up after Stephen was killed, traveled as far as Phenice, Cyprus, and Antioch, preaching the Word only to the Jews. And some of them were those of Cyprus and Cyrene, who after coming to Antioch, spoke to the Grecians, preaching about Christ Yeshua. And the hand of God was with them: and many people believed, and turned to God. Then news of this came to the church that was in Jerusalem, so they sent out Barnabas, to go as far as Antioch. Who, when he came, and had seen God's grace, was happy, and encouraged them all that they should cling to God with all their hearts. He was a good person, and full of the Holy Spirit and of faith: and many people came to God through him. Then Barnabas went to Tarsus, to look for Saul, and when he had found him, he brought him to Antioch. And then for a whole year they gathered with the church, and taught all the people. And the followers were first called Christians in Antioch. And in these days great preachers came from Jerusalem to Antioch. And one of them named Agabus stood up, and said by the spirit that there would be a great drought throughout the whole world, which came to pass in the days of Claudius Caesar. Then the followers, everyone as they were able, decided to send relief to the Christians who lived in Judea, which they did, sending it to the elders by the hands of Barnabas and Saul.

161

Herod Beheads James, Peter Freed From Jail

12 [1-10] Now about that time Herod the ruler used his power to trouble some of the church. And he beheaded James, the brother of John with the sword. And when he saw that it pleased the Jews, he tried to take Peter also, during the celebration days of unleavened bread. And when he arrested him, and put him in prison, he ordered four troops of guards to keep him; intending after Passover to bring him out to the people. So Peter was kept in prison, but the church didn't stop praying to God for him. And the night before Herod was to bring him out, Peter was sleeping between two guards, held with two chains; and the doorkeepers kept the prison tight. And the angel of God came to him, and a bright light shined in the prison. The messenger hit Peter on the side, and woke him up, saying, *"Get up quickly."* And the chains fell off from his hands. Then the angel said, *"Get dressed, and put on your sandals."* And so he did. And then the angel said, *"Throw your coat around you, and follow Me."* And he went out, and followed along; and didn't know that what was happening or the angel was really true; but thought that he was seeing a vision. When they were past the first and the second guards of the prison, they came to the iron gate that leads to the city, which opened up for them all by themselves. And they went out, going down the street; and then the angel was gone.

[11-19] And when Peter came to himself, he said, *"Now I know for sure, that God has sent the messenger, and has taken me out of Herod's hands, saving me from what the Jews were hoping for."* Then when he had thought about it, he came to the house of Mary, the mother of John, whose nickname was Mark; where many were gathered together praying. And as Peter knocked at the door of the gate, a girl named Rhoda came to listen carefully. When she knew Peter's voice, she didn't open the gate, being so happy, but ran in, and told them that Peter was at the gate. They said to her, *"You're crazy."* But she kept on telling them the same thing. Then they said, *"It's his spirit."* But Peter kept knocking, and when they opened the door, and saw him, they were amazed. But Peter, waving to them with his hands to be quiet, told them how God had brought him out of the prison. And they said, *"Go tell this to James, and the followers."* So he left, and went there. Now as soon as it was day, the guards were very upset, and didn't know what happened to Peter. And when Herod called for him, and they couldn't find him, he questioned the guards, and ordered them to be killed. So Peter went down from Judea to Caesarea, and stayed there.

Herod Dies

[20-25] Now Herod was very angry with the people of Tyre and Sidon, but they came with one heart to him, having made Blastus, the ruler's own private assistant, their friend, and wanted peace because their country was supported by food from the ruler's country. Then on a set day Herod, arrayed in royal apparel, sat on his public throne, and made a speech to them. And the people shouted out, saying, *"It's the voice of a god, and not of a man."* And suddenly the angel of God struck him, because he didn't give God due respect, and he was eaten of worms, and died. And the Word of God grew more and more. Then Barnabas and Saul came back from Jerusalem, when they had completed their ministry, and took along John, whose nickname was Mark.

Paul and Barnabas Sent Out

13 [1-13] Now there were in the church that was at Antioch certain great preachers and teachers; Barnabas, Simeon that was called Niger, Lucius of Cyrene, Manaen, which had been brought up with Herod the governor, and Saul. As they ministered to God, and went without food to pray, the Holy Spirit said, *"Separate Me Barnabas and Paul for the work that I've called them."* And when they had gone without food and prayed, and laid their hands on them, they sent them away. So they, being sent out by the Holy Spirit, went to Seleucia; and from there they sailed to Cyprus. And when they were at Salamis, they preached the Word of God in the places of worship of the Jews, having John to help them. And when they had gone past the island to Paphos, they found a certain sorcerer, a false preacher, a Jew, whose name was Bar-jesus, who was with the deputy of the country, Sergius Paulus, who was a careful person and called for Barnabas and Saul, because he wanted to hear the Word of God. But Elymas the sorcerer (this is the meaning of his name) refused to accept them, looking for a way to turn the deputy away from the faith. Then Saul, (who is also called Paul,) filled with the Holy Spirit, set his eyes on him, and said, *"You sneaky and lying child of the devil, you enemy of everything good, won't you stop twisting the right ways of God? And now, the hand of God is on you, and you'll be blind, not seeing the sun for a while."* And suddenly a mist of darkness fell on him; and he went about looking for someone to lead him by the hand. Then the deputy, when he saw what happened, believed, being amazed at the Word of God. Now when Paul and the others left from Paphos, they came to Perga in Pamphylia, where John left them and went back to Jerusalem.

[14-22] But when they went from Perga, they came to Antioch in Pisidia, and went into the Place of Worship on a Day of Worship, and sat down. And after the reading of the Word of God and the great preachers, the rulers of the Place of Worship asked them, saying, *"Do you all have any word of encouragement for the people? If so, say so."* Then Paul stood up, and waving with his hand, said, *"People of Israel, and you who honor and respect God, pay attention. The God of this people of Israel chose our ancestors, and uplifted the people when they lived as strangers in the land of Egypt, and with great strength brought them out of it. And God put up with their ways for*

162

forty years in the countryside. And when God had destroyed seven nations in the land of Canaan, their land was divided to them by lot. And after that God gave them judges for about four hundred and fifty years, until Samuel, the great preacher came. And later when they wanted a ruler: God gave them Saul, the child of Kish, from the family of Benjamin, for forty years. And when God had removed him, God lifted up David to be their ruler; of whom also God said, 'David the child of Jesse, I've found, is someone after my own heart, which will fulfill all My will.'

[23-37] God has raised up a descendant of this person, as promised to Israel, a Savior, Yeshua. John had first preached before the Christ's coming, the baptism of a changed life, to all the people of Israel. And as John finished his work, he asked, 'Who do you think I am? I'm not the one you're looking for. But, there comes One after me, whose shoes I am not worthy to undo.' You people, children of the family of Abraham, and whoever among you respects God, the Word of how to be saved is sent to you now. Those who live at Jerusalem, and their rulers, because they didn't know Yeshua was the Christ, nor even the voices of the great preachers which are read every Day of Worship, they've made to come true by passing judgment on the Christ. And even though they found no reason for a death sentence, they still wanted Pilate to put Yeshua to death. They did everything that was written about the Christ, who they took down from the cross and laid in a tomb. But God raised the Christ from the dead, who was seen for a long time by those who came up with Yeshua from Galilee to Jerusalem. We are the witnesses of Christ to the people, and tell you this happy news. The promise which was made to the ancestors, God has made happen for all of us, who are their children, through this person. God has brought Yeshua back to life again; as it's also written in the second song, 'You're My Child, today I have born you.' And about God raising the Christ from the dead, no more to return to death, God said in this way, 'I'll give you the true promises of David.' Which is why God also said this in another song, 'You won't let your Holy One rot in the grave.' But David, after having served his own people by the will of God, died, and was laid with his ancestors, and rotted in his grave. But the Christ didn't rot, whom God brought back to life.

[38-43] So we want you to know, dear people and loved ones, that through this person, who we've preached to you, you can be saved from your sins. Through Christ, all that believe are made right from everything, from which you couldn't be made right by the Word of God which was given to Moses. So beware, in case what was spoken of in the great preachers comes on you: 'See, you who hate others, wonder and die! I'll do something in your days, something you'll never believe, even if someone tells it to you.' And when the Jews had gone out of the Place of Worship, the other peoples begged them to preach this to them the next Day of Worship. Now when the people left, many of the Jews and religious converts followed Paul and Barnabas, who, speaking to them, proved to them that they should stay in God's grace.

[44-52] When the next day of Worship came, almost the whole city came together to hear the Word of God. But when the Jews saw the crowds, they were jealous, and spoke against what Paul was saying, contradicting him and disrespecting God. Then Paul and Barnabas, having no fear, said, "It was necessary that the Word of God was first spoken to you, but seeing you reject it, and judge yourselves unworthy of everlasting life, we turn to the other peoples. The Christ has told us, saying, 'I've made you to be a light to the other peoples, that you would teach all people how to be saved, even to the farthest parts of the world.'" And when the other peoples heard this, they were happy, and praised the Word of God: and whoever was set apart for everlasting life believed in the Christ. And the Word of Christ was published throughout the whole region. But the Jews stirred up the dedicated and honorable women, and the leading men of the city, and made the people prejudiced against Paul and Barnabas, and forced them to leave out of their coasts. So they shook the dust off of their feet as a witness against them, and came to Iconium. And the followers were joyful, and filled with the Holy Spirit.

Paul Stoned and Left for Dead

14 [1-7] Later, in Iconium, they went both together into the Jews' Place of Worship, and spoke, so that a great crowd, both of the Jews and also of the Greeks, believed. Then the unbelieving Jews stirred up the other peoples, and made them turn against the Christians. But they stayed a long time, speaking without fear in Christ, who gave witness to the Word of God's grace, letting signs and amazing things be done by their hands. So the people of the city were divided, part of them agreeing with the Jews, and part with the followers. And when an attack was planned by both the other peoples, and also by the Jews, along with their rulers, to abuse them shamefully, and kill them, they became aware of it, and ran away to Lystra and Derbe, cities of Lycaonia, and to the region that lies around them. So they preached the New Word there.

[8-18] And there was someone at Lystra, sitting helpless, being a cripple in their feet from birth, who had never walked. This person heard Paul speak, who firmly watching them, knew that this person had faith to be healed, and said with a loud voice, "Stand on your feet." And suddenly this person jumped up and walked. And when the people saw what Paul had done, they called out, saying in the language of Lycaonia, "The gods have come down to us in the likeness of human beings." And they called Barnabas, Jupiter; and Paul, Mercurius, because he was the leading speaker. Then the priest of Jupiter for their city, brought a cow and a wreath to the gates, and would have sacrificed the cow with the people. But when the followers, Barnabas and Paul, heard about it, they tore their clothes, and ran in among the people, calling out, and saying, "People, why are you doing this? We're human

163

beings just like you and have a human nature, and preach to you so that you'll turn from these empty practices to the living God, who made heaven and earth, the sea and everything in it: Who in the past let all nations act in their own ways. Just the same, God left us a witness. God is good, giving us rain from heaven, and fruitful seasons, filling our hearts with food and happiness." And with this, they barely kept the people from worshiping them.

[19-28] And certain Jews from Antioch and Iconium came, who won over the people to stone Paul, and they threw him out of the city, thinking he was dead. But as the followers stood around him, he got up, and went back into the city. The next day he went with Barnabas to Derbe. And when they had preached the New Word to that city, and had taught many, they came back through Lystra, Iconium, and Antioch, proving the souls of the followers, and encouraging them to stay in the faith, and telling them that we must go through many troubles to come into the realm of God. And when they had set apart elders for every church, and had prayed, willingly going without food, they trusted them to God, on whom they believed. And after they had passed through Pisidia, they came to Pamphylia. When they had preached the Word in Perga, they went down into Attalia, where they then sailed to Antioch, and where they were praised for God's grace to them for the work they'd done. And when they had come, and had gathered the church together, they went over everything that God had done with them, and how they had opened the door of faith to the other peoples. They stayed there a long time with the followers.

Questions of the Law

15 [1-11] And some people which came down from Judea told the Christians, *"Unless you're flesh is cut in the way of Moses, you can't be saved."* So when Paul and Barnabas had a big disagreement with them and argued about it, they decided that Paul and Barnabas, and a few more of them, would go to Jerusalem to the followers and elders to ask about it. The church sending them on their way, they passed through Phenice and Samaria, telling how the other peoples were saved: and all the Christians there were very happy about it. And when they had come to Jerusalem, they were welcomed by the church, and the followers and elders, and they told them everything that God had done with them. But some of the sects of the religious leaders who believed got up, saying that they needed to cut the foreskins of the other peoples, and to order them to obey the Word of God by Moses. And the followers and elders came together to decide the matter. After there had been a lot of arguing, Peter got up, saying to them, *"Christians, you know how that a good while ago God chose among us, that the other peoples by my mouth would hear the New Word, and believe. And God, which knows the hearts, gave them witness, by giving them the Holy Spirit, just as God did to us. God put no difference between us and them, making their hearts pure by faith. So now, why are you tempting God, to put restrictions on the new followers, which neither our ancestors, nor we were able to carry? Don't we believe that through the grace of Yeshua the Christ we'll be saved, just as they do?"*

[12-21] Then everyone was silent, and listened to Barnabas and Paul, who told them what wonderful and amazing things God had done among the other peoples by them. And after they stopped speaking, James said, "Christians, listen carefully to me: Simeon has made known how God first visited the other peoples, to take a people out of them for God's name. And the Words of the great preachers agree with this; as the Word says, *"I'll return later, and will rebuild the Place of Worship of David, which is fallen down; and I'll rebuild its ruins, and I'll set it up, so that the rest of the peoples might look for God, and all the other peoples, on whom My Name is called, God said, who does all this".* God knows everything we've done from the beginning of the world. So this is what I think: we shouldn't trouble those who came from among the other peoples who turned to God. We should write to them, and tell them not to worship anything else but God, not to do any sexual sin, and not to eat anything that has been strangled, or still has blood in it. Moses, since long ago, has been made known to them in every city by those who preached, being read in the places of worship every Seventh Day.

[22-35] Then it pleased the followers and elders, along with the whole church, to send some chosen out of their own company to Antioch with Paul and Barnabas; namely, Judas, who was nicknamed Barsabas, and Silas, who were leaders among the Christians. They wrote letters later by them in this way:

> The followers, elders, and Christians send greeting to the Christians which are of the other peoples in Antioch and Syria and Cilicia: So as we've heard that some who went out from us have upset you with their words, weakening your faith, saying, "You must be cleansed, and obey the Word of God": to whom we gave no such word. We thought it best, all of us having one heart, to send some of our people to you, along with our dear loved ones Barnabas and Paul, who have risked their lives for the Name of our Christ Yeshua. So we've sent Judas and Silas, who will also tell you the same things by mouth. It seemed good to the Holy Spirit, and to us, to put on you nothing more than what's necessary; That you don't eat meats offered in false worship to statues, don't eat anything with its blood in it, or that has been strangled, and don't do any sexual sin. If you keep yourselves from these things, you'll do good. Be well.

164

So when they were dismissed, they came to Antioch, and when they had gathered the crowd together, they gave them the letter: Which after they had read it, they celebrated for the comfort it gave them. And Judas and Silas, being great preachers also themselves, encouraged the Christians with many words, and blessed them. And after they had stayed there awhile, they went in peace from the new Christians back to the followers. Silas decided to stay there, and Paul and Barnabas also stayed in Antioch, teaching and preaching the Word of God, with many others also.

[36-41] And a few days later, Paul said to Barnabas, "Let's go and visit the Christians everywhere that we've preached the Word of God, and see how they're doing. And Barnabas decided to take with them John, whose nickname was Mark. But Paul didn't want to take him with them, who had left from Pamphylia, and didn't go with them to the work. And the argument between them was so great, that they separated from one another: and so Barnabas took Mark, and sailed to Cyprus; And Paul chose Silas, and went, being recommended by the Christians to God's grace. And they went through Syria and Cilicia, confirming the churches.

Paul Meets Timothy

16 [1-15] Then they came to Derbe and Lystra, where a certain follower was, named Timothy, whose mother was a Jew, who believed; but whose father was a Greek. They were told of Timothy by the Christians that were at Lystra and Iconium. Paul wanted him to go out with them; and took and cut his foreskin because of the Jews there, all of them knowing that his father was a Greek. And as they went through the cities, they gave them the rules they were to keep, that were set up by the followers and elders which were at Jerusalem. So the churches settled in the faith, and increased in number daily. Now when they had gone throughout Phrygia and the region of Galatia, and were foretold by the Holy Spirit to preach the Word in Asia, after they had come to Mysia, they tried to go into Bithynia, but the Spirit wouldn't let them. And passing by Mysia, they came down to Troas. Then a vision appeared to Paul in the night, in which someone of Macedonia stood, calling them, saying, *"Come over into Macedonia, and help us."* And after he had seen the vision, we quickly tried to go into Macedonia, gathering that God had called us to preach the New Word to them. So leaving from Troas, we came straight to Samothracia, and the next day to Neapolis; And from there to Philippi, which is the leading city of that part of Macedonia, and a colony. We were staying a few days in that city. And on the Seventh Day we went out of the city by a river side, where prayer services were being held. We sat down, and spoke to the women who went there. And a certain woman named Lydia, who sold things dyed purple, of the city of Thyatira, which worshipped God, heard us. God opened her heart that she listened to the things which were spoken by Paul. So after she and her family were baptized, she begged us, saying, "If you've judged me to be faithful to God, come and stay at my house. So she won us over.

[16-24] And then as we went to prayer, a certain girl who was being controlled by an evil spirit, which helped her tell the future, and which made her employers much money by her fortune telling, followed Paul and us, and called out, saying, *"These people are the workers of the Most High God, who will show us the way to be saved."* And she did this for a long time, so Paul, being tired of it, turned saying to the spirit, *"I tell you in the Name of Yeshua the Christ, come out of her."* And it came out as soon as he said it. And when her employers saw that they had no hope of making any more money off of her, they caught Paul and Silas, bringing them into the shopping center to the rulers, and brought them to the courts, saying, *"These people, being Jews, greatly trouble our city, and teach a way of life, which isn't right for us to do, nor to observe, being Romans."* And the crowd gathered together against them, tearing off their clothes, and told the guards to beat them. And when they had beaten them, they put them in jail, charging the jailer to keep them safely: Who, having gotten such a charge, threw them into the inner prison, and put their feet in chains.

Paul and Silas Sing at Midnight

[25-40] And at midnight Paul and Silas prayed, and sang praises to God: and all the prisoners heard them. And suddenly there was a great earthquake that shook the foundations of the prison, and all the doors began to open, and everyone's chains fell open. And the keeper of the prison, awaking out of sleep, and seeing the prison doors open, drew out his sword, and would have killed himself, thinking that the prisoners had run away. But Paul called out, saying, *"Do yourself no harm; we're all here."* Then he called for a light, and came in trembling, and bowed down to Paul and Silas, and brought them out, saying, *"Please, what must I do to be saved?"* And they answered, *"Believe on Yeshua the Christ, and you'll be saved, and your whole house."* And they told him the Word of God, along with all that were in his house. And he took them at the same time of night, and washed their wounds; and was baptized, him and his whole house. And when he had brought them home, he gave them something to eat, and celebrated, believing in God with his whole house. But when the day came, the courts sent the sergeants, saying, *"Let those people go."* And the keeper of the prison told this to Paul, *"The courts have sent to let you go: so you can leave now, and go in peace."* But Paul answered, *"They have beaten us openly uncharged, being Romans, and have put us in jail; and now do they want to kick us out secretly? No! Let them come themselves and get us out."* And the sergeants told these words to the courts, who were afraid when they heard that they

were Romans. And they came, begging them, and brought them out, and asked them to leave the city. And they went out of the prison, and went to the house of Lydia, and when they had seen the Christians, they comforted them, and left.

17 [1-4] Now when they had passed through Amphipolis and Apollonia, they came to Thessalonica, where there was a Place of Worship of the Jews. So Paul, as his way was, for three Days of Worship, went in and explained to them and showed them from the Word that Christ needed to have suffered, and come back to life again from the dead; saying that *"This Yeshua, whom I preach to you, is the Christ."* And some of them believed, and a great crowd of dedicated Greeks and many of the leading women gathered together with Paul and Silas.

[5-9] But the Jews that didn't believe, became jealous, and gathered a crowd of evil people, who stirred up the whole city, and attacked the house of Jason, trying to bring them out to the people. But when they didn't find them, they took Jason and a few other Christians to the rulers of the city, saying, *"These people who have upset the whole world have come here also; Whom Jason has taken in: and they all act against the law of Caesar, saying that there's another ruler, Yeshua."* Both the people and the rulers of the city were greatly upset when they heard this, and when they had taken money from Jason and the others for security, they let them go.

[10-15] And right away the Christians sent Paul and Silas away by night to Berea, where they went into the Jews' Place of Worship. The people there were more understanding than those in Thessalonica, in that they accepted the Word with willing minds, and searched the Words daily, to see whether or not those things were true. So many of them believed; both the honorable women of the Greeks, and many of the men. But when the Jews of Thessalonica found out that Paul preached the Word of God at Berea, they came there also, and stirred up the people there. And then the Christians quickly sent Paul away to go to the sea, but Silas and Timothy still stayed there. And those who led Paul brought him to Athens, and being told to tell Silas and Timothy to come to him as quickly as they could, they went.

[16-21] Now while Paul waited for them at Athens, his spirit was stirred when he saw the whole city falsely worshiped other things. So he argued in the Place of Worship with the Jews, and with the other people who were dedicated, and in the shopping center daily with whoever he met. Then he met certain philosophers of the Epicureans, and of the Stoics. And some said, *"What's this babbler trying to say?"* Others said, *"He seems to be telling us of a strange god;"* because he was preaching about Yeshua and the new life to them. So they took Paul, and brought him to Areopagus, asking, *"Would you please tell us what this new teaching is, which you've been talking about? What you've been saying seems strange to us, so we want to know what it means."* (All the Athenians and the strangers who came there spent all their time either telling, or listening to something new.)

The Unknown God Made Known

[22-33] Then Paul stood in the middle of Mars' hill, saying, "You people of Athens, I realize that you're too superstitious in everything, because as I passed by, and watched your devotions, I found an altar with this inscription, TO THE UNKNOWN GOD. I'll tell you about the One whom you worship without knowing. God, who made the world and everything in it, seeing that this One is the God of all heaven and earth, doesn't live in Place of Worship made with human hands; Neither is worshipped with human hands, as though God needed anything, seeing that God gives life, breath, and everything else to all things; And has made of one race all the nations of humanity that live on the face of the earth, and has decided their times beforehand, and where the borders of their nation was to be; To look for God, if it so happens that they search for God, and find God, though God isn't far from any of us. We live, and move, and have our very being in God; as certain also of your own poets have said, *"We're God's children also."* So then, since we're the children of God, we shouldn't think that God is like gold, or silver, or stone, which is carved by the art work of a human being. And though God winked at these times of ignorance; now God tells everyone everywhere to change their evil ways. God has chosen a day, in which the whole world will be judged rightly by that person whom God has set apart; in which God has given assurance to everyone, in that God has raised the Christ from the dead. And when they heard of the coming to life again of the dead, some mocked him, but others said, *"We want to hear more about this from you."* So Paul left them, but some of them went with him, and believed: Dionysius the Areopagite, a woman named Damaris, and some others, being among them.

Paul Ministers in Corinth

18 [1-6] Later Paul went from Athens, and came to Corinth, finding there a certain Jew named Aquila, born in Pontus, who had just come from Italy, with his spouse Priscilla; (because Claudius had told all Jews to leave Rome:) and came to them. And because they did the same kind of work, he stayed with them, and worked because they were all tentmakers by trade. And they argued in the Place of Worship every Seventh Day, and won over many of the Jews and the Greeks. And when Silas and Timothy had come from Macedonia, Paul was called by the spirit to clearly tell the Jews that Yeshua was the Christ. But when they argued against it, showing disrespect for God, he shook his clothing, saying to them, *"Your blood is on your own heads; I've done what I was supposed to, and now I'll go to the other peoples."*

166

[7-11] And he left there, and went to someone's house, named Justus, who worshipped God, whose house was right next door to the Place of Worship. And Crispus, the leading ruler of the Place of Worship, believed on Christ, along with his whole house; and many of the Corinthians who heard believed, and were baptized. Then God spoke to Paul in a dream by night, saying, "Don't be afraid, but speak, and don't be silent. I am with you, and no one will try to hurt you because I have many people in this place." And he stayed there a year and a half, teaching the Word of God among them.

[12-17] And when Gallio was the deputy of Achaia, the Jews, with one heart, stirred everyone up against Paul, and brought him to the judgment seat, saying, *"This person teaches others to worship in a way that is against the Word of God."* And when Paul was just about to speak, Gallio said to the Jews, *"If it were about some wrong or evil action, Jews, I would put up with you and reason with you. But since it's a question of words and names, and of your law, you see to it! I won't judge these kinds of things."* And he ran them out from the judgment seat. Then all the Greeks took Sosthenes, a ruler of the Place of Worship, and beat him right in front of the judgment seat. And Gallio didn't even care about that.

[18-23] Paul still stayed there a good while, and then took leave of the Christians there, and sailed into Syria, with Priscilla and Aquila going along. Paul had all his hair cut off in Cenchrea because he had made a promise. Then he came to Ephesus, and left them there, but he himself went to the Place of Worship, and argued with the Jews. When they wanted him to stay a little longer with them, he said no; But told them goodbye, saying, *"I must keep the celebration that comes in Jerusalem if at all possible, but I'll come back to you later, if its God will."* And he sailed from Ephesus. And when he had landed at Caesarea, he went up and greeted the church there, then went down to Antioch. And after he had spent some time there, he left, and went over all the country of Galatia and Phrygia in order, strengthening all the followers.

[24-28] And a certain Jew named Apollos, born at Alexandria, a great speaker, and knowledgeable in the Word, came to Ephesus. This person was taught in the way of Christ; and being strong in the spirit, he spoke and taught everything about the Christ perfectly, knowing only the baptism of John. And he began to speak without fear in the Place of Worship, whom when Aquila and Priscilla had heard, they took him aside, and explained to him the way of Christ more completely. And when he wanted to go on to Achaia, the Christians wrote, encouraging the followers to accept him. And when he came, he greatly helped those who had believed through grace, publicly winning over the Jews, and showing Yeshua to be Christ by the Word.

Paul Heals and Preaches at Ephesus

19 [1-12] And then, while Apollos was at Corinth, Paul having passed through the upper coasts, came to Ephesus. Finding some followers there, he asked, *"Have you gotten the Holy Spirit since you believed?"* And they said, *"We haven't even heard that there is any Holy Spirit."* So he asked them, *"Then into what baptism were you baptized?"* And they said, *"Into John's baptism."* Then Paul said, *"The truth is, John baptized with the baptism of a changed life, saying to the people, to believe on the One who would come later, that is, on Christ Yeshua."* So when they heard this, they were baptized in the Name of Christ Yeshua. And when Paul had laid hands on them, the Holy Spirit came on them, and they spoke in another language, and preached. There were twelve of them in all. And they went into the Place of Worship, and spoke without fear for about three months, arguing and proving the things of the realm of God. But when some were doubtful, and didn't believe, but spoke evil of that way to the crowds, he left, and separated the followers, teaching daily in the school of Tyrannus. And this happened for two years; so that all those who lived in Asia heard the Word of Christ Yeshua, both Jews and Greeks. And God did some amazing things by the hands of Paul, so that even handkerchiefs or aprons were brought from his body to the sick, and the diseases were healed, and the evil spirits left them.

[13-20] Then some of the traveling Jews, exorcists, took it upon themselves to call the Name of Christ Yeshua over those who had evil spirits, saying, *"We order you to come out by Yeshua whom Paul preaches."* There were seven children of someone named Sceva, a Jew, and a leader of the priests, which did this. But the evil spirit answered them, saying, *"Yeshua I know, and Paul I know; but who are you?"* And the person in whom the evil spirit was jumped on them, attacking and overpowering them, so that they ran naked and wounded out of that house. And all the Jews and Greeks living at Ephesus found out about it; and great fear fell on them all, so the Name of Christ Yeshua became well known. And many that believed came, and confessed, telling what they had done. Many of them, who used witchcraft, brought their books together, and burned them in front of everyone: and they counted to see what they were worth, and found it to be fifty thousand silver coins. So the Word of God grew more and more and did well.

Ephesus in an Uproar

[21-27] After Paul had passed through Macedonia and Achaia, he decided in the spirit to go on to Jerusalem, thinking, *"After I've been there, I must also go to Rome."* So he sent into Macedonia two of those who had ministered to him, Timothy and Erastus; but he himself stayed in Asia for a while. And at the same time there was a great stir about that way. Someone named Demetrius, a silversmith, which made silver objects of worship of Diana, and helped the salesmen make a lot of money, called together everyone in that occupation, saying, *"People, you know that we make our money by this trade. Besides this, you see and hear, that not just at Ephesus, but almost throughout all of Asia, this Paul has won over and turned many people away from us, saying that the things which are made with hands aren't gods at all. Not only our employment is in danger of loosing its place; but also the Place of Worship of the great goddess Diana will be hated, and her beauty will be destroyed, whom all Asia and the whole world worships."*

[28-41] And when they heard this, they were very angry, and called out, saying, *"Great is Diana of the Ephesians."* And the whole city was in an uproar. Then, having caught Gaius and Aristarchus, of Macedonia, Paul's traveling companions, they rushed together into the theatre. And when Paul would have come to speak to the people, the other followers wouldn't let him. And some of the leading of people of Asia, which were his friends, sent to him, begging him not to go into the theatre. So some cried one thing, and others cried out another because the whole crowd was confused; and most of them didn't even know why they had come together. So they forced Alexander out of the crowd, the Jews putting him forward. Alexander waved his hands to make his defense to the people, but when they knew that he was a Jew, they all called out with one voice for about two hours, *"Great is Diana of the Ephesians."* Then when the town clerk had quieted the people, he said, *"You people of Ephesus, everyone knows that the city of the Ephesians is a worshipper of the great goddess Diana, which came down from Jupiter! Seeing then that this can't be argued against, you should be quiet, and do nothing too quickly. You've brought these people here, which haven't stolen anything from the Place of Worship, nor have spoken evil of your goddess. So if Demetrius, and the others which are with him, have a problem with anyone, court days are held, and there are officers: let them accuse one another. But if you have a problem with anything else, it'll be decided on in a legal gathering. We're in danger of being called into question for today's uproar! There's no reason for us to explain this meeting."* After he had said this, he told the crowd to go.

Paul Raises the Dead

20 [1-12] And after the uproar ended, Paul called the followers, and hugged them, and left to go into Macedonia. After he had gone through it, and had given the Christians there much encouragement, he came into Greece, and stayed there three months. And when the Jews tried to catch him, as he was about to sail into Syria, he planned to return through Macedonia. And Sopater of Berea; Aristarchus and Secundus of the Thessalonians; Gaius of Derbe, Timothy; Tychicus and Trophimus of Asia all went with him into Asia. They had gone on ahead, waiting for us at Troas. And we sailed away from Philippi after the holidays of unleavened bread, and came to them to Troas in five days; where we stayed seven days. And on Sunday, when the followers came together to break bread, Paul preached to them, being ready to leave the next day; and kept talking until midnight. And there were many lights in the upstairs room, where they were gathered together. And there sat in a window a certain young person named Eutychus, who had fallen into a deep sleep. As Paul was preaching for a long time, he fell down as he was sleeping from the third story window, and was found dead. And Paul went down, and fell on him, and holding on to him said, *"Don't worry, he's still alive."* So when they had come up again, and had broken bread, after having eaten, and talked for a long while, even till daybreak, he went. And they brought the young person alive, and were greatly comforted.

[13-16] We went to the ship, and sailed to Assos, intending to take Paul in there, because he had chosen to go there on foot. And when he met us at Assos, we took him in, and came to Mitylene. And we sailed from there, and came the next day across from Chios; and the next day we arrived at Samos, and stayed at Trogyllium; and the next day we came to Miletus. Paul had decided to sail by Ephesus, not wanting to spend time in Asia because he was in a hurry, if it were possible, to be at Jerusalem on the day of Pentecost.

[17-27] And from Miletus he sent to Ephesus, and called the elders of the church. And when they had come, he said, *"You know, from the first day that I came into Asia, how I've lived among you at all times, serving God with a willing mind, and with many tears, and trials, which happened to me by the evil plans of the Jews: And how I didn't keep anything back that was helpful to you, but have told you everything, having taught you publicly, and from house to house. I have told both the Jews, and also the Greeks, about having a changed life in God, and having faith in Yeshua the Christ of God. And now I go to Jerusalem, trusting in the spirit, not knowing what might happen to me there, except that the Holy Spirit witnesses in every city, saying that imprisonment and troubles await me. But none of this changes my mind, nor do I count my life dear to myself, so that I might finish my way with joy, and the ministry, which I've gotten from Christ Yeshua, to tell others of the New Word of God's grace. And now, I know that you all, among whom I've gone preaching the realm of God, won't see me any more. So I tell you today, that I'm innocent of the blood of all people. I haven't neglected telling you any of the Words of God.*

168

[28-38] *So be sure of yourselves, and to all the people, which the Holy Spirit has made you overseers, to take care of the church of God, which has been bought with the Christ's own blood. I know that after I leave, evil people who are as wild wolves will come in among you, tearing the people apart as if they were a flock of animals. Even out of your own selves, some will come, speaking evil things, to lead the followers away after themselves. So watch, and remember, that for three years I didn't stop warning everyone, night and day, with tears. And now, Christians, I give you to God, and to the Word of God's grace, which is able to build you up, and to give you an inheritance among all those who are set apart. I've wanted no one's money or clothes. Yes, you yourselves know, that these hands have worked for whatever I and those who were with me needed. I've shown you in every way, how that by working you should support the weak. And remember the Words of Christ Yeshua, who said, 'It's more blessed to give than to get'."* And when he had said this, he kneeled down, and prayed with them all. And they all cried very much, hugging Paul's neck, and kissing him, being sorry most of all for what he had said about them not seeing him any more. And they walked him to the ship.

Phillip's Daughters Foretell Paul's Arrest

21 [1-14] And then after we had left them, and started out, we sailed straight to Cos, and the next day, on to Rhodes, and from there, on to Patara. Then finding a ship to Phenicia, we boarded it, and set out again. Now when we had seen Cyprus, we left it on the left hand and sailed to Syria, and landed at Tyre, because the ship was to be unloaded of its cargo there. And we stayed there for seven days, and found followers, who said to Paul through the Spirit, *"Don't go up to Jerusalem."* And at the end of those days, we left, and went on our way. The followers walked with us on our way, along with their families, till we were out of the city. Then we kneeled down on the shore, and prayed. And when we had said goodbye to one another, we boarded the ship; and they went back home. And after we left from Tyre, we came to Ptolemais, and greeted the Christians there, and stayed a day with them. And the next day, we that were of Paul's company went, and came to Caesarea: and we went to the house of Philip, the evangelist, which was one of seven; and stayed with him. And this person had four daughters, who had never been sexually active, who preached. And as we stayed there for a long time, there came down from Judea a certain great preacher, named Agabus. And when they came to us, they took Paul's belt, and tied their own hands and feet up, saying, *"The Holy Spirit said, 'The Jews at Jerusalem will tie up the person that owns this belt, and will deliver him into the hands of the other peoples.'"* And when we heard this, both we, and the people of that place, begged him not to go up to Jerusalem. Then Paul asked, *"Why are you crying and breaking my heart? I am ready not only to be tied up, but also to die at Jerusalem for the Name of Christ Yeshua."* And when he wouldn't change his mind, we stopped, saying, *"Let what God wants be done."*

[15-26] And after that, we packed our stuff, and went up to Jerusalem. Some of the followers of Caesarea went with us, and brought with them Mnason of Cyprus, an old follower, with whom we would stay. When we had come to Jerusalem, the Christians gladly took us in. The next day Paul went with us to James; and all the elders were there, also. And when he had greeted them, he told them in detail all the things God had done among the other peoples by his ministry. And when they heard it, they praised God, saying, *"You see how many thousands of Jews there are which believe; and they're all passionate about the Word of God. But they have heard of you, that you teach all the Jews, who live among the other peoples, to turn away from Moses, saying that they shouldn't cut the foreskins of their children, nor to practice that way of life. What then, should we do? The crowd will come together as soon as they hear that you've come. So do what we say to you: There are four people who have made promises; Them take, and purify yourself with them, and pay for them to have their heads shaved: and then everyone will know that the things they were told about you, aren't true; but that you yourself also walk orderly, and obey the Word of God. About the other peoples which believe, we've written and decided that they don't have to do this, except only that they stay away from foods offered in the false worship of other things, and from anything that's been strangled, or still has its blood, and from sexual sin."* Then Paul took the others, and the next day purifying himself with them, went into the Place of Worship, to signify the end of the days of purification, so that an offering could be offered for all of them.

Paul is Arrested

[27-40] And when the seven days were almost ended, the Jews which were of Asia, when they saw him in the Place of Worship, stirred up all the people, and took him, calling out, *"People of Israel, help: This is the person, that teaches everyone every where against the people, and the Word of God, and this place: and has also brought Greeks into the Place of Worship, making it unholy."* (because they had seen Trophimus an Ephesian with him before in the city, whom they thought Paul had brought into the Place of Worship.) And the whole city was upset, and a mob of people came together, taking Paul out of the Place of Worship, and shut the doors. And as they tried to kill him, news came to the captain of the guard that all Jerusalem was in an uproar, who quickly took soldiers and guards, and ran down to them. When the people saw the captain and the guards, they stopped beating Paul. Then the captain came near, and took him, and ordered him to be held with two chains; and demanded to know who he was, and what he had done. And some cried out one thing, and some another, among the crowd. So

169

when he couldn't find out for sure what had started the disorder, he ordered him to be carried into the prison. And when Paul got to the stairs, he had to be picked up and carried off by the guards because the people were so violent. The crowd of people followed them, calling out, *"Take him away!"* And as Paul was to being led into the prison, he said to the captain, *"May I speak to you?"* Who answered, *"Can you speak Greek? Aren't you that Egyptian, which made an uproar not long ago, and led four thousand people who were murderers out into the countryside?"* But Paul said, *"I am a Jew of Tarsus, a city in Cilicia, a citizen of no rough city: I beg you, let me speak to the people."* So when he had given him permission, Paul stood on the stairs, and waved his hand to the people. And when it was silent, he spoke to them in the Hebrew language.

Paul's Defense to the People

22 [1-11] Paul said to them, *"Everyone, hear my defense which I make to you now."* (And when they heard him speaking in the Hebrew language to them, they quieted down: and he said,) *"The truth is, I am a Jew, born in Tarsus, a city in Cilicia, but brought up in this city at the feet of Gamaliel, and taught in the strict way of the ancestors in God's Word, and was as passionate about God, as you all are today. And I abused the people of this Way, even to death, arresting and putting them in jails, both the men and the women. As also the leading priest are my witnesses, and all the court of the elders: from whom also I had gotten letters to the Jews, and went to Damascus, to bring those who were arrested there back to Jerusalem to be punished. And then, as I traveled there, and came near Damascus about noon, suddenly a great light from heaven shined all around me. And I fell to the ground, and heard a voice saying to me, 'Saul, Saul, Why are you trying to hurt me?' And I said, 'Who are you, Christ?' And the Christ told me, 'I am Yeshua of Nazareth, whom you're trying to hurt.' And those who were with me saw the light, too, and were afraid; but they didn't hear the voice of the One who spoke to me. And I said, 'What should I do, Christ?' And the Christ told me, 'Get up, and go into Damascus; and it'll be told you there everything that has been chosen for you to do.' And when I couldn't see because the light was so bright, being led by those who were with me, I came into Damascus.*

[12-21] *And someone named Ananias, someone dedicated to the Word of God, having a good report of all the Jews which lived there, came to me and said, 'Brother Saul, see again.' And as soon as he said this, I could see him. And he said, 'The God of our ancestors has chosen you, that you would know God's will, and see that Holy One, and would hear the voice of the Christ. You'll be the Christ's witness to everyone of what you've seen and heard. And now, what are you waiting for? Get up, and be baptized, and wash away your sins, calling on the Name of God.' And then, when I came again to Jerusalem, even while I prayed in the Place of Worship, I was in a trance; And saw the Christ saying to me, 'Go quickly, and get out of Jerusalem because they won't accept what you say about Me.' And I said, 'Christ, they know that I locked up and beat in every Place of Worship those who believed on You: And when the blood of Your martyr Stephen was shed, I was standing there, too, and agreed to his death, and kept the coats of those who killed him.' And the Christ told me, 'Go and I'll send you far from here to the other peoples.'"*

[22-30] And they listened to him until he said this, and then called out, saying, *"Put a person like this to death because he isn't fit to live."* And as they called out, and took off their coats, and threw dust into the air, the captain told them to bring him into the prison, and question him by beating; in order to know why the people were calling out against him. And as they tied him up with leather straps, Paul said to the soldier next to him, *"Is it right for you to beat someone who is a Roman, and has not been charged with anything?"* When the soldier heard that, he went and told the captain, saying, *"Be careful what you do because this person is a Roman."* Then the captain came, asking, *"Tell me, are you a Roman?"* And Paul said, *"Yes."* And the captain said, *"I got this right with a lot of money."* And Paul said, *"But I was born with that right."* Then suddenly those who were about to question him left: and the captain was also afraid, after he knew that Paul was a Roman, and because they had tied him up. The next day, because they wanted to know for sure why Paul was being accused by the Jews, he let him out and brought him down, and told the leading priests and all their court to appear, and set Paul before them.

Paul Goes to Court

23 [1-9] And Paul, carefully watching the court, said, *"Everyone, I've lived in good conscience to God until today."* And the leading priest Ananias told those who were next to him to hit him on the mouth. Then Paul said to them, *"God will hit you, you whitewashed wall because you sit and judge me in the Word of God, and order me to be beaten, which is against the Word of God."* And those who stood there said, *"Are you accusing God's leading priest?"* Then Paul said, *"I didn't know that he was the leading priest, but the Word says, 'You shouldn't speak evil of the ruler of your people.'"* But when Paul realized that part of them were of one religious sect, and the others were of another religious sect, he called out in the court, *"People, I am a religious leader, the child of a religious leader: because of my belief and hope of the coming to life again of the dead I am called into question."* And when Paul had said this, an argument started between the religious leaders and the ministers from the other religious sects: and the crowd was divided, because one religious sect says that there's no the coming to life again, nor angel, nor spirit: but the religious leaders believe in both. And everyone started calling out: and those who were of the religious leaders' belief stood up, and said, *"We find this person not guilty! If a spirit or an angel has spoken to him, let's not fight against God."*

[10-21] And when everyone started arguing again, the captain, fearing that Paul would have been torn apart by them, told the guards to go down, and take him away from them by force, and to bring him back to the prison. And the night after that, Christ came to him, saying, *"Be happy, Paul! Just as you've told of Me truthfully in Jerusalem, so you must be a truthful witness at Rome, also."* And when it was day, some of the Jews came together, and put themselves under a curse, saying that they wouldn't eat or drink anything till they had killed Paul. And more than forty of them had made this promise. So they came to the leading priests and elders, saying, *"We've put ourselves under a great curse, that we won't eat anything until we've killed Paul. So now you, along with the court, tell the captain to bring him down to you tomorrow, as though you want to ask him more questions: and we, when they come close enough, will be ready to kill him."* But when Paul's nephew heard of their plan to kill him, he left, and went to the prison, and told Paul. Then Paul called one of the guards to him, saying, *"Bring this young person to the captain because he has something to tell him."* So he took him, and brought him to the captain, saying, *"Paul, the prisoner called me, and asked me to bring this young person to you, who has something to say to you."* Then the captain took him by the hand and went with him aside secretly, and asked him, *"What do you want to tell me?"* And he told him, *"The Jews have all agreed to ask you to bring Paul down into the court tomorrow, as though they wanted to ask him some questions. But don't give in to them, because more than forty people have planned to kill him, which have promised, that they won't eat or drink anything till they've killed him: and now they're ready, waiting for a promise from you."*

Paul Sent to Felix

[22-35] So then the captain let the boy leave, and told him, *"Don't tell anyone what you've told me."* And he called two guards, saying, *"Get two hundred guards ready to go to Caesarea, and seventy riders, and two hundred soldiers, at nine o'clock tonight; And give them a horse for Paul, and bring him safely to Felix, the governor."* Later, he wrote a letter:

> *Claudius Lysias to the most excellent governor Felix sends greeting. This person was taken from the Jews, and would have been killed by them: then I came with an army, and rescued him, knowing that he was a Roman. And when I wanted to know the reason why they accused him, I brought him out into their court: Whom I realized then was being accused of questions about their law, but I don't have anything to charge him with worthy of death or even of imprisonment. And when it was told me that the Jews planned to kill this person, I sent him quickly to you, and gave word to his accusers also to tell you what they had against him. Goodbye.*

Then the guards did as they were told and took Paul, bringing him by night to Antipatris. The next day they left the riders to go on with him, and then went back to the prison. When they came to Caesarea, and had given the letter to the governor, they turned Paul over to him. And when the governor had read the letter, he asked what province Paul was from. And when he found out that he was from Cilicia; he said, *"I'll hear you, when your accusers have come, too."* And he told them to keep Paul in Herod's court.

Paul Defends Himself in Court

24 [1-9] And after five days Ananias the leading priest came down with the elders, and with a certain well spoken person named Tertullus, who told the governor of the accusations against Paul. And when he was called on, Tertullus began to accuse him, saying, *"Seeing that we enjoy great peace with you, and that you have done very worthy things for this nation by your generosity, we accept it always, everywhere, most noble Felix, with great thankfulness. But so that I won't be too tiring to you, I ask you to hear a few words from us out of your kindness. We've found this person to be a troublesome person, who starts rebellions among all the Jews throughout the whole world, and a ringleader of the sect of the Christians: Who also has tried to treat the Place of Worship with disrespect: whom we took, and would have judged by our law. But the captain Lysias came on us, and with great force took him out of our hands, ordering his accusers to come to you. You will know this for yourself when you question him about the things we're accusing him of.* And the Jews also agreed, saying that it was true.

[10-23] Then Paul, after that the governor had waved to him to speak, said, *"As I know that you've been a judge to this nation for many years, I'll more gladly, answer for myself: because I know that you can understand that it has been only twelve days since I went up to Jerusalem to worship. And they didn't find me in the Place of Worship arguing with anyone, nor stirring up the people, neither in the Place of Worship, nor in the city. They can't prove anything they're accusing me of now. But I tell you this, that I worship in the Way, which they call heresy, the God of my ancestors, believing everything which is written in the Word of God and in the words of the great preachers: And I have hope in God, which they themselves also allow, that there will be a coming to life*

again of the dead, both of the good and the evil. And in this, I always try to have a good conscience, without doing wrong to God, or anyone else. Now after many years, I came to bring gifts to my nation, and offerings. At which point, certain Jews from Asia found me cleansed in the Place of Worship, not with a crowd, nor with any disorder. Who should have come before you, to accuse me, if they had anything against me. Or else, let these that are here say if they've found me doing anything wrong, while I stood in the court, except maybe for this one thing, that I called out to them, I am being called into question by you today about my belief in the coming to life again of the dead." And when Felix heard this, having a better knowledge of that Way, he told them to wait, saying, *"When Lysias, the captain, comes down, I'll make a decision on your case."* And he told a guard to keep Paul, but to let him have freedom, and not to tell anyone that they can't minister or come to him.

[24-27] And after a few days, when Felix came with his spouse Drusilla, who was a Jewess, he sent for Paul, and listened to him speak about the faith in Christ. And as he spoke to them about goodness, self-control, and the judgment to come, Felix shook with fear, saying, *"Go for now; but I'll call for you again when it's a better time."* He was hoping also that Paul would give him some money to free him, so he sent for Paul more often, and talked with him. But after two years Porcius Festus took the office of Felix: and Felix, wanting to do the Jews a favor, left Paul in prison.

Paul Appeals to Caesar

25 [1-12] Now when Festus came into the province, after three days he had gone up from Caesarea to Jerusalem. Then the leading priest and the other leaders of the Jews told him of the accusations against Paul, and begged him for a favor, that he would send Paul to Jerusalem, while people were waiting down the road to kill him. But Festus said, that Paul would be kept at Caesarea, and that he himself would leave shortly to go there. So he said, *"Let whoever among you that's able, go down with me, and accuse this person, if there is any wrongdoing in him."* And when he had stayed among them more than ten days, he went down to Caesarea; and the next day sitting on the judgment seat, he had Paul brought to him. And when he came, the Jews that came down from Jerusalem stood around, charging Paul with many serious complaints, which they couldn't prove. While he said for himself, *"I haven't done anything against the law of the Jews, nor against the Place of Worship, nor even against Caesar."* But Festus, wanting to do the Jews a favor, asked Paul, saying, *"Will you go up to Jerusalem, to be judged of this by me?"* Then Paul said, *"I'm standing at the court of Caesar, where I should be judged: I have done no wrong to the Jews, as you very well know. If I'm an offender, or have done anything worthy of death, I don't refuse to die: but if I have done none of this that I'm accused of, no one can hand me over to them. I make my appeal to Caesar."* Then when Festus had talked with the court, he said, *"You've appealed to Caesar, so to Caesar you'll go."*

Paul Speaks to Agrippa

[13-22] And after a few days the ruler Agrippa and Bernice came to Caesarea to greet Festus. And when they had been there a long time, Festus told them about Paul's case, saying, *"There's someone left locked up by Felix: About whom, when I was at Jerusalem, the leading priests and the elders of the Jews told me, hoping to have a judgment against him. I answered, It isn't the way of the Romans to deliver anyone to die, before the accused has seen the accusers face to face, and has had a chance to answer for himself about the crime charged against him. So, when they had come here, without any delay, I held court the next day, and told the person to be brought out. When the accusers stood up, they brought none of the accusations I thought they would: But had some questions against him about their own religious beliefs, and of someone named Yeshua, who had died, whom Paul said was alive. And because I didn't really know how to answer those kinds of questions, I asked him if he would go to Jerusalem, and be judged there about it. But when Paul had appealed to be kept until the hearing of Augustus, I ordered him to be kept till I might send him to Caesar."* Then Agrippa said to Festus, *"I would like to hear this person myself."* So he told him, *"Tomorrow, you'll hear him."*

[23-27] And the next day, when Agrippa came, and Bernice, with great show, and was gone into the court, with the captains, and the leaders of the city, Paul was brought out at Festus' word. And Festus said, *"Ruler Agrippa, and people in the court, listen to this person, about whom all the leaders of the Jews have talked with me, both at Jerusalem, and also here, saying that he shouldn't be allowed to live any longer. But when I found that he had done nothing worthy of death, and that he himself has appealed to Augustus, I've decided to send him. But I have nothing to write to my Ruler. So I've brought him out to you, and especially to you, ruler Agrippa, so that, after he's questioned, I might have something to write. It seems to me to be out of the question to send a prisoner, with nothing to signify the crimes against him."*

26 [1-11] Then Agrippa said to Paul, *"You're may speak for yourself, now."* Then Paul reached out with his hand, saying for himself: *"I think myself happy, ruler Agrippa, because I'll answer for myself today to you about everything in which I am accused of by the Jews: Especially because I know you to be an expert in the Jewish way of life and all the questions which we have: so I beg you to hear me patiently. My way of life from my youth, which was at first among my own nation at Jerusalem, which all the Jews know; Those who knew me from the*

172

beginning, if they would tell you, know that I lived the life of a religious leader in the most strict sect of our religion. And now I stand and am judged for the hope I have in the promise made by God to our ancestors: The promise we hope to get, which was made to our twelve families, who sincerely serve God day and night. It's for this hope's sake, ruler Agrippa, that I am being accused by the Jews. Why would you think it an incredible thing, that God would raise the dead? The truth is, I thought myself, that I should do many things against the Name of Yeshua of Nazareth. Which I did in Jerusalem, putting many of the Christians in prison, having gotten power from the leading priests; and when they were put to death, I spoke against them. And I punished them often in every Place of Worship, and tried to get them to dishonor God; and being very angry with them, I chased them even to far off cities, to abuse them.

[12-23] At which point as I went to Damascus with power and orders from the leading priests, at noon, I saw on the road a great light from heaven, brighter than the sun, shining around me and those who journeyed with me. And when we had all fallen to the ground, I heard a voice speaking to me, and saying in the Hebrew language, 'Saul, Saul, why are you trying to hurt me? Isn't it hard for you to fight against my prods? And I said, Who are you, Christ? And the Christ answered, I am Yeshua who you're trying to hurt. But get up, and stand on your feet because I've appeared to you so I can make you a minister and a witness both of what you've just seen, and of the things that you'll see later; I'll deliver you from your own people, and from the other peoples, to whom I now send you, to open their eyes, and to turn them from darkness to light, and from the power of Satan to God, so that they can be saved from their sins, and have an inheritance among those who are set apart by faith in Me.' At which point, Ruler Agrippa, I wasn't disobedient to the heavenly vision: But I went first to those of Damascus, and at Jerusalem, and throughout all the coasts of Judea, and then to the other peoples, to tell them to change their ways and turn to God, and to do right to have a changed life. This is why the Jews caught me in the Place of Worship, and tried to kill me. But having the help of God, I'm still here to this day, witnessing both to small and great, saying nothing other than the faith of the great preachers and Moses said would come: That Christ would suffer, and be the first that would come back alive from the dead, and would give light to our people, and to the other peoples."

[24-32] And as Paul so spoke for himself, Festus said with a loud voice, "Paul, you're beside yourself; all your learning has made you crazy." But he answered, "I am not crazy, most noble Festus; but I speak the words of wisdom and truth. You know of this, and I speak freely to you because I know that none of this is hidden from you, because this thing wasn't done in secret. Ruler Agrippa, do you believe the great preachers? I know that you do." Then Agrippa said to Paul, "You almost prove to me that I should become a Christian." And Paul said, "I wish to God, that not only you, but also everyone who hears me today, were both almost, and altogether such as I am, except for my imprisonment." And when they had said this, the ruler got up, and the governor, and Bernice, and those who sat with them: And when they were gone aside, they talked between themselves, saying, "This person has done nothing worthy of death or of imprisonment." Then Agrippa said to Festus, "He might have been set free, if he hadn't appealed to Caesar."

Paul Sent to Rome

27 [1-8] And when it was time for us to go to Italy, they gave Paul and some other prisoners to someone named Julius, a soldier of Augustus' troop. And going into a ship of Adramyttium, we started, meaning to sail by the coasts of Asia. Aristarchus, a Macedonian of Thessalonica, was with us. And the next day we landed at Sidon. And Julius treated Paul kindly, and gave him freedom to go to friends to refresh himself. And when we had started from there, we sailed behind Cyprus, to protect us from the storm winds. And when we had sailed over the sea of Cilicia and Pamphylia, we came to Myra, a city of Lycia. And there the soldier found a ship of Alexandria sailing into Italy; and they put us in it. And when we had sailed slowly for a long time, and had almost gotten to Cnidus, the winds not letting us, we sailed behind Crete, next to Salmone; And as we almost passed it, we came to a place which is called Fair Havens; near the city of Lasea.

Paul Warns of Shipwreck

[9-15] Now when a long time had passed, and when the sailing was quite dangerous, because the Holiday had already passed, Paul warned them, saying, "Please, I know that this voyage will be hurt and have a lot of damage, and not only the cargo and ship, but our very lives will be in danger." But the soldier was more willing to do what the captain and the owner of the ship said, than what Paul had said. And because the haven wasn't a good place to winter in, most of them wanted to leave there also, if by chance they could get to Phenice, and winter there; which is a haven of Crete, and lies toward the south west and north west. And when the south wind blew softly, thinking that they had gotten their chance, they left there and sailed close to Crete. But not long after a great storm wind blew, called Euroclydon. And when the ship was caught, and couldn't go into the wind, we let it drive.

[16-24] And sailing in the shelter of a certain island called Clauda, we had to work very hard to save the lifeboat: Which when they had brought it up, they used ropes to help support the ship. And fearing they would get stuck in the sand, they raised the sail, and were driven by the wind. And the boat, being greatly rocked by the

storm, the next day, they lightened the ship. And the third day, we threw all the tackling of the ship out with our own hands. And when we couldn't see the sun, nor the stars for a long time, and we were in a very great storm, we lost all hope of being saved. But after a long time without any food, Paul stood in the middle of them, and said, *"People, you should have listened more carefully to me, and not have left Crete, and gotten all this harm and loss. And now I tell you to be calm, because no one's life will be lost, but only the ship. The angel of God, who I belong to and serve, came to me tonight, saying, 'Don't be afraid, Paul; you must be brought to Caesar: And God has given you all those who sail with you.'*

[25-34] *So, please, be calm, because I believe God that it'll be just as it was told me. But we must be put on a certain island."* But when the fourteenth night came, as we were driven up and down in Adriatic Sea, about midnight the ship's crew believed that they were coming near to some land. And when they sounded, they found it twenty fathoms: and when they had gone a little further, they sounded again, and found it fifteen fathoms. Then fearing we would be driven on to the rocks, they put four anchors out of the stern, and prayed for daylight. And as the crew was about to escape out of the ship, when they had let the lifeboat down into the sea, pretending as though they were putting anchors out of the foreship, Paul said to the soldier and to the guards, *"You won't be saved unless they stay in the ship."* Then the guards cut the ropes off of the boat, and let it fall. And just as the sun was rising, Paul begged them all to eat, saying, *"Today is the fourteenth day that you've waited and gone without food, having eaten nothing. I ask you to eat something for your health because not one hair will fall from the head of any of you."*

[35-44] And when he had said this, he ate, and gave thanks to God in presence of them all: and then he began to eat. Then they all felt better, and began to eat, too. And there were two hundred and seventy-six people on board the ship. And when they had all eaten enough, they lightened the ship, and threw the wheat out into the sea. And when it was day, they didn't know what land they were at: but they found a bay with a beach, in which they were hoping, if at all possible, to drive the ship ashore. And when they had brought the anchors up, they let them fall into the sea, and let loose the rudder ropes, and lifted the mainsail into the wind, and tried to reach the shore. And being driven into a place where two seas met, they ran the ship aground; and the forepart stuck in the sand, and couldn't move, but the hinder part was broken by the violence of the waves. And the guards' planned to kill the prisoners, in case any of them swam out, and escaped. But the soldier, wanting to save Paul, wouldn't let them; and told that those who could swim to jump into the sea first, and get to land, and then the rest, some on boards, and some on broken pieces of the ship. And so they all escaped safely to land.

Paul Heals on the Island of Malta

28 [1-6] And when they had escaped, then they found out that the island was called Malta. And the native people were very kind and kindled a fire, and welcomed us all, because of the falling rain, and the cold. And when Paul had gathered a bundle of sticks, and laid them on the fire, a snake came out of the heat, and bit his hand. And when the natives saw the venomous snake hanging on his hand they said among themselves, *"No doubt this person is a murderer, whom, though he has escaped the sea, still justice won't let him live."* But Paul shook it off into the fire, and wasn't harmed at all. But when they thought he would have swollen, or fallen down dead suddenly, and saw after they had watched a great while, that he wasn't harmed, they changed their minds, saying that Paul was a god.

[7-10] A leading person of the island whose name was Publius lived in that area; who had kindly taken us all in for three days. And then when Publius' father was sick with a fever and a bloody diarrhea, Paul came in, and prayed, and laid his hands on him, and healed him. So when this happened, others in the island, who had diseases came also, and were healed. And we were honored with many honors also; and when we left the island, they gave us whatever we needed.

Paul Arrives at Rome

[11-16] And after three months we went in a ship of Alexandria, whose sign was Castor and Pollux, the Twin Brothers, which had wintered in the island. And landing at Syracuse, we stayed there three days. And from there we got a compass, and headed to Rhegium: and after one day the south wind blew, and we came the next day to Puteoli. We found Christians there, and were asked to stay with them for a week: and then we went toward Rome. And from there, when the Christians heard about us, they came to meet us as far as Appii Forum, and Three Inns. When Paul saw them, he thanked God, and took courage. And when we came to Rome, the soldier handed the prisoners over to the captain of the guard: but Paul was allowed to live by himself with a soldier who guarded him.

[17-31] And then after three days Paul called all the leaders of the Jews together: and when they had come together, he said, *"People, though I've done nothing against the people, or the way of life of our ancestors, still, I was taken prisoner from Jerusalem into the hands of the Romans. Who, when they had questioned me, would have let me go, because I had done nothing to deserve death. But when the Jews spoke against it, I had to appeal to Caesar; not that I had anything to accuse my nation of. Because of this, I have called for you, to see*

174

you, and to speak with you. It's for the hope of Israel that I have been made a prisoner like this." And they said, "We haven't gotten any letters from Judea about you, nor have any of those who have come here spoken anything bad about you. But we want to hear from you what you think about this sect, because we know that it's spoken against everywhere." And when they had chosen a day, many people came to where Paul was staying. Then Paul explained and carefully told them everything about the realm of God, proving to them about Yeshua, both out of the Word of God by Moses, and out of the great preachers, from morning till evening. And some believed what was said, and some didn't believe. And when they didn't agree among themselves, they went, after Paul had said this, "The Holy Spirit spoke well by Isaiah the great preacher to our ancestors, saying, 'Go to this people, and say, Hearing you'll hear, and won't understand; and seeing you'll see, and not realize: because the heart of this people has become numb, and their ears are hard of hearing, and their eyes are closed; or they would see with their eyes, and hear with their ears, and understand with their heart, and would be changed, and I would heal them.' So let it be known to you, that the New Word of how to be saved by God is being sent to the other peoples, and they'll listen." And when Paul had said these words, the Jews left, and had many questions among themselves. And Paul lived there two whole years in his own rented house, and took in all that came to him, and taught them about the realm of God, and all the teachings about Yeshua the Christ, without fear, and no one forbidding him.

The wilderness and the lonely place shall be glad for them, and the desert shall rejoice, and blossom as the ROSE. Isaiah 35:1

Paul's Letter to Romans

1 [1-7] Paul, a worker of Yeshua the Christ, called to be a follower, set apart for the New Word of God, (Which God had promised before by the great preachers in the Holy Word,) about the Child of God, Yeshua the Christ, our Savior, who was in human form from the line of David; And by the spirit of faithfulness said to be the Child of God with power, by the coming to life again from the dead. We've accepted, by grace, the membership of the faith among all nations, for the name of Christ. You all that are in Rome are also called of Yeshua the Christ, dear loved ones of God, and called to be Christians. May grace and peace come to you from Yahweh God, and Yeshua the Christ.

Not Ashamed of the New Word
[8-17] First, I thank my God for you all, through Yeshua the Christ, that your faith is being spoken of throughout the whole world. God is my witness, whom I serve with all my spirit in the New Word of the Child of God, that I always remember you in my prayers, never stopping. I ask if, in any way now at last, I might come to you by the will of God and have a good journey. I long to see you, so that I can give you some spiritual gift, so that you'll have what you need; That is, so that I'll be in good spirits along with you by the faith that we now share. I want you to know, Christians, that I planned often to come to you, (but was unable before this,) that I might have some converts among you also, just as I do among the other peoples. I owe it both to the Greeks, and to the other foreigners, both to the wise, and to the unwise. So as much as is in me, I'm ready to preach the New Word to you who are at Rome also. I am not ashamed of the New Word of Christ because it's the power of God to save everyone that believes; first the Jews, and then the other peoples. The goodness of God is made known, which is by faith: as the Word says, "*Those made right will live by faith.*"

No Excuses
[18-22] The judgment of God is revealed from heaven against all the evil and ungodliness of human beings, who hold back the truth with their ungodly actions; What might be known about God, they know, because God has clearly shown it to them. The things that we can't see about God, have been clearly shown to us since the creation of the world, that is, God's everlasting power and Godhead, which is understood by seeing everything that is made, so that they have no excuse. And even when they knew God, they wouldn't praise God as God, nor thank God; but became like unthinking idiots in their thoughts, and their stupid hearts were darkened. They claim to be wise, but they became like unthinking idiots, changing the light of the everlasting God into the false worship of other things, in the form of human beings, birds, animals, and water creatures.

On Homosexuality and Other Sins of the Flesh
[24-32] So God also gave them up to the evil they wanted out of their own hearts, to shame their own bodies among themselves. They changed the truth of God into a lie, and worshipped and served what was created more than the Creator who made them, who is blessed forever. So be it! Because of this God gave them up to the evil they wanted, so that even their women changed the natural way of sex into what is against nature (anal sex): And in the same way the men also, not wanting to have sex with a woman naturally, but wanting to have sex with each other (homosexual anal sex); men with men, doing what is clearly wrong, and getting diseases in themselves from their wrongs, which they rightfully deserved as punishment. And as they didn't like to remember God, God gave them over to an ungodly mind, to do what isn't natural; Being filled with all ungodliness, sexual sin, evil, greed, cruelty; jealousy, murder, arguments, lies, criticism; gossip, back-talkers, God-haters, wanting revenge, proud, braggers, inventors of evil things, disobedient to parents, without knowledge, promise breakers, without natural love, stubborn, and uncaring: Who knowing the judgment of God, that those who do such things are worthy of death, and not only do them, but are happy when others do them.

Everyone will Come to Judgment
2 [1-16] So you're inexcusable, you people, who judge others, because however you judge someone else, you accuse yourself because you who are judging others do the same kinds of things. But we're sure that in truth the judgment of God is against those who do such things. And do you think, you people, who judge those who do such things, and do the same, that you'll escape the judgment of God? Or do you hate the riches of God's goodness, and patient waiting; not knowing that the goodness of God leads you to a changed life? But because of your hardness and unchanged heart, you store up for yourself rage against the day of rage, when the good sense of God will be made known, who will give everyone just what their actions deserve. Everlasting life to them who patiently continue doing good, while looking for victory, honor, and a spiritual body: But God will have resentment and rage toward those who want to argue, and don't obey the truth, but are ungodly. Suffering and sorrow will

come to every soul of those who do evil, of the Jew first, and also of the other peoples; But victory, honor, and peace, to everyone that does good, to the Jew first, and also to the other peoples. God shows no favor to anyone. Whoever has sinned without knowing the Word of God will also be destroyed without the Word of God: and whoever has sinned knowing the Word of God will be judged by the Word of God. Those who only hear the Word of God aren't right to God, but those who act on the Word of God will be made right. When the other peoples, which haven't heard the Word of God, naturally do the things contained in the Word of God, these, not having the Word of God, are a law to themselves. This shows the work of the Word of God is written in their hearts, their conscience also giving proof, and their thoughts either accusing or else excusing them. This will happen in the day when God will judge the secrets of humanity by Yeshua the Christ as my New Word says.

Being a Jew is of the Heart

[17-24] If you're called a Jew, and rest in the Word of God, and brag about your relationship to God, and you know God's will, and approve of the things that are best, being taught from the Word of God; And if you're sure that you yourself are a guide to those who are blind, a light for those who are in darkness, a teacher of the stupid, a teacher of babies, you have, in the Word of God, the spirit of knowledge and the truth. So why do you teach others, but don't teach yourself? You, who preach that someone shouldn't steal, do you steal? You, who say that no one should act in sexual sin, do you act in sexual sin? You, who hate false worship, do you worship falsely? You that brag about yourself in using the Word of God, do you dishonor God by breaking the Word of God? So the Name of God is disrespected among the other peoples because of you, as the Word says. The truth is, if you obey the Word of God, your cleansing is good: but if you break the Word of God, your cleansing is as if you weren't cleansed. So if those who aren't cleansed keep the goodness of the Word of God, won't their uncleanness be as if they were cleansed? And won't those who aren't clean by nature, if they fulfill the Word of God, judge you, who by the written word and by the Jews break the Word of God? Those who are only Jews outwardly aren't really cleansed at all, which are only outwardly cleansed in the body: But it is those who are inwardly cleansed that are Jews; and being a Jew is of the heart, by the Spirit, and not by the letter of the law; whose praise isn't of human beings, but of God.

No One is Good

3 [1-8] So what advantage has the Jew then? or what good is it to be cleansed? It's good in every way: but most importantly, because they were trusted in to be the preachers of God's Word. So what if some don't believe? Will their unbelief make God's faithfulness useless? Never! God speaks truth, but everyone else is a liar. The Word says, *"That all Your words might be proved right, and that You might be found fair when You judge."* But if our ungodliness shows the goodness of God more, what can we say? Is God not good who punishes those who deserve it? (I speak as a human being) Never! Because then, how could God judge the world? Some might ask, *"If the truth of God is shown more by my lie to God's victory; then why am I judged as a sinner?"* And some say, (as we're falsely accused of saying,) *"Let's do whatever evil we want, so that good may come from it."* They'll get just what they deserve!

[9-18] So what then? Are we any better than they are? No, in no way because we've proved to both the Jews and the other peoples, that they're all sinners; As the Word says, *"No one is good, no, not even one. No one understands; no one tries to find God. They've all turned out of the way. They've all together failed to be any good; There's no one that does any good, no, not one. Their mouths are like open graves; they've spoken nothing but lies; their words spread like the poison of a snake. Their mouths are full of anger and cursing. They're quick to murder. Their ways only destroy and hurt others. They don't know how to make peace. They have no fear of God's punishment."*

We are Saved By Faith

[19-31] Now we know that whatever things the Word of God says, it says to those who know the Word of God, so that every mouth can be shut, and all the world will be found guilty before God. So no one will be made right in God's sight by doing the things the Word of God says to do, but the Word of God brings us to the knowledge of sin. But now the goodness of God that comes without doing what the Word of God says, is made known to us, being witnessed by the Word of God and the great preachers; This is the goodness of God which comes by faith in Yeshua the Christ to all those who believe. No one is any different. All have sinned, and fail to measure up to the goodness of God, who are made right freely by God's grace. We are bought back by Christ Yeshua, who God has sent to take our place through faith in the Christ's shed blood, to make known God's goodness for the forgiveness of past sins, which were overlooked by God, to make known, I say, at this time God's goodness. And in order to be fair, to cleanse those who believe in Yeshua. So why do you brag then? You have no reason to brag about the law you follow or of anything you've done. No, but only by following the Word of God, which is of faith. So we conclude that people are made right by their faith, not by doing what the Word of God says. Is God the God of the Jews only? Isn't God also the God of the other peoples? Yes, of the other peoples also! So seeing it's One

177

God, who will forgive those who are cleansed by faith, and those who aren't cleansed by the same faith, do we then make the Word of God useless by our faith? Never! But we prove the Word of God is true.

4 [1-8] So what can we say then, that Abraham, our ancestor, as concerning the body, has found? If Abraham were made right by what he'd done, he'd have reason to brag; but not before God. What did the Word of God say? Abraham believed God, and he was counted as good. Now the pay of those who work isn't a gift, but is earned. But those who don't work, but believe on the One who forgives the ungodly, their faith is counted for good. Just as David also says the person who God calls good without considering what they've done is blessed, saying, *"Blessed are those whose actions are forgiven, and whose sins are covered. Blessed is the person to whom God doesn't count a sinner."*

[9-15] So are those who are cleansed, that is cut in the flesh, the only ones who are blessed, or are those who aren't cleansed also blessed? Don't we say that Abraham's faith was counted for goodness. So when was it counted as good then? When he was cleansed, or before he was cleansed? Not in cleansing, but before then. He got the sign of cleansing, a seal of the goodness of the faith which he had before he was cleansed, in order to be the ancestor of all those who believe, who aren't cleansed, so that they might be counted good also. And the ancestor of cleansing not just to those who are cleansed only, but who also walk in the steps of that faith of our ancestor Abraham, which he had when he was still not cleansed. The promise, to be the heir of the world, wasn't to Abraham, or to his children, through the Word of God, but through the goodness of faith. If those who are of the Word of God are heirs, faith is useless, and the promise would be useless. The Word of God only brings us rage from God. And where there is no law, there's no sin.

[16-25] So it's of faith, that it might be by grace, to the end that the promise might be made sure to all the descendants; not only to those who are of the Word of God, but to those also who are of the faith of Abraham, who is the ancestor of us all. (As the Word says, *"I've made you an ancestor of many peoples."*) Abraham believed God, the very God, who gives life to the dead, and speaks of what hasn't happened yet as though it has already happened. Abraham, who against all hope, in hope, believed in order to become the ancestor of many peoples; just as it was spoken, *"so will your descendants be."* And not at all having a weak faith, he didn't consider that his body was as good as dead, even when he was about a hundred years old, nor even that Sarah's womb was dead: Who never swayed from believing the promise of God by doubting; but had great faith, giving praise to God; And being fully sure that what God had promised, God was also able to do. And so it was counted as goodness for him. Now it wasn't written for Abraham's sake alone, that it was counted for good to him; But for us also, who will be counted as good, if we believe on the God who brought back Yeshua our Christ from the dead; Who died for our sins, and was raised again for our forgiveness.

Christ Brings Us Back to God

5 [1-11] So being made right by faith, we have peace with God through our Christ Yeshua: By whom we also have access by faith into this grace in which we now stand and celebrate in hope of the victory of God. And not only so, but we have victory in our trials as well, knowing that our troubles help us to patiently wait through it; And our patience builds good character; and our character gives us hope. And we aren't ashamed of our hope because God's love flows through our hearts by the Holy Spirit which is given to us. Even when we were still without strength, when the time was right, Christ died for the ungodly. Someone would hardly die for a good person, but still some would even dare to die for a good person. But God shows love for us, in that, even while we were still sinners, Christ died for us. Much more then, being now made right by the blood of Christ, we'll be saved from God's rage through Christ. And if, when we were enemies, we were brought back to God by the death of God's own Child, much more, being brought back, we'll be saved through the new life of Christ. And not only so, but we also celebrate in God through our Christ Yeshua, by whom we've now been bought back.

[12-21] So, as sin came into the world by one person, and death by sin; and so death passed to everyone, because all have sinned: (Until the Word of God came, sin was in the world, though sin isn't counted when there's no law. Just the same, death ruled from Adam to Moses, even over those who hadn't sinned like Adam did when he disobeyed a direct order, who was the likeness of the One who was to come. But the free gift isn't like the sin. But if through the sin of One person many die, God's grace, and the gift by grace, which is by One, Yeshua the Christ, has come much more to many. And the gift isn't like it was by someone who sinned, because the judgment was brought by One to accuse him, but the free gift is given to forgive the sins of many people. If by one person's sin death ruled; how much more will those who get the riches of grace and the gift of goodness reign in life by One, Yeshua the Christ.) So as by the sin of one judgment came on everyone to accuse them; in the same way by the goodness of One, the free gift came to everyone to forgive them and bring them life. As by one person's disobedience many were made sinners, so by the obedience of One, many will become good. Besides this, the Word of God came so that the sin might grow more and more. But where sin grew, grace grew much more. So as sin has ruled to death, in the same way, grace might reign through goodness to everlasting life by Yeshua our Christ.

178

We are Dead to Sin

6 [1-11] So what will we say then? Will we keep on sinning, that grace can grow more? Never! How will we, that are dead to sin, live any longer in it? Don't you know, that as many of us as were baptized into Yeshua the Christ were baptized into the death of Christ? So we're buried with Christ by baptism into death, so that like Christ was brought back from the dead by the victory in God, in the same way, we also will walk in the newness of life. If we've been brought together in the likeness of Christ's death, we'll also be raised up, just like the Christ came to life again. Knowing this, our old person is put to death with Christ, so that the body of sin might be killed, and that we wouldn't serve sin again. Whoever is dead is freed from sin. Now if we're dead with Christ, we believe that we'll also live with Christ. Knowing that Christ, being raised from the dead, dies no more; death has no more control over the Christ. In that the Christ died, Christ died to sin once, but in that the Christ lives, Christ lives to God. Just the same, think yourselves also to be dead to sin, but alive to God through Yeshua, our Christ.

[12-23] So don't let sin reign in your human body, that you would do whatever evil it wants. Don't let your body parts be used as tools of ungodliness to sin, but give yourselves to God, as those that are alive from the dead, and use your body parts as tools of goodness for God. Sin won't have control over you because you aren't under the Word of God, but under grace. What then? Will we sin, because we aren't under the Word of God, but under grace? Never! Don't you know, that to whom you give yourselves as workers to obey, you work for whoever you obey; whether it's sin to death, or obedience to goodness? But God be thanked, that even though you were the workers of sin, you've obeyed from the heart the kind of teachings which was given you. So then, being made free from sin, you became the workers of goodness. I speak as a human being, because of the weakness of your body. Just as you've given your body parts as workers for evil and to sin which led to more sin; in the same way now give your body parts as workers to goodness which leads to faithfulness. When you were the workers of sin, you were free from goodness. What good did you get then from those things in which you're now ashamed? The end result of those things is death. But now being made free from sin, and becoming workers for God, the good you do leads to faithfulness, and in the end to everlasting life. Death is the payment for sin; but the gift of God is everlasting life through Yeshua our Christ.

The Word of God Shows Us Our Sin

7 [1-6] Don't you know, Christians, (for I speak to those who know the Word of God,) how that the law controls a person as long as they live. A person is joined to their spouse by the law so long as they both live; but if one of them dies, the other is set free from the law of marriage. So then if, while the spouse lives, they are married to another person, they would be acting in sexual sin: but if one dies, they are free from that law; so that they aren't acting in sexual sin, though they're married to another person. So, my dear Christians, you also are become dead to the law by the body of Christ; that you would be joined to another, even to the One who is raised from the dead, so that we would bring others to God. When we were acting on the wants of our bodies, the acts of sin, which were made known to us by the law of God, worked in our bodies to bring about death. But now we're freed from the law of God, being dead to that which we were held by; so that we would serve in the newness of the spirit, and not in the letter of the law, which is now old to us.

[7-13] What can we say then? Is the law of God sin? Never! No, but I wouldn't have known sin, but by the Word of God, because I wouldn't have known want, unless the law of God had said, "*You shouldn't want what others have.*" But sin, taking the opportunity by the Word, brought about all kinds of evil wants in me. Before I knew the Word of God, sin was dead. I was alive without the Word of God once, but when the law came, sin was awakened, and I died. And the law, which was given to bring life, I found to bring me death. Sin, taking opportunity by the Word, lied to me, and killed me by it. So the law of God is holy, and the Word holy, and just, and good. So then, was what's good bringing death to me? Never! But sin, that it might be seen as sin, was bringing about death in me by what's good; so that sin by that Word might become very sinful.

The Spiritual Battle Between the Mind and Body

[14-25] We know that the Word of God is spiritual: but I'm earthly, completely sold out by my sin. What I do I don't allow. What I want to do, that I don't do; but what I hate to do, that I do. If then, I do what I don't want to, I admit that the Word of God is good. Now then, it's not me that does it, but it's the sin that lives in me. I know that nothing good lives in me (that is, in my body,) because even though I want to do what's good; I don't know how to do it. The good that I want to do I don't do: but the evil things which I don't want to do, that I do. Now if I do what I don't want to, it's not me that does it, but the sin that lives in me. So then, I find a law, that, when I want to do good, evil is right here with me. I truly want to do the Word of God in my inner person. But I see another law in my body, fighting against the law in my mind, and making me captive to the law of sin which is in my body. Oh what a miserable person I am! Who will free me from this body of death? I thank God, through Yeshua the Christ, our Savior. So then, with the mind I myself serve the law of God; but with the body the law of sin.

179

Those Who Reject Christ, Don't Have God

8 [1-11] So God doesn't accuse those who are in Christ Yeshua, who don't act on what the body wants, but act on what the Spirit wants. The law of the Spirit of life in Christ Yeshua has freed me from the law of sin and death. What the law couldn't do, because it was weak in our bodies, God did by sending Yeshua, God's own Child, in the likeness of a sinful human being. And because of sin, God accused all sin in the body of Christ, so that the goodness that the law calls for could happen in us, who don't act on what the body wants, but act on what the Spirit wants. Those who live for the body act on the things the body wants; but those who live by the Spirit act on the things the Spirit wants. To be bodily-minded brings death; but to be spiritually-minded brings life and peace. The bodily mind is against God because it doesn't answer to the law of God, nor can it. So then those who live by the body can't please God. But you don't live by the body, but by the Spirit, if in fact, the Spirit of God lives in you. Now if anyone doesn't have the Spirit of Christ, they're not of God. And if Christ is in you, the body is dead because of sin; but the Spirit is alive because of goodness. But if the Spirit of the God, who brought back Yeshua from the dead, lives in you, the God who brought back Christ from the dead will also bring your human body back to life by the Spirit that lives in you.

We Owe Ourselves to Christ

[12-17] So, Christians, we owe our lives, not to the body, to live for the wants of the body, because if you live for the body, you'll die; but if you put an end to the actions of the body through the Spirit, you'll live. Those who are led by the Spirit of God are the children of God. You haven't been given the Spirit to be controlled again by fear; but you've been given the Spirit of adoption, by this we cry out to God, who cares for us like a parent. The Spirit itself tells the truth to our own spirit, that we're the children of God. And if we're children, then heirs; heirs of God, and joint-heirs with Christ, that is, if we suffer with Christ, so that we can all be praised together.

Suffering for Christ

[18-30] I think that whatever we suffer now in this time isn't worthy to be compared with the victory which we'll have. The hope and expectation of all creation waits for the children of God to be made known. All creation was made useless, not willingly, but by the will of the One who has subjected it in hope, because even the creation itself will also be freed from the control of evil and given the amazing freedom of the children of God. We know that the whole creation groans and labors as in the pain of childbirth together until now. And not only the creation, but we ourselves also, which have the promise of the Spirit, even we ourselves groan within ourselves, waiting for the adoption, and for our bodies to be saved. We're saved by hope: but hope that is seen isn't hope, because what someone sees, they don't still hope for. But if we hope for what we don't yet see, then we wait for it with patience. Just the same, the Spirit also helps our weaknesses because we don't even know what we should pray for as we ought to. So the Spirit itself speaks up for us with groanings which can't be spoken. And the One who searches the hearts knows what the mind of the Spirit is, because the Spirit speaks up for Christians by the will of God. And we know that God will make everything work out and come together for the good of those who love God and are the called for God's purpose. Those whom God knew before time, God also chose before time to be like God's own Child, who is the firstborn among many Christians. Besides this, those whom God chose before time, God also called: and those whom God called, God has also made right: and those whom God has made right, God has also made known.

[31-39] So then, what can we say about this? If God is for us, who can come against us? And won't God, who didn't spare God's own Child, but gave the Christ up for us all, along with Christ, also freely give us everything? Who will blame God's chosen with anything? It's God that forgives. Who is the One who accuses? It's Christ that died, yes, but instead, that is here back to life again, who is even at the right side of God, who also speaks up for us. What can separate us from the love of Christ? Will troubles, or suffering, or discrimination, or hunger, or nakedness, or danger, or death? As the Word says, *"For Your sake we're killed all day long; we're like animals going to be slaughtered."* No, but we can overcome all this and more through Christ who loves us. And I know without a doubt, that neither death, nor life, nor angels, nor things in spiritual realms, nor powers, nor what's here now, nor the things that are yet to come, nor the heights of the heavens, nor the depths of Hell, nor any other creature, can separate us from God's love, which is in Christ Yeshua our Savior.

The Chosen ones

9 [1-5] I tell the truth in Christ, and am not lying, my conscience also being my witness in the Holy Spirit, that I've great heaviness and continual sorrow in my heart. I could almost wish that I myself could be damned from Christ for my people, my own race in the physical sense. They're the Israelites; to whom the adoption was promised, and the victory, and the promised agreements were given, along with the Word of God, and the service of God, and all the promises. They're the human ancestors of the Christ, who is over all, who God blessed forever. So be it!

[6-13] But it isn't as though the Word of God has no effect. Not all who are descended from Israel, are Israelites. Neither, because they're descended from Abraham, are they all children; but, "*In Isaac will your promised descendents be called.*" That is, those which are the natural children of the body, these aren't the children of God, but the children of the promise are counted for the promised descendents. And this is the Word of promise, "*at this time I'll come, and Sarah will have a child.*" And not only this; but when Rebecca also had conceived the twins by our ancestor Isaac (the children not being born yet, nor having done any good or evil) one was chosen, so that the purpose of God for the chosen ones would come to pass, not because of anything that's done, but because of the God who calls. It was said to her, "*The elder will serve the younger.*" As the Word says, "*Jacob I have loved, but Esau I have hated.*"

[14-21] What will we say then? Is there ungodliness with God? Never! God said to Moses, "*I'll have mercy on whoever I have mercy, and I'll have compassion on whoever I have compassion.* So then, it isn't earned by those who choose, nor of those who try to work for it, but is given by the God that shows mercy. The Word said about Pharaoh, "*I have raised you up even for this very purpose, that I might show my power in you, and that My Name might be made known throughout all the earth.*" So God has mercy on whoever God has mercy, and whoever God wants to harden will be hardened. So then you might say to me, so why does God still find fault? Who can fight against God's will? No, but you who are just a human being, who are you to question God? Will the thing made say to the One who made it, "Why have you made me this way?" Doesn't the potter have power over the clay, to make the same lump a dish for a special purpose, and another for everyday use?

[22-33] What if God, wanting to show God's rage, and make known God's power, waits with much patience for those who God rages against, who are made to be destroyed; And to make known the riches of God's victory on those who have God's mercy, which God had prepared before time for victory? Yes, even us, whom God has called, not out of the Jews only, but also out of the other peoples. As God said also in Hosea, "*I'll call them My people, which weren't My people; and her a dear loved one, which wasn't a dear loved one.*" And it'll happen in the very place where it was said, "*You aren't my people;*" there they'll be called "*the children of the living God.*" Isaiah also cries out about Israel, "*Though the number of the children of Israel be as the sand of the sea, only a few will be saved: because in goodness God will make a quick end to the work, making a quick end with the final judgment on the earth.*" And as Isaiah said before, "*Unless God Almighty had left us a descendent, we would have been like Sodom and Gomorrah.*" So what can we say then? That the other peoples, which didn't follow the ways of goodness, have gotten goodness, even the goodness which is of faith. But Israel, which followed the law of goodness, hasn't reached the law of goodness. Why? Because they didn't follow it by faith, but by what they'd done of the law. They stumbled over that stone, as the Word says, "*I lay in Zion a stone that many will stumble over and a rock that many will be offended by, but whoever believes on the Christ won't ever be ashamed.*"

Claim Christ as Your Savior

10 [1-13] Everyone, what my heart wants and my prayer to God for Israel is, that they'll be saved. I know that they have a passion for God, but not for knowledge. And they, being without knowledge of God's goodness, and going about to prove their own goodness, haven't accepted the goodness of God. Christ is the goodness of the law of God for everyone that believes. Moses tells about the goodness which is of the law of God, "*The person who does those things will live by them.*" But the goodness which is of faith says it this way, "*Don't say in your heart, Who will go up into heaven? (that is, to bring Christ down from above) Or, Who will go down into the depths of Hell? (that is, to bring Christ up again from the dead.)*" But what did it say? "*The word is near you, even in your mouth, and in your heart;*" that is, the Word of faith, which we preach. If you claim with your mouth Christ Yeshua as your savior, and believe in your heart that God has raised the Christ from the dead, you'll be saved. With the heart a person believes for goodness, and with the mouth confession is made in order to be saved. The Word said, "*Whoever believes on the Christ won't be ashamed.*" There's no difference between the Jew and the other peoples because the same God over all blesses all that call on Yeshua the Christ. Whoever calls on the Name of Christ Yeshua will be saved.

[14-21] How then can they call on the One in whom they haven't believed? How can they believe in the One, in whom they haven't heard? How can they hear without a preacher? And how can they preach, unless they're sent? As the Word says, "*How beautiful are the feet of those who preach the New Word of peace, and bring happy news of good things!*" But they haven't all obeyed the Word. Isaiah said, "*Yahweh God, who has believed our report?*" So then faith comes by hearing, and hearing by the Word of God. But I ask, *Haven't they heard?* Yes, the truth is, "*Their sound went into all the earth, and their words to the ends of the world.*" But I ask, *Didn't Israel know?* First Moses said, "*I'll make you jealous by those who are not a nation, and I'll anger you by a nation that doesn't understand.*" But Isaiah has no fear, saying, "*I was found of those who weren't looking for me; I was made known to those who didn't ask about me.*" And said to Israel, "*All day long I've stretched out my hands to a disobedient and arguing people.*"

181

By Grace We Are Saved

11 [1-7] I say then, have the people of God been abandoned? Never! I also am an Israelite, from the line of Abraham, of the family of Benjamin. The people which God foreknew haven't been left by God at all. Don't you know what the Word said about Elijah? How he spoke to God against Israel, saying, *"God, they've killed your great preachers, and torn down your altars; and I am left alone, and they want to take my life."* But what did God answer? *"I've kept for myself seven thousand others, who haven't bowed the knee to that false god Baal."* Just the same then, at this present time also, there's still a few left who are chosen by grace. And if we're chosen by grace, then it's not by what you've done. Otherwise, grace isn't grace at all. But if it's by what you've done, then it's not grace. Otherwise the work that you do isn't work at all.

[7-12] So what then? Israel hasn't found what they are looking for; but the chosen ones have found it, and the rest can't understand. (As the Word says, *"God has given them the spirit of slumber, their eyes don't see, and their ears don't hear;"*) to this day. And David said, *"Let their wealth have control over them, and become a trap, and a problem, and a punishment to them. Let their eyes be blinded, so that they can't see, and may their backs be bent down always."* I say then, have they only stumbled to fall? Never! But through their fall the other peoples are saved, to make them jealous. Now if their fall brings the riches of being saved to the rest of the world, and their loss allows the other peoples to be saved; how much more will their addition bring greater riches to God's realm?

Israel Blinded to Open the Eyes of Other Peoples

[13-24] I speak to you other peoples, because I am a minister to you, but I brag about my ministry so that maybe in some way I can make my own people jealous, and might save some of them. If their being tossed aside brings together the rest of the world, their acceptance will be as the dead coming back to life? If the first fruit is holy, the rest is also holy: and if the root is holy, so are the branches. And if some of the branches are broken off, and you, being like a wild olive tree that's grafted in among them, are nourished by the root with them and are strengthen by the olive tree; don't think that you're better than the branches. But if you brag, know that you don't strengthen the root, but the root strengthens you. You might say then, *"The branches were broken off, that I might be grafted in."* That's true; it was because of unbelief that they were broken off, and you're joined by faith. So don't think yourselves better than them, but fear, because if God didn't spare the natural branches, be careful, in case God doesn't spare you either. So think about God's goodness and strict judgment both. Strict judgment came on those who fell; but God's goodness came to you, that is, if you stay in God's goodness. Otherwise you'll also be cut off. And they also, if they quit living in unbelief, will be grafted back in because God is able to graft them in again. And if you were cut out of the olive tree which is wild by nature, and were grafted in against your own nature, into a good olive tree: how much better will these, which are the natural branches, be grafted into their own olive tree?

[25-32] Christians, I don't want you to be without knowledge of this secret, in case you think yourselves better than you are; that Israel, in part, has been blinded until all the other peoples have come in. And so all Israel will be saved as the Word says, *"The Deliverer will come out of Zion, and will turn ungodliness away from Jacob: This is my promise to them, when I take away their sins."* But as to the New Word, they're enemies of it for your sakes, and as touching the chosen ones, they're loved for their ancestors' sakes. The gifts and calling of God can't be taken back. As in the past you didn't believe God, now you have found mercy through their unbelief. Just the same, they also don't believe now, so that through your mercy, they also can have mercy. God has judged them all in unbelief, in order to have mercy on all of them.

[33-36] How deep are the riches both of the wisdom and the knowledge of God! God's judgments can never be fully understood, and God's ways can't be fully known! Who understands the mind of God? Or who has questioned God? Or who has first given to God, so that it'll be paid back to them again? Everything is of God, and through God, and for God, who will have victory forever. So be it!

Be a Living Sacrifice

12 [1-2] So I beg you, Christians, by the mercies of God, that you give your bodies as a living sacrifice, holy, acceptable to God, which is only reasonable for you to do. And don't accept the ways of the world, but be changed by the renewing of your mind, so that you can know what is the good, acceptable, and complete will of God.

[3-8] And I say, through the grace given to me, to everyone that is among you, not to think of yourselves more highly than you should think; but to think with clear judgment, according to how much faith God has given to each of you. Just as we have many parts in one body, and they don't all have the same purpose; so we, being many, are one body in Christ, and we are all part of one another. So then having differing gifts for the grace that is given to us, whether preaching, let's preach according to our faith; Or ministry, let's serve in our calling; or whoever teaches, let them use the teaching they've been given; Or whoever encourages, let them use the encouragement

182

they have to give; whoever gives, let them do it in sincerity; whoever leads, let them lead with careful thought; and whoever shows mercy, let them show it with cheerfulness.

[9-21] Love in truth, without faking it. Hate what is evil and hold on to what is good. Be loving and kind to one another with the love of friendship, wanting to honor others before yourselves; not having a lack of concern; but being passionate about your work, serving God; celebrating in your hope; being patient in your troubles; praying right away for everything; supplying the needs of Christians; and welcoming others. Bless those who mistreat you: bless, and don't curse them. Celebrate with those who celebrate, and cry with those who cry. Get along with one another. Don't be too proud of yourself, but think of others who are in a lower place. Don't be wise in your own thinking. Don't repay anyone evil for evil. Be honest in the sight of everyone. If it's possible, as much as it depends on you, live peaceably with everyone. Dear loved one, don't try to get someone back, but instead leave room for God's rage because the Word says, "*Revenge is mine; I'll repay, God said. So if your enemy is hungry, feed them; if they're thirsty, give them a drink. If you do this you'll make them burn with shame.*" So don't be overcome by evil, but overcome evil with good.

Respect God's Authority

13 [1-7] Let everyone answer to whoever leads them, because no one comes to power but of God: Whoever has power is put in place by God. So whoever doesn't accept that power, doesn't accept what God has put in place, and those who fight against it will bring judgment on themselves. Rulers aren't a dread to those who do good, but to those who do evil. So why then are you afraid of those in power? Do what is good, and you'll have their praise, because they're the minister of God to you for good. But if you do what is evil, be afraid because they don't hold power for no reason, but because they're the minister of God, to carry out judgment on those who do evil. So you need to accept them, not only because you might be punished, but also for your conscience sake. Because of this, pay your taxes also because they're God's ministers, who give all their time to service. So pay all their dues: taxes to whom taxes are due; payments to whom payments are due; respect to whom respect is due; and honor to whom honor is due.

[8-14] Owe no one anything, but to love one another, because whoever loves another has done what the Word of God says to do. Because of this, "*You shouldn't act in sexual sin, You shouldn't kill, You shouldn't steal, You shouldn't lie about someone, You shouldn't want what others have;*" and if there's any other word, it's briefly understood in this saying, namely, "*You should love others as yourself.*" Love does nothing wrong to another, so love does what the Word of God says to do. And do that, knowing the time, that now it's high time to awake from sleep, because now we're closer to being saved than we ever thought. The night is almost over, and the day is near, so let's put off what we've done in darkness, and let's put on the covering of light. Let's walk honestly, as in the day; not in fighting and drunkenness, not acting in sexual sin and shamelessness, not in arguing and jealousy. But put on the likeness of Yeshua the Christ, and don't satisfy the wants of the body.

Everyone will Acknowledge God

14 [1-11] Allow those who are weak in the faith, but not as far as doubtful arguments. One believes that they can eat everything, but another, who is weak, eats only plants. Don't let those who eat hate those who don't eat; and don't let those who don't eat judge those who eat because God has accepted them. Who are you that judges another's worker? To their own employer they stand or fall. Yes, they'll be held up because God is able to make them stand. Someone respects one day above another and another values every day alike. So let everyone be completely sure in their own mind. Whoever respects the day, respects it in God; and whoever doesn't respect the day, to God they don't respect it. Whoever eats, eats to God, and they give thanks to God; and whoever doesn't eat, to God they don't eat, and they give thanks to God. None of us lives to ourselves, and none of us dies to ourselves. If we live, we live to God; and if we die, we die to God, so whether we live, or die, we're God's. For this reason Christ both died, and rose, and awakened, in order to be Christ both of the dead and the living. But why do you judge one another? Or why do you make one another not important? We'll all stand at the judgment seat of Christ. The Word says, "*As I live, God said, every knee will bow to Me, and every people will acknowledge God.*"

[12-23] Then everyone of us will give account of ourselves to God. So let's not judge one another any more, but decide to do this instead: Don't be a problem to anyone else or give an occasion for another to fall. I know, and am sure by Christ Yeshua, that there isn't anything evil of itself: but to those who believe anything to be evil, to them it's evil. So if another gets upset about your food, then you aren't acting in love. Don't destroy their faith with your food, for whom Christ died. Don't let your good be spoken ill of. The realm of God isn't about food and drink; but goodness, and peace, and joy in the Holy Spirit. Whoever serves Christ in this is acceptable to God, and approved of by others. So let's try to do the things which make peace, and the things that can benefit one another. Don't let what you eat destroy the work of God. To be sure, all food is good; but it's evil for someone to offend others with their food. It's good not to eat meat, nor to drink wine, nor anything else if it makes another stumble, or be offended, or made weak. Do you have faith? Keep it for yourself and for God. We will be happy if we don't

183

bring guilt on ourselves in whatever we approve of. Whoever doubts is damned if they eat, because they don't eat in faith, and whatever isn't of faith is sin.

Love One Another

15 [1-6] We then that are strong ought to be patient with the sins of the weak, and not to please ourselves. Let everyone of us please others for their good to build them up. Even Yeshua didn't please the Christ's own self; but as the Word says, "*The accusations of those who dishonored You fell on Me.*" Whatever things that were written before were written to help us learn, so that we, through the patience and comfort of the Word, might have hope. Now the God of patience and comfort will help you to think of one another in Christ Yeshua, so that you can with one mind and one mouth praise God, the God, who our Christ Yeshua is from.

[7-13] So accept one another, as Christ also accepted us in order to make God known. Now I tell you that Yeshua the Christ was a minister of the Jews for the truth of God, to confirm the promises made to the ancestors, and so that the other peoples might praise God for God's mercy; as the Word says, "*Because of this, I'll praise You among the other peoples, and sing to Your name.*" And again it said, "*Celebrate, you other peoples, with God's people.*" And again, "*Praise God, all you other peoples; Praise God, all you peoples.*" And again, Isaiah said, "*A shoot will spring up from the root of Jesse, One who will rise up to reign over the nations, in Whom the other peoples will trust.*" Now let the God of hope fill you with every joy and peace as you believe, so that you can grow in hope, through the power of the Holy Spirit.

[14-21] And I myself am sure also that you Christians are full of goodness, filled with all knowledge, and able also to warn one another. Just the same, Christians, I've written without fear all the more to you about some things, to remind you, because of the grace that has been given to me by God, so that I would be the minister of Yeshua the Christ to the other peoples, ministering the New Word of God, that the offering up of the other peoples might be acceptable, being set apart by the Holy Spirit. So I have a reason to make known what God has done through Yeshua the Christ in me. I won't dare to speak of anything Christ hasn't done in me, by word and action, to make the other peoples acceptable, through powerful signs and amazing things, by the power of the Spirit of God; so that from Jerusalem to Illyricum, I've fully preached the New Word of Christ. Yes, I have tried hard to preach the New Word, not where Christ was named, in case I might build on another person's foundation, but as the Word says, "*Those to whom the Christ wasn't spoken of, will see: and those who haven't heard will understand.*"

Paul Plans His Journey

[22-29] For this reason I've also been stopped many times from coming to you, but now having no more place in these parts, and having wanted these many years to come to you, whenever I take my journey into Spain, I'll come to you. I trust to see you in my journey, and to be brought on my way there by you, if first I enjoy your company. But now I go to Jerusalem to minister to the Christians. It has pleased them of Macedonia and Achaia to make a certain contribution for those Christians who are poor which are at Jerusalem. It's truly pleased them; and they do owe it to them. If the other peoples have shared in their spiritual things, their duty is also to minister to them with their earthly things. So when I've done this, and have brought to them this blessing, I'll come to you first and then go on to Spain. And I am sure that, when I come to you, I'll come in the fullness of the blessing of the New Word of Christ.

[30-33] Now I beg you, Christians, for Yeshua the Christ's sake, and for the love of the Spirit, that you work together with me in your prayers to God for me; so that I can be freed from those in Judea who don't believe; and that my service for Jerusalem will be accepted by the Christians; And that I can come to you with joy by the will of God, and that I can be renewed with you. Now the God of peace be with you all. So be it!

Paul's Final Greetings

16 [1-16] I entrust to you Phebe our sister, who is a church worker, which is at Cenchrea. I ask that you accept her in God, as Christians should, and that you assist her in whatever business she needs of you because she's helped many people, and myself also. Say hello to Priscilla and Aquila, my helpers in Christ Yeshua, who have for my life risked their own necks: to whom not only I give thanks, but also all the churches of the other peoples. Say hello also to the church that is in their house. Say hello to my dear loved one Epaenetus, who is the first one to be won for Christ in Achaia. Say hello to Mary, who worked very hard for us. Say hello to Andronicus and Junia, my kin people, and my prison mates, who are of note among the followers, who also were in Christ before me. Say hello to Amplias my dear loved one in God. Say hello to Urbane, our helper in Christ, and Stachys my dear loved one. Say hello to Apelles, who is approved in Christ. Say hello to those who are of Aristobulus' family. Say hello to Herodion my kinsman. Say hello to those who are of the family of Narcissus, which are in God. Say hello to Tryphena and Tryphosa, who work together in God. Say hello to my dear loved one Persis, who worked very hard in God. Say hello to Rufus, chosen in God, and his mother and mine. Say hello to Asyncritus, Phlegon, Hermas, Patrobas, Hermes, and the Christians which are with them. Say hello to Philologus, Julia, Nereus, their sister,

Olympas, and all the Christians which are with them. Say hello to one another with a kiss of love. The churches of Christ say hello to you as well.

Stay Away From Those Who Cause Disagreements

[17-20] Now I beg you, Christians, mark those who cause disagreements and upsets against the Word of God which you've learned; and stay away from them. Those who are like this don't serve our Christ Yeshua, but their own way; and by nice words and smooth speeches they mislead the hearts of innocent people. Your acceptance of the word is heard about by everyone. I am so happy on your behalf, but I still want you to be wise about what's good, and innocent about what's evil. And the God of peace will crush Satan under your feet shortly. The grace of our Christ Yeshua be with you. So be it!

[21-24] Timothy, my worker, Lucius, Jason, and Sosipater, my kin people, say hello to you. I, Tertius, who wrote this letter, says hello to you in God. Gaius, my host, and the whole church, says hello to you. Erastus, the officer of the city, says hello to you, and Quartus, a Christian. The grace of our Christ Yeshua be with you all. So be it!

[25-27] Now to the One who has the power to approve you by my New Word, and the preaching of Yeshua the Christ, for the revelation of the secret, which was kept secret since the world began, but is now made known, and by the words of the great preachers, for the Word of the everlasting God, made known to all nations for the acceptance of faith. To the God, who is only wise, be victory through Yeshua the Christ forever. So be it!

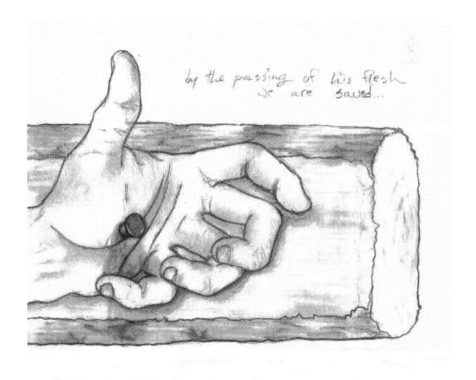

185

Paul's First Letter to the Corinthians

1 [1-3] From Paul, who am called to be a follower of Yeshua the Christ, through the will of God, and Sosthenes, our coworker, to the church of God, which is at Corinth, to those who are set apart in Christ Yeshua, called to be Christians, with everyone everywhere who call on the Name of Yeshua, our Christ, both theirs and ours: May God's grace and peace be with you, from the God we're from, and from Yeshua the Christ.

[4-9] I thank my God always for you, for God's grace which was given to you by Yeshua the Christ; who blessed you in everything, both in all your words, and in all your knowledge. This is proof of what you say about having Christ; so that you don't lack any gift, while waiting for the coming of our Christ Yeshua: Who will also prove you to the end, so that you can be found without fault in the day of our Christ Yeshua. God is faithful, who called you to the church of God's Child, Yeshua our Christ.

Denominations and Sects Forbidden

[10-17] Now I beg you, Christians, by the Name of our Christ Yeshua, that you all speak the same thing, and that there be no disagreements among you; but that you be completely joined together in the same mind and in the same judgment, because it has been told me of you, my Christians, by those who are from the house of Chloe, that there are disagreements among you. Now I say this, that all of you are saying, *"I am of Paul;"* or *"I am of Apollos;"* or *"I am of Peter;"* or *"I am of Christ."* Is Christ divided? Was Paul put to death for you? Or were you baptized in the Name of Paul? I thank God that I baptized none of you, but Crispus and Gaius, in case anyone should say that I had baptized them in my own name. I did baptize the family of Stephanas also, but besides that, I don't know if I baptized anyone else. Christ didn't send me to baptize, but to preach the New Word: not with any great words of wisdom, in case the cross of Christ would have no effect.

The Preaching of the Cross is Stupidity to Unbelievers

[18-31] The preaching of the cross is stupidity to those who are dying; but to us, which are saved, it's the power of God. The Word says, *"I'll silence the wisdom of the wise, and bring to stupidity the understanding of the sensible."* Where are the wise ones? Where are the lawyers? Where are the debaters of this world? Hasn't God made the wisdom of this world stupid? Since the world couldn't know God by it's own wisdom, in God's wisdom, God was pleased to save those who believe by the seeming stupidity of preaching. The Jews want physical proof, and the Greeks want wisdom: But when we preach Christ put to death, it's confusion to the Jews, and pure stupidity to the Greeks; but to those who are saved, of any race, Christ is the power and wisdom of God. And even the stupidity of God is wiser than that of humanity; and the weakness of God is stronger than that of humanity. So you see of your calling, Christians, how that few wise ones, few powerful ones, and few proud ones out of humanity are called: But God has chosen the stupid things of the world to puzzle the wise; and God has chosen the weak things of the world to defeat the things which are powerful; And the dishonorable things of the world, and things which are hated, God has chosen, yes, and things which aren't, to bring to nothing the things that are: So that nobody would be prideful in the presence of God. But by God, you are in Christ Yeshua, who is our wisdom, our goodness, our setting apart and blessing, and our saving; so that, like the Word says, *"Whoever is prideful, let them be proud in God."*

Spiritual Discernment

2 [1-8] Christians, when I came to you, I didn't come with great speech or wisdom, telling you the Word of God, because I decided not to teach anything to you, except Yeshua the Christ, and the Christ put to death. And I was with you in weakness and fear, trembling greatly. My speech and my preaching wasn't with the tempting words of humanity's wisdom, but in the showing of the Spirit and of power: So that your faith wouldn't stand in the wisdom of humanity, but in the power of God. But we speak wisdom to those who have become strong in the faith. Still, not the wisdom of this world, nor of the powers of this world, which will all come to nothing, but we speak the wisdom of God as a secret, yes, the hidden wisdom, which God set apart before the world was created for our victory: Which none of the rulers of this world knew, because if they had known it they wouldn't have put the Christ of victory to death.

[9-16] But as the Word says, *"No eye has seen, nor ear heard, nor the heart of any person imagined what has been prepared for those who love God."* But God has revealed these truths to us by the Spirit because the Spirit knows everything, yes, even the secrets of God. Who knows what is in someone, except the spirit of that person, which is in them? Like this, no one knows the things of God, but the Spirit of God. Now we have, not the spirit of the world, but the Spirit, which is of God; that we might know the things that are freely given to us by God. Which we also speak, not in the Words which human wisdom teaches, but which the Holy Spirit teaches; judging spiritual things against things that are spiritual. But the natural person doesn't accept the things of the Spirit of God

because it doesn't make sense to them. Nor can they understand it, because they're spiritually dead. But whoever is spiritually alive judges everything right, but still, they themselves aren't judged rightly by anyone. *"Who knows the mind of God, that they may teach God?"* But we have the knowledge of the mind of Christ.

Denominations and Sects Forbidden Again

3 [1-7] Christians, I couldn't speak to you as to the spiritually alive, but as to earthly people, just like new babies in Christ. So I've fed you with milk, and not with solid food, because to this point you weren't able to have it, nor are you able to yet, because you're still earthly. While there's jealousy, strife, and disagreements among you, aren't you earthly, and walk as earthly people? While one says, *"I am of Paul;"* and another says, *"I am of Apollos;"* Aren't you still being earthly? So who is Paul and who is Apollos then, but the ministers who brought you to faith, just as God gave to everyone? I've planted, Apollos watered; but God gave the increase. So then the one who plants is nothing, nor the one who waters; but only God who gives the harvest.

[8-17] Now whoever plants and whoever waters are one and the same and will all be rewarded for their own work. We're all coworkers with God: you're God's farmer's, you're God's builders. For God's grace, which has been given to me, as a wise master-builder, I've laid the foundation, and someone else built on it. But let everyone be careful how they build on it. No one can lay any other foundation than what has already been laid, which is Yeshua the Christ. Now if anyone builds on this foundation with gold, silver, precious stones, wood, hay, or stubble; It will become plain what every person's work is because it will be clearly seen on that day, becoming exposed by the fire, which will try everyone's work to see what kind it is. If anyone builds on a work, which isn't burned, they'll get a reward. But if someone's work is burned, they'll lose their reward, though they themselves will be saved; but still as though by fire. Don't you know that you're God's Place of Worship, and that the Spirit of God lives in you? So if anyone makes God's Place of Worship unfit, God will put them to death, because God's Place of Worship is holy, which you are.

[18-23] Let no one mislead themselves. If anyone among you seems to be wise in this world, let them become like an idiot, so that they can be wise; because the wisdom of this world is stupidity with God. The Word says, *"God catches the wise in their own scheming."* And again, "Yahweh God knows that the thoughts of the wise are meaningless." So let no one be prideful about these human beings, because everything is yours; Whether Paul, or Apollos, or Peter, or the world, or life, or death, or things present, or things to come; all these are yours; And you are Christ's; and Christ is God's.

Ministers of Christ

4 [1-7] So let people think of us as the ministers of Christ and managers of the secrets of God. Besides this, it's required of managers to be found faithful. But it doesn't matter to me that I'm judged by you, or by a human system of judgment: yes, and I don't even judge my own self, because I don't know everything myself; still I'm not excused by this: but the One who judges me is God. So don't judge anything before Christ comes, who will bring both the hidden things of darkness out into the light, and will make plain the thoughts of the hearts and then each one of us will be praised by God. And this, Christians, I've symbolically shifted to myself and to Apollos for your sakes; so that you might learn through us not to think in human terms above what is written, that none of you become prideful one over another. And who makes you different from one another? And what do you have that you weren't given? Now if you did accept it, why do you brag, as if you hadn't been given it?

Ministers Made Examples to the World

[8-21] Now you're full and rich, and you've ruled as rulers without us, and I hope to God that you do rule that we might also rule with you. But I think that God has put us followers last, as if we were chosen for death because we're made an example to the world, both to angels, and to human beings. We make ourselves foolish for Christ's sake, but you're wise in Christ; We're weak, but you're strong; You're respectable, but we're disrespected. Even to this day, we hunger, thirst, and are poorly clothed, and are beaten, and have no real home; And we work, working with our own hands; being hated, we bless; being abused, we suffer it; being defamed, we plead. And we're made as the filth of the world, and are the trash of all to this day. I don't write this to shame you, but as my dear loved children, I warn you. Even though you may have many teachers in Christ, still, you've only one who bore you, because in Christ Yeshua, you were born through me through the New Word. So I beg you, follow me. Because of this, I have sent Timothy to you, who is my own Child that I love, and faithful in God, who will bring you into remembrance of my ways which are in Christ, as I teach everywhere in every church. Now some are prideful, as though I wouldn't come to you. But I'll come to you shortly, if God wills it, and then I'll know, not the words of those who are prideful, but the power, because the realm of God isn't in word, but in power. What do you want? For me to come to you with force, or in love, and in the spirit of gentleness?

187

Immorality Destroys the Church

5 [1-5] It's commonly told that there's sexual sin among you, and such sexual sin as isn't so much as named among the other peoples, that one would have the spouse of one of their parents. And you're prideful, instead of crying over this, that the one who has done this might be taken away from among you. The truth is, being absent in body, but present in spirit, I have judged already, as though I were present, about those who have done this. In the Name of our Christ Yeshua, when you're gathered together, and my spirit, with the power of our Christ Yeshua, let Satan have such as this until they ruin their body, so that the spirit might be saved in the day of Christ Yeshua.

[6-8] Your bragging isn't good. Don't you know that just a little yeast leavens the whole lump of dough? So put out the ones who remain in their earthly ways, so that you can become a new lump of dough, as if you're unleavened. Even Christ, our Passover, is sacrificed for us: So let's keep the celebration, not with the leaven of our old ways, nor with the leaven of hatred and evil; but with the unleavened bread of honesty and truth.

Immorality is to be Judged by the Church and Separated from the Assembly

[9-13] I wrote to you before in a letter not to keep company with the sexually immoral: Yet you can't stay away from the sexually immoral of this world totally, or with the selfish, or cheats, or with those who worship falsely, because then you would need to completely leave the world. But I've written to you not to keep company with anyone called a Christian, who is a sexually immoral person, or is selfish, or worships other faiths, or is abusive, or a drunk, or a cheat; so don't keep company with these kinds of people. I've no business judging those that aren't in the faith. I only judge those who are thought of as Christians. But those who aren't in the faith God judges. So separate those evil people from among you.

Taking Legal Actions Against Christians

6 [1-11] If you have something against another, dare you take legal action in the earthly courts, instead of bringing it before the church? Don't you know that the Christians will judge the world? And if the world will be judged by you, aren't you worthy to judge things like this? Don't you know that we'll judge angels? How much more then, should we judge things that concern this life? If then you make judgments of things concerning this life, set them to judge who are least valued in the church. I speak to your shame. Is it so, that there isn't a wise person among you? No, not even one, who will be able to judge between one another? But someone takes legal action against another, and that to the courts of unbelievers! So there's quite a fault among you, because you take legal action against one another. Why don't you instead take wrong? Why don't you instead let yourselves be taken advantage of? But no, you do wrong, and take advantage of one another. Don't you know that the ungodly won't inherit the realm of God? Don't be misled: Neither the sexually immoral, nor those who worship falsely, nor those who are sexually unfaithful, nor cross-dressers, nor those who are homosexual, nor thieves, nor selfish, nor drunks, nor haters, nor cheats, will inherit the realm of God. And some of you were like this, but now you're clean and have a changed life; but now you're set apart; but now you're made right in the Name of Yeshua the Christ and by the Spirit of our God.

Give God Body and Spirit

[12-20] All things are legal to me, but everything isn't good for me. Even though everything is legal for me, I won't be controlled by anything. Food is for the body, and the body needs food: but God will put an end to both. Now the body isn't for sexual sin, but for God; and the body needs God. And God, who has brought Christ back to life, will also bring us back to life with great power. Don't you know that your bodies are the members of Christ's body? Should I then take the members of Christ, and make them the members of a sexually immoral person? Never! Don't you know that whoever is joined to a sexually immoral person is one body? The Christ said, when two are joined, they will become as one body. But whoever is joined to God is one spirit. So run from sexual sin! Every sin that someone does is outside the body; but whoever takes part in sexual sin sins against their own body. Don't you know that your body is the Place of Worship of the Holy Spirit which is in you, which you have from God? You aren't even your own, because you were bought for a price. So give God your body, and your spirit, which are both God's.

On Marriage

7 [1-7] Now about the things in which you wrote to me: It's good for someone not to be sexually active. But just the same, let every man have his own wife, and let every woman have her own husband to keep away from sexual sin. Let the husband give to the wife what is rightfully due her, and the same also the wife to the husband. The wife doesn't have complete control of her own body, but the husband shares it; and the same also, the husband doesn't have complete control of his own body, but the wife shares it. So don't cheat one another out of affection, unless it be with agreement for a specific time, so that you can willingly going without food and pray; then come together again, so that Satan doesn't tempt you for your lack of faithfulness. I give you permission for this, but I don't command it. I wish that everyone were just like I am. But everyone has their own gift of God, one person has one gift, and someone else has another gift.

Live as You are Called

[8-24] So I say to the unmarried, the widows, and the widowers, it's good for them if they can live without being sexually active just as I do. But if they can't control themselves, let them marry because it's better to marry than to be continually tempted with sexual immorality. And I say to the married, but not I, God, the wife shouldn't leave her husband; but if she must leave, let her stay single, or make up with her own husband; and the husband shouldn't divorce his wife. But to the rest, and this is what I think, but it's not God's command: If any Christian man has a wife that doesn't believe, and she is pleased to live with him, he shouldn't divorce her. And the Christian woman who has a husband that doesn't believe, and that is pleased to live with her, let her not leave him. Because the unbelieving husband is set apart by the wife, and the unbelieving wife is set apart by the husband: or else your children would be ungodly; but now they're blessed. But if the unbeliever leaves, let them leave. A Christian brother or sister isn't trapped in such cases, because God has called us to be in peace. And how do you know, wife, whether you'll save your husband? Or how do you know, husband , whether you'll save your wife? But use the gifts that God has given to you, and stay just as you were called by God. And I ordain this in all the churches. If someone is called in a higher social standing, don't let them look for lower social standing. If someone is called in a lower social standing, then don't let them look for a higher social standing. What situation you are in is unimportant, but the keeping of the Words of God is what is truly important. Let everyone live the same way they were called. Are you called being a hired worker? Don't worry about it, but if you can become free to do your own business, then take the chance to do that instead. Because whoever is called in God, being a worker, is free in God. In the same way also, whoever is called, being free, is Christ's worker. You're bought with a price; so don't work for what ungodly people want. Christians, let everyone else live in God just as they were called.

On the Unmarried and the Widows

[25-40] Now about those who have never been sexually active, I have no Word of God, but still I give my judgment, as someone that has found the mercy of God to be faithful. I think that this is good for the present problem, I say, that it's good for someone to be like one who has never been sexually active. Are you married? Don't look to be separated. Are you separated from a spouse? Don't look for a spouse. But if you do marry, you haven't sinned; and if those who have never been sexually active get married, they haven't sinned. Just the same, they'll have trouble in the physical realm, but I would like to spare them that. But I say this, Christians, the time left is short; so those who have spouses should be as though they didn't have one; And those who cry, as though they didn't cry; and those who celebrate, as though they didn't celebrate; and those who buy, as though they didn't have anything; And those who use this world, as not abusing it, because the way of this world is coming to an end. But I wouldn't have you worry. Whoever is unmarried cares for the things that concern God, and how they can please God; but whoever is married cares for the things that are of the world, and how they can please their spouses. There's a difference also between a married person and one who has never been sexually active. The unmarried cares for the things of God, so that they can be holy both in body and in spirit; but whoever is married cares for the things of the world, how they can please their spouses. I say this for your own good; not that I want to limit you, but to tell you what is acceptable, and so that you can serve God without being pulled in two different directions at once. But if anyone thinks that they behaved unwisely toward their promised one, if their youth is passing them by, and their needs demand it, then let them do whatever they have vowed in their heart. But if they can keep the one who has never been sexually active pure, they do well. So then whoever gives themselves in marriage does well; but whoever doesn't give themselves in marriage does better. A spouse is bound by law as long as the other spouse lives; but if one spouse dies, the other is free to be married to whoever they want, as long as they are both Christians. But they'll be happier if they live as I have said: and I think that I do have the Spirit of God.

Don't Use Your Freedom to Harm Others' Consciences

8 [1-13] Now about things used for the worship of other faiths, we know that we all have knowledge. Knowledge is full of self-importance, but love builds up others. And if anyone thinks that they know anything, they don't know anything as they should. But if anyone loves God, this person is known by God. As about the eating of what is offered in worship of other faiths, we know that something worshiped falsely isn't anything in the world but a statue, and that there's no other God but One. Though there are other things that are called gods, whether in heaven or in earth, (as there are many gods, and many saviors,) there's only One God to us, the God, who is the Creator of everything, and we're in God; and have One Savior, Yeshua the Christ, through whom everything exists, and we live through Christ. But everyone doesn't have that knowledge, because some with consciences of the false worship still to this time, eat it as a thing used to worship something falsely; and their consciences being

189

weak are ruined. But food doesn't commit us to God, because if we eat, we aren't any better; and if we don't eat, we aren't any worse. But be careful that this freedom of yours doesn't become a problem in some way to those who are weaker. So if anyone who has knowledge takes a meal in their place of false worship, won't the conscience of those who are weak be encouraged to eat what is offered in false worship; And through your knowledge won't the weak Christian be ruined, for whom Christ died? But when you sin this way against the Christians, and wound their weak consciences, you sin against Christ. So if certain foods makes me offend other Christians, then I won't eat it while the world is still here, because I might offend another Christian.

On the Rights of A Follower of Christ

9 [1-10] Am I not a follower? Am I not free? Haven't I seen Yeshua the Christ, our Savior? Aren't you my work in God? If I am not a follower to others, still doubtless, I am to you, because you're the proof of my work in God. My answer to those who question me is this: Don't we have the right to eat and to drink? Don't we have the right to take with us a spouse, too, as the other followers do, and as the families of Yeshua, and Peter do? Or do only Barnabas and I have no right to take time off? Who goes to fight at their own expense? Who plants a garden and doesn't eat its fruit? Or who feeds a herd, and doesn't drink the milk from the herd? Do I say this as just a person? Or doesn't the Word of God say the same things also? The Word of God says by Moses, "You shouldn't muzzle the mouth of the cow that treads out the grain." Doesn't God take care of the cow? Or was it said for our own sakes? It was said for our sakes, no doubt, because it's written that "Whoever plows should plow in hope; and that "Whoever threshes in hope, should get from what they had hoped."

Give the New Word of Christ without Charge

[11-19] If we've planted to you spiritual things, is it a great thing if we pick your earthly things? If others have this right over you, shouldn't we have more right than they? Just the same, we haven't even used this right; but suffer through everything, so we won't hinder the New Word of Christ. Don't you know that those who minister in holy things live off the things from the Place of Worship? And those who serve at the altar take from what is brought to the altar? Just like this, God has said that those who preach the New Word would live off of preaching the New Word. But I've used none of these rights, nor have written this, that it would be this way to me, because it would be better for me to die, than for anyone to make my bragging of no use. Though I preach the New Word, I don't have anything to brag about, because it's necessary for me; yes, how sorry I would be, if I didn't preach the New Word! But if I do this thing willingly, I'll get a reward, but if it is against my will, I've been trusted with the responsibility of the New Word. What is my reward then? The truth is, that when I preach the New Word, I give the New Word of Christ without charge, so that I don't abuse my power in the New Word. And though I am free from everyone, still I have made myself worker to all, so that my reward will be greater.

On Self-Control

[20-27] And to the Jews I became like a Jew, that I might win over the Jews; to those who are bound by the Law, as though I were bound by the Law, that I might win those who are bound by the Law; And to those who are without law, as without law, (not being without law to God, but under the law to Christ,) that I might win those who are without law. To the weak I became as the weak, that I might win the weak: I become everything to everybody, so that I might in some way save some. And I do this for the New Word's sake, that I might share in it with you. Don't you know that those who run in a race all run, but only one wins the prize? So run to win. And everyone that wants to win is paced in everything. Now they do it to get a prize that won't last; but we work for an everlasting prize. So I run with a purpose; and I fight, not as someone that only swings at the air: But I use self-control, in case in some way, after I've preached to others, I myself would be rejected.

Examples of Sin from the Old Agreement

10 [1-13] Besides this, Christians, I want you to know of how all our ancestors walked under the cloud, and walked through the sea; And all of them were baptized to Moses in the cloud and in the sea; And all of them ate the same spiritual food; And all drank the same spiritual drink because they drank of that spiritual Rock that followed them: and that Rock was Christ. But God wasn't pleased with many of them so they died out in the countryside. Now these were our examples, so that we wouldn't want the evil things that they wanted. So don't be like those who worship falsely, as some of them were; as the Word says, *"The people sat down to eat and drink, and got up to play around."* So don't join in sexual sin, as some of them did, and twenty-three thousand of them fell in one day. And don't tempt Christ, as some of them did, and were killed by snakes. And don't whisper complaints, as some of them did, and were killed by the One who destroys all. Now all this happened to them for our example: and they're written for our warning, on us who the end of the world now comes. So let those who thinks they stand be careful in case they fall. You will face no temptation but what is common to all humanity; but God is faithful, who won't let you be tempted more than what you're able to handle; but will make a way for you to escape along with the temptation, so that you'll be able to handle it.

On False Worship

[14-24] So, my dear loved ones, stop worshiping falsely. I speak as to the wise; so judge what I say. Isn't the sharing of the blood of Christ the cup of blessing which we bless? Isn't the sharing of the body of Christ the bread which we break? And we being many are one bread, and one body, because we're all one who have taken part of that One bread. Look at Israel. Aren't those who eat of the sacrifices those who have taken part in the worship at the altar? What am I saying then? That something worshiped falsely is anything, or what is offered in sacrifice to statues is anything? But what I am saying is that the things which the other peoples sacrifice, they sacrifice to evil spirits, and not to God; and I don't want you to have anything to do with evil spirits. You can't drink the cup of Christ, and the cup of evil spirits. You can't share in God's table, and in the table of evil spirits. Aren't we provoking God to jealousy? Are we stronger than God? I have a right to do anything, but everything isn't needed; And though I have a right to do anything, everything isn't for the best. Don't look out only for your own good, but everyone should look out for the good of one another.

Do Your Best to Offend No One

[25-33] So eat whatever is sold in the meat market, and for the sake of your conscience, don't ask any questions, because the whole earth is God's, and everything in it. And if any of those who don't believe call you to a celebration, and you want to go; eat whatever is set before you, and don't ask any questions for the sake of your conscience. But if anyone says to you, *"This is offered in sacrifice for false worship;"* don't eat it for the sake of the one who told you, and for conscience sake, because the earth is God's, and everything in it. When I say conscience, I mean the other person's, because why should my freedom be judged by another person's conscience? Because if I, by grace, am one who has shared, why am I evil spoken of for what I give thanks? So whether you eat, or drink, or whatever you do, do it all in praise of God. Do your best to offend no one, not the Jews, nor the other peoples, nor the church of God, just as I try to please everyone in everything, not looking out for my own good only, but for the good of many, so that they might be saved.

On Order of Public Worship

11 [1-16] Be followers of me, just as I am of Christ also. Christians, I praise you because you remember me in everything, and willingly do what I have told you. But I want you to know, that man's power comes from Christ; and the woman's power comes from the man; and Christ's power comes from God. Every man praying or preaching, having their head covered, dishonors their authority. But every woman that prays or preaches with her bare head dishonors her authority, because that is just as if her head was shaved. If the woman isn't covered, she may as well be shaved. So if it's shameful for a woman to have her head shaved, she should be covered as well. Men shouldn't cover their head, because they're a picture and reflection of God: but woman is the reflection of man. The man isn't from the woman; but the woman from the man. And the man wasn't created for the woman; but the woman to be the helper of the man. Because of this, the woman should have a symbol of authority on her head when she prays or preaches because of the angels who are present. Just the same, the man isn't free from the woman, nor the woman free from the man, in God. Just as the woman is of the man, in the same way the man is also by the woman; but everything is of God. Judge for yourselves: is it good for a woman to pray to God with her head bared? Doesn't even nature itself teach you, that, if a man has long hair, it's shameful? But if a woman has long hair, it's a praise to her because her hair is her covering. But if anyone wants to argue about it, we don't practice this way of life, nor do any of the churches of God.

On the Celebration of the Last Supper

[17-34] In this that I tell you now, I don't praise you, because you come together for bad, rather than for good. First of all, when you come together in the church, I hear that there are disagreements among you; and I only know part of it. But there must be differences among you, to show clearly which of you are approved by God. So when you come together into one place, this isn't to eat the Christ's supper, because when you eat, everyone takes their own supper before the others: and one is hungry, and another is drunk. Don't you have homes to eat and drink in? Or do you hate the church of God, and want to shame those who don't have anything? What should I tell you? Should I praise you in this? No, I don't praise you. I've gotten from Christ what I have given to you, that the same night in which Christ Yeshua was handed over, the Christ took the bread, gave thanks, then broke it, saying, *"Take and eat: this is the symbol of my body, which is broken for you: do this to remember Me."* Then the Christ also took the cup, after they had eaten, saying, *"This cup is the New Word written in my blood: do this, as often as you drink it, to remember Me."* And as often as you eat this bread, and drink this cup, you show Yeshua's death till the Christ comes again. So whoever eats this bread, and drinks this cup of Christ, being unworthy, will be guilty of the body and blood of Christ. But everyone should question themselves, before they eat of that bread, or drink of that cup, because whoever eat and drinks, being unworthy, eats and drinks damnation to themselves, not understanding Christ's body. This is why so many of you are weak and sickly, and many more are dead. If we

judged ourselves, we wouldn't be judged by others. But when we're judged, we're corrected by God, so that we won't be punished with the rest of the world. So, Christians, when you come together to eat, wait for one another. And if anyone hungers, let them eat at home, so that you don't come together and bring judgment on yourselves. And I'll set everything else in order when I come.

Different Spiritual Gifts, Same Spirit

12 [1-11] Now about spiritual gifts, Christians, I wouldn't have you without knowledge. You know that when you were like the other peoples, you yourselves were swayed by these dumb statues, just as you were led to believe. So I want you to understand that no one speaking by the Spirit of God can curse Yeshua, and that no one can say that Yeshua is God but by the Holy Spirit. Now there are differences in your spiritual gifts, but you all have the same Spirit. And there are differences in the ways you worship, but you worship the same Christ. And there are differences in the way you serve, but it's the same God who works in everything in all Christians. But the appearance of the Spirit is given to each of you for the good of all Christians. The Word of wisdom is given to some by the Spirit; to others the Word of knowledge by the same Spirit; To others faith by the same Spirit; to others the gifts of healing by the same Spirit; To others the working of amazing things; to others the Word of things to come; to others the understanding of spirits; to another different kinds of languages; to another the interpretation of languages: But the same Spirit does all of these things and gives to everyone as the Christ wants to.

Different Members, Same Body

[12-18] As there are many parts in one body and all the members of that one body, being many, make up the body, so also is Christ. By One Spirit we're all baptized into One body, whether we're one race or another, whether we work for someone else or for ourselves; and we have all been made to drink into One Spirit. So the body of Christ isn't just one member, but many different members. If the foot says, *"because I am not the hand, I am not part of the body;"* is it not still part of the body? And if the ear says, *"because I am not the eye, I am not part of the body;"* is it not still part of the body? If the whole body were an eye, how would it hear? If the whole body were an ear, how would it smell? So each member has been put in the body, just as God pleased. And if everyone was the same part, how would there be a body?

[20-31] But now there are many parts, but still one body. And the eye can't say to the hand, "I don't need you;" nor the head to the feet, "I don't need you." No, but those members of the body, which seem to be less needed, are still necessary. Those members of the body, which we think to be less needed, we take better care of; and even our private parts are given special treatment and our exposed parts don't need anything. So God has put the body together, in such a way as to give more honor to those parts which lack it, so that there would be no separation in the body; but that the members would have the same care for one another. And if one member suffers, all the members suffer; or when one member is honored, all the members celebrate. Now you're all the body of Christ, and members in particular. And God has set some in the church, first traveling messengers, second preachers, third teachers, after that, those who do amazing things, then those who can heal, then helpers, then overseers, and finally those who speak in different languages. Can they all be traveling messengers? Can they all be great preachers? Can they all be teachers? Do all do amazing things? Do all have the gift of healing? Do all speak in different languages? Do all interpret them? You should want the best gifts, but still I'll show you a better way.

Love Lasts, Other Gifts will End

13 [1-3] Though I speak with both human and spiritual languages, if I don't have love, I'm just making noise. And though I have the gift of preaching, and can understand all secrets, and all knowledge; and though I have great faith, so that I could move mountains, but don't have love, I'm nothing. And though I give all my earthly goods to take care of those who are poor, and though I give my body to be burned, but don't have love, it does me no good.

[4-13] Love puts up with much suffering, and is kindhearted; love doesn't get jealous; love doesn't use force and doesn't consider itself better than others, doesn't behave poorly, doesn't try to get its own way, isn't easily aggravated, doesn't blame others wrongly; doesn't approve of sin, but of the truth; takes responsibility in everything, believes everything, hopes for everything, lasts through everything. Love always lasts. Preaching will come to an end; languages will come to an end; and knowledge will come to an end. All our knowledge is incomplete, and even our preaching is incomplete. But when what is complete is here, then what is incomplete will come to an end. As a child, I spoke like a child, I took things in like a child, I thought like a child: but as an adult, I gave up those childish ways. Now we see as if through a piece of darkly tinted glass; but then we'll see Christ face to face. Now I know only partly; but then I'll know just as I am known. And now these three are what will really last: faith, hope, and love; and the greatest of these is love.

192

On Speaking in Unknown Languages

14 [1-19] Ask for love, and ask for spiritual gifts, but more than that, ask that you may preach. Whoever speaks in an unknown spiritual language doesn't speak to humans, but to God, because no one understands them; even though they speak secrets in the spirit. But whoever preaches speaks to others to make them strong, to encourage them, and to comfort them. Whoever speaks in a spiritual language makes themselves strong; but whoever preaches makes those of the church strong. I wish that all of you could speak with spiritual languages, but I would rather that you preach, because the one who preaches is more important than the one who speaks with spiritual languages, unless it can be interpreted, so that the church may be made strong. Now, Christians, if I come to you speaking with all kinds of languages, what good will I do you, unless I speak to you either by revelation, or by knowledge, or by preaching, or by teaching? And even things without life giving sounds, like a flute or a harp, unless it makes a difference in its sounds, how can we know what is played? If the trumpet gives an unknown sound, who will know to get ready for the battle? So in the same way, unless you speak words that are easy to understand, how can anyone know what you speak? You may as well speak into the air. There are, it can be, so many kinds of voices in the world, and none of them are without significance. So if I don't know the meaning of the voice, I'll be like a foreigner to those who speak, and whoever speaks will be like a foreigner to me. Just the same, since you're passionate of spiritual gifts, be sure to pray for those which build up the church. And let those who speak in a spiritual language pray that they can interpret, because if I pray in an unknown language, my spirit prays, but I don't understand what I pray. So what am I saying then? I'll pray in the spirit, and I'll pray with understanding also; I'll sing in the spirit, and I'll sing with understanding, also. Or else, when you bless with the spirit, how will those in the room who haven't heard the Word say *"So be it"* at your giving of thanks, seeing they don't understand what you say? The truth is, you gives thanks well, but they aren't helped at all. I thank my God that I speak with these languages more than you all. Yet in the church, I would rather speak five words with my understanding, that by My voice I might teach others also, than ten thousand words in an unknown language.

[20-25] So, everyone, don't be like children in understanding, even though you should be like children in anger; but in understanding, be adults. In the Word of God it says, *"With those of other languages and other lips I'll speak to this people; but in the same way, they won't hear Me, God said."* So these languages are for a sign for unbelievers, not to those who believe. But preaching is for those who believe, and not for unbelievers. So if the whole church has come together, and everyone speaks in an unknown spiritual language, and those that haven't heard the Word before, or are either unbelievers come in, won't they say that you're crazy? But if everyone preaches clearly, and someone comes in that doesn't believe, or hasn't ever heard the Word before, they'll be won over by everyone, and they'll be judged by everyone. So the secrets of their hearts are made clear; and they will bow their heads and worship God, and say that God is truly in you.

On Orderly Worship, speaking in Spiritual Languages, Women

[26-40] How is it then, Christians, that when you come together, everyone has a song, a word, a spiritual language, a revelation, or an interpretation? Let everything be done to benefit of all. If anyone speaks in an unknown language, let it be by two, or at the most three, and that in turn; and let someone interpret it. But if there isn't an interpreter, let them not speak out in the church; but let them speak quietly to themselves, and to God. Let two or three preachers speak, and let someone else judge what they speak. If anything is made known to someone else there, let the first speaker be quiet. Now, you can all preach one by one, so that everyone can learn, and be in good spirits. And the spirits of the preachers are responsible to the preachers. God doesn't bring confusion, but peace, as it should be in all churches of the Christians. And your women shouldn't speak out in a disorderly manner in the churches either, because it isn't permitted for them to speak out this way; but they're told to be helpful, as the Word of God says. And if they have questions, they should ask their husbands about it at home because it's a shame for women to speak out disorderly in the church. Did the Word of God come from you? Or did it come to you only? If anyone thinks of themselves as a preacher, or spiritual, let them acknowledge that the things that I write to you are the Words of God. But if anyone is without knowledge, let them be without knowledge. Christians, you should want to preach, and don't forbid anyone to speak in spiritual languages. But let everything be done properly and in order.

The Evidence of Christ Coming to Life Again

15 [1-11] Besides this, Christians, I tell you the New Word, which I preached to you, and which you've accepted, and in which you take your stand; And you'll be saved by it, if you keep in mind what I preached to you, unless you really didn't believe it. And I've given you only what I was given first of all, how that Christ died for our sins as the Word says; And Who was buried, and rose again on the third day, as the Word says: And that the Christ was seen by Peter, then by the twelve: And after that, the Christ was seen by more than five hundred Christians at once; of whom most are still with us today, though some are now dead. After that, the Christ was seen by James; then by all the followers. And last of all, I saw the Christ myself, at just the right time. And I am the

193

least important of the followers, who has no right to even be called a follower, because I abused the church of God. But by God's grace, I am what I am; and the grace which was given to me wasn't meaningless because I have worked more than all of them. Still, not I, but by God's grace, who was with me. So, whether it was me or them, we preached, and you believed.

Our Hope is in Christ

[12-23] Now, if it's preached that the Christ rose from the dead, how do some of you say that there's no coming to life again from the dead? If there is no coming to life again from the dead, then is Christ not raised? And if Christ isn't risen, then our preaching is meaningless, and your faith is also meaningless. Yes, and we're found false witnesses of God because we've told you that God brought Christ back to life: whom God hasn't raised up, if it is true that the dead don't come to life again. If the dead don't come to life again, then Christ hasn't been raised: And if Christ hasn't been raised, your faith is meaningless and you're still in your sins. Then those who have died in Christ have been destroyed forever. If our hope is in Christ for this life only, we're the saddest of all people. But Christ has come back to life, and is the first fruits of those who died. Since death came by one human being, new life came by a human being for the dead. Just as all die in Adam, everyone who is in Christ will live. But everyone in their own time: Christ the first fruits; Later, those who are in Christ at the Christ's second coming.

[24-34] Then the end will come, when Christ will give up the realm to Yahweh God; when the Christ puts down all right, rule, and power. And Christ must reign, till all enemies are in Christ's control. Then, the last enemy that the Christ will put an end to, is death itself. *"Because God has put everything in Christ's control."* But when God said, everything is in Christ's control, it's plain that God isn't included in this, who put everything in Christ's control. And when everything is under Christ's control, then the Christ will be responsible also to the One who put everything in the Christ's control, so that God may be Ruler over everything. Or else why would some be baptized for the dead, if the dead don't come to life again at all? Why are they then baptized in the place of those who are dead? And why do we put ourselves in danger all the time? I say by the joy which I have in Yeshua our Christ, I die daily. If I follow after the way of a human being only, and I fight with animals at Ephesus, how does that help me, if the dead don't come to life again? *"Let's just eat and drink, because tomorrow we die."* Don't be misled: evil people make good people do bad things. Awake and be good, and don't sin, because some of you don't really know God. I say this to your shame.

The New Body

[35-44] But some are asking, *"How are the dead brought back? And what kind of body will they have?"* You idiot, what you plant isn't brought back to life again, unless it dies: And what you plant, isn't the body that will be, but it's like bare grain, maybe wheat, or some other grain, but it is given a body as it pleases God, and every seed will have its own body. Every physical body isn't the same: but the human body is of one kind, the body of animals is another kind, fish have another, and birds have another. There are also heavenly bodies, and earthly bodies: but the light of the heavenly is one kind, and the light of the earthly is another. The sun has one kind of light, and the moon has another, and the stars have another kind, because one star differs from another in its strength. So is the new life also of those who come to life again from the dead. Though it's planted in sinfulness; when it's raised it will be sinless: It's planted in disgrace; but will be raised in victory: it's planted in the weakness of death; but will be raised in the power of everlasting life: It's planted a natural body; but will be raised a spiritual body. So there's a natural body, and there's a spiritual body.

Christ Gives the New Life

[45-58] And so the Word says, *"The first human being, Adam, was given life by the Spirit; the last Adam, the Christ, was given a Spirit that gives life."* But what is spiritual didn't come first, but what is natural came first; and then what is spiritual. The first person was of the earth, and made of earth: the second person is God from heaven. As the earthly one was, so are those who are earthly: and as the Heavenly One is, so also will be those who are heavenly. And as we're like the earthly, we'll also be like the Heavenly One. Now I say this, Christians, that our human bodies can't go into the realm of God; nor do evil people get spiritual bodies. I'll tell you a secret; We won't all die, but we'll all be changed, in a split second, in the blink of an eye, at the last sounding of the trumpet, the dead in Christ will be raised to everlasting life, and we'll all be changed. This sinful body must put on a sinless one, and this human body must put on a spiritual body. So when this sinful body has put on a sinless one, and this human body has put on spiritual one, then this saying that is written will come true: *"Death is swallowed up in victory. Where is the sting of death? Where is the victory of the grave?"* The sting of death is sin; and the strength of sin is the Word of God. But thanks be to God, who gives us the victory through our Christ Yeshua. So, my dear Christians, be firm and unmoved, always doing well in the work Christ gives you, so that you know your work isn't meaningless in Christ.

194

Offerings and Support of Ministers and Other Christians

16 [1-9] Now, about the collection for the Christians, as I've told the churches of Galatia, do this as well. Every Sunday, let everyone of you bring the money you have to give, as God has given you, so that there won't have to be a collection when I come. And when I come, whoever you approve by your letters, I'll send to bring your kindness to Jerusalem. And if it's possible that I go also, they'll go with me. Now I'll come to you, whenever I pass through Macedonia, because I'll go that way. And it may be that I'll stay, yes, and even spend the winter with you, so that you can send me on my journey wherever I go next. So I won't see you now on the way, but I trust to stay with you for a while, if God allows it. But I'll stay at Ephesus until Pentecost because a great chance for useful ministry has come to me, and there are many enemies.

[10-18] Now if Timothy comes, make sure he has nothing to fear while with you, because he is doing the work of Christ, as I am. So make sure he's not rejected and send him away in peace, so that he can come back to me, because I'm waiting for him to come with the other Christians. Now about our coworker Apollos, I really wanted him to come to you with the other Christians, but he didn't want to come at all right now; but he'll come when he has the time. So watch, stay in the faith, act like adults, and be strong. And do everything in love. I beg you, Christians, because you know that those of the family of Stephanas are the first Christians of Achaia, and that they've completely given themselves to the ministry of the Christians, that you cooperate with people like this, and to everyone else who helps us, and does the work of Christ. I'm happy about the coming of Stephanas, Fortunatus, and Achaicus, because they've given me what you couldn't. They've awakened both my spirit and yours, so accept people like this.

Final Greetings

[19-24] The churches of Asia say hello to you. Aquila and Priscilla say hello to you most lovingly in Christ, along with the church that meets in their house. All the coworkers in Christ say hello to you. Say hello to one another with a kiss of love. This is the greeting of me, Paul, written with my own hand. If anyone doesn't love Yeshua the Christ, let them be damned! Come, Christ Yeshua! May the grace of our Christ Yeshua be with you. I send my love to you all in Christ Yeshua. So be it!

Untitled

by

Rob Hatfield

195

Paul's Second Letter to the Corinthians

The God of Every Comfort

1 [1-11] From Paul, a follower of Yeshua the Christ, by the will of God, and Timothy our coworker in Christ, to the church of God, which is at Corinth, and all the Christians, which are in all Achaia: May you have the grace and peace from Yahweh our God, and from Yeshua the Christ. May Yahweh God be blessed, the God our Christ Yeshua comes from, the God all mercies come from, and the God all comforts come from; Who comforts us in all our troubles, so that we may be able to comfort those, who are in any kind of trouble, with the same kind of comfort that we ourselves have been comforted with by God. As we have suffered much for Christ, so we'll be comforted much by Christ. And if we're troubled, it's for your comfort and to help you to be saved, which is what helps us to keep going in what we suffer: or if we're in good spirits now, it's for your comfort and to help you to be saved. And our hope for you is strong, knowing that just as you've taken part in the suffering, so you'll be comforted. Christians, we want you to know of our trouble which came to us in Asia, that we were troubled more than ever, more than our own strength, so that we even lost all hope of life. We had a death sentence in us, so that we wouldn't trust in ourselves, but in God who raises the dead: Who saved us from such a great a death, and so saves us: in whom we trust that even now, will still save us. You've also helped by praying for us, that many more people will give thanks in our place, for the gift given to us by the answered prayers of many of you.

We Have a Clear Conscience

[12-24] Our joy is that our conscience tells us by God's grace that we've lived in the world with simple and godly honesty, not with earthly wisdom, and even more so with you. We write to you no other faith than what you've read or already know; and I trust you'll know this even to the end of your days; As in a way, you've also accepted that we're your joy, just as you'll also be our joy in the day of Christ Yeshua. And in this trust, I was thinking of coming to you, so that you might have a second chance to do a good thing; And to pass by you into Macedonia, and to come back out of Macedonia to you, and to be sent on my way again by you to Judea. Do you think I thought of this without thinking it through? Or do the things that I plan, come from my own human thinking, that I would say both yes and no at the same time? But as God is true, our word to you wasn't unreliable, saying both yes and no at the same time. The Child of God, Yeshua the Christ, who was preached among you by us, even by me, Silvanus, and Timothy, wasn't yes and no, but in Christ, was always yes. And all the promises of God are "Yes" in Christ, and in Christ, we say "So be it" to the praise of God. Now the One who creates all of us in Christ, and has chosen us is God; Who has also put the proof of ownership on us, and given us this proof by the Spirit in our hearts. Besides this, I call on God for a defense of my soul that the reason I didn't come to you was to spare you. Not that we have any control over your faith, but that we could help you to have joy, because it's by faith that you keep on going.

Overcome with Love, not Sorrow

2 [1-7] But I decided on this in myself, that I wouldn't come back to you in sorrow. If I make you sorry, who can make me happy, but the ones who are made sorry by me? And I wrote this to you, in case, when I came, I would have sorrow from the very ones I should have joy in; having trust in you all, that my joy is the same joy that you all have. In much suffering and heartbreak, I wrote to you in tears; not that you would be upset, but that you might know the great love that I have for you. But if anyone has caused sorrow, in a way, they haven't caused me sorrow, as much as they've caused you sorrow: not to put it too unkindly. And they have had enough punishment from you all. So instead, you should forgive and comfort them, or they may be overcome with too much sorrow.

[8-17] So I beg you to prove your love to them. It was for this reason that I wrote, that I might know for sure if you do what you should. And whoever you forgive, I forgive also, and if I forgave anything, I forgave it for your sakes in Christ; Just in case Satan would get a hold on us, for we know of the ways of evil. And when I came to Troas to preach Christ's New Word, and a door was opened to me by God, my spirit would not rest, because I didn't find Titus, my coworker in Christ: so I left there, and went on to Macedonia. Now thanks to God, who always helps us to have victory in Christ, and spreads the scent of the knowledge of the Savior by us everywhere. We're like a sweet scent of Christ to God, in those who are saved, and in those who are destroyed: To one we're the scent of death that leads to death; and to the other the scent of life that leads to life. And who is enough for this? We aren't like many, who sell the Word of God for money, but we're sent from God in truth, and in the sight of God we speak in Christ.

We Are Ministers Not of the Letter of the Law, but of the Spirit of the Law

3 [1-11] So should we start to say good things about ourselves again to you? Or do we need, as some others do, letters of approval to you, or letters of approval from you? Our letter is you, written in our hearts, known and read by everyone. So you're clearly told to be like a letter from Christ written by us, but not written with ink on pieces of paper, but with the Spirit of the living God, written in the pages of the human heart. And we have this trust through Christ in God: Not that we're enough in and of ourselves to think anything much of ourselves; but we're enough in God; Who has also made us able to be ministers of the New Word; not of the letter of the Law, but of the spirit of the Law, because the letter kills without mercy, but the spirit of grace gives life. But if the way of death, which was written and carved in stones, was so amazing that the children of Israel couldn't hardly look at the face of Moses for its brightness; which was already beginning to fade away: Won't the way of the spirit be even more amazing? And if the way of judgment is so amazing, how much more amazing will the goodness of grace be. And even what was amazing then isn't amazing at all compared to the amazement of the goodness of the grace we have now. And if what passed away was amazing, how much more amazing is that grace that we have forever.

[12-18] Seeing then that we have such hope, we speak as plainly as we can: And not as Moses, who put a covering over his face, so that the children of Israel couldn't hardly see him until the brightness had faded away: But their minds were blinded because even to today, the same covering is still there when the Old Word is read; which is only taken away in Christ. Even to today, when Moses is read, the covering stays on their hearts. But in the same way, when someone turns to Christ, the covering is taken away. Now Christ is that Spirit: and where the Spirit of Christ is, there's freedom. But we all, with uncovered faces, as if looking in a mirror, see the light of Christ in us, as we're changed into the likeness of Christ with more and more goodness, as we're given by the Spirit of Christ.

We Don't Give Up

4 [1-12] So seeing that we've been given this ministry by the mercy of Christ, we don't give up; But we've given up the secret ways of dishonesty, not being tricky, nor handling the Word of God falsely; but by clearly stating the truth entrusting ourselves to everyone's conscience in the sight of God. But if our New Word is covered, only those who are lost can't see it: The god of this world has blinded the minds of those who don't believe, unless the light of the amazing New Word of Christ, who is the picture of God, shines on them. And we don't preach about ourselves, but Yeshua the Christ as being God; and ourselves your workers for Yeshua's sake. And God, who told the light to shine out of the darkness, has shined in our hearts to give us the light of the knowledge of the victory of God in the face of Yeshua the Christ. But this wealth of knowledge is kept in human beings, so that others can know that this great power is of God, and not us. And though we're troubled from all sides, still we're not greatly upset; We're confused, but not hopeless; Mistreated, but not left alone; pushed down, but not broken; We're always suffering the death of Christ Yeshua in our human bodies, so that the life of Christ might also be known in our human bodies. And we who live are always giving ourselves up for dead for Yeshua' sake, so that the life of Yeshua also might be known in our human bodies. So then death is working in us, so that life can work in you.

[13-18] And having the same spirit of faith, just like the Word says, *"I believed, and so I speak;"* we also believe, and we speak; Knowing that Yahweh God, who brought back Christ Yeshua, will also raise us up by Yeshua, and will offer us, along with you. And everything is for your sakes, that the amazing grace, having come to many people, would let their thankfulness overflow in the praise of God. And so we don't give up; but though our outward lives are destroyed, still the inward life is renewed each and every day. And our suffering, which lasts only a little while, gives us a victory that far outlasts anything we go through now; So we don't look at the things which we see, but at the things which we don't see, because the things which are seen are only temporary; but the things which aren't seen will last forever.

The Judgment Seat of Christ

5 [1-10] And we know that if our earthly body that we live in were to be destroyed, we have a heavenly body in God, which isn't like our human bodies, but will last forever in heaven. But in this body we cry, actively hoping to be clothed with our heavenly body: So if it's true that we're clothed, we won't be without it. And though we that are in this body cry, being greatly troubled: not that we want to be unclothed, but clothed with our heavenly body, so that our human body might be completely covered with life. Now the One who has created us for this same reason is God, who has also given to us the Spirit as proof. So we're always sure, knowing that, while we're in our bodies, we're separated from God, but because we walk by faith, and not by sight, we're sure, I say, instead to even be willing to leave this body to be with God. So we work, that, whether here or there, we can be accepted by God, because we all have to appear at the judgment seat of Christ; so that everyone can get back what they're owed for the things they did in their body, whether it was good or bad.

[11-16] So knowing the fear of God, we try to change the minds of others; and though it's clear to God who we are; I trust also that in your consciences we are made clear. And we don't approve of ourselves again to you, but we want to give you a chance to be proud of us, that you can have something to answer those who take pride in appearances, but not in the heart. And if we're crazy, it's for God's sake: or if we use good sense, it's for your sake, because the love of Christ makes us believe that if One died for all, then all are dead: And that One died for

197

all, so that those who live wouldn't ever live for themselves again, but for the One who died for them, and rose again. So now, we see no one as they are in the body: and yes, though we've known Christ in the body, still now we don't know the Christ that way any more.

[17-21] So then, if anyone is in Christ, they're a new creature, putting their old ways in the past until everything becomes new to them. And we are brought back to God, who has done all this by Yeshua the Christ, and has given to us the ministry of bringing others back to God; That is, that Yahweh God was in Christ Yeshua, bringing the world back to a relationship with God, not counting their sins against them; and has trusted to us the Word, which brings others back to God. Now then, we're spokespersons for Christ, and as though God was begging you through us: we beg you in Christ's stead, to come back to God, who has made Christ to be sin for us, who knew no sin; so that we might become the goodness of God through Christ.

Being Patient Survivors

6 [1-10] We then, as workers together with Christ, beg you also not to accept God's grace without purpose. God says, *"I've heard you at just the right time, and in the day you were saved I have helped you;"* so now is the right time; now is the day to be saved. We try not to offend anyone in anything, so that the ministry won't be blamed: But in everything we approve of ourselves as the ministers of God, being patient survivors in our troubles, in our needs, in our suffering, in our beatings, in our imprisonments, in our chaos, in our work, in our willingness to go without sleep and food; By our purity of heart, by our knowledge, by our patience, by our kindness, by the Holy Spirit, by our heartfelt love, by the Word of Truth, by the power of God, by the protective covering of goodness which surrounds us, in honor and dishonor, in bad news and good news: as misleaders, and yet true; as unknown, yet still well known; as dying, yet still living; as punished, yet not killed; As sorrowful, yet always with joy; as poor, yet making many rich; as having nothing, yet still possessing everything.

Have Hearts filled with Love and Separate from the Ungodly

[11-18] You Corinthians, we speak clearly to you, and our hearts are filled with love for you. You aren't kept from loving by us, but you're kept from loving in your own souls. Now return our love to us, (I speak as to my children,) be heart-filled also. And don't come together with unbelievers, to be married unmatched, because what can goodness have to do with ungodliness? And how can light blend with darkness? And what agreement has Christ made with Satan? Or what does one who believes have to do with an unbeliever? And how can God's Place of Worship be filled with the worship of other things? And it's your own innermost soul, which is the Place of Worship of the living God; as God has said, *"I'll live in them, and be active in them; and I'll be their God, and they'll be my people. So come out from among the ungodly people, and separate yourselves from them, says Yahweh God, and don't touch anything that's evil; and I'll accept you, and I'll be like a parent to you, and care for you as my sons and daughters, says the Almighty Yahweh God."*

Cleanse Ourselves Before God with Godly Sorrow

7 [1-8] So having these promises, dear loved ones, let's cleanse ourselves from everything filthy, in both the body and the spirit, making ourselves completely clean in the fear of God. Accept us, because we've wronged no one, we've ruined no one; we've taken advantage of no one. I don't speak this to accuse you, because I've already said to you, that our hearts are filled with love for you, whether we die or live for you. I speak to you without fear, and my hopeful pride in you is great: My heart is filled with comfort; I'm very joyful even in all our troubles. And when we had come into Macedonia, we had no rest, and we were troubled everywhere; outside were fightings, and inside were fears. But in the same way, God, who comforts those that are put down, comforted us by the coming of Titus; And not by that only, but by the comfort that he was comforted in you, when he told us of your great hope, your sorrowful crying, your great concern for me; so that I was even more joyful. And though I hurt you with my letter, I'm not sorry for writing it, though I am sorry, realizing that the letter hurt you, though it was only for a little while.

[9-16] Now I am full of joy, not that you were sorrowful, but that you were sorry enough to change your life because you were sorrowful in a godly way, so that you weren't really hurt by us in any way. And you can't be sorry for the godly sorrow that changed your life and helped you to be saved, because the kind of sorrow brought by the world only brings a hopeless death. See for yourselves what I'm saying; how that you sorrowed in a godly way, in order to make you truly care; Yes, look how you tried to clear yourselves; Yes, look at the anger you had; Yes, look at the fear you had; Yes, look at your longing to see me; Yes, look at the passion you had; And yes, what justice you wanted! In all this you've cleared yourselves of wrongdoing in this matter. So even though I wrote to you, I didn't do it for the one who had done the wrong, nor for the ones who had suffered wrongs, but so that our care for you in the sight of God might be seen by you. So we were comforted in your comfort: and yes, had even more joy for the joy of Titus, because his spirit was awakened by you all. So if I've said anything prideful to him about you, I'm not ashamed; but as we spoke everything to you in truth, in the same way our prideful bragging, which I made to Titus, is the truth. And he has more love for you, because he knows how you all

accepted him, how with fear and trembling you truly accepted him. And now I celebrate because I can trust you in everything.

On Giving Graciously

8 [1-9] Besides this, Christians, we want you to know of the grace God has given to the churches of Macedonia; How that in a great test of suffering, most of their joy and their deep poverty was found in the riches of their freedom in giving. They gave what they were able to, I say, and yes, even more than they were really able to, giving of their own free will; Asking and begging us to take the gift, and let them share in the blessing of helping the Christians. And they did this, not as we had hoped, but first gave their own selves to God, and then to us by the will of God. So much so, that we wanted Titus, just as he had begun, to pass on the same acts of grace to you also. So, as you grew fruitful in everything else, in faith, in words, in knowledge, and in all your concern and love for us, see that you grow fruitful in your acts of grace in giving as well. This isn't a command, but I speak on account of the gracefulness of others, and to prove the honesty of your love. And you know the grace of our Christ Yeshua, who was rich, and still for your sakes became poor, that you might become rich through Christ's own poverty.

[10-15] And in this I give my advice because this is necessary for you, who have begun to not only want to do, but also to do it over a year ago. So now act on your wanting to do it; so as there was a willingness, your actions can follow also out of what you have to give. If there is a willing mind first, then whatever you've to give is acceptable, and it doesn't matter what You haven't got to give. I don't mean that other people shouldn't give at all, and you to be overly troubled by giving: But give on an equal basis, so that now in the time of your plenty you can give whatever they need, and that when they are able they can also give you what you need: so that there is a balance: As the Word says, *"Whoever took in richly had nothing over; and whoever took in little didn't go without anything they needed."*

[16-24] And I thank God, who put the same true care that I have for you into the heart of Titus. And to be sure, he not only accepted this responsibility; but being so excited about it, went to you of his own accord. And another Christian coworker, whose is praised in the work of the New Word throughout all the churches is coming along; And not that only, but this is the one who was chosen by the churches to travel along with us for this responsibility, which is overseen by us to the praise of Christ, and to prove your willingness to give: We want to stop anyone from blaming us falsely in this responsibility which we oversee: Trying to do what is honest, not only in the sight of God, but also in the sight of humanity. And we've also sent with them our Christian coworker, whom we've proved to be careful in many things many times, but now how much more careful in this great trust, which I have in you. If anyone asks about Titus, he's my coworker and helper to you: or if anyone asks about these Christian coworkers, they're the angels of the churches, and the praise of Christ. So show them, and the churches the proof of your love and of our bragging about you.

The Gift Better than Words

9 [1-7] So as touching the ministering to the Christians, it's really not needed for me to write to you, because I know you're willing to do this, which is why I brag of you to those of Macedonia, that Achaia was ready a year ago; and your passion has stirred up a very many more into action. Yet I have sent these Christian coworkers, in case our bragging of you in this way is for nothing; and that, as I said, you can be ready in case it so happens that those of Macedonia decide to come with me and find you unprepared, and that both we and you would be ashamed that we bragged about you so surely. So I thought it necessary to encourage these Christian coworkers to go ahead to you, and take up your willing gift, in which you had already known about, so that it might be ready, as a free-will offering, and not be given unwillingly. But I say this, those who give sparingly will also bring in sparingly; and those who give graciously will also bring in graciously. So let everyone give as they plan in their heart; not complaining about it, or because they feel they have to, because God loves those who give joyfully.

[8-15] And God is able to make all things be gracious to you; so that you'll always have everything you need, and can share graciously in every good work: (As the Word says, *"The goodness of those who scatter out and give to those who are poor lasts forever."* Now the One who gives seed to the farmer gives both bread for your food, and multiplies your seed that is planted, and increases the fruits of your goodness; Being enriched in everything so you can give more graciously, which causes us to give thanks to God. And the overseeing of this service not only supplies the needs of the Christians, but also causes many people to give thanks to God; And by the test of this help, they praise God for your full acceptance of the New Word of Christ, and for your heartfelt gift to them, and to everyone else; And by their prayer for you, whose hearts are filled with love for you, for that very grace of God that's in you. I Thank God for the gift that's much better than any words could say.

Spiritual Warfare

10 [1-6] Now I, Paul, beg you myself by the humbleness and gentleness of Christ, who am humble when I am with you, but not being there face to face, I have no fear of you: But I beg you, so that I won't have to be so

199

fearless when I come, with that sureness that I expect to have against some, who think of us as if we lived for the things of the earthly realm. And even though we live in the earthly realm, we don't fight with earthly swords. The swords of our warfare aren't earthly, but have the power in God even to pull down spiritual strong holds; targeting thoughts, and any imagination that raises its head against what we know about God, and keeping every thought in agreement with Christ; And being ready to fight back all rebelliousness, when you've come into full agreement with Christ.

Defense of Our Ability and Area of Work

[7-11] Do you look at things as they appear outwardly? If anyone trusts in themselves that they belong to Christ, they should seriously think again, that even as they belong to Christ, so do we also belong to Christ. And though I speak somewhat more freely of our ability, which God has given us for building you up, and not for tearing you down, I won't be ashamed, even if I seem to scare you by my letters. And though my letters are said to be very serious and powerful; and my bodily presence is said to be weak, and my speech is disgraceful, let them seriously think about this, that is, just as we are in the words of our letters when we're not there, we'll be just as powerful in action when we are there.

[12-18] But we dare not compare ourselves to, or make ourselves as one of those, who think themselves to be something: but really they know nothing because they measure and compare themselves by people just like themselves. But we won't brag about things outside our limits, but within the limits of the ability, which God has given us, which includes what we do with you. We don't stretch ourselves beyond our limits, as though we didn't have the ability to reach you, because we have come even as far as you in preaching the New Word of Christ. We don't brag of things outside our limits, that is, of other's work that may have been given to us; but having the hope that when your faith grows, our area of work will grow greatly by you, and that we can preach the New Word in other areas besides where you are, and not to brag in another person's line of work. But whoever brags, let them brag in God, because it isn't those who approve of themselves that are approved, but those whom God approves.

Don't be Misled by Those Who Try to Make a Profit Off The Word of God

11 [1-15] I hope to God you'll put up with me even when I do speak a little bit crazy: and you have put up with me. But I am crazy over you with a godly passion because I've promised you to Christ so that I can present you as a faithful spouse to Christ. But I fear, in case by some means, as the snake fooled Eve with half-truths, so your minds would wander from the pure truth that is in Christ. I'm afraid that if someone comes and preaches something different about Yeshua that we haven't preached, or if you accept another spirit, which You haven't accepted before, or hear another New Word, which You haven't accepted before, you might very well believe it. But I think that I haven't followed the least bit behind the very first followers. And though I am not very well trained in my speech, yet I am in knowledge; but we've been thoroughly open among you in everything. What sin have I done in humbling myself so that you might be lifted up, so I could preach to you the New Word of God freely and without pay? What support I took from other churches, I took to help you. And when I was with you, and needed anything, I was supported by none of you, because what I needed I was given by the Christians, who came from another place. I've kept myself from asking you for any help for anything, and so I'll keep myself from ever asking you for anything. As the truth of Christ is in me, no one there will stop me from saying this. And why? Do you think it's because I don't love you? God knows that I do. But what I do, that I'll keep on doing, so that I can cut off any chance for those who want a chance to make something of themselves, so that they can appear to be just as we are. And people like this are false followers, false workers, changing themselves into the appearance of followers of Christ. And no wonder, even Satan changes into an angel of light. So it's not strange if their ministers also are changed into the ministers of goodness; who will be punished for what they do.

The Many Sufferings

[16-33] I say again, let no one think of me as crazy; but if otherwise, still accept me as a crazy person, so that I can talk about myself a little. What I speak, I don't speak for God, but as in stupidity, in this self-confident bragging. Seeing that many brag about their earthly lives, I'll brag also. And you gladly accept thoughtless ones, seeing that you yourselves are wise! And you even allow it, if they control you, if they use you, if they take from you, if they say they're better than you, or even if they hit you on the face. And I speak about our own dishonor, as we had been weak in this way, too. Just the same, whatever anyone wants to brag about, though I speak stupidly, I'll brag about it, also. Are they Jews? So am I. Are they from Israel? So am I. Are they the descendants of Abraham? So am I. Are they ministers of Christ? I speak as a crazy person, but I am more! I have worked harder; I have been beaten more times than I can count; I have been locked up more often; I have escaped death more often. The Jews beat me five times with thirty-nine licks. I was beaten with sticks three times; I was attacked with stones once; I was shipwrecked three times, and spent a night and a day in the sea; I have traveled often, and have been in danger of drowning, in danger of thieves, in danger of my own people, in danger of other people, in danger in the city, in danger in the countryside, in danger in the sea, in danger among false Christians; I have

been tired and aching, often with no sleep, hungry and thirsty, often willingly going without food, cold and going without clothes. And besides all this, my daily concerns, which is the care of all the churches. Who is more weak than I am? Who is offended, and I am not burning with anger? So if I need to brag, I'll brag about all my weaknesses. The God, who Yeshua, our Christ is from, which is blessed forever, knows I'm not lying. Even in Damascus, the governor under Arttas, the one who guarded the city of the Damascus, wanted to arrest me, but I was let down through a window in a basket by the wall, and escaped from them.

Visions and Revelations

12 [1-10] Doubtless, it does no good for me to brag like this, so I'll come to visions and revelations of Christ. I knew someone in Christ more than fourteen years ago, who was taken up to the third heaven, (whether in the body, I can't tell; or whether out of the body, I can't tell: only God knows.) And I knew how this person, (whether in the body, or out of the body, I can't tell, only God knows,) was taken up into the Garden of Paradise, and heard things words can't describe, which no one is able to tell. I'll brag about this kind of person, but I'll only brag about myself in my weaknesses. And even if I wanted to brag, I wouldn't be crazy, because I'll tell the truth: but now I don't brag, in case anyone would think more of me than what they see me to be, or that they hear of me. And in case I were to be more proud than I ought, because of the many revelations, I was given a thorn in my side, the angel of Satan to keep me down, in case I were to become more proud than I ought. I prayed to Christ three times because of this thing, that it might leave from me. And Christ told me, *"My grace is enough for you because My strength is seen in your weakness."* So most gladly, I'll brag about my weaknesses instead, so that the power of Christ can be seen by all. So I have joy in my weaknesses, in accusations, in times of need, in discriminations, in all kinds of troubles for Christ's sake, because when I am weak, that is when I'm really strong.

[11-21] I am crazy for bragging like this; but you've made me do it because I ought to have been approved of by you. I have followed not the least bit behind the very first followers, though I'm nothing. The truth is I've done the signs of a follower among you with much patience, in signs, and amazing things, and powerful actions. And how is it that you were treated any lesser than the other churches, unless it's because I myself didn't ask you for anything? Forgive me this wrong! This is the third time I am ready to come to you; and I won't ask you for anything because I don't want anything that's yours, except you, because the children shouldn't save up for their parents, but the parents for their children. And I'll very gladly use up all that is mine and even be used up myself to save your souls; though the more greatly I love you, the less I am loved. But anyway, I didn't trouble you, but being the sneaky way that I am, I caught you in my sneakiness. Did I get anything from you by any of those I sent to you? I wanted Titus to go, and sent with him the other Christians. Did Titus get anything from you? Didn't we both have the same spirit? Didn't we both go the same way? Once again, do you think that we're making excuses for ourselves to you? What we say, we say before God in Christ, and everything we do, dear loved one, is to help you. I fear that when I come, I won't find you as I want to, and that I'll be found by you as you wouldn't want me. I'm afraid that there'll be arguments, jealousy, anger, making fun of me, bad-mouthing, gossiping, arrogant pride, or chaos. And in case, when I come back, my God will humble me among you, and that I'll be upset by many who have sinned, and haven't changed from their evil ways, sexual sins, and filthiness.

Last Warning

13 [1-4] This is the third time I am coming to you, so in the presence of two or three witnesses every word will be settled. I told you before, and warned you the second time, as if I were present; and not being there now, I write to those who up to now have kept on sinning, and to all others, that when I come back, I won't show mercy to you, since you look for proof that Christ is speaking in me, which isn't weak to you, but is powerful in you. And even though the Christ was put to death through weakness, yet by the power of God, Christ still lives. And if we also are weak in Christ, by the power of God we'll still live with Christ for you.

[5-10] So examine yourselves, and see whether you're in the faith or not; prove it to your own selves. Don't you know your own selves, how that Yeshua the Christ is in you, unless, in fact, you are unsaved? But I trust that you'll come to know that we aren't unsaved. Now I pray to God that you don't do anything evil; not so that we would appear approved of, but that you would do what is right, even if we were unsaved. We can't do anything against the truth, but only for the truth. And we're happy, when we're weak, and you're strong: and we pray for godly actions to follow your faith. So I write this, while not there, in case when I am there, I am too angry with you, and use the power which God has given me to tear you down instead of building you up.

[11-14] Finally, Christians, goodbye. Let godly actions follow your faith, be in good spirits now, be of one mind, live in peace, and the God of love and peace will be with you. Say hello to one another with a kiss of love. All the Christians here say hello to you. May the grace of Yeshua the Christ, and God's love, and the relationship of the Holy Spirit, be with you all. So be it!

Paul's Letter to the Galatians

1 [1-5] From Paul, a follower, (not made so by others, nor by any human action, but by Yeshua the Christ, and Yahweh God, the God who raised the Christ from the dead;) and all the Christians which are with me, to the churches of Galatia: May you have grace and peace from Yahweh God, and from our Christ Yeshua, who willingly died for our sins to free us from the evil that is in this world now, for the will of God, who we are from: May God be made known forever without end. So be it!

[6-9] I can't believe that you're so quickly leaving your faith in the One who called you into the grace of Christ to another New Word: which isn't really another New Word at all; but there are some that are troubling you, and would change the truth of the New Word of Christ. But though we, or even an angel from heaven, were to preach any word to you other than what we've already preached to you, let them be damned forever. As we said before, I say so now again, if anyone preaches any other New Word to you other than what you've already heard, let them be damned forever.

Paul's Call is from Christ

[10-14] Now, am I trying to convince others, or to please God? Or am I trying to please other people? If I still wanted to please others, I wouldn't be the worker of Christ. But I tell you, Christians, that the New Word which was preached by me isn't from the mind of any human being. I didn't get it from a person, nor was I taught it, but it was made known to me by Yeshua the Christ. You know of my lifestyle in the Jewish religion, how that in the past, I abused those of the church of God more than anyone, and tried to stop it: And in that religion I moved ahead of many of my equals in my own nation, being more passionate of my ancestors' way of life.

[15-23] But when God, who decided even before my birth to call me by grace, was pleased to make Christ known in me, so that I might preach the Christ to the ungodly; I didn't first go to talk it over with human beings, nor did I go up to Jerusalem to those who were followers before me; but I went straight to Arabia, and came back to Damascus later. Then after three years I went up to Jerusalem to see Peter, and stayed there fifteen days. But I saw none of the other followers, except for James, Christ's brother. Now I say before God that I am not lying about the things which I write to you. Then later I came into the regions of Syria and Cilicia; And I wasn't personally known to the churches of Judea, which were in Christ, even though they had heard that the one who had abused them in the past was now preaching the faith which I had tried to put an end to. And they praised God for me.

False Teachings Creep In

2 [1-5] Then fourteen years later I went with Barnabas up to Jerusalem again, taking Titus along with me as well. And I knew to go up by the Spirit of revelation, and told them the New Word which I preach to the other peoples, but secretly to those who were well known, in case in some way I might be working, or had been working, for no reason. But not even Titus, who was with me, being a Greek, was required to keep the tradition of having the foreskin cut off: And that was only brought up because of false believers who had unexpectedly come in, having come in secretly to see the freedom we have in Christ Yeshua, and to try to make us do what they wanted us to: To whom we didn't give in, even for an hour; so that the truth of the New Word might stay with you.

[6-10] But these, who seemed to think themselves something, (whatever they were, it doesn't matter to me: God doesn't accept anyone by their place in this world:) though they seemed to be highly respected, they gave me nothing to add to my message: But instead, when they saw that the New Word to the other peoples was trusted to me, just as the New Word to the Jews was to Peter; (because the One who worked effectively in Peter to the Jews, was the same One who was powerful in me toward the other peoples.) And when James, Peter, and John, who seemed to be the most important, realized the grace that was given to me, they accepted me and Barnabas by shaking hands on our partnership; so that we could go to the other peoples, and they to the Jews. They only wanted us to remember those who are poor; which was the same thing that I wanted to do.

[11- 21] But when Peter came to Antioch, I stood up to him face to face, because he was wrong in that before certain ones came from James, he ate with the other peoples, but when they had come, he had withdrawn and separated himself, fearing those who were Jews. So all the other Jews did the same; and even Barnabas was also fooled by their show of tradition. But when I saw that they didn't walk rightly in the truth of the New Word, I said to Peter in front of them all, if you, being a Jew, live like the other peoples, and not as the Jews do, why are you trying to get the other peoples to live like the Jews? We, who are Jews by nature, and not like the ungodly ones of the other peoples, know that people aren't made right by the what they've done in the Word of God, but by their faith in Yeshua the Christ, just as we've believed in Yeshua the Christ, so that we might be made right by our faith in Christ, and not by anything we've done out of the Word of God, because no one is made right by what they've done out of the Word of God. But if, while we're being made right by Christ, we ourselves are also found to

be sinners, does that show that Christ is spreading sin? Never! For if I do again the things which I have already stopped doing, I make myself a sinner. So I die through the Word of God, so that I might live for God. And even if I am put to death with Christ: I live; though not I, but it's Christ who lives in me: and the life which I now live in the body I live by my faith in the Child of God, who loved me, and willingly died for me. So I don't make God's grace to have no purpose, because if my goodness were to come by my obedience to the Word of God, then the death of Christ would be meaningless.

We are Saved by Faith, not Works

3 [1-6] You stupid Galatians, who has tricked you into not obeying the truth, who have already been shown that Yeshua the Christ has been put to death for you? I only want to know this: Did you receive the Spirit by what you've done out of the Word of God, or by the hearing of faith? Are you so stupid? Having begun in the Spirit, are you now completed by what you do with your body? Have you suffered so many things for nothing? If it was, in fact, for nothing. So does the One who gives to you the Spirit, and does the amazing things among you, do it because of what you do out of the Word of God, or by the faith that you have in what you hear? It is just like when Abraham believed God, and God thought of him as good because he believed.

[7-14] So don't you know that only those who have faith are the children of Abraham. And the Word, knowing ahead of time that God would forgive the ungodly because of their faith, preached the New Word to Abraham, saying, *"In you every race of people will be blessed."* So then those who have faith are blessed along with Abraham, who believed God. Whoever thinks they are made right by what they do are cursed because the Word says, *"Everyone that doesn't continue to do everything which is written in the book of the Word of God is cursed."* It's clear that no one is made right by the Word in the sight of God, because *"Those made right will live by faith."* But outwardly obeying the Word of God isn't from faith, but *"The person that obeys it will live by it."* Christ has saved us from the curse of the Word of God, by being made a curse for us because the Word says, *"Anyone who hangs on a cross is cursed:"* so that the blessing of Abraham might come to all the other races through Yeshua the Christ; and so that we might get the Spirit that was promised by our faith.

[15-22] So, everyone, what I am saying is like when other people make agreements; even though it's only a human agreement, still if it's confirmed, no one can take away from it, or add anything to it. Now it was to Abraham and "the seed" that the promises were made. The Word didn't say seeds, meaning many descendants; but One descendant, "And to your seed," which is Christ. And what I am saying is this, that the promised agreement, which was confirmed by God in Christ, can't be taken away from, making the promise have no purpose, by the Word of God, which came over four hundred years later. For if the inheritance is by the Word of God, it's no longer by the promise: but God made the agreement with Abraham by promise. So why then do we have the Word of God? It was given to us to show us what sin is, till the Christ came, whom the promise was spoken of; and it was given by angels to a human go-between, Moses. Now there is One God, and One party doesn't need a go-between. Does the Word of God then go against the Promises of God? Never! Because if there had been given a law which could have given life, the truth is, goodness would have come by that Word. But the Word has put all under the curse of sin, so that the promise by faith in Yeshua the Christ might be given to those who believe.

[23-29] But before faith in Christ came, we were kept by the Word of God, waiting for the faith which would later be made known. So the Word of God was like our schoolteacher to bring us to faith in Christ, so we could be made right by faith. But now that faith is here, we no longer need to be taught by a schoolteacher. For you're all the children of God by faith in Christ Yeshua, and whoever has been baptized into the faith of Christ has put on the likeness of Christ. There's no difference between races, there's no difference between workers or those who are free, there's no difference between males or females because you're all one and the same in Christ Yeshua. And if you're Christ's, then you're of Abraham's lineage, and heirs of the promise.

Adoption of the Children of God

4 [1-10] Now I say, that as long as the heirs are children, they're no different than a worker, even though someday they'll have control of everything; But they're under the control of teachers and managers until the time the parent gives them control. Just the same, when we were children, the things of the world controlled us: But when the right time came, God sent the Child, born of a woman, born under the rule of the Word of God, in exchange for those who were under the rule of the Word of God, so that we might be adopted like children. And because you're children, God has sent the Spirit of the Child into your hearts, which cries out to God, who cares for us like a Parent. So you're not a just a worker anymore, but you're a child; and if you're a child, then you're an heir of God through Christ. Then again, when you didn't know God, you worked for those things that aren't really gods. But now, after you've come to know God, or rather, after God knows you, why do you want to turn back and be controlled by the weaker things of this world? You're still keeping the rules of your traditional holidays, and special months, times, and years. I'm afraid that I've wasted my work on you for no reason at all.

[12-19] Everyone, I beg you, be as I am because I'm just like you. You haven't hurt me at all. You know how at first, through the weakness of my body, I preached the New Word to you. And you didn't hate or reject the weakness of my body; but took care of me as an angel of God, just as you would Christ Yeshua. So then, where is the blessing that you spoke of? I tell you that if it had been possible, you would have even taken out your own eyes, and given them to me. So have I become your enemy now, because I tell you what is true? They eagerly try to convince you, but not for your good; yes, they would keep you out, so that you might want to go along with them. But it's always good to be eager in good things, and not only when I'm there with you. My little children, I'll have the pains of birth over and over again until the life of Christ is created in you! I want to be there with you now and to change the way I have to speak to you because I question whether you really have the truth or not.

[21-31] Tell me, you that want to be controlled by the Word of God, don't you know the Word of God? The Word says that Abraham had two children, one by a worker, the other by a freewoman. But the one who was born of the worker was born in the normal way, while the one who was born of the freewoman was given by the promise of God. These things are a symbol to us because these are two promised agreements; The first one came from Mount Sinai, which is controlled by that agreement, which is symbolized by Hagar. Hagar is a symbol for Mount Sinai in Arabia, and is like Jerusalem is now, that is, she and her children are under the control of the first agreement. But the spiritual Jerusalem, which is from above, is free, and is the spiritual mother of us all. The Word says, "*Celebrate, you who can't have children; break out and cry, you who have never had the pain of birth, because the deserted one has many more children than she who has a husband.*" Now Christians, as Isaac was, we're the children of promise. Just as it was then, those who are born the normal way abuse those who are born in the Spirit, now. But in the same way, what does the Word say? "*Throw out the worker and her child because the child of the worker won't be heir along with the child of the free woman.*" So then, Christians, we aren't children of the first agreement, but of the promise.

Love Others

5 [1-8] So stay in the freedom that Christ has given to make us free, and don't be caught up again by being controlled by the first agreement. I, Paul, say to you, that if you're living by the first agreement, Christ will do you no good. I say again to everyone that is living by that agreement, that they must keep every point of that whole agreement. Christ means nothing to you, who are trying to be made right by the first agreement; and you're not living by grace. We, through the Spirit, wait for the hope of goodness by our faith, because in Yeshua the Christ, neither those who live by that agreement, nor those who live by the promise are really changed unless they're living by faith, in love. You were doing well; so who stopped you from obeying the truth? The influence they have on you doesn't come from the One who calls you.

[9-15] A little untruthful leaven makes the whole lump a lie. But I trust in you that through God, you won't change your minds: but the ones who trouble you will take their punishment, whoever they are. And I, Christians, if I'm still preaching from the first agreement, why do I still suffer discrimination? Then those who are offended by the cross would stop. I wish that they would even cut themselves completely off which trouble you. Christians, you've been called to freedom; but don't use your freedom for an excuse to live in ungodly ways, but to serve one another in love. Because all the Word of God is completed in this one word, which is "Love others as you love yourself." But if you snap at each other and hurt one another, be careful that you aren't completely destroyed by one another.

Fruits of the Spirit

[16-26] So what I'm saying then is this: Walk in the Spirit, so you won't do the sinful things you would naturally want to do. For what you naturally want to do fights against what the Spirit wants you to do, and the Spirit fights against what you naturally want to do: and these are fighting against one another: so that you aren't able to do the things that you want. But if you're led by the Spirit, you aren't controlled by the Word of God. Now the things that you've done in your natural self are clear: Adultery and other kinds of sexual sins, all kinds of evil and filthy things, worshiping other things falsely, witchcraft, hateful differences, cruel jealousy, thoughtless anger, fighting and rebellion, untruthful beliefs, envious greed and murders, drunken partying, and other things like these: of which I tell you as I've also told you in the past, that those who do these kinds of things won't inherit the realm of God. But the fruits of the Spirit are love, joy, peace, patience, kindness, goodness, faithfulness, helpfulness, and self-control. There's no law against these kinds of things. Those who are Christ's have put to death what they naturally want and like in their physical bodies. So if we live in the Spirit, let's also do what the Spirit wants us to do. Let's not want the meaningless recognition we get from others, stirring up each other, and being greedy for what others are or have.

Help One Another

6 [1-6] Everyone, if someone is being controlled by a fault, you who are spiritual, try to bring them back with a gentle spirit; carefully remembering that you may also be tempted. Help one another with your problems, and you'll do the Word of God by your faith in Christ. And if some are proud of themselves, when they have no reason to be, they mislead themselves. So let everyone judge their own actions, and then they can be proud of themselves without thinking of themselves as better than others. So let everyone take care of themselves as they are able. And let those who are taught by the Word share with those who teach them all the good things they have been given.

[7-10] Don't be misled; God's Word won't be taken lightly, because whatever someone does, they'll get back more of the same things. Whoever does whatever evil they want to do will get back whatever evil they do; but whoever does what the Spirit wants will get everlasting life from the Spirit. So let's not get tired of doing good because we'll get what we work for in due time, if we don't give up. So let's do good to everyone as much as we can, especially to those who are in the family of faith.

[11-16] You see how large the letters are that I've written to you with my own hand. Those who want to be seen by what they do outwardly, are those that are trying to convince you to live by outward rules; but only because they would suffer discrimination for the cross of Christ. Those who do these things don't even obey the Word of God; but they want you to obey it, so that they can brag about making you do it. But may I never brag about anything but the cross of our Christ Yeshua, by whom the ways of the world are put to death in me, and I die to the world. In Christ Yeshua neither those who live by the first agreement, nor those who live by the promise are changed at all unless they are changed into a new person. And whoever lives by this rule, peace and mercy be on them, and on the new people of God.

[17-18] So let no one give me trouble from now on because I have on my body the scars of Christ Yeshua. Everyone, May the grace of our Christ Yeshua be with your spirit. So be it!

205

Paul's Letter to the Ephesians

1 [1-7] From Paul, a follower of Yeshua the Christ by the will of God, to the Christians which are at Ephesus, and to all the faithful who are in Christ Yeshua: May grace and peace be with you, from Yahweh God, and from Yeshua the Christ. May Yahweh God be blessed, the God of our Christ Yeshua, who has given us every blessing in the spiritual realm in Christ. God has chosen us in Christ even before the creation of the world, that we would be set apart and without blame before God. We were chosen before time to be the adopted children of God through Yeshua the Christ, out of God's love and favor for us; in order for God's grace to made known to us, in which God has accepted us in the Dear Loved Christ. The cost was the blood of Christ Yeshua, which has bought us back, in order to save us from our sins, for the riches of God's grace.

Marked by the Holy Spirit
[8-14] In this, God has greatly blessed us in all wisdom and foresight, having made known to us the secret of what God truly wants, which was decided by God for God's own happiness: That in the right time everything would be brought together to be completed in Christ, both that which is in heaven, and that which is on earth; everything in Christ. So we have an inheritance in Christ, being chosen before time for the purpose of the One who works everything out by God's own plan, so that we, who first trusted in Christ, would make God known by our praise. And you have also trusted in Christ, after you heard the Word of truth, the New Word that saves you. After you believed, you were also marked with that Holy Spirit of promise, which is the proof of our inheritance until the possession is bought back, and we will make God known by our praise.

[15-23] This is why, after hearing of your faith in Christ Yeshua, and your love for all the Christians, I give thanks for you always, remembering you in my prayers. I pray that the God of our Christ Yeshua, the God, who we make known, will give to you the spirit of wisdom and revelation to know God, and that the eyes of your understanding will be opened. I pray that you can know the hope of God's calling, and the riches of making known God's inheritance in the Christians, the very greatness of God's power to us who believe, according to the working of God's great power, which God did in Yeshua the Christ. I pray that you know the Christ was raised from the dead, and sat beside God in the heavenly realm, far above all other spiritual realms, or power, or stronghold, or control, and every name that is named, not only in this world, but also in that which is to come. And that everything was put under the Christ's control, and Christ became Ruler over everything in the church, which is the body of Christ, which completes the One who completes everyone in everything.

We are Brought back to Life
2 [1-10] And God has brought you back to life again, who were dead in your uncontrolled actions and sins. In the past you did this, walking in the ways of this world, for the ruler of the power of the air, the spirit that works now in those who refuse to be controlled by God. In the past, our lifestyle suited the wants of our body, fulfilling what the body and the mind wanted; and we were by nature the children of rage, just as others are now. But God, who is rich in mercy, for the great love that God has for us, even when we were dead in our sins, has brought us back to life again together with Christ, and by grace you're saved. God has raised us up together, and made us sit together in spiritual realms in Christ Yeshua, so that in the time to come the very riches of God's grace would be shown in God's kindness toward us through Christ Yeshua. By grace you're saved, through your faith. You're not saved of yourselves, it's the gift of God. You've done nothing to deserve it, in case anyone wants to brag. We're all God's handiwork, created in Christ Yeshua to do good works, which God has previously set apart for us to do, so that we would do them at the right time.

We Worship God in Spirit
[11-22] So remember, that you once lived like the other people, who are called unclean by those who call themselves clean, because of that which is done in the physical body by human beings. Remember that at that time, you were without Christ, kept from being a citizen of Israel, and were strangers to the promised agreements, having no hope, and without God in the world. But now in Christ Yeshua you who were then far away are now brought near by the blood of Christ. Christ is our peace, and has brought both together, and has broken down the wall that separates us; having put an end to that rage of the Word of God in the Christ's body, which was only about following rules, in order to make one new people of the two in Christ, and so making peace. And this happened to bring back both people to God in one body by the cross, having put an end to the rage by this word: The Christ came and preached peace to those who were far away, and to those who were near. Through Christ we are both joined by One Spirit to the God we came from. So now you're not strangers and foreigners anymore, but citizens along with the other Christians, and are now part of the family of God. You're built on the foundation of the followers and great preachers, Yeshua the Christ being the first corner stone in whom all the building is

perfectly fit together to grow into a holy Place of Worship in God. You also are built together in Christ to be a Place of Worship of God, through the Spirit.

Other Peoples Share Israel's Promise

3 [1-9] Because of this, I Paul, am the prisoner of Yeshua the Christ for you other peoples, if you've heard of the privilege of God's grace which I have been given for you. That is, that Christ made known to me the secret by revelation, as I wrote before in a short letter, by which, when you read it, you can understand how I know the secret of Christ. In other times this wasn't made known to the children of humanity, as it has been made known to God's holy followers and great preachers now by the Spirit. But it was made known so that the other peoples could be part of the same body, sharing in the promise of Israel in Christ by the New Word. And I was made a minister of this New Word, for the gift of God's grace which was given to me by the purposeful activity of the power of God. I have been given this grace, who am the least worthy of all Christians, so that I would preach the unimaginable riches of Christ to others, and to make everyone see the purpose of this secret, which from the beginning of time God has kept secret, who created everything by Yeshua the Christ.

The Endless Boundaries of Christ's Love

[10-20] And this has happened so that the great wisdom of God would be made known to the rulers and powers in spiritual realms by the church, for the everlasting purpose which God has worked out in Yeshua, our Christ. In Christ, we have no fear, who we can go to with trust by our faith. So I don't want you to give up because of my troubles for you, which is really for your victory. So, I bow my knees to the God of our Christ Yeshua, for whom the whole family in heaven and earth is named. I pray that God will give you strength, out of the riches of God's victory, with the power of the Spirit in the inner person so that Christ can live in your hearts by faith; And that you, being rooted and grounded in love, may be able to understand, along with all Christians, the endless boundaries of Christ's love, which is wider, and longer, and deeper, and higher than anyone can know, so that you might be filled with everything God has for you. Now God is able to do so much more than anything we can ask or even think of by the power of the Spirit that acts in us. May God have victory in the church by Christ Yeshua to the end of time, and forever. So be it!

Christ Gives Gifts to Humanity

4 [1-10] So, I, the prisoner of God, beg you to walk worthy of the work that you're called to do, in humility and gentleness, and with patience, forgiving one another in love. Try to be as one in the Spirit, coming together in peace. There's one body, and one Spirit, just as you've been called in one hope; There's One Christ, one faith, one baptism; One God, the same Yahweh God we are all from, who rules over everything, and is everywhere, and is in every one of you. And Christ has measured out gifts to everyone of us by grace. This is why it is said, "*The Christ went up to heaven leading a long line of freed prisoners, and gave gifts to humanity.*" So now that the Christ has gone up, the Christ must also have come down first to the earth? So the One who came down is the same One also that has gone up to the highest heaven, in order to complete everything.

[11-16] And the Christ chose some of us to be followers, some great preachers, some evangelists, some pastors, and some teachers; And Christ gave these gifts to complete the Christians, for the work of the ministry, and for the good of the body of Christ until we all come together in the same faith, and the same knowledge of the Child of God. This is so we can become a complete person, that is, so we can become mature like Christ. We shouldn't act like children anymore, getting confused by, and being swayed by every new teaching, by those who would fool us with their evil lies, who are only waiting for a chance to mislead us. But we should always tell the truth in love in everything we do, so we can grow up in Christ, which is the head of the body. In Christ, the whole body is perfectly joined and held together by everyone that does their own work and helps the body to do its work, which helps the body to grow for its own good in the love of Christ.

Be a New Person

[17-24] So I tell you, in the name of Yahweh God, that you must not keep on living as other people live, with their useless thinking. They don't understand, being strangers to the life of God, because they refuse to accept the truth. These people, having no sense of shame, have given themselves over to living filthy lives, always wanting to do something more evil. But those in Christ haven't learned to be this way, if you've really heard the truth, and have been taught by the truth that is in Yeshua. That truth tells you to put off your former lifestyle, which is the old person that is ruined by the evil it wants. You must change the way you think, putting on the new person, which is created by God in true goodness and right living.

[25-32] So everyone of you tell the truth to others, and stop lying, because we all belong to the same body. Be angry, but don't sin. Don't let the day come to an end with your rage still in your heart, or you'll give the devil a way to destroy you. Those of you who have stolen must not steal anymore, but instead work with your hands the things which are good, so that you can have enough to give to those in need. Don't say anything evil, but say only

what's good for the benefit of others, your words being graceful to whoever hears it. Don't grieve the Holy Spirit of God, by which you're marked till the day we're saved. Don't become bitter, angry, or full of rage, yelling and talking evil, and hating; but be good and kind to one another, forgiving one another, just as God for Christ's sake has forgiven you.

Walk as Children of Light

5 [1-10] So be followers of God, as dear children; and walk in love, as Christ also has loved us, and has died for us as an offering and a sacrifice to God for a sweet-smelling scent. And don't let any sexual sin, or any evil thing, or greed, be named among you, as Christians shouldn't live this way; nor immorality, nor stupid talking, nor joking around, which aren't right to do; but instead give thanks. You should know that no sexually immoral or evil person, nor a selfish person, or someone who worships falsely, has any part in the realm of Yeshua the Christ and of Yahweh God. Don't let anyone mislead you with meaningless words, for because of this, the rage of God is on those who refuse to be under God's control. So don't take part in it along with them. You once lived in darkness, but now you live in the light of God; so walk as children of light, because the fruit of the Spirit lives in everything right, and good, and true; and proves what is acceptable to God.

[11-21] So don't have anything to do with the meaningless actions of darkness, but instead expose them for what they are. It's a shame even to speak of what's done by them in secret, but everything that is disapproved of is made clear when it's brought to light and whatever makes it clear is light. This is why God said, *"Awake, you who are sleeping, come to life from the dead, and Christ will give you light."* See then, that you walk carefully, not as thoughtless people do, but as wise ones, using your time wisely, because the days are evil. So don't be unwise, but understand what God wants you to do. And don't be getting drunk on alcohol, which is excessive; but be filled with the Spirit. Speak to yourselves in sayings and hymns, and spiritual songs, singing and making melody in your heart to God. Always give thanks to the God we are from for everything in the Name of our Christ Yeshua; accepting one another out of respect for God.

Wives and Husbands Live in Love and Respect

[22-33] Wives, accept the leadership of your husbands, as you would accept God's leadership, because the husband is the head of the wife, just as Christ is the head of the church; and the savior of the body. So just as the church is responsible to Christ, so you wives should be responsible to your own husbands in everything. But you husbands, be sure to love your wives just as Christ also loved the church, and unselfishly died for it; In order to set it apart and cleanse it with the washing of water by the Word, and in order to present it to Christ's own self an amazing church, not having any fault, or blame, or any such thing; but that it would be holy and without a flaw. So you men should love your wives as your own bodies. Whoever loves their wife loves themselves. No one has ever hated their own body; but they take good care of it and value it, just as God does the church. We're all members of the Christ's body, and of the Christ's bones. Because of this, a man will leave his parents, and will be joined to his wife, and the two of them will be as one body. This is a great secret; but I am speaking about Christ and the church. So in the same way let everyone of you in particular love your own wife just as you love yourself; and the wife should see that she shows respect for her husband.

Children Respect Your Parents

6 [1-9] Children, accept what your parents say, who are in God, because this is right. Show respect for your parents; (which is the first word with a promise;) so that things will go well with you, and you can live a long life here on the earth. And you parents, don't make your children angry; but bring them up right, teaching and warning them about God. Workers, be acceptable to those who are your overseers in the physical body, with fear and trembling, with an undivided heart, as if you worked for Christ; and not just when they see you, as people-pleasers; but as the workers of Christ, doing the will of God from the heart. Do your work with good will, as to God, and not only to others, knowing that whatever good anyone does, they'll get the same of God, whether they're workers or work for themselves. And you who are overseers, do the same things to them, not threatening them, knowing that your Overseer is also in heaven; and there is no favor toward anyone with the Christ.

The Whole Armor of God

[10-20] Finally, my dear Christians, be strong in God, and in the power of God's strength. Put on the whole armor of God, so that you'll be able to stand against the lies of the devil. We don't struggle against human beings, but against spiritual realms, against powers, against the rulers of the darkness of this world, against spiritual evil in high places. So take the whole armor of God, so that you can be able to withstand in the evil day, and having done all you can, to keep standing. So stand, putting around your waist the belt of truth, and having on the protective covering of goodness; And prepare your feet to march with the New Word of peace; Above all, taking the shield of faith, so that you'll be able to stop all the burning arrows of the devil. And take as your helmet the fact of being saved, and the sharp blade of the Spirit, which is the Word of God, praying always with all your prayers

and requests in the Spirit. Keep on watching, praying for all the Christians, and for me, that words will be given to me, so that I can speak without fear, to make known the secret of the New Word, for which I am locked up as a spokesperson, so that I can speak without fear in it, as I should.

[21-24] But so that you also can know my affairs, and how I am doing, Tychicus, a dear loved one, a Christian and faithful minister in God, will make everything known to you: Whom I've sent to you for that purpose, that you might know how we're doing, and that he will comfort your hearts. Peace be to all the Christians, and love with faith, from the God who we are from and Yeshua the Christ. May God's grace be with all those who love our Christ Yeshua in truth. So be it!

Paul's Letter to the Philippians

1 [1-11] From Paul and Timothy, the workers of Yeshua the Christ, to all those in Christ Yeshua, which are at Philippi, along with the overseers and helpers of the church: May God's grace and peace be with you, from Yahweh God, and from Yeshua the Christ. I thank my God every time I remember you in prayer, always asking for what I need with joy, for your friendship in the New Word from the first day until now; I am so sure that Yahweh God, who has begun a good work in you will do it until the day Yeshua the Christ comes again. It's right for me to think this way of you all, because you're in my heart. You all have shared of my grace, both while I have been locked up, and as I have defended and proven the New Word. God knows how greatly I long for you all in the spirit of Yeshua the Christ. And I pray that your love can grow more and more in knowledge and in good judgment, so that you can know what's best; and that you can be honest and without blame till the day of Christ; which ends in the acts of goodness that come from Yeshua the Christ, to the victory and praise of God.

Suffering for Christ

[12-30] But I want you to understand, dear Christians, that the things which happened to me have worked out to spread the New Word; So that it's plain to all in the government, and everywhere else that I have been put in jail for Christ; And being more sure because of my being locked up, many of those in Christ speak the Word much more boldly and without fear. It's true that some preach Christ even out of jealousy, causing trouble; but some also out of good will: The first ones preach Christ because of a disagreement, not honestly, but wanting to add to my suffering while I am locked up: But the other out of love, knowing that I am here for defending the New Word. So what then? In spite of this, whether in lies, or in truth, Christ is preached in every way; and I celebrate in this, yes, and will keep on celebrating. I know that I'll be freed through your prayers, and by the Spirit of Yeshua the Christ. It's my deep belief and hope that I won't be ashamed of anything, but will act without fear, as always, so Christ will be made known by my life now also, whether it is by living, or by dying. To me, to live is to live for Christ, and to die is to get everlasting life. But if I keep on living in my body, I'll have more time for my work, still, I don't even know what I would choose. I can't choose between the two, wanting to go to be with Christ; which is so much better. But just the same, to keep on living in the body is more needful for you. And trusting this, I know that I'll live and stay with you all for your personal growth and joy in the faith; so that by my coming to you again, you'll have greater joy in Yeshua the Christ, for me. Only let your lifestyle be as the New Word of Christ says it should, that whether I come and see you or not, I'll hear all about you, that you have one spirit, working together with one mind for the faith of the New Word. Don't be afraid of those who come against you, because this clearly shows them that they're damned, but shows you that you're saved by God. On behalf of Christ, God has let you, not only believe in the Christ, but also suffer for the Christ's sake. You are now going through the same kinds of troubles which you saw me having, and hear that I'm having right now.

Be Humble

2 [1-11] So if you have hope in Christ, if you have any comfort of Christ's love, if you have any relationship with the Spirit, if any tender care and mercy, make my joy complete, having the same mind, the same love, the same purpose, and the same spirit. Don't let anything be done with fighting or for selfish reasons; but in a spirit of humbleness, let everyone think of others as better than themselves. Don't just think about yourselves, but also think of others. Think the same way that Christ Yeshua did: Who, being in the form of God, thought nothing of being the same as God. But the Christ, having no known name, became as a hired worker, coming in the form of a human being. Then being found as a human being, the Christ was humble, and accepted death, even the death of the cross. So God has also put the Christ in the highest place, and given the Christ a name above all names: That at the name of Yeshua every knee would bow, all those in heaven, all those on earth, and all those buried in Hell; And that every mouth would admit that Yeshua the Christ is Christ, to the praise of the God we are from.

[12-17] So, my dear loved one, just as you've always done, and not just when I'm there, but now much more while I'm away, keep on working toward being saved yourself with a shivering fear. It's God who works in you, both to make you want to do God's will, and to do God's will. So do everything without whispering complaints or arguing about it, so that you can't be blamed for anything. Be harmless children of God, without fault, in a world of twisted and evil people. Then you'll shine out as a light in the night sky when you share the Word of Life with others, and I'll celebrate in the day of Christ, that I haven't done all this for nothing. Yes, and even if I have to sacrifice myself as a drink poured out in service for your faith, I'm happy, and celebrate with you all. For the same reason you're also happy, and celebrate with me.

[19-30] But I trust in Christ Yeshua to send Timothy to you shortly, so that I can be in good spirits also, when I know how you are. I don't have anyone else who thinks like me, who will naturally care about you, as I do.

210

Everyone looks out for their own well being, and not for the well being of those who belong to Yeshua the Christ. But he has proven to you, that, as a child with a parent, he has served along side me in the New Word. I hope to send him quickly, as soon as I see what's going to happen to me. I trust in God that I'll come shortly myself. Yet I thought it necessary to send Epaphroditus to you, my Christian brother, and coworker, and soldier for Christ, but also the angel you sent to take care of my needs. He longed after you all, and missed you terribly, because you had heard that he had been sick. And he truly was so sick he was near death, but God had mercy on him; and not only on him, but on me also, or I would have had one sorrow added to another. So I sent him all the more carefully, so that, when you see him again, you can celebrate, and so that I can be less sorrowful. So accept him in Christ with great happiness; and respect those like him. He came in your place to help me for the work of Christ, being near death, and not thinking of his own life.

Reach for What's Ahead

3 [1-10] Finally, my dear Christians, celebrate in God. It isn't any trouble for me to write the same things to you again, because it's to keep you safe. Beware of those dogs, the evil people who only want to cut you to pieces. We're the ones who are clean, which worship God in the spirit, and celebrate in Christ Yeshua, and have no trust in what we do in the body, though I might have reason to trust what I've done in the body. If anyone thinks that they have reason to trust in what they've done in the body, I have more: My flesh was cut on the eighth day after my birth; I am of the family of Israel, of the family of Benjamin, a Hebrew of the Hebrews; And as to the Word of God, a religious leader; As to passion, I treated the church shamefully; as to being good as is in the Word of God, I was without blame. But whatever I might have gained from this, I think as nothing but loss for Christ. Yes, no doubt, and I think of everything as loss for the greater knowledge of Yeshua, my Christ, for whom I've suffered the loss of everything, and think of it all as nothing more than the waste of the body, so that I can be found in Christ. I no longer have my own goodness from doing the Word of God, but what is through the faith of Christ, the goodness which is of God by faith. Now I know Christ, and the power of Christ's coming to life again, and have shared in the Christ's sufferings, being made acceptable by the Christ's death.

[11-21] By this way, I hope I might come to new life from the dead. It's not as though I've already gotten there, or were already complete: but I chase after it, so that I can hold on to that for which I am also held on to by Christ Yeshua. Christians, I don't think myself to have made it: but I do this one thing; I forget the things that are in the past, and reach for things that are ahead of me, I run for the finish line to win the prize of the high calling of God in Christ Yeshua. So whoever wants to be complete should do this same thing: and if you think another way about anything, God will reveal even this to you. Just the same, those who are being completed, should walk by this same rule, and should think in the same way. So, Christians, be followers along with me, and watch those who walk in the way of Christ, so that you have us for an example. I've told you often and now tell you again with tears, that many are enemies of the cross of Christ. Those who live only to eat, and who celebrate in their shameful behaviors, who think only of earthly things will be destroyed in the end. But we live for heaven, where we'll also find the Savior, Yeshua the Christ: Who will change our sinful body, so that it can become like the amazing body of the Christ. And the Christ, by this power, is even able to control everything for the Christ's own purpose.

Don't Worry, Pray

4 [1-9] Christians, my dear loved ones, who I long for, you are my joy and my crown. So keep yourselves in Christ, my dear loved ones. I beg Euodias, and Syntyche to come together in Christ. And I beg you also, my true coworkers, help those women who worked with me in the New Word, along with Clement also, and with my other coworkers, whose names are in the Book of Life. Celebrate in Christ always: and again I say, Celebrate! Let your self-control be seen by everyone. Christ is here. Don't worry about anything; but pray about everything, making known whatever you need to God, with thankfulness. And the peace from God, which is greater than anyone can ever understand, will keep your hearts and minds through Christ Yeshua. Finally, dear Christians, whatever is true, whatever is honest, whatever is right, whatever is pure, whatever is lovely, whatever is spoken well of; if there's anything good, and if there's anything worthy of praise, think about these kinds of things. Those things, which you've learned, and been given, and heard about, and seen me doing, do them and the God of peace will be with you.

[10-20] But I celebrate in Christ greatly, that now, at last, your care for me is growing again; I know you cared for me, even when you couldn't show it. I'm not saying this out of need, because I've learned to be at peace, however I am. I know how to do without, and how it is to have more than I need. I've learned through everything, both to be full and to be hungry, both to have more than enough and to suffer with needs. I can do anything in Christ, who gives me strength. Just the same, you've done well, in that you understood why I suffered. Now you Philippians know also, that in the beginning of the New Word, when I went from Macedonia, that no church talked with me about giving and receiving, but only you. Even in Thessalonica, you sent for my needs once again. I'm not saying this because I want a gift, but because I want the results of what helps you grow. But I have all I need, and am satisfied. I have plenty, having gotten from Epaphroditus the things which you sent, the scent of a sweet smell,

an acceptable sacrifice, well pleasing to God. And my God will give you everything you need out of the riches that have been made known by Christ Yeshua. Now may our God, who we're from, be made known forever and ever. So be it!

[21-23] Say hello to every Christian in Christ Yeshua. Those who are with me say hello to you. All the Christians say hello to you, and most importantly those who are of Caesar's family. The grace of our Christ Yeshua be with you all. So be it!

The wilderness and the lonely place shall be glad for them, and the desert shall rejoice, and blossom as the ROSE. Isaiah 35:1

Paul's Letter to the Colossians

1 [1-17] From Paul, a follower of Yeshua the Christ by the will of God, and Timothy our Christian brother, to the Christians and all the faithful ones in Christ which are at Colosse: May grace and peace be with you, from Yahweh God and Yeshua the Christ. We give thanks to God, who Yeshua the Christ is from, praying always for you, since we heard of your faith in Christ Yeshua, and of the love which you have for all the Christians. The hope which is laid up for you in heaven, in which you heard in the words of truth of the New Word, which is here for you, as it is in all the world, is growing, as it does also in you, since the day you heard it, and knew God's grace in truth. Epaphras our dear coworker, who is a faithful minister of Christ for you, told us of your love in the Spirit. Because of this, we also, since the day we heard it, don't stop praying for you, and wanting you to be filled with the knowledge of what Christ wants with wisdom and spiritual understanding. We hope that you might please God, growing in every good work, and increasing in the knowledge of God; strengthened with all strength, for the amazing power of Christ, in patience and suffering, with joyfulness; giving thanks to God, Who has made us right in order for us to take part of the inheritance of the Christians in light: Who has taken us from the power of darkness, and has brought us into the realm of God's Own Loved Child. We've been bought through Christ's blood to save us from our sins; Who is the living example of the invisible God, the firstborn of every creature. By Christ everything was created, that is in heaven and earth, both visible and invisible, whether it's thrones, or areas of control, or spiritual realms, or powers. Everything was created by Christ, and for Christ: And Christ was before everything, and by the power of Christ everything exists.

Christ is the Head of the Body

[18-29] And Christ is the head of the body, the church: who is the beginning, the first to be raised from the dead; in order to have the most important place in everything. It pleased God that all of the Godhead would be in the Christ; And having made peace through the blood of the cross, by Christ, to bring everything back to God by Christ, I say, whether it's things in earth, or things in heaven. And you, who were at odds at one time and enemies in your minds by the evil that you've done, still now Christ has bought back: In the flesh of Christ's body through death, to set you apart without blame, being unconvictable in God's sight: If you stay in the faith, being well grounded and settled, and don't move away from the hope of the New Word, which you've heard, and which was preached to every creature which is under heaven. I, Paul, am made a minister and now gladly accept my sufferings for you, taking on the troubles of Christ in my body for the body's' sake, which is the church. I am a minister of the church for the privilege of God, who is given to me for you, to fulfill the Word of God; Even the secret which has been hid from ages and from generations, but now is made known to the Christians. God wants to make known the wealth of the victory of this secret among the other peoples; which is Christ in you, the hope of victory: Whom we preach, warning everyone, and teaching everyone in all wisdom; so that we can present each one complete in Christ Yeshua. This is why I also work, striving for the work of God, which works greatly in me.

Cleansed in Christ

2 [1-5] And I wish you knew what great struggles I have for you, and for them at Laodicea, and for whoever hasn't seen me face to face. I hope that their hearts might be in good spirits now, coming together in love, and to have all the wealth of the full assurance of understanding, to know the secrets of God, both of Yahweh God, and of Yeshua the Christ; in whom are hidden all the treasures of wisdom and knowledge. And I say this, in case anyone tries to fool you with tempting words. Because though I am absent in the body, still I am with you in spirit, with joy and watching over you, and seeing the strength of your faith in Christ.

[6-10] So as you've gotten Christ Yeshua, the Savior, walk in Christ, rooted and built up in Christ, and settled in the faith, as you've been taught, prospering in it with thankfulness. Beware, in case anyone tries to ruin you through certain ways of thought and meaningless lies, in the way of human beings, after the ways of the world, and not after Christ. Because all the fullness of the Godhead is in the body of Christ, and you're complete in Christ, which is the head of all spiritual realms and power.

[11-15] And you're cleansed in Christ with a spiritual cleansing, in putting the sins of the flesh out of the spirit by Christ. You're buried with Christ in baptism, and also raised with Christ through the faith of the work of God, who has raised Christ from the dead. And you, being dead in your sins and the uncleanness of your body, have been brought back to life again together with Christ, who has forgiven you all your sins. Christ crossed out the writing of rules that were against us, which were hard for us to follow, and took it out of the way, nailing it to the cross; And having destroyed spiritual realms and powers, Christ made a show of them openly, triumphing over them in it.

[16-19] So let no one judge you in what you eat or drink, or in respect of a holiday, or of the new moon, or of Days of Worship, which are only a shadow of things to come. The body is freed through Christ, so let no one

cheat you out of your reward by tricking you into thinking salvation can be gained by yourselves, or through the worship of angels. They're intruding into what they haven't seen, filled with useless pride by their earthly minds, and not holding on to the Head, from which all the body gets nourishment ministered to it and comes together by joints and ligaments, and grows with the nourishment of God.

[20-23] So if you're dead with Christ from the ways of the world, as though living in the world, are you still subjecting yourselves to rules, (Don't touch; don't taste; don't hold; which are all about things that are gone when they are used;) the rules and teachings created by human beings? And these things do appear to be wise in the worship of human willpower, false humility, and the neglecting of the body, but aren't of any value against the selfishness of the soul.

All are Accepted in Christ

3 [1-4] If you then are risen with Christ, look for what is above, where Christ sits on the right side of God. Place your love on things above, not on things on the earth. Because you're dead to the world, and your life is buried with Christ in God. When Christ, who is our life, appears, then you'll also appear with Christ in victory.

[5-11] So put to death in your bodies, which are on earth, sexual sin, all evil, unnatural affection, evil passions, and greed, which is false worship, because the judgment of God comes on the children of rebelliousness for these very things. And you also once did these kinds of things, when you lived in that way. But now you should also get rid of all these; anger, rage, hatred, disrespect, and filthy talking coming out of your mouth. And don't lie to one another, seeing that you've gotten rid of the old person with your past actions; and have put on the new person, which is renewed in knowledge in the likeness of the One who created you. There's neither one race nor another, cleansed nor uncleansed, foreigner nor uncivilized, worker nor free: but Christ is all that counts, and in Christ, all are accepted.

[12-17] So put on, as the chosen of God, holy and dear loved ones, souls of mercy, kindness, humbleness of mind, gentleness, patience; waiting for one another, and forgiving one another. And if anyone has a problem with someone, just as Christ forgave you, so you should forgive others, too. And above all this, put on love, which is the perfect bond. And let the peace of God rule in your hearts, to which you're called in one body; and be thankful. Let the Word of Christ live richly in you in all wisdom; teaching and warning one another in sayings and songs and spiritual songs, singing with grace in your hearts to God. And whatever you do in word or action, do all in the Name of Christ Yeshua, giving thanks to Yahweh God through Christ.

Family Life

[18-25] Wives, show respect to your own husband, as you would to God. Husbands, love your wife, and don't be abusive with her. Children, obey your parents in everything, which is pleasing to God. Fathers, don't stir up anger in your children, or they will become discouraged. Workers, work hard for your employers at all times as for the physical body; not just when you're seen by them, as people-pleasers; but in the trueness of the heart, as in respect to God. Whatever you do, do it wholeheartedly, as to God, and not just for those you serve; knowing that you'll get the reward of the inheritance from God because you serve Yeshua the Christ. Whoever does wrong will be punished for whatever they've done: and God shows no partiality between persons.

Know How to Answer About Your Faith

4 [1] Employers, pay your workers an equal wage that is fair; knowing that you also have a Boss in heaven.

[2-6] Stay in prayer, and watch in the same with thankfulness; while also praying for us, that God would open to us a door to speak the New Word, so we can tell the secrets of Christ, for which I'm in jail, also. I want to make it plain, as I should speak. Walk in wisdom toward those who are outside the church, buying your time. Speak always with grace, seasoned with salt, so that you can know how you should answer everyone.

[7-9] Tychicus will tell you how I'm doing, who is a dearly loved brother, and a faithful minister and coworker in Christ: Whom I've sent to you for the same purpose, to know how you are, and to comfort your hearts; with Onesimus, a faithful and dearly loved brother, who is one of you. They'll let you know everything that's happened here.

[10-17] Aristarchus, my jail mate says hello to you, and Mark, the cousin of Barnabas, (the one about whom you've already gotten word: if he comes to you, take him in;) And Jesus, which is called Justus, who are Jews. These are my only coworkers in the realm of God, which have been a great comfort to me. Epaphras, who is one of you, a worker of Christ, says hello to you, always praying hard for you, so that you can stand completely perfect in everything God wants. I tell you, that they have a great passion for you, along with those who are in Laodicea, and those in Hierapolis. The dearly loved, Dr. Luke, and Demas say hello to you. Say hello to the Christians which are in Laodicea, and Nymphas, and the church which is in their house. And when this letter is read among you, let it be read also in the church of the Laodiceans; and you read the letter from Laodicea. And say to Archippus, "Be true to the ministry which you've gotten in Christ, so that you complete it."

[18] The Greeting is by my own hand, Paul. Remember I am in jail. May grace be with you! So be it!

214

Paul's First Letter to the Thessalonians

1 [1-10] From Paul, Silvanus, and Timothy, to the church of the Thessalonians, which is in Yahweh God and in Yeshua the Christ: May grace and peace be with you, from Yahweh God, and Yeshua the Christ. We give thanks to God always for all of you, mentioning you in our prayers; never forgetting your work of faith, and work of love, and patience of hope in Yeshua, our Christ, in the sight of Yahweh God. And we know, Christians, dear loved ones, that you were chosen of God, our New Word not coming to you only in word, but also in power, and in the Holy Spirit, and in much promise. You know by others what kind of people we were among you for your sake. And you became followers of us, and of Christ, having gotten the Word in much suffering, but with joy of the Holy Spirit. You were examples to all that believe in Macedonia and Achaia. From you the Word of God sounded out, not only in Macedonia and Achaia, but also everywhere your faith toward God has spread, so that we don't need to say anything. They themselves say of us how we came to you, and how you turned to God from worshiping other things to serve the living and true God; And to wait for Yeshua, God's Child from heaven, whom was raised from the dead, which keeps us from the punishment to come.

Give up Your Life for Others

2 [1-12] You yourselves, Christians, know our coming to you wasn't for nothing. Even after we had suffered, and were shamefully treated, as you know, at Philippi, in our God, we weren't afraid to speak to you the New Word of God with a lot of argument, because our encouragement wasn't a mistake, nor of evil, nor in untruthfulness. We were trusted by God with the New Word, in the same way we speak; not as pleasing others, but God, which tries our hearts; Nor did we ever use flattering words, as you know, nor a coat of greed; God is our witness: Nor did we look for praise from humanity, not from you, nor from anyone else, when we might have asked for help, as the followers of Christ. But we were gentle among you, just as a breastfeeding mother loves her own child. So lovingly hoping for you, we were willing to have given to you, not only the New Word of God, but also our own lives, because we loved you so much. And you remember, Christians, our work and pain because we worked night and day, so we wouldn't be a hardship to any of you, and we preached to you the New Word of God. You're witnesses, and God also, how faithfully and justly and unblameably we behaved ourselves among you that believe. You know how we encouraged and comforted and told everyone of you, as a parent does their children, to walk worthy of God, who has called you to victory in the realm of God.

[13-16] Because of this, we never stop thanking God also, because, when you had gotten the Word of God, which You heard from us, you didn't take it as a word from just humans, but as it is in truth, the Word of God, which actually works in you who believe, as well. And you, Christians, became followers of the churches of God which are in Judea in Christ Yeshua, because you also have suffered the same kinds of things from your own people, just as they have from the Jews: Who both killed the Christ Yeshua, and their own great preachers, and have abused us. They don't please God, and are against everyone else, forbidding us to speak to the other peoples so that they can be saved, to complete their sins always because the judgment is on them here to the full.

[17-20] But we, Christians, being taken from you for a little while in presence, but not in spirit, tried all the more to see you face to face with great love. We would have come to you, even I, Paul, once again; but Satan stopped us. But what is our hope, or joy, or crown of joy? Isn't it you, in the presence of our Christ Yeshua, at the second coming? Yes, you're our victory and joy.

Grow and Prosper In Love

3 [1-13] So when we could no longer wait, we thought it best to be left at Athens alone. So we sent Timothy, our Christian brother, and minister of God, and our coworker in the New Word of Christ, to teach you, and to comfort you in your faith: That no one would be upset by these troubles because you yourselves know that we're chosen to be like this. The truth is, when we were with you, we told you to that we would suffer troubles, just as it happened, and you know. And because of this, when I could no longer wait, I sent to know your faith, in case by some means the tempter had tempted you, and our work was meaningless. But now, when Timothy came from you to us, and brought us the good news of your faith and love, and that you remember us well, always hoping to see us, as we also hope to see you. So, Christians, we were comforted about you in all our suffering and sorrow by your faith, because now we live, if you stay in God. And what thanks can we give to God for you, for all the joy that we have for your sakes before our God? Night and day, we pray greatly that we might see your face, and might give you what is lacking in your faith. Now may God, who we're from, and Yeshua, our Christ, guide us to you. And God make you grow and prosper in love toward one another, and toward everyone, just as we do toward you: To the end that God can keep your hearts without blame in faithfulness to God, even our God, at the coming of our Christ Yeshua with all the Christians.

Work Hard, Walk Honestly

4 [1-12] So we beg you, Christians, and encourage you by Christ Yeshua, that as you've gotten from us how you should walk to please God, so you would prosper more and more. And you know the Words we gave you by Christ Yeshua, because this is what God wants, that you be set apart and blessed. God wants you to give up sexual sin, so that everyone of you would know how to keep their body set apart, with blessing and honor; Not in the need of excitement, like other people who don't know God. No one should go beyond this and take advantage of another in any matter, because God is the punisher of everything like this, as we also have warned you and told you truthfully. God hasn't called us to evil, but to faithfulness. So whoever hates this, doesn't just hate the person who brought it, but God, who has also given to us the Holy Spirit. But as to the love of friendships, you don't need me to write to you because you yourselves are taught of God to love one another. And though you do this toward all the Christians, which are in all Macedonia, we beg you, Christians, that you let your love grow more and more; Try to lead a quiet life, and to mind your own business, and work hard with your own hands, as we told you; so that you can walk in honesty with those who are outside the faith, and that you can lack nothing.

The Dead in Christ Rise First

[13-18] But I want you to know, Christians, about those who are dead, so that you don't sorrow, as others which have no hope. Because if we believe that Yeshua died and rose again, in the same way God will bring with Christ those who are dead in Yeshua. And we say this to you by the Word of God, that we, who are alive and stay here to the second coming of Christ, won't keep those who are dead from coming to life before us. Christ will come down from heaven with a shout, with the voice of the archangel, and with the trumpet of God. The dead in Christ will rise up first, and then we which are still alive and here will be taken up together with them in the clouds, to meet Christ in the sky: and so we'll be with Christ forever. So comfort one another with these words.

Christ Comes Unexpectedly

5 [1-11] But of the times and the seasons, Christians, you don't need me to write to you, because you yourselves fully know that the day of Christ comes as a thief in the night. And when they say, "Peace and safety;" then punishment will come on them suddenly, as pain on a woman in labor; and they won't escape. But you, Christians, don't live in darkness that the time would take you by surprise. You're all children of light, and children of the day: we aren't of the night, nor of darkness. So let's not sleep, as others do; but let's watch and use good sense. Those who are sleeping sleep in the night; and those who are drunk are drunken in the night. But let us, who are of the day, use good sense, putting on the body armor of faith and love; and for a helmet, the hope of being saved. Because God hasn't chosen us for punishment, but to be saved by our Christ Yeshua, who died for us, so that, whether we're still alive or are dead, we would live together with Christ. So comfort yourselves together, and help one another, just as you're doing.

Respect the Leader's in Christ

[12-22] And we beg you, Christians, to acknowledge those who work among you, and are over you in Christ, and warn you; Think of them very highly in love for their work's sake. Be at peace among yourselves. Now we encourage you, Christians, warn those who don't act right, comfort the mentally ill, support the weak, and be patient toward everyone. See that no one gives evil for evil to anyone. Always try to do what is good, both for yourselves, and for everyone else. Celebrate always, and never stop praying. In every thing give thanks because this is what God wants in Christ Yeshua for you. Don't hold back the Spirit. Don't hate the preaching. Prove everything; hold on to what is good. Give up anything that even appears to be evil. And the very God of peace will wholly set you apart; and I pray to God that your whole spirit, soul, and body be kept safely without fault to the coming of our Christ Yeshua. Faithful is the One who calls you, who also will do it.

[25-28] Everyone, pray for us. Say hello to all the Christians with a kiss of love. I tell you by God to read this letter to all the faithful Christians. May the grace of our Christ Yeshua be with you. So be it!

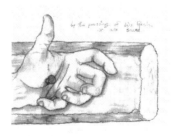

216

Paul's Second Letter to the Thessalonians

1 [1-2] From Paul, Silvanus, and Timothy, to the church of the Thessalonians, in Yahweh our God and Yeshua the Christ: May you be blessed with grace and peace, from Yahweh, our God, and Yeshua the Christ.

[3-12] We must thank God for you always, Christians, as is right, because your faith grows greatly, and the love of everyone of you all toward each other grows. We ourselves have success in you in the churches of God for your patience and faith in all your abuses and trials that you keep on going through. This is clear proof of the fairness of God's judgment, that you can be found worthy of the realm of God, for which you also suffer. It's a good thing with God to repay troubles to those who trouble you. And so you, who are uneasy, can rest with us when Yeshua the Christ comes from heaven with God's powerful angels to punish in flaming fire those who don't know God, and that don't obey the New Word of Yeshua the Christ. These will be punished with endless destruction and put out of the presence of God, and from the light of God's power when the Christ comes to be known in the Christians, and to be admired by all those who believe (because our profession among you was believed) in that day. So we also always pray for you, that our God would count you worthy of this calling, and complete all the joy of God's goodness, and the work of faith with power, so that the Name of our Christ Yeshua, can be made known in you, and you in God, for the grace of our God and Yeshua the Christ.

A Loss of Faith Before Christ Comes Again

2 [1-12] Now, Christians, about the coming of our Christ Yeshua, and about our gathering together to be with Christ, we beg you not to be quickly upset in your mind, nor to be uneasy, not by spirit, not by word, and not by letter, as if from us, as if the day of Christ had already come. Let no one mislead you by any means, because that Day won't come, unless a great loss of faith comes first, and that *soul of sin* becomes known, the child of Hell; Who opposes and praises them self above all that is called God, or that is worshipped; so that as God, they will sit in the Place of Worship of God, believing that they are God. Don't you remember that when I was still with you I told you this? And now you know what is keeping this from happening, and that they will become known in their own time. Because the secret of sin is already working, only the One who now lets this happen will let it happen, until that one is taken out of the way. And then that evil one will become known, whom God will burn up with the blast of Christ's breath, and will destroy with the brightness of Christ's coming. This is the one, whose coming is after the working of Satan, with all power, amazing signs, things without truth, and all the ungodly lies in those who are to be destroyed; because they didn't accept the love of the truth, in order to be saved. And for this reason, God will send a strong sense of false belief on them, so that they'll believe the lie, and that they'll all be damned, who didn't believe the truth, but enjoyed ungodliness.

[13-17] But we must thank God for you always, Christians, dear loved ones of God, because God has chosen you from the beginning to be saved by the blessing of the Spirit and by your belief of the truth. You were called by our New Word, in order to get the light of our Christ Yeshua. So, Christians, stand your ground, and keep the way of life which you've been taught, whether by word, or our letter. Now may our Christ Yeshua, and Yahweh God, who we are from and who has loved us, and has given us everlasting reassurance and a good hope through grace, comfort your hearts, and approve you in every good word and work.

Stay Away from Disorderly Christians

3 [1-5] Finally, Christians, pray for us, that the Word of God will have free reign, and become well known, just as it's known by you: And that we'll be spared from unreasonable and evil people, because some of them don't have faith. But God is faithful, who will approve you, and keep you from the evil one. And we have trust in God about you, both that you do and will do the things we tell you to do. And may Christ guide your hearts into God's love, and into patient waiting for Christ.

[6-16] Now we tell you, Christians, in the Name of our Christ Yeshua, that you stay away from every person that calls themselves a Christian that walks disorderly, and not in the way of life which they learned from us. You yourselves know how you should follow us, because we weren't disorderly among you; Neither did we eat anyone's food for nothing; but worked with sweat and hard work night and day, so that we wouldn't be chargeable to any of you: Not because we don't have the right, but to make ourselves an example for you to follow us. Even when we were with you, we told you this, that if anyone wouldn't work, neither would they eat. And we hear that there are some who are walking disorderly among you, not working at all, but being busybodies. Now those who are such people, we tell and advise by our Christ Yeshua that they work without arguing, and eat their own food. But you, Christians, don't get tired of doing good. And if anyone doesn't obey our word by this letter, note that person, and stay away from them, so that they will be ashamed. Yet don't think of them as an enemy, but warn them as a Christian. Now may the God of peace give you peace always and by all ways. God be with you all.

217

[17-18] I write the Greeting of Paul with my own hand, which is the sign in every letter. May the grace of our Christ Yeshua be with you all. So be it!

Paul's First Letter to Timothy

1 [1-2] Paul, a follower of Yeshua the Christ by the Word of God, our Savior, Yeshua the Christ, which is our hope; To Timothy, a true child in the faith: Grace, mercy, and peace from Yahweh God and Yeshua our Christ.

The Word of God for the Disobedient

[3-11] Now do as I said when I begged you to stay at Ephesus, and I went on to Macedonia. Tell your people not to teach any other teachings, nor to pay attention to stories and endless genealogies, which only cause questions, instead of building them up in their faith in God. Now I said this out of love from a pure heart, and a good conscience, and a heartfelt faith. But some of you, having changed their way, have turned aside to meaningless talking, wanting to be teachers of the Word of God, but they don't understand what they say, nor what they uphold. But we know that the Word of God is good, if used rightly; So we know that the Word of God wasn't given for good people, but for the lawless and disobedient, the ungodly and sinners, the unholy and disrespectful, for murderers, for those who are sexually unfaithful, or homosexual, kidnappers, liars, and anything else that's against the good teachings of the amazing New Word of the blessed God, with which I have been entrusted.

[12-20] I thank Yeshua our Christ, who has enabled me, who thought of me as faithful, putting me into the ministry. Before I was someone who spoke evil of the church, mistreating, and hurting those in it: but I found mercy, because I did it unknowingly in unbelief. And great was the grace of our Christ with faith and love, which is found in Christ Yeshua. Christ Yeshua came into the world to save sinners; of whom I'm the greatest. This is a faithful saying, and worthy of acceptance. But I found mercy so that Yeshua the Christ might show complete patience in me first, as an example to those who would believe on the Christ later to have everlasting life. Now to the invisible, everlasting Ruler, who can never be destroyed, the only wise God, be honor and victory forever and ever. So be it! I'm entrusting to you everything that I tell you, my child Timothy, according to the word which was spoken of you before, that by these things you might fight a good fight, holding on to your faith with a good conscience. But some having lost their faith, have become like those who are shipwrecked. I've given over Hymenaeus and Alexander to Satan, so that they might be taught not to speak evil of God.

The Beauty of Women of Godliness

2 [1-7] So, I encourage, that, first of all, our prayers, both for what we need and speaking up for others, and the giving of thanks, be made for everyone; Both for the rulers, and for all that are in power; so that we can lead a quiet and peaceable life in every godly way and in all honesty. This is good and acceptable in the sight of God our Savior, who wants everyone to be saved, and to come to the knowledge of the truth. There's One God, and One who speaks up for us to God for humanity, the person Christ Yeshua; Who willingly died to pay for the sins of all, to be shown to us in truth at the right time. I am set apart to be a great preacher, and a follower, (I speak the truth in Christ, I'm not lying;) to teach the other peoples in faith and truth.

[8-15] So I want people everywhere to pray, worshiping with uplifted hands, being holy, without rage and doubting. Just the same, women should dress themselves properly in acceptable clothing, with self-control; not with fancy hairdos, or fine jewelry, or high-priced clothes; But with what really beautifies women of godliness, that is, with the good things that they do. Allow the women to learn quietly, accepting the Word of God. But I don't allow a woman to teach, nor to have power over her own husband, but to be quiet in this case. Because Adam was first formed, then Eve. And Adam sinned knowingly, but the woman, being lied to, came into sin. Just the same, a woman will be saved through the birth of a child, if they keep the faith in love and faithfulness with seriousness.

Guidelines for Overseers and Leaders

3 [1-10] It's true, if anyone wants the office of an overseer, they want a good thing. An overseer then must be without fault, the spouse of one spouse, watchful, self-controlled, having good behavior, welcoming to strangers, able to teach, not a heavy drinker, nor an abuser, not greedy for money, but unselfish, patient, and not argumentative; Someone that leads their own home well, having their children well disciplined, and showing respect; (if someone doesn't know how to lead their own home, how can they take care of the church of God?) It must not be someone new in the faith, in case being lifted up with pride they fall into the same judgment as the devil. Besides this, they need to have a good report of those not in the church; in case they're dishonored and are tempted by the devil. In the same way, the ministers of the church must be serious, not saying different things to different people, not a heavy drinker, not greedy for money, holding the secret of the faith in a pure conscience. And these should also be proved first and if they are found without fault, then let them serve the office of a minister.

[11-16] In the same way, the women who lead must be serious, not gossipers, watchful, faithful in everything. Let the ministers of the church be the spouse of one spouse, leading their children and their own homes well. Those who serve the office of a minister well must have a good standing for themselves, and great courage in the faith which is in Christ Yeshua. I write this to you, hoping to come to you shortly, but if I stay long, so that you can know how people should act in the house of God, which is the church of the living God, the strength and foundation of the truth. And without a doubt, the secret of godliness is great: God was made known in the body, made complete in the Spirit, seen of angels, preached about to the nations, believed on in the world, and taken up in victory!

The Latter Times

4 [1-10] Now the Spirit openly says, that in the latter times some will leave the faith, being led away by tempting spirits, and teachings of evil spirits; Pretending to be what they aren't and lying; having their conscience ruined; Forbidding people to marry, and telling them to give up eating meats, which God has created to be eaten with thankfulness by those who believe and know the truth. Every creature of God is good, and nothing is to be refused, if it's eaten with thankfulness. It's set apart by the Word of God and prayer. If you remind the Christians of this, you're a good minister of Yeshua the Christ, grown up in the words of faith and in the good teachings, which you've followed. Don't believe godless myths and old fairytales, but instead train yourself to be godly. Training the body does a little good, but godliness is good for everything, holding promise for the life that you have now, and for your life to come. This is a faithful saying and worthy to be accepted. So we both work and suffer dishonor, because we trust in the living God, who is the Savior of everyone, especially of those who believe.

[11-16] Tell this and teach it and let no one find fault with you for your youth; but be an example to believers, in word, in lifestyle, in love, in spirit, in faith, in purity. Take care of the reading, the preaching, and the teaching until I come. Don't neglect the gift that is in you, which was given to you by word, which was told you before, when the elders laid hands on you. Think about these things; giving your full attention to them; so that your spiritual growth will appear to all. Be careful of yourself, and of the Word of God; stay in it, because in doing this you'll both save yourself, and those who hear you.

Treatment of Elders and Widows

5 [1-16] Don't accuse an elder, but treat them as a parent; and the younger ones as siblings; The elder women as mothers; the younger women as sisters, with all decency. Honor widows that are true widows, but if any widow has children or other family, let them first show their faith at home by repaying their parents because that is good and acceptable to God. Now those who are true widows, having no one to care for them, trust in God, and keep on praying and asking God for help night and day. But those who live richly in pleasures are dead even while they live. Tell them these things, so that they can be without fault. So if anyone doesn't give for their own, and especially for those of their own home, they have no true faith, and are worse than an unbeliever. Don't let a widow be counted, who is under sixty years old, and only if she has been the spouse of one person, spoken well of for the good she's done; if she's brought up her children, if she's taken in strangers, if she's taken care of the needs of Christians, if she's helped the troubled, if she's done everything good with care. But the younger widows refuse because when their physical needs turn them against following Christ, they'll remarry, bringing judgment on themselves, if they break their promises to God. And besides this, they learn to be lazy, going from house to house; and not only to be lazy, but to gossip and to mind other peoples' business, telling things which they shouldn't. So I'd rather that the younger women remarry, have children, keep the house, give the enemy nothing to speak evil of. Some have already followed after Satan. So if anyone believes they have widows, let them take care of them, and don't let the church be troubled; so that the church can take care of those who are really in need.

[17-25] Let the elders that lead well, especially those who preach and teach the Word, be thought of as worthy of double honor. The Word says, "Don't muzzle the cow that grinds the grain;" And "The worker is worthy of their pay." Don't accept an accusation against an elder, unless there are two or three witnesses. Those who sin should be accused before the church, so that others will fear also. I tell you, before God, and Yeshua the Christ, and the chosen angels, to do this without prejudice, not doing favors for anyone. Don't lay hands on anyone too quickly, nor take part in the sins of others: keep yourself pure. Don't drink water only any longer, but use a little wine for your stomach's sake and your sicknesses, which comes often. Some people's sins are clearly seen even before they go to judgment; and some aren't known till later. It's the same also with the good that's done; Some good things are clearly seen now; and those things that aren't seen, won't be hidden forever.

If We have Food and Clothing, Be Happy

6 [1-10] Let all the workers who are forced to work for someone else count those they work to be worthy of the most respect, so that the Name of God and these teachings aren't spoken evil of. And those who work for believers, shouldn't show them any less because they're Christians, but should work harder for them, because the one who has been helped by the work is a faithful and dear loved one. Teach this and encourage it. If anyone teaches otherwise, and doesn't accept these good words, which are the Words of our Christ Yeshua, and the Word of God, which are for godliness; That person is proud, knowing nothing, but loves to argue and fight about words, which only bring jealousy, fighting, abuses, evil imaginings, and unreasonable arguments by those with ruined minds, who don't have the truth. They think that a show of religion brings financial gain, so stay away from these kinds of people. But true godliness with peace is a great gain. We bring nothing into this world, and we certainly can't take anything out of it, so if we have food and clothing, let's be happy with that. But those who want to be rich fall into temptation and a trap, wanting many stupid and hurtful things, which ruin them and send them to Hell. The love of money is the root of all evils. Some, being greedy for it, leave the faith, and give themselves a world full trouble.

The Good Fight of Faith

[11-16] But you, dear one of God, escape this; and follow after goodness, godliness, faith, love, patience, and gentleness. Fight the good fight of faith. Hold on to the everlasting life, to which you've been called. You've made a good confession to many witnesses. I tell you, in the sight of God, who gives life to everything, and to Christ Yeshua, who made a good confession to Pontius Pilate, to keep this word without fault, blameless, until the appearing of our Christ Yeshua. The Christ will be made known at just the right time, who is the blessed and only Supreme One, the Ruler of rulers, and the Savior of saviors; Who is the only Everlasting Spirit, which lives in the light which no one can come near to; whom no one has seen, nor can see: to whom be everlasting honor and power. So be it!

[17-21] Tell those who are rich in this world, not to think themselves as better than others, nor trust in uncertain riches, but to trust in the living God, who richly gives us everything to enjoy; That they do good things, that they be rich in good behavior, ready to give, willing to share; Saving up for themselves a good treasure for the time to come, so that they can take hold of everlasting life. Timothy, keep what has been put in your trust, keeping away from ungodly and mindless arguments, and disagreements about what is falsely called knowledge, which some have accepted and left the faith. Grace be with you. So be it!

221

Paul's Second Letter to Timothy

1 [1-18] From Paul, a follower of Yeshua the Christ by the will of God, for the promise of life which is in Christ Yeshua; To Timothy, a dearly loved child: Grace, mercy, and peace from Yahweh God and Yeshua our Christ. I thank God, whom I serve with a good conscience as my ancestors did, that I've always remembered you in my prayers, both night and day. When I think of your tears, I greatly hope to see you, that I can be joyful when I remember the heartfelt faith that is in you, which lived first in your grandmother Lois, and your mother Eunice. I am sure that it's in you also. I want to help you remember so that you'll awaken the gift of God, which is in you from the time I laid my hands on you. God has given us a spirit of self-control, of good mental health, and of love, and not a spirit of fear. So don't be ashamed to speak of our Christ, nor of me the prisoner of Christ: but share in the troubles of the New Word for the power of God; Who has saved us, and called us with a holy calling; not for what we've done, but for God's own purpose and grace, which was given us in Christ Yeshua before the creation of the world. This is now made known by the appearing of our Savior, Yeshua the Christ, who has put an end to death, and has brought everlasting life to light through the New Word. I am chosen to be a great preacher, a follower, and a teacher of the other peoples, for which I also suffer. But I'm not ashamed because I know who I believe in, and am sure that God is able to keep what I've trusted Christ with until that day. Hold on to what you've heard from me as an example of good teachings in the faith and love, which is in Christ Yeshua. Keep that good thing which was trusted to you by the Holy Spirit which lives in us. You know that all those who are in Asia have turned away from me; of whom are Phygellus and Hermogenes. God give mercy to the house of Onesiphorus because they often awakened my spirit, and wasn't ashamed of my being locked up. He searched hard for me until he found me when he came to Rome. God allowed him the gift of mercy in that day: you know very well how many times he ministered to me at Ephesus.

Keep On Going Through Everything

2 [1-14] So, my child, be strong in the grace that is in Christ Yeshua. The things that you've heard from me among many witnesses, entrust the same to faithful ones, who will be able to teach others also. Keep on going, even in troubles, as a good soldier of Yeshua the Christ. No one who fights gets themselves mixed up with the pleasures of this life; so that they can please the one who has chosen them to be a soldier. And if someone wins a race, aren't they awarded a winner's crown, if they follow the rules. Also the farmer that works hard is the first one to get a share of the crops. Consider what I say; and God will give you understanding in everything. Remember that Yeshua the Christ, from the line of David, was raised from the dead according to the New Word. I suffer troubles because of this, even to the point of my being locked up as an evil doer; but the Word of God isn't locked away. So I keep on going through everything for the sake of those who are chosen, so that they can also be saved in Christ Yeshua with everlasting victory. Here's a faithful saying: If we die with Christ, we'll also live with Christ: If we suffer, we'll also reign with the Christ: if we disown the Christ, the Christ will also disown us: If we don't believe, still the Christ is faithful, who can't disown the Christ's own self. Help them remember this, telling them before God, not to argue about words, which is to no good, but only to the weakening of those who hear.

Study and Know God's Word

[15-26] Study, to show yourself that you're approved by God, a worker who need not be ashamed, correctly understanding the Word of Truth. But ignore ungodly and meaningless talk because it only brings more ungodliness. The words of Hymenaeus and Philetus eat away like a cancer; Who have left the truth, saying that the new life has already come; and have overcome the faith of some. But the foundation of God stands true, having this seal, *"God knows those who belong to Christ."* And *"Let everyone that names the Name of Christ stop sinning."* But in a great house there aren't just bowls of gold and of silver, but also of wood and clay, some being for more graceful purposes, and some being for disgraceful purposes. So if a person cleanses them self from disgraceful uses, they'll be like a graceful bowl, set apart, right for the owner's use, and made to do good things. Quickly run away from the wants of youth: but follow after goodness, faith, love, and peace, along with those who call on God out of a pure heart. Ignore stupid questions about things that haven't been taught, knowing that they only start arguments. The worker of God must not argue; but be gentle to everyone, able to teach, patient in evil times, teaching those who are against themselves in gentleness. God may give them a changed life in coming to know the truth; And then they can get themselves out of the trap of the devil, who are taken captive at Satan's will.

The Last Days

3 [1-17] Know this also, that many dangers will come in the last days. Human beings will be lovers of their own selves, greedy for money, full of themselves, proud, speaking evil, disobedient to parents, unthankful, ungodly, without love, breaking peace, liars, without self-control, abusers, haters of what's good, spies, impulsive, self-righteous, lovers of pleasure more than lovers of God; Appearing to be godly, but not having the power of true godliness: Turn away from everything like this. It's this kind of people that sneak into homes, holding captive, and misleading those who are unlearned in the New Word, who have many sins, and are led away by all the things they want. They always want to learn something new, but never accept the knowledge of the truth. Now just as Jannes and Jambres stood against Moses, so do these also fight against the truth: having ruined minds, unacceptable in the faith. As theirs was also, these will go no further because their stupidity will be made known to everyone. But you fully know all my teachings, my way of life, purpose, faith, willpower, love, and patience. You know the discriminations I've suffered through and my troubles, which came to me at Antioch, at Iconium, at Lystra: but God brought me out of them all. Yes, and all that will live godly in Christ Yeshua will suffer discrimination. But evil people and liars will grow worse and worse, lying, and being lied to. But keep the things which you've learned and have been assured of, knowing of whom you've learned them; And that you've known the holy Words from your childhood, which are able to save you and make you wise through faith which is in Christ Yeshua. Every part of the Word is breathed by God, and is good for teaching, for discipline, for correction, for teaching good behavior, so that the people of God can be complete, carefully trained to do what's right.

A Crown of Goodness Waits for Us

4 [1-8] So I tell you before God, and Yeshua the Christ, who will judge the living and the dead at the Christ's appearing and reign; Preach the Word; be ready at any time; convict, correct, and encourage with great patience and good teachings. The time will come when people won't keep on living by godly principles; but they'll take to themselves teachers, who teach them what they want to hear. They won't listen to the truth, but will turn to make believe stories. Watch in everything, keep on going in your troubles, do the work of one who tells others the New Word, giving full proof of your ministry. I'm ready now to be offered up, and the time for me to leave is here. I've fought a good fight, I've finished my race, I've kept the faith: Now a crown of goodness is waiting for me, which the God who judges those who do good, will give me at that time: and not just to me, but also to all those who wait for the Christ's appearing.

[9-18] Do your best to come to me shortly, because Demas has left me, having loved this present world, and went to Thessalonica; Crescens to Galatia, Titus to Dalmatia. Only Luke is with me, now. Take Mark, and bring him with you because he's of use to me in the ministry. Tychicus I have sent to Ephesus. Bring with you the coat that I left at Troas with Carpus, when you come, along with the books, but especially the parchments. Alexander, the metalworker, did me very wrong: God will repay him for what he's done: Whom you should beware of also because he has greatly fought against our words. At my first defense, I stood alone, no one coming to my defense: I pray God won't hold it against them. But Christ stood with me, and gave me strength; that by me the New Word might be fully known, and that all the other peoples might hear: and I was taken out of the mouth of the lion. And God will deliver me from every evil work, and will bring me safely to the Christ's heavenly country. Let Christ be known forever and ever. So be it!

[19-22] Say hello to Prisca and Aquila, and the family of Onesiphorus. Erastus stayed at Corinth: but Trophimus I've left at Miletum sick. Do your best to get here before winter. Eubulus says hello to you, and Pudens, and Linus, and Claudia, and all the Christians. May Yeshua the Christ be with your spirit. May God's grace be with you. So be it!

Paul's Letter to Titus

1 [1-4] From Paul, a worker of God, and a follower of Yeshua the Christ, for the faith of God's chosen, and the acknowledging of the truth which works for godliness; In hope of everlasting life, which God, who can't lie, promised before the world began; But has at just the right time made known the Word of God through preaching, which is trusted to me according to the Word of Christ our Savior; To Titus, my own child in the common faith: Grace, mercy, and peace from Yahweh God and Yeshua the Christ, our Savior.

Ordain Overseers and Elders

[5-16] Because of this, I left you in Crete, that you would set in order the things that still need to be done, and ordain elders in every city, as I had chosen you: If a person is without blame, the spouse of one spouse, having faithful children not accused of rebellion or unruliness. Because an overseer must be without fault, as a manager of God; not selfish, not getting angry too quickly, not a heavy drinker, not abusive, and not greedy for rich living; But has a love for hospitality, a love for good people, serious, fair, holy, and reasonable; Keeping the faithful word as they have been taught, that they can be able by good principles both to encourage and to convince those who argue. There are many unruly and empty talkers and misleaders, especially those of the Jews: Whose mouths must be stopped, who weaken whole homes, teaching things which they shouldn't, for the sake of money. One of them, even a great preacher of their own, said, "The Cretians are always liars, evil animals, lazy pigs." This witness is true. So accuse them sharply, so that they can be firm in the faith; not paying attention to Jewish stories, and words of people, who turn from the truth. To the innocent everything is innocent: but to those who are ruined and unbelieving nothing is innocent; even their mind and conscience is ruined. They say that they know God, but by what they've done they disown Christ, being sickening, and disobedient, and not fit for any good work.

Instructions On How to Live

2 [1-15] But say the things which agree with good principles: That the older men use good sense, be respectful, reasonable, sensible in the faith, in love, and in patience. And the same with the older women, that they be in action as agrees with faithfulness, not liars, not drinking too much alcohol, and teachers of good things; so that they can teach the young women to use good sense, to love their husbands, and to love their children, to be careful, faithful, homemakers, good, respectful to their own husbands, that the Word of God won't be disrespected. Just the same encourage the younger ones to use good sense. Be an example with the good that you do in everything: showing reliability, thoughtfulness, and honesty in the Word, along with good speech, that can't be accused; that whoever argues with you will be ashamed, having nothing bad to say about you. Encourage workers to be acceptable to their own bosses, and to please them well in everything; not talking back; not stealing, but showing themselves trustworthy; that they can beautify the Word of God our Savior in everything. Because God's grace that saves has appeared to humanity, teaching us to reject ungodliness and earthly wants, and to live seriously, with right and godly actions in this present world; Looking for that blessed hope, and the amazing appearance of our great God and Savior Yeshua the Christ; Whose own self was given for us, to free us from all sin, and to cleanse us for Christ's own self, a special people, passionate to do good things. You have every right to speak these things, and encourage, and warn, so let no one resent you.

We are Made Right by God's Grace

3 [1-11] Remind them to respect rulers and powers, to obey the courts, to be ready for all good works, to speak evil of no one, to not be abusive, but gentle and humble with everyone, because we ourselves were also sometimes stupid, disobedient, believing lies, self-serving with different kinds of wants and pleasures, living in hatred and jealousy, being hateful, and hating one another. But after the kindness and love of God our Savior toward humanity appeared, not by any goodness that we've done, but for Christ's mercy we were saved, by the washing of rebirth, and the renewing of the Holy Spirit; Which God shed on us greatly through Yeshua the Christ, our Savior; that being made right by God's grace, we would become heirs for the hope of everlasting life. This is a faithful saying, and I want you to say this often, so that those who have believed in God might be careful to maintain what good they've done. These things are both good and profitable for everyone. But keep away from stupid questions, genealogies, arguments, and disputes about the Word of God because they're useless and mean nothing. Reject those who are rebellious after the first and second warning; knowing that those who are like this are weakened, and sinful, being damned of themselves.

[12-14] When I send Artemas or Tychicus to you, be careful to come to me in Nicopolis because I've decided to winter there. Bring Zenas, the lawyer and Apollos on their journey carefully, so that they will have everything they need. And let our people also learn to keep doing the good things that they've done, meeting necessary needs, so that they won't be unfruitful.

[15] Everyone here with me says hello to you. Say hello to those who love us in the faith. God's grace be with you all. So be it!

Paul's Letter to Philemon

1 [1-7] I Paul, a prisoner for the sake of Yeshua the Christ and Timothy our Christian coworker, to Philemon our dear loved one and coworker, and to our dear loved ones Apphia, and Archippus, our friends, and to the church in your house: May the grace and peace of Yahweh God, our Creator, and Yeshua the Christ, come to you. I thank my God, always mentioning your name in my prayers, because I've been hearing of your love and faith, which you have for Christ Yeshua, and for all Christians. I pray that your faith can be shared successfully by seeing everything that is good in you, which is in Christ Yeshua. We have great joy and comfort in your love, because the souls of the Christians are awakened by you, friend.

[8-20] Though I might be fearless in Christ to tell you what I think is right, yet for love's sake I ask you instead, being old as I, Paul, am, and now also a prisoner for Yeshua the Christ. I ask you for my child, Onesimus, who I converted while locked up, which in the past was useless to you, but now is useful both to you and me. I've sent him back: so please accept him, as if he were me. I would like to have kept him with me, so that he could have ministered to me in the work of the New Word in your place. But without knowing what you think about it, I didn't want to do anything; so that whatever you do wouldn't be because you have to, but because you want to. Maybe he went the wrong way for a little while, so that you would accept him forever. Now, he isn't like a forced-worker, but more than a worker, he's a dear loved one and Christian, especially to me, but how much more to you, both in the physical realm, and in the Spirit of Christ? If you consider me as a friend, accept him as you would me. And if he has wronged you in any way, or owes you anything, let me take care of it. I, Paul, have written this with my own hand, so I'll repay it: not to mention the fact that you owe me much, and besides this, even your own self. Yes, my Christian brother, give me joy in God: let my soul be awakened in God.

[21-25] Being completely sure of your agreement, I wrote to you, knowing that you'll also do more than I ask. But get a place ready for me to stay because I trust that through your prayers I'll be allowed to come back to you. Epaphras, my prison mate in Christ Yeshua, says hello, as do Mark, Aristarchus, Demas, and Luke, my coworkers. May God's grace in Yeshua the Christ be with your spirit. So be it!

A Letter to the Hebrews
(Author Unknown)

1 [1-14] God spoke to our ancestors in the past many different times and in many different ways by the great preachers, and has in these last days spoken to us by God's Child, who has been chosen to be heir of everything, and by whom also the world was made; Who being the perfect reflection of God's glory, and the exact picture of who God is, and keeping everything going by the power of God's Word, when the Christ Yeshua had forgiven our sins, the Christ sat down in honor beside the Glorious God in the Highest Heaven. And being made so much better than the angels, the Christ has a much better name than they by inheritance. To which of the angels has God ever said, *"You're My Child, today I have born you?"* Or, *"I'll be like a Parent to You, and You will be to me as a Child?"* And again, when the Firstborn was brought into the world, God said, *"And let all the angels of God worship the Firstborn."* And God said about the angels, *"Who makes the angels fly like the wind, and the ministers burn like a flame of fire?"* But God said to the Child, *"You are God, and Your reign is forever and ever: You'll rule with a reign of goodness. You've love goodness, and hate sin; so I, Your God, have anointed You with the oil of happiness more than any of Your people. And You, Christ, have made the earth's matter at creation; and the heavens are Your creation: They'll be destroyed; but You'll live forever; and they'll grow old as a piece of clothing; And like an old coat you'll fold them up, and they'll be changed for a new one: but you'll stay the same, and live forever."* And to which of the angels has God ever said, *"Sit beside Me, until I make those who come against you a place to rest your feet?"* So the angels are just ministering spirits, sent to help those who will be saved.

Christ Became Human for Us

2 [1-4] So we ought to pay more attention to the things we've heard that are our proof, in case we should ever let them slip away from us. If God's Word given by angels is true, and every sin and disobedience gets a fair punishment; How can we escape, if we neglect to be saved in such a great way? And God told us of this even at the first, which was confirmed to us by those who heard it; And God wanted to give us proof, both with wonderful signs and amazing things, and with many different miracles, and gifts of the Holy Spirit.

[5-11] God hasn't put the world to come, in which we speak, in the power of the angels. But in a certain place someone told us truthfully, saying, *"What is a human being that You'd think of them? Or the child of a human being that You'd come to them? You made them a little lower than the angels; You crowned them with victory and honor, and set them over all of Your creation: You've put everything in their control."* Because God put everything in our control, God didn't leave anything out. But for now we don't yet see everything in our control. Now we see Yeshua, who was made a little lower than the angels for the suffering of death, crowned with victory and honor; that the Christ, by God's grace, would taste death for everyone. And God, for whom everything is, and by whom everything is, chose to bring many children to victory, and to make Yeshua, through suffering, the perfect leader of those who are saved.

[12-18] Both the One who sets apart and those who are set apart are all of One, who isn't ashamed to call them My people, saying, *"I'll make known Your name to My people, in the middle of the church I'll sing praise to You."* And again, *"I'll put my trust in God."* And again, *"I and the children which God has given Me."* So then as the children are one, who have shared in the body and blood, Christ, taking part of the same through death, overcame the one who had the power of death, that is, the devil; And delivered those, who through fear of death, were enslaved their whole lives. The truth is, Christ didn't take on the nature of angels; but Christ took on the humanity of Abraham. In everything Christ was required to become like humanity, in order to be a compassionate and faithful leading priest in things concerning God, to bring others back to God for their sins. Since Yeshua the Christ has suffered being tempted, the Christ is also able to help those who are tempted.

Keep the Faith

3 [1-11] So, holy Christians, who have taken part in this heavenly calling, think about the Savior and Leading priest that we claim, Christ Yeshua; Who was faithful to and chosen by Yahweh God, as also Moses was faithful in all that house, and who was thought more worthy of being made known than Moses, just as the one who has built the house has more honor than the house. Every house is built by someone; but the One who built everything is God. And the truth is, Moses was faithful in his whole house, as a worker, who could speak about what would be spoken later; But Christ is the Child over God's own home; and whose house we belong to, if we hold on tightly to the trust and the joy of our hope to the end. So as the Holy Spirit said, *"Today if you'll hear My voice, don't be hard-hearted, as when I was made angry in the time of temptation in the countryside: When your ancestors tempted Me, proved Me, and saw what I had done forty years; so that I was grieved with that people, saying, 'They're always wrong in their hearts; and they haven't known My ways.' So I swore in my rage, 'They won't come into my rest.'"*

227

[12-19] So be careful, Christians, in case any of you have an evil heart of unbelief, and leave your faith in the living God. But encourage one another daily, while it's still today; in case any of you become doubtful, listening to the lies of sin. We'll be with the Christ, if we hold tightly to the faith we had at the beginning and keep it to the end; So like it's said, "Today, if you'll hear My voice, don't be hard-hearted, as when I was made angry." Some, when they had heard, made God angry, even though not all of them did, who came out of Egypt by Moses. But who was God angry with for those forty years? Wasn't it with those who had sinned, whose bodies died in the countryside? And to whom did God swear that they wouldn't come into God's rest, but to those who didn't believe? So we see that they couldn't come in because of their unbelief.

The Word No Good Without Faith

4 [1-7] So be careful, in case any of you would seem to come short of the promise of going into God's rest that was given to us. The New Word was preached to us, too, just as to them: but the Word preached didn't do them any good because they had no faith in it. But we who believe will come into rest, just as God said, "As I've sworn in My rage, they won't come into My rest;" although the work was finished from the beginning of time. God spoke in a certain place of the Day of Worship in this way, "And God rested on the Seventh Day from all the work", and in another place again, "They won't come into my rest." So seeing that some must yet come into it, and that those to whom it was first preached didn't come in, it was because of their unbelief. Again, God limits it to a certain day, saying in David, "Today," after so long a time; as it's said, "Today, if you'll hear God's voice, don't be hard-hearted."

[8-16] If Yeshua had given them rest, then wouldn't another day, been spoken of later? So there is still a rest for the people of God. Whoever has gone into their rest, has also stopped doing their own work, just like God did. So let's work till the day of our rest, in case anyone falls into that same kind of unbelief. The Word of God is quick, and powerful, and sharper than any two-edged blade, piercing deep enough to divide the soul and spirit in two, separating even bones and marrow, and understanding even the very thoughts and intents of the heart. There's no creature that isn't plainly seen in God's sight: everything is bare and plain to the eyes of the One to whom we answer. Seeing then that we have such a great leading priest, who has gone on into heaven, Yeshua, the Child of God, let's hold on to what we have said. We don't have a leading priest which can't understand how we feel in our weaknesses; but the Christ was tempted just like we are, yet without ever sinning. So let's come without fear to the throne of grace, so that we can find mercy and grace to help us in our time of need.

Yeshua is our Leading Priest

5 [1-4] Every leading priest is chosen from the people and set apart to act for them in the things of God, so that they can offer both gifts and sacrifices for sins: Who can understand and care about those without knowledge and those who are out of the way because they themselves also have weaknesses. And for this reason, they ought to make an offering for their own sins, as well as for the people. And no one takes this honor on themselves, but whoever is called of God, as was Aaron.

[5-10] So also Yeshua wasn't made a leading priest by the Christ's own self; but by the One who said, "You're My Child, today I have born you." As God said also in another place, "You're a priest forever after the order of Melchisedec." When in the body, Christ Yeshua, had offered up prayers and requests, crying many tears, to the One who was able to save the Christ from death, and was heard because of the Christ's acceptance of God's will. The Christ was the Child of God, yet still learned to accept what God wanted by the things which the Christ suffered; So being completed, became the way of being saved forever to all those who accept the Christ; who was called of God to be the leading priest after the order of Melchisedec.

[11-14] We have many things to say about the Christ, but they are hard to say clearly, since you don't listen well. By this time you ought to be teachers, but you still need someone to teach you again the first things that we believe in God's word; and are like those who need milk, and not solid food. Those who still need milk have not practiced the teachings on being good much because they're like a new born. But solid food is for those who have grown, those who have practiced being good and learned to tell what is good from what is evil.

Don't Give Up but Wait on God

6 [1-7] So moving past the first principles of the Word of Christ, let's go on to completion; not going back to things like changing your life from doing things which lead to death, and of your faith in God, of the Word of God about baptisms, of the laying on of hands, of the coming to life again from the dead, and of everlasting judgment. And we'll do this, if God allows us. It's hopeless for those who once understood, and have experienced the heavenly gift, and shared in the Holy Spirit, and have experienced the good things of the Word of God, and the powers of the realm to come, if they leave the faith, to renew them again to a changed life; seeing that they have put the Christ of God to death anew in themselves, making a public disgrace of Yeshua. The garden which makes use of the rain that often falls on it, and grows plants that are good for the one who takes care of it, gets blessed

228

by God: But the one that grows thorns and briers is useless, and is near being rejected; and will be burned in the end.

[9-12] But, dear loved one, we believe better things of you, the things that come with being saved, even though we speak of this. God isn't so unfair as to forget what you've done and your work of love, which you've done in the name of God, in that you've ministered to the Christians, and still minister. And we want for every one of you to give the same attention to the full promise of hope to the end: so that you won't give up, but do just like those who through faith and patience got the promises. When God made the promise to Abraham, who could swear by nothing greater, so swore by God's Own Self, saying, *"Surely with blessing I'll bless you, and with many descendants I'll multiply you."* And so, after patiently suffering through, Abraham got what was promised. The truth is, people swear by something greater than themselves. To them, a promise is proof enough and puts an end to all doubt. Like this, God, wanting to better show to the heirs of the promise the absolute truth of the Word of God, strengthened it with a promise, so that by these two undeniable things, in which it was impossible for God to lie, we might have a strong comfort, who have run away for a place of safety to take hold of the hope we have been given. This hope we have as an anchor of the soul, both sure and safe, which comes into the presence of God in the Most Holy Place, where Yeshua, who came before us, was made a leading priest forever just like Melchisedec.

Christ is Our Melchisedec

7 [1-10] This Melchisedec, Ruler of Salem, priest of the Most High God, met Abraham returning from the defeat of the rulers, and blessed him. Abraham gave this Priest a tenth of everything. First the name Melchisedec means Ruler of goodness, and then also Ruler of Salem, means, Ruler of Peace. This Priest had no parents, no descendants, had no beginning of days, nor end of life; but was like the Child of God; a Priest that lives continually. Now consider how great this person was, to whom even the patriarch Abraham gave the tenth part of all he had taken. The truth is, those who are of the children of Levi, who have the office of the priesthood, are told to take a tenth of everything by the Word of God, that is, from their own people, though they are all descendants of Abraham: But the Priest who didn't come from Levi got a tenth part from Abraham, and blessed the one who had the promises. And without a doubt the greater One blessed the lesser one. And in our case the tenth part is given to people who die; but in that case the One who still lives gets it. So I might say that the descendants of Levi, who get a tenth part, also paid a tenth part through Abraham's gift, because they were still in the body of their ancestors, when Melchisedec came.

[11-28] So if we could be made perfect by the acts of the Levitical priesthood, under which we got the Word of God, why would there need to be another Priest who would come in the likeness of Melchisedec, and not be called after the usual order of Aaron? But because the priesthood was changed, a change also needed to come to the Word of God. And the One of whom this is spoken belongs to another family, of which no one has ever served as priest. It's clear that our Christ came from the family of Judah; of which Moses said nothing about having a priesthood. And it's still even clearer because after the likeness of Melchisedec another Priest came, who came not by the law of the earthly Word, but by the power of a life without end. God said, *"You're a Priest forever in the likeness of Melchisedec."* The truth is, the first Word was incomplete because we are weak and it was useless for us. The Word of God couldn't make any of us right, but the coming of a better hope did; by which we come near to God. And the Christ was not made our Priest without a promise, like those who are made priests without a promise; but it was with a promise by the One who said, *"God promised and won't go back on it, You're a priest forever in the likeness of Melchisedec."* So Yeshua came as proof of a better Word by this promise. The truth is, there were many priests, because they weren't able to keep serving because of death: But Yeshua, who lives ever, has an everlasting priesthood. So Yeshua is able to completely and finally save those that come to God by the Christ, who lives forever and speaks up for them. The Christ is a leading priest that became for us One who is holy, innocent, without fault, never having sinned, and is in the highest heavens; Who doesn't need to offer sacrifices daily, as those priests did, first for their own sins, and then for the people's, because Yeshua did this once and for all, who offered up the Christ's own self. The first Word gave us priests who sinned; but the Word of the promise, which came later, gave us the Child of God, who is set apart as our Priest forever.

The New Agreement

8 [1-6] Now what we are saying is this: We have a leading priest like this, who sits in a place of honor beside the throne of the Great God in the heavens; A minister of the sanctuary, and of the true Place of Worship, which God made, and not any person. Every leading priest is set apart to offer gifts and sacrifices: so it was needed for this One to have something more to offer. If Yeshua were still on earth, the Christ wouldn't be a priest, seeing that there are already priests that offer gifts for that Word of God: Who serve as the example and shadow of the heavenly things, as Moses was warned of God when he was about to make the Place of Worship, God said, *"See to it that you make everything just as it was shown to you on the Mountain."* But now the Christ has the more perfect ministry, who speaks up for us in the better agreement, which was settled for us by better promises.

229

[7-13] If that first agreement had been found faultless, then there would be no need for the second. But finding fault with those who followed it, God said, "*The time is coming, God said, when I'll make a new agreement with the family of Israel and with the family of Judah: Not like the one that I made with their ancestors in the time when I took care of them to lead them out of the land of Egypt; because they didn't keep their part of My promised agreement, and I didn't accept them, God said. But this is the New Word that I'll give to the families of Israel later, God said; I'll put My Word in their thoughts, and mark them in their spirits: and I'll be to them a God, and they'll be to Me a people: And no one will teach their neighbor or a family member, saying, 'Know God' because everyone will know Me, from the youngest to the oldest. I'll be forgiving of their ungodliness, I won't ever remember their sins and uncontrolled acts again.* So when God said, a New Word, the first became the old One. Now what is replaced becomes old and is about to end.

Christ's Death Needed for the New Agreement

9 [1-10] The truth is, the first agreement had rules of divine service, and also an earthly sanctuary. There was a Place of Worship made; in which the first part had the candle holder, and the table, and the bread; which was the sanctuary. And in the second part, the Place of Worship which is called the most Holy Place; which had the golden censer, and the golden box of the first agreement, which held the golden pot that had the bread from heaven, and Aaron's rod that budded, and the carved stones of the first agreement; and on the lid of the golden box the angels of praise that overshadowed the mercy seat; of which we can't fully speak of now. Now when this was set apart this way, the priests always went into the first part of the Place of Worship, to do the service of God. But only the leading priests went into the second part once a year, and not without blood, which was offered for both themselves, and for the sins of the people: The Holy Spirit shows us that the way into the Most Holy Place wasn't yet opened up, while the first Place of Worship was still standing: Which was just an example for that time, in which were offered both gifts and sacrifices, that couldn't make those who did the service right, as concerning the conscience; Which was only for the rules about foods and drinks, and different washings, and earthly rules, imposed on them until the time of the New Word.

[11-15] So the Christ became our leading priest in the good things that were to come, with a greater and more complete Place of Worship, not made with human hands, that is, not of this nature; Neither by the blood of animals, but by the Christ's own blood, who came into the Most Holy Place once and for all, saving us for all time. If the blood of animals, and the ashes of a cow could be sprinkled for the sinner to bless and cleanse the body: How much more will the blood of Yeshua, who through the Holy Spirit offered the Christ's own self to God, who had never sinned, clear your conscience from the things you've done that lead to death to serve the living God? And for this cause the Christ, who died in our place, can speak up for us in the agreement of the New Word, to save us from the sins that were done under the first agreement, so that those who are called might get the promise of an everlasting inheritance.

[16-28] Where this kind of agreement is made, there must out of necessity be the death of the One making the will, because a will only comes into effect after the person has died. Otherwise, it has no value at all while that person still lives, so not even the first agreement came into effect without blood. So when Moses had spoken every Word of God to all the people, he took the blood of animals, along with water, and scarlet-dyed wool, and hyssop branches, and sprinkled both the Word of God, and all the people, saying, "*This is the blood of the agreement which God has made with you.*" Besides this, he sprinkled both the Place of Worship, and all the bowls of the ministry with blood, because God's Word says almost everything is cleansed with blood; and without the shedding of blood there is no forgiveness. So it was necessary that the examples of things which are in the heavens would be cleansed like this; but the heavenly things themselves are cleansed with better sacrifices than these. Christ didn't go into the holy places made with human hands, which are only examples of the true ones; but the Christ went into heaven itself, and now stands in the presence of God in our place: Who doesn't offer the Christ's own self often, like the leading priest who comes into the holy place each year with blood of animals; because then the Christ would have suffered many times since the beginning of the world: but now once in the end of this time Yeshua has appeared to do away with the consequences of sin by the Christ's own sacrifice. And just like others must die once, but later face the judgment, the Christ was once offered for the sins of many; and will appear the second time for those who look for the Christ, not for their sin, but to save them.

Christ's Blood Given Once and For All

10 [1-10] The Word of God, being a shadow of the good things to come, and not the actual picture of the things, can never with the sacrifices which they continually offered year by year make those who came complete, or they wouldn't have stopped being offered and the worshippers, once forgiven, would have had no more guilty conscience from their sins. But in those sacrifices they remember their sins again every year. It isn't possible for the blood of animals to take away sins. So when the Christ came into the world, who said, "*You didn't want sacrifice and offering, but you've prepared Me a body: You took no pleasure in burnt offerings and sacrifices for sin. Then I said, see, I have come (in part of the book the Word says of Me,) to do what You want, God.*" So before when the Christ said, *"Sacrifice and offering and burnt offerings and offering for sin You didn't want, nor took pleasure in it;"* which are offered by the Word of God; Then the Christ said, *"See, I come to do what You want, God."* The Christ took away the first, so that the second could be set up, by whose will we're set apart through the offering of the body of Yeshua the Christ once and for all.

[11-18] And all the priests stand daily ministering and offering the same sacrifices many times, which can never take away sins: But this person, who had offered One sacrifice for sins forever, afterwards sat down in the place of honor beside God; From then on waiting for God to take control of the Christ's enemies. And by this One offering the Christ has forever completed the work for those who are being set apart. Of which the Holy Spirit is also a witness to us because after what the Christ had said before, *"This is the promised agreement that I'll make with them after those days, God said, I'll put my teachings into their hearts, and I'll write them in their minds; And their sins and uncontrolled actions I'll remember no more."* Now where these have been taken away, there's no longer any need to make offering for sin.

Don't Forget to Worship Together

[19-25] So, Christians, we can have courage to come into the holiest place by the blood of Yeshua, by a new and living way, which the Christ has offered for us, through the curtain, that is, the Christ's body; And we have a leading priest over the house of God; so let's come near with a true heart that fully trusts our faith, having our hearts cleansed from a guilty conscience, and our bodies washed with pure water. So let's hold on to the faith we have claimed to have without doubting; (for the One who promised is faithful;) And let's think about how we can encourage one another to love and to do good things: Not forgetting to come and worship together, as some do; but encouraging one another: and even more, as you see the day getting nearer.

[26-31] And if we willfully keep on sinning after we understand the knowledge of the truth, there is no more covering for sins, but a fearful waiting for judgment and the fiery rage, which will destroy the enemies. Whoever disobeyed Moses' law died without mercy with two or three witnesses against them, so how much worse will the punishment be, do you think, for those who'll be thought worthy, who have rejected the Christ of God, and has thought the blood of the promised agreement that the Christ has given for us an unholy thing, and has done this in spite of the Spirit of grace? We know the One who has said, *"Punishment is for Me to do and I'll repay, God said. And again, God will judge the people."* It's very fearful to fall into the judgment of the living God.

[32-39] But remember in the past, when, after you accepted the truth, you suffered through great troubles; Partly, while you were publically accused in great troubles; and partly, while you became friends of those who were treated like this too. And you even cared for me when I was locked up, and gracefully took the taking of your things, knowing in yourselves that you have better and more lasting things in heaven. So don't give up your trust, which will be greatly repaid. You need to have patience, so that, after you've done what God wants you to do, you might get the promise. *"In just a little while, the One who is coming will come, and it won't be long. Now the good will live by faith: but if anyone turns away, My soul will have no pleasure in them."* But we aren't of those who turn away to be punished; but we are of those who believe to the saving of the soul.

Examples of Faith

11 [1-16] Now faith is the spirit of what we hope for, what we know is true, but don't yet see. By it, the elders were well spoken of. Through faith we understand that the worlds were framed by the Word of God, so that the things which are seen weren't really made of things which appear. By faith, Abel offered to God a better sacrifice than Cain, by which it is said that he was good, and God tells us of his gifts: and by it, he still speaks even though he is dead. By faith, Enoch was changed, not seeing death; and wasn't ever found, because God had changed him. And before he was changed, it was said of him, that he pleased God. So without faith, it's impossible to please God. Whoever comes to God must believe that God exists, and that God rewards those who carefully look for God. By faith, Noah, being warned of God of things not seen yet, acted with fear, built a large boat to save his family; by which the world was found guilty, and became heir of the goodness, which is by faith. By faith Abraham, who was called to go to a place he would later get for an inheritance, obeyed; and went out, not knowing where he was going. By faith, they traveled in the land of promise, in a foreign country, living in tents with Isaac and Jacob, who were also heirs of the same promise: because they wanted a place with a foundation, whose builder and maker is God. Also, through faith, Sara was made strong enough to have a baby, and was given a child when she was too old to have one, because she decided that the One who had promised was faithful. So from that one couple, who were as good as dead, were born as many descendants as the stars of the sky in number, and as uncountable as the sand by the sea shore. These all died in faith, not having gotten the promises, but having seen them in the future, and were sure of them, and accepted them, admitting that they were strangers and aliens on the earth. And those who say such things clearly say that they're looking for a place of their own. And the truth is, if they had cared for the country they came out of, they could have gone back. But they wanted a better country, that is, a heavenly one: so God isn't ashamed to be called their God, who has prepared for them a place to call home.

[17-31] By faith, Abraham, when he was tested, offered up Isaac. The one who had gotten the promises offered up the only child born to him, of whom it was said, "*In Isaac will your descendants be called*," figuring that God was even able to bring him to life, even from the dead, from which he also got him back in a sense. By faith, Isaac blessed Jacob and Esau about the things which would happen in the future. By faith, Jacob, who was dying, blessed both the children of Joseph; and worshipped, leaning on the top of his walking cane. By faith, Joseph, when he died, made mention of the leaving of the children of Israel; and gave word about his bones. By faith, Moses, when he was born, was hid three months by his parents, because they saw that he was a good child; and they weren't afraid of the ruler's word. By faith Moses, when he grew up, refused to be called the child of Pharaoh's daughter; choosing instead to suffer with the people of God, rather than enjoy the amusement of sin for a while. He prized the dishonor of Christ more valuable than the wealth in Egypt because he saw the profit of his future reward. By faith, they left Egypt, not fearing the ruler's punishment, and suffered through, as if seeing the invisible God. Through faith, they kept the Passover, sprinkling the blood, so the angel who killed the firstborn wouldn't touch them. By faith, they walked through the Red sea on dry land, in which the Egyptians who tried to do this were drowned. By faith, the walls of Jericho fell down, after they were surrounded for seven days. By faith, Rahab, a sexually immoral person, wasn't destroyed along with those who didn't believe, because she had taken in the spies with peace.

[32-40] And what more can I say? Time would fail me to tell of Gideon, and Barak, and Samson, and Jephthae; of David also, and Samuel, and of all the great preachers, who through faith took over countries, worked for goodness, got promises, closed the mouths of lions, put out the heat of fire, escaped the edge of the blade, were made strong out of their weakness, became fearless in fighting, made the armies of alien peoples turn and run. Women got their dead raised to life again and others were tortured, not taking the chance to escape; in order to obtain a better life in the spiritual realm. And others had tests of cruel mockings and beatings, yes, and were even locked up and put in chains. Some were stoned to death, sawed in half, tempted to give up on their faith and escape, and some were stabbed with the blade. They wandered around wearing animal skins for clothing, being needy, troubled, and suffering. The world wasn't worthy to have them, some of them wandering around in deserts, and in the mountains, hiding in dens and the caves of the earth. And through faith, all of them, though having lived good lives, didn't get the promise because God, having given something better for us, wanted them to be completed along with us.

Christ Yeshua, the Beginning and End of our Faith

12 [1-10] So seeing that we also are surrounded by so many witnesses, let's get rid of everything that weighs us down, and all the sin which so easily overcomes us, and let's run the race that we've been called to with patience, looking to Yeshua, the beginning and end of our faith. The Christ, for the joy to come, suffered through the cross, despising its shame, and is now at the place of honor beside the throne of God. So consider the One who suffered through such opposition from sinners, in case you get so tired that you want to give up in your minds. In your fight against sin, you haven't yet fought to the point of loosing your life blood. And you've forgotten the encouragement which speaks to you as to children, "*My child, don't hate the discipline of God, nor give up when you're under God's control: because God loves whom God disciplines, and punishes every child that is accepted by God.*" So don't get discouraged when you're disciplined, because God is dealing with you as with children. What child doesn't a parent discipline? But if you're not disciplined, in which all are one who have taken part, then you're bastards, and not legal children. Besides, our physical parents corrected us, and we respected them, so shouldn't we instead allow ourselves to be even more under the control of God, the source of our spirits, and live? The truth is, our parents, for a short time, punished us as they thought was best for us; but God punishes us for our good, so that we might share in God's goodness.

[11-24] Now no discipline seems good at the time, but very hard to deal with: but later it brings peace and goodness to those who are trained this way. So lift up your hands which are hanging down, and strengthen your weak knees; Run straight in the path, so your feet won't be broken; but well. Try to have peace with everyone, and be good, which without goodness no one will see God. Carefully watch so no one fails to receive God's grace; or in case any root of bitterness springs up to trouble you, and ruins many others by that example; Or in case there be any sexually immoral, or disrespectful person, such as Esau, who for one meal sold his birthright, because you know how that later, when he would have inherited the blessing, he was rejected because he didn't change his way of thinking, though he begged for the blessing with many tears. And you aren't coming to the physical mountain that can be touched, that burned with fire, nor to black skies, darkness, and eruptions, along with the sound of a trumpet, and the voice speaking with words with which those who heard begged that they wouldn't be spoken to any more because they couldn't handle what was told them, "*and if so much as a creature touches the mountain, it must be stoned, or killed with an arrow.*" And the sight was so terrible that Moses said, "*I am shaking with fear.*" But you come to Mount Zion, and the heavenly Jerusalem, where God lives, and to a countless number of angels, to the gathering together of the church of the Firstborn, whose names are written in heaven, and to God, the Judge of All, and to the spirits of good people who are spiritually completed, and to Yeshua, the One

who speaks up for us in the new promised agreement, whose sprinkled blood speaks of better things than the blood of Abel.

[25-29] So see that you don't refuse the One who speaks, because if the ones who refused the One who spoke on earth didn't escape, how will we ever escape if we turn away from the One who speaks from heaven: Whose voice shook the earth then, but now God has promised, saying, *"Yet once more, I won't shake the earth only, but also heaven."* And this word, *"Yet once more,"* signifies what can be shaken will be removed, that is the physical world, so that only what can't be shaken will be left. Since we're going to a spiritual place which can't be moved, let's be graceful, so that we can serve God acceptably with respect and godly fear, because our God is like an uncontrollable fire.

Love Each Other Like Family

13 [1-6] Keep loving each other like a family. Don't forget to take care of strangers because in this way, some have unknowingly taken care of angels. Remember those who are locked up, as if you were a prisoner with them; and those who suffer hard times, as you yourselves also suffer in the body. Marriage is to be respected in all ways, and the marriage bed kept pure and holy. God will judge those who practice sexual sin and are sexually unfaithful. Let your lifestyle be without selfishness; and be happy with what you have because Christ has said, *"I'll never leave you, nor turn away from you"*. So that we can say without fear, *"God is my helper, so I won't fear what anyone will do to me."*

[7-17] Remember the leaders who have spoken the Word of God to you. You should follow their faith, thinking about what kind of lifestyle they have. Yeshua the Christ, is the same yesterday, today, and forever. So don't let all different kinds of strange teachings change your mind. It's good for the heart to depend on grace; not on eating certain foods, which haven't helped those who have been controlled by them. We have an altar, from which those who serve in the Place of Worship have no right to eat. Just as the bodies of the animals, whose blood is brought into the sanctuary by the leading priest for sin, are burned outside the camp, so Yeshua also, in order to set apart the people with the Christ's own blood, suffered outside the gate. So let's go to the Christ outside the camp, being dishonored as the Christ was. Here we have no everlasting city, but we look for the one to come. So by the Christ, let's offer the sacrifice of praise to God continually, that is, the fruit of our lips giving thanks to the name of Yahweh God. But don't forget to do good things and to share because God is very pleased with such sacrifices. Obey your leaders, and accept what they say because they watch out for your souls, as those who must give account. Do this so that they can lead you with joy, and not with grief, because that isn't good for you.

[18-25] Pray for us because we believe we have a good conscience, and are willing to live honestly in everything. But I beg you instead to pray that I can come back to you sooner. Now the God of peace, that brought our Christ Yeshua back again from the dead, that Great Keeper of the animals, through the blood of the everlasting promised agreement, make you complete in every good work to do what God wants, working in you what is pleasing in the sight of God, through Yeshua the Christ; who will be made known forever and ever. So be it! And I beg you, Christians, accept this word of encouragement because I've written this letter to you in just a few words. I want you to know that our Christian brother Timothy has been freed and if he comes shortly, I'll see you with him then. Say hello to all those who lead you, and all of the Christians. All those of Italy say hello to you. May grace be with you all. So be it!

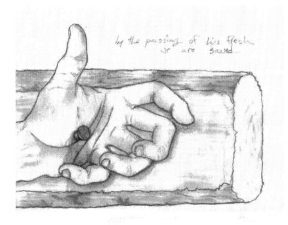

233

A Letter from James

1 [1] From James, a worker of Yahweh God and of Yeshua the Christ; Hello to the twelve families which are scattered out.

[2-18] My Christians, be happy when you're tested by all kinds of temptations, knowing that the testing of your faith brings patience. Let the work of patience outlast the temptation, so that you can be complete and whole, not needing anything. If any of you lack wisdom, ask God for it, who gives freely to all who ask, and doesn't scold them; and it'll be given to them. But ask in faith, not doubting. Whoever doubts is like a wave of the sea blown by the wind and tossed around. Don't think that you'll get anything from God that way. A doubtful person is unsure of them self in everything. Let the Christian of low social status celebrate in the fact that they're rich in Christ: But the rich, in that they're humbled in Christ: Like a flower of the grass they'll all come to an end. As soon as the sun comes up with its burning heat, the grass wilts, and the flower falls off it, and its beauty is gone: so the rich person will also fade away even as they go about their business. Blessed are those who outlast their temptations because after they're tested, they'll get the crown of life, which Yahweh God has promised to those who love God. No one should say when they're tempted, "*I am being tempted by God*" because God can't be tempted with evil, nor does God tempt anyone. When someone is tempted, they're lured away by what they want, and are sure that they need it. Then when they get what they want, they sin; and when they sin, death follows. Don't go wrong here, my dear Christians. Everything good and every perfect gift is from above, and comes from the Light we are from, with whom is no shade, nor fading shadows. God chose to make us with the Word of truth, so that we would be the best of all God's creatures.

Act on what You Hear

[19-27] So, my dear Christians, let everyone first listen, then answer carefully, and not get angry so fast because a person's anger doesn't bring about the goodness of God. Put away everything evil that is unnecessary, and with gentleness, accept the Word growing in you, which is able to save your souls. Do what the Word tells you to do, not just hearing it only, lying to your own selves. If anyone only hears the Word, but doesn't do it, they're like someone looking at their face in a glass, who sees them self, and then goes on their way, quickly forgetting what they just saw. But whoever looks into the complete Word of freedom, and lives by it, not being a forgetful hearer, but does what it says, this person will be blessed in what they do. So if anyone among you is religious, but doesn't control what they say, misleading their own heart, this person's religion is meaningless. True religion, which is holy to Yahweh God, is to go to those without a parent and the single parents in need, and to keep yourself without fault from the world.

Don't be Prejudiced

2 [1-12] My Christians, have the faith of our Christ Yeshua, God of victory, without prejudice. If someone comes to your church with a gold ring, in nice clothes, and also a poor person comes in with raggedy clothes, and you show more respect to the one who wears the nice clothes, and say to them, "*Sit here in the best place;*" and say to the one who is poor, "*Stand over there, or sit here at my feet;*" Then aren't you being prejudiced in your heart, and haven't you judged them with your evil thinking? Listen carefully, my dear Christians, hasn't God chosen those who are poor in this world who are rich in faith, and heirs of the realm of God which has been promised to those who love God? But those who are poor, you hate. Don't people, who are well off, keep you down and take you to court? Don't they dishonor and disrespect that worthy name of Christian, by which you're called? If you follow the law of God as the Word says, "*Love others as you love yourself;*" you're doing what's right: But if you're disrespectful to some people, you're sinning, and are found guilty by the Word of God as sinners. Whoever keeps the whole law, but breaks it in one area, is guilty of breaking it all. Didn't the One who said, "*Don't sin sexually,*" also say, "*Don't kill.*" Now if you don't sin sexually, but you kill someone, you have broken the law of the Word of God. So speak and do, as those who will be judged by the Word of God, which frees us from sin.

Faith Without Action is Dead

[13-26] Those who have shown no mercy will also be judged without mercy. It is much better to have mercy on someone than to judge them. What good does it do, my Christians, if someone says they have faith, but doesn't follow up their faith with actions? Can their faith save them? If a Christian brother or sister is unclothed, and doesn't even have their daily food, and one of you says to them, "*Go in peace, I hope you get warm and full;*" but in spite of this you don't give them what they need for the body; what good did it do? Just the same, faith, if not followed by actions, by itself, is dead. Yes, even though someone might say, "*You have faith, and I have actions:*" I say show me your faith without doing anything about it, and I'll show you my faith by what I do. You believe that there's One God and this is good, but even the evil spirits believe, and shake with fear. But do you want proof, you

thoughtless person, that faith without your actions is dead? Wasn't Abraham our ancestor made right by what he did, when he had offered Isaac, his child, on the altar? Do you see how faith worked along with his actions, and by actions, faith was made complete? And the Word was completed which said, "Abraham believed God, and it was credited to him for goodness:" and he was called the friend of God. You see then that a person is made right by what they do, and not by faith only. Just the same also, wasn't Rahab, a sexually immoral person, made right by what she did, when she took in the spies, and helped them escape. So as the body without the spirit is dead, so faith that is not followed by actions is dead also.

The Untamable Tongue

3 [1-18] My dear Christians, many of you shouldn't be leaders, because leaders will be held to a stricter judgment. We all do many things that are wrong. If a person doesn't offend anyone with their words, they are a complete person, and able also to keep their whole body under control. We put bits in the mouths of horses, so that they'll obey us; and with it we turn their whole body. And also the ships, which are so big, and are driven by very strong winds, are still turned around with a very small helm, wherever the captain wants it to go. Just the same, the tongue is a very small part of the body, but brags about a great many things. See what a great fire a little spark kindles! And the tongue is like a fire, a world of sin. Just the same, the tongue is the worst of our body parts, because it makes the whole body filthy, and changes the whole course of a person's life, setting it on fire by Hell. Every kind of creature, bird, snake, and even the things in the sea, can be tamed, and has been tamed by humanity: But no one can tame the tongue. It's an unruly, evil thing, full of deadly poison. With our tongue we bless the God we come from; and with the same tongue we curse others, who are made in the very likeness of God. Out of the same mouth comes blessing and cursing. My dear Christians, it shouldn't be this way. Does a creek give out both good water and bad at the same place? Can the fig tree, my dear Christians, make olive berries? Or a vine, figs? No creek will have both salt water and fresh. So who is wise and has knowledge among you? Let them show by their good lifestyle that their actions are done with the gentleness of wisdom. But if you have jealousy and resentment in your hearts, don't praise yourself, and lie about what is true. This wisdom doesn't come from above, but is based on feelings, which are earthly, and devilish. Where there is jealousy and resentment, confusion and evil actions will follow. But the wisdom that is from above is first without any evil, then peaceful, gentle, willing to give in, full of mercy and good actions, without any partiality, and without any falsehood. And those who make peace do acts of goodness in peace.

A Friend of the World is an Enemy of God

4 [1-12] Where do these wars and fights among you come from? Don't they come from the things you want, which fight within you? You want, but you don't have: you kill, and want to have, but can't get what you want, so you fight and war. Still, you don't have, because you don't ask. And when you do ask, you don't get what you want, because you ask wrongly, so that you can use it only for the things that you want. You're like sexually unfaithful people. Don't you know that to love the world is to hate the things of God? So whoever wants to be a friend of the world is the enemy of God. Do you think that the Word said for no reason, "The spirit that lives in us is very jealous for us?" But God gives us more grace, which is why it was said, "God doesn't accept the proud, but gives grace to the humble." So accept what God says. Fight the devil, who'll quickly go away from you. Come closer to God, and God will come closer to you. Wash your hands of your evil acts, you sinners; and get your hearts right, you doubting ones. Mourn, grieve, and cry: let your laughter turn into crying, and your joy into sadness. Humble yourselves in the sight of God, who will lift you up. Don't speak evil of one another, Christians. Whoever speaks evil of another, and judges with prejudice, speaks evil of the Word of God, and judges the Word of God. If you judge the Word of God, you're no longer a follower of the Word of God, but a judge. There's only One Lawgiver, who is able to save and to kill: so who are you that you should judge one another?

[13-17] Now listen, you that say, "Today or tomorrow we'll go into a certain city, and stay there a year, buying and selling, and make some money:" when you don't even know what tomorrow will bring. What is your life? It's just a breath, which is here today and gone tomorrow. But you should say instead, "If it's God will, we'll live, and do this, or that." You celebrate with your bragging, but all this kind of celebrating is evil. Those who know to do well, and don't do it are sinning.

Be Patient in Suffering

5 [1-6] Now listen, you rich people, cry and scream for the miseries that will come on you. Your riches are all gone, and all your clothes are moth-eaten. Your gold and silver is corroded; and the rust of them will be a witness against you, and your body will be consumed as by a fire. You've selfishly kept your wealth for yourself in the last days. You haven't paid the workers who worked your fields; you kept back their pay by your lies. The cries of those who worked for you have been heard by the God of All. You've lived in excess and pleasure on the earth, fattening your hearts, as in a day of slaughter. You've accused and killed the good, who didn't fight you back.

[7-12] So be patient, Christians, until Christ comes again. As the farmer waits for the precious fruit of the earth, and has great patience for it, until the early and latter rains come, you be patient also. Settle your hearts because Christ's coming is very near. Don't be unforgiving toward one another, Christians, or you won't be forgiven. The Judge stands at the door. My dear Christians, the great preachers, who have spoken in the Name of God, are a good example of patient suffering. We consider them blessed who kept on going. You've heard about the patience of Job, and seen what God did in the end; God is very forgiving, and tenderhearted. But above everything else, my Christians, don't swear, not by heaven, nor by the earth, nor by any other promise: but say exactly what you mean, either yes or no; or you'll fall into judgment.

Pray for One Another

[13-20] Is anyone among you troubled? Let them pray. Is anyone happy? Let them sing songs. Is anyone among you sick? Let them call for the elders of the church; and let them pray over them, anointing them with oil in the Name of Yeshua the Christ. When you pray in faith, the sick will be saved, and Christ will heal them; and if they have sinned, they'll be forgiven. So be honest and admit your faults to one another, and pray for one another, so that you can be healed. The heartfelt prayer of a good person is very powerful. Elijah was a person with the same nature as us, who prayed passionately that it wouldn't rain: and it didn't rain on the earth for three and a half years. And when he prayed again, the heaven gave rain, and the earth gave its food. So all of you remember, if any of you do go astray from the truth, and someone changes their mind; Let them know, that whoever helps the sinner change from their wrongful ways will save a soul from death, and will bury a great deal of sins.

236

The First Letter from Peter

1 [1-2] From Peter, a follower of Yeshua the Christ, to the Christians, who are scattered throughout Pontus, Galatia, Cappadocia, Asia, and Bithynia, the chosen ones by the foreknowledge of Yahweh God, through the setting apart and blessing of the Spirit, in the acceptance and cleansing power of the blood of Yeshua the Christ: May God's grace and peace be given to you.

[3-9] May Yahweh God be blessed, the God of Yeshua the Christ, who for the great mercy of God, has given us a new life to live out our hope through Yeshua the Christ, who came to life again from the dead, to an honorable and everlasting inheritance that won't ever disappear, waiting for you in heaven, who are kept safe by the power of God through faith, ready to become known in eternity. You greatly celebrate in this, though now for a little while, if need be, your spirit is depressed by the many temptations you face. But the test of your faith, being worth much more than gold that will be destroyed, though it be tested with many troubles, will be found with praise, honor, and victory at the appearance of Yeshua the Christ: Whom you love without seeing; and even without seeing, you still believe, and celebrate with a joy beyond words, full of victory. For this, you'll get the end reward of your faith, even the saving of your souls.

[10-12] This saving, being what the great preachers have asked and searched carefully for, who preached before of the grace that would come to you. They searched for the meaning of what would happen, or when it would happen, when the Spirit of Christ, which was in them, truthfully told us ahead of time about the sufferings of Christ, and the victory that would follow. To whom it was revealed, so that they didn't work for themselves, but for us in the things, which are now told to you by those who have preached the New Word to you by the Holy Spirit sent to us from heaven; which things, even the angels wanted to know.

Be Holy

[13-16] So let your mind be ready, use good sense. Hope till the end for the grace that is to be brought to you when Yeshua the Christ is made known. Be acceptable children, not acting on what you wanted before you knew Christ: But as the One who has called you is holy, be truly good in everything you do. The Word of God says, *"Be holy because I am holy."*

[17-21] Call on the God, who judges each person for their actions without respect to who they are, and act with respect to God in the time of your stay here. You know that your freedom wasn't bought from your meaningless lifestyle, which you got from your ancestors' way of life, with things that will disappear like silver and gold; but with the precious blood of Christ, as of a lamb with no flaw or fault: Who was really set apart at the beginning of the world, but was made known in these last times for you, who by the Christ believe in God, who brought back Yeshua from the dead, and gave the Christ victory; so that your faith and hope might be in God.

[22-26] Seeing you've cleansed your souls in accepting the truth through the Spirit to the heartfelt love of all Christians, see that you continue to love one another with a true heart: Being born anew, not of human origin, but of everlasting origin, by the Word of God, which lasts forever, because *"All humanity is like the grass, and all the glories of humanity like the flowers of the grass. The grass wilts, and its flowers die: But the Word of God lasts forever."* This is what is preached to you by the New Word.

We are Chosen by God

2 [1-5] So stop all hatred, untruthfulness, pretending, jealousy, and all sinful talking, but as newborn babies, crave the true milk of the Word, so that you can grow by it: that is, if you've truly tasted that God is gracious. Come to God as to a living stone, really being unaccepted by others, but chosen by God, precious. You also, as living stones, are built up to be a spiritual house, a holy priesthood, to offer up spiritual sacrifices, acceptable to God through Yeshua the Christ.

[6-10] This is why it's in the Word, *"I lay in Zion the first corner stone, chosen, precious: and whoever believes on this One won't be ashamed,"* for those who believe that the Christ is precious: but to those who are disobedient, *"The stone which the builders wouldn't accept, the same One is made the first cornerstone,"* and *"A stone to be stumbled over, and a rock to be offended by,"* to those who stumble at the Word and don't accept it, for which they were also chosen. But you're a chosen people, a royal priesthood, a holy nation, God's own special people; that you would tell of the praises of the One who has called you out of darkness into God's amazing light. In the past they weren't even a nation of people, but are now the people of God, which hadn't found mercy, but now have found mercy.

[11-12] Dear loved one, I beg you as strangers and foreigners in this world, give up the sinful things your physical body wants that fight against your soul. Have an honest lifestyle among the other peoples, so that even though they speak against you as being evil, they can see the good that you've done, and praise God in the day of Christ's coming.

237

Suffer for Good, Not Evil

[13-25] Accept every human law for God's sake: whether it be to the highest ruler; or to governors, as to those who are sent to punish those who are evil, and to praise of those who do good. This is the will of God, that by doing good you can silence the ignorance of stupid people. As free people, don't use your freedom as a cover-up for sin, but as the hired workers of God. Respect everyone. Love the Christians. Honor and respect God. Respect the rulers. Workers, be responsible to your employers with respect; not only to those who are good and gentle, but also to the ones who are difficult. This is praiseworthy, if someone for conscience toward God keeps on going in sorrow, suffering wrongfully. And what good does it do, if, when you're punished for your own faults, you take it patiently? But it's praiseworthy with God if when you do good things and suffer for it, you take it patiently. And this is why you were called: because Christ also suffered for us, leaving us an example to follow: Who never sinned, nor was untrue: Who when hated, didn't hate back; who when suffering, didn't threaten; but trusted in the One who judges rightly. The Christ's own body took on our sins on the cross, so that we, putting our sins to death, would live in goodness. By the Christ's wounding you were healed, you being like animals going astray; but have now come back to the Keeper and Overseer of your souls.

The Beauty of a Wife's Peaceful Spirit

3 [1-4] In this way, you wives, accept your husbands' leadership, so that if any of them don't obey the Word, they can, even without the Word, be won by your actions, by seeing your godly lifestyle, along with your respect. Don't let your beauty be just the outward beauty of your hairstyle, of the jewelry you wear, or of your clothing, but let it also be the unseen spirit of your soul, which can't age or die, even the beauty of a peaceful spirit, which is very precious in the sight of God.

[5-7] It was in this way, in the old days, that the holy women also, who trusted in God, beautified themselves, accepting the leadership of their own husbands: Just as Sarah accepted what Abraham told her, with respect: whose daughters you are, as long as you do good, without being threatened with any great fear. And in this way, you husbands, live with your wives with understanding, giving respect to your spouses, as caring for someone physically weaker than you are, and as being heirs together of the grace of life; so that your prayers will be heard by God.

Stay Away From Evil and Do Good

[8-12] Finally, all of you be of the same mind, caring for one another, loving each other as a family, be merciful, be considerate: Not repeating evil for evil, or abuse for abuse: but instead be a blessing; knowing that you're called to be so, so that you'll inherit a blessing. *"Whoever loves life, and wants to see good days, let them stop speaking in sinful ways, and let them speak no untruthfulness. Let them stay away from evil, and do good; let them search for peace, and walk in it, because God watches over those who do good, and hears their prayers: but the face of God turns away from those who do evil."*

[13-22] And who would harm you, if you do what is good? But if you do suffer for the sake of doing good, be happy, and don't be afraid of them, nor be uneasy. Have great respect for Yahweh God in your hearts: and always be ready to give an answer to everyone that asks you a question about the hope that is in you, with gentleness and respect. Then you'll have a good conscience; and while they speak badly of you, as if you were evil, those who falsely accuse your good lifestyle in Christ will be ashamed. It's better, if the will of God be so, that you suffer for doing good things, rather than for doing evil things. Just as Christ also has once suffered for sins, the good for the evil ones, in order to bring us to God, being put to death in the body, but brought back to life again by the Spirit. Then the Christ went also and preached to imprisoned spirits, which were disobedient, when once the patience of God waited in the days of Noah, while the ark was being built, in which few, that is, only eight souls were saved by water. And like that, baptism now saves us (not by the washing of filth from the body, but because we have a good conscience toward God) by the new life of Yeshua the Christ: Who has gone into heaven, and now sits beside God; with all the angels, authorities, and powers being put under the Christ.

Watch and Pray

4 [1-6] So then as Christ has suffered for us in the body, in this way, get yourselves ready with this mind because whoever has suffered in the body has stopped letting sin control them; that they no longer live the rest of their time in the body giving in to their human wants, but to the will of God. We have spent enough of our past life doing what other people do, when we lived in filthiness, physical wants, drunkenness, partying, pleasurable feasts, and the sickening worship of other things. In this, they think it's strange that you don't go along with them in their uncontrolled behavior, speaking evil of you. They'll have to give account to the One who is going to judge the living and the dead. This is why the New Word was preached to those who are dead, too, so that they would be judged in the body for their humanity, but live for God in the spirit.

[7-11] But the end of everything is here, so use good sense. Watch and pray. And above everything, have great love among yourselves, because love will overlook many sins. Welcome and serve one another without complaining. As each one has gotten a gift from God, in this way, use it to serve others, as good managers of the many graces of God. If anyone speaks, let them speak as the preachers of God; if anyone ministers, let them do it with the ability that God gives them: so that in everything God can be praised through Yeshua the Christ, to whom praise and power is given forever and ever. So be it!

Trials and Tests to be Expected

[12-14] My loved ones, don't think these hard tests which try you are strange, as though something unusual happened to you. Celebrate, because as much as you've suffered with Christ, you can be happy with just as much joy when the Christ's victory comes. If you're unfairly blamed for your faith in the Name of Christ, you should be happy because the spirit of victory and of God rests on you. Even though Christ is evil spoken of by their actions, Christ will be praised.

[15-19] So let none of you suffer as a murderer, or as a thief, or as someone who does evil, or as a busybody, minding other people's business. Yet if anyone suffers as a Christian, don't let them be ashamed; let them praise God because of it. The time has come for judgment to begin at the house of God: and if it begins with us first, what will happen to those who don't obey the New Word of God? *"And if those who do good things can hardly be saved, how can the ungodly and the sinner?"* So let those who suffer for the will of God entrust their souls in doing good, in the safe keeping of the faithful Creator.

Be Willing to Serve God Without Being Paid

5 [1-5] I encourage the elders which are among you, as I am also an elder, and a witness of the sufferings of Christ, and also one who has shared in the victory that will be known. Take care of the flock of God that is among you, overseeing it, not because you have to, but because you want to; not for money, but be willing to do it for nothing; not giving orders to God's people, but being examples to the flock. And when the Great Keeper appears, you'll get a crown of victory that will never disappear. In this way, you young people, accept the lead of the elders. Yes, all of you accept the lead of one another with humility because *"God doesn't accept those who are proud, and gives grace to those who are humble."*

[6-11] So humble yourselves under the powerful hand of God, who will lift you up when the time is right. Give God all your worries, because God cares about you. Use good sense and be watchful; because your enemy, the devil, walks around like a roaring lion, looking for someone to eat up: Whom you should fight back, being firm in the faith, knowing that the same troubles are happening to others in the world. But the God of all grace, who has called us to everlasting victory in Christ Yeshua, after you've suffered a while, will make you complete, getting you started, strengthening, and settling you in your work. May God have victory and control forever and ever. So be it!

[12-14] I've written briefly by Silvanus, a faithful friend to you, as I think of him, encouraging you, and tell others that this is the true grace in which you stand. The church at Rome, which is chosen along with you, says hello to you; and so does Mark, my child. Say hello to one another with a kiss of love. Peace be with you all that are in Christ Yeshua. So be it!

239

The Second Letter from Peter

1 [1-11] From Simon Peter, a worker and a follower of Yeshua the Christ, to those who have come to the same treasured faith as us by the goodness of our God and Savior, Yeshua the Christ: May grace and peace be given to you by the knowledge of God, and of Yeshua our Christ, as the power of God gives us everything we need for life and godliness, by the knowledge of the One who has called us to victory and goodness. By this, amazing and treasured truths were given to us, so that by these you might have a godly nature, having been freed from wanting what is evil in the world. And besides this, give all your attention to adding goodness to your faith; and knowledge to goodness; and self-control to knowledge; and patience to self-control; and godliness to patience; and friendly care and concern to godliness; and love to friendly care and concern. So, if you have these things and grow in them, your life won't be meaningless or unrewarding in the knowledge of our Savior, Yeshua the Christ. But whoever doesn't have these things can't see what's ahead, and has forgotten that they've been freed from their old sins. So dear Christians, be careful to make sure you were chosen and called, because if you do these things, you won't fall: So your way will be fully cleared into the everlasting realm of our God and Savior, Yeshua the Christ.

God's Word Not of Human Origin
[12-21] I won't forget to remind you of this always, though you know it, and are now settled in the truth. Yes, I think I'm right, as long as I'm in this body, to wake you up by reminding you; knowing that shortly I must leave this body of mine, just as our Savior, Yeshua the Christ has told me ahead of time. Besides this, I'll try to make sure you'll always remember this after my death. Because we haven't followed made-up story tales, when we made known to you the power and coming of our Savior, Yeshua the Christ, but we saw for ourselves Yeshua's greatness. And the Christ received from Yahweh God honor and victory, when the voice of the One worthy of praise came to Yeshua, saying, *"This is My Child, who I love, and I am so pleased with You."* And we heard this voice from heaven for ourselves, when we were with the Christ in the holy mountain. So we're sure of the Word, which was given ahead of time; and you'll do good to think of it as a light that shines in the dark, until the dawn of day when the sun rises in your hearts. You know that no Word, which was given ahead of time in God's Word, is of any human origin. And the Word, which was given ahead of time in the old days, wasn't created by the mind of any human being: but the holy ones of God spoke as they were led by the Holy Spirit.

Beware of False Teachers Who Only Want Money
2 [1-11] But there were false teachers among the people then, just as there are among you now, who secretly teach damned falsehoods, even disowning the very Christ who paid the price for them, and who bring on themselves a quick ruin. And many will follow their evil ways, who will cause the way of truth to be spoken of as evil. And through greed they'll get rich off of you with their false words, whose judgment has left them along time ago, and their damnation won't end. If God didn't even spare the angels that sinned, but threw them down to Hell, and put them into chains of darkness, to be kept until the judgment; And didn't spare the old world, but saved Noah, one of only eight people, a great preacher of goodness, sending the flood on the world of the ungodly; And turning the cities of Sodom and Gomorrah into ashes, damned them to complete ruin, making them an example to those who live ungodly lives now; And saved Lot, who was good, but suffered greatly from the filthy acts of those evil people: (because living among them, that good person's soul suffered daily by seeing and hearing their uncontrolled actions). But God knew how to save the godly from those temptations, and how to keep the evil ones to be punished until the day of judgment: But most importantly those who follow their physical instincts in their greed for evil things, and hate to be told what they should do. They are full of self-importance, and selfish, and they aren't afraid to speak evil of those in power, while angels, which are stronger and more powerful, won't even accuse them to God.

[12-16] But these people, like animals, made to be hunted and killed, speak evil of the things that they don't understand; and will be completely destroyed by their own evil actions. They'll pay for their ungodliness, as those who think it a pleasure to sin openly in broad daylight. They're ruining your celebrations, openly sinning while they keep them with you, lying to themselves. They look on others with sexual sin in their hearts, and can't stop sinning; tempting unstable souls with a heart that's used to selfish actions. They're cursed children, who have left the right way, and have gotten lost, following the way of Balaam, the child of Beor, who loved to be paid for ungodly actions; But he was scolded by a dumb donkey speaking with a human voice for his sin, which stopped the stupidity of the great preacher.

[17-22] These are wells without water, clouds that are carried by a stormy wind, for whom is kept the blackest of darkness forever. When they speak very nice words full of empty promises, they shamelessly tempt others with the sexual sins of the body, even those who had already been freed from living in sin. While they promise them

240

freedom, they themselves become controlled by their sin, because by the sin which a person is overcome, they are controlled by that same sin. And if after they've been freed from the sins of the world through the knowledge of our God and Savior, Yeshua the Christ, they're trapped in it again, and overcome, with the latter end being worse than they were in the beginning. It would have been better for them not to have known the way of goodness, than, after they've known it, to turn from the Holy Word that was given to them. But they do just like this truth says, "The dog goes back to its own vomit again; and the pig that was washed goes back to wallowing in the mud."

Atheists will Come in the Last Days

3 [1-7] This second letter, dear loved one, I now write to you; both of which I hope stirs up your pure minds by reminding you to remember the Words which were spoken by the holy ones, and our words, the followers of Christ our Savior. Know this first, that there will come in the last days those who will mock us, doing whatever they want to, and saying, *"Where is the promise of the Christ's coming? Since our ancestors died, everything continues as it was from the beginning of creation,"* because they want to forget that by the Word of God the heavens were created long ago, and the earth surrounded by water: By which the world that was back then, being flooded with water, was destroyed. But the heavens and the earth, which are now, by the same Word are kept waiting, until the ungodly ones suffer the fire of the day of judgment and the punishment of Hell.

A New Heaven and A New Earth

[8-13] But, dear loved one, don't be without knowledge of this one thing, that with God, one day is as a thousand years, and a thousand years as one day. God's promise is not forgotten, as some say; but God is very patient with us, not wanting anyone to be destroyed, but wanting everyone to change their ways. But the day of God will come as a thief in the night. The heavens will come to an end with a great noise, and even the very elements will melt with great heat, and the earth too, along with everything in it, will be burned up. Seeing then that all this will disappear, what kind of people should you be in all holy behavior and godliness, looking for and hurrying the coming of the day of God, in which the heavens, being on fire, will disappear, and the elements will melt with great heat? Just the same, because of God's promise, we look for the new heavens and a new earth, in which only goodness lives.

[14-18] So, dear loved one, seeing that you look for these things, be careful that you can be found by God in peace, without fault or blame. And know that we're saved by the patience of our Christ; just as our dear loved one, Paul, for the wisdom given to him has also written to you, who has in all his letters spoken of this, too. These things are sometimes hard to understand, which those who are untaught and unstable in the Word struggle, as they do also the other Words, to their own ruin. So you, dear loved one, seeing that you know this, beware in case you also, being led away with the wrongs of the evil ones, fall from your own faithfulness. But grow in the grace and knowledge of our God and Savior, Yeshua the Christ. To whom be victory both now and forever. So be it!

Untitled
by
Rob Hatfield

241

The First Letter from John

1 [1-4] About the Christ, the Word of Life, which was from the beginning, which we've heard, and which we've seen and looked on with our own eyes, and that our hands have touched. The Life was made known to us, and we've seen it, and are eye witnesses, and tell you about that Everlasting Life, which was with Yahweh God. What we've seen and heard we tell to you, so that you also can become one of us. The truth is, our relationship is with God, and with Yeshua the Christ of God. And we write this to you, so that you can have complete joy.

God Forgives Our Sin if We Admit It

[5-10] So this is the Word which we've heard from them, and that we tell to you, that God is light, and there's no darkness at all in God. If we say that we know God, and yet live in the darkness of sin, we lie, and don't act truthfully: But if we walk in the goodness of light, as Christ is in the light, we have a relationship with one another as well, and the blood of Yeshua the Christ of God, washes out all the stains of our sin. If we say that we don't sin, we're only lying to ourselves, and the truth isn't in us. If we admit our sins, God is faithful and fair in forgiving our sins, and washes us from all our ungodliness. If we say that we haven't sinned, we call God a liar, and God's Word isn't in us.

Christ Speaks Up for Us

2 [1-6] My little children, I write this to you, so that you don't sin. But if anyone does sin, we have One who speaks up for us with Yahweh God, Yeshua the Christ, who never sinned. The Christ took the punishment for our sins: and not for ours only, but also for the sins of the whole world. If we do what God's Word says, we know that we know the Christ. But whoever says, *"I know God,"* and doesn't do what God's Word says, is a liar, and the truth isn't in them. And whoever keeps the Word, God's love is truly complete in them. By this, we know that we're in God: whoever says they live in Christ should act like the Christ acted.

[7-17] People of God, I'm not writing a New Word to you, but the same word which you had from the beginning. This same word is the Word which you've heard from the beginning. But in the same way, I do write a New Word to you, which is true in Christ and in you. The darkness of sin is over, and the true light of Christ now shines. Whoever says they're in the light, and hates someone, is still in darkness even now. Whoever loves others lives in the light, and there's no reason for them to stumble. But whoever hates another is in the darkness of sin, and lives in that darkness, and doesn't know where they are going, because that darkness has blinded them to the truth. I write to you, little children, because your sins are forgiven in Christ's name. I write to you, parents, because you've known Christ, who is from the beginning. I write to you, young people, because you've overcome the devil. I write to you, little children, because you've known Yahweh God, as a parent. I've written to you, parents, because you've known Christ, who is from the beginning. I've written to you, young people, because you're strong, and the Word of God lives in you, and you've overcome the devil. So don't love the world, or anything that's in it. If anyone loves the world, God's love isn't in them. Everything that is in the world, every sinful thing you do, and every sinful thing you want, and all your sinful pride, isn't of God, but is of the world. And the world will come to an end, along with all its wants: but whoever does the will of God will live forever.

The Antichrist will Come

[18-29] Little children, the last days are here! As you've heard that the Antichrist will come, even now there are many antichrists; so we know that it's the last days. They left us, but they weren't of us, and if they were of us, they would no doubt have stayed with us: but they left, so that it would be plain that all of them weren't of us. But you're anointed by the Holy Spirit, and you know everything. I haven't written to you because you don't know the truth, but because you know it, and that no lie is of the truth. But whoever denies that Yeshua is the Christ is a liar! Whoever denies Yahweh God and Yeshua the Christ is an antichrist. Whoever denies the Christ, doesn't have God either: but whoever accepts the Christ has God also. So let that live in you, which you've heard from the beginning. If what you've heard from the beginning stays in you, you'll also stay in the Christ, and in God as well. The promise that the Christ has promised us is everlasting life. I have written this to you about those who lie to you to lead you away. But the anointing of the Spirit, which you've been given by Christ lives in you. You don't need anyone to teach you, because this same Spirit teaches you everything, and is the truth, and no lie. Just as it has taught you, you'll live in Christ. So now, little children, live in Christ Yeshua; so that when the Christ appears, we can be sure of ourselves, and not be ashamed at the coming of the Christ. If you know that Christ is good, you know that everyone who lives a godly lifestyle is born of the Christ.

We're called the Children of God

3 [1-12] Look at the love that God has given to us, that we're called the children of God! The world doesn't know us, because it didn't know God. My loved ones, now we're the children of God, and though we don't yet know what we'll be like, we know that when Yeshua appears, we'll be like the Christ. Then we'll see who the Christ really is. And all those who have this hope in Christ wash themselves, to be as pure as Christ. Whoever is doing sinful things disobeys the Word of God also, because sin is the rebelliousness of the Word of God. And you know that the Christ appeared to take away our sins; and there's no sin in Christ. Whoever lives in Christ doesn't keep on sinning. Whoever keeps on sinning hasn't seen Christ and doesn't know Christ. Little children, let no one mislead you. Whoever does goodness is good, just as Christ is good. Whoever is doing sinful things is of the devil because the devil has sinned from the beginning. For this reason, my loved ones, the Child of God was made known, in order to destroy what the devil has done. Whoever is born of God doesn't keep on sinning because the seed stays in them: and they can't keep on sinning, because they're born of God. By this, the children of God, and the children of the devil are made known. Those who don't act with goodness, nor love others aren't of God. So to love one another is the message that you heard from the beginning. Not as Cain, who was of the devil, and killed Able. And why did Cain kill Able? Because Cain's own actions were evil, and Abel's actions were good.

We'll Be Hated by the World

[13-24] Don't be surprised, my children, if the world hates you. We know that we've passed from death to life, because we love all Christians. Whoever doesn't love others lives in death. Whoever hates others is a murderer, and you know that no murderer has everlasting life in them. By this we know God's love, because the Christ's life was given for us, and we also ought to give up our lives for all Christians. Whoever has the things of this world, and sees another who has a need, and doesn't care for them, how can God's love be in them? My little children, let's not love just in the words of our mouths; but in the truth of our actions. And by this we know that we're of the truth, and will assure our hearts in Christ. But if our heart makes us feel guilty, God is greater than our heart, and knows everything. My loved ones, if our heart doesn't make us feel guilty, then we're sure that we're in God. And whatever we ask, we'll get from God, because we do the Word of God, and do what's pleasing in the sight of God. God's Word tells us to believe on the Name of the Child of God, Yeshua the Christ and to love one another, just as God told us to. Now whoever obeys the Word of God lives in God, and God lives in them. And we know that God lives in us by the Spirit that God has given us.

The Spirit of the Antichrist

4 [1-6] My loved ones, don't believe every spirit, but test the spirits to see whether they're from God. Many false teachers have gone out into the world. Know the Spirit of God by this: Every spirit that says that Yeshua the Christ has come in a physical body is of God: And every spirit that doesn't say that Yeshua the Christ has come in a physical body isn't of God: and this is the spirit of the antichrist, which you've heard was to come; and even now is already in the world. You're of God, little children, and have overcome them. Greater is the God who is in you, than the one who is in the world. They're of the world, so they speak from the knowledge of the world, and the world hears them. We're of God. Whoever knows God listens to us; and whoever isn't of God doesn't listen to us. By this we know the spirit of truth, and the spirit of evil.

Love One Another

[7-21] My loved ones, let's love one another because love is of God; and everyone that loves is born of God, and knows God. Whoever doesn't love, doesn't know God because God is love. In this God's love toward us was made known, because God sent the only One Born of God into the world, that we might live through Yeshua the Christ. In this is love, not that we loved God, but that God loved us, and sent the Christ to take our place for the punishment of our sins. My loved ones, if God loved us like this, we also ought to love one another. No one has ever seen God, but if we love one another, God lives in us, and God's love is shown in us. By this we know that we live in God, and God in us, because God has given us the Holy Spirit. And we've seen and tell others that God sent the Christ to be the Savior of the world. Whoever says that Yeshua is the Child of God, God lives in them, and they live in God. And we've known and believed the love that God has for us. God is love; and whoever loves, lives in God, and God in them. In this, our love is fully shown, that we can have no fear in the day of judgment, because as Christ is, so are we in this world. There's no fear in love; but complete love puts fear away because fear has suffering. Whoever has fear doesn't know love. We love God, because God first loved us. If someone says, I love God, and hates another; they're a liar. Whoever doesn't love others whom they have seen, how can they love God whom they haven't seen? And this word we have from God, that those who love God must love others also.

243

Our Faith will Overcome the World

5 [1-5] Whoever believes that Yeshua is the Christ is born of God: and everyone that loves the One who gave the Christ also loves the Christ, who is born of God. And we know that we love the children of God, when we love God, and obey the Word of God. This is God's love, that we obey the Word of God: and these words aren't hard. Whoever is born of God overcomes the world: and our faith is the victory that overcomes the world. Whoever believes that Yeshua is the Child of God will overcome the world!

Three Witnesses, One God

[6-10] This is Yeshua the Christ, the One who came by the baptism of water and of blood; not by the baptism of water only, but by water and the suffering of blood. And it's the Spirit that tells the truth about it, because the Spirit is the Spirit of Truth. And there are three that are truthful witnesses in heaven, Yahweh God, the Word, and the Holy Spirit: and these three are One God. And there are three that are truthful witnesses in earth, the Spirit, and the water, and the blood: and these three agree as One. If we accept the witness of human beings, the witness of God is greater because this is the witness of God who has told us truthfully of the Christ. Those who believe in the Christ of God have the witness in themselves: and those who don't believe God have made God a liar; because they don't believe the Word that God gave of the Christ.

No Life Without Christ

[11-15] And this is the Word that God has given to us, everlasting life, and this life is in God's Christ. Whoever has the Christ has life; and whoever doesn't have the Christ of God doesn't have life. I've written this to you who believe on the Name of Yeshua, the Child of God; so that you can know that you have everlasting life, and so that you can keep on believing in the Name of the Child of God. And this is how we can be sure that we have the Christ, that is, if we ask anything that agrees with what God wants, God will hear us. And if we know that God hears us, whatever we ask, we know that we'll get what we wanted from God.

[16-21] If anyone sees someone do something which is a sin, but doesn't lead to death, if they'll ask, God will give them life for those who don't sin a sin which leads to death. There's a sin that leads to death, so I'm not saying that they should pray for freedom from that kind of sin. All ungodliness is sin, but all sin doesn't lead to death. We know that whoever is born of God doesn't sin this kind of sin; but whoever is born of God has self-control, and the devil doesn't touch them. And we know that we're of God, but the whole world is tempted by evil. And we know that the Child of God has come, and has given us an understanding, that we can know the One who is true. So we're in the One who is true, even in God's Child, Yeshua the Christ. This is the true God, and everlasting life. Little children, keep yourselves from worshiping anything else. So be it!

244

The Second Letter from John

1 [1-3] From John, the elder, to the chosen lady and her children, whom I love in the truth; and not just I, but all those who know the truth, as well; Because of the truth's sake, which lives in us, and will be with us forever. May grace, mercy, and peace be with you from Yahweh God, and from Yeshua the Christ, the Child of God, in truth and love.

Love is to do what Christ's Words Say

[4-6] I celebrated greatly that I found your children walking in the truth, as we've been told by God. And now I beg you, lady, not as a New Word to you, but as a reminder of what we were told from the beginning, that is, that we love one another. Love is to do what Christ's words say. This is the Word that you've heard from the beginning, so that you would do it.

The Antichrist

[7-11] There are many misleaders in the world, who say that Yeshua the Christ didn't come in a physical body. This is a liar and an antichrist. Be careful, so that we don't lose what we've worked so hard for, but that we get our full reward. Whoever sins, and doesn't live by the Words of Christ, doesn't have God. Whoever lives by the Words of Christ, they have both the God we're from and the Christ. If anyone comes to you, and doesn't bring Christ's New Word, don't take them home, nor welcome them with a blessing of God, because whoever welcomes and blesses them takes part in their evil ways.

[12-13] I have so much to say to you, I can't write it all on paper, but I trust I'll come to you shortly, and speak face to face, that our joy can be complete. The children of your chosen sister say hello. So be it!

The Third Letter from John

1 [1-4] From John, the elder, to my loved one, Gaius, whom I love in the truth of Christ. My loved one, I wish more than anything that you can do well and be in good health, just as your soul does well! I celebrated greatly, when the Christians came and told me of the truth that is in you, just as you walk in the truth. It'll be my greatest joy to hear that my children walk in the truth.

Whatever You do, Do Faithfully

[5-8] My loved ones, whatever you do, do it faithfully for both the Christians, and for strangers. They have told of your love to the church, whom if you send them on their way with this godly action, you do well: Because they went for Christ's name's sake, taking nothing from other people. So we ought to accept and give for them, that we might be coworkers for the truth.

[9-10] I wrote to the church, but Diotrephes, who loves to have the most important place among them, won't accept us. So if I come, I'll remember what he does, speaking against us with hateful words: and not content with that, he doesn't accept any of the faith either, and stops those who do, and puts them out of the church.

Whoever does Evil doesn't know God

[11-12] My loved ones, don't do what is evil, but what is good. Whoever does good is of God, but whoever does evil doesn't know God. Demetrius has a good reputation with everyone, and the truth itself speaks well of him. Yes, and we also say he has a good reputation; and you know that what we speak is true.

[13-14] I had many things to write, but I won't write to you on paper, but I trust I'll see you shortly, and we'll speak face to face. May Christ's peace be with you. Our friends say hello. Say hello to all my friends by name.

A Letter from Jude

[1-2] From Jude, the worker of Yeshua the Christ and the brother of James, to those who are set apart by Yahweh God, and saved by Yeshua the Christ and called by the Holy Spirit: May God's mercy, peace, and love, come to you many times over.

Actively Promote the Faith

[3-11] My loved ones, when I gave my full attention to write to you about our shared salvation, I needed to write to you to encourage you to actively promote the faith that was once given to all Christians. Because certain people have snuck in, being overlooked by us, who were long ago set apart for their guilt, ungodly ones, making a mockery of the grace of our God, and disowning the only true Savior and God, Yeshua, our Christ. So I'm reminding you, though you already know this, how that God, having saved the people out of the land of Egypt, later punished those who didn't believe by death. And also the angels who chose not to stay with God, but left their own place to follow Satan, God has kept in everlasting chains in darkness until the great day of judgment. Just as Sodom and Gomorrah, and the people of the cities around them are an example, having given themselves over to sexual sin, went after those of the same sex, and suffered the punishment of everlasting fire. In this way, too, these filthy people, who don't know the truth and destroy their own bodies, hate the authority of the Word, and speak evil of those in authority in the church. Yet Michael, the archangel, who was battling with Satan when they argued about the body of Moses, didn't dare bring an accusation even against the devil, but only said, *"May God accuse you."* But these people speak evil about what they don't understand confusing themselves in what they should naturally know, as physical beings. Sorrow will come to them! For they've followed the path of Cain, and have made the same selfish mistake of Balaam, looking for a profit, and will be destroyed as in the rebellion of Korah.

False Teachers will be Judged

[12-16] These are marks in your love celebrations, when they celebrate with you, eating without fear. They're clouds with the promise of rain, but carried away by the winds; trees whose fruit dies, with no harvest, completely dead, and pulled up by the roots; Raging waves of the sea, foaming and speaking out about their own shame; wandering stars, who are kept in the blackest darkness forever. And Enoch also, the seventh from Adam, preached about these kind of people, saying, *"God comes with countless thousands of the chosen ones, to carry out judgment on all of them, and to prove to all those who are ungodly all the ungodly things they've done, and of all the cruel things, which these ungodly sinners have spoken against our God."* These people are rebellious complainers, doing whatever they want to do. They speak very nice words to get other's praises in order to get ahead.

Our Faith Mocked in the Last Days

[17-23] But remember, my loved ones, the words which were spoken by the followers of Yeshua, our Christ; How that they told you there would be people who would mock our faith in the last days, who would do whatever ungodly things they want to do. These are the ones who separate themselves from the truth, living by their physical drives, and not having the self-control of Spirit. But you, my loved ones, keep encouraging yourselves with your most holy faith, praying by the Holy Spirit. Stay in God's love, looking forward to the mercy of Yeshua, our Christ, in order to receive everlasting life. And care for those who choose to change their actions. Save the rest with fear, pulling them out of the heat of sin; hating even the outward appearance of their sin.

[24-25] Now to the One who is able to keep you from falling into sin, and to present you with great joy, unflawed, in the presence of Christ's victory, and to the only One with God's wisdom, Yeshua, our Savior, be victory and greatness, authority and power, now and forever. So be it!

247

The Revelation of John

1 [1-8] This is the Revelation of Yeshua the Christ, which God gave to the Christ, to show to God's people all the things which must soon happen. It was sent and signified by God's messenger to God's worker John, who has told us the Word of God, and the truth of Yeshua the Christ, and of everything that he saw. Whoever reads it will be blessed, along with those who hear the message of this word which was given ahead of time, and keep what is written in it, because it's time for it to be known. I, John, write to the seven churches of Asia: May God's grace and peace be with you, from the One Who Is, and Who Was, and Is To Come; and from the seven spirits which are in front of the throne of God; And from Yeshua the Christ, who is the faithful witness, and the First Born of the dead, and the Ruler of the rulers of the earth. To the One who loved us, and washed us from our sins in Christ's own blood, and has made us to be rulers and priests to Yahweh God, who Christ is from; May Your victory be known and Your reign be forever and ever. So be it! When the Christ comes back in the clouds of the sky, everyone will see it, and those who killed the Christ and all the families of the earth will cry when they see the Christ. It will happen in this very way! *"I am the First Word and the Last Word, the beginning and the ending,"* said the Christ, *"Who Is, Who Was, and Who Is To Come, the Almighty God."*

[9-20] I, John, who also am your friend and companion in troubles, in the realm of God and in the patient waiting for Yeshua the Christ, was in the island of Patmos, being punished for telling the truth about the Word of God, and for telling the truth about Yeshua the Christ. I was in the Spirit on a Sunday, when I heard behind me a loud voice, like the sound of a trumpet, saying, *"I am the First Word and the Last Word, the beginning and the ending. Write what you see in a book, and send it to the seven Asian churches; to Ephesus, to Smyrna, to Pergamos, to Thyatira, to Sardis, to Philadelphia, and to Laodicea."* And when I turned to see the voice that spoke with me, I saw seven golden candle holders; And in the middle of the seven candle holders Some one like the Christ, clothed with a robe down to the foot, and with a golden belt around the waist; Whose head and hair were white like wool, as white as snow; and whose eyes shined like a flaming fire; And whose feet shown like fine brass, as if they were on fire; and whose voice sounded like a great rushing water; And who had seven stars in one hand: and out of whose mouth came something like a sharp two-edged sword: and whose appearance was like the sunshine in its full strength. And when I saw the Christ, I fell down as if I were dead. And the Christ, whose hand touched me, told me, *"Don't be afraid; I am the first and the last: I am the One who lives, and was dead; and I am alive forever, so be it; and now I have power over Hell and death. Write everything you've seen, all the things which are now, and the things which will happen later; I tell you the secret of the seven stars which you saw in my hand and the seven golden candle holders. The seven stars are the messengers of the seven churches: and the seven candle holders which you saw stand for the seven churches.*

Letters to the Seven Churches

2 [1-7] *To the angel of the church of Ephesus write: The One who holds the seven stars in one hand and who walks among the seven golden candle holders says to you: I know what you've done, your work, and your patience, and how you can't stand those who are evil: how you've tested those who say they're followers, but really aren't, and you know they are liars: And what you've patiently gone through, and because of My Name have worked, and haven't quit. But even so, I still have somewhat against you, because you've left your first love. So remember where you've come from, and change your evil ways, and do what you did at first; or else I'll come to you suddenly, and will take your candle holder from out of its place, unless you change your evil ways. But you have hated the actions of the followers of Nicolas, which I also hate. Whoever will listen, let them hear what the Spirit says to the churches; I'll give those who overcome fruit to eat from the tree of life, which is in the middle of God's Garden of Paradise.*

[8-11] *And to the angel of the church in Smyrna write: The first and the last, which was dead, and is alive says this to you; I know what you've done, and your troubles, and your poverty, (but you're really rich in spirit) and I know the disrespect of those who say they're followers, but really aren't. In truth, they're the followers of Satan. Don't fear anything that you'll suffer: the devil will put some of you in jail, so that you can be tested; and you'll have a great time of troubles: but be faithful, even to death, and I'll give you a crown of life. Whoever will listen, let them hear what the Spirit says to the churches; Whoever overcomes won't be harmed by the second death.*

[12-17] *And to the angel of the church in Pergamos write: The One who has the sharp blade with two edges says this to you: I know what you've done, and where you live, even the very place where Satan reigns: and you still hold on to My Name, and haven't denied My faith, even in the days that Antipas was My faithful martyr, who was killed among you, where Satan reigns. But I still have a few things against you, because those who, like Balaam, who taught Balac to compromise the faith of the children of Israel, to eat things sacrificed in false worship, and to act in sexual sin, so you also have those who practice what the followers of Nicolas do, which I hate. Change your evil ways; or else I'll come to you suddenly, and will fight against them with the blade of my*

mouth, the Word of God. Whoever will listen, let them hear what the Spirit says to the churches; To those who overcome, I'll give some of the hidden bread from heaven to eat, and will give them a white stone, with a new name written in it, which no one knows except whoever gets it.

[18-29] And to the angel of the church in Thyatira write: This says the Child of God, whose eyes are like a flame of fire, and whose feet are like fine brass; I know what you've done, your love, work, faith, and patience, and all the little things you've done; and the last is more than the first. But even so, I still have a few things against you, because you let that woman like Jezebel, which calls herself a great preacher, to teach and to seduce my workers to sin sexually, and to eat things offered in false worship. And I gave her time to change the sinful way of unfaithfulness; but she didn't change her ways. So I'll put her, and those who sinned with her, into a bed of great troubles, unless they change their evil ways. And I'll kill her children with death; and all the churches will know that I am the One who searches the mind and the heart: and I'll give to everyone of you whatever you deserve. But I say to you, and to all the rest in Thyatira, whoever hasn't accepted this teaching, and which hasn't known the depths of Satan, as they speak: I'll put on you no other problem. But what you already have, hold on to till I come. And whoever overcomes, and keeps on doing My work till the end, I'll give them power over the nations just as I got of the One I am from: And they'll rule them with a strong hand; and they'll be broken to shivers like the jars of a potter. And I'll give them the morning star. Whoever will listen, let them hear what the Spirit says to the churches.

3 [1-6] And to the angel of the church in Sardis write: The One who has the seven Spirits of God, and the seven stars says this: I know what you've done, and that even though you have a name that's alive, you're dead. Be watchful, and strengthen those you have left that are ready to die, because I haven't found what you've done to be without fault before God. So remember how you've gotten and heard the Word, and hold on to it, and change your evil ways. And if you won't watch, I'll come on you like a thief, and you won't know when I'll come to you. You still have a few people left in Sardis which haven't ruined the clothes they walk in. They'll walk with Me in white clothes because they're worthy. Whoever overcomes will be clothed in white clothing; and I won't take their name out of the Book of Life, but I'll call their name before the One I am from, and before the angels. Whoever will listen, let them hear what the Spirit says to the churches.

[7-13] And to the angel of the church in Philadelphia write: This said the One who is holy, the One who is true, the One who has the power of David, the One who opens what no one can shut; and shuts what no one can open; I know what you've done: I've given you an open door, which no one can shut, because you only have a little strength left, and have kept My Word, and haven't denied My Name. I'll make those who follow Satan, which say they're My followers, but aren't, and lie about it, to come and fall at your feet, and to know that I have loved you. You've kept the Word of My patience, so I'll also keep you from the time of temptation, which will come to the whole world, to test all those who still live on the earth. I'll come suddenly, so hold tight what you have, so that no one can take your crown. Whoever overcomes I'll make a leader in the Place of Worship of My God, and they won't go out any more. I'll write on them the Name of My God, and the Name of the City of My God, which is New Jerusalem, which will come down out of heaven from My God: and I'll write on them My New Name. Whoever will listen, let them hear what the Spirit says to the churches.

[14-22] And to the angel of the church of the Laodiceans write: This said the Last Word, the faithful and true witness, the beginning of the creation of God; I know what you've done, and that you're neither cold nor hot. I wish you were either cold or hot, but because you're only lukewarm, and not cold or hot, I'll spew you out of My mouth. You say, 'I am rich, and have lots of things, and don't need anything.' But you don't know that you're a useless and miserable person, poor, blind, and naked. I tell you to buy of Me gold tried in the fire, so that you can really be rich; and wear white clothing, that you can be covered, so that the shame of your nakedness doesn't show; and anoint your eyes with medicine, so that you can see. Whoever I love, I judge and discipline, so be very careful, and change your evil ways. I stand at the door, knocking, to see if anyone hears My voice, and opens the door. Then I'll come in and eat with them, and they with Me. I'll allow those who overcome to sit with Me in My throne room, just as I also overcame, and am now sitting with the One I am from, in the throne room of Yahweh God. Whoever will listen, let them hear what the Spirit says to the churches."

Heaven Opened

4 [1-5] Later, I looked and a door was opened up in heaven: and the first voice which I heard was like a trumpet talking with me; which said, "Come up here, and I'll show you the things which must happen later." And suddenly I was in the spirit: And there was a throne in heaven, and the One who sat on the throne shined like a dark green jasper stone and a blood red chalcedony stone: and there was an emerald green rainbow shining around the throne. And there were twenty-four seats around the throne, where twenty-four elders sat, all wearing long white robes and golden crowns. And lightning and voices like thunder came out of the throne: and there were seven lamps of fire burning in front of it, which are the Seven Spirits of God, the Holy Spirit.

[6-11] And in front of the throne there was a great bowl made of glass as clear as crystal: and in the middle of the throne, and around the throne, were four living things, which were full of lights, both in front and in back. And

249

the first one was like a lion, the second one was like a calf, the third one had the face of a human, and the fourth was like a flying eagle. And each the four living things had six wings around them, which were full of lights. They rest neither day nor night, saying, *"Holy, holy, holy, Highest God Almighty, which was, and is, and is to come."* And when they gave praise and honor and thanks to the One who sat on the throne, who lives forever and ever, the twenty-four elders bowed down to the One who sat on the throne, and worshiped the One who lives forever and ever, and put out their crowns toward the throne, saying, *"You're worthy, God, to get praise, honor, and power because You've created everything, and for Your pleasure they live and were created."*

Christ Can Open the Book

5 [1-10] And I saw in the hand of the One who sat on the throne, a book written on front and on back, marked with seven seals. And I saw a strong messenger calling out with a loud voice, *"Who is worthy to open the book, and to loose its seals?"* But no one either in heaven, or in earth, or in Hell, was able to open the book, nor to even look on it. And I cried so much, because no one was worthy enough to open and read the book, nor to look on it. But one of the elders told me, *"Don't cry: the Lion of the family of Judah, the Root of David, has done well and can open the book, and loose its seven seals."* And I watched, and a Lamb stood in the middle of the throne room and of the four living things, and in the middle of the elders, as if it had been put to death, having seven horns and seven eyes, which are the Seven Spirits of God sent out into all the earth, who came and took the book out of the hand of the One who sat on the throne. And when Christ, the Lamb had taken the book, the four living things and twenty-four elders bowed down to Christ, the Lamb, every one of them having harps, and holding golden bowls full of incense, which are the prayers of all the believers. And they sung a new song, saying, *"You're worthy to take the book, and to open its seals, because you were put to death, and have paid our ransom for God by your blood, for every family, language, people, and nation; And You have made us rulers and priests to our God: and we'll reign on the earth."*

[11-14] And as I watched, I heard the voice of many angels around the throne, along with the living things and the elders: and there were so many you couldn't count them all; And they said with a loud voice, *"Worthy is Christ, the Lamb that was put to death to get power, riches, wisdom, strength, honor, praise, and blessing."* And every creature which is in heaven, on the earth, and in Hell, and those that are in the sea, and all that is in them, I heard saying, *"Blessing, honor, praise, and power, be to the One who sits on the throne, and to Christ, the Lamb forever and ever."* And the four living things said, "So be it!" And the twenty-four elders bowed down and worshipped the One who lives forever and ever.

The Seven Seals

6 [1-8] And I saw when Christ, the Lamb opened one of the seals, and I heard a voice like the noise of thunder, one of the four living things saying, *"Come."* And I looked and saw a white horse: and the rider had a bow; and wore a crown: and went out taking control, and to take control. And when Christ, the Lamb had opened the second seal, I heard the second living thing say, *"Come."* And another horse went out that was red: and power was given to the rider, who was given a great sword, to take peace from the earth, and to make people kill each other. And when Christ, the Lamb had opened the third seal, I heard the third living thing say, *"Come."* And I watched, and saw a black horse; and the rider had a pair of balances. And I heard a voice in the middle of the four living things say, "A loaf of wheat bread for a day's pay, and three loaves of barley bread for a day's pay; and see that the oil and the wine stay available." And when Christ, the Lamb had opened the fourth seal, I heard the voice of the fourth living thing say, *"Come."* And I looked, and saw a pale horse: and the name of its rider was Death, and Hell followed behind. And power was given to them over a fourth part of the earth, to kill with war, hunger, death, and with the animals of the earth.

[9-17] And when Christ, the Lamb had opened the fifth seal, I saw under the altar the souls of those who were beheaded and put to death for the Word of God, and for their belief: And they called out, saying, *"How long, Christ, holy and true, until You judge and punish those who live on the earth for our blood?"* And they were all given white robes and were told to rest a little while longer, until all the other Christians would be killed as they were. And I watched when Christ, the Lamb had opened the sixth seal, there was a great earthquake; and the sun became as black as cloth made of goat's hair, and the moon became as red as blood; And the stars of heaven fell to the earth, just as a fig tree drops its out of season figs, when its shaken by a strong wind. And the sky moved together as a scroll when it's rolled up; and every mountain and island were moved out of place. And the rulers of the earth, and the great people, the rich people, the leaders, and all the other powerful people, both workers, and free people, hid themselves in the caves and rocks of the mountains; And said to the mountains and rocks, *"Fall on us, and hide us from the face of the One who sits on the throne, and from the judgment of Christ, the Lamb, because the great judgment day is here; and who is able to stand?"*

250

144,000 Jews Marked for God

7 [1-8] And then I saw four angels standing at the four quarters of the earth, holding the four winds of the earth, so that no wind would blow on the land, or on the sea, or on any tree. And I saw another messenger going up from the east, having the seal of the living God: who called out to the four angels, who were given power to hurt the land and the sea, saying, *"Don't hurt the land, nor the sea, nor the trees, till we've marked the workers of our God in their foreheads."* And I heard the number of those who were marked: and a hundred and forty-four thousand were marked of all the families of the Jews. Twelve thousand were marked of the family of Judah. Twelve thousand were marked of the family of Reuben. Twelve thousand were marked of the family of Gad. Twelve thousand were marked of the family of Asher. Twelve thousand were marked of the family of Naphtali. Twelve thousand were marked of the family of Manasseh. Twelve thousand were marked of the family of Simeon. Twelve thousand were marked of the family of Levi. Twelve thousand were marked of the family of Issachar. Twelve thousand were marked of the family of Zebulun. Twelve thousand were marked of the family of Joseph. Twelve thousand were marked of the family of Benjamin.

[9-17] Then I saw a great crowd, which no one could count, out of every nation, family, people, and language, who stood in front of the throne, and before Christ, the Lamb, clothed with white robes, and palms in their hands, who called out with a loud voice, saying, *"We are saved by our God who sits on the throne, and by Christ, the Lamb."* And all the angels stood around the throne, and around the elders and the four living things, and fell on their faces before the throne, and worshipped God, saying, *"So be it: May God have blessing, praise, wisdom, thanks, honor, power, and strength forever and ever. So be it!"* And one of the elders asked me, *"Who are these clothed in white robes? And where did they come from?"* And I answered, *"I don't know, but you do."* And the elder told me, *"These are those who came out of the great time of troubles, and have washed their robes, and made them white in the blood of Christ, the Lamb. So they stand before the throne of God, and serve day and night in God's Place of Worship: and the One who sits on the throne will stay with them. They'll never be hungry any more, nor be thirsty any more; nor will the sun shine on them, nor burn them any more, because Christ, the Lamb which is in the middle of the throne will take care of them, and will lead them to the source of life giving waters: and God will brush away all the tears from their eyes."*

The Seven Trumpets

8 [1-6] And when Christ, the Lamb had opened the seventh seal, there was silence in heaven for a short time. And I saw the seven angels which stood before God; and seven trumpets were given to them. And another messenger came and stood at the altar, having a golden censer, who was given a lot of incense, to offer with the prayers of all the Christians on the golden altar which was before the throne. And the smoke of the incense, which came up with the prayers of all the Christians, went up to God out of the angel's hand. And the angel took the censer, and filled it with coals from the altar, and threw it into the earth: and there were voices, thundering, lightning, and an earthquake. And the seven angels who had the seven trumpets go ready to sound.

[7-13] The first messenger sounded, and hail and fire mingled with blood followed, and were thrown on the earth: and a third of trees was burnt up, and all the green grass was burnt up. And the second messenger sounded, and something like a great erupting volcano was thrown into the sea: and a third of the sea filled with blood; And a third of all the creatures in the sea that had life, died; and a third of all the ships was destroyed. And the third messenger sounded, and there fell a great star from heaven, burning like a lamp, and it fell on a third of the rivers, and on all the sources of water; And the name of the star is called Wormwood: and a third of the waters became bitter; and many people died from drinking it, because it became poison. And the fourth messenger sounded, and a third of the sun was put out, and a third of the moon, and a third of the stars; so a third of them was darkened, and the daylight didn't shine for a third of the day, and no light shined for a third of the night. And I watched, and heard an angel flying through the middle of heaven, saying with a loud voice, *"Sorrow, sorrow, sorrow is coming to the inhabitants of the earth because of the other voices of the trumpets of the three angels, which are still yet to sound!"*

9 [1-12] And the fifth messenger sounded, and I saw an angel that shined like a star fall from heaven to the earth: which was given the power to open up the bottomless pit. And the bottomless pit was opened; and smoke came up out of the pit, as the smoke of a great burning fire; and the sun and the air were darkened by all the smoke that came up out of the pit. And something like locusts came out of the smoke on the earth: and they were given the power to sting like a scorpion. And it was told them *"Don't hurt the grass of the earth, nor any green thing, nor any tree; but only those people who don't have the mark of God on their foreheads."* And they were told, *"Don't kill them, but make them suffer five months."* And those people suffered with the great pain of a scorpion sting, when it strikes someone. And in those days people will look for death, but won't find it; and will want to die, but death will escape them. And the demonic locusts were armored like horses prepared for battle; and they had something like golden crowns on their heads, and their faces were like the faces of people. They had long hair like a woman's hair, and their teeth were as fierce as lion's teeth. And they had strong protective breastplates, like

251

breastplates of iron; and the sound of their wings was as the sound of many horses running to battle. And they had tails like scorpions, and there were stings in their tails: and their power was to hurt human beings for five months. And their ruler is the angel of the bottomless pit, whose name in the Hebrew language is Abaddon, but in the Greek language has the name of Apollyon, which means "*destroyer*." When this sorrow is over, there are still two more to come.

[13-21] And the sixth messenger sounded, and I heard a voice from the four horns of the golden altar which is before God, saying to the sixth angel which had the trumpet, "*Let loose the four angels which are waiting at the great river Euphrates.*" And the four angels were set free, which had been waiting for this hour, this day, this month, and this year to kill a third of all human beings. And I heard the number of the army of riders, which was two hundred million. And I saw the horses in the vision, and their riders, which had breastplates of bright red, dark blue, and pale yellow: and the heads of the horses were as fierce as the heads of lions; and fire, smoke, and sulfur shot out of their mouths. A third of the human beings were killed by these three troubles, by the fire, the smoke, and the sulfur, which shot out of their mouths. Their power to hurt is in both their heads, and in their tail ends because their tails were like snakes with heads, which they hurt people with. And the rest of the people who weren't killed by these troubles still didn't change their minds or their evil actions, and kept on worshiping evil spirits, and false gods of gold, silver, brass, stone, and wood, idols which can't see, hear, or walk. Nor did they ask forgiveness for their murdering and thieving ways, their witchcraft, or their sexual sins.

Seven Thunders Sealed

10 [1-7] And I saw another powerful messenger come down from heaven, surrounded by a cloud: and crowned with a rainbow, whose face shined like the sun, and whose feet glowed like two pillars of fire: Who held a little book open: and set one foot on the sea, and the other foot on the earth, and called out with a loud voice, like a lion roars. When the messenger called out, seven thunders spoke with voices. And when the seven thunders had spoken with the voices, I was about to write, when I heard a voice from heaven saying to me, "*Don't write what the seven thunders spoke, but keep it to yourself.*" And the angel which I saw stand on the sea and on the earth lifted up a hand toward heaven, swearing by the One who lives forever and ever, who created heaven, and everything in it, and the earth, and everything in it, and the sea, and everything in it, that time would be no longer: But in the days when the voice of the seventh angel begins to sound, the secret of God would be finished, just as God has told the great preachers.

[8-11] And the voice which I heard from heaven spoke to me again, saying, "*Go and take the little book which is open in the hand of the angel, which stands on the sea and on the earth.*" So I went to the angel, saying, "*Give me the little book.*" And the angel told me, "*Take it, and eat it; It'll make you sick to your stomach, but it'll taste as sweet as honey.*" So I took the little book out of the angel's hand and ate it; and it tasted as sweet as honey, but as soon as I had eaten it, it made me sick to my stomach. Then the angel told me, "You must go and preach again to many peoples, nations, languages, and rulers."

Two Witnesses

11 [1-10] And I was given a measuring stick: and the angel stood, saying, "*Go, and measure the Place of Worship of God, and the altar, and count those who worship in it. But leave out the court which is outside the Place of Worship. Don't measure it because it's for the other peoples who will trample the holy city for 42 months. And I'll give power to My two witnesses, and they'll preach 1,260 days, clothed in mourning clothes. These are the two olive trees, and the two candle holders standing before the God of the earth. And if anyone tries to hurt them, fire will come out of their mouths, and burn up their enemies: Those who try to hurt them must be killed in this way. These two have power to shut heaven, so that it doesn't rain as long as they preach. They also have power over the waters to turn them to blood, and to bring diseases on the earth as often as they want to. And when they've finished preaching, the creature that comes up out of the bottomless pit will fight against them, and will overcome them, and kill them. And their dead bodies will lie in the street of the great city of Jerusalem, where our Christ was put to death, which is called in the spiritual realm Sodom and Egypt. And every people, family, language, and nation will see their dead bodies three and a half days, and won't allow their dead bodies to be buried. And those who live on the earth will celebrate over them, and party, sending gifts to one another; because these two great preachers had hurt those who lived on the earth.*"

[11-19] And after three and a half days, the Spirit of life from God went back in them, and they stood up; and great fear fell on all those who saw them. And they heard a great voice from heaven saying to them, "*Come up here.*" And they went up to heaven in a cloud as their enemies watched them. And at that same time there was a great earthquake, and a tenth of the city was destroyed, and seven thousand people were killed in the earthquake. Then all the rest were afraid, and praised the God of heaven. The second sorrow is over, and the third sorrow will come suddenly. And the seventh angel sounded; and there were great voices in heaven, saying, "*The realms of this world have become the realms of Yahweh God, and of God's Christ; who will reign forever and ever.*" And the twenty-four elders, which sat before God on their seats, dropped to the ground, and worshipped

252

God, saying, *"We give you thanks, Highest God Almighty, who is, and was, and is to come; because You've taken Your great power, and have ruled. And the nations were angry that Your rage is here, and that the time is here for the dead to be judged, and that You would give rewards to Your workers the great preachers, and to the Christians, and to all those who fear Your Name, small and great; and for You to kill those who destroy the earth."* And the Place of Worship of God was opened in heaven, and the Ark of the Promise was seen in the Place of Worship. Then there were lightning, thundering, and voices, and an earthquake, and great hailstorm.

The Devil Thrown Out of Heaven to the Earth

12 [1-9] And a great sign appeared in heaven; a woman clothed with the sun, and the moon under her feet, and wearing a crown of twelve stars: And she, being about to have a baby, cried out in pain as she was in labor, and about to give birth. And another sign appeared in heaven; and it was a huge red dragon, having seven heads and ten horns, and seven crowns on the seven heads. And the dragon's tail drew a third of the angels of heaven, and threw them to the earth: and the dragon stood waiting for the woman who was ready to give birth, to eat up her Child as soon as it was born. And she had the Child, who was to rule all nations with a rod of iron: and her Child was caught up to the throne of God. And the woman ran away into hiding, where God had prepared a place to take care of her for 1,260 days. And there was war in heaven: Michael and the angels fought against the dragon; and the dragon fought along with a third of the angels, but they didn't win; nor could they have their place in heaven any more. And the great dragon was thrown out, who was that old snake, called the Devil, and Satan, who misleads the whole world. So the devil was thrown into the earth, along with a third of the angels, who were also thrown out.

[10-17] And I heard a loud voice saying in heaven, *"Now the way to be saved, and strength, and the realm of our God is here, and the power of God's Christ because the accuser of all the Christians is put down, who accused them day and night to our God. But they overcame the devil by the blood of the Christ, the Lamb of God, and by telling the story of how Christ saved them; and they didn't love their lives so much that they even risked death. So all who live in heaven, celebrate! But sorrow will come to the inhabitants of the earth and of the sea! The devil has come down to you, having great rage, knowing that there's only a little while left."* And the devil was thrown to the earth and tried to hurt the woman which had the child. But the woman was given two wings of a great eagle, so that she might fly into the countryside to her place, where she was taken care of for three and a half years, out of reach of the devil. And the snake spewed out a flood of abuse after the woman to cause her to be overcome by it. But the earth helped the woman, and opened up, and swallowed the flood which the dragon spewed out. And the dragon was angry with the woman, and went to fight against the rest of her children, which keep the Words of God, and claim Yeshua as their Christ.

The Creature and it's Clone

13 [1-10] Then I stood on the sea shore, and saw a creature come up out of the sea, having seven heads and ten horns, and on the horns ten crowns, and on the heads a disrespectful name. The creature that I saw was like a leopard, with feet like a bear, and a mouth like a lion. Satan gave it its power, and its government seat, and great control. And I saw one of the heads wounded to death; but the deadly wound was healed. So the whole world was amazed at the creature and worshipped the dragon which gave power to it: and they worshipped the creature, saying, *"Who is like the creature? Who is able to fight against it?"* And the creature was allowed to speak great and disrespectful things against God; and it was given the political power to rule for forty-two months. It spoke disrespectfully against God, to dishonor and disrespect God's Name, and Place of Worship, and those who live in heaven. And it was allowed to fight against the Christians, and to overcome them. It was given power to govern all the families, languages, and nations. And all who live on the earth will worship it, whose names aren't written in the Lamb's Book of Life, that is, of the Christ, who was to be put to death from the beginning of the world. Whoever will listen, let them hear. Whoever takes another's freedom will have their own freedom taken away and whoever causes another to be killed, must be killed themselves. The patience and the faith of the Christians wait for God's justice.

[11-18] And I watched another creature coming up out of the earth; which had two horns like a lamb, but spoke like a dragon. And this religious leader uses all the political power of the first creature that came before it, and causes the earth and those who live in it to worship the first creature, who had come back to life. And this creature does amazing things, making fire come down from heaven on the earth in the sight of all humanity, and misleads all those who live on the earth by the things which it had power to do as long as it rules with the first creature. It told all those who live on the earth, to make a clone of the creature, which had been beheaded, and yet lived. And it had power to give life to the clone of the first creature, so that the clone of the first creature could both speak, and cause whoever wouldn't worship it to be killed. And it causes all, both small and great, rich and poor, free and not free, to get a mark to identify them in their right hand, or in their foreheads. And no one could buy or sell anything unless they had a mark, something like a computer chip with the name of the creature or the number of

its name. This is wisdom. Let those who understand count the number of the creature's name because it's the number of a human being; and the number is 666.

The 144,000

14 [1-5] And I looked, and Christ, the Lamb stood on the mountain of Jerusalem with 144,000 having Yahweh God's Name written in their foreheads. And I heard a voice from heaven, as the sound of rushing waters, and as the sound of the roll of thunder. Then I heard the sound of harpers playing their harps and they sang a new song before the throne, and before the four living things, and the elders. No one could learn that song but the 144, 000 who were saved from the earth. These are those who have kept themselves innocent from the false worship of the world. These are those who follow Christ, the Lamb. These were saved from among human beings, being the first gifts to God and to Christ, the Lamb. And in their mouth was found no untruthfulness and they're without fault before the throne of God.

[6-13] And I saw another messenger fly in the middle of heaven, having the everlasting New Word to preach to those who live on the earth, to every nation, family, language, and people, saying with a loud voice, *"Honor and respect Yahweh God, and give praise to Yahweh God because the time of judgment is here. Worship the One who made heaven and earth, the sea, and all the sources of waters."* And a second messenger followed the first, saying, *"Rome is fallen, is fallen, that great city, because it made all nations drink of the cup of the judgment of its false worship."* And the third messenger followed them, saying with a loud voice, *"If anyone worships the creature and its clone, and takes their mark in their forehead, or in their hand, this person will drink of the cup of the judgment of God, which is poured without being watered down into the cup of God's anger; and they'll suffer, burning with fire and sulfur in the presence of the holy angels, and in the presence of Christ, the Lamb. And the smoke of their suffering will go up forever and ever: and they'll have no rest day nor night, who worship the creature and it's clone, and who take the mark of their name.* So here is the patience of the Christians, who keep the Words of God, and the faith of Yeshua. And I heard a voice from heaven saying to me, *"Write: Blessed are the dead who die in Christ Yeshua from now on: Yes,"* said the Spirit, *"so they can rest from their work; and what they've done will go with them."*

[14-20] And I looked, and saw One sitting on a white cloud, who was like the Child of humanity, wearing a golden crown, and holding a sharp sickle. And another messenger came out of the Place of Worship, loudly calling out to the One who sat on the cloud, *"Swing in your sickle, and harvest! It's time now for you to pick because the harvest of the earth is ripe."* And the One who sat on the cloud swung the sickle in the earth; and harvested the earth. And another messenger came out of the Place of Worship which is in heaven, which also had a sharp sickle. And another messenger came out from the altar, which had power over fire; and loudly called out to the one who had the sharp sickle, saying, *"Swing in your sharp sickle, and gather the clusters of the vine of the earth because her grapes are fully ripe."* And the angel swung that sickle into the earth, and gathered the vine of the earth, and put it into the great winepress of the judgment of God. And those in the winepress were trampled outside the city, and blood came out of the winepress, even up to the horses' bridles, for about two hundred miles.

The Seven Last Horrors

15 [1-4] And I saw another sign in heaven, great and amazing, seven angels having the seven last horrors because God's judgment is to completed by these. And I saw something like a huge sheet of glass shining like fire: and those who had gotten the victory over the creature, and over its clone, and over their mark, and over the number of their name, will stand on the glass, having the harps of God. And they'll sing the song of Moses, the worker of God, and the song of Christ, the Lamb, saying, *"You've done great and amazing things, Highest God Almighty. Just and true are Your ways, and You're the Ruler of the Christians. Who won't fear You, God, and praise Your Name now? You're the only Holy One and all nations will come and worship You because Your judgments are made known.*

[5-8] And after that I looked, and the holiest part of the Place of Worship, which holds the Ark of the Promise was opened in heaven: And the seven angels came out of the Place of Worship, having the seven horrors, clothed in pure white linen, and wearing golden belts around their waists. And one of the four living things gave to the seven angels seven golden vials full of the judgment of God, who lives forever and ever. And the Place of Worship was filled with smoke from the light of God, and from God's power; and no one was able to come into the Place of Worship, till the seven horrors of the seven angels were over.

The Seven Dishes of Punishment

16 [1-7] And I heard a loud voice coming out of the Place of Worship saying to the seven angels, *"Go now, and pour out the seven dishes, which hold the judgment of God, on the earth."* And the first went, and poured out the first dish on the earth; and horrible and painful sores came on those which had the mark of the creature, and on those who worshipped its clone. And the second messenger poured out the second dish on the sea, which became as the blood of a dead person, and every living thing in the sea died. And the third messenger poured out the third dish on the rivers and all the sources of waters, which also became as blood. And I heard the angel of the waters say, *"You're right, Christ, which is, and was, and is to come, because You've judged them for shedding the blood of the Christians and the great preachers, and You've given them blood to drink, which they rightfully deserve."* And I heard another out of the altar say, *"Yes, Highest God Almighty, Your judgments are true and right."*

[8-14] And the fourth messenger poured out the fourth dish on the sun; and power was given to that angel to scorch humanity with fire. And all people were scorched with great heat, and disrespected the Name of God, which has power over these horrors: but they didn't change their ways to give God praise. And the fifth messenger poured out the fifth dish on the seat of power of the creature; and that place was full of darkness; and they gnawed their tongues for pain, and disrespected the God of heaven because of their pains and their sores, and didn't change their minds nor their actions. And the sixth messenger poured out the sixth dish on the great river Euphrates; and all the water dried up, so that the way of the rulers of the east might be cleared. And I saw three frog-like demons come out of the mouths of the dragon, the creature, and its clone. They're the spirits of demons, which do amazing things, and go out to the rulers of the earth and of the whole world, to gather them to the battle of that great day of God Almighty.

[15-20] *"Watch, I come as a thief. Whoever watches will be blessed, if they keep their clothes on, so that they don't walk naked, and expose their shame."* And the demons gathered together those from the east into a place called *"Armageddon"* in the Hebrew language. And the seventh angel poured out the seventh dish into the air; and there came a great voice out of the Place of Worship of heaven, from the throne, saying, *"It's done."* And there were voices, thunders, lightning; and then there was a great earthquake. And it was so powerful an earthquake, and so great, such as never before, since humans lived on the earth. And the great city was divided into three parts, and the cities of the nations fell. Then great Rome was given the cup of the wine of the fierceness of God's rage. And every island disappeared, and the mountains were leveled. And a great hail fell out of heaven on humanity, every hailstone weighing about seventy-five to a hundred pounds each: and the people disrespected God because of the horror of the hail and because its damage was so great.

Rome, The Whore

17 [1-7] And one of the seven angels came, which had the seven dishes, and talked with me, saying, *"Come here; I'll show you the judgment of the great whore that sits on the great waters, with whom the rulers of the earth have falsely worshiped, and the people of the earth have been made drunk with the wine of its false worship."* So I was carried away in the spirit into the countryside, where I saw a woman sitting on a scarlet red creature, full of names that were disrespectful of God, having seven heads and ten horns. And the woman was dressed up in the colors of purple and scarlet, and wore jewels of gold, precious stones, and pearls, having a golden cup in her hand full of the evils and filthiness of her false worship. On her forehead was a name written, *Secret, Rome the Great, The Mother of Whores and Disgraces of the Earth.* And I saw the woman drunken with the blood of the Christians, and with the blood of the martyrs of Yeshua: and when I saw her, I was greatly amazed.

[7-14] And the angel asked me, *"Why are you so amazed? I'll tell you the secret of the woman, and of the creature that carries her, which has the seven heads and ten horns. The creature that you saw was, but isn't now; and will come up out of the bottomless pit, and go on to be finally destroyed: and those who live on the earth will wonder, whose names weren't written in the Book of Life from the beginning of the world, when they see the creature that was, but isn't now, and yet still is. And the mind that has wisdom will know this: The seven heads are the seven mountains of Rome, on which the woman sits. And there are seven rulers: five have fallen, and one rules now, and the other hasn't come yet; and when that ruler comes, that reign will be short. And the creature that was, but isn't now, is the eighth, and is the clone of one of the seven, and will go on to be finally destroyed. And the ten horns which you saw are ten more rulers, which haven't gotten their place of rule yet; but they will get power as rulers for one hour with the creature. These will all have one mind, and will give their power and strength to the creature. These will fight against Christ, the Lamb, but the Lamb will overcome them, who is the Savior of saviors, and the Ruler of rulers: and those who are with the Christ are called, and chosen, and faithful.*

[15-18] Then the angel told me, *"The great waters which you saw, where the whore sits, are crowds of peoples, nations, and languages. And the ten horns which you saw on the creature, these will come to hate the whore, and will strip her naked of everything, and will destroy everything she has, and burn her with fire, because God has put it in their hearts to do what God wants them to do, and to agree to give the rule of their countries to the creature, until the Words of God happen. And the woman which you saw is Rome, that great city, which reigns over the rulers of the earth."*

Rome Falls

18 [1-10] And then I saw another angelic messenger come down from heaven, having great power; and the earth shown with its brightness. And it cried mightily with a strong voice, saying, *"Rome, the great, has fallen, has fallen, and has become the place of demons, and every evil spirit, and a prison for all those evil and hateful birds, because all nations have drunk the wine of the judgment of its false worship, and the rulers of the earth have taken part in this sin with it, and the merchants of the earth have became wealthy through all of its riches."* And I heard another voice from heaven, saying, *"Come out of her, My people, so that you don't share in her sins, and that you don't get punished with her horrors, because her sins have reached to heaven, and God has remembered her unmerciful actions. Give back to her just as she gave to you, and give her double for what she's done. Pour her double into the cup which she's filled. Give her as much suffering and sorrow as she's given praise to herself, and lived richly, because she said in her heart, 'I am a queen, and not a widow, and I'll see no sorrow.'"* So will the horrors of death, crying, and hunger come in one day; and she'll be completely burned with fire because Yahweh God is a powerful judge. And the rulers of the earth, who shared in its sin and lived richly with it, will mourn, and cry, when they see the smoke of its burning. And standing far off for the fear of its judgment, they'll say, *"How sad! How sad! That great city of Rome, that powerful city! In one hour you have been judged."*

[11-20] And the merchants of the earth will cry and cry over the city of Rome because no one can buy its sales goods any more: The sales goods of gold, silver, precious stones, pearls, fine linens of purple, silks of scarlet, all kinds of citrus trees, all kinds of things made from ivory, precious woods, brass, iron, marble, all kinds of cinnamon and spices, scented oils, perfumes, incense, wine, oil, fine wheat flour, wild animals, farm animals, horses, vehicles, workers, and even the souls of human beings. And everyone will say, *"All the things that it wanted are gone now, and everything that was rich and beautiful are gone now, and will never come in it again."* The merchants of this city, which were made rich by her, will stand far off for fear of its judgment, and they will cry and cry, saying, *"How sad! How sad! That great city of Rome, that was clothed in fine linens of purple and scarlet, and wore jewels of gold, precious stones, and pearls! In one hour such great riches has come to nothing."* And every ship owner, and all the ships' companies, and sailors, and whoever traded by sea, stood far off, and called out when they saw the smoke of its burning, saying, *"What city is like this great city of Rome!"* And they put dust on their heads, and called out, crying and crying, saying, *"How sad! How sad! That great city, in which everyone who had ships in the sea was made rich because of its riches! In one hour it's been left empty."*

[20-24] Celebrate over it, all who are in heaven, and all you holy followers and great preachers, because God has taken revenge on it for you. And a powerful messenger took up a stone like a great millstone, and threw it into the sea, saying, *"With this same violence that great city of Rome will be thrown down, and will never be found again. And the sound of harpers, and musicians, and flutists, and trumpeters will never be heard in you again; and no craftsman of any kind will ever be found in you again; and the sound of a millstone will never be heard in you again; And the light of a candle will never shine in you again; and the voices of a bridal party will never be heard in you again, because your merchants were the great people of the earth from all the nations who were tricked by your evil sorceries."* And that city was punished for the blood of all the great preachers, and of all the Christians, and of all that were put to death on the earth.

The Great Supper in Heaven

19 [1-8] And then I heard a loud noise of many voices in heaven, saying, *"Praise Yahweh! May victory, honor, and power be Yahweh God's who saved us! True and right are God's judgments, which have judged the great whore who ruined the earth with her false worship, and which have taken revenge for the blood of God's people at her hand."* And again they said, *"Praise Yahweh!"* And the smoke of that city went up forever and ever. And the twenty-four elders and the four living things bowed down and worshipped God who sat on the throne, saying, *"So be it; Praise Yahweh!"* And a voice came out of the throne, saying, *"Praise our God, all you who are God's people, you that fear God, both small and great."* And I heard the voice of a great crowd, as the voice of rushing waters, and as the voice of powerful thundering, saying, *"Praise Yahweh! Highest Almighty God reigns. Let's be happy and celebrate, and give honor to God because the marriage of Christ, the Lamb is here, whose spouse has made herself ready. And she was allowed to be clothed in pure white fine linen, because the fine linen is the acts of goodness of the Christians."*

[9-16] And I was told, *"Write, Blessed are those who are called to the wedding supper of Christ, the Lamb."* And I was told, *"These are the true Words of God."* And I fell down to worship the angel who spoke, but I was told, *"See that you don't do it: I am your coworker, and of those that tell how Yeshua changed their lives: Worship God because telling how Yeshua changed my life is the spirit of the Word, which was given ahead of time."* And I saw heaven opened, and saw a white horse; and the One who sat on it was called *"Faithful and True,"* and the Christ is right to judge and fight against evil. The Christ, who had eyes like flames of fire, wore many crowns; and had a name written, that no one knew, but only the Christ. And the Christ was clothed with a coat dipped in blood: and the Christ's name is called *"The Word of God."* And all the forces of heaven followed along on white horses, clothed in pure white fine linen. And out of the Christ's mouth went a sharp blade, which is the Word of God, so

256

that the nations would be struck with it. The Christ will rule them with a rod of iron and trample the winepress of the fierceness and rage of Almighty God. And the name, *Ruler of rulers, and Savior of saviors,* is written on the Christ's coat and thigh.

[17-21] And I saw an angel standing in the sun; who called out, saying to all the birds that fly in the heavens, *"Come and gather together to the supper of the great God; so that you can eat the bodies of rulers and captains, and the bodies of powerful people, and their soldiers and horses, and the bodies of everyone else, both free and not free, both small and great."* And I saw the creature, and the rulers of the earth, and their forces, gathered together to fight against the One who sat on the horse, and against all the Christ's forces. And the creature was taken, along with the clone that did the amazing things for the creature, with which they lied to all those who had gotten the mark of the creature, and worshipped the clone of the creature. These were both thrown alive into a lake of fire and burning sulfur. And all the rest were put to death with the blade of the One who sat on the horse, which went out of the Christ's mouth: and all the birds were filled with their bodies.

The Reign of Christ

20 [1-6] And I saw an angel come down from heaven, having the power to open the bottomless pit and a great chain in the angel's hand. And the angel took the dragon, that old snake, which is the devil, who is called Satan, which was chained a thousand years, and thrown into the bottomless pit, and shut it up. And the angel marked the devil so that he couldn't mislead the nations any more, till the thousand years were over. After that, the devil must be freed for a little while. Then I saw thrones, and those who sat on them, and judgment was given to them. Then I saw the souls of those who were beheaded for telling about Yeshua, and for the Word of God, and which hadn't worshipped the creature, nor its clone, nor had gotten their mark in their foreheads, or in their hands. These lived and ruled with Christ a thousand years. But the rest of the dead didn't come to life again until the thousand years were over. This is the first coming to life again. Blessed and holy are those who take part in the first coming to life again: the second death will have no power over them, but they'll be priests of Yahweh God and of Yeshua the Christ, and will reign with the Christ a thousand years.

The Judgment

[7-10] And when the thousand years are over, Satan will be freed out of the pit, and will once again go out to mislead the nations which are in the four quarters of the earth, both the creature and the people, to gather them together for the battle: the number of which is as uncountable as the sand of the sea. And they went up on the breadth of the earth, and surrounded the forces of the Christians, and the greatly loved city of Jerusalem, but fire came down from God out of heaven, and burned them to death. And the devil that lied to them was put into the lake of fire and burning sulfur, where the creature and the clone of it are, and will suffer day and night forever and ever.

[11-15] And I saw a great white throne, and the One who sat on it, in whose presence the earth and the sky broke up and disappeared. And I saw the dead, small and great, standing before God; and the books were opened. Then another book was opened, which is the Book of Life: and the dead were judged out of what was written in the books, for all the things they had done. And the sea gave up the dead who were in it; and death and Hell gave up the dead who were in them: and they were all judged for what they had done. And death and Hell were thrown into the lake of fire. This is the second death. And all those whose names weren't found written in the Book of Life were thrown into the lake of fire.

A New Heaven and Earth

21 [1-8] And I saw a new heaven and a new earth because the first heaven and the first earth were destroyed; and there was no sea anymore. And I, John, saw the holy city, New Jerusalem, coming down out of heaven from God, like a bride who has made herself beautiful for her husband. And I heard a loud voice out of heaven saying, "God's Place of Worship is now with humanity, and God will be with them. They'll be God's people, and God will be with them, and be their God. And God will wipe every tear away from their eyes; and there won't be any more death, sorrow, crying, or pain because all these things from before are ended. And the One who sat on the throne said, *"I have made everything new."* And I was told, *"Write all this down, because these words are true and faithful. It's done, now. I am the First Word and the Last Word, the beginning and the end. I'll freely give to those who are thirsty from the source of the water of life. Whoever overcomes will inherit everything; and I'll be their God, and they'll be my child. But those who are afraid, unbelieving, sickening, murderers, those who practice sexual sin, those who do witchcraft, those who worship falsely, and the liars, will have their part in the lake of fire and burning sulfur, which is the second death."*

The New Jerusalem

[9-14] Then one of the seven angels, which had the seven dishes full of the seven last horrors, came to me, and talked with me, saying, *"Come here, and I'll show you the bride of Christ, the Lamb."* And I was carried away in the spirit to a great and high mountain, and shown that great holy city, the New Jerusalem, coming down out of heaven from God, having the light of God: and its light was like a very precious stone, even like a jasper stone, clear as crystal; And the city had a huge high wall, and had twelve gates, with angels at each gate, and names written on it, which are the names of the twelve families of the children of Israel. One name was on each of the three east gates; on the three north gates; on the three south gates; and on the three west gates. And the wall of the city had twelve foundations, and in them the names of the twelve followers of Christ, the Lamb.

[15-27] And the angel who talked with me had a golden reed to measure the city, its gates, and its walls. And the city was built in a cube with the length the same as the width: and the angel measured the city with the reed, and it was one thousand four hundred miles. Its length, width, and height are all equal. And the wall measured about two hundred feet thick, according to the measure of a human being, that is, of an angel. And the building of its wall was made of jasper: and the city was made of pure gold, as clear as glass. And the foundations of the city's walls were decorated with all kinds of precious stones. The first foundation was clear jasper; the second, blue sapphire; the third, a bloodstone; the fourth, an emerald; the fifth, red carnelian; the sixth, ruby; the seventh, indigo chrysolite; the eighth, aquamarine; the ninth, gold topaz; the tenth, yellow green chrysoprasus; the eleventh, orange jacinth; the twelfth, purple amethyst. And the twelve gates were twelve pearls; each gate was made of one large pearl: and the street of the city was pure gold, as clear as glass. And I saw no Place of Worship in it because Yahweh God Almighty and Christ, the Lamb are the Place of Worship. And the city won't need the sun or the moon to shine in it because the light of God and Christ, the Lamb will shine in it. And the nations of those who are saved will walk in its light: and the rulers of the earth will bring their riches to honor it. And its gates won't be shut at all by day and there'll be no night there. And they'll bring the riches and honor of the nations into it. And nothing will ever come into it that's filthy, or sickening, or tells a lie: but only those who are written in the Lamb's Book of Life.

Christ is Coming

22 [1-5] And I was shown a pure river of the water of life, which was as clear as crystal, flowing from out of the throne of God and of Christ, the Lamb. The tree of life was in the middle of its street, and on both sides of the river, which made twelve different kinds of fruits, and yielded its fruit each month: and the leaves of the tree were used for the healing of the people. The curse will be over, so the throne of God and of Christ, the Lamb will be in it; and God's people will serve them. They'll see God's face; and God's Name will be in their foreheads. And there won't be any night there; and no one will ever need a candle, or sunlight, because Yahweh God gives them light, who will reign forever and ever.

[6-15] And the angel told me, *"These things are faithful and true: and Yahweh God of the great holy preachers sent this messenger to show to God's people the things which will happen very soon. 'I'm coming soon: blessed is whoever keeps the sayings of the Word, which was given ahead of time in this book.'"* And I, John saw and heard all of this. And after I had heard and seen all this, I bowed down to worship at the feet of the angel, who told me, *"Make sure that you don't do that because I am one of your coworkers, and of the great preachers, and of those who keep the sayings of this book. Worship God."* And the angel told me, *"Don't hide the sayings of the Word, which was given ahead of time in this book because the time for it to be known is here now. Whoever is evil, let them still be evil: and whoever is filthy, let them still be filthy: and whoever is good, let them still be good: and whoever is holy, let them still be holy. 'I'm coming soon; and I have rewards to give to everyone for the work they've done. I am the First Word and the Last Word, the beginning and the end, the first and the last. Blessed are those who do My Words, so that they can have the right to the tree of life, and can come in through the gates into the city. Outside the city are whores, those who do witchcraft, those who practice sexual sin, murderers, those who worship falsely, and those who love to tell lies.*

[16-21] *I, Yeshua, have sent My messenger to tell you all this in the churches. I am both the Root and the Descendant of David, and the Bright and Morning Star. Let the Spirit and the church say, "Come." And let those who hear say, "Come." And let those who are thirsty come. And whoever wants it, let them freely take from the water of life. I tell everyone that hears the message of the New Word, which was given ahead of time in this book, if anyone adds to the meaning of the things in this book, God will add to them the curses that are written in this book: And if anyone takes away from the meaning of the book of this New Word, which was given ahead of time, God will take away their part out of the Book of Life, and out of the holy city, and from all the blessings which are written in this book. The Christ who testifies of this said, 'The truth is, I'm coming soon.'"* So be it! Yes, come soon, Christ Yeshua. May the grace of our Christ Yeshua, be with you all. So be it!

So don't have anything to do with the useless actions of darkness,
but instead expose them for what they are.
This is why God said,

Awake,

you who

are sleeping

Come to life from the dead

And

Christ

will give

you light.

Ephesians 5:14

Personal Notes

Personal Notes

Personal Notes

Personal Notes

Personal Notes

Personal Notes

Personal Notes

Personal Notes

Personal Notes

Personal Notes

Personal Notes

80 Day Summer Reading Plan

40 Days		40 Days	
Through the New Word		**Through the Sayings and Hymns**	
Day 1	Matthew 1-7	Sayings 1-5	
Day 2	Matthew 8-14	Sayings 6-10	
Day 3	Matthew 15-21	Sayings 11-15	
Day 4	Mathew 22-28	Sayings 16-20	
Day 5	Mark 1-8	Sayings 21-25	
Day 6	Mark 9-16	Sayings 26-31	
Day 7	Luke 1-6	Hymns 1-5	
Day 8	Luke 7-12	Hymns 6-10	
Day 9	Luke 13-18	Hymns 11-16	
Day 10	Luke 19-24	Hymns 17-20	
Day 11	John 1-7	Hymns 21-25	
Day 12	John 8-14	Hymns 26-30	
Day 13	John 15-21	Hymns 31-35	
Day 14	Acts 1-7	Hymns 36-41	
Day 15	Acts 8-14	Hymns 42-45	
Day 16	Acts 15-21	Hymns 46-50	
Day 17	Acts 22-28	Hymns 51-55	
Day 18	Romans 1-8	Hymns 56-60	
Day 19	Romans 9-16	Hymns 61-67	
Day 20	I Corinthians 1-8	Hymns 68-72	
Day 21	I Corinthians 9-16	Hymns 73-78	
Day 22	II Corinthians 1-6	Hymns 79-85	
Day 23	II Corinthians 7-13	Hymns 86-89	
Day 24	Galatians 1-6	Hymns 90-95	
Day 25	Ephesians 1-6	Hymns 102-106	
Day 30	Philippians, Colossians	Hymns 107-110	
Day 31	I and II Thessalonians	Hymns 111-118	
Day 32	I and II Timothy	Hymns 119 1-56	
Day 33	Titus, Philemon	Hymns 119 57-96	
Day 34	Hebrews 1-7	Hymns 119 97-128	
Day 35	Hebrews 8-13	Hymns 119 129-160	
Day 36	James, I and II Peter	Hymns 119 161-176	
Day 37	I, II, and III John, Jude	Hymns120-130	
Day 38	Revelation 1-7	Hymns 131-137	
Day 39	Revelation 8-13	Hymns 138-145	
Day 40	Revelation 14-22	Hymns 145-150	

The Beatitudes

Mathew 5:3-12

"*Blessed are those whose spirits are disheartened because the power of heaven is now theirs. Blessed are those who grieve because they'll be in good spirits now. Blessed are those who are gentle because the earth will be given to them. Blessed are those who hunger and thirst for goodness because they'll be filled with it. Blessed are those who have compassion because they'll be given compassion in return. Blessed are those whose hearts are innocent because they'll see God. Blessed are those who are peacemakers because they'll be called the children of God. Blessed are those who are abused for the sake of goodness, because the power of heaven is now theirs. Blessed are you, when people hate you, and mistreat you, and say all kind of evil things against you falsely, for My sake. Celebrate, and be very happy because your reward in heaven will be great because they also abused the great preachers who came before you.*

Yeshua's Prayer

Yahweh,
our God
in heaven,
Your Name is Holy.
May Your everlasting realm come soon.
May Your will be done on earth, just as it's done
in heaven. Give us what we need for today.
And forgive our sins,
as we forgive those
who sin against us.
Help us not to sin
when we're tempted,
but free us from evil,
because the power
and the victory
of Your Realm
is forever. So be it!

About the Author

Sis. Kimberly Marie Hartfield is an Ordained Minister in the Evangelical Faith, and has received a Master of Science Degree in Christian Counseling from William Carey University in 2009. She received her Bachelor of Science in Psychology in 2004 with minors in both Religion and English. She lives in Hattiesburg, MS, and is a mother of eight children. She is the founder and president of Go Fish Ministries, Inc. an advocacy group for victims of sexual and domestic violence. **Go Fish Ministries, Inc** is primarily for victims of sexual and domestic violence, but is also a ministry for the unchurched and churched population in general, as Jesus said, *Follow me and I'll teach you to fish for others.* She believes that as many biblical writers were less than perfect, ordinary people with a strong faith, that with her own strong faith, God can and will do something extraordinary in her less than perfect, ordinary life. She began this paraphrase shortly after receiving her first degree from WCU. It was the result of many months of study and comparisons of other versions, which for one reason or another didn't seem quite satisfactory for ease of reading and keeping the basic Scriptural intent. After searching through most available common versions, she was led to begin a paraphrase of the Psalms and Proverbs as a beginning for the paraphrase of the New Testament. Kim has been called to the homeland mission field of North America and hopes to be able to use this unique and easily readable paraphrase of the New Testament and the Psalms and Proverbs as a tool for the ministry of witnessing to the grace of God and comforting God's people with the truth of God's mercy. She claims II Corinthians 3 & 4 as her calling, which states: *"May Yahweh God be blessed, the God our Christ Yeshua comes from, the God all mercies come from, and the God all comforts come from; Who comforts us in all our troubles, so that we may be able to comfort those, who are in any kind of trouble, with the same kind of comfort that we ourselves have been comforted with by God."* She believes that the Christian community's ultimate authority is the guidance of the human heart by the Holy Spirit and the Word of God.

For more information about her ministry write to:
Go Fish Ministries, Inc. 76 MIMS Road, Hattiesburg, MS 39401
Or visit our website at *http://gofishministries.wordpress.com*

G.O. F.I.S.H.

A General Outreach & Free Interpretation of the Sayings and Hymns

Jesus Said: Follow Me and I'll make you fishers of others.

Special Features:

A unique and easily readable paraphrase of the New Testament and the Proverbs and Psalms

Easy to read print

Art work by Rock Hartfield

Unique Paraphrases of The Beatitudes, The Lord's Prayer, and the Ten Commandments

Brief Bio of the Author

A Go Fish Ministries Publication, Hattiesburg, MS Printed in U.S.A.

Cover Design by Sister Kimberly M. Hartfield